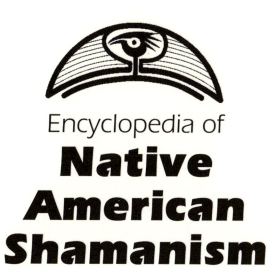

Encyclopedia of
Native
American
Shamanism

Encyclopedia of
Native American Shamanism

Sacred Ceremonies of North America

William S. Lyon

ABC-CLIO

Santa Barbara, California
Denver, Colorado
Oxford, England

Maps 1–15 are adapted from George Peter Murdock and Timothy J. O'Leary, *Ethnographic Bibliography of North America* (New Haven, CT: Human Relations Area Files Press, 1975). Reprinted by permission.

Library of Congress Cataloging-in-Publication Data
Lyon, William S., Ph. D.
    Encyclopedia of Native American shamanism : sacred ceremonies of
North America / William S. Lyon.
        p.   cm.
    Includes bibliographical references and index.
    1. Indians of North America—Medicine—Encyclopedias.   2. Indians
of North America—Rites and ceremonies—Encyclopedias.   3. Indians
of North America—Religion—Encyclopedias.   4. Shamanism—North
America—Encyclopedias.   I. Title.
E98.M4L98   1998
615.8'82'08997—dc21   98-34582
                                                                                            CIP

ISBN 0-87436-933-9

05   04   03   02   01   00   99   98   10   9   8   7   6   5   4   3   2   1

ABC-CLIO, Inc.
130 Cremona Drive, P.O. Box 1911
Santa Barbara, California 93116-1911

Typesetting by Letra Libre

This book is printed on acid-free paper ∞.
Manufactured in the United States of America

To William M. Bass, professional anthropologist par excellence, for swaying me to become an anthropologist in the first place and then instilling in me the scientific aspects of fieldwork; and also to Wallace H. Black Elk, Lakota holy man par excellence, for teaching me the importance of "going native" during fieldwork. It is through the blending of their yin/yang understandings of the universe that I was able to produce this work. To both of them I will always be most grateful for the balance they have brought to both my career and my life.

Contents

Illustrations

The decorative illustrations on the first page of each chapter for letters A–L are from the following publications: *Decorative Art of Indian Tribes of Connecticut*, Anthropological Series, no. 10, Memoir no. 75 (Canadian Department of Mines Geological Survey, 1915); *Navajo Medicine Man Sandpaintings* by Gladys A. Reichard (New York: Dover Publications, Inc., 1977); *Crow Indian Beadwork* by William Wildschut and John C. Ewers (New York: Museum of the American Indian, Heye Foundation, 1959); *Quill and Beadwork of the Western Sioux* by Carrie A. Lynford (Washington, D.C.: Bureau of Indian Affairs, United States Department of the Interior, 1940); *Iroquois Crafts* by Carrie A. Lynford (Lawrence, Kansas: U.S. Indian Service, 1945); *Southwest Indian Designs* by Caren Caraway (Owing Mills, Maryland: Stemmer House Publishers, Inc., 1983); *Southwestern Indian Designs* by Madeleine Orban-Szontagh (New York: Dover Publications, Inc., 1992). The illustrations on the first page of each chapter for letters M–Z are from *Decorative Art of the Southwest* by Dorothy Smith Sides (New York: Dover Publications, Inc., 1961).

Each illustration, listed by chapter and position on the page, is briefly described below.

A

Top　　Apache basket design [Orban-Szontagh 1992: Museum of the American Indian, Heye Foundation, New York]

Bottom　Body designs from Mohegan painted baskets [Canadian Department of Mines Geological Survey 1915]

B

Top　　Mimbres design on bowls

Middle　Crow beadwork [Wildschut and Ewers, 1959]

Bottom　Iroquois design used on metallic ornaments and brooches [Lynford 1945]

C

Top　　Mimbres design on pottery

Middle　Iroquois Celestial Tree design

Bottom　Apache basket design [Orban-Szontagh 1992: Museum of the American Indian, Heye Foundation, New York]

D

Top　　Iroquois design used on metallic ornament [Lynford 1945]

Middle　Sacaton design

Bottom　Apache basket design [Orban-Szontagh 1992: Museum of the American Indian, Heye Foundation, New York]

E

Top　　Hopi kachina design [Caraway 1983]

Bottom　Apache basket design [Orban-Szontagh 1992: Museum of the American Indian, Heye Foundation, New York]

F

Holy Man, Navajo Shooting Chant sandpainting [Reichard 1977]

G

Top　　Quill work, Western Sioux [Lynford 1940]

Middle　Classic Mimbres bowl design

Bottom　Quill work, Western Sioux [Lynford 1940]

H

Top   Quill work, Western Sioux [Lynford 1940]

Middle   Hopi kachina design [Caraway 1983]

Bottom   Quill work, Western Sioux [Lynford 1940]

I

Top   Mohegan painted baskets [Canadian Department of Mines Geological Survey 1915]

Bottom   Hopi pottery design [Caraway 1983]

J

Top   Sacaton design [Canadian Department of Mines Geological Survey 1915]

Middle   Crow beadwork [Lynford 1940]

Bottom   Scatticook painted design [Canadian Department of Mines Geological Survey 1915]

K

Top   Hopi kachina design [Caraway 1983]

Middle   Mohegan painted design [Canadian Department of Mines Geological Survey 1915]

Bottom   Quill work, Western Sioux [Lynford 1940]

L

Feathered snake, Navajo sandpainting [Reichard 1977]

M

Top   Pottery decoration from a Sikyatki ruin, Arizona [Sides 1961]

Middle   Pottery decoration, American Southwest [Sides 1961]

Bottom   Pottery decoration from a Sikyatki ruin, Arizona [Sides 1961]

N

Top   Pima basket design, Arizona [Sides 1961]

Middle   Hopi pottery decoration, Arizona [Sides 1961]

Bottom   Pima basket design, Arizona [Sides 1961]

O

Top   Pima basket design, Arizona [Sides 1961]

Middle   Pottery design from Acoma, New Mexico [Sides 1961]

Bottom   Pima basket design, Arizona [Sides 1961]

P

Top   Pottery design from San Ildefonso, New Mexico [Sides 1961]

Bottom   Bird design on painted pottery, Pecos Pueblo, New Mexico [Sides 1961]

Q

Top   Papago basket design, Sonora, Arizona [Sides 1961]

Middle   Stylized bird on painted pottery, Zuni Pueblo, New Mexico [Sides 1961]

Bottom   Papago basket design, Sonora, Arizona [Sides 1961]

R

Top   Painted ceramic decoration from a Sikyatki ruin, Arizona [Sides 1961]

Middle   Pottery decoration from a Sikyatki ruin, Arizona [Sides 1961]

Bottom   Pottery decoration from Four Mile ruin, Arizona [Sides 1961]

S

Top   Pottery design from Homolobi ruin no. 1, near Winslow, Arizona [Sides 1961]

Middle   Pottery decoration from Santo Domingo Pueblo, New Mexico [Sides 1961]

Bottom   Design on painted pottery, Homolobi ruin no. 1, near Winslow, Arizona [Sides 1961]

T

Top   Painted snake design on pottery, Shongopovi ruin, Arizona [Sides 1961]

Middle   Pottery decoration from Pecos Pueblo, New Mexico [Sides 1961]

Bottom   Prehistoric pottery decoration from the Mimbres River Valley, New Mexico [Sides 1961]

Preface

This encyclopedia marks the first major introduction to the anthropological study of Native American medicine powers as they have been recorded over the past three centuries. In addition, the text is written from the point of view of the natives themselves, that is, in the belief that shamans can do what they say they can do. Professional anthropologists have long avoided this approach because the roots of shamanism reach into the realm of living magic, a place most academicians fear to tread. In fact, to date, there has been no overview of Native American shamanism in North America based on the point of view expressed herein.

Our initial studies of Native American shamanism began only in the last century. In the beginning, anthropological research focused on the different forms in which shamanism was manifested, individually and in ritual societies. At that time there was great interest in tracing the tribal lineages along which certain ceremonies had migrated through time. Anthropologists were also interested in the processes by which simple rituals had evolved into more complex rituals over time. These ethnographers were most fortunate because shamanism was still thriving, and much was recorded.

By the 1920s research on shamanism had begun to shift to the psychology of shamans. The popular notion of shamanism being some form of hysteria appeared during this period. However, by the 1960s research no longer validated this stance, and it was reversed. In fact, shamans came to be seen as superadjusted within their own societies.

By the 1950s Åke Hultkranz and others had set into motion the comparative study of Native American religions. Also by then ethnographic research, given the loss of traditional ways, had

given way to a focus on ethnological theory. In both cases these studies tend to ignore the medicine powers of shamans and focus mainly on ritual organization, content, design, change, and symbolism. When certain mysterious aspects of shamanism are considered, they are often still seen as invalid and labeled "preposterous" or "eccentric" [e.g., Hultkrantz 1992:82].

As such, only within the past two decades has a small group of anthropologists begun to take shamans seriously. All of the old ethnographic records were purposely written to show the writers' disbelief in shamanism. The first field ethnographers were impressed by the abilities of shamans, as were the even earlier voyagers who came into contact with them, be they priests, trappers, traders, or army generals. However, academic pressures were such that these early ethnographers had to make it clear in their writings that they didn't really believe in the shamans' medicine powers. Those anthropologists who did believe in the reality of such medicine powers kept their knowledge secret out of fear that their publications would be condemned as rubbish, that is, not seen as "scientific." (For an excellent example of this issue, see the account of Dr. William Tufts Brigham [M. Long 1936:52–58], the first Hawaiian ethnographer.)

The major problem has always been the fact that shamanism does not lend itself to "scientific" scrutiny. There are several good reasons for this. For one, in a shamanic ritual any disbelieving observer attending the ceremony biases the results—a well-known fact based in quantum mechanics. Therefore, disbelieving scientists automatically skew the shaman's results in any experimental situation. Furthermore, real shamans are not willing to conduct "placebo" healing sessions felt to be necessary in establishing the proper "scientific controls" for any study on the efficacy of shamanic healing. Perhaps the most important reason is that shamans tend to see our "scientists" as simply naive people. That is, we are the ones who have lost the precious know-how to make shamanism work. As such, shamans tend to be unwilling subjects. They most often view cooperation in "scientific studies" as a waste of their time.

Despite this avoidance of the magic issue, it is interesting to note that over the past century the term "medicine," when used in anthropology regarding Native America, did come to be equated with mystery, magic, and holy matters versus prescribed drugs. A mystery aspect to anything was its medicine power. For example, whiskey was termed "medicine water" not because it cured you in any way but because it somehow mysteriously made you act in an abnormal way. That is, it had a mysterious power over one's mind. Thus, early on, whiskey is known to have been used by shamans during their vision quests.

In the past two decades there are many reasons why shamans have gained credibility. For one, there is a growing awareness and body of evidence about the efficacy of certain rituals such as the Sun Dance and sweat lodge ceremonies. Sweat lodge ceremonies are now in common use in drug treatment programs across the United States, and the number of Sun Dance participants increases annually, as do the number of dances. Furthermore, modern physicists are beginning to link certain aspects of shamanism to recent findings from quantum mechanics (for example, see Fred Allen Wolf's The Eagle's Quest). Thus, a new scientific understanding is emerging that explains some of the earlier mysteries of shamanism. Finally, there is a growing number of anthropologists who realize the importance of "going native" and honestly participating in shamanic rituals. As anthropologist Edith Turner, wife of the late Victor Turner, recently wrote, "To reach a peak experience in a ritual, sinking oneself fully in it really is necessary. Thus for me, 'going native' achieved a breakthrough to

an altogether different world view, foreign to academia, by means of which certain material was chronicled that could have been gathered in no other way" [Turner 1997:22].

In this encyclopedia I have tried to avoid the use of the inherently ethnocentric and disassociative qualifiers that plague our literature. Statements such as "They believe that . . . ," "It is purported that . . . ," or "They claim that . . ." are to be found only in direct quotations. It is unfortunate that field anthropologists have been forced to publicly deny the reality of Native American medicine powers lest they lose their professional reputations. Interestingly enough, however, the earliest recorded beliefs in the reality of shamanic medicine powers are to be found among the records of the French Jesuit priests of the sixteenth century. A careful reading of these early Jesuit records reveals an interesting pattern. The first priests on the scene initially believed that the shamans were simply frauds, using some form of deception or stage magic. Eventually, however, the Jesuits began to realize that the shamans' medicine powers were often quite real. Thereafter one reads of medicine powers being demonstrations of the "work of the devil." Now, some 300 years later, anthropologists are also admitting their reality.

This encyclopedia is a continuation of ABC-CLIO's Encyclopedia of Native American Healing (EONAH). In the first work the focus was on medicine powers used for healing, the main task of shamans. Here the focus is on all the other various ways in which medicine powers are manifested; the book also includes some additional material on healing. The two works are designed to complement each other and form a very thorough coverage of Native American shamanism in North America. For example, terms used in this encyclopedia that are defined in the first encyclopedia are referenced as "(EONAH, p. —)." Readers should refer to the given page number(s) if they are unfamiliar with such terms. Also, a general term used in shamanism that is missing from one encyclopedia is apt to be found in the other one. For terms that do not appear as entries herein, check the index for their possible location within the text. Many Native American terms that do not appear as entries are used and defined elsewhere. In addition, each encyclopedia focuses on a different aspect of the known literature on shamanism. For that reason nearly 85 percent of the references in this encyclopedia represents new material on shamanism that is not listed (or covered) in the previous encyclopedia.

When it comes to ethnographic data on shamanism, the North American ethnographies are a vast and unique treasure. Nowhere else in the world will one find so much material recorded on shamanism among so many different cultures within a specific geographical region. We arrived in great numbers with field notebooks in hand as shamans were fading from the scene, and we have many wonderful accounts of their astounding feats of power. So I am the first to admit that there are still many works on shamanism not listed in either bibliography. At the same time, I believe that well over half of the data on Native American shamanism in North America is to be found between these two bibliographies. Furthermore, I have attempted to cover all of the different manifestations of Native American shamanism and shamans' associated medicine powers as recorded for North America. As such, the two encyclopedias together constitute the largest coverage to date of the subject.

Presently there is no clear taxonomy of shamanism, and such a thing may not be possible. To begin with, there is the problem of whether a person of power has enough power to be designated a shaman within any culture. That is not a problem that is dealt with in this volume, and as such, many of the entries herein include persons who would normally not be called shamans within their own culture. Those persons of known powers are variously referred to as shamans, holy men, medicine men, priests, and so forth. Also included are accounts of the evil users of medicine powers—the witches and sorcerers. The reason for this is that the same rules for handling medicine powers apply to all situations.

Within the realm of bona fide shamans, one finds that each shaman has a different set of medicine powers. Furthermore, each medicine power is limited to certain uses and most often carries specific taboos regarding its use. Thus, one shaman may have the power to heal war wounds while at the same time having the power to find lost objects, while another shaman may specialize in stomach problems while also having the ability to alter the weather. To complicate matters, a single spirit, such as the Bear spirit, might confer different medicine powers to different shamans. Therefore, it is somewhat easier to classify the power uses of shamans than it is to classify the shamans themselves. Here again, there is no standard system of classification or taxonomy simply because medicine powers have not been the subject of much investigation to date. This means that readers should be on the lookout for such entries as horse medicines, war medicines, weather medicines, or hunting medicines that are, for the most part, unknown taxonomic categories.

This work is also designed to aid researchers in locating original materials on all aspects of shamanism. For that reason, much of the text consists of direct quotations. Within each quotation, material added by the original author is included in parentheses, while material added by me is included in square brackets. Furthermore, each entry most often contains several bibliographic references that are designed to lead one to more detailed works and thus to more information on the subject at hand. The index is also designed to aid researchers. It is especially useful in cross-referencing the individual entries when one's focus is on a particular subject or culture. In addition, many of the encyclopedia entries contain cross-references to other entries that provide the reader with additional data.

As with the last encyclopedia, this encyclopedia does not cover plant usage by Native American shamans and herbalists. However, a new and much larger bibliography on the ethnobotany of North America appears as a separate appendix. To this end I am most grateful to Professor Dan Moerman of the University of Michigan for allowing me to extract the bibliography from his recent Timber Press publication titled *Native American Ethnobotany.*

Finally, I want to particularly thank Peter Falt and Sean Heard for their tremendous assistance in editing the manuscripts of both encyclopedias and Eric Falt for his untiring assistance with this manuscript. Also, I wish to thank all the people at ABC-CLIO who have worked on both of these projects over the past three years—in particular Todd Hallman for asking me to initiate this project in the first place and his close work with me on producing it and Susan Ficca for her creative artwork, cover designs, and interior layouts. Others at ABC-CLIO include Liz Kincaid, Mary Kay Jezzini, Alicia Merritt, Connie Oehring, and Kristi Ward. Last, and perhaps most important, I want to thank all those Native American medicine men and women who, in the face of extreme opposition, persisted in devoting their life to upholding the sacred traditions of Native America. Without their perseverance this magical aspect of Native America would have disappeared long ago.

User's Guide

Entry Format

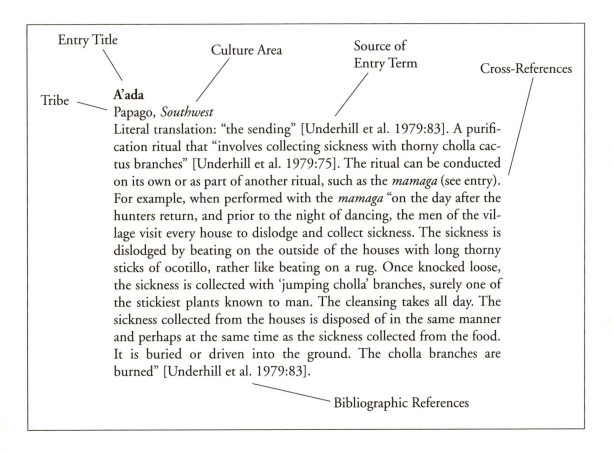

Entry Title

Culture Area

Source of
Entry Term

Cross-References

Tribe

A'ada
Papago, *Southwest*
Literal translation: "the sending" [Underhill et al. 1979:83]. A purification ritual that "involves collecting sickness with thorny cholla cactus branches" [Underhill et al. 1979:75]. The ritual can be conducted on its own or as part of another ritual, such as the *mamaga* (see entry). For example, when performed with the *mamaga* "on the day after the hunters return, and prior to the night of dancing, the men of the village visit every house to dislodge and collect sickness. The sickness is dislodged by beating on the outside of the houses with long thorny sticks of ocotillo, rather like beating on a rug. Once knocked loose, the sickness is collected with 'jumping cholla' branches, surely one of the stickiest plants known to man. The cleansing takes all day. The sickness collected from the houses is disposed of in the same manner and perhaps at the same time as the sickness collected from the food. It is buried or driven into the ground. The cholla branches are burned" [Underhill et al. 1979:83].

Bibliographic References

Entry Title: Every entry in the encyclopedia is headed with a word or phrase that is intended to most fully and accurately reflect the content. Because of the diversity and complexity of the information in many entries, an adequately representative title is not always possible. To provide readers access to the significant information in entries not adequately reflected in the titles, we provide entries under other significant titles that direct the reader, by means of cross-references, to these entries. Most of the entry titles are in Native American languages. We recognize that many of these terms will be unknown to most users of this work. Still it is by this means that we are able to retain cultural identity and integrity of the information presented. The information in these entries is intended to be accessible through other entries with more familiar entry titles by following the cross-reference suggestions. Often users of this work will want to follow a series of cross-references, even chains of cross-references, to find the information they seek. We also hope that, for many users, this cross-referencing technique will stimulate a process of exploration. We hope that readers will be interested in comparisons, compilations, and connections among the entries in the encyclopedia.

Tribe and/or *Culture Area:* Entry titles are followed by the identification of the tribe and/or culture area where relevant. Typically a tribe, a list of tribes, or a tribal grouping is listed first followed by the culture area (identified in italic type) in which this tribe, list of tribes, or tribal grouping (Algonquian, Teton, Pueblo, etc.) is located. The culture areas are in turn keyed to a set of detailed maps.

Unfortunately, the division of Native American culture areas has not been standardized in anthropology, and several different systems have been devised throughout this century. In this work, the division into areas as set forth by Murdock and O'Leary (1975) has been adopted.

Cross-References: There are terms found in the text of the entries that are also the titles of other entries where related information is presented. These cross-references are in italic type and the reader is then referred to that entry with the phrase "see entry" in parentheses.

Many terms used in this encyclopedia have been previously defined in the *Encyclopedia of Native American Healing* (EONAH). These terms are cross-referenced as "EONAH, p. —" in parentheses.

Cross-references listed at the end of an entry provide additional details or examples for that entry.

Bibliographic References: Because the information in this encyclopedia represents only a small fraction of a veritable mountain of available material, bibliographic suggestions are provided for

most entries. This feature, along with the extensive bibliography, enhances the usefulness of this encyclopedia for scholars and specialists, as well as for the general reader seeking greater detail.

As a general rule, the first reference cited in an entry usually contains that particular entry term. Persons wanting more linguistic detail for an entry term, such as number of syllables, word division, syllable accent, and so forth, should consult such reference works.

Maps

Maps are provided for fifteen culture areas to assist in locating tribes. Tribe and/or culture area designations are given in entries where relevant.

References

The references section is in alphabetical order by the last name of the author. Works by the same author are organized chronologically by the year of publication. Multiple publications for the same year for a given author are arranged alphabetically by title and an alphabetic character is appended to the year. References to the bibliography are made throughout the encyclopedia by the author's last name and the year of publication. For duplicate last names, the first initial of the author's first name is included in the citation.

Index

An index to the entries has been provided to facilitate research on specific tribes or tribal groupings. It is a standard subject index that includes tribes or tribal groupings, culture areas, and key concepts germane to Native American shamanism.

The index also contains Native American terms used in the text that do not appear as entries. Persons searching for a particular Native American term that does not appear as an entry should consult the index.

Native American Languages

More than 150 Native American languages are represented in the titles of entries in this encyclopedia. Native American languages have come to be written primarily through the introduction by linguists and others of orthographic systems that assign a symbol or alphabetic character to the phonemic structure "the distinguishable sounds" of a language. For many Native American languages several different orthographies have been used. Further complexity is introduced by the abilities and eccentricities of various persons who have recorded these Native American terms. Some hear a "b" sound where others hear a "p" sound; some hear "ts" where others hear "s." The linguistic and orthographic complexities of any Native American language are fully understood only by the specialist in that language. Though ideally every Native American word used in the encyclopedia would be presented so that the orthography would most closely reflect Native American pronunciations, this is not even possible, much less practical, and it would require

readers to engage a minicourse in phonetics to use the encyclopedia. We have decided to do all we can to avoid misrepresentation and confusion, yet we recognize that it is essential for the encyclopedia to be "user-friendly." Native American words are presented either in the most commonly used Anglicized forms, where known, or exactly as they appear, plus most diacritical markings, in the sources we have used. Common alternative spellings and dialectical variants of entry terms are also given. Readers should be aware that pronunciations of the terms based on the simplified presentation likely only generally resemble how the word would sound if pronounced by a speaker of the language. Many of the ethnographic documents contain discussions of language and orthography. Readers interested at this technical level are encouraged to consult these works, as well as dictionaries on the relevant languages.

Maps

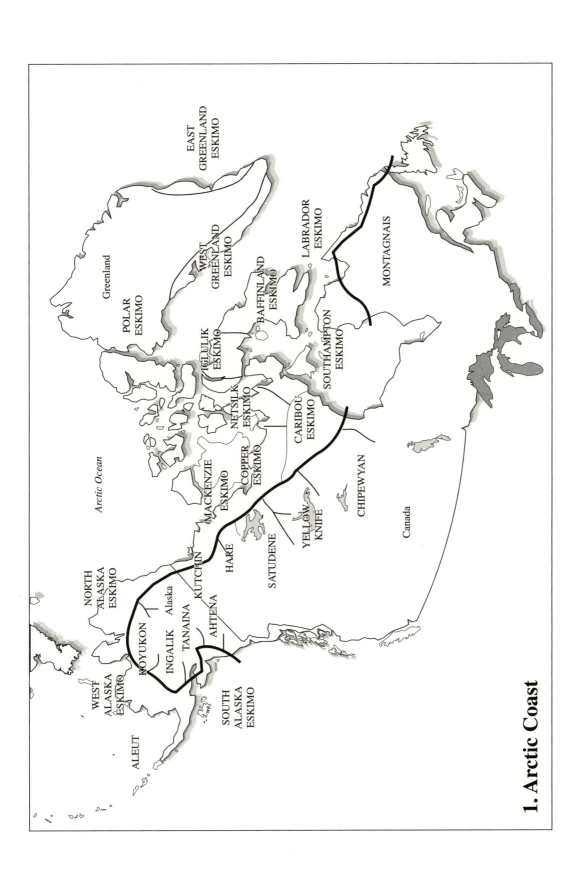

1. Arctic Coast

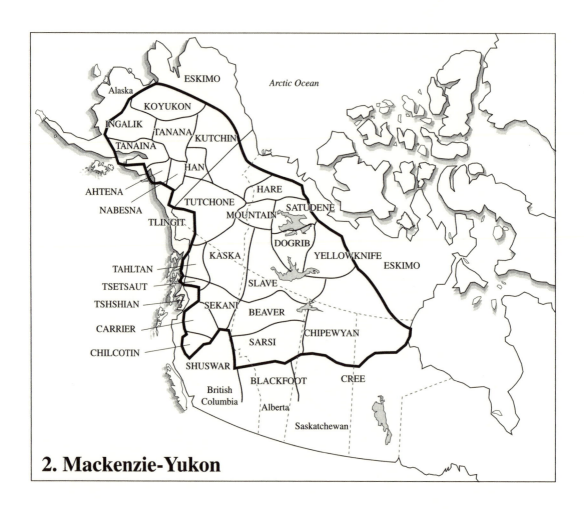

2. Mackenzie-Yukon

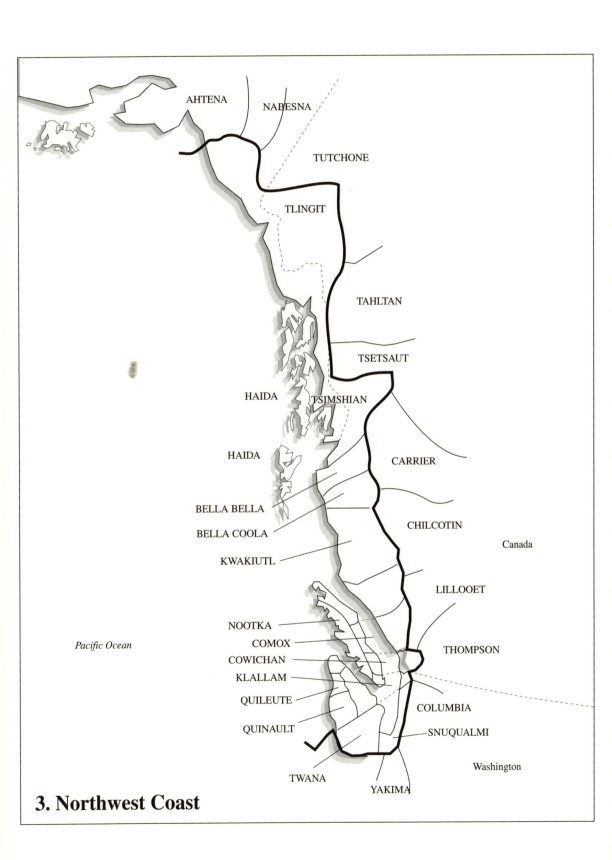

AHTENA

NABESNA

TUTCHONE

TLINGIT

TAHLTAN

TSETSAUT

HAIDA

TSIMSHIAN

HAIDA

CARRIER

BELLA BELLA

CHILCOTIN

BELLA COOLA

Canada

KWAKIUTL

LILLOOET

NOOTKA

COMOX

Pacific Ocean

COWICHAN

THOMPSON

KLALLAM

QUILEUTE

QUINAULT

COLUMBIA

SNUQUALMI

TWANA

Washington

YAKIMA

3. Northwest Coast

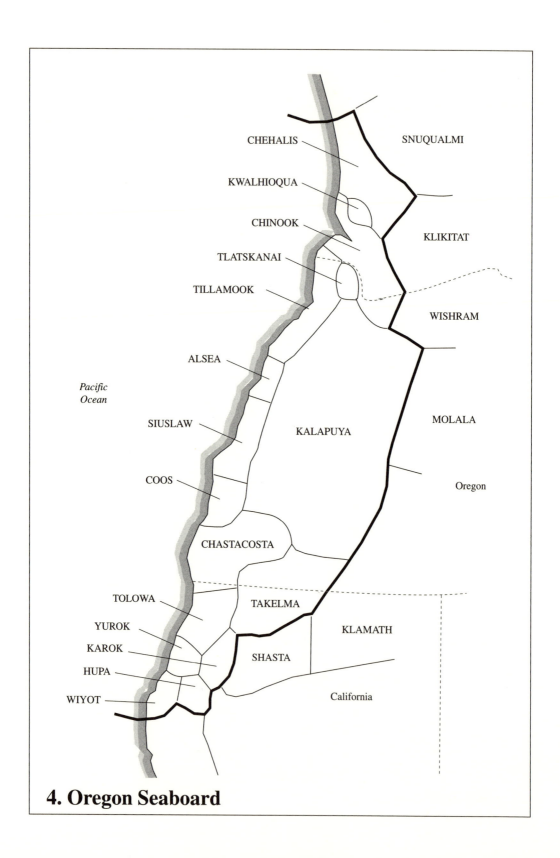

4. Oregon Seaboard

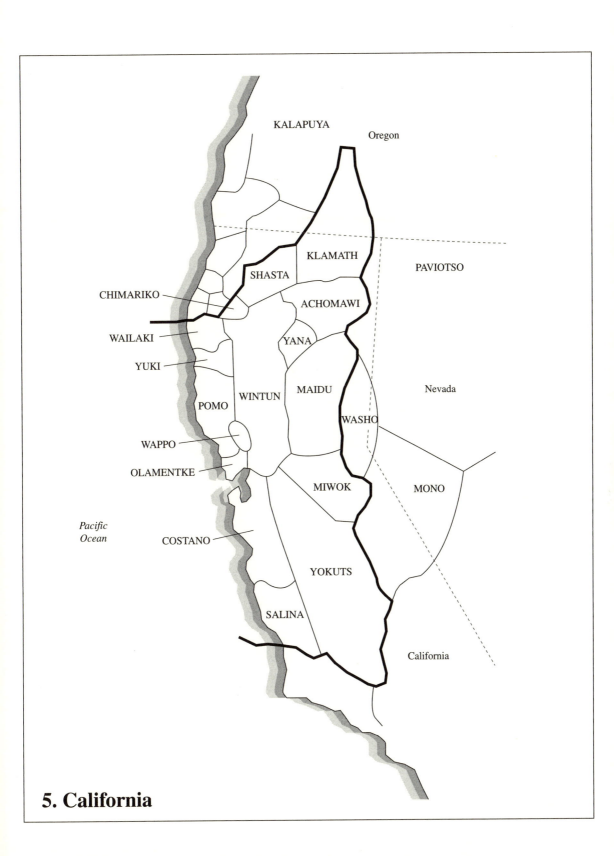

KALAPUYA

Oregon

KLAMATH

PAVIOTSO

SHASTA

ACHOMAWI

CHIMARIKO

YANA

WAILAKI

YUKI

WINTUN

MAIDU

Nevada

POMO

WASHO

WAPPO

OLAMENTKE

MIWOK

MONO

Pacific
Ocean

COSTANO

YOKUTS

SALINA

California

5. California

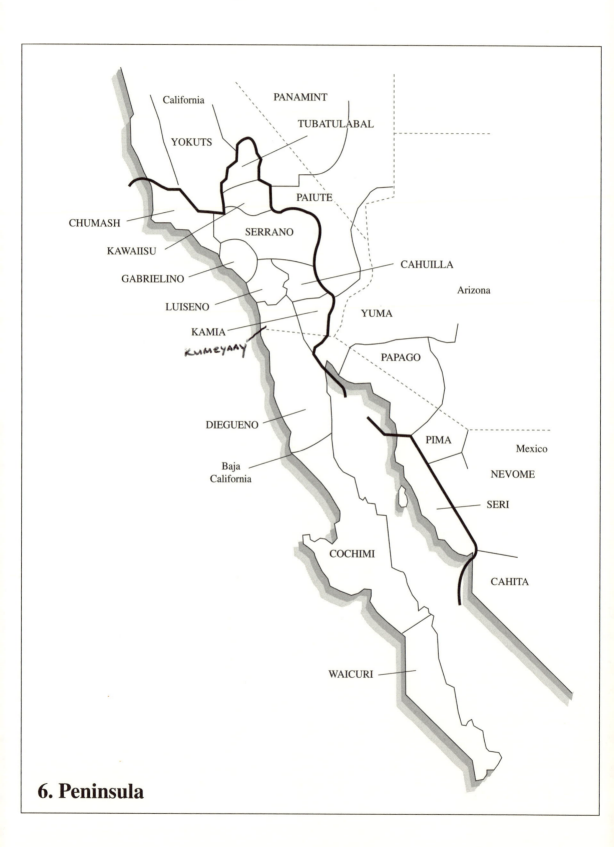

California

PANAMINT

YOKUTS

TUBATULABAL

PAIUTE

CHUMASH

SERRANO

KAWAIISU

GABRIELINO

CAHUILLA

Arizona

LUISENO

YUMA

KAMIA

KUMEYAAY

PAPAGO

DIEGUENO

PIMA

Mexico

Baja
California

NEVOME

SERI

COCHIMI

CAHITA

WAICURI

6. Peninsula

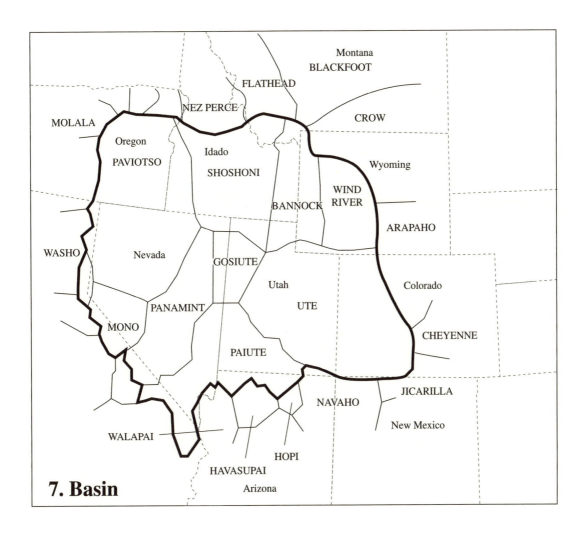

Montana
BLACKFOOT
FLATHEAD
NEZ PERCE
CROW
MOLALA
Oregon
Idado
Wyoming
PAVIOTSO
SHOSHONI
WIND
RIVER
BANNOCK
ARAPAHO
WASHO
Nevada
GOSIUTE
Utah
Colorado
PANAMINT
UTE
MONO
CHEYENNE
PAIUTE
JICARILLA
NAVAHO
New Mexico
WALAPAI
HOPI
HAVASUPAI
Arizona

7. Basin

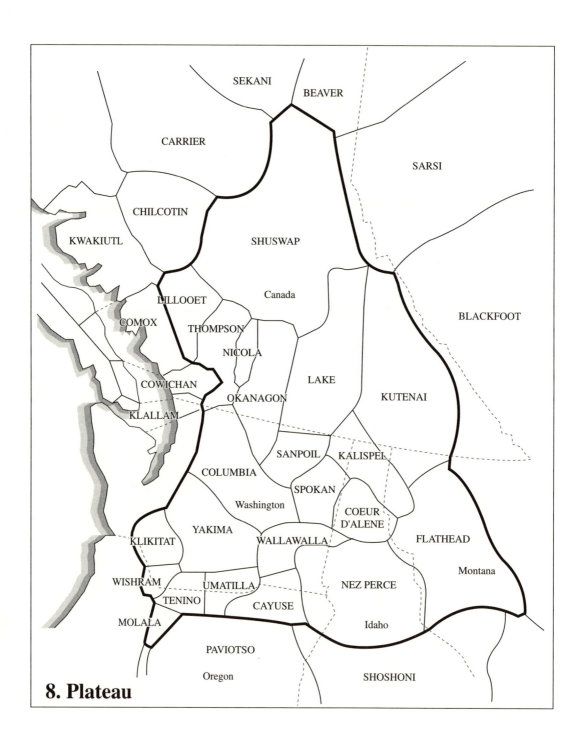

8. Plateau

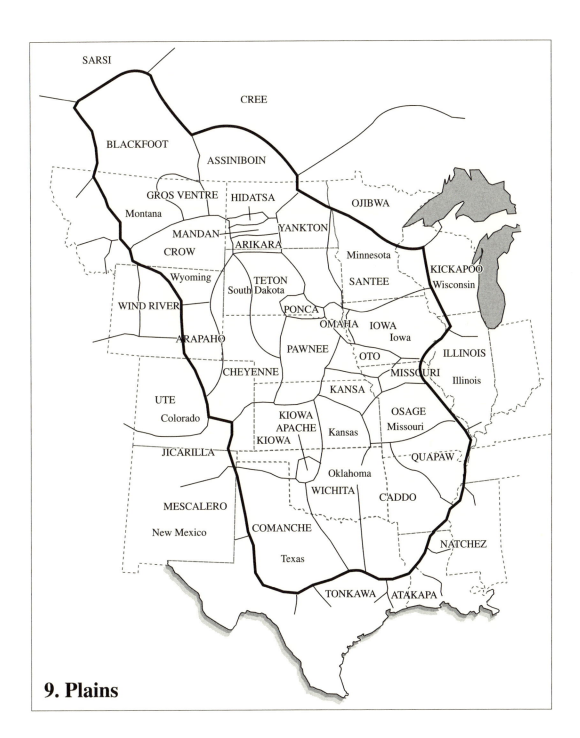

9. Plains

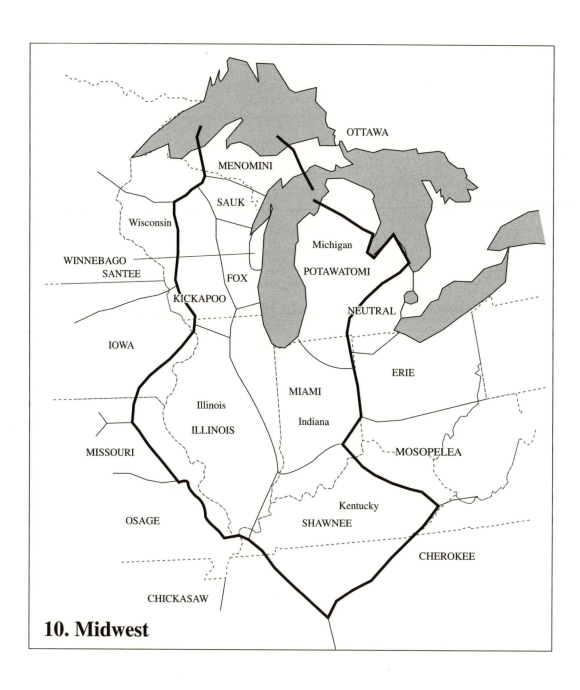

10. Midwest

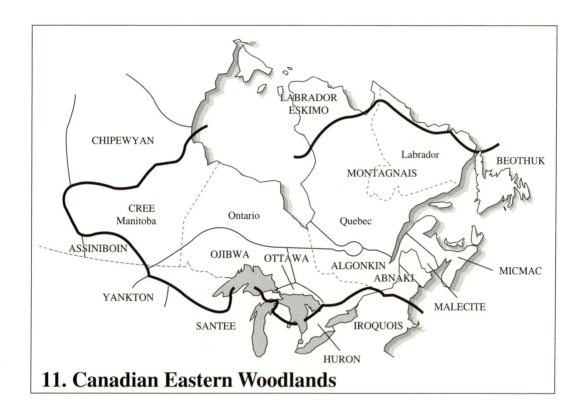

11. Canadian Eastern Woodlands

12. Northeast

13. Southeast

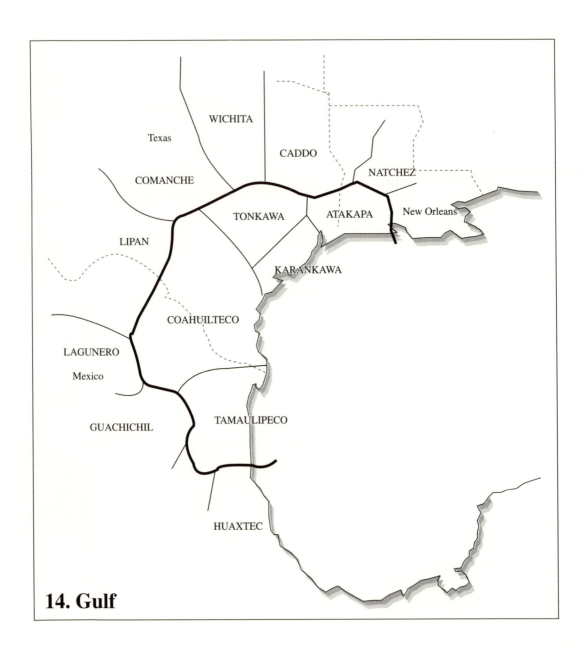

14. Gulf

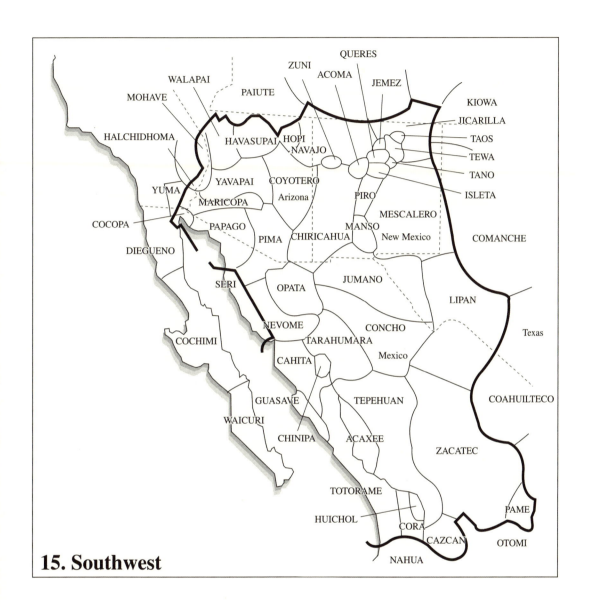

15. Southwest

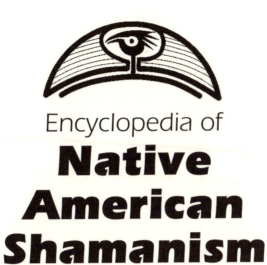

Encyclopedia of
Native
American
Shamanism

A'ada
Papago, *Southwest*

Literal translation: "the sending" [Underhill et al. 1979:83]. A purification rite that "involves collecting sickness with thorny cholla cactus branches" [Underhill et al. 1979:75]. The ritual can be conducted on its own or as part of another ritual, such as the *mamaga* (see entry). For example, when performed with the *mamaga* "on the day after the hunters return, and prior to the night of dancing, the men of the village visit every house to dislodge and collect sickness. The sickness is dislodged by beating on the outside of the houses with long thorny sticks of ocotillo, rather like beating on a rug. Once knocked loose, the sickness is collected with 'jumping cholla' branches, surely one of the stickiest plants known to man. The cleansing takes all day. The sickness collected from the houses is disposed of in the same manner and perhaps at the same time as the sickness collected from the food. It is buried or driven into the ground. The cholla branches are burned" [Underhill et al. 1979:83].

The *a'ada* is also performed to remove from a village any "'poison' *(hiwhoina)* enclosed in a small tube [which] lodges itself somewhere within the ground of the victim village" [Underhill et al. 1979:87]. The shaman "works through the night to the accompaniment of other people's singing. . . . Once the sickness is located, usually near dawn, the medicine man goes to extract and destroy it. . . . Ocotillo sticks and cholla branches are used to extract sickness from every house, the idea being that a good deal of poison has escaped from the hidden tube. At the end of the day, this collected sickness is disposed of with the *a'ada* speech" [Underhill et al. 1979:87–88].

In all cases the *a'ada* ends by sending away the gathered sickness through the recitation of a specific prayer.

Aciwani
Zuni, *Southwest*

Zuni priests [Bunzel 1932b:549]. The religious life of a Zuni "is exclusively a series of participations in group rituals. No avenue is left open for individual approach to the supernatural" [Bunzel 1932a:544]. As such, through long years of training within their different sacred societies, some of these priests eventually become shamans. However, unlike the shamans of most other Native American cultures, the Zuni shamans do not operate outside the group ceremonial context.

Adówen

Iroquois, *Northeast*

Seneca personal chant [Tooker 1970:29]. "The rite of personal chant (adówen') is ancient with the people of the longhouse, who say it is one of the Four Ceremonies given them by the Creator" [Fenton 1942:18]. These are personal power songs. "The Personal Chant is composed of individual thanksgivings for one's wife, one's family, or the life of a 'friend,' and the singing of one of many songs which are to some extent the property of one's family and possibly of the clan. It is the last song sung by a warrior before death" [Fenton 1936:16]. That is, this is the death song sung by a warrior as he is being tortured to death by the enemy [Fenton 1942:19].

During certain periods of their annual religious ceremonies, such as the New Year Ceremony at midwinter and the Green Corn Festival at midyear, the Iroquois hold the *adówen* rite of personal thanksgiving and singing. For example, during the New Year Ceremony, the *adówen* is the second of four ceremonies held on the eighth day of this nine-day ritual.

Aglirktok

Mackenzie Eskimo, *Arctic Coast*

Kittergaryuit word meaning that something is under a taboo.

> In certain things a man may be aglirktok at birth and will have to remain so forever by reason of the tribe to which he belongs. . . . In other cases a man may become aglirktok automatically, as it were, by attaining a certain age or by having certain things that are in the nature of natural development happen to either himself or some relative or intimate associate. All these cases are fairly definite and are easily known and kept in mind with the result that offenses against the aglirktok condition are rare and the consequent misfortunes and

punishments assigned to a breach of conduct are not likely to occur.

> Under certain conditions, however, a man may become aglirktok without knowing it [e.g., contact with ghosts]. . . . It is in connection with a misfortune that comes without assignable cause that the shamans go into seance and inquire who it is that is aglirktok and why. . . . The shaman will usually after the performance of suitable ceremonial rites of the summoning of his familiar spirit find out that some hitherto unsuspected thing is really aglernaktok to the man in question and he announces this fact. . . . Aglernaktok is generally applied to things, conditions, and actions but may also apply to persons [Stefánsson 1914:126–127].

Agriculture medicine

Any prayer or ceremonial ritual that is performed to evoke supernatural powers to aid in the planting, growing, and harvesting of crops. Not all Native American cultures grow crops, but those that do most often have various rituals to ensure success. Such rituals are very prevalent in the arid Southwest, where growing conditions are nearly impossible.

In observing the success of the Zuni agriculturists, Cushing wrote in the last century: "We may smile at the superstitious observances of the Indian agriculturist, but when we come to learn what he accomplishes, we shall admire and I hope find occasion to imitate his hereditary ingenuity" [Cushing in Green 1979:253–254]. Every Zuni farmer has resorted to a corn priest who "is keeper of the sacred 'medicine' of his clan or order" [Cushing in Green 1979:254]. At the request of each farmer, the different corn priests (shamans) use special pigments prepared in a special manner to symbolically mark a prayer stick (see entry), which is then decorated with feathers, and to paint a small "section of cane filled with wild tobacco supposed to have been planted by rain, hence sacred" [Cushing in Green 1979:254]. Once the prayer stick is prepared, the shaman blows his breath upon the prayer plume and the sacred "cigarette" to imbue them with power and then gives them to the farmer.

> Taking them carefully in his left hand, the latter goes forth to his new field. Seeking a point in the middle of the arroyo below all his earthworks [irrigation dams], he kneels, or sits down on his blanket facing east. He then lights his cane cigarette and blows smoke toward the North, West, South, East, the Upper and the Lower regions. Then, holding the smoking stump and the plumed stick near his breast, he says a prayer. From the substance of his prayer. . . . We find he believes: that he has infused the consciousness of his prayer into the plumed stick; that with his sacred cigarette he has prepared a way "Like the trails of the winds and rains" (clouds). . . . Having taken the cloud-inspiring down of the turkey, the strength-giving plume of the eagle, the water-loving feather of the duck, the path-finding tails of the birds who counsel and guide Summer, having moreover severed and brought hither the flesh of the water-attracting tree [the prayer stick per se], which he has dipped in the god-denizened ocean, beautified with the very cinders of creation [smudged?], bound with strands from the dress of the sky-born goddess of cotton— he beseeches the god-priests of earth, sky and cavern, the beloved gods whose dwelling places are in the great embracing waters of the world, not to withhold their mist-laden breaths. . . . Thus thinking, thus believing, thus yearning, thus beseeching, (in order that the seeds of earth shall not want food for their growing, that from their growth he may not lack food for his living, means for his fortune) he this day plants, standing in the trail of the waters [arroyo], the smoke-cane and prayer-plume [Cushing in Green 1979:254–255].

See also *ckoyo, Ìsáné, Ivaxi, mamaga, sdanc gohat, tsanati, Uwanami,* weather shamans.

Ahalbŏcî
Seminole, *Southeast*
Literal translation: "little box" [Sturtevant 1954b:159]. Specially woven baskets, shaped like two flat envelopes, that were once used by shamans to store their medicine plants.

Another term for such a container is *ahălbóc-náknósî,* meaning "old little box." This second term is also used for the shamans' sacred cere-monial medicine bundle. "About seventy-five years ago there were nine different medicine bundles of various sizes in existence. Three of these were accidentally destroyed in fires, two of them together about 1895, and the other about 1908. Of the remainder, one is Cow Creek, as it always has been. The other five are today held by three Mikasuki medicine men, but this is a recent development. For a long time each was held by a different medicine man, who could if he wished hold an indepen-dent busk" [Sturtevant 1954a:33].

Within each of these bundles are up to six or seven hundred different medicines, each individ-ually wrapped in a piece of buckskin or white cloth. "The number of items in the bundles varies, since each was originally made up from the smaller individual war bundles of from one to five or six owners" [Sturtevant 1954a:34]. All of the contents are kept wrapped together in a complete deerskin (with head and legs attached) with the hair to the outside.

Ahayuta tikä
Zuni, *Southwest*
The Zuni Gods of War Society. The *Ahayuta* so-ciety is responsible for war medicine. The leader-ship of this society is delegated to the Bow Priests, and membership to the society requires the killing of an enemy. In fact, anyone who kills an enemy must join this society in order to pro-tect himself from the ghost of the deceased vic-tim. *Paetone* is this society's patron war *etowe* (fetish—see EONAH, p. 71), in the form of a shell. In addition there is also a sacred scalp at-tended to by the scalp chief. Heading this society is both a society chief and a battle chief.

The *Ahayuta* society also has powers for footraces and gambling.

Aheki
Shasta, *California*
Pain (see *pains*). This is also the term for a shaman's helping spirit [Kroeber 1925:302]. Since a "pain" is considered a form of power, it is

not unusual to find the same word being used for a spirit.

Ăhlukaĭliñgûk

West Alaska Eskimo, *Arctic Coast*
Literal translation: "the one who knows everything" [Nelson 1899:427]. Unalit term for a shaman who has the power to foretell the future.

Ahtcak

Cree, *Canadian Eastern Woodlands*
A force present in all living things. Mandelbaum [1940:251] translated the term as "soul." In this case it is the free soul (EONAH, p. 84)—the soul that enters the body at birth and leaves at death. It is also the soul that travels during a visionary experience and speaks with spirits. It resides along the nape of the neck.

Aichmudyim

Beothuck, *Canadian Eastern Woodlands*
Black Man or Red Indian Devil [Winter 1975:134–135]. This term is taken from a drawing rendered by Shananditti, the last survivor of the Beothuck culture in Newfoundland. It was one of several sketches drawn by her in the winter of 1828–1829. According to her note the man wore a beaver skin suit and had a large beard, even though the drawing itself depicted no beard. It is not clear whether this was a real person, such as a priest, or a supernatural being.

Aikha

Kwakiutl, *Northwest Coast*
Kitimat term for shaman [Lopatin 1945:63]. See also *hasha*.

Aishiuwinen

Ojibwa, *Canadian Eastern Woodlands*
Chippewa fetishes. These are described as

> sacred, personal articles kept by a person throughout his life as guardians against any harm or misfortune. They are made or obtained according to instructions received by a person in

his own fasting dream, or through a dream of a close relative or a we′e who presents the article to the person in infancy or childhood. An aišiu′winən may also originate as the result of a intelligence received by a conjurer at a shaking-tent seance. Such objects receive special care and handling, being hung on the loop of the cradle-board of a child and commonly hung over the bed of an adult. The person must never part with the object, and if it is accidentally destroyed, or worn out, it must be replaced with a counterpart. These articles were commonly taken to religious ceremonies or might be carried on a long journey, and upon the death of the person they were buried with him [Ritzenthaler 1953b:210–211].

See also *Wimesin Shkibijigen.*

Aithukatukhtuk

South Alaska Eskimo, *Arctic Coast*
Great Feast to the Dead [Hawkes 1914:31, 33]. This ceremony, sponsored by the relatives of a deceased person, requires the gathering of many gifts and much food, and it is therefore not conducted at regular intervals but rather when the relatives have completed their preparations. The ceremony may be conducted for more than one deceased person.

Another ceremony, the *Ailigi,* the Annual Feast to the Dead, is a yearly ceremony conducted right after the Bladder Feast (see *Tcaúiyuk*) in December to appease the spirits of those departed in the preceding year until their individual *Aithukatukhtuk* can be conducted.

The *Aithukatukhtuk* is attended by many outside of the village and lasts for four days. The excessive giving of gifts and feasting is done so that "the ghost [of the deceased] is furnished with such an abundance that it can never want in the world below" [Hawkes 1914:31] but also serves as a great incentive for guests to attend. Once the feast is started, no one can leave the village until the ceremony is complete. At the conclusion each *näskuk* (feast giver) calls out the name of his deceased relative, bidding that the individual be gone to the afterworld. As a final act of the ceremony, each of the visitors receives many gifts, usually new clothing made from the finest furs.

Aiyas kumomli
Washo, *Basin*

Antelope chief. This title is given to shamans who lead the deer and jackrabbit hunts. By 1926 no Antelope chiefs were living, but their use of hunting medicine was remembered and reported:

The Antelope chief sees some antelope in a dream. He reflects about it and goes to the place dreamt about in the mountains. He sees two or three head, then he knows his dream is true. He begins to talk to them. He does not tell anyone as yet, but keeps his own counsel and studies the matter himself. He continues dreaming three or four times. Then he begins talking to the antelope, taking a pipe. He wants to see what he can do. He looks at the antelope, he lets them see him walking alongside of them; they do not run away. He does this two or three times. Soon he tells the people to come together and says, "My people, I have dreamt truly or falsely, I don't know which. In the place I dreamt truly, you'll see them there this morning." He sends two boys to the place as scouts. They look for game and see ten or fifteen head feeding there together. The boys do not let the antelope see them. They go back and tell the chief, "Your dream is true, we saw a herd right there." That evening he studies the matter again while in bed. He dreams again and tells his people, "Well, I dreamt last night, I dreamt right before. I dreamt of two antelope last night, you fellows drove them into the corral, we all killed them and had something to eat." The old people answer: "Yes, if you dreamt right, we'll have meat, we'll try tomorrow to go after them."

The corral (mə´dap) is about an acre in size, with a chute leading to the entrance. Sagebrush is piled so high that the antelope cannot jump out. The men go to drive the antelope in. The chief stands just back of the corral, smoking his pipe. He says, "I'll stay home behind the corral. If I dreamt right, you'll drive them in and we'll kill them. If they get scared at you fellows, we can't help it; but I think we'll kill them easily in the corral." When the antelope are near, he says to the beasts, "Don't get scarred, come on easily now, don't get discouraged, listen to my words. We are making a home for you, you have come a great way." The antelope stop and look toward him. They are not afraid at all, but keep quiet, like sheep driven into a pen. Instead of scattering, they come into the sagebrush pen. He says to the people, "When I tell you, then is the time to shout." When all are in the pen, the people close up, and the chief bids them commence killing [Lowie 1939:324–325].

Aiyik-comi
Seminole, *Southeast*

Mikasuki (earlier: Miccosukee) shaman. This is the term used for "a common doctor" [Greenlee 1944:318]. The most powerful Mikasuki shamans are called *yaholi*. Other designations exist, such as *aiyik imifosi,* meaning "medicine grandfather" [Greenlee 1944:318]. The Mikasuki also distinguish between a "doctor" and a "medicine man." The latter are men who possess

a fragment of the old war medicine which [they] inherited from some clan member. . . . This war medicine is so powerful that it is not kept at the camps but is hidden away at the Green Corn dance grounds. It is used only at this festival. The medicine is a sort of powder, silverish in color, and kept in small buckskin bags. Some of the medicine is also clay-colored. The number of bags possessed by each medicine man varies, some having twelve, some only two. If the medicine should become scattered when the bags are opened at the Green Corn dance, it cannot be touched by hand but must be gently scraped into a neat pile with the quill taken from the wing of a buzzard. This is the war medicine which is taboo to women. . . . If a woman approached too near this strong medicine it would certainly knock her down. When this special medicine passes into new hands at the death of the medicine man, the old buckskin bags are destroyed and it is transferred to new ones. The inheritance of the sacred medicine bundles just referred to is strictly a clan affair [Greenlee 1944:317].

A boy who displays a willingness to undergo training is taught by an older shaman, even if they are not from the same clan. Shamans who train to heal undergo a lengthy period of instruction that is gradational. The levels of training are linked with the lunar calendar. For example, the first degree is known as *fubli hasi* (wind moon), named after the first month, and the tenth degree is known as *yobi hasi* (calm moon, no wind), named after the tenth month. It is not unusual for a shaman to train for ten years to advance only one degree [Greenlee 1944:318].

Illness is often diagnosed as soul loss. Soul loss usually occurs during dreaming. Certain types of dreams may also cause illness, such as dreams of fire or a bear, which cause fever. Dreams of certain animals are used to diagnose a patient's condition.

Healing treatments most often involve: (1) the use of an herbal concoction prepared by the shaman (administered in three ways—ingested by the patient, inhaled by the patient via steam, or blown on the patient through a tube; sometimes two or more methods are combined); (2) the singing of medicine songs when using this concoction on the patient; and (3) adherence to prescribed ritual procedures (for example, when gatherng medicine leaves from a bush, the picker must get leaves only from the north and east sides of the bush). In cases of severe illness a healing treatment may last as long as one week. Normal treatments range from one to three days.

Some herbs are used directly for power purposes. Tobacco, for instance, is used in a pipe to change the course of a hurricane. (This same usage is known among the Lakota of the Plains and many other Native American cultures as well.) A splinter taken from a tree recently struck by lightning contains "strong thunder medicine" [Greenlee 1944:324].

Akaka
Yavapai, *Southwest*
Dialectical variant: *kakaka* (Western Yavapai) [Gifford 1936:308]. Northeastern Yavapai an-thropomorphic spirits. This is a class of dwarf spirits, around 3 feet in height, that aid shamans. They are often heard at night but seldom seen, although one often sees their tiny footprints. They live in underground caves. "To see an akaka' go up vertical wall was sign someone would die shortly" [Gifford 1936:308].

The *akaka* travel through the air and can be heard drumming at night. "Kakaka' had power over deer; sometimes helped hunter, told him to go to certain place for deer" [Gifford 1936:308]. They also come to the aid of a shaman during a healing ceremony.

See also *basemacha*.

Akikita
Oto, *Plains*
A nineteenth-century shaman who acquired supernatural powers from a bullet, a Wolf, and four Buffalo spirits. All of his visions came as waking visions and were unsolicited. For this reason Whitman [1937:92, n. 2] noted that "had Akikita not been a great warrior who had proved his 'power,' his visions would have been received with reserve."

A bullet came to him as a youth shortly after he married. Of this incident his *hitakwa* (grandson) reported: "There was a big tree there, and he [Akikita] lay against it, thinking that he was hungry. Akikita was facing east. He heard a gun go off, way off. He could just barely hear it. Then he heard the bullet coming whistling, hum, hum. It said to Akikita, 'Akikita, I'm coming.' While he was sitting there the bullet rolled in front of him. It said: 'Akikita, I pity you. If you have any difficulty, any hard trouble, you must think about me. If you are in battle and think about me, they won't kill you. Get a little bell and tie it to your wrist'" [informant J. P. in Whitman 1937:88]. (Note: J. P. spoke very little English and had "priestly knowledge" [Whitman 1937:xvi]; therefore, his designation as *hitakwa*, mentioned above, was more an indicator of his spiritual relationship to Akikita, especially in light of the fact that, as Whitman mentioned,

J. P.'s father was Akikita's nephew [Whitman 1937:88, n. 3].)

From a white Wolf Akikita received doctoring powers. He got lost for four days trying to find his way home. After four days without food, he had a waking vision in which a white Wolf gave him a sacred wolfskin.

> He [Akikita] said the white wolf told him that if there was any sickness, he was to hang the hide up and the wind would blow four days and blow the sickness away. He told his people the white wolf said: "Whenever you are in war, put on the hide and go and fight." . . . After the war he came home. They found four bullets in each of the four corners of the hide, but not one had pierced it.
>
> And one time the whole tribe had small-pox. People died and died. They got Akikita to hang his hide up. It blew for four days hard. It blew away the sickness, and after that there was no more. That is proof of what had happened to him. The small-pox went no further [informant J. P. in Whitman 1937:90].

Thus both the bullet and the white wolf hide served as amulets to protect Akikita in warfare. From four Buffalo spirits he received additional healing powers, in particular for those shot in warfare. He would use special plants that had been shown to him in his vision when using his Buffalo powers [J. P. in Whitman 1937:92].

Alchuklash
Chumash, *Peninsula*
A type of shaman among the Chumash who has the acquired ability "to interpret the movements of the sun, moon and stars and utilize their power to influence the course of cosmic events" [B. Miller 1988:121]. The *alchuklash* act both as astronomers and astrologers by "studying both the heavens and the effect the heavens had on the life and destiny of the Chumash people" [B. Miller 1988:121]. Both men and women serve in this capacity.

Alektca
Creek, *Southeast*
Shaman (priest or doctor). These shamans are also known as *hilis-haya,* "medicine makers" [Swanton 1928:615]. They undergo a special training called the *poskita,* meaning "to fast," and they form a special class of men collectively called *isti poskalgi,* or "fasting men" [Swanton 1928:617]. Their training is usually conducted during the summer, and there are several courses of instruction, leading to greater powers. "After the fifth or sixth 4-day period [training] one could ask the teacher to put him through the 8-day session, and after that he could ask the teacher to put him through the 12-day session, which was the last" [Swanton 1928:618]. The shaman leading the training is called *Istepuccauchau thlucco,* "great leader" [Swanton 1928:620].

One of the first things they learn is how to treat gunshot wounds. Gunshot treatments are divided according to whether the injury is a flesh wound, a bowel wound, or a head wound. Eventually the *Istepuccauchau thlucco* will "teach the novice the proper treatment for any disease that the latter might desire to learn about" [Swanton 1928:618]. Those who become skilled wear certain items that indicate their powers. For example, a shaman proficient in treating gunshot wounds wears a buzzard feather, while one able to cure snakebites wears a fox skin. "The fox skin is worn because foxes catch and eat snakes showing that they, like the wearer of the fox skin, can conquer them. A person who can cure a snake bite also has a tobacco pouch made of opossum skin, because an opossum can kill and eat a snake like a fox" [Swanton 1928:618–619]. A shaman with extraordinary night vision wears an owl feather in his headdress. Those who can see anything in the dark also are known to paint a black circle around each eye in imitation of a raccoon. "If a man had been killed at night a doctor having this power would paint these circles about his eyes and track the murderer right to his own house. He could see his tracks 'like a spider's web' and follow them. . . . According to Silas Jefferson, a man with a 'skunk's pouch' was considered a great medicine man capable of charming any kind of animal" [Swanton 1928:621].

"At the head of the priesthood in each town was the hilis-haya or 'medicine maker,' who communicated the necessary spiritual qualities to the medicines at the annual busk, had general charge of the public health, protected all from ghosts, and so on" [Swanton 1928:620]. With regard to healing ceremonies, there are indicators that "the method of bestowing medical treatment seems to have changed progressively after first contact with the whites, the religious [shamanic] features becoming less and less pronounced and the features connected with the administration of the medicine more and more important" [Swanton 1928:622]. That is, more importance was given to the recitation of prescribed formulas that went with the administration of each herbal medicine and details such as the direction the patient should face during a healing, the shaman blowing his power into the medicine before administering it, etc. This same pattern applies to other cultures of the Southeast area, such as the Chickasaw, Natchez, and Cherokee.

"In earlier times it is said that the doctors claimed to have intercourse with good or bad spirits, but this personal side of the influences which they controlled appears to have gradually fallen out so that they were later of a general magic nature rather than through personal assisting spirits" [Swanton 1928:626]. Nevertheless, certain shamanic elements remain. For instance, cupping horns (see entry) and suction by mouth on the afflicted area are used to heal patients in addition to administering herbal concoctions. When a disease object is removed, it is displayed for all present to see.

Alexis
Natchez, *Southeast*

Late-seventeenth-century term given by M. Dumont (or Butel-Dumont) for shamans [Swanton 1911:80]. Dumont arrived in the Natchez area

in 1687 and later observed a Natchez "bleeding" treatment. He reported: "The *alexis* never use lancets to draw blood, but when they have a sick person who they think needs to be bled they take a splinter of flint with which they make many incisions into the flesh of the sick person in the place where he feels the pain. After that they suck the blood, either with the mouth or with the end of a bison horn, which they have sawed off and of which they have made a kind of cone *(cornet)* which they apply to the place. This is what they call a bleeding" [Dumont in Swanton 1911:80–81]. Of course, it can be assumed that the shaman was more than likely sucking out an intrusive disease object or evil spirit in this case. In observing their overall shamanic medicine, Dumont said that "they many times cure their sick as surely as the most skilled physicians could do" [Dumont in Swanton 1911:80].

In 1758 Le Page du Pratz also reported that similar techniques were being used by Natchez shamans. He observed patients being cut with splinters of flint and noted the cuts were always of a size that the shaman's mouth could cover. In fact, du Pratz himself, after a long period of suffering, submitted to treatment by Natchez shamans. His thigh pains were treated by incision and sucking, followed by the application of a poultice. He reported: "At the end of eight days I was in condition to go to the fort. I was entirely cured, for from the time I felt nothing more. What a satisfaction for a young man who finds himself in perfect health after having been compelled to keep to his house for the space of four months and a half, without having been able to go out for an instant!" [du Pratz in Swanton 1911:81].

Du Pratz was healed a second time by a Natchez shaman. A French physician had recommended a treatment with fire for his "lachrymal fistula in the left eye." Fearing this treatment, he seized upon the opportunity to be treated by a Natchez doctor instead. In this instance the shaman treated his eye daily for eight days, putting a compound steeped in water into the eye. And once again the Natchez treatment was effective. Subsequently, du Pratz echoed Dumont's earlier observation, especially after seeing several Frenchmen healed when French doctors had failed: "These physicians have made a great number of other cures, the narration of which would demand a special volume; I am satisfied to report only these three, which I have just cited [not included here], to let it be seen that the maladies which are elsewhere [among French physicians] regarded as almost incurable, which are cured only at the end of a long period and after great suffering being experienced, maladies of this kind, I say, are cured without painful operation and in little time by the native doctors of Louisiana" [du Pratz in Swanton 1911:83].

Praise for the shamans' healing abilities was also reported by de la Vente: "I have seen many who have received 4 or 5 bullet or arrow wounds through the stomach and who are so perfectly cured of them that they do not suffer any inconvenience. . . . Through the knowledge of simples which they have received from their fathers they will cure hands, arms, and feet that our best surgeons would not hesitate to cut" [de la Vente in Swanton 1911:83].

Alini
Miwok, *California*
Literal translation: "people different from us" [Gifford n.d. a:24]. Central Miwok general classification for shamans. Shamans are classified according to their abilities or powers. Some examples recorded by Gifford [n.d. a:24] in 1914 are:

1. *alinī nukai*—shaman who has powers to control rain (sings accompanied by cocoon rattles). (See *sokot*.)
2. *alinī mohlemeh*—shaman for bear songs (sings).
3. *alini tshipamalu*—shaman who is possessed by the spirit of a grizzly bear (does not sing).
4. *alini hiwehyi*—shaman who diagnoses diseases (sings and dances).
5. *alini aselmeh*—coyote shaman (sings).

6. *alini wakelmeh*—rattlesnake shaman (sings).
7. *alini hiwaiyasi*—shaman who has the power to find lost objects (sings).
8. *alini ulemeh*—shaman who has the power to increase the acorn productivity.
9. *alini uwemeh*—shaman who has the power to increase the deer productivity.

These different types of shamans are called upon when needed. For example, the *alinī nukai* is called upon to help the Miwok grow vegetables out of season. A one-night singing and rattling ceremony brings four days and nights of rain. These shamans can also bring wind.

The following is an account of how Susie Williams's father became an *alinī aselmeh*. He had been sick for about a month and under the treatment of a *koyabi* (sucking doctor—see EONAH, p. 138) before dying one day around noon.

He seemed dead all night. They were crying. Next day about 9 they were going to burn [him]. Everybody ready. Wood piled. They took him to pile to burn him. Put him on top pile ready to burn. They lit fire from four sides. Wood started to blaze. When wood near him started to burn he started to move shoulders. Hands and feet tied. Tom's uzumati brother got there and said, "Hurry up and get him out, he is alive." They got him out of fire as told. After they took him out and laid him beside fire he sat up. . . . When he got up he told his mother, "Go open that ground over there, and water and rattlesnake will come out. Hurry up. You'll see rattlesnake come out of dry ground as soon as you open." His mother scratched ground with fingers, and while she was scratching it, water just jumped out. Right after it came rattlesnake. As soon as rattlesnake came after water, Susie's father jumped up and ran. He ran all over hills hollering like crazy man. His father and brothers chased him but couldn't catch him. Blood coming out of nose like water. They finally caught him after a while, on that same day. . . . After they caught him he sing coyote song. He raise up his left hand after they caught him. He was inside the umutshu. As soon as he raised up his hand, something, a devil or coyote [spirit], threw a sokossa [also *sohkosa*—see *sokot*], cocoon rattle, into his left hand. As soon as he caught that he sang right away. He sang that all night. While he was singing, coyotes came and walked around the umutshu by Harvard [name of location]. Next morning he went out into hills singing. Lots of coyotes following him, running behind him calling. . . . Everybody was afraid of him on account of the coyotes following him. Four big, ugly coyotes were following him with blood all over them. . . . After he stopped singing he commenced to talk to captain [of Kohtohplana]. He said, "I'm just doing this singing to shake the dust off myself. I did not know what was going to happen to me before till they got me dead and got me back again." . . . He said nothing when he got up to go home. Just got up singing, and went out. Soon as he got out, other coyotes holler and jump around. They come right up to him and follow him home. . . . After he got home, he went out next day and got those black rocks (*sikā*) which set people crazy if they catch them. They are also called coyote rocks. These rocks move from one house to another during the night, but return to Susie's father's house before morning. In each house they make a hissing noise, or noise like cat spitting. Sometime the rock would not go back, but would stay in other house. Then people go tell Susie's father his rock there and he go over and get him. That's what he did when he got started [John Kelly translating for Susie Williams in Gifford n.d. a:18–20].

This particular shaman could cure sicknesses caused by the coyote. In addition, because he had dreamed of the rattlesnake while on his funeral pyre, he could handle those snakes without harm. "Whenever he saw rattlesnake he used to grab it; used to keep him. They never hurt him. First one he keep a long time. After a while he turned them loose and then catch more. When people did not believe he could handle rattlesnake he used to go out and get them. Susie and Tom [Williams] don't know how he got power over coyote. He did not know himself" [John Kelly translating for Susie Williams in Gifford n.d. a:21].

An *alinī wakelmeh* can also handle rattlesnakes and can doctor people for rattlesnake bites. In doctoring, he sings over the patient and touches the patient's body all over with a long string of rattlesnake rattles. However, *alinī wakelmeh* do not have the power to keep people from being bitten by rattlesnakes.

During some of the Miwok large ceremonials, such as the four-day *Kaleha* Dance, these shamans display their ability to control rattlesnakes. Their songs used to charm the rattlesnakes are different from their curing songs. Tom Williams spoke to Gifford [n.d. a:25] of a cousin who was such a shaman. This man could call to a rattlesnake and have it come to him and coil up in his lap. In order to retain his rattlesnake power, he had to abstain from eating meat, which is a common taboo for an *alinī wakelmeh*. When somebody killed a rattlesnake, blood would come out of this man's nose, and he would cry and say, "My friend got killed" [Gifford n.d. a:26]. Eventually he was killed by another shaman. "Tuyuku put rattlesnake poison on him. He had no doctor. But the way they found out afterwards was that his belly swelled up and broke, and lots of rattlesnakes, large and small, came out of his belly. Those who were holding him when he died and crying over him all ran when the snakes came. They buried him at Kôtôplana" [Gifford n.d. a:26–27].

Tom Williams also told of another cousin who had received rattlesnake medicine from a two-headed rattlesnake.

At the house where he is stopping when he has that breakfast there are rattlesnakes hanging all over the place; little ones and big ones—the house is just full of them. When he sings, all rattlesnakes come together toward him, all come to him. He had elderberry cane with 2 headed rattlesnake wrapped around it all the time. He handles cane with either hand. When he holds cane, one head is at top of cane, other on his wrist, wrapped around. It is a black rattlesnake. . . . Then he kneeled down, took the largest rattlesnake he had and threw him 20 feet from him. He had a rattle of 6 cocoons tied on chaparral. After throwing snake he sings and shakes rattle. The rattlesnake stands up on his tail, waves back and forth, and rattles at same time. He comes back to the boy slowly, with half his length in air. When he gets to him he coils up between his legs, stops rattling [John Kelly translating for Tom Williams in Gifford n.d. a:36–37].

Susie Williams's aunt was an *alini ulemeh* who received her powers in a dream. "She got song in dream. After she sang she went to sleep again that same night. Then she dreams again about that [acorn] tree. 'That tree you can get acorns on that tree any time you want, summertime or wintertime, year around.' The people did not know where she was getting acorns. They could not find any place, yet she was still getting them. People were asking where she got them. She won't tell. She say, 'I get them here and there on the ground under each tree.' She did that the year around. . . . She used rattle sokosa when she sang at night. She sang four times in night" [John Kelly translating for Susie Williams in Gifford n.d. a:27–28].

Allen, Frank
Twana, *Northwest Coast*
A Skokomish man born circa 1858 of a Skokomish father and a Dungeness Klallam mother. He died on April 25, 1945. The following is his account of how, around the age of fourteen, he obtained Loon power for gambling:

I have found tamánamis [power] by myself. When I was a boy my father trained me hard. My back is scarred today from where they took me out of bed early in the morning and broke a hole in the ice in the wintertime and put me in to bathe. You have to get up early when you are young and keep clean to get tamánamis. And then they would take me to lonely places and leave me.

Well, I was at Rock Point one time, and a loon *[qoola]*, came right up to me and I went to sleep. And that loon took me to a lake . . . where he had

a big house. And he took me in the house. . . . And he went and got four slaha' bones and gave one pair to his wife and one pair to himself. And he gave me a song. . . .

But I always had fine luck at slahal with that power. Qoola brought me lots of goods at one time. . . . He looked like a person in my vision, when I went to sleep. . . . He comes to me once in a while and talks to me, summer or winter. When I fell down and hurt my back last winter [circa 1936] I thought I was going to die. But my qoola came to me when I lay sick . . . my power came and lit to me, and his voice was just like a person. He told me, "You're not going to die." And then I knew I'd get well. Power doesn't come and talk to you that way if you're going to die. When you're hurt and going to die your power won't come near you however much you want it [Frank Allen in Elmendorf 1993:182–183].

Aɬxelay
Wishram, *Plateau*
Literal translation: "moves himself" [Spier and Sapir 1930:239]. This term refers to the training a youth goes through in preparation for a vision quest. Training begins around six to twelve years of age when the youth is sent out to spend a night in isolation—a process that is repeated over time.

"Many of them got more than one spirit at a time; this made them especially ill and unstrung. But they were accordingly stronger in the future, and correspondingly greater shamans. A shaman was respected according to the number of spirits he had, and paid in proportion. Some had as many as five or six familiars" [Spier and Sapir 1930:240].

Amulet
A readily portable and usually small object worn or carried by its owner, with the understanding that it possesses the power to bring him good fortune, protect him, and imbue him with powers or qualities not naturally his own. The amulet is a symbol or token of a supernatural being, who

is pleased by seeing it worn and grants his protection and aid to the wearer.

Amulets can also consist of some body part of an animal, worn with the understanding that the wearer will obtain the desirable characteristics of that animal to supplement his own abilities.

Unlike the fetish (see entry), an amulet is generally not considered to be either alive or the dwelling place of a spirit. The nature of an amulet most often depends on the vision instructions received by the maker, but this is not always the case. For example, "the amulets of the Inuit are efficacious not of their own right but through their association with spirits. In most Inuit cases, the spirits are the ghosts of the animals from which the amulets have been made" [Merkur 1987:172].

An individual typically obtains his amulet from a shaman, who empowers it. I observed one Lakota shaman "catching" an amulet from the air. In this instance, the shaman had the person, who asked for an amulet, roll fresh sage into a ball, about the size of a tennis ball. This was handed to the shaman, who held it above his head in his right hand and prayed. When he brought the ball of sage back down and opened it, it contained a small rock in the center; this rock was now sacred. In a similar manner it has been noted that the Inuit (Eskimo) shamans living along the Kobuk River in Alaska, when asked for a powerful amulet, often pull it from their body for the recipient [Lantis 1947:88, n. 24].

Some examples of Eskimo amulets were described by Merkur: "At Point Barrow, on the northern Alaskan coast, the skin of a golden eagle was considered an excellent whaling amulet. Rather than an empty skin, a stuffed eagle might be carried in the boat. When the hunt was successful, the eagle skin was stuck in the stern on the voyage back to shore. Similar data obtain from Canada and Greenland. The Copper Inuit, in the western portion of the Northwest Passage, believed that parts of an eagle's beak or claws give good fortune in all kinds of hunting. In West Greenland, the beak

of an eagle served as an amulet that was customarily attached to the harpoons used in whaling" [Merkur 1987:173–174].

"The amulet ideology is indicated in a tradition from Repulse Bay in the central Canadian Arctic that tells of a man who prepared arrows from caribou-antlers in a special fashion which made the arrows impossible to extract once they were embedded in his enemy's flesh" [Boas in Merkur 1989:13].

From among the Tanaina in southern Alaska, Osgood [1937:176] reported: "Amulet-stones are described as being alive; as a rock with a rattle; a smooth stone with a flattened stomach and a rounded back which if put on a table would roll about. They have two little holes for eyes and another as an anus. They leave a track when they move.... One amulet, seen in the Kachemak Bay area, has passed through several generations into the owner's hands. It is of worn, irregular shape, has the appearance of stone but is apparently not, since it is light and has something rattling inside of it which is said to be a young one born about twenty-five years ago. Another, at Kenai, is more obviously stone and the owner said that it is dead probably as he had not fed it for over two years."

Rasmussen [1969:184] reported that among the Eskimo "the longer an amulet has been worn, the greater is its power." Moreover, "the mystic power of an amulet is not invariably at the service of the person wearing it; the actual object for instance, may be given away to another, but its inherent activity will not operate on his behalf unless he has given something in return.... There are amulets for various qualities, such as making the wearer a good walker, preserving him from danger on thin ice, keeping him warm in the coldest weather, giving extra stability to his kayak, and so on" [Rasmussen 1969:136]. He observed young girls wearing amulets for their children yet to come—a swan's beak to ensure that the first child is a male; the head of a ptarmigan to ensure her son will have speed and endurance in hunting caribou; a bear's tooth for powerful jaws and sound digestion; an ermine pelt (with skull attached) for strength and agility; and a little dried flounder to protect against strangers. Rasmussen collected hundreds of amulets during his many expeditions in the Arctic region. Other examples he noted included parts of the tern for skill in fishing; the foot of a loon for skill in handling a kayak; the head and claw of a raven for a good share of meat in all hunting; the teeth of a caribou for skill in hunting the caribou; and a strip of skin from a salmon for producing fine, strong stitches when sewing [Rasmussen 1969:185–186].

For other examples see *Akikita, angoak, ârnuaq, chikauvasi, hodui, inugwak, ipétes, ize, okawafe, talbixw*.

Amuukyat
Yavapai, *Southwest*
An early-nineteenth-century shaman who received his power mainly from two spirits named Komwidapokuwia and Skatakaamch. On one occasion Christ appeared to him in a vision. During another vision the Sun spirit "cut little holes in the right side of my chest, and put medicine in the holes" [Amuukyat in Gifford 1936:312]. When he returned from this vision, he said "[I] knelt on the ground, and pressed with my knees and hands as I sang a song. When I lifted my hands, green sprouts of isimakanyach [dark-medicine] plant came out of the ground" [Amuukyat in Gifford 1936:312].

He wore a *chikauvasi* (see entry) of glass beads that were made according to instructions received from Skatakaamcha. He used this in his healing ceremonies. (In former times such necklaces were used for war medicines.) From Komwidapokuwia he received a song "for curing all kinds of illness" [Gifford 1936:311]. Eventually she taught him many songs, and he also learned songs from Skatakaamcha. Skatakaamcha is one of the principal guardian spirits of all shamans throughout their history, and therefore during this vision Amuukyat reported that "all these old shamans appeared to instruct me" [Amuukyat in Gifford

1936:312]. Skatakaamcha taught him to use a drum and rattle during his healing ceremonies.

"In 1932, Amuukyat had bullroarer [EONAH, p. 42] made from pine struck by lightning which he no longer used. Formerly used it to treat sick. When summoned, he whirled bullroarer to send his power ahead to sick person. Then went himself, taking bullroarer. Swung it outside sick person's house, and clouds, lightning, and thunder came from east" [Gifford 1936:309].

During a healing ceremony he would sing and shake his gourd rattle with his right hand. He would hold his left hand aloft and then touch the sick person with it to make him well. "Singing for a sick person takes four nights. I sing songs Komwidapokuwia taught me. She taught me many songs. At San Carlos I sang for people nearly dead with heart trouble and other troubles. When they were nearly dead and had only two or three breaths more, I sang and revived them" [Amuukyat in Gifford 1936:311].

"Amuukyat did not scarify in curing except for a boil or carbuncle, which he washed with decoction of juniper leaves. He cured by singing, not by sucking. Chorus of singers which assisted him was 'new invention' old shamans did not have" [Gifford 1936:313]. In 1932 he recorded many of his songs on phonograph cylinders, which are now at the Museum of Anthropology, University of California, Berkeley.

See also *basemacha*.

Anaalutaa
East Greenland Eskimo, *Arctic Coast*
Ammasalik (or Angmagsalik) shaman's spirit-calling stick. During shamanic ceremonies the shaman usually has an assistant play the *qilaain* (drum, see entry), while he taps out a rhythm on the floor. This tapping, typically made with a simple wooden stick, is used both to call the spirit and to send the spirit away.

In other cases the shaman makes a tapping noise with a *makkortaa* [Thalbitzer 1914:642]. "It consists of a round, flat piece of black skin, from five to five and a half centimeters in diameter, which is held tightly in the hollow of the hand, while it is struck or rapped-on with a carved wooden stick with the other hand. By the aid of this little instrument the angakok [EONAH, p. 15] produces a loud rhythmic knocking" that calls forth his guardian spirits [Thalbitzer 1931:434].

Ane himu
Hopi, *Southwest*
Literal translation: *ane,* "hard, well, strongly, very," and *himu,* "something" (or "what" when used to ask a question) [Loftin 1986:181]. This term is translated as "very something" but can also be translated as "Mighty Something" given the fact that the Hopi consider *ane himu* to be the foundation of all creation. "*A'ne himu* refers to that which the Hopi experience as anonymous and autonomous or, as Kennard notes, that which is 'powerful but unknown'" [Loftin 1986:181].

Prayers of supplication are offered to *ane himu,* and, when experienced, *ane himu* is felt to be sacred. However, "the Hopi may participate in the sacred only to the extent that they align their breath with the cosmic breath that is 'very something'" [Loftin 1986:183]. At the core its attributes remain a mystery, and the Hopi are thus intentionally vague when commenting on *ane himu.*

Angakussarfiks
Polar Eskimo, *Arctic Coast*
Power caves. These are special caves in the Smith Sound area to which a novice shaman, male or female, goes to acquire a helping spirit. Such caves are located through mystical means. The novice "goes alone at night to a place where the rock is hollow, and resounds when trod upon: that is, to a cavernous cliff. He walks straight toward this. If he is to be an angakoq [shaman—see EONAH, p. 13], he will walk into a hole or cave in the hill; if not, he will strike the face of the cliff. When he has entered, the cavern closes upon him. When it re-opens, he must go out, else he will be shut up forever" [Kroeber 1900:303].

Within this cave there is "a stone with an even surface and a smaller one; the angakok apprentice having to grind the first with the second until Tornarsuk [see entry; see also *tornrak,* EONAH, p. 286] announced himself in a voice arising from the depths of the earth" [Rink in Kroeber 1900:304].

Angalkuk
Yupik, *Arctic Coast*
Shaman. These shamans are renowned for their shamanic flights. "One or two [informants] have said that they saw a shaman literally soar into the sky during the course of a séance, while others have described feats of levitation that would carry a shaman from one end of a kashim [ceremony house] to the other or cause him to float and fall in spurts across the ground outside, like a ptarmigan in flight. Elders have described to me other feats as well—sitting unharmed in a pot of boiling water, for example, or shitting icicles, or causing walrus tusks to soften into a malleable sort of plastic, or causing boulders too heavy to be moved by ordinary men to come crashing through the skylight of a kashim" [Carey 1992:137–138].

Angaxkox
West Alaska Eskimo, *Arctic Coast*
Dialectical variant: *angatkok* (EONAH, pp. 15–16). Nunivak shaman. A person became a shaman via dreams.

> A young man would begin to see spirits in his night dreams, or he would encounter them as he traveled alone across the tundra. As the disturbing dreams increased, he became more and more ill. He seemed to waste away. Then the old people would get their heads together and decide that he was becoming a shaman. An old man would give the young person, male or female, a drum and would help him to practice his new powers. How much formal instruction there was and just what it consisted of could not be learned. . . .
> When a shaman, young or old, saw one or more of the spirits, he often received a song, but

not always. Normally he would receive some specific power: to drive away bad weather, to prevent illness or witchcraft, to bring the herring, and so on. He would carve an amulet or make up a song to represent the spirit and its power. He would give amulets with curative power to patients as part of his doctoring [Lantis 1946:200].

Male shamans often give public demonstrations of their powers, but female shamans rarely do. Shamanic feats include: "being burnt, flying up, going under the ground (via the fire pit), going under the sea, putting a stick through his flesh, getting loose when tied, sucking through a walrus tusk as through a hollow horn, bending stone arrow points and knife blades, extracting an arrow point without leaving a scar. . . . One demonstration by a mature shaman went as follows: He 'died,' that is, went into a trance or became unconscious in the kazigi [ceremonial house]. He was taken out and shavings heaped all around and over him. While he was being burnt, his voice could be heard like that of a walrus. After the people had returned to the men's house, the shaman tapped on the skylight and came in, whole again" [Lantis 1946:201].

Anggou
Delaware, *Northeast*
"The generic designation for the condition of being blessed with a spiritual revelation through a vision" [Speck 1931:51].

Angoak
North Alaska Eskimo, *Arctic Coast*
Tikerarmiut (at Point Hope) term for charm [Rainey 1947:274]. The *angoak* is usually carried (for example, in a hunting bag) or stored in a special place, such as the bow of a whaling boat or attached to a towline. A charm worn on one's clothing or body (an amulet) is called *tupitkaq* (or *tupitqaq*) and consists of such items as the nose skin of a polar bear, the head of a loon, the skin of a weasel, the tail of a wolverine, beads, etc. [Rainey 1947:253, 272]. However, the terms are now used interchangeably.

It is interesting to note that the Tikerarmiut have two classes of *angoak*—charms that "work with things of dead people" and charms that "work with things of a woman at childbirth." A person obtains charms from only one class, for the other class is harmful or *kiruq* (taboo). "One whose charms are beneficially affected by women's belongings might die if a bit of blubber taken from a grave were placed in his food. One whose charms are derived from the property of the dead would become ill if he entered a house where a woman had recently had a child, or would be unsuccessful in a whale hunt if a menstruating woman had sewed his whale boat skin" [Rainey 1947:272].

Animism
A philosophical term used to refer to the belief that objects can be animated by being occupied by a spirit or are themselves spiritual beings. Early anthropologists assigned animism to their category of "primitive" people, and it was seen as an early stage in the philosophical evolution of human beings. Consequently, this term also carries with it the derogatory connotation that Native American cultures were less developed because of their belief in animism.

In dealing with Native Americans, some scholars also use the term *animatism* to refer to the belief, found among many Native American cultures, that all inanimate objects themselves have consciousness. Animatism is "a doctrine of universal vitality" or "a general animation of nature" [Osgood 1937:169].

Ansote
Kiowa, *Plains*
A nineteenth-century shaman. Parsons wrote of an incident in which Ansote was called upon to ward off an impending tornado: "He put the cord attached to *taime* [Grandfather, referring to their Sun Dance ceremonial bundle] around his neck, and carried it in his arms. Wearing a buffalo robe,

Edward S. Curtis, Prayer to the Mystery, *1907. Photogravure.*

buffalo moccasins, he held his buffalo robe from his body, both arms widespread, and ran around his tipi four times, and sat down at the tipi entrance; again he did this. He spoke to Red Horse [a spirit], holding out his arms [palms downward]. It hailed and rained. Not a tipi was left standing (except one little one). Mother shoved us children under the beds. It would have been worse had not Ansote made his medicine" [Pitdogede in Parsons 1929:109].

Antu
Yokuts, *California*
Also: *angtu* [Kroeber 1925:511], *antuw* (EONAH, p. 16). Shaman. Shamans receive their power through a series of dreams in which a guardian spirit appears and gives the novice instructions on certain songs to sing, certain talismans to use, etc. Most persons receive some minor power via dreams. However, the more a person dreams, "the greater his knowledge of the occult would become, and the bond between the individual and the supernatural world increasingly strengthened. In other words, the difference between a shaman's power and that of a non-professional was one of quantity rather than of quality" [Gayton 1930:389].

With regard to healing, most illnesses are diagnosed as being caused by object intrusion. For that reason Yokuts shamans are continually suspected of causing illnesses, especially if they lose several patients. In most cures the shaman makes an incision on the body at the location of the disease object and then sucks out the object. "The intruding object was always exhibited upon its extraction by the curing shaman; it might be a few hairs, finger-nail clippings, insects, a blood clot, the moustache of a mountain lion, and so on" [Gayton 1930:390].

Anukite ihanblapi
Teton, *Plains*
Literal translation: "they dream of face-on-both-sides" [Powers 1977:58]. The Double-Woman society of the Oglala. This is a society of women

that have dreamed of the Double-Woman spirit. Men who dream of Double-Woman and join the society live as berdaches (EONAH, p. 30). "The Double-Woman appears in a number of conventional forms [in vision]: as a person with two faces, one beautiful, the other ugly; a single beautiful woman, most often a temptress; or two women who represent alternative answers to a single question, often of a divinatory nature. The two women often change into black-tailed deer at the conclusion of dreams. Thus a synonym for Double-Woman is *Sinte sapela win* ['black-tailed woman']" [Powers 1977:58–59].

The female shamans of this society "are wakan [holy—see EONAH, pp. 305–306], but not regarded as exactly normal; they are always running after men and have unusual powers to seduce them" [Wissler 1912b:93]. These shamans are particularly adept at *wakan* quill work. "This is a powerful cult and many women when in the trance get power to make very effective shields and other war medicines" [Wissler 1912b:94].

Aouten
Micmac, *Canadian Eastern Woodlands*
See *oüahich*.

Aoutmoin
Micmac, *Canadian Eastern Woodlands*
An early-seventeenth-century term for shaman [Mavor and Dix 1989:141]. See also *bohinne*.

Äpaxkumikäk
Potawatomi, *Midwest*
See *pextcigosan*.

Aperketek
East Greenland Eskimo, *Arctic Coast*
See *Tornarsuk*.

Apershaq
Iglulik Eskimo, *Arctic Coast*
Plural: *apershät* [Rasmussen 1929:113]. Literal translation: "one that exists to be questioned." A term used to refer to a shaman's helping spirit.

However, such spirits are more often referred to as *torngraq* (see entry).

(Note: This term, taken from a secondary source, was incorrectly given as *aperfat* in EONAH, p. 16.)

Arnagtoq

West Greenland Eskimo, *Arctic Coast*
A special term used for a shaman who has the power to transform himself into the guise of any animal he chooses. Birket-Smith [1924:452] told of a man who had turned himself into a reindeer, a fish, a seal, and a dog, among other things.

Ârnuaq

West Greenland Eskimo, *Arctic Coast*
Dialectical variants: *arnoaq* (East Greenland Eskimos) [Thalbitzer 1914:629]; *arngoaq* (Labrador); *anruaq* (Kangianermiut and Ungalardlermiut); and *änroq* (Nunivârmiut) [Rasmussen 1941:23 and 36]. Plural: *ârnuat* [Birket-Smith 1924:447]. Personal amulet (see entry). Before being used, an amulet must be consecrated with a spell, and then it is treated as a living person. Amulets are given to children early on to wear as protection and to give them special abilities. Most adults have several. Any item can serve as an *ârnuaq* as long as it has magical power. The teeth of a fox, the claws of an eagle, and the dried fetus of a dog are said to contain special power. Often Eskimo amulets are wooden human figures. The most common stone amulets are made from beadlike stones or pebbles and are called *kalilernerit* [Thalbitzer 1914:630].

One acquires the characteristics of the animal or object from which the amulet is made. From the fox amulet one obtains the ability to be cunning; straps used to tie up shamans during power ceremonies are used as amulets to make young hunters able kayakers; pieces of whetting stones make one invulnerable; and a raven's beak makes one lucky at finding drifting carcasses.

Among the Ammasalik (or Angmagsalik) of East Greenland, the *teaawta* is a common amulet worn on the arm; it is usually made from a strip of seal skin and decorated with beads. Women wear the amulet on their right wrists, while men wear one on the upper part of each arm. "Similar objects are known from the other Eskimo regions" [Thalbitzer 1914:627].

The Ammasalik have many different types of amulets. For example, the "nail of the fourth finger of a dead man might also be used as amulet if placed on the breast or back; on the approach of a disease during sleep, i.e., the attack of an evil thought or spirit, the nail grows unseen and on account of its hardness and sharpness prevents the disease from penetrating within. . . . [Or] when people become ill, one may help them by putting into their amulet-harness, armlets or hair-tops, certain small Crustacea (*eqitartin*) from the beach or bees. . . . owing to the death of a near relative [women] insert amulets under the armlet [mentioned above] or ankleband [another amulet], either the dried gum from a fox's jaw or whiskers of foxes. Against evil words or slander they also use amulets which are stuck into the hairtop. . . . When a woman is with child an amulet is inserted right above her vulva in order to protect the child" [Thalbitzer 1914:627].

These are but a few of the personal amulets found among these people. Amulets also appear in houses, in tents, on kayaks and umiaks (multipassenger boats), on hunting weapons, and in other such places. In some cases a song is sung while the amulet is used, as when a harpoon containing an amulet is launched.

As a general rule amulets work only if they are present. However, among these Eskimos a man who finds himself in a dangerous situation without his *ârnuaq* may call upon it for aid nonetheless. These medicines differed from ordinary amulets in that there was a special bond between the *ârnuaq* and its owner, such that the owner did not have to have physical possession of his *ârnuaq* in order to use it; rather, he could call upon its power from any place at any time. In addition, an "*ârnuaq* might do duty as a *pôq,* or guise, and enable its owner to assume the guise of the *ârnuaq*" [Birket-Smith 1924:447]. Thus there was more of an alliance between the spirit of the *ârnuaq* and its owner than is found in most amulet use.

For other examples see *oka wafe.*

Arrow swallowing
Pueblo, *Southwest*
See *Shotikianna.*

Asbathlqo
Twana, *Northwest Coast*
A type of ritual impurity caused by "contact with menstrual blood" [Elmendorf 1960:492]. Such "contact" can be as slight as the mere sight of or physical nearness of a menstruant. This type of impurity is "intensely distasteful to guardian spirits" [Elmendorf 1960:493], such that it puts "a temporary stop to any activities concerned with or requiring support from supernatural powers" [Elmendorf 1960:437]. In order to purify oneself, one must resort to intensive bathing and scrubbing of the body with doubled-up yew (or other conifer) boughs, fasting, and/or purging. The desired purification is usually accomplished within one or two days.

Asenapäneniwagi
Fox, *Midwest*
Rock spirits. This word is a compound of *aseni,* meaning "stone," and *neniwagi,* meaning "men," where "-äpä- would seem to mean 'male' in accordance with the general principles of Algonquian philology; but would seem to be redundant" [Michelson 1927:123].

Because spirits appeared in human guise to shamans, the Fox often simply added the source of the spirit to the stem "men." For example, *metegwineniwagi* literally means "tree men" and refers to the spirits of the trees.

Asetcuk
North Alaska Eskimo, *Arctic Coast*
A renowned Tikerarmiut shaman who died around the turn of the twentieth century. He was capable of making shamanic flights through the air. Around 1880 while visiting the Diomede Islands, Asetcuk was asked to take a shamanic flight to St. Lawrence Island to check into the whereabouts of a man named Ungoariuk who had gone there to trade but had not returned on time. "To do this, he chose a certain evening, instructed all the people of the camp to remain indoors and to keep their dogs tied. Then he had his host tie him up in his usual manner when flying. He always removed his trousers and parka and arranged one of his reindeer socks in the position of a gee-string. Then he put a boy's trousers over his shoulders, and had his hands tied behind him, with one end of the binding thongs attached to some heavy object like an adze head. The lights were dimmed and he 'got his power' by walking around his drum. But this first night he did not actually fly to St. Lawrence. It would be dangerous to expose too much of one's power in the presence of other *angatkoks* [shamans]. However, bound in readiness for flight and in possession of his power, he was able to see what was happening on St. Lawrence. He reported that the boy was all right" [Rainey 1947:277].

However, the next day the lost man's father saw an ill omen, and Asetcuk decided to make a real flight that evening.

On this occasion he was so anxious to start that he wasted no time. When one of the supposedly extinguished lamps in the house flared up the people saw him already in the air. Of course he then dropped back again. After another false start, when his dangling adze head caught on a pan near the skylight, he finally was off through the ventilator shaft. He always flew with one knee drawn up and arms outstretched; in the air wings sprouted from his shoulder blades and his mouth grew to extend outward and up to his tattoo markings. . . . Later Asetcuk reached St. Lawrence Island. After circling the houses to peer in through the skylights he saw Ungoariuk lying on the floor of one of them. Asetcuk placed his face close to the skylight so that Ungoariuk could recognize him.

When Asetcuk returned to the Diomedes, his power was so strong he could not descend. He had to fly around inside the house so that the breath of all the people inside "who had no spirits" could help him "get down." After that he was unconscious for a while, but the people put his drum into his hands and gradually he restored himself to his normal condition by beating it. Asetcuk told the one-eyed man that his son was all right and would return. Very soon he did arrive at the Diomedes. When he saw Asetcuk he said he had seen his face in a vision at the skylight of the house on St. Lawrence. So everyone knew he was a great *angatkok*. News of him spread all over the region [Rainey 1947:277–278].

Like most powerful shamans Asetcuk could also use his powers to kill a person. In order to do this, he "stroked his own left arm, pulled it inside himself, and thrust it out through his own mouth. If he pointed this hand at anyone that person would be killed at once" [Rainey 1947:278].

Ashiwanni
Zuni, *Southwest*
Collective term for this culture's fifteen different rain societies [Parsons 1933:16]. However, not all weather shamans (called "rain priests" among the Zuni) are members of a rain society. In her 1918 census of the Zuni, anthropologist Elsie Parsons found that only 22 of the 49 weather shamans belonged to one or more societies [Parsons 1933:19].

For the society affiliations of the Zuni *Ashiwanni,* see *formulistic magic.*

Ashuta
Kwakiutl, *Northwest Coast*
Kitimat term for a shaman's guardian spirit [Lopatin 1945:66]. See also *hasha.*

Askîpûkagokesi
Potawatomi, *Midwest*
This is the name of a certain type of wood used in making the model dugout canoe employed in curing. Water is poured into the canoe and allowed to stand until it acquires the taste of the wood. The water is then drunk as a medicine.

"In olden times nearly everyone used to have a canoe model made of this wood, and a paddle to go with it. They also made little wooden medicine bowls of it, and small stirring ladles, and miniature wooden pestles. These were all used to flavor medicine water. The usual dose was, according to prescription, one, two, or four times the contents of the canoe or bowl" [Skinner 1924:209].

This medicine comes from a spirit named *Pakotcinîni,* translated as "Wild-Man," or "Woods-Elf" [Skinner 1924:209].

Askwitit
Kalapuya, *Oregon Seaboard*
Power sticks [Boyd 1996:124] among the Tualatin Kalapuyas. These were shamans' sticks, usually made from cedar wood and about 3 feet in length. They were usually carved and painted, and infrequently decorated with feathers.

During ceremonial rituals, Kalapuya shamans would cause their *askwitit* to dance about the room. (See *tamanowash sticks* for details.)

Among the neighboring Chinookan peoples, the *askwitit* took the form of painted and carved flat boards.

Aslabatab
Twana, *Northwest Coast*
A particular diagnostic technique known as "being looked at by a vision-acquired spirit" [El-

mendorf 1960:496]. Frequently, after the death of a person with an acquired power, the power would seek out a living member of the family. In so doing, the power would make the person it sought ill. A shaman would then effect a cure, which would bring this power to the individual so that he could use it.

Aspergill

Any device, most often a branch of a bush, that is used to ceremonially sprinkle consecrated water. For example, in a Lakota Sweat Lodge Ceremony, the water to be used is first consecrated by touching the water container to the hot rocks within the lodge each time it is brought into the lodge. Thereafter the shaman often uses a wrapped bundle of sage as an aspergill, dipping it into the container and sprinkling the water therefrom onto the hot rocks in the center pit.

Various forms of aspergills are particularly prevalent in the ceremonies of the Southwest area.

Astalax

Twana, *Northwest Coast*

Land-mammal hunting powers. Such powers usually came from some type of animal spirit such as a wolf. This was a *cshalt* (see entry) form of power.

Asthla

Twana, *Northwest Coast*

A type of ritual impurity in a person caused by "emission of or contact with semen" [Elmendorf 1960:492]. To rid oneself of such impurity, intensive bathing, fasting, and/or purging is used. This form of impurity is not as dangerous as *asbathlqo* (see entry).

Atámántán

Quinault, *Northwest Coast*

Weather spirit. This is the name of the spirit used by Quinault shamans to control the weather. In

this region, weather shamans are used to stop the rain rather than bring it. Although these shamans can stop the rain, it is reported that they have no control over snowfall [Olson 1936:150].

Atámántán is a particularly powerful spirit, such that shamans must handle this spirit with great care lest it kill them.

For an example of a Quinault weather shaman, see *Old Tom Mouse*.

Atekata

East Greenland Eskimo, *Arctic Coast*

Ammasalik (or Angmagsalik) term for a person's name. A person's name is considered to have a power in this and many other Native American cultures. When a person dies all others bearing the same name must assume a different name until an infant is born into whom the name of the deceased can be imbued. "The word drops out of the language, and is replaced by a circumlocution, a derivative, or a synonyme, so that the language is considerably modified by this process" [Jesuit priest in Kroeber 1900:310]. When a newborn arrives who will be given the name of the deceased person, the infant "is rubbed about the mouth with water, while the names of the dead after whom it is named are pronounced" [Jesuit priest in Kroeber 1900:309]. The name of a deceased person is not even mentioned in casual conversation. If the dead person's name happens to be the name of some object as well, that object is also "not spoken of for some time" after the person's death [Kroeber 1900:309].

"On Davis Strait the infant is always named after the persons who have died since the last birth took place. If a relative dies while the child is younger than four years or so, his name is added to the old ones, and becomes the proper name by which it is called" [Boas in Kroeber 1900:309].

Athlashi

Zuni, *Southwest*

Sacred stone fetishes (see entry) used in ceremony. These are ancient stones that emerged with the first people. Many society members have more than one *athlashi*. Like most fetishes they require "feeding" to keep the spirit in them active; otherwise "they would disappear" [Parsons 1939:329]. During the performance of the Big Firebrand Society's ritual, the Zuni shaman drops them into a bowl of medicine water. In other cases they are used in an altar display (EONAH, p. 11).

Such sacred stones are used by other Pueblo cultures as well, such as the Hopi, Sia, and Isleta. "The Isletan stones are kept by the medicine man in the bag with their corn fetish or bundled in a buffalo-skin bag. Some are said to look like and to represent birds and the animals; others represent the mountains where bird or animal stones are found" [Parsons 1939:329].

Atikomaskiki
Cree/Ojibwa, *Canadian Eastern Woodlands*
Caribou's medicine [Cooper 1930:514]. This term refers to any bezoar taken from a caribou. It brings good luck to the finder. There are few records of bezoar use on the American continent.

Atishwin
Chumash, *Peninsula*
Personal charm (see entry). Among the Chumash charms often come in the form of "small cylindrical stones with tapered ends rather like plummet stones. Chumash shamans used these ritual objects for a variety of purposes including curing the sick, making oneself invisible to arrows, for sorcery, and to bring rain. Shamans might also employ large quartz crystals which were sometimes attached to wands and were associated with rainmaking" [B. Miller 1988: 125–127]. These charm stones are most often made of steatite or serpentine and are about 3 inches in length.

Charms worn as amulets (see entry) come in the form of "various animal parts such as bear claws, bird talons, rattlesnake skulls, and bits of human hair" [B. Miller 1988:127].

Augury
The art or practice of divination; prophecy. Most shamans practice some form of augury; however, this medicine power is not limited to shamans. For example, Muwaini ("drinks-from-spring-without-cup"), a Chemehuevi layman, made predictions for his people during the 1930s [Kelly 1936:136].

Among the Southern Paiute a special song is sung to find out about someone who is not present: "Sometimes a person would want to know about a friend or relative who was far away or who was missing. Then he would go to a certain man and ask him to sing and tell him if the person were alive. The singer was not a doctor but he dreamed and had a song. The latter was called kɔtɔ´tɔ-xuviïb (travel-song). A man had to be something like Coyote to have this (?); as he sang something like Coyote traveled over the country and saw what had happened" [unnamed informant in Kelly 1936:136].

Augury plays a major role in most war medicines, in which it is used to determine the number and movement of one's enemies.

See also *divination*.

Aumakua
Hawaiian, *Pacific*
Spirit. Helping spirits appeared to shamans mainly through dreams, and they bestowed special powers. Once acquired, a spirit could then be used via dreams to obtain information. For example:

> When a man found a fine *koa* tree he went to the *kahuna kalai waa* [EONAH, p. 127] and said, "I have found a *koa* tree, a fine large tree." On receiving this information the *kahuna* went at night to the *mus* (men's quarters), to sleep before his shrine *(kuahu),* in order to obtain a revelation from his deity in a dream as to whether the tree was sound or rotten.
>
> And if in his sleep that night he had a vision of someone standing naked before him, a man

The ritual robes and equipment of a Tsimshian, Northwest Coast, shaman are displayed on a model (National Museum of Man, Ottawa, Ontario, Canada).

without a *malo* [loincloth], or a woman without a *pau,* and covering their shame with the hand, on awakening the *kahuna* knew that the *koa* in question was rotten *(puha),* and he would not go up into the woods to cut that tree [Malo in Handy 1968:119].

In this case the nudity suggests that the tree is unsound and should not be used.

When a spirit appears in human form, it is often called *kupuna,* meaning "ancestors" [Handy 1968:123]. This seems to be the case today, but in former times a guardian spirit often appeared in its animal, plant, or other such form, collectively known as *kino lau,* "innumberable bodies" or "leaf bodies" [Handy 1968:123]. For example, one spirit known as *Kamapuaa,* "Hog-child," which is the spirit of sweet-potato planters, appears in many different forms—as human, pig, small fish, foliage of the candlenut tree, a certain wild grass, and the *lipehu* seaweed.

Powers given by spirits are associated with certain taboos, such as not eating the flesh of one's animal spirit. "The large elekuma crab was the aumakua of a family in Kohala, on the island of Hawaii. A woman of that family, after eating this crab, broke out in great ulcerous sores that nothing could heal. They sapped all her vitality. When hope for her life had been given up, a relative came to call, and, knowing about such sickness, he recognized the cause of the trouble instantly. With prayers and medicine, the sores were gone in less than a week" [M. K. Pukui in Handy 1968:123].

The *aumakua* can also be the source of an illness, such that certain animals are associated with certain diseases. For instance:

> For sickness caused by the displeasure of the caterpillar spirit *(aumakua peelua)*. The *aumakus* causing this sickness can be identified by the rolling movement of the patient's body and in a caterpillar-like manner of walking. Take eight sweet potato leaves *(palula)* and wrap in a *ti* leaf packet. Make five of these packets. Take a whole sweet potatoe *(u'ala)* vine and let the patient wear it around his neck a whole day. . . .
>
> For sickness caused by the displeasure of the eel spirit *(aumakua puhi)*. The *aumakua* causing this sickness may be recognized by the appearance of the patient. His body perspires freely, his mouth is slimy, his skin is reddened, and his general appearance suggests that of an eel. Sprinkle him five times with salt water and turmeric (an agent used to exorcise any spirit), take five tender leaves of the *manini* variety of taro, tear each of them up into small pieces and wave them before the eyes of the patient, while reciting (the proper prayer) [quoted from an old manuscript in Handy 1968:123–124].

The most important animal *aumakua* is that of the shark. "But shark aumakua differ from all others in this, that whereas in other cases a species

of plants or animals are the kino lau of the spirit and all have to be respected, with the shark aumakua it is a matter of intimate personal relationship with a particular shark frequenting a given locality, recognized by color or markings, and called by its own name" [Handy 1968:124]. This spirit, most often associated with a family of fishermen, leads the fishermen to good fishing spots while driving off marauders of its own species.

Autni
Wishram, *Plateau*
See *iauni*.

Avenarï
Paiute, *Basin*
A renowned Las Vegas (Southern Paiute) weather shaman around the turn of the twentieth century who spent most of his life among the Chemehuevi at Wianekat (a site along the Colorado River, between Fort Mohave and Cottonwood Island). He received his power through dreams.

> To bring rain he did not sing but used crystals *(pi'utovï)* which looked like diamonds. These he alone could find at a place that had been struck by lightning. He seldom sang to bring rain, but instead touched one of the crystals to the surface of a bowl of water. Immediately it began to rain. If he used a large crystal the storm continued many days.
>
> To stop the rain he sang; or he gathered rain water from the leaves of trees and drank it (similar to the reputed Kawaiisu practice).
>
> Once a party of Mohave were on their way to Mohave station (Kawaiisu) for clamshell beads. They stopped near the camp of Avena'rï. They taunted him, saying, "This man cannot bring rain." But before they left Avena'rï brought a rain so heavy that the country was flooded. There was so much water that the Mohave said, "Have we not crossed the Colorado River already?" They went on their way but two or three of them were drowned [Kelly 1939:165–166].

Unlike some weather shamans Avenarï could bring rain at any time of the year, "although in summer it would be only a light shower" [Kelly 1939:166].

Awtpamá
Wishram, *Plateau*
The Columbia River Sahaptin word for tobacco *(Nicotania attenuata)* [Boyd 1996:126–127]. This word comes from the roots *awt,* meaning "to be sacred, holy, to purify," and *pamá,* meaning "for belonging to."

Native American cultures in this area often used native tobacco to induce altered states of consciousness, i.e., trance, in which they would become "dead." In such states shamans would then communicate with their helping spirit(s). Thus, because tobacco helps them access a "holy" state of being, it is also considered sacred.

Axwecama
Yuma, *Southwest*
Enemy dreamer. One class of war dreamers among the Yuma. The other class was the war leader dreamer, called *kwánámicama* [Forde 1931:181]. These shamans were responsible for war medicine and were called upon to appeal to their helping spirits for aid. They often sought out their enemies' location in order to ambush them or at least attain a tactical advantage. "War prayers had a set form, were in a 'different' language, and were received from one of the animal spirits" [Forde 1931:181].

Aya
Hopi, *Southwest*
Rattle. Although ceremonial rattles come in several forms, most of them are made from gourds—dried, filled with pebbles through a hole made in the top, and with a stick placed into the hole. Others include the *paaya,* "water rattles" [Stephen 1936:110], which contain no water per se and are used on the altar of the Flute Society; the *wupa aya,* "long rattles" [Stephen 1936:747], which are actually prayer sticks (see *prayer feathers/sticks* entry) stuck in cones on the altar of the Snake Society; and rattles made from

bunches of scapulae, usually from deer, antelope, or mountain sheep, referred to as *würwüryom aya* or *kala haiinniadta* [Stephen 1936:432]. Most often such rattles are used to accompany the singing of ceremonial songs.

Ayahadilkah
Navajo, *Southwest*
Literal translation: "underneath burning" [Wyman and Bailey 1944:329]. A healing ceremony known in English as bison fumigation (because of the use of bison genitals) or fumigant-burning. This ceremony is conducted as part of the Lifeway ceremonial and is used to treat "sexual excess, adultery, or breach of ceremonial continence" [Wyman and Bailey 1944:329]. Known symptoms are headache, chronic head or eye trouble, and "pain in bones." *Ayahadilkah* is also closely associated with the Flintway ceremonial.

The treatment includes pouring an infusion of mixed herbs and animal parts from a turtle-shell cup onto hot rocks in a pit, over which the patient sits underneath a blanket. Following this the blanket is removed, and the patient is bathed in the infusion from head down by the shaman. The patient is also given some of the infusion to drink.

Ayikcmífosî
Seminole, *Southeast*
Literal translation: "medicine's owner" [Sturtevant 1954b:89]. One of two terms used by the Mikasuki division for a shaman. The other term is *ayikcahicâcî,* or "medicine keeper" [Sturtevant 1954b:89]. The Mikasuki term *ayikcomí* (EONAH, p. 23) is used for any male or female who has medicinal knowledge, such as an herbalist.

Shamans undergo formal periods of training conducted exclusively in January or early February. Only males are formally trained, usually beginning around the age of ten to fifteen. They cannot be married. Female shamans learn from other men or women, and most of them act as midwives and treat menstruating women.

Through formal training men obtain different degrees, named after the months. In some cases a novice receives from the teacher "a living 'medicine' in their bodies which enables them to doctor more effectively than others. . . . A teacher will not give it to [just] any student, but only a few—it is said that he can tell by watching a pupil's eyes whether he is worthy of it" [Sturtevant 1954b:143–144]. Once this internal medicine is obtained, the shaman must keep it alive and strong through monthly ritual procedures that involve fasting and taking emetics.

The men are usually specialists in ritual, but most shamans are also capable of doctoring illnesses. Only men are trained as doctors, and substantial training and experience are required. Successful doctors "have considerable power and are able to cure many conditions including the more serious ones" [Sturtevant 1954b:91]. Healers and diagnosticians are not differentiated. Diagnosis is not done by supernatural or clairvoyant means and "seems to be the weakest part of Seminole medicine" [Sturtevant 1954b:136].

Shamans are also in charge of the Mikasuki sacred ceremonial medicine bundles, each called *ahǎlbócnáknósî* ("old little box") [Sturtevant 1954b:159], that have been handed down through many generations. These bundles are used in conducting community ceremonies such as the Busk Ceremony (EONAH, p. 42). In fact, "one of the main purposes of the annual busks is to renew and preserve the power of the [Seminole medicine] bundles. The medicine bundles are the symbols and the powers around which Seminole ceremonial and political life are organized, are believed necessary for the existence of the group, and can in this sense be considered the 'soul' of the Seminole 'body.' The medicines [contained in the bundles] are capable also of doing great harm or of losing their potency, so must be treated carefully and protected from potentially harmful influences" [Sturtevant 1954a: 42]. Consequently, they must be given proper care by the attending shamans to protect the community from danger.

Healing ceremonies consist of the use of various healing songs, prayers, and plants by the shaman. Most plants used are different parts of trees, with bay leaf the most frequently used medicine, followed by cedar [Sturtevant 1954b:161]. When medicine plants are used their efficacy is initially increased through the shaman blowing his breath on them. The association of a plant with a medicine bundle also increases its power. Such ritual actions cause these plants to become medicine [Sturtevant 1954b:168]. The songs and prayers are usually recited in the Creek language [Sturtevant 1954b:149]. In addition "the songs are always sung over a pot of [plant] medicine, except for the few cases where no medicine is used at all" [Sturtevant 1954b:119]. Moreover, each medicine must be prepared and administered to the patient in a ritually prescribed manner. When administered, these plant medicines are usually drunk by the patient, sprinkled and/or blown from the mouth onto the patient by the shaman, and/or rubbed onto the patient's body. In all cases songs accompany their use. In fact, the "songs or spoken spells [prayers] which are used in curing are considered by the doctor to be much more important than the medicinal plants" [Sturtevant 1954b:119].

"All treatments involve songs or spoken spells and blowing into or on the medicine" [Sturtevant 1954b:186]. If several treatments by one shaman do not bring success, another shaman will be called in by the family. Although there are no prearrangements made with the shaman for his payment [Sturtevant 1954b:281], in all cases the shaman must be paid, usually with a cow, hog, chickens, a few yards of cloth, a tanned skin, etc.; money is rarely used since the shaman "did not pay to acquire his skills" [Sturtevant 1954b:142]. The treatments themselves are conducted in a ritualistic manner, common to the Southeast area, and the healing ceremonies do not evoke the direct aid of helping spirits to effect a cure. Like the ceremonies of the Southwest, the power of the spirits is evoked through the proper performance of the healing ceremony. Sturtevant [1954b:142] concluded that "Seminole medicine is quite mechanical in its operation, in that cures follow automatically from the proper diagnosis, use of the correct herbs, and perfect performance of the appropriate songs or spells [prayers]."

It should be noted that in former times, the Seminole did indeed have shamans who demonstrated the use of spirit powers. They were known as the *owǎlǎlhî* (see *owǎla*).

Ayxya
Kwakiutl, *Northwest Coast*
Kitimat term for shaman [Lopatin 1945:63]. See also *hasha*.

Badger blood divination
Cree, *Canadian Eastern Woodlands*
A divining technique used by the Plains Cree. Coming Day reported:

If you kill a badger, lay it on its back. Take the entrails out, but leave the blood in, and you can tell something the next morning. If a man looks into it he can see himself there. I knew of four young men who did it. One saw a black faced man, just skin and bones. He died after a long sickness. Another saw a very old man with many wrinkles and hair white as snow. He lived to an old age. One saw a man who had been scalped. He was killed in battle shortly afterward. The last saw a young man with his eyes closed. He died at an early age.

These men were all young. The old men told them not to do it, for it is the one certain way of knowing how you would die. . . . This badger blood looking was discovered accidentally once when a man was out hunting [Coming Day in Mandelbaum 1940:262].

Bagijiganatig
Ojibwa, *Canadian Eastern Woodlands*
Chippewa Offering Tree. This is a community-constructed fetish that is used to ward off disease. In a typical scenario,

[a shaman] is warned by his guardian spirit that a sickness is about to visit the community. The person sends invitational tobacco to a number of people by a runner who tells the people to come to a certain place at a certain time "to make an offering" of clothes. At the appointed time the people assemble with tobacco, food, and articles of clothing. The food is laid out, and tobacco passed, both of which are offered to the ma´nidog [see *manitou*, EONAH, p. 164] of the air, particularly the thunder-birds (bine´siwəg) by the dreamer, or someone he has asked to speak for him. The dreamer relates his dream to the people, tells the ma´nidog that this offering of clothing is being made to them imploring their intercession to keep that sickness away. After the feast the clothing brought by the participants is assembled and hung on a tree or pole along with tobacco. In the one case I saw the clothing was tied in bunches and hung about two-thirds of the way up a slender, eighteen-foot tall pine tree from which all the branches had been trimmed except for a few at the top. In other instances a slender pine tree is cut down, peeled, and trimmed just leaving a tuft of branches at the top.

The clothing and tobacco are tied near the top and the pole either leaned up against the house, or set upright in the ground. It is said that the clothing should be articles worn close to the body, not overcoats or the like. The usual articles hung on the pole or tree include underwear, pants, shirts, dresses, and aprons. They must be left hanging for at least four days, and during that time they are accepted by the ma´nidog. In some instances they may be left up until they disintegrate; in other cases they are taken down on the fifth day and used for dish-rags. The former seems to be the older practice. Occasionally a Chief Dance will follow the ceremony of clothes hanging [Ritzenthaler 1953b:214].

Basemacha
Yavapai, *Southwest*
Literal translation: *ba,* "person," and *semacha,* "helping spirits" or "deities" [Gifford 1936:309]. Curing shaman. Curing shamans most often receive their power for healing via two spirits, Komwidapokuwia and her grandson Skatakaamcha, the latter of whom bestows upon the shaman his gourd rattle for curing. Healing ceremonies usually last for four days. The shaman sings over the patient, holding the "edge of left hand against face, palm forward" [Gifford 1936:309]. Some shamans smoke tobacco in clay pipes and blow the smoke over their patient. "Sometimes shaman placed pinches of tule pollen on patient. Shamans of old school used 4-holed flageolet (ordinary flute six holed) and rattle. Those coming from San Carlos used only rattle. Shaman sang to find seat of pain, put flageolet against it and played" [Gifford 1936:309]. He then makes an incision in the patient's skin with a sharp flake of white or black stone. He sucks on this incision to remove the disease object, which is usually "blood with [a] lump or worm-shaped clot" [Gifford 1936:309].

"Shaman did not always locate seat of illness by singing. Then sometimes Skatakaamcha came to his aid, and his patient recovered. If Skatakaamcha did not come, patient died. Sometimes, in Verde Valley region, shaman sang very long time until an akaka´ [see entry] came carrying stick, often of cottonwood, with green leaves on end. Akaka´ pressed sick person, then went away. Person recovered.... To summon aid of Skatakaamcha or akaka´, shaman sometimes secretly swung bullroarer [EONAH, p. 42] at night before sucking in morning" [Gifford 1936:309].

If a shaman dreams of heavy wind or a rainstorm, it is a sign that a disease such as smallpox or measles is coming. In such cases a *kitiye sware* (singing shaman) is used to ward off the illness. This shaman will make a *matkinyur* (sand painting) of white earth, about 20 feet square. He sings at the sand painting while other men sing as well, and "women and some men danced or marched in approaching and retreating lines" [Gifford 1936:310]. Sand paintings are also used during the initiation ceremony for novice shamans.

For other types of Yavapai shamans, see *pokwia*.

Baswadash
Twana, *Northwest Coast*
Shamans who doctor illnesses. See *swadash*.

Batapuis
Yavapai, *Southwest*
Dialectical variant: *tipuyi* (Western Yavapai) [Gifford 1936:316]. Literal translation: *ba,* "person," and *tapuis,* "witch" [Gifford 1936:317]. Northeastern Yavapai sorcerer. The sorcerer would use his *bakina* (power) to shoot *batapui* or *banei* (poison) into his victim through an incantation. To heal the victim a curing shaman would be called upon to send the sorcerer's *bakina* back to him.

Bathon
Omaha, *Plains*
Smell. Because smell is invisible, this term is also used to indicate a supernatural influence. In this context it also means:

1. The essence in food offerings to ghosts that ghosts eat from the offerings.
2. The influence in a medicine bundle.
3. The influence in a menstruating woman.

4.   The influence in a doctor. [Fortune 1932:29]

Bathon may be either beneficial or harmful, but it is most often conceived of as being dangerous. Beneficial *bathon* comes in the form of the power to cure illnesses.

The concept of *bathon* is extended by the Omaha to what might be called "vibes" in contemporary English. For instance, someone who prays for the recovery of a sick individual is seen as extending good *bathon* upon the sick person. Or a person might not be allowed to be around a sick person because his bad *bathon* would harm the sick person. In addition the Omaha believed that *bathon* travels on the wind, and therefore, they would avoid walking downwind from a powerful shaman.

Batsawe
Hidatsa, *Plains*

Hot Dancers' ceremony. They performed a special fire-handling dance that spread in the Central Plains area during the latter part of the nineteenth century. It more than likely originated among the Arikara and spread to the Hidatsa, Mandan, Crow, Oglala, and other areas. In most instances "the performers danced barefoot on glowing embers and took out meat from a pot of boiling water. The hands, as well as a part of the forearms and the feet, were painted red" [Maximilian in Lowie 1913b:252]. Among the Hidatsa "when a dance was held, a big fire was built and slices of half-dried meat were boiled in a kettle suspended over it. A hide scraped clear of hair was stretched out flat behind the fire. The officer who was painted black came to the fireplace, chewed some medicine, and spat it first on his hands, and then into the kettle. Then he plunged his hand into the vessel, extracted a piece of meat, and threw it on the hide. The other members followed suit until all the meat had been taken out. No one ever burned his fingers. By way of joking a man sometimes put a piece of hot meat on a friend's back, for he knew the medicine would prevent scalding" [Lowie 1913b:253].

Among the Oglala this feat was performed by the *heyóka* (EONAH, p. 104–105) [Lowie 1913a:113; Wissler 1912b:82]. For example, the *heyóka* society of the eastern Dakota perform a Hot Dance ritual that consists of "the performers' plunging their arms into a kettle of boiling water without being scalded. . . . [It] was also practiced by the Ojibwa Wabeno and the Hot Dancers of the Mandan, Hidatsa, and Arikara. . . . Whale [a Santee] states that only the head man knew the medicine and he would not reveal the secret to anyone; he it was that chewed the medicine and put it on the performers' arms" [Lowie 1913a:113, 116]. In addition the dancers also would take boiling water from the kettle and throw it upon their bare backs [Eastman in Lowie 1913a:116].

The Santee also perform a *peta nasnipi watcipi,* or Fire-Walkers' Dance: "They extinguish fire with their feet" [Lowie 1913a:125, n. 2].

> The performers removed their moccasins. They piled up wood high, to the length of thirty feet. Before the fire-walk the head man [shaman] would inspect the wood pile, and in my informant's opinion, he sprinkled some medicine on it, probably the same as that used by the heyoka. . . . The men chosen mixed tallow with vermilion, and rubbed it on their bare feet. They waited until the wood was kindled into a blazing fire. Then they fell to singing and drumming, and the fire-walkers started across the fire, three-abreast. The head man merely looked on. They went the entire length of the fire, then they retraced their steps. Sometimes they succeeded in putting out the fire on the second trip; it never took more than four trips. After the last walk neither ashes nor any other trace of the fire remained visible [Lowie 1913a:125–126].

Among the Mandan members of their Crazy Dog Society performed the Hot Dance. "After a large fire had been built, a number of glowing embers were scattered about, and then the boys, stripped of all clothing, danced on them with their bare feet. The hands, forearms, and feet of the performers were colored red. Sliced meat was boiling in a kettle over the fire. When the meat had been well done, the dancers put their hands into the boiling water, took out some of the meat, and ate it at the risk of scalding themselves. Those coming last to the kettle had the worst of it, for they were obliged to dig down deeper into the water than their predecessors. During the dance the performers carried weapons and rattles in their hands" [Maximilian in Lowie 1913b:308–309].

Among the Crow it was also members of their Crazy Dog Society who became the first Hot Dancers. "Before long [early 1870s] practically all the Crazy Dogs became Hot dancers" [Lowie 1913b:148]. Eventually, four different Crow societies—the Night Hot dancers, Big-Ear-Holes, Last dancers, and Sioux dancers—performed the Hot Dance. However, "the dance does not correspond to the Hot dance of the Mandan, Hidatsa, and Arikara described by Maximilian, but is identical with the Omaha or Grass dance of other tribes" [Lowie 1913b:200].

Bear Butte
See *hanblecheyapi.*

Bear ceremonialism
See *bear medicine/possession.*

Bear-knife bundle
Blackfoot, *Plains*
A form of war medicine. This medicine most often takes the form of a large dagger-like knife that has the jaws of a bear attached to it. Wissler [1912a:131] reported that the bear-knife medicine was "on the verge of extinction" and that Maximilian had observed a similar knife among the Gros Ventre circa 1840.

It was the only weapon the owner was allowed to use during warfare. Among the Blackfoot this particular war medicine was considered extremely powerful, such that "its owner was seldom killed, for its appearance frightened everyone into submission, after the manner of bears" [Wissler 1912a:134]. At the same time, the transference rit-

ual associated with this medicine was so torturous to the recipient that few men ever sought out this particular medicine power. Of this ritual Wissler [1912a:132] wrote: "The recipient must catch the knife thrown violently at him and is also cast naked upon thorns and held there while painted and beaten thoroughly with the flat of the knife."

Black Bear, from the Piegan division, reported that he had received a bear-knife medicine bundle around 1870 that was said to have originated among the Sarsi. Prior to the transfer ceremony for this bundle, he held seven sweat lodges on seven different days for the owner of the medicine bundle. Wissler [1912a:133] detailed the transfer ritual::

At first some rose bushes or thorns were stuck in a row close together near the rear of the tipi. The owner sat on the left and the buyer on the right of the thorns. Some red paint and gunpowder mixed with water were put into cups, placed near the owner. Then a smudge was made with parsnip root near the bushes. The two men were naked. When Black-bear was getting this knife there were many men in the tipi. Seven drums were used. When the singing began all those in the tipi made all the noise possible, shouting and shaking all the tipi poles.

The owner moved about in his seat as a bear does, moving backward and forward. When the owner was about to paint the purchaser, seven men stood outside of the tipi each with a gun. The owner sprang upon the purchaser, threw him on the thorns and painted him. At the same time the guns were fired. The owner turned the purchaser first on one side and then on the other while painting him, holding him against the thorns all the time. The shooting of the guns is to represent shooting at bears when they are in the brush.

After the man had been painted with the seventh paint, scratched down with the fingers, and the marks with gunpowder made over the eyes and mouth, another smudge was made. The knife, still in its wrappings, was passed four times over the smudge and taken out of its coverings. The owner, holding the knife in his right hand, went through the motions of stabbing. Meanwhile, singing and drumming was going on. The owner again threw the purchaser on the thorns and slapped him on the breast with the flat of the bear knife, turned him over, and slapped him on the back. The two men crawled along on hands and knees to the north side of the fireplace where the owner again sprang on the purchaser and again slapped him on the breast and back with the knife. They crawled to the west side and he repeated the same movements. Thus the purchaser became the owner of the bear knife."

Following this ritual Black Bear spent four successive nights learning the songs that went with his newly acquired medicine bundle. (For some reason the traditional knife-catching requirement was overlooked in his ceremony.) Immediately thereafter he went to sleep out in the hills alone with his bundle until he dreamed about it. This was required of all recipients of the bear-knife medicine, and their quest usually lasted from four to seven nights.

As mentioned above, Black Bear could use no weapon during warfare other than this knife. Furthermore, he could "never turn back from the enemy, but [had to] go directly forward singing songs from the ritual, take an enemy by the hair and stab him" [Wissler 1912a:133]. In addition to its use, this medicine knife needed to be protected from certain taboos. For instance, "Dogs must not come inside while the owner is there and no one should strike on iron while he is smoking" [Wissler 1912a:133]. Finally, its care was also ritually prescribed. Of this Wissler [1912a:134] reported: "During the summer the knife is kept unwrapped and fastened to one of the tipi poles inside near the owner's seat, that it may be at hand when needed. Late in the fall, it is taken down and placed in its bundle where it remains until spring, thus imitating the bear. During this time, the bundle is suspended on a tripod behind the tipi through the day. A smudge of parsnip root is made three times daily."

Bear medicine/possession

Bear medicine is usually envisioned as a particularly powerful form of healing medicine. Bear ceremonialism is found throughout North America and in the Old World as well. Men who receive visions from the Bear spirit, particularly the grizzly bear, or dream of the Bear spirit often become powerful doctors. Bear shamans are prominent in California, particularly in central California among the Penutian-speaking people. They are also found among the Zuni, Tanoan, and Keresan (Pueblo) people of the Southwest area, where shamans are commonly referred to as "Bears." For example, "Bear medicine" is found in the Flint and Fire Medicine Societies (see entries *chayan* and *hakan*) [Parsons 1939:133]. The Keresan "impersonated bears and could be transformed into bears. They were thought to be very dangerous because they could kill anyone. They were invulnerable and could travel great distances in an instant. Among many of these tribes the dangerous and malevolent aspects of the Bear shamans were more prominent than their curing powers. In this area

A Tlingit shaman's charm. A bear figure is seated at the back to the right. The large head is that of a wolf, with devilfish tentacles on the ears.

also Bear shamans were organized into sodalities. Among the Shoshonean-speaking Cupeños, Gabrieleñ, and Cahuillas, especially powerful Bear shamans are said to have existed but were not organized into sodalities" [Levy 1994:317].

In 1914 anthropologist E. W. Gifford recorded the following unusual account given by Tom Williams, a central Miwok. It concerns his older brother, who had been possessed by a Bear spirit but did not become a shaman. The account was translated for Gifford by Williams's grandson, John Kelly:

> Tom's old brother was going along trail home about sundown when big grizzly bear grabbed him and carried him home at big cave (Hiyawula) in Table mountain near Rawhide. Brother dead, bear had killed him by pressing his heart. Bear took out his heart, intestines, etc., and put his own in place, in other words, traded. Brother four days and four nights dead. Indians look for brother, can't find him. Lots of bear sing by brother all time in bear's hole or hangi. Brother's wife and two girls cry all the time. Bears put big stick in pile of dirt. Bears try to get brother up, but he can't get up, all the same dead. Three times they tried, but no use. Bears say "Go home" fourth time. Brother gets up, bites way through door, just like cut with axe. He go home, bears following. He lives this side Tuttletown. He go along saying 'Ha-a-ha-a-a,' like bear. Brother finds house. Indians try to catch him but can't. He disappears each time. They catch him at Wüyü. Indians all singing. Take him home. Bear hair on upper arms. All Indians sing four nights and days. When he well he talk [to] mother. He says "One bear catch me [at] Tuttletown." That all right; they say nothing. He go to Supêmô, this side Springfield. They make big hangi for big dance. Lots Indians come. Brother he says he show them [his powers]. He says you go get bark live oak, pile it up inside, burn it. After all people are inside of hangi he comes up from outside and goes in door. No one sees him. He looks like a bear. He goes in [and] walks across fire. He was really a bear. People then saw him. He sat in middle of fire. No burn him. He laid down in fire growling like bear; he grovels around and makes hole. He stays in fire and plays for three or four hours. Then he goes

outside just like bear. He goes in river and washes off. No more play. When he go inside hangi, he laugh at all Indians. 'What's matter you fellows,' he says. That's [the] way one time [with] my brother. He no doctor, he no sing. White man afraid [of] brother. They think he crazy. They see fire he go in, no hurt him. . . . When brother go rancheria the bears follow him, three or four. Bears sit in house. Brother tells bears to go, motioning with right hand. Brother no doctor. Never dream about bear" [John Kelly translating for Tom Williams in Gifford n.d. a:1–2].

Steward [1933:309–310] reported that the Bear shamans of the Owens Valley Paiute can not only transform themselves into bears (see *ünü*) but also cause a bear to kill a person. This ability of Bear shamans to transform themselves into the shape of a bear is a widely reported phenomenon [i.e., V. Miller 1979:25].

Bear ceremonialism is also widespread in the Plains area. Among the Oglala (Sioux), shamans who acquired a Bear helping spirit became members of the Bear Society of shamans.

> The shamans of this cult were held in very great regard because of their power in healing wounds. . . . At the [society] feast the medicines are displayed. Sometimes a shaman displays his abilities by suddenly hitting the earth upon which a turnip or a small cedar tree springs up. An informant heard of a shaman putting up a plum tree, a juneberry, or cherry tree, and when the singers were singing and beating the drum, he sat there with his face painted up wakan [holy] and suddenly shook the tree upon which the fruit fell to the ground. The members usually each ate a little of the fruit and saved some for medicine. A shaman at Standing Rock, it is said, would first hit the earth, then put his hands to his mouth when all would see his canines protruding like a bear. If anyone is badly wounded in battle he is taken to the tipi and the bear cult called in [Wissler 1912b:88–89].

Although bear ceremonialism is known to have ancient origins, in some cultures it has come to be classified by anthropologists as a "social" dance rather than a religious ritual or ceremony. However, even in these "social" dances, one might expect to find the remnants of ancient shamanic ritual. For instance, the Bear Dance among the Southern Ute of Colorado (conducted annually following "the first thunder in spring" [Opler 1941b:28]) was classified as a "social" dance in 1936 by anthropologist Marvin Opler. However, in their closing dances, which "have a special significance" [Opler 1941b:27], we find the following shamanic actions of the "wise song leader" [Opler 1941b:28], who leads the occasion:

In the last dance, if a woman falls down, that means she is in danger of losing her sight. If a man falls down, it merely stops the dance and no immediate danger is attached thereto. In either case, the fallen member of the band does not rise at once, but calls out the song leader who must walk around the fallen person clockwise. He then places his rasp over the knees of the prostrate dancer and then touches it first to the right, and then the left shoulder of the person. Then the back is touched and lastly, the head. With each gesture, the rasp is raised to the lips [of the song leader] after touching the body, and the leader draws it from the lips to the air, blowing out the evil. This is to bless the person, to give him good health and good luck. It is believed to be a special cure for rheumatism or backache, and for a woman concerned it prevents the impending blindness, "so she can be a good sewer of buckskin," while for the man concerned, it will prevent him from being attacked by bear in the mountains, "so he can continue to be a good hunter." Even if no one should fall in the last swift movements of the dance, anyone with these fears or afflictions may ask the wise song leader to manipulate the rasp [Opler 1941b:27–28].

In this account the rasp used by the shaman is "a notched stick two and a half feet long, painted with red ochre

and sometimes decorated with other colors. The ankle bone of any animal was used in rubbing over the notches and a deep hole covered with a basket, upside-down, was used as a resonator. The basket of twined ware is about two feet in diameter" [Opler 1941b:26]. The use of this rasp for ceremony was taught to the Ute via the Bear spirit in a dream. "In former days, the rasps were buried in the resonator pit after the ceremony" [Opler 1941b:29]. Given the sacred nature and handling of this rasp, coupled with the Southern Ute shamanic healing practice of blowing on the patient [Kelly 1936:138] and use of the shaman's lips [Kelly 1936:133], it can readily be seen that this "social" dance still contained viable shamanic components in the 1930s.

Opler [1941a:290] also described a Bear shaman among the Chiricahua (Apache) who "cured many diseases." Also given was an account of this shaman successfully healing a case of severe pneumonia with a four-day bear ceremony [Opler 1941a:290–291].

Among the Inuit (Eskimo) *angakut* (shamans, see *angakoq*, EONAH, pp. 13–15), a shaman with advanced powers is designated *angakoq pulik* (or *puliq, poglit,* etc.) [Merkur 1991:237–239]. These shamans undergo a special initiation associated with the bear and walrus in which the shaman experiences a shamanic death and subsequent resurrection. Typically the shaman is bound hand and feet, and once the lights have been extinguished "a white bear [always a polar bear] immediately enters by the door, bites the Magician in the big toes, drags him to the sea,

Tlingit forehead mask representing a bear.

and leaps with him into the water. A sea elephant [walrus], which is found there at the designated place, seizes him by his genital parts, and eats both him and the bear. A moment later, his bones are thrown on the pavement of the house where the magic is done; and when all are found there, his soul leaves the earth and unites with his bones, in such a fashion that he regains life, and now he is an *Angekkok Poglik*" [Egede in Merkur 1991:237].

Of these two spirit helpers the Bear is the most powerful as Rasmussen reports: "The mightiest and most influential of them all was Nanoq Tuliorialik ("The Bear with the fangs"). This was a giant in the shape of a bear, who came as often as he was called. . . . When that particular spirit deigned to occupy his body, he, Unaleq, could transform himself into a bear or a walrus at will, and was able to render great service to his fellow men by virtue of the powers thus acquired" [Rasmussen in Merkur 1991:239].

See also *chayan, kopati, Matcogahri, Notwita, Unaleq, ünü, Wanke, White Bear.*

Bear's Belly
Arikara, *Plains*

A shaman during the first part of the twentieth century who was a member of the Bear Medicine Society and leader of the Arikara Medicine Lodge Society. He was renowned for his power displays. "He would mount to the top of the lodge, face the people, beat his breast and throw out his abdomen, sitting with his arms spread out and abdomen protruding. A fellow member would ascend, bearing with him a war axe or tomahawk. With this he would strike Bear's Belly a heavy blow on the protruding abdomen and then retire, leaving the axe sticking in the wound. Bear's Belly would groan and cry for a time, then descend from the roof still carrying the axe in the wound. A group of the medicine men would surround him, withdraw the axe, and he would appear uninjured, and unscarred" [Will 1934:47].

Also see *Shunáwanùh.*

Beautiful Feathers
Cree, *Canadian Eastern Woodlands*

A shaman from the West People band of the Plains Cree during the nineteenth century. The following is an account of one of his power duels with an old Saulteaux shaman:

One year he [Beautiful Feathers] was camping there [near Edmonton]. There was an old Saulteaux who had caused a lot of trouble through bad magic. When the Cree saw him they said, "Here's where we have trouble." Sure enough, before long a man came around announcing that the Saulteaux was challenging the Cree medicine men to a contest in his tipi. They all had to go lest the old Saulteaux work even more harm on them if they stayed away.

Beautiful-feathers waited until the last when the Saulteaux's large tipi was full of men. He entered and took a seat near the door. Next to the Saulteaux was a barrel of whiskey, a case of twist tobacco, ammunition, and a brand new gun. These were to go to the winner of the contest.

The Saulteaux began by lighting the pipe and passing it on. But when the next man took it, a snake head darted out of the stem. The man passed it on and so it was passed around until it reached Beautiful-feathers. He just took the snake's head between his teeth, drew it out, threw it away, and smoked the pipe. Then the pipe was smoked around.

"Aha," said the old Saulteaux, "Things are beginning to become interesting. Young man, you and I are going to play a little. You begin, young man." But Beautiful-feathers said, "No, old man, you are the challenger, you begin."

Then the Saulteaux put his thumb in the rifle barrel, ripped it open, and handed it over. Beautiful-feathers grasped the barrel, drew his hand up, and the gun was whole again.

"Aha," said the Saulteaux, "things are interesting." He took an eagle feather, smoothed it, and said, "Young man, watch out." He hurled the feather at Beautiful-feathers who caught it. Beautiful-feathers also smoothed the feather and said, "Old man, watch out." He hurled the feather and it pierced the old Saulteaux until only the tip was showing.

The old Saulteaux fell over, but he had provided four singers for just such a time. One singer began and the old Saulteaux stopped bleeding. The second joined in and the Saulteaux began to breathe. When the third and fourth sang, he was all right. Then he rolled the whiskey, the tobacco, the gun, outside of his tipi and said, "Young man, you win." When the Saulteaux went back to his country, he died [Pierre La Cree in Mandelbaum 1940:256].

Beaver medicine bundle

Blackfoot, *Plains*

See *kosksstakjomõpista.*

Bekikiak

Fox, *Midwest*

A medicine used to ward off sorcerers. This is a powdered medicine that is chewed every night to keep away "night travelers" or witches [M. R. Harrington 1914:222].

Benedict, Ruth

Ruth Fulton was born in 1887. Her father died when she was two, and a childhood case of the measles left her partially deaf [Babcock 1993:108]. She graduated as a Phi Beta Kappa scholar in English from Vassar in 1909. In 1914 she married Stanley Benedict, a research chemist at Cornell Medical College [Babcock 1993:109]. She began her training in anthropology under Franz Boas (EONAH, pp. 36–37) at Columbia University, having been recommended to him by Elsie Parsons (see entry), whom she first met in 1919 when she took a course taught by Parsons at the newly established New School for Social Research [Babcock 1993:109–110]. Benedict became a lecturer at Columbia in 1923 in the Department of Anthropology. In 1931 she was appointed assistant professor, in 1937 associate professor, and finally in 1948 full professor. (Delays in promotion for women were typical of academia during this period.)

Most of her work on Native America was done during the early part of her career, with her first major work being her Ph.D. dissertation from Columbia University in 1923 entitled *The Concept of the Guardian Spirit in North America,* which was published in that same year as Memoir No. 29 of the American Anthropological Association. During the 1920s she did fieldwork in the Southwest area, publishing *Tales of the Cochiti Indians* in 1931 as Bulletin No. 98 of the Bureau of American Ethnology.

Thereafter she turned toward theoretical anthropology, publishing her classic work, *Patterns of Culture,* in 1934. Toward the end of her career, she focused on the culture of Japan, publishing *The Chrysanthemum and the Sword* in 1946. During the 1940s she became the second woman ever to be elected president of the American Anthropological Association (E. C. Parsons was the first), and she is currently honored with her picture on the 36-cent U.S. postage stamp.

Big Bill

Twana, *Northwest Coast*

A Skokomish man whose native name was Stlha. Around 1865 to 1870 he received *tiwatayin* war power.

He first met that tiwatayin power in the mountains back of Quilcene, one time when he was looking for tamánamis [see entry]. . . . And he took sick and his uncles, the Charleys, doctored him. And Tenas Charley found out what was the matter with him. He stopped his doctor song and said, "Tiwatayin wants to talk to his master. Tiwatayin wants to come to this man." So Tenas Charley brought that power to Bill now and as soon as it came to him he hollered, "Ho ho!" and roared. And the doctors said, "Put a rope around him now! Tie him!" So they tied a rope around his waist and two men held on to it. And now Bill started to sing. . . . And blood started pouring out of his mouth [a sign of catching power]. And he danced around the room, those two men holding him by ropes tied to the one [rope] around his waist. And Bill took great big leaps, and at last he jumped up to one of the rafters and stood there and then jumped down again. And two or three times he did that.

The reason they tied ropes to him was that people with that power . . . sometimes break out of the house and that power takes them and they don't come back again. They just keep on going [Elmendorf 1993:183].

In another instance Big Bill was told by his spirits to carry a specific-named, large, round boulder from one village to another.

And that [rock] was an old, old thing with the Skokomish people. In the old days way back, men had been able to lift it, but for generations back no one had been able to raise it higher than his knees. And now Bill's power had told him to lift that rock and carry it [to another village 2 miles to the north]. . . .

I wasn't there but people told me what happened. Bill lifted that rock a little first and put it on his feet, and then rolled it right up his body and balanced it on his shoulders. And then he set out. . . . They say he rested only once on the way. And he packed that rock to where the village was and put it down. And now he is done [Elmendorf 1993:184].

Big Canoe, Frank
Kalispel, *Plateau*
One of the last Upper Pend d'Oreilles to conduct the Jumping Dance during the first part of the twentieth century. The participants of this dance were men who had received a song from a spirit via a vision quest. (These quests are most often conducted on McDonald Peak in the Mission Range of mountains in Montana.) "At the conclusion of the dance, those whom the One Above had taught a song raised their right hands and prayed, not only for themselves, but for their children so that the One Below would not interfere with their destiny" [Dusenberry 1959:56].

Big Cloud
Hidatsa, *Plains*
A shaman during the first part of the nineteenth century. One of his medicine powers was a mys-

tery song that he received from a large bird during a dream; singing this song, he gained protection from being wounded in battle. In addition, he could also bring rain. His grandson, Wolf Chief (see entry), gave the following account of this power:

Once we had no rain. Our gardens and corn-fields and crops were all dry and suffering for rain. The villagers gathered and brought presents to my grandfather and asked him to make rain come. So my grandfather put the black-bear's foot-bone and the snares on the ground, and tied the black bear-skin about him like a blanket; he had also a whistle. My grandfather sent me to the river for a bucket of water, and bade me sprinkle the water over the medicines and on the floor. He walked around the medicines on his toes, in a crouching position, blowing his whistle. My grandfather began thus about noon; about sunset a heavy cloud appeared in the west. The song my grandfather sang the meanwhile was not the one he had received from the bird, but another one.

It rained all that evening, all night, and till nearly noon the next day. The ground was moistened deep, and pools stood on the low ground.

Then my grandfather said: "I shall now take the presents the villagers have brought." If he had not brought the rain he would not have taken the presents [Wolf Chief in Pepper and Wilson 1908:318].

Big Ike
Yurok, *Oregon Seaboard*
A weather shaman during the latter part of the nineteenth century who was locally known as "the Rainmaker." During the winter of 1889–1890, gold miners along the lower Klamath River became concerned by the lack of rain, which was needed for their gold mining operations. No gold had yet been taken out, and they decided to hire Big Ike to make it rain. "Whereupon Big Ike told them he would make rain enough for them to work all winter, that much and no more. . . . He agreed to make rain for twenty dollars paid to him by each miner, they to

pay him when the rain began to fall, and the bargain was made" [Graves 1929:69].

Big Ike then went up to a cave on Medicine Rock and made rain medicine. He told them that it would begin to rain in three days, and "on the afternoon of the third day the clouds began to gather and before night it began to rain" [Graves 1929:70]. However, on the following day, when Big Ike went to collect his fee, one of the miners refused to pay. "The last one he [Big Ike] called on was a new-comer and not very well known to the other miners, and was working a claim that he had jumped while the owner was away. He refused to pay, and told Big Ike that he had nothing to do with making rain; called him a savage and his wife a squaw" [Graves 1929:70].

Disgruntled by this degrading treatment, Big Ike returned to his cave on Medicine Rock and proceeded to make even more rain. Soon it began to rain harder than ever, and several fellow Yuroks went to him to pursuade him to stop, fearing that their village would soon be inundated. "He told them to go back, that this rain was going to fall until such time as the paleface miners were willing to pay him in full; that even though he was, in the eyes of the white man, a savage and his wife a squaw, they would have to come to him there at Medicine Rock before the rain would stop" [Graves 1929:74].

The Yuroks hastened back to the miners and told them "that the Rainmaker was in an ugly mood; that their homes were about to be carried away; that if the rain was not stopped soon the mountain-side would surely go; that there would not be a mine left" [Graves 1927:74].

The miners then went up to Medicine Rock to pursuade Big Ike to cease his rain making. However, they also failed, Big Ike telling them,

Go back to your claims and make that white man, who said that I did not make this rain, pay for the trouble that you have all been to, and when you are through, tell him to leave this camp and never return. I am Big Ike, the Rainmaker, and no

savage, neither is my wife a squaw. Tell that white man to sharpen one hundred stout stakes and drive them into the ground. I see that the mountain has started to slide already. You will have to hurry before the slide gains momentum, otherwise, the stakes will not hold back the slide.

The miners went back to where the one who had refused to pay was at work, and told him what the rainmaker said, telling him to get busy making and driving the stakes, and to be sure that he drove each stake down until it would hold, and to drive them until there would be no further danger of a slide. He started to object, telling the miners that was nothing but Indian talk, that if the Indian rainmaker wanted the mountain-side staked down he would have to do it himself. A few choice "cuss words" from the miners soon convinced him that he had better get to driving stakes, and so soon as the last stake was driven, to leave camp for all times.

If he had not driven the stakes when he did the mountain-side would be bare of ground today. As it is, the stakes are still holding it. The dishonest miner left, never to return [Graves 1929:75–76].

However, the flood did wash away the houses that had been built on the flats along the river.

Billie, Josie
Seminole, *Southeast*

A shaman who was born in 1885 and became one of the most important shamans of the Mikasuki division of the Seminole. He received four years of shamanic training under Billie Motlow (also recorded as Motlo), an older shaman who had advanced to the tenth degree of their shamanic training (see *aiyik-comi*). Josie Billie began to practice shamanism around the age of twenty-nine, but he "presented a difficult problem in social control. He was often drunk and violent, but since he was a shaman, his misdeeds were overlooked. Finally he was ostracized and threatened with death by the Trail Indians and moved to the Big Cypress Reservation" [Covington 1993:151]. By fifty-four, Josie Billie had advance only to the first degree of training.

He knew many herbal formulas and treated many different ailments such as fevers, headaches, broken bones, etc. He was also known to refer "cases to white doctors that his medications could not cure" [Covington 1993:232], and sometimes he would purchase his herbs, such as barks and roots, from wholesale drug firms. When administering his herbs Josie Billie would either chant or sing prescribed power phrases, often in the Creek language. To ward off a camp fever, Josie Billie was once observed using two tablespoonfuls of tobacco. "He took turns in singing a chant and blowing his breath on the tobacco. He then wrapped it up for a while and held it. During the course of the night he repeated this process. At daybreak some tobacco was placed in a pipe and smoked. Then Josie solemnly declared that the fever would never molest his camp" [Greenlee 1944:324].

In addition to healing, Josie also had other shamanic powers. He was sought out, most often by young girls, for the preparation of love medicines (see entry). In preparing such a medicine, Josie would repeatedly chant the name of the intended "victim" of the girl's affection. He was also capable of causing someone to have a fever. At night he would sing a calling song to call away the soul of the sleeping person. Once the soul came to him, he would grab it and throw it into a fire. "This severe treatment can be given to anyone in any camp no matter how far away the camp is from the one where the medicine man prepares his malevolent spell. On the next day the victim thus cursed will have a fever which he cannot dispel. He will die in a short time. His only chance to escape the effect of the spell is to employ a medical practitioner to devise a counter-spell which will remove the baneful influence" [Greenlee 1944:324].

Around 1940 he became a practicing Baptist and "turned over possession of the medicine bundle to his brother Ingraham Billie" [Covington 1993:258].

Bini
Carrier, *Mackenzie-Yukon*

An early-eighteenth-century shaman/prophet who instigated a widespread religious movement throughout the Northwest from Haines, Alaska, in the north to Vancouver Island and Rivers Inlet in the south, and interiorly among the Babine, Tahltan, and the Tinneh. "Many feats of magic were attributed to him, including the defeat of some very powerful witches. . . . Bini was noted for the use of a strange tongue and a strange manner of singing. While singing and dancing, he carried a cross and made something like the sign of the cross over his head and breast" [J. Miller 1984:142–143]. Although this was seen by historians as a "religious movement," one Port Simpson informant "felt that this was actually not a new religion, but rather it was a new form of *haleyt* (see entry) dance which also included unintelligible songs, dancing, and rolling on the floor" [Beynon in J. Miller 1984:143].

Birchbark medicine
Cree, *Canadian Eastern Woodlands*

A medicine used to gain the goodwill of friends and relatives so that they would be liberal in the giving of gifts to the bearer of this medicine. Typically, to obtain this type of medicine, an individual would make a drawing on birchbark. A description of one such drawing follows: "The drawing represents a tipi with many radiating lines representing ropes drawing on other people's property, such as, horses, saddles, guns, clothing, etc. As these many lines all lead to his tipi they symbolize his power to draw in or acquire such property. When a man has one of these birchbark medicines all visitors are strongly moved to make handsome gifts to the host. In using the medicine, the owner first rubs the birchbark with the contents of the small medicine bag then secretly places it at the lower inside of the tipi cover behind one of the rear poles. Then everyone entering the tipi falls under the spell of its secret influence. The bark is described as being about one foot square and must be held in a smudge of sweetgrass every time the tipi is moved" [Wissler 1912a:90].

Bītshāwī
Miwok, *California*
A type of central Miwok shaman who cures by pressing on the patient with his hands [Gifford n.d. a:25]. These shamans do not sing, but they use a *sohkosa*, cocoon rattle, during their healings. A *bītshāwī* can be either male or female.

Black-covered-pipes
Blackfoot, *Plains*
Two special pipes that were owned by members of the Catchers Society in 1910 and considered by them to be very powerful medicines [Wissler 1912a:159].

Black-tailed Deer Dance
Blackfoot, *Plains*
A hunting medicine ceremony. The Blackfoot culture obtained this ceremony from the Kutenai during the latter part of the nineteenth century. Members of the society wear a string of deer ankle bones painted red to symbolize that the wearer "holding these bones is likewise holding the feet of the deer" [Wissler 1913:441]. In addition, some members, during the deer hunt, wear a pair of yellow-painted rabbit ears "to give speed and endurance" [Wissler 1913:441].

Members of this society learned hypnotism. Tailen Ashley, who introduced the ceremony to the Piegan, reported that "those who do not believe in the dance and ridicule it, are thrown into a trance by those who have the power, and are then awakened and become followers. Each man and woman member has a [power] song of his or her own and some have more. The songs are bought from members and a horse or other property paid for them. Sometimes new songs are dreamed" [Tailen Ashley in Wissler 1913:441].

When the ceremony is held for hunting, medicine members usually dream the whereabouts of deer. "One member told us that in his dreams three catholic nuns always appeared and gave the information" [Wissler 1913:440]. Other members have the power to charm game. However, the ceremony, which usually lasts one night, can also be used for healing. In serious cases of illness, the ceremony may last as long as four nights.

Wissler [1913:442] also noted that "some members have power to give ill luck."

Black Wolf
Ponca, *Plains*
A renowned prophet/shaman during the latter part of the nineteenth century. "Whenever the Poncas entertained the Osages at a social, religious, or political gathering, Black Wolf presided" [Draper 1946:18]. He was a weather shaman, locator of game, and best remembered as a healer for having saved his people from an epidemic. He was much disliked by the local whites for his tenacity in instructing his people to retain their old ways rather than accept the ways of Western civilization.

His walk to death was witnessed and reported by journalist William R. Draper and covered in an issue of the *Christian Herald:*

Black Wolf came forth [from his lodge], bleeding from fresh cuts on his arms and legs. His face, dark and sullen, was drawn with pain. He lifted his arms and began to talk, making a farewell speech reciting all the good things he had done for his people. . . .

Crossing his left hand over the right hand and holding them both to the front, he turned and marched slowly toward the river bank. Humming a song of death, as indicated by the position of his hands, he did not stop on the sandy bar, but waded into the swirling waters, and was soon lost to view.

When his body was recovered, a few hours later, the Indians wailed, and mourned, and gave the old man a stylish funeral [Draper 1946:19–20].

Blue Bird
Arikara, *Plains*
A powerful shaman who was a member of the Ghost band of Arikara and died around 1921.

He was renowned for his power feats. He "used to fasten a thong to a long slender split or skewer. With the splint he would pierce his head, thrusting it in at one ear and pulling it out of the other, then pulling the cord through after it. He would then seize the string at either end and pull it back and forth through his head, meantime groaning and crying. The string would then be withdrawn and he would be in his normal condition again. This man's specialty was the treatment of earache and pains in the head" [Will 1934:48].

See also *Bear's Belly, Paint, Running Wolf, Shunáwanùh*.

Bohinne
Micmac, *Canadian Eastern Woodlands*
Shaman. This is Father Chrétien Le Clerq's late-seventeenth-century rendering of the term for shaman. The modern term is *buówin* (EONAH, p. 42) or *buoin* [Wallis and Wallis 1955:134].

At the beginning of the seventeenth century, Marc Lescarbot reported that a Micmac shaman was known as *aoutmoin,* and Father Pierre Biard, who came from France in 1611, also used the term *aoutmoin* for shaman. Similarly, the shaman's helping spirit was called *aouten* [Wallis and Wallis 1955:146].

The practice of the Micmac shaman is known only through early writings. Treatment for illnesses included the shaman blowing on the patient's body and sucking a disease object from it. However, Lescarbot observed an unusual form of treatment in which the disease object was pulled out by means of a cord. "The medicineman dug a deep hole and within it burried a stick tied to a protruding cord. He chanted, danced, and howled over the hole and alternately, over the sick man who lay nearby. He then entered into active combat with the evil, slashing about so furiously or pulling so hard at the rope that he broke out in sweat. Suddenly he roared out that the moment of peril was at hand. . . . Now the crowd pulled at the rope; but in vain. More howls and slashes from the medicineman, more

tugs at the rope. Little by little the stick was uncovered and torn out. On the end were some decayed bones or a piece of skin covered with dung. This was the evil" [Lescarbot in Wallis and Wallis 1955:135].

"In addition to treating the sick . . . the medicineman was called upon to predict the future, to answer whether a missing person was alive or dead, to name the place to hunt for game, and to approve or disapprove of war plans. . . . Medicinemen seem to have been adept illusionists, raising up visions of spirits and 'snakes and other beasts that go in and out of the mouth while they are talking'" [Baird in Wallis and Wallis 1955:147].

Bôla
Wintun, *California*
One of two types of shamans, the other being the *yomta* (EONAH, p. 329). Although the *bôla* employs sucking in his healing ceremonies, he only sucks out blood; by contrast the *yomta* draws out a disease-object. The *bôla* works by dreaming and has less prestige than the *yomta*.

This particular type of shaman is most likely associated with the Bole or Maru cult [Meighan and Riddell 1972], the California version of the widespread Ghost Dance cult.

Brown, Fanny
Wintun, *California*
A Wintu shaman of wide repute from the Upper Sacramento subarea. In 1935 she was estimated to be 65 years old. Her healing powers were acquired from the guardian spirits of her brother and sister, which came to her slowly over time after their deaths. However, she had the reputation of being a "poisoner and is rarely called to attend a patient" [Du Bois 1935:92]. She was also known to have clairvoyant abilities, as this report reveals: "Fanny's boy was killed. He was found in the river (Sacramento). They said he had been drowned. Fanny went into a trance and told all that had happened. She said he had been murdered and that his body had been kept under

the house for two days. Then it was thrown in the river. She told where the body would be found in the river between Kennett and Keswick. People looked for the body and found it just where she said it would be. Ever since then she has sent poison to us here a lot" [Wash Fan in Du Bois 1935:92].

Brown was primarily a sucking doctor who removed *pains* (see entry) by sucking on the patient's body. Her parents were not doctors. Of the spirits she obtained later on from her brother and sister, she reported: "I got all their powers and their spirits. They came to me little by little. My brother had two spirits. My sister had two—a sucker spirit and a human one. I don't know what two my brother had. I don't know what human soul my sister had. I was a little girl then. My mother told me about her. My sister and brother got to be doctors by dancing in a sweat house" [Fanny Brown in Du Bois 1935:93].

In this case we seem to have a very unusual instance of a shaman knowing from whom she inherited spirits but not knowing what type of spirits they were. However, since Wintu shamans go into trance during a healing, they never really know what or how many spirits come to them (e.g., see *Charles, Nels*).

Of her own doctoring she reported:

I have a bunch of feathers to use in doctoring. It was hidden in the mountains by a great old-time doctor. My brother found it and brought it in the house to me and left it there. The feathers should all come from the wings of eagles. Tail feathers are too short. If a man who isn't a good doctor holds a bunch of these feathers, he will get a headache. It is dangerous for him to handle them. I made my own headdress (yellow-hammer) and necklace (of rattlesnake rattles). I killed my own rattlesnakes. A person who is a good doctor isn't afraid of rattlesnakes.

I don't know what a "pain" looks like. Some people say it looks like a sliver of bone. . . . When I suck out a pain I chew it up and kill it with my teeth, then I spit it out into a bundle of grass. I

never swallow it. I hide the bundle of grass in the bushes. Once I doctored a man three days and nights and I got out a pain every time I sucked. . . .

When you doctor, the interpreter [shaman's assistant] asks the doctor [who is in trance] questions and gets answers. When a doctor is in a trance he talks another language. I don't know how or when I learned doctor's language. It is just my spirit talking to my heart [Fanny Brown in Du Bois 1935:93–94].

Here again, by way of clarification, it should be noted that Brown is in a trance when she removed a pain and therefore really never remembered seeing it.

Brush Dance
Yurok, *Oregon Seaboard*

This is a healing ceremony held for a child. "The dance is held in the living house, but the roof and most of the walls of this are taken down for the occasion. On the first night young men dance about the fire for a few hours. They wear no ornaments but hold boughs of foliage up before them. The following night is an intermission, and on the third or fourth night the dance proper takes place from dark until dawn" [Kroeber 1925:61–62].

"Two formulas are in use for the dance, or, it would be better to say, two types of ceremonial action in connection with the formula, since the latter is always somewhat different according to the individual reciting it. The *umeleyek* formula is spoken on the first and third nights; the alternative *worero*, which is considered stronger, on the first and fourth, and is followed by the waving of pitch-pine brands over the child" [Kroeber 1925:62].

The terms *umeleyek* and *worero* are used by the Yuroks to refer to this ceremony, while *Brush Dance* is the American term for it [Kroeber 1925:55].

Charles S. Graves witnessed this ceremony on several occasions. He wrote:

I first witnessed the "Brush Dance" over fifty years ago. The last time I witnessed it was July 4th, 1927, at Orleans. They dance all night for the purpose of saving the life of a little child; they were not dancing for amusement. When they want amusement they dance "white man dance."

All of the members of the tribe, and Indians from all other tribes were there, as were also many palefaces, and I was among the number. And with one accord, we asked the Great Spirit to spare the life of this child; and the baby's life was spared.

Yes, I do believe in Indian ceremonies, especially one like the "Brush Dance," where the ceremony has to do with saving the life of a baby [Graves 1929:22–23].

Buffalo doctors
Plains

Many of the Plains cultures had societies of shamans associated with the buffalo. The Oto, for instance, had the Buffalo Doctors' Lodge. "Although not all the members of the society practiced doctoring, the Buffalo Doctors' Lodge was primarily a society of doctors. But it also had functions other than curing. It was associated with the cultivation of corn. . . . But the primary purpose of the society was curing" [Whitman 1937:105]. The Oto also referred to this society as the Buffalo Way [Whitman 1937:106].

The Oto Buffalo shamans were very effective. "They were especially effective in cases of wounds, broken bones, and delayed childbirth, though they doctored other illnesses as well. In general they employed a special curing technique. The doctors chewed medicine, herbs known only to the doctors, and would then spray it over the patient's wound. If the patient were severely wounded, several doctors would effect the cure. The proof of a good doctor was that he made people well" [Whitman 1937:105]. Those who were cured by the Buffalo society became eligible for society membership. In addition, "small boys were selected as members, their entrance fees being paid to the leader of the group they were to join. Women were also eligible for membership" [Whitman 1937:108].

The Buffalo society among the Omaha was also devoted primarily to healing. It was known as the *Te ithaethe* society, from *te,* meaning "buffalo," and *ithaethe,* meaning "to show compassion." That is, it was a society of "those to whom the buffalo has shown compassion, by coming to them in a vision and giving power" [Fletcher and La Flesche in Fortune 1932:60]. Like the Oto, this society was also associated with the cultivation of corn. One informant reported: "When the corn is withering for want of rain the Buffalo Society have a dance. They borrow a large vessel, which they fill with water, and put in the centre of their circle. They dance four times around it. One of their number drinks some of the water, spurts it up into the air, making a fine spray in imitation of a fog or misting rain. Then he knocks over the vessel, spilling the water on the ground. The dancers then fall down and drink up the water, getting mud all over their faces. Then they spurt the water up into the air, making fine misting rain, which saves the corn" [Pathinnanpaji in Fortune 1932:59].

In his later analysis of the Omaha *Te ithaethe,* Fortune [1932:73–74] concluded that, due to similar patterns in the visions of the society members, "it seems clear that the vision is a society owned privilege which is handed down. . . . For a doctor always tells a vision as if it were his own experience. . . . What actually happens in other cases is that the father tells the son a traditional vision account, much as a myth is told, which is then reset by the son as if it were his personal experience." However, Fortune's conclusion was conjecture because, as he admitted, "we are dealing, of course, with difficult material where information is hard to come by" [Fortune 1932:73] and for which he secured no direct evidence.

See also *Mowitihagi.*

Buffalo rock bundle
Blackfoot, *Plains*
See *iniskim.*

Buffalo stones

Hidatsa, *Plains*

The name given to three personal medicine stones belonging to Big Cloud (see entry). He obtained the first and largest stone during a vision quest by placing a yellow grasshopper under his sagebrush pillow, which then turned to stone. He took the stone and placed it into a pouch; when opened several years later, the pouch contained a second, smaller stone. In turn, after two more years a third stone appeared in the pouch. These stones were Big Cloud's personal medicine that enabled him to become a great leader and warrior among his people [Pepper and Wilson 1908:324–325].

Bunzel, Ruth

Ruth Bunzel graduated from college in 1918 and by 1924 was working as Franz Boas's (EONAH, pp. 36–37) secretary at Columbia University when he suggested that she do a project on Native American pottery. Subsequently, with virtually no training as an anthropologist, she traveled to the Southwest with Ruth Benedict (see entry), where she lived during the 1920s with the family of a major Zuni potter named Catalina Zuni, in particular with Catalina's daughter Flora [Hardin 1993:262]. Between 1924 and 1929 she spent five summer seasons and two winters among the Zuni, learning to make pottery. She, along with Matilda Coxe Stevenson (see entry), was one of the first women in anthropology to use the field technique known as "participant observation." This work resulted in her first major publication, entitled *The Pueblo Potter*, which appeared in 1929. This manuscript was concerned with the social limitations imposed on artistic expression within a culture, and it demonstrated how pottery designs are passed from mother to daughter through time. She was also one of the first anthropologists to claim that pottery designs were not always symbolic in nature.

During the 1930s she published a wealth of information on Zuni ceremonialism, myths, etc., often much to the surprise of her Zuni informants. In the latter part of her career, she did fieldwork in Guatemala and also edited a book, *The Golden Age of American Anthropology*, with Margaret Mead.

During her career she was a lecturer, research associate, and adjunct professor at Columbia University, which was remarkable given the discrimination against women in academia in that era. Indeed, it was a well-known fact that "in anything a woman has to be twice as good and work twice as hard as a man to be recognized" [Spicer in Fox 1993:305].

Buoin

Micmac, *Canadian Eastern Woodlands*

See *bohinne*.

Caiyaik

Keres, *Southwest*

Members of the *Cikame* or *Shikame* (see entry) society who often operate as hunting shamans [White 1930:612]. The *Cikame* also serves as a curing society.

Calf Shirt

Blood, *Plains*

A war leader, shaman, and chief of the Lone Fighters band during the 1800s. As a youth he acquired spirit power from the grizzly bear through the sacrifice of the youngest of his four wives. The power given was "that henceforth no bullet, arrow, or knife could penetrate his body" [Dempsey 1994:48]. Accordingly he received the second name of Impervious to Bullets. However, because Calf Shirt was subject to wild bouts of drinking and a terrible temper, he also acquired the nickname of Miniksee, or Wild Person [Dempsey 1994:51].

In December 1873 he was gunned down at Fort Kipp, Montana. Accounts of his death indicate that he entered the fort in a rage, dressed as a warrior, to seek revenge for an insult by the traders there. "As the chief approached the trading room, he continued to sing his war song, then paused to perform a few steps of the war dance. . . . Kipp shouted to his men to kill the offending Indian. They promptly opened fire, and although Calf Shirt was peppered with lead balls, he just stopped, then slowly turned around and strode out the main gates of the fort. He made no attempt to return their fire" [Dempsey 1994:56, 57]. He continued to walk for 100 yards before collapsing into a deep excavation from which earth sodding had been taken for the roof of the fort. "There were sixteen bullet holes in his body, every one of them a fatal shot; he had evidently possessed the vitality of a grizzly bear" [Schultz in Dempsey 1994:57].

Calf Shirt had a nephew by the same name who was also a shaman. This Calf Shirt received his powers from the rattlesnake during a vision. "The snakes were his brothers and did his bidding. If he whistled, they slithered through the grass to his feet; if he made a sign, they quietly slipped away" [Dempsey 1994:140]. "By some peculiar method he was able to go alone upon the prairie and secure very large rattlesnakes, one of which he would carry inside of his blanket coat" [Maclean in Dempsey 1994:141]. This Calf Shirt would show his powers to the whites for money. One journalist reported, "Calf Shirt claims to have some subtle power over snakes and to see him take his present specimen up, she measuring about three feet long, catch it by the neck and cram about eight inches of it, the deadliest reptile in America, head first down his throat, is calculated to make the marrow in any man's bones shiver" [unidentified journalist in Dempsey 1994:145]. He died in 1901.

Calumet Dance
See *Peace Pipe Dance*.

Cangkdeska wakang
Teton, *Plains*
Literal translation: "sacred hoop" [Howard 1984:103]. Santee (Canadian Sioux) term for medicine wheel. Often the medicine wheel appears in the symbolic form of a limb bent into the shape of a hoop with a cross superimposed upon it. This equal-armed cross symbolizes the four winds or four directions. These "fur covered hoops are sometimes carried by dancers as symbols of the medicine wheel, and small versions, cut from rawhide and wrapped with quillwork, are often worn as hair ornaments or tied to deer tail 'medicine brushes' attached to Grass Dancers' deer hoof bandoliers" [Howard 1984:103].

Caxwu
Twana, *Northwest Coast*
A wooden figure, about 4 feet in height, in the image of the Little-Earth (dwarf) spirits used by the Chehalis people. Elmendorf [1993:242–249] reported on their use in an attempt to find some gold hidden by the former dead wife of a man named Lighthouse Charley around 1870. By using the *caxwu* they were able to locate two of her hiding places and recover some of the lost gold.

In ceremonial use the *caxwu* is held by an individual but becomes animated of its own accord. It turns quite hot, often blistering the hand of the person who holds it. When not in use it is kept wrapped in cedar bark.

Chantway
Navajo, *Southwest*
See *hatáál*.

Charles, Nels
Wintun, *California*
A Wintu shaman who was born around 1887 and began to doctor around 1912. He began dreaming around 1908 or 1909 and underwent a six-month training in shamanic doctoring beginning in early 1912 under two other Wintu shamans, Charlie Klutchie and Tilly Griffen. Until he began dreaming he always went to church, and as a result his initial guardian spirit "looked like church pictures of God. He wore a crown" [Nels Charles in Du Bois 1935:95]. Within two years after he began his practice, many spirits came to him. Of these spirits and his doctoring, he reported:

I never knew how many spirits came, though some doctors might. . . . I dreamed songs too and could then get up and sing them. In my dreaming the spirit which came to me was light. . . . Sometimes a spirit is too strong for a doctor, so another doctor must be called in. Some spirits are vicious and abuse you. They make you run out in the hills, where you have a trance. Spirits look you over first. If you aren't right they won't stay with you. . . .

Before doctoring, I got other doctors to strengthen me by singing. I went to Charlie Klutchie and Tilly Griffen. I paid them to sing for me. In order to keep a spirit, you must take care of yourself. You must keep away from women who are having their monthlies. . . . My power is not so great because my spirits worry. They don't know what to do with themselves. When they were strong, I was strong and could cure patients. But after I lost my sister and some aunts, I was worried and that bothered my spirits. I was weakened. My spirits aren't sure whether they can cure a sick person and they are weakened by not being sure. If a person abuses me I mustn't wish him to be sick, or die, or have bad luck. That would ruin me. My spirits might think differently and that would weaken my power. Spirits talk to my heart and know what I think. Different doctors have different ideas. Spirits protect a doctor from sickness. I haven't been sick since I began dreaming even though I have been around smallpox, measles, and influenza. . . .

When you go into trance—when spirits come to a doctor—the doctor and the people hear a whizzing noise. Then the doctor feels a hotness. I always feel mine in my head. When you doctor, if one spirit doesn't work, another comes to help it. You smoke tobacco to call a spirit. A doctor has just a certain number of spirits. Four or five is a large number to have. The doctor never knows what spirits come to him. It is the interpreter who calls the spirits and knows how many come. The doctors speak in a language that has higher words in it. One word can mean many things. I never learned this language. I can't even talk Wintu well, but when a spirit enters me the spirit talks and they say I talk Wintu perfectly well. It is just like talking with unknown tongues and getting the spirit in the Pentecostal church. A doctor may sing for several hours and not locate a sickness. During the singing he tells what happens, what happened a few days ago, what will happen by and by. While he is singing he is in a trance. All this time the doctor's spirit is watching for the poison.

Today doctors sing more. In the old days they sucked more. You are in a trance when you suck. When you suck you might extract a stone. The spirit in the doctor sees the bad blood, and shows the doctor where to suck. I have sucked people, but I never know what I extract. . . . To pull a poison out with your hand is harder than when the sickness just needs sucking. The doctor's spirit kills the poison.

My spirits travel about all the time, they know everything. . . . In the old days doctors would find things by singing. For instance, if a dog were lost while hunting, a doctor would sing and talk to the dog and tell him where his master was.

A Tlingit shaman's ivory charm carved to represent a wolf's head.

I don't feel weak or tired after doctoring. I don't know how many people I have doctored [Nels Charles in Du Bois 1935:95–97].

Charm

Objects, substances, or mixtures of herbs and other items that, by their inherent properties, either can compel the spirits or forces of nature to aid the manipulator of the charm in some particular, invariable way or can bring about the desired results without the intervention of any spirit simply through the power of the charm itself. A charm that carries good fortune is known as a talisman.

Charm making is common throughout Native North America, and the most commonly sought after charm is the "love medicine" charm, which is used to attract another individual. However, charms come in many different forms for many different purposes, and the anthropological literature is replete with examples of them.

Quite often charms are associated with some form of animal. In these cases the power of the charm parallels the power of that particular animal spirit. For example, a Mountain Lion charm would be more powerful than a Ground Owl or Mole charm.

The variety of charms is virtually endless, as the following examples suggest. Among the East Greenland Eskimos, "charred moss from the lamps is put on the lash of the whip to keep it from flying off when the whip is cracked" [Kroeber 1900:308]. Charms also come in the form of songs among the Eskimo. "They consist mainly of fragments from old songs, handed down from earlier generations. They can be bought, at a high price, or bequeathed by the 'owner' on his deathbed to another. But they must never be heard by any save the one who is to use them, or their power will be gone" [Rasmussen 1969:137].

One of the most common forms of charms are the prayer offerings (see *offerings* entry) that often accompany individual prayers. These offerings are made to improve the efficacy of an individual's prayer, and they come in many different forms. In addition the offering of tobacco to "feed" the spirit of a ritual mask, drum, etc., is also a form of charm. Corn pollen offerings (see entry) are another common form of charm used in the Southwest.

Songs and incantations (spells) can also serve as charms. The Hopi have a purification or discharming song known as *náwuhchi tawi.* "The Powamu priest takes an eagle wing feather in his left and some ashes in his right hand, sprinkling some of the ashes on the feather and beats time with it to the singing. . . . This song [joined in by all present] has six verses, and at the end of each verse the Powamu priest brushes the ashes from the feather towards the hatchway [of the kiva], all the others circling their right hand before themselves and throwing the ashes, which they hold between thumb and forefinger, and also at the same time spitting in the same direction. After the sixth time they all beat and rub off the ashes from their hands and bodies, blow the ashes from their hands and they are then considered to be purified of the peculiar charm or 'taboo' of the Popwamu" [Voth 1901:109]. Among the Hopi any uninitiated person who observes the secret ceremonies of any society must undergo such a purification since observing the ceremonies is taboo. In the case of the *Popwamu* society, breaking this taboo causes the knee area to swell and the tendons about the knee to contract. In other societies different society-associated, physical ailments manifest themselves.

For other examples see *angoak, atishwin, Chüawimkya, dukud,* *etsoul, huuku, kahimtcine, kusabi, kxói, mole, mushkiki, nakwakwosi, nauühic, nawuhchingwu, One Spot, otterskin war medicine, paho, qolo-gogolog, sáwanikia, serrat, siwín, talasi, tihu, túkosiwäwûs, tupilak, war bridle charm, watawe, xosi.*

Chayan
Keres, *Southwest*
Dialectical variant: *cheani* (Laguna) [Parsons 1926: 108]. Plural: *chaiañi* [Lange 1959:254]; *chayani.* Cochiti Pueblo term for medicine man or shaman. The leaders of this group's medicine societies are generally known as the *cacique,* a Spanish term that is often shortened to *kasik* by the inhabitants of Cochiti [Lange 1959:240]. This office is held by a shaman who has demonstrated medicine powers. As such, the *cacique* is also addressed according to his powers or the society he heads. For example, the *cacique* who heads the Flint Society may also be known as *hishtanyi chayan,* "flint medicine man." Other examples are the *shui chayan,* "snake medicine man," of the Snake Medicine Society and the *hakanyi chayan,* "fire medicine man," of the Fire Medicine Society [Bandelier in Lange 1959: 237]. All other shamans are members of one or more medicine societies. Thus, for these people, shamanism generally operates within the confines of a medicine society. In cases of minor illness, a shaman may go alone to the house of a patient to treat him, but most often a medicine society is convened to conduct a healing.

The major functions of the Cochiti medicine societies "are the curing of disease, retreats for rain, and the selection of pueblo officers, of which the first is the most fundamental. . . . The medicine-men are re-

A Tlingit shaman's headdress, a mask with a protruding tongue used in ceremonies to heal wounds; attached to the mask is a walrus ivory charm in the form of a land otter.

ally secondary at solstices; although they carry much of the burden, it is really the cacique [head shaman] who is in charge. The assistance of the medicine-men at masked dances is, too, a rather minor function, as well as their custody of masks" [White 1930:618].

Of particular importance is the power received from the Bear spirit, such that shamans are often referred to as "Bears" [Lange 1959:256]. Bear-claw necklaces (and bracelets) and dried bear paws are common ritual paraphernalia.

Shamans of the Fire Medicine Society (now extinct) treated burns and fevers. During their healing ceremonies the shamans handled fire with impunity if "the 4 or 5 days [of] rigorous and absolute fasting which precedes such a cere-mony . . . is done with perfect free will and car-ried out fully" [Bandelier in Lange 1959:266–267]. During the ceremony a little broomlike tuft of grass, called *popote,* was set on fire, and the head shaman took bites of the flaming grass and chewed it. In addition the other shamans of the society performed a fire dance in which "one after another jump into a flaming pyre and dance, in the very center of the flames" [Bande-lier in Lange 1959:267].

Other power feats of shamans were reported by Bandelier:

Some of the Chayani placed a white screen in the background of a darkened room. Behind it and on the floor they placed a round disk painted yellow, representing the *Sun.* Then they began to sing and at the song the disk began to rise on the East corner of the screen, like the sun would in the heavens. When it reached the highest point of the curve (which corresponded with the middle of the screen) the song was interrupted,—and the sun also stopped. When the singing began again the sun resumed its motion gradually declining toward the West until it touched the floor at the corner of the screen. He [Bandelier's informant] attributes this clever performance to the efficacy of the Song exclusively.—Another very pretty trick is also done with an empty gourd, the top of which is perforated and has four Eagle's plumes

fastened to it. The bottom of the gourd is of course convex and cannot stand. Nevertheless, as soon as the song of the Chayani begins, one of them gives it a very slight blow with the hand and this causes it to stand up and remain thus as long as the singing lasts, while the plumes quiver in a dancing motion [Bandelier in Lange 1959:267].

Chesakkon
Ojibwa, *Canadian Eastern Woodlands*
Shaking tent [Coleman 1937:52]. The lodge used in the performance of the Shaking Tent Ceremony (EONAH, p. 246–249).

Chidid
Twana, *Northwest Coast*
"Power of eye"; to supernaturally "electrocute" [Elmendorf 1960:503]. When a novice first re-ceived power from a helping spirit during a vision quest, the power was uncontrolled. One manner in which this uncontrolled power manifested itself through the novice was *chidid.* "To satisfy them-selves as to the power of their newly acquired shaman spirit novices often gave their 'power of eye' full rein while returning home after their vi-sion encounter. By merely gazing at them they could kill small animals or birds, crack rocks, or wrench limbs out of trees" [Elmendorf 1960:503].

Related to this is a condition known as *chiditeb,* which occurred during a vision quest if the novice became frightened and ran from an approaching spirit power. The spirit then "elec-trocuted" the novice for his or her fear [Elmen-dorf 1960:506–507]. This "electrocution" by the spirit "resulted in the novice going into convul-sions, either immediately or a day or two after his return home, and dying with twisted and contorted limbs" [Elmendorf 1960:502].

Chikauvasi
Yavapai, *Southwest*
Medicine necklace. These necklaces, made of stone or glass beads, are used by shamans and imbued with power. Different beads are named for different powers. For example, "one turquoise bead *(kahauvashua)* gave power, a black stone

bead *(pukinyacha)* was deer hunter's amulet. . . . Beads for natural powers called by Skatakaamcha [a spirit], musakikauwa, foggy talk" [Gifford 1936:310]. The necklace is worn under one's shirt or otherwise hidden from view at all times.

"[The] necklace [is] used by some shamans [i.e., *ikwivchisiwe,* weather shaman] to make wind, rain, hail. One who understood all uses of necklace was powerful; his knowledge was bestowed by Skatakaamcha. He might accompany war party. Could foretell outcome of campaign by feather divination" [Gifford 1936:310].

See also *basemacha* and *pokwia.*

Chindi
Navajo, *Southwest*
Ghost. "The ghost of an individual is a malignant influence, released at death and capable of return to earth as an apparition" [Wyman et al. 1942:11]. The source of this "malignant influence" is "a little thing, small as a grain of dust, which Changing Woman places in the back of a person's head (where you see the depression) immediately after birth when the infant makes the first sound" [D. S. in Wyman et al. 1942:11]. When a person dies this "little thing" goes (north) to the afterworld, where after four days it become a *chindi.* A *chindi* is similar to the modern Western concept of an evil spirit, but this spirit was once a living person rather than a supernatural being. However, other Navajos believe that *chindi* encompasses all the evil in the world and that at death a person's own evil joins the *chindi* but remains capable of emerging from it in apparitional form. These forms include a coyote, owl, mouse, spot of fire, whirlwind, indefinite dark objects, and human forms. In addition, these forms may visibly change in shape or size, and they usually make sounds, such as whistles.

Personal contact with such ghosts results in sickness or misfortune. Consequently, the Navajos have many different shamanic procedures and ceremonies, such as Evil Way and Enemy Way, to combat this evil influence in people's lives.

Choñotkya
Hopi, *Southwest*
Plural: choñotki. Ceremonial reed cigarettes [Stephen 1936:75]. Made from sections of reed filled with tobacco, they are used in various ceremonies, such as the *Powamu,* for blowing smoke on certain *kachinas.* They are always lit using a cedar-bark fuse called *kopichoki.* In addition the Hopi use several different types of ceremonial pipes for smoking during ceremonies.

Chüawimkya
Hopi, *Southwest*
Snake Society. From *chüa,* "he of the earth," the Hopi word for snake [Stephen 1936:1211]. This society is renowned for its Snake Dance, which is performed every other year (alternating with the Flute Ceremony) along with the *Chübwi-wimkyamu,* or Antelope Society [Stephen 1936:1212], in the Snake-Antelope Ceremony. The Snake-Antelope Ceremony begins eight days before the official beginning with the making of *pahos* (see entry), and, once started lasts for nine days, followed by four days of activities. In the nineteenth century the medicine powers of the Snake-Antelope Ceremony were used to control the Hopis' enemies; today the ceremony is performed to control rain [Parsons 1939:1148].

Prior to the Snake Dance per se,

> there is a ceremony when the snakes are released in the kiva, the men sitting chanting with their eyes closed, while the serpents in their multitude react to the sound like wheat in the wind and climb in the men's laps and look into their faces and—this is well attested—coil in the laps of those with open hearts who have grown beyond human hate and fear. And sleep there. . . . That is a minor point of the dance.
>
> The major point is rain. Here the nature of sympathetic magic seems obvious. We know from pueblo paintings and petroglyphs of all periods that snakes are associated with lightning and with

Snake Dance at Oraibi (photograph by Adam Clark Vroman, 1898).

the descending rain itself. They also penetrate the earth and seek out its springs. . . . [During the dance] the snakes are making the same squirming pattern in the dust that the washes take as they wriggle out and away into the plain. Rain is being brought to the plaza in this way [Scully 1975:342].

The Snake Dance is performed on the afternoon of the ninth day. In former times, "all the Pueblos had the rattlesnake-dance, and carried snakes in their mouths" [Bourke 1884:197]. The first published account of this ceremony came from John G. Bourke [1884], who watched it at Walpi on August 12, 1881. Since then many recorded observations of the dance have appeared. One observer described it as "an elaborate series of prayers . . . to send life-giving rain

to save their corn and peaches, beans and squashes, and other crops that mean life to the Hopis. Rattlesnakes, bullsnakes, gartersnakes, and any snakes they can capture are believed to be messengers that will carry the prayers" [Forrest 1961:18].

The most spectacular part of the ceremony occurs when the Snake Society dancers release their captured snakes and proceed to pick them up, place them in their mouths, and dance with them. Voth described the scene: "The dancer having been handed a snake, placed it between his lips *(kahchanglawu)* and moved slowly forward being accompanied by another priest who had placed his arm around the dancer's neck *(má-wokngwu)*, occupying, as it were, with his snake whip, the attention of the snake, warding off the latter's head from the dancer's face as much as possible. As soon as these two had described the circuit in front of the *kisi* the snake was dropped and picked *(pungñimani)* up by the third man. The two again approached the *kisi,* received another reptile and went through the same performance. The gatherers held sometimes as many as four, five and even more snakes in their hands, and it has been observed that on several occasions a dancer would take more than one reptile at a time between his lips" [Dorsey and Voth 1902:251]. "Occasionally a big rattler did coil ready to fight as soon as released, but a few motions of a snake whip [held by the dancers] caused it to uncoil, and the gatherer, with a sudden grab, snatched it up" [Forrest 1961:62]. Even white observers have been overwhelmed during this aspect of the ceremony. Hamlin Garland (see entry) watched the performance in the summer of 1895 and wrote: "For an hour I had been carried out of myself" [Garland in Underhill and Littlefield 1976:15; originally appeared in the August 1896 issue of *Harper's Weekly*].

One of the little-known difficulties of this dance is the fact that a dancer may not spit. Voth [1903:346] reported: "I have been told by a Snake priest that they are not allowed to expectorate during the whole performance outside of the kiva, but have to swallow any sputa that may collect in their mouths, even while holding the snakes. They say if any one should step on their sputa or in any way whatever come into contact with it, he would be affected by the peculiar snake charm; i.e., some part of his body would swell up and if not discharmed, burst." In fact, all persons attending this ceremony who are not initiates of the Snake Society are susceptible to this ailment. For that reason all of the observers, at the conclusion of this nine-day ceremony, hum together the discharming song known as *náwuhchi tawi* (see *charm*) [Voth 1903:348]

On the altar of the Snake-Antelope Ceremony sit the *chamahia* (also *chamahiya* [Parsons 1939: 333])—celt-shaped, stone fetishes. The spirits of the *chamahia* are evoked during the ceremony. Rather than dancing with snakes in their

mouths, the *chamahia* swallow the snakes. "The snake went down into the stomach and was drawn up again, and rain speedily followed" [Stephen 1936:707].

Many other rituals are performed during the nine days of the Snake-Antelope Ceremony. For instance, on the eighth day there is a footrace. The ritual beginning of this race was observed in the 1890s:

Namurztiwa then took a particle of clay from the stone which had been lying at the left of the cloud symbols, and smeared a small portion of it on the bottom of the foot of each of the runners, the explanation of this being, so it was said, to induce the rain clouds to come more quickly, the mud having been taken from a spring. While the men who were soon to take part in the race now stood in line awaiting the signal, Namurztiwa began walking toward the village, passing over successively the second and third set of cloud symbols, until he reached the fourth, or the one nearest the village. While he had been doing this, the two Kalehtakas had twirled their bull roarers [EONAH, p. 42] and shot their lightning frames over the shrine. They now started in the direction of the fourth set of symbols, but one went at one side of the path and the other at the other side. . . . Their arrival at the fourth cloud symbol, where Namurztiwa was awaiting them, was the signal for the start of the race, all of the runners starting forward simultaneously, yelling vociferously as they passed each set of cloud symbols [Dorsey and Voth 1902:231].

Chúharipiru
Pawnee, *Plains*
Skidi medicine bundle. This term is derived from *chuhuru,* "rainstorm," and *ripiru,* "wrapped up." Sometime this bundle is known more affectionately as *atira,* "mother," referring to the "two ears of corn kept in each bundle and symbolically spoken of as the mother of the people. The reference to rain is due to the conception that the important powers of the world reside in the west, the home of the thunderers, from whence

the powers of the bundles come. . . . Thus at the sound of the first thunder in spring, the keeper of each bundle must immediately open it with the proper procedure and make an offering of dried buffalo meat to the powers in the west" [Murie 1914:550]. Each of the thirteen Skidi villages had one such bundle in its possession, with the original and most sacred or powerful bundle being the Evening Star (or Red Calf) bundle held at Tuhrikakuh (the center village).

"At the time of the federation of these [13] villages, powers were delegated to four special or main bundles which in turn served as the basis of the governing power" [Murie 1914:551]. These four bundles, representing the powers of the four directions and kept at Kitkahapakuhtu (the old village), were: the Yellow Tipi (or Yellow Star) bundle (northwest), the Mother-Born-Again (or White Star) bundle (southwest), the Leading Cornstalk (or Red Star) bundle (southeast), and the Big Black Meteoric Star bundle (northeast). The four shamans in charge of these bundles were the highest authorities among the Skidi. If any other bundle was to be opened, the keeper of the Evening Star bundle had to be present, "and the conductor [of the opening ceremony] is either he or one of the four leading priests, as the ritual may require" [Murie 1914:555].

Cicäwuskw
Fox, *Midwest*

Hunting medicine. This particular hunting medicine consists of the dried head of an ivory-billed woodpecker (called *mämäwu*) to which a bag of paint (called *wäcihon*) is attached; a small bag of purification incense (called *nothigun*) is contained within the *mämäwu*. The use of this medicine was described as follows:

The hunter who wishes to use this medicine must purify himself by taking a sweat-bath every day for four days; then the next morning he goes out to some spot not frequented by women and builds a new fire, upon which he throws some of the compound of tobacco and herbs [in the *nothigun*],

fumigating his body, hunting pouch, blankets, bullets, everything he is to use, in the resulting smoke. Then he lays tobacco on the woodpecker's head and asks or prays that he may kill a spike buck or a yearling doe, which are said to be the hardest to find and kill. If I understood correctly, each man who is to hunt does all these things, and then the leader, if there is a party, ties the woodpecker head to his scalp lock. They go the first day to their hunting ground and make camp, then at dawn the next day they sally forth, the leader, wearing the woodpecker, to the east, the others different directions. One of them will kill the spike buck or young doe, because they asked for it. Whoever accomplishes the feat cuts the head off and throws it to the east, then skins and cuts up the carcass, leaving a strip of hide and hair on the breast. When this is cut loose and pulled back the blood inside is thrown to the four directions, in this order: E., S., W., N., after which the breast is given to the owner of the medicine to make a feast. After this everything becomes easy for the hunters [M. R. Harrington 1914:226–227].

(Note: The sacred bundle referred to in this account is Bundle 2/7812 of the Heye Collection that is now housed in Washington, D.C., at the National Museum of the American Indian.)

Cicikwanani
Fox, *Midwest*

Gourd rattles [Fisher 1939:90]. Gourd rattles are frequently used to accompany the songs of sacred ceremonies among the Fox.

Ciwa
Comox, *Northwest Coast*

The term used by the Sechelt division for a clairvoyant [Barnett 1955:150]. See *kwaneman*.

Cixax
Twana, *Northwest Coast*

The process of shooting some form of *swadash* (see entry) into a person in order to harm him.

[A] doctor can also take a sharp stick or a sharp bone and cixax it into you, even if you are some distance away. It goes into you without marking your skin and makes you sick. The doctor duku'd [puts power into] that stick, "electrifies" it, by making it invisible when he sends it. . . . The doctor who treats a person for this sickness sees the thing inside of him when he diagnoses. . . .

Then the doctor lays the patient down and draws a blanket up to his chest and sings for his own doctor power. He uses his swa´daš like an x-ray eye, to see into the sick person and tell what is the matter with him. Then, when he has found where the shot swa´daš is in the patient's body, he puts his lips over that part and sucks. When it comes out in his mouth he grabs it in both hands and plunges it into a basket half full of water at his side. He holds it there and groans and sobs. He has to hold it hard or it will get away.

I have also seen a doctor spit out the swa´daš into a little . . . bundle that he held in his hands at the moment he sucked out the bad power. . . .

When he brings the power out of the water, the doctor holds both hands closed, backs up and thumbs and forefingers together. He holds it that way in his two fists so it can't get away. Then he backs up and gets someone with a knife to cut the little bundle in two between his fists. When they do that the bundle bleeds. That kills the swa´daš and the doctor who sent it. . . .

Then, after he throws the tamánamis [swadash] away or kills it, the doctor picks up water in two hands and goes "bu bu" at it and turns it into an icicle, and shoots it into the sick man, right at the place the swa´daš came out. That is a sore spot. He shoves the icicle in, and that heals the soreness. Then the ceremony is over [Henry Allen in Elmendorf 1993:217–218].

Sometimes a shaman sends the harmful swadash to the "Little-Earths" (dwarf spirits) instead of cutting it in two. To do this, the shaman throws the swadash in their direction and then motions his hands as if fanning it toward them. This procedure causes the guilty sorcerer to go crazy.

In cases where the victim could not be saved, he "was sometimes wrapped up in blankets and buried alive or laid in a burial canoe in the grave-yard. They call that ptɑ´qs (tied at both ends), and it refers to smothering . . . that smothers the swa´daš and the doctor who shot it. Of course it kills the sick person, who had that power shot into him, but they only do this when he's nearly dead anyway. He's just buried and dies. It's only done when the case is hopeless" [Henry Allen in Elmendorf 1993:220].

Ckoyo
Keres, *Southwest*

Giant Society. This medicine society consists of powerful shamans who are able to control the weather and heal illnesses caused by witches (*kanatyaiya*—see entry). At San Felipe the "women members of the Giant Society are called Shiwanna" [Parsons 1939:900], meaning "Thundercloud" [White 1930:607]. However, at Acoma, Laguna, Santo Domingo, and Cochiti, the *Shiwanna* [see entry] form an independent society of men [White 1930:604].

Every February at Cochiti, the Flint (*Hictiani*—see EONAH, pp. 105–106) and Giant Societies conduct a one-night general healing for the entire village. "All are treated with medicine water and aspersing, and noxious things are withdrawn from the body" [Parsons 1939:534]. Cochiti's Giant Society has a recipro-cal relationship with the Kachina Dance Society as well. "The Giants make prayer-sticks for the Kachina society who keep their masks in the house of the Giants" [Parsons 1939:901]. The Giants also have masks, including a mask of Buz-zard [Parsons 1939:346]. During the summer solstice the Giant Society, along with other med-icine societies, goes into retreat for rain ceremo-nials. The society is also called into play during the planting of blue corn [Parsons 1939:790].

Coacoochee
Seminole, *Southeast*

Also: *Kowákocî* [Sturtevant 1954b:376]. Literal translation: "wildcat." An early-nineteenth-cen-tury shaman who became famous for leading the

1837 escape of twenty Seminoles who were imprisoned in the fort in St. Augustine. He used his medicine powers to effect the breakout. According to one account Coacoochee "magically decreased the size of himself and the others so that they could pass through the small hole in their cell wall, put their guards to sleep magically, and once they were outside, made the ground move backward under their feet to hasten their flight; another version says that he managed the escape by means of his ability as a sorcerer to pass through solid walls and locked doors" [Sturtevant 1954b:376; also in Sturtevant 1955].

Corn pollen offerings

See *hatawe, oneane, talasi.*

Coyogo

Pomo, *California*

A shaman of the *qoobakiyalxale* (see entry) type who lived around the turn of the twentieth century; his English name was Fred Hogan. The following account describes how he healed a woman who had fainted after going out in the night for a few minutes:

> For twenty minutes she didn't breathe at all. Cɔ´yɔgo (Fred Hogan) was there . . . and [he] had his outfit. . . . He thought maybe the woman had seen a ghost. Usually they dress up for a ghost with black and white paint, and maybe green leaves, but he just fixed up in some woman's clothes. He got his father, who was there, to sing for him, and to hold the woman up and prop her eyes open as he came in. Then her back went off like the crack of a gun and she began to shake all over. Fred performed a little, and then he said, "You heat some water and we'll wash her face. She'll get over

that shock soon." He put medicine in the water and washed her face and arms and hands. He took her hands and feet and pulled them and stroked them. He pulled her fingers and toes and her legs and arms and stroked her back, and then he stretched her out and left her. He sang prayer songs. Next day she was all right [William Benson (or Ghalganal, "wampum pursuer") in Freeland 1923:67].

Crazy Horse

Teton, *Plains*

This renowned Oglala Sioux chief and war leader, whose Lakota name was Ta Sunka Witko, was known to use war medicines in his raids. "Before entering a fight Crazy Horse painted his face with white spots by dipping the ends of his fingers into the paint and lightly touching his face here and there. Some warriors painted their faces like that to show they had been brave in some fight in a snow storm or when snow was on the ground, but Crazy Horse used that paint for his protection in battle" [Minniconjou Chief Joseph White Bull in Vestal 1934:320–321].

Medicine headdress of the Sioux chief Crazy Horse.

In addition Crazy Horse carried a bulletproof medicine made for him by Woptuka, or Old Man Chips (often mistaken in the literature for Horn [Charles] Chips, who was Woptuka's son). "He was the first man who made a sacred ornament for Crazy Horse to use in the war and probably this is where Crazy Horse was made bullet-proof and got his (bullet-proof) power" [Black Elk in DeMallie 1984:157]. The Chips family contends that when Crazy Horse was killed in 1877, he had given this medicine to Woptuka for renewal. In battle Crazy Horse carried this medicine in a small leather bag worn on a string around his neck and under one arm.

Crowi
Keres, *Southwest*

Snake Society, whose members are one of four general types of shamans found among the Keres. The other three are the Lightning shamans (see *Shiwanna*), the Ant medicine men (see *Sii*), and those who cure ailments caused by witches (see *kanatyaiya*).

The *Crowi* operates as a regular society in the pueblos where it is found, except that "at Acoma the Snake medicine men are simply an aggregation (not an organized society) of doctors who treat snake bites. . . . The snake shamans do not have the paraphernalia nor the 'power' (derived from beast gods) which the regular medicine societies possess. They do not cure as a group; a single shaman treats his patient. They are simply snake doctors" [White 1930:606]. At Zia the Snake Society is also used for rain-making ceremonies. "At Chochiti, the Snake society is part of the Flint group, i.e., in order to be a Snake shaman one must also be a Flint medicineman" [White 1930:607]. For the most part, members of the Snake Society treat bites from poisonous animals.

Cshalt
Twana, *Northwest Coast*

Also: *csált*. Dialectical variants: *sthlkeyin* (Klallam); *skelaletut* (Puget Sound Salish) [Elmendorf 1960:487]. Spirit power. From the Twana *cashalt*, meaning "dream, dreaming." Among the Twana "all human success and failure, skill and mediocrity, received their explanation in terms of personal relations or lack of relations with supernatural beings" [Elmendorf 1960:481]. Given this belief, almost everyone sought out his or her own form of *cshalt*. There are many different kinds of spirit powers, collectively called *tamánamis* (see entry), and many different ways in which they manifest themselves to an individual. "Some kinds you never see and some kinds come to you as animals you can see—bear, wolf, crow, and so on. That animal will come right up to you when you're tamánamis hunting and you'll ulixw [get him for tamánamis]. And he'll show you things in a vision and give you a song and give you orders what to do, what kind of food he wants and so on. But some kinds of tamánamis are things you can't see" [Frank Allen in Elmendorf 1993:186]. Most often one acquired a *cshalt* either through direct contact with a spirit or by inheriting a *cshalt* that had been obtained by a now-deceased relative.

Cshalt and *swadash* (see entry) are the two general forms of *tamánamis*. Swadash (also *swádas*—EONAH, p. 267) is shamanic power used mainly for diagnosing and healing, while *cshalt* is any other kind of power [Elmendorf 1993:199] obtained by a layperson. That is, these two forms of power are distinguished according to their users, with the shaman having more power acquired from stronger guardian spirits. Therefore, a shaman is described as *beswadash* (literally "having guardian spirit power"), where *swadash* is "power" of the type that comes to shamans from guardian spirits, while a layperson is *becshalt* ("having guardian spirit power"), which is the "power" that is for the layperson. "Furthermore, the most general key native terms covering the conceptual domain of power and the uses of power do not distinguish between guardian spirit as a power-conferring entity and the power obtained from a guardian spirit" [Elmendorf 1984:284]. The other major difference between these two forms of power is that *cshalt* comes to a person only in the winter, at which time the person is required to "feed" his power by performing certain ceremonies. *Swadash* power, by contrast, is available to the shaman all the time. Both males and females can obtain *cshalt*.

The variety of powers that manifested were almost endless—powers for hunting, gambling, fighting, freedom from fleas, eating large quantities without suffering, etc. Sometimes one's power would only be evidenced during ceremonies by the exhibition of certain dance steps or the singing of certain songs. But whatever the manner in which these powers manifested, they were always associated with a particular kind of helping spirit. "Some spirits, however, conferred two or more distinct kinds of power, usually on different human owners. It was the powers conferred by spirits [i.e., not the spirits per se] that were grouped in named classes in this culture" [Elmendorf 1960:482].

For examples of different forms of *cshalt,* see *astalax, lahul, qwaxq, sadada, sbetedaq, schalaq, schucus, siyalt, skuykwi, slahal,* and *yalbixw.* However, it should be noted that "many lay guardian spirits, although these were usually minor ones with weak powers, did not fall under any named power category, other than the general one of cshalt" [Elmendorf 1960:490]. That is, the Twana tend to name only the more powerful forms of *cshalt.* In addition, these weaker powers are "characterized by simpler, less elaborately complex, and less definitely characterized ceremonial forms" [Elmendorf 1960:490].

Ctcuitaua
Keres, *Southwest*
The name given to a particular power spot atop Mt. Taylor (which Boas [1928:294] called "the prophetic hole"), to which both Pueblo and Navajo people make sacred journeys. Among the Laguna Pueblo people the journey is made by four shamans—the head *kurena, kashare, hictcianyi* (see *Hictiani,* EONAH, pp. 105–106), and *kapina* (see entry)—and three assistants. The

four shamans approach the *ctcuitaua,* where they remain one night and then return to tell what they have seen.

The relationship between the *kurena* and *kashare* and the other Laguna shamanistic societies is not clear [Boas 1928:293], but it was reported that the *kurena* are "in charge of all the shamanistic societies" [Boas 1928:292]. Also, the *kurena* and *kashare* lead the warrior's dance and also the Parrot clan when they greet those returning from gathering salt.

Cuns
Beaver, *Mackenzie-Yukon*
The term for the medicine lodge in which this group's variation of the Shaking Tent Ceremony (EONAH, pp. 246–249) is performed [Goddard 1916:263].

Cupping horn
One of the most common forms of the cupping instrument (EONAH, p. 55) found in North America. In most instances the horn of a buffalo is used. The shaman places the larger end of the horn over the afflicted area of the patient's body and sucks through the hollow center of the horn during a healing ceremony. In some cases the shaman first makes small incisions in the patient's skin in the area over which the horn will be placed.

In the Southeast area the cupping horn is widely used by shamans in various cultures, including the Choctaw, Creek, Natchez, Catawaba (who use a turkey wing bone), Chickasaw (who use a 4-inch cane tube), Cherokee, and Seminole shamans [Sturtevant 1954b:176]. Among the Mikasuki Seminole, for instance, a treatment for alligator bites features the use of a cupping horn: "The doctor first speaks a short spell, then sucks blood from the wound with the horn, then, holding the edges of the cut together, sings a song. . . . For a severe wound, for example an axe cut on the foot which will not stop bleeding, a doctor may sing a short song and then apply white clay or mud to the wound, which stops the bleeding" [Sturtevant 1954b:300]. The Seminole also use this cupping horn to remove "the Little People sickness, which is caused by certain supernaturals shooting a cobweb into their victims. The cobweb appears in the blood which is removed, thus establishing the diagnosis and curing the patient" [Sturtevant 1954b:121–122]. "The horn was originally that of a buffalo, according to tradition, but nowadays a section of horn from domestic cattle is used" [Sturtevant 1954b:173].

Among the Creek "Jackson Lewis said that pricks were sometimes made over the affected part with a little piece of glass. The large end of a short piece of cow horn was then placed over them and a quantity of blood sucked out through a hole pierced in the small end. . . . But unlike the former European practice, blood letting was not resorted to in cases of fever" [Swanton 1928:625].

Cupping horns are also found among the Plains cultures. For instance, Whitman [1937: 103] mentioned their use among the Oto.

It should be noted that the use of a cupping horn for bloodletting is not always associated with shamanism. Among the Chippewa in Minnesota and Wisconsin, for example, women specialists known as *bepeshwejikwe,* "cutting or scratching women" [Ritzenthaler 1953b:193], are called upon to treat ailments such as headaches, blood poisoning, dizziness, soreness, swelling, and rheumatism through the use of a cupping horn. "There is no cult or supernatural practices connected with it. The knowledge and technique is taught to an apprentice for a fee" [Ritzenthaler 1953b:193]. The treatment may also be revealed to an individual through dreams: "One male informant claimed he was taught how to do it by a mosquito and horse-fly, through a dream" [Ritzenthaler 1953b:193]. Basically, the technique used by these "specialists" differs little from that used by shamans elsewhere. A small incision is made on the patient with a sharp object (razor blade, sliver of glass, etc.), and the cupping horn, made from the tip of a cow horn, is placed over the cut and sucked through by the *bepeshwejikwe.* (For additional details see *papaicoang,* EONAH, p. 212).

See also *alexis.*

Dâki
Kiowa, *Plains*
Guardian spirit [Parsons 1929:116].

Daxwchaluxw
Twana, *Northwest Coast*
A form of compulsive magic used to attract another person.

> This is not tamánamis [see entry] itself; it is a way of using tamánamis, but only a few people know how to use daxwchaluxw. If you want to use it yourself, you have to go to one of those people and buy the use of it. The owner will tell you the use of it, but that won't make it yours for good, you won't be able to sell it to somebody else, or use it any time. There are special songs that go with daxwchaluxw, and the man who has it will pass the song to you, and give you the ability to use it, give you the right directions to use it.
> The way to use this song is to go to a waterfall or to a beach where there are loud breakers. You have to be all alone. Then you sing against the noise of the water, all alone, you and the waves. You may have to sing for hours. But finally, where you pull your breath in, you start yourself to cry. Then you're answered. That means your loved one is crying too, starting to long for you [Henry Allen in Elmendorf 1993:252–253].

Dâyumki
Kiowa, *Plains*
Shaman [Parsons 1929:137]. Most of these shamans are sucking doctors. In diagnosing a sickness the shaman often covers his head with a black cloth, and when doctoring the patient he often sprinkles him with a bunch of sage dipped into hot water. Blowing on the patient is another technique used in healing.

Deganawidah
Huron, *Northeast*
Also: *Dekanawida* [Hewitt 1917:322]. Literal translation: "two river-currents coming together" [Hewitt in Hodge 1907:383(Part 1)], or "man, the thinker" [Grinde 1977:3]. The great shaman/prophet of a period circa the fifteenth century (sometime between A.D. 1000 and 1450). Circumstantial evidence suggests he was born near Kingston in Ontario, Canada, which was

then the territory of the Huron. At some point he had a powerful vision that transformed his life. He "perceived the vision as a message to him from the Master of Life to bring harmony into the human condition and unite all peoples into a single family" [Grinde 1977:4]. However, "because he was fatherless, an outcast with no standing" [Grinde 1977:4], it is believed that, at an early age, he went to live among the Iroquois. It was there that Deganawidah, along with his devotee Hiawatha, used his great medicine powers to form the historical Iroquois confederation known as the *Oñgwanonsioñni,* meaning "we are of the extended lodge" [Hewitt in Hodge 1907:617(Part 1)]; (English variants: Iroquois League, Five Nations, Iroquois Confederation, etc.). One account described how, when about to be overtaken by his enemies, Deganawidah simply used his medicine powers to transform himself into a tree.

Although Deganawidah "stammered so much, he could scarcely talk . . . his handsome face was said to have reflected the soul of a mystic" [Grinde 1977:4]. After meeting Hiawatha, who became his messenger and spokesman, Deganawidah found that his efforts for unity would finally meet with great success. The bringing together of five, mutually hostile nations (Cayuga, Mohawk, Oneida, Onondaga, and Seneca) by one (Huron), born of their enemies no less, indicates Deganawidah's powerful influence over the people of his times and, more than likely, of their great respect for his medicine powers.

So great were those powers that everything said of him suggests the miraculous, even in regard to his birth. "Omens foreshadowed his birth, and portents accompanying this event revealed the fact to his virgin mother that Dekanawida would be the source of evil to her people, referring to the destruction of the Huron confederation by that of the Iroquois. Hence at his birth his mother and grandmother, with true womanly patriotism, sought to spare their country woes by attempting to drown the

new-born infant by thrusting it through a hole made in the ice covering a neighboring river. Three attempts were made, but in the morning after each attempt the young Dekanawida was found unharmed in the arms of the astonished mother" [Hewitt in Hodge 1907:383(Part 1)]. More conservative scholars tend to view these accounts as "a composite of myth and legend that approaches native history" [Jennings et al. 1985:15].

Renowned not only for his great medicine powers but also for his great wisdom, Deganawidah laid out the principles of operation for the new league, sometimes called the "Constitution of the Five Nations" [Jennings et al. 1985:15]. He named this document *Kaianerekowa,* "The Great Law of Peace" [Weatherford 1991:286], and in it set forth teachings with regard to "righteousness, civil authority, and peace" [Jennings et al. 1985:14]. A century (or more) later, in July 1744, the Iroquois chief Canassatego, during a Native American–British assembly in Pennsylvania, became the first person on record in U.S. history "to propose a union of all the colonies and to propose a federal model for it" [Weatherford 1988:135]. Of course, he suggested Deganawidah's model. A decade later Benjamin Franklin, then commissioner of Indian affairs for Pennsylvania, echoed this same proposal before the Albany Congress by advocating "that the new American government incorporate many of the same features as the government of the Iroquois" [Weatherford 1988:136]. Three decades later in writing the U.S. Constitution, the founders "followed the model of the Iroquois League not only in broad outline but also in many of the specific provisions of their *Kaianerekowa*" [Weatherford 1988:138].

Thus did Deganawidah, more than any other single individual in U.S. history, personally contribute to the final structure of the Constitution. Given these facts, one might well say that the true "Father of America" is Deganawidah. It is not surprising to learn that "when Deganawidah finally succeeded in bringing peace to the tribes, he planted a new tree to commemorate the alliance of friendship and to remind future generations of the precepts of the Good Mind. The tree had four large white roots, each of which grew in a different direction. Deganawidah prophesied that the roots of the tree would eventually grow to the far parts of the world, *that in time the four roots would grow to include new nations of people not yet known. From many nations they would create one*" (italics added) [Weatherford 1991:287].

Devil doll
Tanaina, *Mackenzie-Yukon*
A miniature human figure, often completely dressed in caribou clothing, that is carved by a shaman and used by him as one means to extract diseases from his patients.

> When a shaman is called upon to save a patient in serious condition, he darkens the room and begins to dance to the accompaniment of a drum, holding the "doll" close to his breast. At the very height of the ceremony, when the drumming is deafening and the shaman ecstatic with emotion [i.e., in a trance], he suddenly thrusts the "devil doll" at the patient. When the noise has died away and the shaman sinks in exhaustion to the ground, the "devil doll" has disappeared. It can have gone no place, it is said, but into the body of that one for whom the performance was being made.
>
> On the following night, the shaman comes again to the same house and dances in a mad fury while his assistants pound wooden pestles heavily on the drum boards. Again at the climax of the proceeding, the shaman thrusts his hands at the patient's chest. When he has finished, the "devil doll" is once more clasped in his arms, having returned from the body of the sick person whose evil tormentor has been forced by the superior power of the "doll" to evacuate its victim [Osgood 1937:179].

Dew Eagles
Iroquois, *Northeast*
See *oshadageaa*.

Dikwa
Wiyot, *Oregon Seaboard*
A shaman's helping spirit. "The sex of the guardian spirit is usually the opposite of that of the shaman" [Kroeber 1907:348]. Because these spirits resided in the nearby hills, they were referred to as the *wishi-dikwa,* "inland spirits" [Kroeber 1925:117].

In other contexts the word *dikwa* means supernatural. For example, a woman's menstrual period is known as *dikwa-laketl.* The term is also used for magical poison. Earlier the term was also applied to whites.

Disease-object
The actual object associated with object intrusion (EONAH, p. 199), one of the major causes of disease among Native Americans. In this case the patient's illness is caused by some object located within his or her body. The task of the shaman is to locate this object and remove it. This is most often done by sucking on the patient's body at the location of the object, thus the term *sucking shaman* (EONAH, pp. 264–266). Most often the shaman applies his mouth directly to the patient's body, but in some cases a cupping instrument (EONAH, p. 55) is used. The shaman may also remove the disease object by means of a feather or some other implement.

The forms taken by these objects vary considerably. Most often they are small in size, and sometimes are living creatures, such as spiders, centipedes, toads, etc., that are seen to move about. In some cases the object may appear as a black slime or other viscous matter. In most all cases the disease-object is ritually destroyed in some manner almost immediately after its removal—being thrown into a fire, buried in a hole in the ground, placed into a bowl of medicine water, etc. However, before destroying the object, the shaman usually displays it to the audience at hand.

See also *pains*.

Divination

A form of magic in which mystical means are used to seek answers to specific questions. "Divinatory techniques use the unpredictable to predict the unpredictable" [Aberle 1966:229]. In Native North America the most common form of divination is the diagnosis of a patient's illness. Another common form of divination involves finding lost objects or missing persons by shamans. Divination is also frequently used in hunting medicine (see entry) and war medicine (see entry).

One of the simplest and most readily available ways to answer one's question is by smoking the sacred pipe [EONAH, pp. 238–240]; in the Southwest this takes the form of smoking tobacco (rolled in a cornhusk) in the form of a large, thick cigarette. Thus the sacred pipe serves as a portable prayer altar for the individual seeking divine inspiration and intuitive knowledge. As such, the sacred pipe could be put to many uses. For example, Charley Olney [in Hines 1992:292–304] gave an interesting account of how he hurriedly rounded up a party of ten Yakima men to help him rescue a boy named Abe Lincoln, who, while horseback riding with Olney, had fallen into an ice crevasse on Mt. Adams during August 1869. Before the rescue party left their horses for foot travel across the snow pack, they sat down and smoked a sacred pipe together. (This was typical of all important undertakings. If there are dangers ahead, one will be alerted through praying with a sacred pipe.) Furthermore, one day later, once they reached the site where the boy had fallen into the crevasse, they again sat down to smoke their sacred pipe in order to determine if the boy was dead or alive. While they sat quietly smoking it, they heard Abe yell out and immediately set down the pipe and proceeded to rescue him.

Quite often various parts from an animal are used for divination purposes. A scapula may be held close enough to a fire to become scorced, for instance, and then it is "read" according to the burn marks and cracks on it. In anthropology this divination technique is termed *scapulimancy*

A painting on cloth of a shaman using tobacco as part of a divination ceremony.

(see entry). The Ojibwa of Lake of the Woods and Rainy Lake use scapulimancy, calling it *masinisawe* (see entry). In addition they use bear patellae and beaver innominates. "The knee cap of a bear is put on red hot sand [near a fire]. If it moves, good luck will follow; if it does not, no luck will come" [Cooper 1936:11]. At Rainy Lake the shaman often points his sacred pipe at the patella. "One old man so pointed his pipe, and the patella made a complete revolution; the next day the old man killed another bear" [Cooper 1936:27]. "A beaver hip-bone is held in one hand and lifted up over the diviner's head out of range of his vision. With a finger of his other hand he aims at the bone. If his finger penetrates the foramen in the bone, he will, when next hunting beaver, come out in his trail at a beaver lake; if he touches the bone at the socket, at a beaver dam" [Cooper 1936:11–12]. Among the Algonquian otter paws are tossed into the air and read according to whether they land with the palms or backs turned upward.

Divination is often accomplished by the shaman gazing into a crystal or a bowl of water; this is particularly common in the Southwest area. This technique is known in anthropology as *scrying* (see entry). In the Basin area the shaman often covers his head with a black cloth when scrying. Other shamans elsewhere simply drum, rattle, or both during a divination ceremony.

In the Northeast area one of the most common forms of divination is the Shaking Tent Ceremony (EONAH, pp. 246–249).

See also *badger blood divination, chikauvasi, Doctor Black Chicken, dodeuks, hasha, horse medicine, Igluhuk, Keseruk, kila, kiła, kiluxin, Kimvuanipinas, kwaneman, ma caiyogo, masinisawe, Medicine Snake Woman, Mikenak, Millak, onawabano, qilijog, Sea Lion, seer, sketotsut, Thekenendatetco, tlahit, Two Wolves, ulunsata, Wahwun, Wakiasua, Wallace, Emma, waptashi, widaldal, wodi,* and *Yupa.*

Diyin dineé
Navajo, *Southwest*
Literal translation: "Holy People" [Lamphere 1969:280]. A class of spirits. The term *diyin* "connotes sacredness in the sense of super-human abilities and potentially dangerous powers rather than purity, reverence, or holiness" [Lamphere 1969: 280, n. 3]. Kluckhohn [1959:437] suggested "charged with positive spiritual electricity" as a suitable definition and noted that in other contexts this term translates as "immune."

Holy People appear in many different forms. Some, such as Thunder People, Snake People, and Buffalo People, are associated with natural phenomena, while others, such as Changing Woman, Holy Man, and Holy Boy, are spirits who originated in mythic times when they emerged from "lower worlds."

These spirits have human attributes, such as maleness or femaleness, and like humans each has a soul and a breath. In addition, "they can participate in human-like social relationships (marriage, child-rearing, and acting in terms of kinship roles)" [Lamphere 1969:280].

Djesikon
Ojibwa, *Canadian Eastern Woodlands*
The cylindrical tent used in the Shaking Tent Ceremony (EONAH, pp. 246–249). Although this lodge is used primarily for divination purposes, some shamans do shoot "needles or porcupine quills with medicine a long distance through the air at intended victims" [Cooper 1936:9], which is a form of sorcery.

Djoklonos
Modoc, *California*
Literal translation: "Black Sage-Brush Head" [Spier 1930:117]. The name of a very powerful shaman who lived around the turn of the twentieth century. As was the custom his earth-lodge was filled with the skins of animals he used in his practice. He "had little cottontail rabbits hanging in his earth-lodge. Sometimes they would run around as though alive; they were spirits. He had a stuffed butterball duck skin hanging on the south side. Sometimes this spirit made blood flow from the duck's bill and at other times it flew about in the lodge" [Spier 1930:117].

He also used a stone pipe. "Whenever he wanted to smoke, the pipe lit itself, or rather a spirit did it. He visited Ctai´is, a Klamath shaman living at the mouth of the Williamson river, and exchanged pipes with him. After his return home, Ctai´is found the pipe missing. Later they had word from the Modoc that the pipe had returned to him" [Spier 1930:120].

Doctor Black Chicken
Teton, *Plains*
A Hunkpapa shaman residing at Fort Peck, North Dakota, during the latter part of the nineteenth century. He had several different medicine stones that he used as power sources. "The large stone he called 'Beats the Drum.' When horses are stolen, the doctor made a tipi in his house under which he placed his drum with this stone. After a time the rock would beat the drum and reveal the thief and the location of the horses. When a person was very sick and his

death anticipated, he painted the two smaller stones. These he called the 'Large and Small Doctor'" [Culin 1901:171].

Doctor Charley
Twana, *Northwest Coast*

A shaman during the latter part of the nineteenth century whose special power brought food. The following is an account of his use of this power circa 1875:

> We come to a tamánamis [see entry] that Doctor Charley had. It was called xwanathlcha yakwalash, a Skokomish name (probably Chehalis), that doesn't mean anything. That power brought food.
>
> Now Doctor Charley got sick one winter, five feet of snow, and he lay that way quite a while. And one of his wives . . . said, "Well, we'll have to do something . . . we'll have people in and have a big dance. That will wake him up." So they sent me and some other young fellows around to invite people to Doctor Charley's place. . . .
>
> And my great-uncle sustx did the talking for Doctor Charley. He got up and said, "Tonight we're going to show something. Stay here, people." So that night Bob Burns and I took hold of those two [canoe] poles, and Doctor Charley came up to us and hollered "co'co'co'co" at those poles. And I remember that pole I held gave two or three jumps, and then it got hot in my hands and it was just like electricity going up my arms. I don't remember very clear what happened, but they told me those poles danced up and down in the house with us, from one end of the house to the other. And when Doctor Charley quit and the poles stopped, I let go and sat down and my hands were all blistered on the inside where I had held that pole.
>
> And now we stopped and ate. Everybody in the house ate. And now Doctor Charley got up and said, "There's one out there in that direction and another outside over there. Go out and get them." And two fellows went out and pretty soon they came back with a deer apiece. And now Doctor Charley told Duke Williams to get a net and they

took the net down to the river and caught lots of steelhead salmon (skwawal). Now they've got lots of food, xwanathlcha yakwalash is feeding them now.

> And after everybody ate, Doctor Charley gave away things to all the people there, a few little things to everyone. They gave me a dollar and a half for holding that pole [Frank Allen in Elmendorf 1993:184–185].

Dodeuks
Klamath, *California*

Literal translation: "to dream" [Spier 1930:122]. This term is used for the shaman's clairvoyant ability to find lost objects or see events at a distance. "Lost articles are found through the dog spirit. The people are lined up in two opposing rows—an excellent psychological expedient for discovering guilt—while the shaman passes along searching for the suspect. He sees the stolen object shine in the thief's upraised palm. This takes place in the open" [Spier 1930:122].

Dokos
Wintun, *California*

The disease object removed from the body of a shaman's patient, usually said to have come from a sorcerer. In the literature *dokos* is most often translated as "a pain" (see *pains*). During the diagnosis of a patient, "a doctor, if the spirit is in him when he comes to see a sick man, is able to look right through the body of the patient and see where the dokos lies. Sometimes he is not able to draw it out; he can see where the dokos is, that is all; but if his spirit were stronger than the one who put it there, he could draw it out and cure the patient" [Curtin 1898:513].

Dubrieswehi
Oto, *Plains*

Ghost doctors. Shamans who treat patients possessed by ghosts. "The Oto make a linguistic distinction between ghosts and spirits. In English, however, they use the terms interchangeably" [Whitman 1937:120].

Dudl
Maidu, *California*
Also: *dul.* Dialectical variant: *kilem* (Placer area Nisenan) [Beals 1933:398]. Term used by the Eldorado area Nisenan (Southern Maidu) for drum.

Dukud
Twana, *Northwest Coast*
To affect the behavior or shape of things in a magical way [Elmendorf 1960:526]; a charm (see entry). This is accomplished through the use of magical spells known as *duxwchaluxw,* incantations that are sung or recited. These spells can be inherited or bought from their current owner. Most often "the person affected by duxwchaluxw magic was compelled, often against his will, to the actions desired by the practicer of the magic. This condition was termed dukutab, 'magically compelled, betwitched'" [Elmendorf 1960:526].

Dumalaitaka
Hopi, *Southwest*
Helping spirit or spirit guide [Titiev 1972:57].

Eagle-hunting medicine
Hidatsa, *Plains*

Eagle feathers were prized for their medicine powers, and many different cultures had elaborate hunting methods to procure them. The Hidatsa used the pit-trap method (for details see G. Wilson 1928) to procure eagles. In so doing, they also used medicine powers. A Hidatsa named Small Ankle considered his eagle-hunting medicine to be one of his greatest powers. He instructed his son, Wolf Chief, in its use: "When you see an eagle flying high in the sky as you lie in the pit, take the snare I have given you—the first I presented to you—and motion with it, casting it up in the air, drawing it back, at the same time singing this mystery song, and the eagle will fly down soon and seize your bait. So, too, the two mystery songs of the sun and the moon. If you sing them at night in your eagle-hunting lodge, or if while you lie in your pit no eagles are in sight, sing one or both of these songs, casting the snares that go with them; soon eagles will appear" [Wolf Chief in Pepper and Wilson 1908:315].

Echul
Diegueño, *Peninsula*

Sexual disorder. The Diegueño divide psychological sexual disorders into two major categories. The less serious *kimilue* diagnosis is based on such symptoms as violent sexual dreams, loss of appetite, and general apathy. *Kimilue* in a more extenuated form, a sort of "sexual hysteria," is diagnosed as *echul* [Moriarty 1965:11]. In both cases the cure is performed by a "dream doctor" (*kwisiyai*—see EONAH, p. 145).

Accounts of shamans operating as psychoanalysts are rare in the literature, but there is no reason to believe that this was not and is not still a normal function of their office (for example, see Lyon 1996). The following account, fully published in 1936, speaks to the treatment of *eschul:*

A young girl came to the dream doctor for treatment shortly after her engagement had been broken. At first she dreamed constantly of her lover, took no interest in her household duties, and behaved, according to the doctor, in a "fitsy" manner. The episode which brought her to the dream specialist was a fall from her horse during a fit. She

Edward S. Curtis, Placating the Spirit of the Slain Eagle—Assiniboin, *1926. Photogravure.*

rolled on the ground "as if a man was with her." Her mother, weeping hysterically, seized a club with which to beat off the *echul* bird-lover who was thought to be with her, and inflicted severe wounds upon the girl. Doctor X.'s psychotherapy consisted of having her relate to him episodes in her love life and recent dreams. He advised a change of scene followed by marriage to anyone of the right clan. He also did some blood letting and recommended such nourishing foods as acorn gruel and pinole mush to build up her strength.

It is interesting to observe that the dream doctors of the Diegueño had so clearly formulated the pattern of "love dreams" that once a doctor heard the key symptoms of a mental disorder, he proceeded to draw upon his experience as a [shamanic] practitioner in breaking down the initial resistance of his patient by stating at the outset of the treatment, "You can't be ashamed in front of me because I know all about your dreams," intimating that it was useless for the patient to conceal anything from a man trained in magic and dreams. He thus gained the confidence of his patient who narrated the details of his experience and dreams, the narration of which is so important in therapy. Then the dream doctor fitted the general pattern of the treatment to the individual needs of his patient [Toffelmier and Luomala 1936:207, 209].

Ehtskinna
Blackfoot, *Plains*

Horns. Term for members of the Horn Society, a group of very powerful men and women. All of their ceremonies are held in secret, and non-members consider it dangerous to even speak about the society. "The power of members is so great that to wish anyone ill or dead is all that is needed to bring the realization" [unnamed Blood woman in Wissler 1913:411]. During their secret rituals all others in the camp remain in their lodges.

The society is headed by two male members. During ceremonies all members don special regalia, consisting of weasel tail shirts and leggings and head bonnets bearing horns and tails. The dance leader wears a special bonnet with an arrow sticking straight out from the center of the forehead. Two other members wear the special "straight-up-bonnets" fringed with weasel tails. Other ceremonial items include small bulb rattles with streamers of ribbon attached to the end, hooked lances (pine with a birch hook sinewed to the top and made new for each ceremony) wrapped with otter fur and trimmed with swan skin, owl tails (tied in the hair), red face paint, caps made of swan skin, ceremonial drums, etc.

Horns are feared for their power.

Our informant [a Horn] once killed a buffalo by the power of the horns. In chasing a herd of buffalo, he began to fall behind. Then he rode back and forth across their trail four times, whipped the ground and shouted. Setting out again he saw a fat cow, down but still kicking. At another time he used the same formula to cause a rider's horse to fall. Again at a horse race between some Piegan and Flathead Indians, he spat four times upon a stone and placed it in the hoof print of the opposing racer, which soon became lame.

When a horn member wishes to kill a person, he sharpens one end of a small stick, paints it red, names the victim and casts the stick into the fire. Once when the horns were assembled, a man came in and denounced them vigorously. No one said anything in reply, but within four days the defamer took sick and died [Duvall in Wissler 1913:416].

Ekaskini
Blackfoot/Blood, *Plains*

A great shaman and warrior who was born around 1822. As a child he went by the name of Atsitsi (Screech Owl), and at the age of thirteen he completed a successful vision quest in which he acquired "the song of the thunder spirit and could sing it when he needed help. [Shortly thereafter he also] acquired the holy songs of the sparrow hawk, rabbit . . . and mouse" [Dempsey 1994:28, 29]. The following year, he first began to use his medicine powers as a warrior. During his first battle (with the Cree), Atsitsi, afoot and with only a small tomahawk in hand, took on three warriors who were armed with flintlocks and on horses and slew all three. Thereafter his named was changed to Ekaskini (Low Horn) [Dempsey 1994:32].

Ekaskini had great powers of stealth and became wealthy through his ability to steal from his people's enemies. However,

> Low Horn gave away all the horses he had taken. His father, his cousins, and others in the camp benefited from his exploits on the war trail.
>
> His powers seemed to make him immune from danger. Time and time again he entered a Cree or Assiniboine camp to take a prized buffalo runner or race horse. Wearing his sparrow hawk feathers and quietly chanting his holy songs, he seemed to move through the camps like a shadow, leaving his enemies angry and afoot [Dempsey 1994:32].

He died in battle in 1846 at the age of twenty-four. But at this point the story of Ekaskini takes a mystical turn, for it is reported that as he lay dying on the battlefield, he actually reincarnated into a young boy who was born among the Blood Nation some 150 miles to the south. This child was named Only Person Who Had a Different Gun and went by Different Gun. At the age of six, while on a trip to Fort Edmonton, Different Gun and his party happened across a Blackfoot woman named Deer Old Woman, who was the widow of Low Horn. Different Gun recognized her and told a playmate that "she was my sweetheart when I was young" [Dempsey 1994:41]. On the following day, as they crossed the battle site where Low Horn had been killed, Different Gun began to cry and told his father, "I'm crying because this is the place where I was attacked and killed by the Crees. I am Low Horn" [Dempsey 1994:41].

The elders, however, did not believe Different Gun, so the boy told them where he had hidden his whip and skinning knife just before he was killed. On the following morning they went to the two different locations and found the items located exactly where Different Gun had said they would be. "The whip was lying there [under a rock] just as Low Horn had left it, but when they tried to pick it up, it was so rotten that it fell to pieces in their hands. Then they went to the hollow and dug away the earth and leaves in the shallow trench. There they found Low Horn's old skinning knife. It was so rusty that it had holes in it" [Dempsey 1994:42].

At that point Different Gun was once again named Low Horn. "When Low Horn was young, everyone knew of his strange reincarnation and believed that he would become a holy man. Therefore, no one was surprised in the 1870s when he began visiting with the medicine men of the tribe, listening to them, and gradually learning their ways" [Dempsey 1994:42]. Eventually he became a renowned healer, adding the white-headed eagle's power to the powers of the former Low Horn, which he also possessed. His most famous cure took place on October 19, 1891, when he began doctoring a Blood warrior named Steel, who had been shot through the chest and given up for dead by the white physicians. "Using four of his most sacred paints and the power of the mouse inherited from the Blackfoot Low Horn, he performed his rituals. Twelve days later, after constant attention from Low Horn, the wounded man was strong enough to ride a horse to the medicine man's camp so that he might continue to be treated. Steel did not die as predicted; in fact, he lived for another fifty years" [Dempsey 1994:44]. During this healing Low Horn "took a bone whistle, cutting the air with its sharp and penetrating sounds. Finally, he bent down close to the man's body and blew into his wound. He placed his hands over the area, paused, then threw himself back with a flourish. . . . Not a sound was heard. The medicine man had obviously drawn the evil spirit from Steel's body and now he held it in his fist. Then, carefully and dramatically, he opened his hand and held up the object for everyone to see. It was a live white mouse" [Dempsey 1994:157].

Upon breaking one of his spirit taboos, Low Horn foresaw his own death, which occurred in June 1899 when he was fifty-three years of age.

Enatcûggedi
Beaver, *Mackenzie-Yukon*
Literal translation: "leave something ready for somebody coming along there" [Goddard 1916:228, n. 2]. A medicine pole erected by a shaman for help from "the one who helps him in dreams" [Ike in Goddard 1916:228, n. 2]. In some cases the *enatcûggedi* is a straight pole set into the ground; in other cases two poles are erected in the form of a cross. They are usually from 5 to 8 feet in height and may be painted. To these poles offerings are attached.

The following is an account of the use of an *enatcûggedi* by a nineteenth-century shaman trying to save his people from starvation: "He made a medicine pole, painted it, and set it up. He had a man stand beside the pole and made it as high as the man. He then began to sing, and although it was the middle of the winter it thundered and began to snow. The snow fell until it was as high as the top of the pole. Then they could kill all the game they needed. Just the heads of the moose were sticking out of the snow and they could be killed with spears" [Fournier in Goddard 1916:260].

These medicine poles are also used by the Cree and Slave.

Endóbniwat
Potawatomi, *Midwest*
Literal translation: "to challenge (another tribe) in war" [Ritzenthaler 1953a:159]. Sacred bundle. By the 1950s only four bundles were known to remain: two Buffalo bundles, one Crow bundle, and one Thunderbird bundle. One of the Buffalo bundles and the Thunderbird bundle "apparently are no longer honored by regular ceremony, although a year ago the bundles were repaired, the sacred objects therein fumigated by burning cedar boughs, and a deer meat feast held by a group of six persons" [Rithzenthaler 1953a:158].

The other two bundles are held by one person who conducts "fairly regular ceremonies for the buffalo and crow bundles in his possession.

These ceremonies should be held twice a year, in spring and fall." [Ritzenthaler 1953a:158]. Little is known about these bundles because "the Sacred Bundle ceremonies . . . are attended with much secrecy. Even the purpose of the ceremony remains vague, although I was informed that it was held to honor the animal spirits represented by the bundle, that it was sometimes held to cure the sick, and that it could be held to renew or repair the bundle" [Ritzenthaler 1953a:156–157].

Ensgänye gainqgáyonka
Iroquois, *Northeast*
Seneca Traditional Women's Dance. Literal translation: "women-their-feet-shuffle song-of-an-ancient-type" [Fenton 1936:16, n. 23]. This was a religious ceremony in which women gave thanks to the "three sisters"—the corn, the beans, and the squash.

Etsarav
Yuma, *Southwest*
The Yuma's general category of sickness [Forde 1931:183]. Anthropologist Daryll Forde [1931: 185] determined there were four major causes of sickness among the Yuma:

1. Sickness from natural causes. . . . Massage and blowing of saliva on the injured part are used to aid the cure.
2. Dream poisoning by spirits in which the poison must be sucked out by the doctor. The seat of the poison may also be brushed with feathers and pointed at with the finger or a short stick [see *icâma xekwir*].
3. Soul loss consequent on a severe blow resulting in unconsciousness, or due to the efforts of ghosts (i.e., the spirits of the dead) to carry off the soul of the patient, especially when weakened by other sickness. The blowing of tobacco smoke and the spraying of saliva frothed up in the mouth are devices employed to aid the recovery of the soul [see *xelyatsxamcáma*].
4. Bewitchment, in which one individual, generally a doctor, induces sickness in

another by magical means with the aid of a spirit [see *metudhauk*].

Each Yuma shaman receives power to cure only certain illnesses, so the patient must find the shaman who has the proper power to handle his case. The following is an unusual account of a woman, identified only as "Pat's wife," whose spirit advised her about which shaman to seek out: "She has never seen it, for it always speaks from behind, but it is a female spirit. She has no name for it. Once it saved her life, for she was very sick and unconscious and no one could do her any good. As they sat around her, suddenly a voice was heard speaking through her mouth, very gently but strong, saying, 'Go and get onyakalak,' a doctor who lived some distance away. The voice was different from her ordinary voice. Her father tried to make it speak again, but it didn't answer. They sent for the doctor, who came a long distance and cured her, after everybody had thought that she would die" [Manuel Thomas in Forde 1931:184].

Etsatcev
Yuma, *Southwest*
Sickness curer [Forde 1931:183]. A general term for a healing shaman. See *tcev* for specific types.

Shamans receive their power through spirits and dreams of spirits. "The River Yumans . . . believed that power-bringing visions come by chance, in natural sleep, and, though an individual's whole success in life depended upon his dreams, he was powerless to induce them. Stated in modern terms, this reflects a belief in the innate superiority, perhaps also superior luck, of certain individuals. The subject of the dream was not an animal, as with the Papago, but a mountain or a supernatural being; sometimes merely a prophetic experience" [Underhill 1939:172].

For powerful shamans "the spirit appears before the man is born, when he is only one or two months in the womb" [Manuel in Forde 1931:182], while other men may not "dream any

power" until they are over forty. The spirit gives the shaman instructions with regard to the range of sicknesses and misfortunes he can treat as well as how cures are to be achieved. A shaman cannot treat patients until his spirit tells him he may begin. Consequently, the relationship between the shaman, his guardian spirit, and the patient differs from individual to individual. "In general the spirit merely instructs the doctor to undertake treatment and gives him the strength to effect the cure" [Forde 1931:183].

Undertaking a cure not only involves having the ability to do so but also depends on the shaman's state of mind. For example, Manuel, a shaman who began dreaming at the age of twelve but did not try to cure until he was "an old man," reported in the 1920s:

If I hear of a sick person something tells me whether his illness is one I would be good for. This may happen even if I have not had a dream and power especially for his sickness. If I feel right I know that if they have come for me I will be able to cure the man. When I have a good feeling I am very strong and light inside and any other doctor who works on the sick one usually fails. The patient and his relations know too, for I seem to draw the sick man to me. Always, I think, I have been asked to cure when I felt strong for it, and on these occasions I am always successful. . . . When I work on the patient it does not tire me at all and it makes me very happy. Generally I can cure very quickly then, maybe in a few hours or in a day or two.

Sometimes I feel quite different about it, I don't get any good feeling and though I do my best I do not often cure then. I don't get any feeling of lightness and when I go away from the sick man I don't want to return to him. I feel heavy and tired and very sleepy at night. . . . I know it is really no good me trying to help him even if I have had a dream for his sickness.

But I do not always know how things are going to be. Sometimes I do not feel really good until I begin to cure. Other times I lose a lot of strength when I start to work on the patient and it does not go well [Manuel in Forde 1931:184].

Etschechuk

Hupa, *California*

Literal translation: *ets* refers to any material used in constructing a fish dam, and *chechuk* means "bring out" [Gifford 1940:28]. This term refers to shamans who have the proper medicine for building a fish dam. Such dams are always constructed by males. The *etschechuk* must fast before he begins his construction, and the procedure is ritually prescribed. Most often his medicine was passed down through family lineage. Of course, the Hupa also construct fish dams without the use of an *etschechuk*.

See also *wilohego*.

Etsoul

Yuma, *Southwest*

Charm. There are many different types of charms among the Yuma—charms for attracting women, charms for gambling, charms for war, charms for causing sickness, etc. Most often these are special stones either worn on the body or ground to powder and rubbed on the body. For example, *kwats humuk* is a charm made from a crystal, and *icima* is a pebble charm found in the desert. The following is an account of the Yuma *toul haxnåk,* a sickness charm: "An Indian goes into the hills to find charm stones; they are colored or transparent, but can have any shape. The stones must be ground up very fine into powder and mixed with red paint and, if possible, the intestines of some animal or bird. The lizard is very good. Men used this a great deal to weaken their enemies in fights and their competitors in races. The odor of the charm substance afflicts those who approach the charmer. In a race the runner with the most powerful charm goes ahead and the odor of his charm causes those behind to sweat and breathe with difficulty. Without knowing the cause they are tired out and get cramps. If the charm works for a long time it causes boils over the body, swellings filled with watery substance which itch badly" [Manuel Thomas in Forde 1931:195].

On occasion, when a victim underwent a cure for charm sickness, the bearer of the charm would die. "Sometimes when a person has a powerful charm his relatives about the house die off in consequence" [Manuel Thomas in Forde 1931:195].

Eyum

Maidu, *California*

See *yomuse*.

Fan, Ida
Wintun, *California*

A shaman during the 1930s. During Wintu sacred ceremonies shamans often enter into trance and are possessed by their helping spirit. In this state, the shamans frequently deliver prophetic speech. The following description of one such occasion was provided by Ida Fan and recorded and translated by anthropologist Dorothy Lee. The Wintu understood that the spirit was speaking to all those present through Fan's mouth. It seemed to be warning them about their loss of the old, sacred ways:

> You who call yourself Wintu, when you look west toward the mountains, look not at one another with glowering eyes. The world is growing desolate. The people who were here but a few days ago, they who had a Wintu body-smell, when they went about to the north, when they went about to the south, all was well. But now you are not like Wintu; we see you transformed into something strange when, coming up behind you, we see you. Do not say to yourselves, "I am a true Wintu." You have been transformed into something queer. As for us, we live wandering to the north, wandering to the south. When we look back and see our children, we say, "*hehe,* our children arouse compassion, speaking as they do in a strange tongue."
>
> The world is approaching its end. And you people here live drifting to the north, drifting to the south. We see you; so he-who-is-above sees you, looking down; for it is he who planted you below [Lee 1941:411].

Fetish

Also: fetich (nineteenth-century form). Any object that (1) is regarded as a living being, possessed of supernatural power, and endowed with consciousness and volition, or (2) is the dwelling or representation of such a being and possesses its magical powers, wholly or in part. A fetish is most often the property of an individual, who speaks to it and makes regular sacred offerings to it.

Regarding fetishes used by the Eskimo, Hawkes [1916:136] noted that "the assistance of the individual spirit [associated with the fetish] is given grudgingly, and often the owner has to chastise it by stripping the fetish of its garments, subjecting it to blows, and by other forceful means until it grants good fortune again. If it proves obstinate, it is given away.... It is said to

F

lose its power when taken off the person, and to regain it when put on, which may be due to the idea that it derives a certain vitality from the body of its owner." In the latter case the fetish technically serves as an amulet (see entry).

"The Netsilik, in the eastern part of the Northwest Passage, may make a bear out of snow and bring it to life by placing bear's teeth in its mouth. The artificial bear will then cause disease, accidents, or even death to occur

Cheyenne buffalo effigy, c. 1860–1880. Carved wood, tufted fiber tail. Gift of Mr. and Mrs. Edward C. Lawson.

to the enemy of its maker. . . . Shamans might make a doll out of lamp-moss or a snow-beater. The doll was placed inside a bag. A magic formula was pronounced. The bag was struck, and something inside it would move about 'just like a dog.' Struck twice more, the bag disappeared and the doll ran off. It had a human or a canine head, and sometimes the legs of a caribou" [Merkur 1989:14–15].

The Zuni runners place a stone arrow point in their hair as a running medicine. They also attach an arrowhead to their corn fetishes "to keep off witch sickness" [Parsons 1939:331].

The Fox in the Midwest have a fetish addressed as "Neniwa (man) who owns the medicine" [M. R. Harrington 1914:232]. It is a 10-inch, hardwood fetish, obtained by a female shaman in the early 1800s, that is shaped like a man. It was obtained from the spirits during a vision quest. "Six days she fasted, and on the night of the sixth it seemed as if somebody, some supernatural being, had taken pity upon her, for she was granted a vision in which she was told to go to a certain place at a certain time if she wished to find something that would help her. Going to that place as appointed, she saw what seemed to

be a crow flying toward her carrying some object in its claws which it dropped near where she stood. When she ran to pick it up she found it to be this little figure of a man" [M. R. Harrington 1914:231].

Each year a feast is held to empower this figure, which must be dressed in new clothes as soon as it is unbundled. During the feast a dog is sacrificed, and tobacco offerings are given to this fetish.

This power object is used for many different purposes—gambling, love medicine, good health, long life, etc. "In case of sickness the owner of the fetish, arriving on the scene, opens the bundle and speaks to it, sprinkling tobacco the while, and begs it to help the ailing one. A piece of broadcloth or a good blanket or some other expensive piece of goods is then folded and placed on the rack above the sick person or else near his head, and the image laid upon it to remain all night. When the owner comes for her fetish in the morning, she takes the goods upon which it has rested as her fee" [M. R. Harrington 1914:232].

Because fetishes are considered to be living spirits, special rules must be followed when they are handled. Typically, they must be regularly "fed" in some manner, usually through prayers and offerings. They also must be guarded from contamination in any form; they may, for instance, be sheltered from vulgar language used around them, wrapped in special bindings when not in use, regularly smudged to keep evil spirits away from them, etc. Lantis [1947:32–33] noted that "on Kodiak Island and the north Bearing Sea area, the whalers kept their whaling implements, amulets and the mummies or human images [fetishes] that gave them their power in secret places away from the settlements."

For other examples, see *aishiuwinen, athlashi, bagijiganatig, caxwu, devil doll, ge´estein, iariku, ingukh, Issiwun, iyatiku, kue, Mahuts, masutïkï, medicine bundle, mirarackupe, Never-Sits-Down shield, patash, pauborong, pogok, samahiye, Tenektaide, tohópko, tuavitok, ulunsata, Wimesin shkibijigen, yugûk.*

Fewkes, Jesse Walter

J. W. Fewkes received his Ph.D. in marine biology from Harvard in 1877 and began work in the university's Museum of Comparative Zoology, where he was in charge of the lower invertebrates section. In the spring of 1887, Fewkes went to the islands along southern California on a collecting trip for the museum, and on his return he met his first Native Americans, the Pueblo. Much fascinated by them, he returned in 1889 or 1890 to make the first wax cylinder recordings of Hopi songs in northeastern Arizona. "In 1891 he succeeded Frank Hamilton Cushing as leader of the Hemenway Southwestern Archaeological Expedition—a research project for New Mexico and Arizona that began in 1886 and was terminated in 1894 with the death of its benefactress, Mrs. Mary Hemenway, of Boston" [Judd 1967:27]. During 1891 Fewkes began his lifelong work on Hopi ceremonials. The Hopis admired Fewkes and initiated him in 1891 into the priesthoods of both the Flute and Antelope Societies (see *Chüawimkya*). Fewkes was one of the few self-trained anthropologists that pioneered anthropological fieldwork in North America. It was also during this period that he founded the *Journal of American Archaeology and Ethnology.*

In 1895 he joined the staff of the Bureau of American Ethnology at the Smithsonian as an ethnologist; however, his first work for the bureau involved archaeological excavations north of Hopi country in the Southwest area. It was there that he first became acquainted with the subsequently renowned potter Nameyo, who "daily visited the site to copy designs from discarded potsherds and hold lengthy discussions over surface finish. They used every scrap of paper available, even wrappings from packaged soda crackers, as Fewkes related years later, and charcoal when pencils were lacking" [Judd 1967:27–28]. By 1896 he returned to the Hopi to again conduct ethnographic fieldwork there.

Over the years Fewkes also continued his work in archaeology. He is best remembered for his excavation and restoration of Mesa Verde National Park in southwestern Colorado, which began in 1908.

On March 1, 1918, Fewkes became the director of the Bureau of American Ethnology. Although he was a prolific writer (with some 130 articles published on Native America), after assuming the directorship he found little time for publishing his work. For example, although he also excavated in Cuba, Puerto Rico, the Lesser Antilles, Florida, and Colorado after 1918, he wrote nothing for the bureau except one small publication (BAE Bulletin 70) on the ruins of southwestern Colorado. However, he was one of only two bureau directors ever to be elected to the National Academy of Sciences (William H. Holmes was the other).

Fewkes remained in office until January 15, 1928, when he resigned due to ill health. He died on May 31, 1930, at the age of eighty.

Fire-handling medicine

Fire handling is a common element in the shamanic practices of Native North America. It was first noted by Jesuit priests in the early 1600s, and I have seen it myself among the Navajo. In fact, there is a continuous record of fire handling in the anthropological literature. Walking on hot coals, a recent fad among Americans, is nothing new to Native America, as the following examples illustrate:

[Father Pierre] Pijart reported to [Father Paul] Le Jeune that, in May of 1637, he had attended an *aoutaeroki* feast at Ossassané among the Hurons—a ritual held to bring health to those for whom it was done. Dancing and shouting were carried on for much of the night; but, in the midst of this, a shaman took into his mouth a rather large red-hot coal which he proceeded to convey to the sick, one by one, each of whom was some distance away from him. Beside each patient he made growl-like noises, all the while distorting his face as he blew upon them. Soon the coal broke in his mouth, and the shaman declared the feast a failure and that another must be done the next night. After the first feast, a French lay assistant to the Jesuits went forward to inspect the shaman's mouth, . . . but the lay assistant reported finding the shaman's mouth free of burns.

On the ensuing night, stones were again heated in a fire which Pijart declared "was hot enough to burn down the cabin," and that he almost withdrew except that he was determined to see if all he had heard about such events were true. As the stones were being heated in the fire, about two dozen singers chanted in a fashion that the missionary described as extremely "lugubrious" and "frightful." To Pijart's amazement, as the red-hot stones were removed from the fire, several sorcerers came forward, took them between their teeth and went to the patients to repeat the growling and blowing Pijart had seen the previous night. One of these stones, with the teeth marks, was the one sent on to Le Jeune in Quebec.

"You will be astonished that a man can have so wide a mouth; the stone is about the size of a goose egg. Yet I saw a savage put it in his mouth so that there was more of it inside than out; he carried it some distance and, after that, it was still so hot, that when he threw it to the ground sparks of fire issued from it."

This apparent immunity to fire on the part of certain shamans and their devotees is recounted a number of times by the missionaries and shown to have manifested itself in several ways. Jaques Buteux, while working among the various tribes who moved in and out of Three Rivers in 1640–41, wrote that during one three-day feast, particularly grand in scope, the women and girls began to dance while certain men took the shaman and caused him to walk over red-hot embers; he was not burned, reported the missionary [Moore 1982:85–87].

Around 1796 the fire-handling abilities of the Menomini and Ojibwa shamans were incorporated into a religious revitalization movement known as the *Wabeno* (see *wábano; wabeno,* EONAH, p. 303) complex, and by the early 1800s the term *wabeno* was being used for these shamans. In 1896 Hoffman [1896:151] reported that the *wabeno* was able "to take up and handle with impunity red-hot stones and burning brands, and without evincing the slightest discomfort it is said that he will bathe his hands in boiling water, or even in boiling sirup. On account of such performances, the general impression prevails among the Indians that the wâ´beno is a 'dealer in fire,' or a 'fire handler.'" As incredible as it may seem, these early anthropologists actually believed that the *wabeno* simply used a plant, which he rubbed on his skin, to make him impervious to fire.

The *wabeno* also used fire for divination purposes. This was reported by Father Peter Jones in 1861 (in his *History of the Ojebway Indians*) as follows: "It is pretended [in the opinion of this priest] that all the Algonquins and Abenaquis formerly practiced a kind of pyromancy, the whole mystery of which is as follows: They reduced to a very fine powder some charcoal, made of cedar; they disposed this powder in their own manner, and afterwards set fire to it, and by the form which the fire took whilst it ran along this powder, they pretended to discover what they wanted to know" [Jones in Hoffman 1896:153].

Among the Quinault on the Northwest Coast, it was reported that a "person who had Raven (tocà´n or kwa´k̓) for a spirit could eat fire and hold live coals in his mouth 'because raven eats blood' which is the same color as fire" [Olson 1936:150]. And the Kwantlen tribe of the Halkomelem (Cowichan) in the Puget Sound area had "a noted old shaman among them who [was] reported by the natives and white settlers to have been able to do many strange and mysterious things, such as dancing on hot stones, handling live coals, and drinking or otherwise mysteriously disposing of enormous quantities of liquids, such as oils or water" [Hill-Tout 1903:405].

Regarding the Tanaina of southern Alaska, Osgood [1937:180] reported: "Various accounts are found of shamans walking through fire, picking up hot rocks, and swallowing burning knives. The latter are said to feel like icicles. There was the case of a shaman who without any clothes sat down on some bath-stones which were heating in the middle of a fire. It did not bother him for the rocks were cold. . . . One shaman made a fire by putting shavings in his armpits and dancing around counterclockwise. He burned tobacco in the same way."

The Eskimo shamans at the head of Norton Sound in Alaska also

caused themselves to be burned to ashes and then returned to life, not even their clothing showing a trace of fire. . . . The following description of burning a shaman is from a village south of the Yukon mouth, and was obtained from a fur trader who knew the circumstances: The shaman gathered all the villagers into the kashim [ceremonial house] and, after putting on his fur coat, told them that he wished to be burned and return to them in order that he might be of greater service to the village. He directed that a crib of drift logs should be built waist high, in the form of a square, with an open space in the center, where he could stand. He chose two assistants, whom he paid liberally to attend to the fire and aid him in other ways. His hands and feet were bound and a large mask, covering his face and body to the waist, was put on him. Then the people carried him out and set him inside the crib, after which everyone except the assistants returned to the kashim and the assistants set fire to the pyre in front. Smoke and flames rose from the logs so that the inside of the crib was rendered slightly indistinct; the assistants called out the people, who, when they saw the mask as they had left it, facing them through the smoke, were satisfied. After they had seen it they were ordered to remain within doors until the next morning upon pain of calling down upon them the anger of the *tunghät* [spirits]. . . . I was told that this ordeal of fire was supposed to endow the person enduring it with the power to cast off or assume

the bodily form at will and to greatly increase his power in other ways [Nelson 1899:433, 434].

(Nelson claimed that such feats were actually tricks effected by the assistants.)

The Maidu residing in the mountain area of El Dorado County (at Camino) in California conducted initiation ceremonies in which the novices "danced, picked up hot rocks, rubbed on hands, placed in armpits, rubbed selves all over" [Jane Lewis in Beals 1933:388]. Dixon [1905:279] also mentioned that the Northern Maidu shamans could "walk through fire unharmed." In nearby northwestern California there was a male shaman "who was distinguished by his ability to handle hot stones and to eat live rattlesnakes" [Posinsky 1965:231].

Fire-handling medicine is also known among the Santee (in this case the Canadian Sioux): "Charles Padani (Standing Buffalo) spoke of a famous Santee fire-walker. This man, he said, first boasted that he could perform the feat and that he would stage it for such and such a day. A crowd gathered. The magician appeared and built a large fire, and when it had burned down he raked the coals into a great rectangle. The man then bet some whites who were in the crowd that he could walk through the coals barefoot. He not only did this, but then walked back over the flaming surface a second time, and won a large sum of money" [Howard 1984:115].

The Rabbit Medicine society (also variously called Mother Night, Young Dog, Blackbird, Dakota, "Sioux"—see *Shunáwanùh*) of the Arikara is skilled in fire medicines. As Will recorded: "A large flat stone would be placed in the fireplace and a brisk fire kept burning upon it for several days. The stone would become so hot as to almost glow by the end of that time. The fire was then raked off, leaving many hot coals on the hot stone, and the members of the band would dance barefoot on the stone and the hot coals for several minutes at a time with no apparent injury to their feet. Members of the band [medicine society] would also thrust their arms to the shoulder in boiling water, and even jump bodily into large kettles in which the water was briskly boiling. My informants state that there was never any appearances of injury nor sign of pain after such performances. As might be expected, the specialty of this band [medicine society] was the treatment of burns" [James Young Eagle in Will 1934:45–46].

There are also reports of shamans who could turn themselves into fire. Discussing the Alaskan Inuit, for example, Rasmussen noted that

> the most feared form of [shamanic] metamorphosis was from man to fire—a shaman could turn himself into a ball of fire and fly through space, spreading death and destruction around him.
>
> Shamans were particularly active in autumn, during the first dark nights, and one could see fire-ball after fire-ball rushing through the sky [Rasmussen in Ostermann 1952:131].

In addition to fire-handling medicines, there is a genre of power feats that are associated with fire. For instance, Father Chrétien Le Clerq, the French Jesuit missionary to the Micmac on Gaspée Peninsula, noted during the latter part of the seventeenth century that "shamans could make trees appear all on fire without being consumed" [Mavor and Dix 1989:143].

For other examples of fire handling, see *angalkuk, batsawe, chayan, Hadihiduus, Hakan, hasha, haxa, Iruska, Kawenho, kiuks, Klislah, Lahatcanos, Onayanakia, Petcuduthe utakohi, puhagüm, siaiuklw, sukwiya, Taiwetälem, tcuyaliclofor, Thomas, Albert, tuyuku, wábano, Yayatü society.*

Fish
Blackfoot, *Plains*

A Piegan man who, around 1910, originated the Stick Game Dance, which came to him in a dream. Central to the ceremony is a stick game bundle containing a set of sticks used in the game. One informant reported of this particular ceremony: "The stick game dance or ceremony is regarded as a powerful medicine. In it prayers are offered to God only and not to the stars, moon, sun, and other Blackfoot deities [spirits]. In case of sickness the head of the family may make a vow to provide a feast for the owner of the stick game bundle if the sick one recover[s]. Then some time after the recovery he invites everybody, old and young, to the feast. The ceremonies are held at night. . . . Fish dreamed of a man who came to give him the stick game bundle [power]. . . . Fish claims the stick game bundle to be very powerful. If a person be sick he may vow to play with the stick game owner in order that he may recover. . . . There are three stick game bundles now" [Eagle Child in Wissler 1913:448–450].

Formulistic magic

A scholarly term first used by anthropologist Ruth Bunzel (see entry) to describe Native American shamanic and religious ceremonies that focus on ritual perfection and include the lengthy reciting and singing of ritual formula without verbal error. This term is used to differentiate along a continuum from individual shamanic ceremonies to ceremonies in which shamans use one or more assistants to highly complex rituals that are lengthy and include many official shamans and their assistants—in other words, to differentiate between individual and highly complex social means of handling and manipulating supernatural powers.

In North America formulistic magic is most highly developed in the Southwest area, particularly among the Navajo, Pueblo, Hopi, and Zuni. In these societies shamanic performances are the responsibility of various religious societies. The head shaman of each society is usually known as either "chief" or "priest," and members of the society are often referred to as "the priesthood."

The complexity of the Zuni religious societies is reflected in the fact that they are divided into two groups—twelve curing societies, known as the *Shumakwe* (see entry), and fifteen rain societies, known as the *Ashiwanni* (see entry). To add to their complexity, Zuni religious societies belong to lineages within the clan. During the 1920s field research by anthropologist Elsie Parsons [1933:80–81] revealed the complex society affiliations of the fifteen *Ashiwanni* (numbered below):

	Society Membership
Town Chieftaincy (Kyakweamosi) (1) (Rain Priesthood of the North)	
Tsa'tsana	Pechasilokwe (Bedbug)
	Ne'wekwe
	Uhuhukwe
Chiko	Chikyalikwe (Snake-medicine)
	Snake-medicine
Tsi'autiwa	
Paltowa(2) (Rain Priesthood of the East)	
Waihusiwa	Shuma'kwe
Laya'tisi	Bedbug
	Makyełannakwe (Big Firebrand)
	Shuma'kwe
Hina	Big Firebrand
	Halokwe (Ant)
Tsaihusiluñkya	
Onawa (3) (Rain Priesthood of the South)	
1. Justito (Okash)	
2. Kuyatsaluhti	
3. La'usi	
4. Mikyela	
5. Itsełkai	Big Firebrand
6. Mother of 1, 4, 5	
7. Ts'annatsaiti'ts'a	
8. Daughter's daughter of 6	
Koyemshi or Hekiapawa (Rain Priesthood of the West) (4) (5)	
Lemi	Shi'wannakwe [see entry]
Huluati	
Nałashi	
Tseyi'i	
Shintanni	
Pekwin Kyakyalikwe (Eagle People) (6)	
Mayawe	
Haliana	Big Firebrand
	Bedbug
Kwaletshi	Big Firebrand
Pa'tela	
Upts'anawa (7)	
I'tailuhsi	Makye tsannakwe (Little Firebrand)
	Ant
	Lewekwe (Wood)
Tshaliwa	Big Firebrand
Monta	
Chikwa	
Towakwe (8) (Corn People)	
Pontashi	Shi'wannakwe
	Bedbug
	Shuma'kwe
Shi'tshiwini	

Kolowisi (9) (Horned Water Serpent)
Kanawihti   Snake-medicine
                                                 Ko'chikwe (Cactus)
Kahtshanni   Uhuhukwe
Kwihma
Paulita   Uhuhukwe

Shuma'kwe (10—actually a curing society the chiefs of which operate as a rain society)
Ma'sewi   Little Firebrand
Ta'kyakwekwe
Meli

Yatokwe (11) (Sun People)
Tu'ky'ats'o'ta   Shuma'kwe
Kuyalu
Kuhimats'a

Kya'nakwe (12) or Towakwe (13) (Corn People)
Lonhose
Lomansito
Sha'lako   Snake-medicine
La'silu
Kanawuli   Shuma'kwe

Hewimosikwe (14) of Lemaltishilowa (15)
Lanuitsawi (personal name, Tsawasi)   Snake-medicine
Hu'pa
Lemałtishilowa
sister of Hu'pa   Ant

Gabe, Charlie
Kalispel, *Plateau*

A renowned shaman who died during the winter of 1936–1937. As a youth he had received powers from the Little People, "persons who look very much like Indians except for their very dark skins and their diminutive stature of about two feet and one-half to three feet" [Turney-High 1937:13]. Gabe was a seer, weather shaman, medicine dance leader, and trainer of novice shamans, among other things. He was well known for his ability to see things at a distance and look into the future. For example, whenever someone came to visit him, Gabe would know the identity of his visitor and call out the person's name before opening his door. Many tried to sneak up on him. "They would take off their shoes. They would make friends with the dogs. But every time Charlie called out their names and opened the door for them" [Turney-High 1937:31]. He even knew what people afar were saying about him.

> The winter of 1927 was most severe. The shaman had several head of cattle in those days, and feed was getting so depleted that his wife came to him and told him something had to be done to save the herd. Charlie said, "All right, we will start tonight." He had only his wife with him to aid in the singing, but they sang and sang for the Chinook wind while the shaman danced. When the evening of the fourth day came no change in the weather had been effected. But the shaman said, "When morning comes you look out on the ridge just northeast of here and tell me what you see." When morning came the wife went to the door but soon came flying back to Charlie's bed and asked him to come and look. "No," said he, "I sent you to look. You tell me what you see."
>
> "I see a rainbow on that little hill," she reported. Two hours later the Chinook wind came and melted all the snow away so that the cattle could eat grass [Turney-High 1937:32].

Gagohsa
Iroquois, *Northeast*

Literal translation: "face" [Fenton 1941:405]. Term used by the Seneca for their ceremonial false-face masks, usually carved from basswood. The power to make such masks is given directly to individuals by a spirit known as *Shagodjiowengowa* (or *Shagodjowéhgowa* [Fenton 1937:224]), the

Helper, who is addressed among the Seneca as "Our Grandfather." These masks are "emblematic portrayals or representations of spiritual powers assigned to combat and overcome all malignant influences" [Keppler 1941:17].

A person receives a vision in which a spirit directs him to carve a certain type of mask; once this is done, the mask transfers the power of that particular spirit to the individual when it is worn in ceremony.

Consequently, these masks are treated as sacred objects and carry with them certain taboos with regard to their handling and care. A contaminated mask is called *odgoh gahneegondahgoh*. Such a mask must be "scraped with a white stone knife and kept in 'hiding' until it was believed to have been purified by its seclusion, or until all ill effects were thought to have worn away through the penitence of the offending party" [Keppler 1941:39]. When returned to use, a small bag of sacred tobacco, *unjengwa onweh*, is attached to the mask "partly to appease, partly to insure its future goodwill and the preservation of its inherent powers" [Keppler 1941:39]. Fenton [1937:230] noted that when a mask is transferred from one person to another, the new owner also adds such a pouch of tobacco to the mask. In addition, "sometimes the masks become hungry and the owners rub their lips with mush and anoint their faces with sunflower oil, which after many years imparts a rich luster" [Fenton 1937:230].

For details see *False-Face Society,* EONAH, pp. 79–82.

Gaguwara
Iroquois, *Northeast*
Literal translation: "face" [Fenton 1941:405]. Term used by the Mohawk for their ceremonial false-face masks. See *gagohsa.*

Gahan
Mescalero, *Southwest*
The Apache Mountain Spirits Ceremony. During the performance of the *Gahan* ritual, which in recent times has been combined with this group's puberty ceremony for girls, "masked beings who live in the caverns of the sacred mountain come forth in power for the healing of the tribe" [Scully 1975:351]. Costumed dancers impersonate the various spirits. "The mountain spirits start coming in after sundown. . . . As the first spirits come in from the east, emerging, so they say, from their mountain cavern home, they move straight toward the still glowing west and seem to be blessing that direction and the new night. . . . The mountain spirits are painted black, with crosses and other shapes very bold in white on their backs, chests, and arms. They wear black hoods with vast, abstracted tree or antler shapes of slatted Spanish Bayonet (yucca) rising from their heads. Sticks of the same material are held like swords in each hand, and are striped like the arms that wield them with white snake or lightning shapes" [Scully 1975:360].

Gahnohgwahsehnah
Iroquois, *Northeast*
Literal translation: "sacred medicine" [Keppler 1941:26]. Powdered herbs used in the healing ceremonies of the Seneca *Niganägaah* society. During a healing ceremony *gahnohgwahsehnah* is added to water and given to the patient to drink. If the mixture stays on top of the water, this indicates to the shaman that the patient will not recover. If it sinks into the water, it indicates that the patient will heal.

Gakil
Maidu, *California*
The term used by the Southern Maidu for spirits of the dead. These are the spirits called upon in a shamanic séance to answer questions. The shaman conducts the ceremony at night. "The interior of the dance house *(kum)* was without a fire, and dark. For five or ten minutes the shaman shook his cocoon rattle *(wososa).* Then a roaring sound was heard outside, at which the shaman lay down and ceased shaking his rattle.

After a few minutes the spirit arrived, picked up the rattle, shook it a little, and mumbled. The spirit told the assembled people what was happening at the place he came from; he also told them to be kind to one another; and he would foretell whether the acorn and other crops would be good. The spirit would discourse thus for half an hour, then drop the rattle, and depart with the same roaring sound with which he arrived. Several spirits would come in the course of one evening's performance" [Gifford 1927:245–246].

Gambling medicine

One of the primary uses for supernatural power is in gambling medicines, and many different examples of gambling medicines are reported in the literature. These medicines are normally acquired from a particular spirit or spirits by an individual, usually via some form of vision questing; however, in some cases such a medicine is acquired from a shaman. Gambling medicines are more often owned by an individual than by a shaman since anyone can acquire supernatural powers.

Among the Quinault on the Northwest Coast, we know of five different spirits that brought gambling power, named according to the bodily posture assumed by the gambler:

> làa´opàt ("sit down"), who sat down;
> tsele´utnisam ("kneels"), who knelt;
> towłḱala´xuts ("collar bone"), who was headless;
> cḱwała´łopàt ("lie down"); and xwiḱla´lasuk ("stand up"), who stood up. The owners of the first two always assumed the pose of the spirit (sitting or kneeling) while gambling. The last was the type W. M.'s mother controlled. It came to her in the form of a salmonberry bird (skwit) in a canoe. She heard its song and its directions to turn around. Then she saw two marked beaver teeth dice lying in the canoe of the spirits. She always gambled with these and seldom lost, and during her lifetime became quite rich from her winnings. She once staged a gambling bout with the most famous woman

gambler of the Puget Sound. The game was played at Elma and onlookers bet large sums on the outcome. Each woman started with 100 tally sticks. A half day passed before the contest was over. W. M.'s mother would prepare for an important contest such as this by singing her spirit songs for two or three days [Olson 1936:150–151].

Both foot and horse racing are widespread forms of gambling in North America. The Zuni hold footraces between different pueblos, and each pueblo assembles a four-man team to compete in the event. One such race, on April 16, 1932, was recorded: "Each team of four men is led single file by their overnight ceremonialist, in this case a War chief for one team, and an Ant society man for the other. The leader casts a handful of prayer-meal in front of his team before he leaves them at the edge of town. He is 'opening the road.' The racers continue on . . . into a stretch of greasewood where they stoop to pray and sprinkle prayer-meal. The teams scatter, evidently each man is praying on his own. Then in single file the runners come over to the starting-line, the arms of each folded tightly across his bare chest, as if holding in something. As indeed they are doing, the powers of four swiftly flying birds—anethlauwa or hawk, shokyapissa or red-shoulder hawk, akwatsu'ta, and tse'wia or McGillivray's warbler" [Parsons 1939:822]. The night before the racers had also gone through a ceremony to receive "powers for 'abdomen and back'" [Parsons 1939:823].

In mythic origins the Papago received power from the Cranes to play their "kick-ball" game, in which teams of runners kick a ball from the starting point to a mountain some 15 miles in the distance and back. Thus the real goal of the game is to endure the entire 30-mile course. "The challenging visitors always sing for their hosts, and the hosts pay 'because they have come so far and have suffered on the way, and because they have entertained us with beautiful singing'" [Underhill

1938:152]. However, what is most unusual about this race for competitive-oriented Westerners is the fact that "sometimes the visitors sing songs extolling the names of prominent men in the challenged village. As a rule, no man lightly mentions another man's name, for fear of using up its magic power; but to use it in this auspicious connection is to bring the owner luck, and each man sung for responds with a gift" [Underhill 1938:154].

Among the Papago the most successful gamblers are those who have acquired supernatural gambling power. In regard to their hidden-ball guessing game, in which a scarlet bean is hidden in one of four reed tubes, one report noted that the best gamblers "had usually had a supernatural experience which gave them the requisite power. One informant, after killing an eagle, had been visited by the dead bird, who promised him success and told him always to fling down the tubes with their openings toward the east. He never lost" [Underhill 1939:142]. Before the reed tubes are thrown down, they are filled with varying amounts of sand in order to hide the bean. In the instance just cited, the openings of the tubes were also to be pointed to the east when being filled. In addition the eagle spirit gave the informant specific instructions for making a power-imbued set of four reed gaming-tubes, which he followed, and he always won with them [Underhill 1939:170].

Some forms of foot racing are ritualized, and, therefore, gambling is not the main incentive in these activities. For an example, see *Chüawimkya*.

See also *Ahayuta tikä, lahul, masutikï, micaduskwe, Suwi, tamánamis, ukemauwûsk*.

Ganohwa

Iroquois, *Northeast*

Seneca term for the turtle-shell rattle used by the False-Face Society (EONAH, pp. 79–82) during their ritual performances. Another rattle, known as *osnoh ganohwa*, is made from hickory bark and filled with wild cherry pits [Keppler 1941:28].

"Rubbing the turtle-shell rattle, *ganohwa*, upon the bark of a tree or against any wooden surface symbolically invoked its eternal life spirit and absorbed from it the mystic powers of both the 'Below-' and 'Above-world' which were connected by the Great Tree's deep roots and sky-reaching branches. The Great Tree, *gaindowane*, was most important in Seneca beliefs. Its branches sheltered in peace and security, its trunk symbolized strength and unity, and its roots reached far and deep to the foundations of the earth supported on the carapace of the turtle" [Keppler 1941:24].

Garland, Hamlin

Hamlin Garland was born on September 14, 1860, in West Salem, Wisconsin. In 1884 he went to Boston, where he began his writing career. He "was a first-rate man of letters, a very meticulous observer, and a talented writer, who, in all of his associations with the American Indian, was an active and careful note-taker. His notebooks contain great quantities of raw materials relating to the American Indian during the period 1895 through 1905" [Underhill and Littlefield 1976:8]. In addition, he was "not only enlightened for the time but more sympathetic toward the Indian than typical American public opinion in any period of our national history" [Meyer in Underhill and Littlefield 1976:8].

His firsthand experiences with Native Americans began in 1895 during a trip to the Southwest area, where he visited the Utes, Tiwa (at Isleta), Keres (at Laguna and Acoma), Zuni, and Hopi (Moki). During his visit with the Hopi, he met Jesse W. Fewkes (see entry) and Frederick W. Hodge (see entry) from the Smithsonian, who were there to observe the Hopi Snake Dance (see *Chüawimkya*). Garland later wrote of this tour that it "turned out to be the most profitable season of my whole career. It marks a complete 'bout face. . . . In truth every page of my work thereafter was colored by the expressions of this glorious, savage, splendid summer" [Garland in Underhill and Littlefield 1976:17–18].

In the years to follow, he traveled throughout the West interviewing Native Americans, including the Sioux, Cheyenne, Crow, Flathead, Nez Perce, Yakima, Assiniboin, Gros Ventre, Navajo, Arapaho, Wichita, Comanche, Blackfoot, and others. In all of his writings, he tried to portray the Native American point of view. Subsequently he became involved in "Indian reform," as it was known at the turn of the century, and in April 1902 he met with President Theodore Roosevelt to discuss his views on the matter. Following this, from about 1903 to 1913, his writing on Native Americans decreased as he settled in to family life and did little or no more traveling. His writings on Native Americans came to an end, for the most part, with the 1923 publication of *The Book of the American Indian,* which was illustrated by Frederick Remington, of whom Garland was not particularly fond. This was his most elaborate publication but not necessarily his best work. Much of his work remains unpublished and is currently located in the Hamlin Garland Collection at the University of Southern California Library in Los Angeles.

Geakâmpiugea
Kiowa, *Plains*
Literal translation: "life food" [Parsons 1929:95]. Before going into battle, a warrior often requested assistance for success from one of the women's societies. In so doing he vowed to provide a feast upon his return from battle. When he came back the warrior then gave the women the food for the feast, and they would take it and "withdraw into their tipi, allowing none in. Sounds of bears would be overheard. They beat a drum. Should any one trespass during this retreat of an hour or so, something would happen to him, he would be bewitched" [Parsons 1929:95]. During this ceremony the food was blessed, and when finished the women took some of the food to the warrior. He in turn received a blessing from this *geakâmpiugea.*

Ge·estcin
Coyotero, *Southwest*
The generic term used by the White Mountain Apache for painted fetishes. This term "applies to anything bearing ceremonial designs: sand paintings, hoops and staffs, painted buckskin objects, ga·n masks, etc. Ge'estcin are holy and prayed to because [they are] endowed with supernatural power and are personifications of it. They must be addressed before they can exert full influence. Even ga·n masks are prayed to by the dancers before being donned. Only certain ceremonies include the right to make ge'estcin. Eventually these objects must be disposed of in some cave or rock crevice, with appropriate prayers and under instruction of the shaman who directed their making. Some ge'estcin made to use in a single ceremony must be put away shortly afterwards; others made for an individual may be kept by him as long as their powers last" [Goodwin 1938:33].

Genius locus
Plural: genii loci. This phrase is used infrequently in anthropology to refer to spirits that are known to inhabit certain geographical locations, such as mountains, caves, lakes, etc. The genius locus is one type of possible guardian spirit for a shaman.

Geronimo
Apache, *Southwest*
This famed Chiricahua war leader gained political power because of his abilities as a powerful shaman. "Geronimo got political power from the religious side. He foresaw the results of the fighting, and they used him so much in the campaigns that he came to be depended upon. He went through his ceremony, and he would say, 'You should go here; you should not go there.' That is how he became a leader" [unidentified informant in M. E. Opler 1941:200].

As a shaman he had many powers. For healing he had ghost powers (for ghost sickness) and coyote powers. The following account of a four-day healing ceremony described how Geronimo used his coyote powers to cure an old man:

The ceremony began in the evening, as soon as it became dark. It took place in an arbor outside of

A photograph of Geronimo, the famed Chiricahua war leader who gained political power because of his abilities as a powerful shaman

Geronimo's home. There was a fire. Geronimo and the patient were on the west side of the fire. Geronimo sat facing the east, and the patient lay stretched out before him. . . .

Geronimo had an old black tray basket before him filled with things he used for the ceremony. He had a downy eagle feather in it and an abalone shell and a bag of pollen. All these things were wrapped up in a bundle before the ceremony began.

He rolled a cigarette and puffed to the directions first of all. . . . After smoking, he rubbed the patient with pollen. He dropped pollen on the patient, just on certain parts of the body. He prayed to the directions as he did this. These prayers referred to Coyote and were on the same order as the songs which followed.

He started to sing. There were many songs, and the songs were about Coyote. They told how Coyote was a tricky fellow, hard to see and find, and how he gave these characteristics to Geronimo so that he could make himself invisible and even turn into a doorway. They told how the coyote helped Geronimo in his curing. Geronimo accompanied his singing with a drum which he beat with a curved stick. At the end of each song he gave a call like a coyote [unidentified informant in M. E. Opler 1941:40].

Among Geronimo's war medicines was a "gun ceremony" used to make one invincible to bullets [M. E. Opler 1941:311], and the ability to control daylight: "When he was on the warpath, Geronimo fixed it so that morning wouldn't come too soon. He did it by singing. Once we were going to a certain place, and Geronimo didn't want it to become light before he reached it. . . . He wanted morning to break after we had climbed over a mountain, so that the enemy couldn't see us. So Geronimo sang, and the night remained for two or three hours longer. I saw this myself" [unidentified informant in M. E. Opler 1941:216].

See also *war medicine*.

Gichimanido
Ojibwa, *Canadian Eastern Woodlands*
Also: *gichimanidoo* [Vizenor 1981:84]. A Chippewa variant of *Kitche Manitou* (EONAH, pp.

135–136), being their term for the Creator [Ritzenthaler 1953b:189]. They also use the expression *midemanido* for the Creator.

Gidahim
Papago, *Southwest*
A planned war raid expedition conducted most often by several villages [Underhill et al. 1979:114]. War was usually waged in a ritual manner and involved the use of medicine powers to ensure success. In the Papago case the journey to the enemy involved four stops along the way for prayers. On the night before the attack, the warriors would gather around a campfire and give orations. Also during this night "medicine men divined the location of the enemy and worked to render them defenseless" [Underhill et al. 1979:120]. The final phase of the *gidahim* took place upon the return of the warriors. This was a purification rite in which a "cure speech" was given and the shamans doused the warriors with water and blew upon them (*wúsot*, see EONAH, p. 320) for purification purposes [Underhill et al. 1979:131].

Gifford, Edward Wilson
Ethnologist Edward Gifford was born in Oakland, California, on August 14, 1887. He became the curator for the Museum of Anthropology at the University of California, Berkeley, where he remained throughout his career. Although he did some fieldwork in various Pacific islands, he is best remembered for his outstanding work among the Native Americans of California. He excelled both as a field ethnologist and as a linguist.

Gogimish
Ojibwa, *Canadian Eastern Woodlands*
An unidentified plant, described as about 2 feet in height with black bark and clusters of small red flowers, that is used in *mide* (EONAH, p. 173) medicines. Hoffman [1891:226] reported that it was used in "magic remedies" to ward off the influence of sorcerers and evil charms. The

root of this plant is also used in a special mixture that produces a paralysis of the mouth, known as the "twisted mouth" [Barnouw 1977:178]. Once administered this mixture takes about a week to achieve its full effect, and then it goes into remission within six to twelve weeks [Hoffman 1891:227]. People are careful not to provoke a shaman partially out of fear that he may retaliate by sending "twisted mouth" [Lantis 1968:63].

Grass Dance

Also: Omaha Dance. Originally a Warrior Society dance, today it is a widespread social dance found among the Sarsi, Blackfoot, Gros Ventre, Assiniboin, Crow, Teton (Dakota), Omaha, Iowa, Ponca, Kansa, Hidatsa, Pawnee, Arikara, Arapaho, Menomini, Ojibwa, Plains Cree, Plains Ojibwa, Shoshoni, Winnebago, Cheyenne, Flathead, Kiowa, Osage, and Oto [Wissler 1916:862]. The Teton Sioux received it in the early 1860s from either the Ponca or Omaha and call it the *Omáha Wacípi* (the Sioux use the same term for both the Ponca and Omaha nations) [Howard 1984:146]. The Ponca and Omaha called it *Hethúshka*. Subsequently it became known among the Canadian Santee as both *Heyúshka* and *Pejí Wacípi*, "Grass Dance" [Howard 1984:146], of which they have two variations—the Big Grass Dance and the Young Men's Grass Dance. Among the U.S. Santee it is known as *Hotángka Wacípi*, "Winnebago Dance" [Howard 1984:146]. Among the Assiniboin it is known as *Pejíng Wacípi*, "Grass Dance," and *Pejíng Miknáka*, "Grass Tucked-in" [Ernest White Eagle in Howard 1984:165].

Central to the performance of the Grass Dance is the ritual preparation of and feasting on a sacred soup made from a puppy "that had not been allowed to become a family pet" [Howard 1984:156]. The ritual sacrifice of a puppy is common among the Sioux. For example, a particularly difficult healing ceremony might require the preparation of dog soup. In all cases it is considered an honor to receive the animal's head in one's serving.

Hachtad
Twana, *Northwest Coast*

Hate magic. This term comes from *hachad,* "hating someone" [Elmendorf 1960:523]. This is a form of sorcery in which a person uses his or her helping spirit power to harm someone. *Hachtad* is practiced in secrecy. Most often it is performed by a shaman who is hired to hurt an enemy, but a layman might do this job if his *cshalt* (see entry) is strong enough. *Hachtad* is most often directed against enemy villages as a substitute for war raids.

Hadigonsashoon
Iroquois, *Northeast*

Term used by the Seneca for their original False-Face Society, from which others eventually sprang, such as the *Idos* and the *Niganägaah* societies [Keppler 1941:22]. The function of this society is to perform "ministrations to the sick as individuals and invocations to the propitiation of malignant forces which might visit or were visiting their fury upon the whole tribe" [Keppler 1941:21].

For details see *False-Face Society,* EONAH, pp. 79–82.

Hadihiduus
Iroquois, *Northeast*

The Onondaga term for "singing the songs of the Medicine Men's Society" [Fenton 1942:20]. The Iroquois grow their own gourds to be made into rattles for this ceremony. Consequently, their meetings are colloquially called "pumpkin shakes" [Fenton 1985:9]. The Onondaga songs are secret and are not to be sung outside of the medicine lodge. These songs, handed down over many generations, are the source of the power for healing. Onondaga shamanic healing takes place in both individual practices and in the efforts of organized, shamanic-based societies such as the *Hadihiduus.*

The *Hadihiduus* has a suborder known as *Hadinegwáis,* "the fan strikers" [Fenton 1942:29]. The members of this society consist of "individuals having large birds as familiars [guardian spirits], those who have dreamed of large birds (or chickens nowadays), and individuals who have been cured of 'eagle sickness,' a neurotic complaint of the shoulders, back, and legs" [Fenton 1942:29].

In former times, "perhaps a thousand years ago, men of each Iroquois nation had these songs for contesting magic power. Only magicians belonged to this society, and only magicians danced. All the old songs which they used referred to their powers. While they were dancing they demonstrated these powers by 'throwing' or 'shooting sharp objects,' such as 'horns' (antler), which gives to part of the ritual the names of 'sharp point' (*gai"don*), or one would sing 'something (like a bear) is running around.' The magician would then transform himself into a bear and run around there in the room. Another would make a twig stand of itself in the center of the room while the other medicine men danced around it. Still another would in turn go to the fire and remove red hot stones and juggle them. A man lacking this kind of power could not do this" [Chief Joseph Logan in Fenton 1942:21].

A performance of the *Hadihiduus* is divided into two parts. The first part is called "Throwing In a Song," and the second part is the round dance, "the so-called Medicine Dance (ganony-áhgwen)" [Fenton 1942:22, 24]. "[The term] 'gahii'dohon', 'sharp point,' possibly, is an obscure archaic word which is used as a name for the [round dance] ceremony. It refers to sharp objects which shamans shoot" [Fenton 1942:24, n. 6].

Hadjamuni
Keres, *Southwest*
Also: *hächamoni* (EONAH, p. 97) (Sia), *hachaminyi* [Parsons 1939:270], *hachamuni* (Acoma) [Parsons 1926:124]. Prayer stick. See *offerings*.

Hadui
Iroquois, *Northeast*
Literal translation: "hunchback." Term used by the Onondaga for their carved basswood ceremonial false-face masks. These masks are symbolic carvings of specific spirits, each of which carries with it specific powers. They serve as amulets, in the sense that when the owner of a mask dons it during a ritual, the particular spirit represented by the mask possesses the wearer and comes to the aid of the people. As a result, each mask is treated as a sacred object.

For details see *False-Face Society,* EONAH, pp. 79–82.

Haguks
Iroquois, *Northeast*
Cayuga and Onondaga term for Dew Eagles [Fenton 1942:29]. See *oshadageaa* for details.

Haha
Thompson, *Plateau*
See *haxa*.

Hahagil
Comox, *Northwest Coast*
Shaman [Barnett 1955:148]. See *siaiuklw* and *snäem* for details.

Hakan
Keres, *Southwest*
Fire Society; sometimes referred to in the literature as the Firebrand Society [Parsons 1939:441]. This is a medicine society of fire handlers found at Acoma, Santa Ana, Cochiti, and Zia pueblos. "It has become extinct at Laguna" [White 1930:605], but at Cochiti, "the Fire society is included within the Flint [*Hictiani*—see EONAH, pp. 105–106] society together with the Snake group" [White 1930:605, n. 1]. Among the neighboring Tewa, the "Flint and Fire are the 'Bear medicine' societies" [Parsons 1939:133]. The Fire Society is most likely of ancient origin. In the Acoma creation myth "the rattle of the first shaman, the Fire society chief, was made of the scrotum of elk, filled with agave seeds" [Parsons 1939:384, n.*].

The Fire society functions primarily as a curing society, and many of its rituals are, of course, associated with fire. For example, "the Fire society chief of Acoma uses lightning-riven wood" when making prayer sticks [Parsons 1939:274]. In addition society members

perform fire and hot-water tricks, also sword-swallowing at initiations. . . . Sia Fire shamans walk on live coals or eat them, and in their dance the following day they swallow long sharp sticks. Cochiti Fire shamans take burning straw, put out the flame, and put the ashes into their mouth. After a four-day retreat Acoma Fire shamans dig a shallow pit. . . . A fire is built in the pit. . . . Women members bring out four pots of water and build fires under them. From their baskets they throw meal into the boiling water, stirring it with their bare hands. They take out the mush and throw balls to the people on the housetops. All the members dance in anti-sunwise circuit around the pit, while they sing four songs. The chief stirs the live coals and ashes with his hands, then he and the other men jump into the pit. . . . This fire performance is followed at Acoma as at Sia by an exhibition of stick-swallowing. Some of the "sticks" are saplings whittled down with the foliage left at the top, others are flat, painted boards. (Both types are used by Zuni and Hopi. The Zuni stick is somewhat curved and is surmounted with feathers). Women accompany men in their stick-swallowing dance, but do not swallow sticks. At Zuni women formerly did swallow sticks. . . . It is reported that death has resulted from stick-swallowing [Parsons 1939:441–442].

During the summer solstice the Fire society, along with other Kersan medicine societies, goes into retreat to hold rain-making ceremonies.

Haldaugit

Tsimshian, *Northwest Coast*

Also: *haldawit* (EONAH, pp. 101–102). Witchcraft. "Personal belongings were the most potent means of producing ill effects. Hair, nail parings, or soiled clothes were secured and combined with plants and objects believed to have an evil influence. Incantations were said over these, and the specific evil intended for the individual was mentioned. For illnesses caused by witchcraft, the patient could only be cured if the shaman secured the personal belongings that had been used and washed them clean of the harmful intent" [J. Miller 1984:141].

Haleyt

Tsimshian, *Northwest Coast*

Supernatural power obtained from spirits. This term also implies that the power is controlled and "expressed through simulations of desired state" [J. Miller 1984:137]. This is the power of shamans. Supernatural power expressed in an uncontrolled manner is *naxnox* (see entry).

See also *samhalait*.

Hamatsa

Northwest Coast

Cannibal. The *Hamatsa* Dance, a widespread ceremony along the Northwest Coast, incorporates powerful cannibalistic rituals [McDowell 1997:133]. It was a secret society into which members were initiated, usually during the winter ceremonial. "According to Boas, in ancient times, slaves were killed for an ecstatic *hamatsa* and he devoured them" [McDowell 1997:137]. Later the *Hamatsa* Dance substituted ritual can-

Kwakiutl Hamatsa society visor mask. Such masks were worn in Hamatsa society dances and were associated with the man-eating spirit, a bird monster known as hokhokw.

nibalism for actual human sacrifice. Kwaikiutl informants reported in the 1890s that the *Hamatsa* Dance was acquired by them from the Heiltsuk (Bellabella) to their north (from Gardner Canal to Rivers Inlet) in 1835. However, by 1914 Boas had received information that the Kwakiutl living at Smith Inlet had acquired the *Hamatsa* Dance from the Nakwaxdaxw, a southern Kwakiutl branch from Blunden Harbour in Nugent Sound, around 1575 to 1600 [McDowell 1997:133–134, 221]. Thus the one acquired in 1835 was a new *Hamatsa* Dance [McDowell 1997:210].

During their initiation new *hamatsa* enter an ecstatic state and become crazed for the taste of human flesh; they run amuck in the village and take bites out of people [McDowell 1997:135]. Flesh from corpses was also soaked in salt water and smoked by a female shaman before being eaten during this initiation ceremony. By the 1890s "dogs were substituted for corpses and, instead of biting bits out of people the *hamatsa* merely shaved off a sliver of skin and sucked it" [Tannahill in McDowell 1997:211]. A variant of the *Hamatsa* Ceremony is still performed in such places as Alert Bay during winter ceremonies [McDowell 1997:133].

Hänäsish
Klamath, *California*

Also: *hänäs*. A special type of medicine arrow used by shamans in their healing ceremonies. These arrows are about 3 to 4 feet in length and have no arrow points attached to their tips. Their use in treating patients is as follows:

> The spirit of the medicine-tools [arrows], múluasham sko´ks, has to call for them through the conjurer, ki´uks, and the conjurer then sticks them into the ground, one on each side of the sufferer's couch. The office of the arrows is to keep the person's soul there, to scare away the disease, or to pin it down and kill it, and therefore they are given the shape of a weapon. When one or more pairs [they are used only in pairs] of the

hänä´sish are seen sticking around a patient's bed, the public may rest assured that the conjurer has very strong hopes of restoring the person to health. When the arrows are handled in the correct manner, the patient will recover within a short time; but pulling them up before he or she is entirely well would kill the sufferer, or make him as sick as he was before. Any kind of songs can be sung to them while they stand there for days and days; either the song of the spider, lightning, cloud, or wind, for instance. The utüssusá-ash song-medicine, which is of help against all distempers, sometimes calls for these arrows [Gatschet 1893:112].

When using a pair of *hänäsish,* the shaman must also use another special medicine arrow called *tchúpash*. This arrow is normally somewhat longer, upwards of 3 feet, and cigar-shaped, tapering off at both ends. Feathers are attached to one end. "Its purpose is to improve the medical power of the conjurer by calling up other defunct animal spirits to assist him in becoming a 'strong doctor.' Its employment prescribes a dance lasting five days and five nights. The tchúpash, being a *weapon* also, catches the disease of the patient and brings it to a deep earth-pit, called shlokópash, where it is fastened and destroyed" [Gatschet 1893:112].

Hanblecheyapi
Teton, *Plains*

Dialectical variant: *hamdéciya* or *hamdéjapi* (Santee) [Howard 1984:125]. Lakota vision quest. From *hanblecheya,* meaning "crying for a vision" [Howard 1984:125]. Lakota vision questing is the major avenue to power for the Lakota shamans. The quest is performed in isolation for several days, usually up to four, at a known power spot, typically located at a high elevation (i.e., the top of a butte). Eagle Butte north of Martin in south-central South Dakota and Bear Butte just northeast of Sturgis, South Dakota, are currently two of the most frequently mentioned Lakota vision quest sites. The latter, called *Mato Paha* ("Bear Mountain") in Lakota, is 1,400 feet high (actual elevation is 4,422 feet above sea level) and is an ancient vision quest site for other Native American cultures as well. "Of all the tribes, the Cheyenne attach the most importance to the mountain. They call him Nowah'wus—Where the people are taught, or simply, Bear Tipi" [Schukies 1993:288]. Others who use this sacred site are the Mandan, Kiowa, Arapaho, and Kiowa-Apache. Unfortunately for the Native Americans, however, Bear Butte was made into a state park in 1961 and is currently, along with 8,000 acres of surrounding land, on the National Register of Historic Places as a point of natural history [Schukies 1993:288]. Now that a tourist trail has been constructed to the summit, vision quests are more difficult to conduct, given the lack of isolation afforded the quester.

Both men and women *hanblecheya,* or go on vision quests, for the purpose of obtaining supernatural power from a guardian spirit. Abstinence from food or water during the quest is the norm. Those who are visited by a powerful spirit usually go on to become shamans or at least sweat lodge leaders, herbalists, Sun Dancers, etc. As a rule, shamans periodically *hanblecheya* throughout their lives.

Hanhepi
Teton, *Plains*
Literal translation: "night"; the Power of the night, its spirit or mystery [Buechel 1970:165]. "Any cult meeting held at night, usually between dust and midnight" [J. L. Smith 1967:17]. This term is used for Lakota shamanic performances. When the performance of a *hanhepi* involves binding the shaman in a blanket wrapped with rope, the ceremony is then known as *yuwipi* [EONAH, p. 331]. The *yuwipi* is primarily a healing ceremony, but it is also used for divination purposes, such as finding lost objects, predicting the outcome of certain events, etc.

Hasha
Kwakiutl, *Northwest Coast*
Also: *aikha* (ay´xya) [Lopatin 1945:63]. Dialectical variant: *hasà* (Haisla) [Olsen 1940:197]. The

Kitimat term for shaman. There are two kinds of shamans among the Kitimat—the *hasha* (xa´ca) and the *hailikila* (xayli´kila) [Lopatin 1945:63]. The *hasha* is an independent practitioner, and the *hailikilas* are only nobles who are organized into a subdivision of their Secret Society.

Persons who manifest "a fit of epilepsy, stammering, extraordinary sleepiness, or some other nervous disorder" [Lopatin 1945:64] are considered potential shamans. To become a shaman, one must acquire an *ashuta,* or guardian spirit. This is most often done via a vision quest, but "sometimes an ashuta came to a man of its own will and commanded the man to become a shaman" [Lopatin 1945:66]. "In practice, however, the gift of shamanhood has been transmitted from one to another member of the same family for many generations. Usually after a

A cherry-wood and cedar-bark shaman's rattle with a carved wooden head.

shaman's death his nephew became a shaman. . . . The Kitimat believe that the ashuta (acu´ta), or spirit of the shaman, might be willed by a shaman before his death to his heir, usually his nephew, together with his property" [Lopatin 1945:65]. Once a shaman, he remains unmarried [Lopatin 1945:79].

As in other cultures Kitimat shamans perform various functions. "Healing of the sick was his most important duty for the benefit of his clan. He located lost objects or persons, foretold the future, multiplied game, controlled the weather, and averted catastrophe. The shaman also took care of all spirits who had wandered into the neighborhood of the village" [Lopatin 1945:64]. When performing a ceremony he wears an elaborate costume, usually consisting of, among other things, a fringed bearskin cloak; a decorated apron made of woven mountain-goat hair to which rattling shells, bear teeth, whalebones, etc., are attached; a 6-inch-wide cedar-bark collar; decorated armbands; facial painting; a maple- or juniper-wood carved rattle; and, in some cases, an elaborately carved and painted staff.

Powerful shamans seek many spirit helpers, both the *ashuta* and "roving idle spirits" [Lopatin 1945:67]. "The shaman gathered such spirits together and gave them food and entertainment. In return the thankful spirits helped him in his shamanistic affairs. They became allies in his contests with other spirits. Thus there was a kind of symbiosis between the shaman and the spirits. The shaman lived with these spirits, keeping them always near him. The spirits when fed, employed, and entertained by the shaman brought the people no harm; so the shaman rendered great service to the people by keeping hungry and idle spirits from troubling them" [Lopatin 1945:64].

Once a shaman acquires an *ashuta*, he has to gain public confidence in his shamanic powers, usually by publicly demonstrating them. "Besides, he had to give at least two potlatches—one to his clan, the other to the whole tribe—in order to be legitimized in the office. These potlatches gave him a license to practice. Thus the two tasks for becoming a shaman were, first, to win the confidence and affection of the public and, second, to accumulate property for distribution at the potlatches. For the accomplishment of these two tasks several years were required" [Lopatin 1945:68]. When demonstrating his abilities the shaman first enters into trance possession. "In this trance the shaman performed several feats. He might jump into the large and brightly blazing fire and walk there. He guessed at once where things hidden by people of the audience were and performed other 'miracles'" [Lopatin 1945:70]. Other such "miracles" include eating glowing-hot embers and stabbing oneself with a knife without harm [Lopatin 1945:77].

Most cases of serious illness are diagnosed either as soul loss or object intrusion. Less frequent is the diagnosis of spirit possession. For soul loss the shaman goes on a shamanic journey to recover, bring back, and reinsert (sometimes several days later) the lost soul into the patient. For object intrusion massage and sucking methods are employed on the patient's body. For spirit possession the evil spirit is exorcised from the body. In this latter case "it might happen that the intruder was a more powerful spirit than the ashuta, in which event the ashuta in its own behalf invited some other powerful spirit to help banish the evil spirit" [Lopatin 1945:74]. Most healing ceremonies last from three to five days.

Less frequently women become shamans, and in order to practice they must remain unmarried. "A woman shaman reached a state of ecstasy more readily than a man shaman; she was also more violent and hysterical [during trance] than a man shaman; yet a woman shaman was looked upon as inferior to a man shaman" [Lopatin 1945:76].

The Secret society of the *hailikila* consists of eight degrees. The fourth degree, the *Doodukhula (dudu'xula),* is "a conclave of the shamans. . . . Sometimes they were called upon to cure a person who was very ill" [Lopatin 1945:85]. The seventh degree, *Noolnsista (nulntsi´sta)*, is the fire eater's degree. During the fire eaters' performances, "having ordered the people to make a large fire, they threw into it whatever happened to be at hand, such as boards, wooden tools, boxes. They then stripped and leaped into the blaze. To the great wonder of the crowd, they walked in the fire and ate the burning embers" [Lopatin 1945:85].

Hashtélnéh
Navajo, *Southwest*
Literal translation: "again it is being fixed up" or "re-making is done" [Sapir and Hoijer in Wyman and Bailey 1944:332, n. 9]. Repairing ceremony. "The repairing ceremony may be required and may be performed in connection with *any* ceremonial (including Blessingway and Enemyway)" [Wyman and Bailey 1944:333]. It is used to treat several conditions but especially hysteric catalepsy. When anyone attending a ceremony is seized with catalepsy, this ceremony is immediately performed on the victim.

The treatment involves the use of male and female lightning symbols drawn in the earth, fumigation with cornmeal (yellow corn for females and white corn for males), and rubbing and massaging the patient with hands, a bullroarer, and a mountain sheep's horn. Songs from Windway and Nightway accompany the procedures.

Hatáál
Navajo, *Southwest*
Sings [Lamphere 1969:279]. Navajo ritual practices are organized around various "sings," also called chants. Each chant is a system of ritual procedures, and many chants are grouped together into chantways (EONAH, pp. 47–49). In turn, each different chantway is given a name, which becomes the name of a particular ceremony, such as Blessing Way, Male Shooting Way, Beauty Way, etc. (also sometimes written as Blessingway, Male Shootingway, and so forth). Each chantway has a specific set of power applications. For example, the Beauty Way is designed to correct: aching and swollen joints; skin irritations; a pain across the waist; an aching spine; loss of consciousness; and any sickness "that comes to those who have lain 'in a snake's bedding,' or those who have killed a snake" [Opler 1943:93].

The *hatáál* are among the most lengthy and complicated ceremonies known to Native Americans. For healing alone there are over sixty chantways. Some of them take upwards of nine days to perform and include hundreds of songs, all of which must be sung precisely if the ceremony is to succeed. Thus it often takes many years for a person to learn a particular chantway, that is, to become a qualified "singer" *(hataałi)* [Lamphere 1969:279]. In addition the performance of a chantway is extremely expensive to undertake. For example, Bill Morgan mentioned that, circa 1930, one man paid $1,500 for a Night Chant performance and another man paid the same for a Mountain Chant performance, both at a time when "three hundred and fifty dollars will support a family of five in comparative comfort for one year" [Morgan 1931:391]. Obviously, a serious illness is also a serious financial burden on the family.

In an overview of the many different *hatáál*, one finds that "Navajo ritual constitutes a system of interrelated symbols which are repeatedly patterned in a particular manner" [Lamphere 1969:283]. In particular, "a fourfold pattern using sex, color, and direction distinctions structures these [Navajo] ritual procedures" [Lamphere 1969:301–302].

Hatawe
Keres, *Southwest*
Cochití Pueblo term for corn pollen. This same term is also used at Laguna [Parsons 1926:127]. *Hatawe* is gathered by women from the corn while it is still green. "Its use is restricted primarily to adults, especially the medicine men or male and female members of the various secret societies" [Lange 1959:231]. Its use invokes super-

natural assistance, and therefore, it is a common item in every Pueblo ritual. Offering it to sacred objects is referred to as "feeding" the fetish.

Hatawe is also used by other cultures of the Southwest, such as the Navajo, Hopi, Zuni, and Apache. For other examples see *oneane, talasi*.

Hatetsens
Iroquois, *Northeast*
Seneca medicine man [Pinnow 1964:58].

Haxa
Thompson, *Plateau*
Also: *xaha, haha*. "A mysterious person; anything composed of mystery, or having powers above the ordinary, and which cannot be readily understood or imitated" [Teit 1898:57; 112, n. 185]. This term was given for the Nkamtcinemux and Cawaxamux divisions, but most likely it applies to all shamans of the Thompson River cultures in British Columbia. Two other forms of the term are *haxaôimux,* which Teit [1898:116, n. 255] translated as "land mystery or spirit," and *xahaoimux,* "a place which is mysterious, or in which some 'mystery' or supernatural or being dwells" [Teit 1898:117, n. 264]. When referring to a shaman, the term is *xahatîk losqayux,* meaning "an Indian versed in 'mystery,' 'medicine,' or magic" [Teit 1898:117, n. 264]. Also, the term *xahastêm* means "to regard with mysterious awe or care" [Teit 1898:117, n. 264].

"The frequent occurrence of guardian spirits that are only part of an animal or weapon, [such] as a deer's nose, the nipple of a gun, the left or right side of any thing, the head, the hand, the hair, the tail of an animal, is remarkable. Some Indians had guardian spirits of unusual color or of some particular color,—a gray tree, a white stump, a white horse, a black dog, a spotted dog or fish, a black fox, a blue sky, a red cloud, a black fog, a red fish, etc." [Teit 1900:355]. Guardian spirits that are the sole property of shamans include fog, blue sky, feet of a man, hands of a man, private parts of a man, private parts of a woman, and the bat, among others.

All individuals seek power through the aid of such guardian spirits but for different reasons. However, "the ceremonial training necessary for becoming a shaman extended over a much longer period—sometimes years—than that necessary for becoming a warrior, hunter, fisherman, or gambler. Among the Lower Thompsons a shaman who desired to obtain a dead person for his guardian spirit placed a skull in front of his private sweat-house, and danced and sang around it. Then he took it into the sweat-house, where he kept it all night. He sang and prayed to the soul of the deceased person to whom the skull belonged to impart to him the desired knowledge" [Teit 1900:354]. Both males and females become shamans, although the majority are males. "Some shamans have staffs (especially old shamans), which are painted symbolically, representing lightning, snakes, etc., or their guardian spirits. Figures of these are also carved or painted on their pipes. They were believed to have the power of causing and curing diseases due to witchcraft or to the loss of the soul" [Teit 1900:360].

A shaman uses his guardian spirits both in diagnosing and in treating a patient. "It is said that some shamans were able to ascertain the cause of sickness, only after their guardian spirits had entered their chests. If the first guardian spirit whom they called did not give the desired information, the shaman called another one. If the guardian spirit refused to enter the shaman's body, but jumped back as soon as he approached him, it was a sure sign that the patient would die" [Teit 1900:362]. In treating the patient the shaman often paints his own hair, hands, and chest red before beginning. He then seats himself by the patient. "He had a small basket standing near him, in which he kept some water, which he put into his mouth, and sprayed it either over or in front of the patient's body. Some shamans were said to be able to make the water in their basket increase or decrease, or boil, by supernatural means. Others had a small fire burning near them. They swallowed glowing embers and burning sticks" [Teit 1900:362].

The cure is most often effected by sucking a disease object from the patient's body. "When a person was believed to be bewitched, a powerful shaman was summoned, who sucked the disease out of the person's brow. A hole or mark was left in the brow, from which blood flowed. Then the shaman showed the bone [sorcerer's 'arrow'] he had removed, with bloody deer's hair twisted around it. He threw it a long distance away, and before long the shaman who had shot the bone was taken sick. In other cases the shaman, after pulling out the disease, turned towards the west, threw it in that direction, and blew at it four times" [Teit 1900:363].

"Sometimes shamans were called upon to treat horses and dogs, but only valuable or favorite ones. They proceeded in the same manner as when treating people" [Teit 1900:364].

Helikila
Kwakiutl, *Northwest Coast*
Literal translation: "spirit owner" [Olson 1940:197]. The Haisla term for shaman. Most often shamans are males.

Another term used by the Haisla for shaman is *hasà* (see *hasha*).

Hesi
Maidu and Wintun, *California*
Dialectical variants: *akit* (Valley Nisenan), *saltuke* (Salt or Northern Pomo) [Kroeber 1932:Table 1, foldout insert between pp. 394–395]. Spirit Impersonation society. The *Hesi* is a widespread, central California society of shamans who impersonate different spirits for different functions. For example, the *Sili* spirit, who comes from the ocean in the south, is impersonated for healing [Kroeber 1932:337].

Heswombli
Klamath, *California*
One of two terms used by the Klamath for a cure. The other term is *tcota* [Spier 1930:122]. See *kiuks*.

Hewitt, John Napoleon Brinton
Anthropologist J. N. B. Hewitt was born in Lewiston, New York, in 1859. His mother was part Tuscarora, and his father was a Scottish physician. Hewitt attended school with the intention of also becoming a physician but was swayed to anthropology in 1880 by anthropologist Erminie A. Smith, who hired Hewitt to assist her in collecting Iroquois legends.

In 1886, subsequent to Smith's death, Hewitt was employed by the Bureau of American Ethnology. He became an expert on Iroquoian dialects and traced their connection to the Cherokee language. He also studied the history and political structure of the Iroquois League (see *Deganawidah*), which resulted in his 1918 Smithsonian publication, *A Constitutional League of Peace in the Stone Age.*

He died in 1937.

Hikwsi
Hopi, *Southwest*
The Hopi concept of the Creator is "Giver of the Breath of Life." This "Breath" that the Creator bestows into each living thing is the "spark" of life known as *hikwsi.* The Creator remains basically a mystery and is therefore conceived of as *ane himu* (see entry), "very something." Thus *hikwsi* and *ane himu* are one and the same, and both are "perceived by Hopi as 'the very heart of the Cosmos itself'" [Whorf in Loftin 1986:183].

Hilishaya
Creek, *Southeast*
Literal translation: *hilis,* "medicine," and *haya,* "makers" [Swanton 1928:615]. See *alektca.*

Hilyulit
Yuki, *California*
Singing doctors [V. Miller 1979:25]. See *iwilhiltat.*

Hisákidamissi
Creek, *Southeast*
Taskigi division term for Creator. Literal translation: "Master of Breath," from the words

hisákida, meaning "act of breathing," and *imíssi,* meaning "its controller" [Speck 1907:134].

Hitáktákxe
Nootka, *Northwest Coast*

Makah term for power; "any type of power that a person receives" [Colson 1953:249]. Men and older boys seek power via vision quests at specific power spots in nearby woods. These quests normally last for four days. Usually a specific power is sought—power for whaling, power for gambling, power for war, power for doctoring, etc.—but sometimes the quester receives an unsought power. However, because families used the same power spot through many generations, "it was rare for a person to receive a type of power which his immediate relatives had not obtained" [Colson 1953:250].

Once power is received, the new shaman is usually ill for several months until he learns to properly carry out the instructions of his power. Each power carries with it specific rules for its use, and the shaman must obey these rules if he is to control the power. It is not until the new shaman begins to sing his power songs, given to him by his helping spirit, that others come to know what his power actually is. At this point a shaman who also has the same power is called upon to "fix" this power within the proper place of the new shaman's body. Powerful shamans acquire many powers, but the final proof of them always rests upon the shaman's successes.

Power is always potentially dangerous. Shamans can "throw" their power into others (sorcery), and a chance encounter with a strong power can kill a person. For instance, one report noted that "a china slipper [small sea animal used for food] seen in the woods is a manifestation of power so great that those who handle it are likely to die from the effects" [Colson 1953:255]. One informant recalled an incident that occurred in 1932 while he was in the woods surveying the Makah Reservation:

There were three of us always used to work together all the time and never work with anybody else. We was running control lines, and about noon when we were having lunch—after we got through, we heard something hitting the tree. A cedar tree. It must have been about nine, ten feet off the ground. It was one of those china slippers. And one of the fellows, the tallest of us, took and pried it off the tree with an axe. And the other fellow got it and sliced it in half. I didn't want to bother it. Just stood and watched. And this didn't look like china slipper. Just all blubber inside, fat. Looked like cream of some kind, but wasn't solid either. And this fellow who pried it off the tree died that same week. . . . And the other fellow who cut it open, he suffered [a] long time before he died. That's all I've seen, and they died pretty close together [Fisher in Colson 1953:256].

In more recent times, due mainly to the influences of Christianity, many shamans have been reticent about discussing their abilities. The following is an unusual account (circa the 1940s) of a Makah woman (a Presbyterian) who was given a shamanic healing by her husband, James, who was from another tribe:

James said to me, "You're the kind that doesn't believe in things. I can see that in you. You were brought up that way, and you don't believe in the Indian ways. You fight against it." I told him I always had been that way, that was true. Then he came back in [in] a little while and told me that in spite of it he'd try to help and he knew he could do it. I told him I'd like him to try. He started in to wash his hands. Sick as I was, I noticed that. He washed and washed his hands using soap and water. Then he used alcohol and rubbed his hands with that. It was night, and we were alone here. He came over to me and held his hands in front of me—not touching me, but moving them in front of me. It felt hot. Then he laid his hand on my forehead. I was sitting up. He put his hand on the back of my head, right where my brain sits on the spine, and the other hand right here on my nose. He wasn't pressing heavily but just holding his hands there. Then he said, "You're feeling in great pain, aren't you? I can feel that." I told him it was terrible pain, that I felt sick everywhere from it. He told me that he wasn't going to press hard and that I wasn't to feel frightened but I might begin to feel paralysed. Sure enough, in a little while I began to feel it all through my head and spine. I felt just like I wanted to lie down. Then he was finished. He washed his hands just as carefully as he had before—just as though I were full of germs. Then he went out and started to get supper for me. I don't know what it was, but by the time he finished, I was able to get up and go out there and eat my supper. I felt as well as I ever do [unnamed informant in Colson 1953:243–244].

Another form of Makah power is known as *kxói* (see entry).

Hmuga

Teton, *Plains*

Dialectical variant: *hmunga* (Lakota) [Buechel 1970:194]. The Santee (Canadian Dakota) term for sorcerer, from the stem *hmu* or *hmun,* meaning a humming sound like that made by the flapping of the wings of a bird. *Hmuga* "could change into an owl. They would fly to a scaffold where someone was buried and steal the corpse's tongue. They would dry these tongues and use them in their black magic. This one man had a complete necklace of these tongues to show how many people he had killed. . . . We call these people *kingyángpi* ('flyers') because they can fly around in bird form and work their magic" [Wood Mountain in Howard 1984:114].

Hobáya

Creek, *Southeast*

Shaman, prophet [Speck 1907:118]. This is the term used by the Taskigi division whose members call themselves the Maskogalgi [Speck 1907:106]. These shamans were often associated with war medicines. The *hobáya* would accompany a war party on a raid carrying with him a bundle of sacred herbs and medicines. One of the medicines used was a part of the horns of a mythical snake, which would make a warrior immune to wounds. If a warrior was wounded, however, the *hobáya* would make an emetic from cedar leaves and give it to him to drink to ensure recovery. During the battle the *hobáya* would sing his power songs or shout certain formulas to confuse and frighten the enemy. In addition he would use his powers to "weaken the enemy and blind the eyes of their warriors. He could also foretell events and determine whether raids or hunting excursions would be successful or not" [Speck 1907:114].

Another Taskigi term for shaman is *owála* (see entry).

Hochañi

Keres, *Southwest*

See *Hotshanyi.*

Hodge, Frederick Webb

Frederick W. Hodge was born in England in 1864. He began as a stenographer at the U.S. Geographical and Geological Survey in 1884 and subsequently became the field secretary to the Hemenway Southwestern Archaeological Expeditions, beginning in 1887 (see *Matilda Coxe Stevenson*). After three years with the expedition, he transferred to the Bureau of (American) Ethnology at the Smithsonian in 1889, where he worked for Chief Clerk J. C. Pilling. Later he became the librarian and also accompanied Dr. Jesse Fewkes (see entry) as a field assistant. He did undertake some archaeological excavations of Zuni ruins, such as Hawikuh, where he became known among the Zunis as Teluli, "the mouse who digs holes."

During his work as the bureau librarian, he undertook his monumental work, eventually published (in 1907) as the *Handbook of American Indians North of Mexico,* a two-volume work totaling 2,093 pages (part two was first published in 1910). Issued as Bulletin 30 of the bureau's series, it was so popular that on August 12, 1912, Congress ordered a second printing of the work totaling 6,500 copies, of which Congress ordered 6,000 for personal distribution. Between 1907 and 1930 Hodge also spent time editing the twenty-volume work of Edward Curtis's photographic study of Native Americans entitled *The North American Indian.*

In addition to his work at the bureau, Hodge was also the editor of *American Anthropologist* for thirteen years (1902–1914). On January 1, 1910, he became the director of the Bureau of American Ethnology. During his tenure as the director of the bureau, he was known as "ethnologist-in-charge" rather than "chief." He remained in that office until 1917, when he was invited to become the director of the Museum of the American Indian, supported by the Heye Foundation in New York City. He remained there for the next fifteen years before moving to Los Angeles in 1932, where he became the director of the Southwest Museum for the remainder of his career. He retired in 1956 and moved to Santa Fe, New Mexico, where he died that same year. Throughout his career Hodge was one of the most prolific writers and publishers on Native America, producing 350 published works.

Hoffman, Walter James

Ethnologist W. J. Hoffman was born in Weidasville, Pennsylvania, on May 30, 1846. His family included several generations of physicians, and in 1866 he himself graduated from Jefferson Medical College, where he had studied under his grandfather. In 1870 he enlisted as a staff surgeon in the Franco-Prussian War. During this time he invented an improved bullet extractor for use in the military service. He returned to the United States in May 1871, where, although hired as a U.S. acting assistant surgeon in the U.S. Army, he was detailed as a naturalist and mineralogist to a geological expedition in Arizona and Nevada, headed by Lieutenant Wheeler. In 1872 he became post surgeon at Grant River, Dakota, where he studied the language and mythology of the Sioux. In 1873 he accompanied the Yellowstone Expedition, and by

1877 was hired by Professor F. V. Hayden, chief of the U.S. Geographical and Geological Survey of the territories, to take charge of the organization's ethnology and mineralogy collections.

On September 10, 1879, the Bureau of Ethnology was founded, and Hoffman was appointed assistant ethnologist in charge. Thereafter he spent several years traveling throughout the United States researching Native American sign language and pictographic writings. In 1887 he began a study of the Ojibwa Grand Medicine Society, or *Midewiwin* [EONAH, p. 174], in Minnesota, which resulted in his most important ethnographic contributions. After five years Hoffman became the first white man ever to be admitted to this society.

Throughout his life Hoffman was an avid scholar not only in ethnology but also in mineralogy and natural history. He belonged to more than forty leading scientific and historical societies both in the United States and in Europe. He published widely and diversely, including one paper on the ethnography and philology of the Pennsylvania Germans. By the time of his death on November 8, 1899, at Reading, Pennsylvania, he had received many medals, diplomas, and honors not only from the United States but also from Germany, Portugal, Venezuela, Patagonia, Norway, and Sweden.

Hohoyaüh

Hopi, *Southwest*

Also: *hohoyawûh, hohoyawû, and hohoyowû* [Stephen 1936:1218]. The term for the stinking black tumble (dung) beetle used as a medicine both for warriors and in the performances of the *Chüawimkya* (see entry). The warriors called upon the *hohoyaüh* "to come out and crawl over and obscure their trail, so that any enemy coming in the rear and seeing their trail would think it an old one" [Stephen 1936:96]. In making prayers to the *hohoyaüh,* the beetle was bound up in a *tiponi* (see entry). The *hohoyaüh* was also placed into small, white, clay pellets that were attached to the warrior's *tozriki* (see entry). It was spoken of as the "warrior's tame animal" [Stephen 1936:96].

In the performances of the *Chüawimkya,* two handfuls of these beetles are added, among other things, to a boiling pot of medicine water that is subsequently drunk by all members of the society. "If the Snake men did not drink this antidote, their bellies would swell up and burst" [Stephen 1936:765].

In actuality, two different beetles are used, the "*Hoho'yaüh* or *hoho'yawuû,* said to be blind, and the *ta'la hoho'yaüh,* or stinking tumble bug" [Stephen 1936:765].

Hokitta
Miwok, *California*
A power object used by an *ālini uwemeh* (deer shaman). It is a ball, about 1.5 inches in diameter, that is sometimes found within a deer. Deer shamans also use a *mohleh,* which is a rock shaped "like a deer's foot, or like a deer heart with fat and kidneys on each side" [John Kelly translating for Tom Williams in Gifford n.d. a:39]. Deer shamans receive their deer-hunting medicine via songs that come to them in dreams from the Deer spirit.

Hoktitasha
Zuni, *Southwest*
Mountain lion. This animal plays an important role in hunting medicine. A hunter who issues the cry of the mountain lion while hunting can cause the deer to become nervous, such that they can be hunted without weapons. In addition, while the hunter is away, his wife brings out an image of Mountain Lion each morning to pray for success in the hunt. She draws a line from the image in the direction her husband went hunting and also "feeds" this image. When the hunter returns, the blood from the deer is smeared on the mouth of the image [Parsons 1939:335, 362].

Holy Turnip Bonnet
Blackfoot, *Plains*
See *natoas.*

Hopini
Mandan, *Plains*
Medicine power obtained from a guardian spirit. Power is most often obtained via a vision quest. "Fasting, practiced in the hope of receiving visions, was an almost universal activity among the Mandans, though women engaged in it less than men. A young man would fast in the expectation of receiving a guardian spirit who would direct his conduct; he might experience a vision that would serve as a guide on his next war expedition" [Meyer 1977:79].

Such power is then used, for example, in "ceremonies designed to bring the buffalo near enough so that they might be readily killed or to ensure adequate rainfall for the corn crops" [Meyer 1977:78].

Horqarnaq
West Alaska Eskimo, *Arctic Coast*
An Agiarmiut shaman during the early part of the twentieth century. Ethnographer Knud Rasmussen observed, in January 1923, a ceremony performed by Horqarnaq to stop a storm that had been raging for three days. Among his helping spirits were the spirit of his deceased father, one of his father's former spirits (a giant with claws), a snow figure in the form of a human being, and a red stone he called Aupilalanguaq [Rasmussen 1969:272]. During the ceremony Horqarnaq went into trance and battled the spirit of the storm in the person of his drummer, named Kingiuna, whom he "killed" three times during the performance [Rasmussen 1969:275–276]. The following morning the sky was sunny, and the storm was gone.

Horse medicine
Plains
Horse medicine in some form is used by all Native American cultures that have horses. It comes in many different forms, and many different rituals surround the making of horse medicine. For example, the Kiowa have a specific medicine for finding a lost horse. Their shaman erects a small, buffalo-

A horse stick (club), 1870 (Ellis Soper Collection, gift of the University of Tulsa).

robe tipi within the confines of a larger tipi. Four pipes are displayed on the ground before the shaman enters the tipi, and during the divination many voices are heard emitting from this tipi [Parsons 1929:113]. The shaman then describes to the owner his horse and its present location.

The following is a detailed account, given by Red Plume, of the use of horse medicine among the Blackfoot:

Horse medicine is considered very powerful. Should one who has not the right, sing the horse songs, his horse will fall with him and he will be injured. The owner of the horse medicine must never have a shin bone broken in his tipi, for if he does, his horse will break its leg. Those who have the power of the horse medicine can use it in many ways. It gives them luck in obtaining horses. If a horse should become exhausted while on the road, the owner of the medicine would give the horse some of it, put some into his nostrils, and rub it on his nose, his mane, and down his back to his tail. He then grasps the end of the tail and shakes it four times. The horse is then allowed to eat a little and is as strong as ever and will not again become exhausted.

When a horse has the colic the owner of the horse medicine brews some of it and gives it to the horse. With it he then wets the breast and a spot near the kidneys. Finally, he rubs it on the nose, the mane, and the back to the tip of the tail which he shakes four times. After this he dips a willow switch into the medicine and makes three passes with it as if to whip the horse and with the fourth, whips him, the horse getting well at once.

Before a horse is run the rider sings a song to prevent it from falling. Sometimes, while on the warpath, if he is uneasy about getting horses, he will make a vow that he [will] give the horse medicine owners a feast. When such a vow is made a horse is sure to be obtained. When inviting the horse medicine owners to the feast, the first one invited gives the host a few tail feathers and tells him to give one to each of the horse medicine owners invited. As soon as a horse medicineman receives a feather he knows at once that he is to attend a feast since this is the custom when the horse medicine ceremony is to be held. In most ceremonies invitations are shouted out by a herald, but in the horse medicine [ceremony] they must not even be spoken. In the dance [of this ceremony] the pledger carries a rope and whip making pawing motions with the hands.

At the beginning of the ceremony a smudge of sweetgrass is made [after erecting the horse medicine altar]. The horse medicinemen with their wives are seated at the left of the tipi, leaving the right or guest side vacant. The only outsider allowed to partake in the ceremony is the man who made the vow to give the feast. About the close of the ceremony he dances and then serves the horse medicinemen with a berry soup. He is the only one who dances during this ceremony. All their medicine bundles, consisting of powders tied up in small buckskin bags, are placed in a row in the rear of the tipi. Two red plumes are stuck in the corners of the smudge place [i.e., the horse medicine altar] while two black plumes stuck in opposite corners are their medicines. All those taking part in the ceremony have their own drums, some have horses painted on them, and some have horses' hoofs. After the smudge is made, the man sitting nearest the right of the tipi sings four of his songs, the others join him and he is followed by the man next to him. All present join in the singing. Each one sings four songs, thus ending the ceremony. The face of the man who made the vow is painted red. Before singing, each man prays that the one making the vow [will] have luck in procuring horses during his lifetime, etc. After this, berry soup is served and the ceremony ends.

When a horse medicine owner wishes to cause a horse to lose a race it must be done without the knowledge of the owner. The horse is stolen the night before the race is to be run and the horse medicine owner sings, and rubs his powder on the hoofs and nose of the horse and turns it loose. Should he wish to win the race in another way he tells the rider on which side to run. If he wishes the doctored horse to fall he rubs some of the medicine on a switch which the rider uses. As the race starts, the rider lets the doctored horse lead for a while. He then crosses back and forth before the leading horse and throws the switch in front of it, causing it to fall. Thus, the other rider will pass him in the race. On the other hand, the horse may not be made to fall at all but [he will] make him unable to run past so his horse will win the race. The songs are: "My horse is going to run. May my horse run all right."

During the horse medicine ceremony no outsiders may be present. There are less than twenty horse medicinemen [circa 1903]. Another way in which the horse medicinemen may exert

their power is when running buffalo in the winter when the ground is icy and they use their power to prevent their horses from slipping on the ice. There is still another way to show their power. When a man wishes to go to war to steal horses he goes to one of the horse medicinemen with a pipe filled with tobacco and asks for help. The horse medicineman paints him and gives him a small buckskin bag containing powdered medicine, tells him how it is to be used, and what songs to sing. The man desiring the power does not paint until the war party is within sight of the enemy's camp. He must not let anyone cross his tracks. . . . If this does happen, the person doing it would at once become crippled in some manner. The one using the medicine usually drags his rope and never fails to procure a horse. During the trip a marrow bone must not be broken in the war lodge nor be heated by the fire while he is in it. For catching a wild horse the formula is to carry some of the medicine and ride about the animal in a circle. As soon as the horse scents the medicine he will stand and permit himself to be taken.

One time two men who were known for their great horse medicine power decided to see which had the greater power. They, on their horses, ran a race over a frozen pond. Going at full speed, the two riders went along side by side, neither of the horses showing any signs of slipping. As they came to the edge of the ice, one man whipped the other horse causing him to slip a little, proving that he had a trifle more power than the other [Red Plume in Wissler 1912a:108–111].

Anthropologist Clark Wissler reported a "Horse Cult" among the Oglala Sioux that was "probably the *Shunkwakan wacipi* 'horse dance,' a reenactment of a vision related to dreaming of thunder" [Powers 1977:59]. According to a shaman named Calico, his maternal grandfather, Sits-in-Wallow, originated this medicine.

They had medicines to restore exhausted horses. These were carried in small bags. When a pinch of the medicine was placed on the tongue of a horse, he would shake himself, then roll and rise fresh for another dash. If a horse is sick, there are particular medicines for each ailment. As wild, or "outlaw," horses cannot be given medicine, a special kind is tied on the end of a root digger and set up on the range. The horse will be attracted by the smell and grow fond of the odor, so that he will approach a person holding some of the medicine in his hand. Brood mares were often treated with all of the above medicines to produce fine colts. For a horse that balks, runs to one side, or bolts, when charging the enemy or running buffalo, a medicine is chewed by the rider and spit upon the fore-top, mane, tail, and nostrils. This also makes him fleet of foot. For racing medicines are rubbed upon the feet and body. The end of a willow switch is chewed, dipped in medicine, and used as a whip in the race and for touching an opposing horse to make him slow [Wissler 1912b:97].

Only shamans can empower such medicines, and therefore, each rider who wants one must make his formal request to a qualified shaman.

In addition to having medicine powers for horses, some shamans actually receive their supernatural powers from the Horse spirit. Lowie [1909:44] gave a brief account of this rather unusual form of treating the sick as performed by an Assiniboin shaman:

> Some singers entered the lodge and sang according to the shaman's directions. After several songs, the performer walked to the horse, untied him, and brought the rope to the lodge, the horse still remaining in the same position. The shaman unpinned the front of the lodge, so that the horse could enter. At the next intonation of the song, the horse walked into the lodge, and began smelling the sick man, who was not even able to turn from one side to the other. Whenever the horse drew a breath, smoke of various colors— blue, red, black—issued from his nostrils. He placed his mouth over the sick man, and several round objects fell on the patient's breast. The shaman ordered the man to swallow them which he did. The horse walked out to the pole and stood facing the lodge-entrance. The patient suddenly felt like rising. First he sat up, then he rose unaided, stepped out of the lodge, walked around the camp, returned, and sat down. He said

that he no longer felt weak, but was inclined to walk about. Previously he had not been able to eat, now he was hungry.

The Las Vegas band of Southern Paiutes also have horse shamans who treat injuries from horses. They are called *waarïvpuaxantï* (see entry).

See also *haxa, Horse Society Dance, White Man*.

Horse Society Dance
Assiniboin, *Plains*

A two-day ceremony held about once every two years in which initiated members acquired horse medicines. The ceremony began with the leaders slowly entering and sitting down. These men were then asked to pray for the new members, and a sacred pipe was filled and smoked by all present. Following this introduction the leaders prayed, often for many hours, and were then presented with gifts for the powers to be conferred on the new members. Once the gifts had been distributed, the other members of the society were then invited in. "For the first two hours, the members sat still, not uttering a sound. They then rubbed his [an initiate named Medicine Boy's] head and body with various sacred herbs that they had made by pointing to the ground with their finger and they gave the power to make these roots to Medicine Boy. Each root that they made had different curative powers. One could make a horse gentle; while another could cure a certain specific horse sickness. . . . All things could be cured by these members. Medicines were made by these to refreshen tired horses, that they would never become exhausted. If a horse were to break its leg, a member could have that horse running within a week. Snowblindness could be cured by any member" [Rodnick 1938:50, 52]. When these powers had been given to the various initiates, food was then offered to the spirits of the society. This was followed by additional prayers, songs, and gift giving.

At the conclusion of the ceremony, various members would display their powers for the spectators. "One old woman had a pair of horse ears tied to her moccasins. Instead of leaving footprints of the moccasins, all that could be seen were hoof tracks. Some had the power to place sticks in the ground as they started to sing their sacred songs, the sticks prancing around as if they were living horses" [Rodnick 1938:51].

Following the ceremony each new initiate was given a special set of instructions to follow. For instance, Medicine Boy, mentioned above, "was told to be very careful with his bridle, saddle and whip and under no conditions to loan them to any of his friends or relatives. No one was supposed to ride his own horse. For four years after being admitted to the society, he alone could use his horse and riding equipment. At the end of four years, he was to paint red circles on the shanks of his horse and with white clay paint lines representing lightning over the horse's back, while the horse's eyes were to be painted with white circles. Four days later he was to wash this paint off and then he would be able to loan his horse to others" [Rodnick 1938:51]. According to other instructions, he had to burn any of his hair found on his comb in a small hole in the ground, and he and his wife could not use one another's blanket.

In addition to transferring horse medicines to the new initiates, the ceremony also included the healing of diseases. For those wishing to be healed, "a special type of pemmican was eaten at this time. Each member stretched forth his hand and all types of unknown medicinal plants appeared, plants that did not grow in the natural state. These were then pounded and mixed with the pemmican by a young virgin, of about fourteen. This medicine when eaten was able to cure all types of diseases, but only a member of the Horse Society had the power to procure the plants and roots to be used for this pemmican" [Rodnick 1938:51–52].

Hotshanyi

Keres, *Southwest*
Also: *Hishtanyi-Chayan,* "Flint medicine man" [Bandelier in Lange 1959:237], Hochañi. The head of the Flint society at Chochiti. The

shaman who headed this society was in charge of the group's war medicines. Prior to battle he conducted rituals to secure success in battle. The night before the campaign he personally put sacred paint on the warriors and their weapons. (Sometimes this was done by one of his approved assistants.) He prepared and gave out herbal mixtures "which strengthened his warriors and struck terror in the hearts of the enemy" [Lange 1959:250–251].

In the Flint society's *kiva* he also prepared a secret war medicine, called "fire-eating" medicine, that involved the use of a sacred stick known as *Potroesht* (also *Potshoäsht*), meaning "lightning" [Bandelier in Lange 1959:238].

Upon the return of the war party, the *Hotshanyi* led the Scalp Dance and purification of the warriors. He also attended to healing their wounds. Afterward he was the keeper of the enemy scalps and in charge of "feeding" them with a periodic sprinkling of cornmeal and pollen to ensure no supernatural harm came from them [Lange 1959:249].

Humbleness

One clear aspect of shamanism is the humble attitude a shaman must assume in the presence of his helping spirits. Consequently, much of a shaman's speech during sacred ceremonies involves belittlement of the self and an understating of his powers. The following is a typical example, taken from a healing ceremony performed by the Wintu shaman Qorit in 1937: "So now he drank. And again he chanted, for a long time. 'Of the people I can attend to no one: because I am a person who has not been perfected. I who am a little child, how could I know anything? Thus when people approach my flat [i.e., come to me for help], how can I attend to them? For I am a child, personified body-dirt" [Wintu Sadie Marsh quoting Qorit in Lee 1941:409].

Hunting medicine

The use of supernatural powers to increase one's ability to acquire game. Hunting medicines came

A Kitksan (Tsimshian) *shaman's charm carved from a moose horn, representing a killer whale.*

in many different forms, many of which are discussed in this encyclopedia and are widely known. It is highly likely that they occurred in some form in every North American culture that hunted game. Hunting medicines also aided in the acquisition of the fattest or largest game, the game with the finest pelts, etc. It should be noted that hunting per se was most often highly ritualized. For example, a hunt was usually preceded by a sweat-lodge purification rite not only to increase the efficacy of the medicines but also to rid the body of the human scent. In addition,

there were ritual procedures for approaching game, for what should be done upon killing game, for how the game was to be butchered, for what parts should be offered to the spirits, for who could eat what parts, and so forth. As such, hunting medicines were at the core of every successful hunt.

In its most simple form hunting medicine was simply a charm or some form of fetish (see entry for examples) worn or carried by the hunter. Charms made by shamans or bestowed by spirits were considered more powerful than charms found by the hunter himself. Even the hunting weapons were often subjected to hunting medicine. For instance, the Central Miwok of California used a special charm stone to sharpen their arrows [Gifford n.d. a:4]. The medicine could also be a song or a certain prayer. In more complex forms the hunter underwent training in hunting medicine and sometimes even became a shaman himself.

Hunting medicine included all the rituals performed to bring success in hunting. Thus for a single hunt many different rituals may have been performed. The following illustrates the different rituals performed to ensure success in a whale

A nineteenth-century lithograph of a buffalo hunt on the plains.

hunt, as found among the Inuit (Eskimo) at Cape Prince of Wales:

> When the new cover was on the boat, it was placed on the rack. The woman threw food over it to boys who scrambled for it. After everything was refurbished, the crew in new clothing had a feast and dance.
>
> A few days later when they were ready actually to go whaling, each man brought his amulets, harpoon-heads, etc., from his secret cache on the mountain [see *fetish*] and stowed them in the boat. "New and curiously painted paddles" were also taken. A stuffed seal was placed in the bow looking toward the sea. The shaman held a head-lifting performance [*krilaq*—see EONAH, p. 139, entry *qilajoq*] to determine whether everything was propitious. The day before the launching, the crew fasted and sang ceremonial songs. That night boat-owner and harpooner remained outside, the others inside singing the umialik's [a large boat] songs.
>
> Next morning the boat was carried to the shore, turned upside down over the implements. Boys sang, again the woman threw food over the umiak to the boys who scrabbled for it. The boat was launched to an accompaniment of chanting. It was allowed to drift out, the crew in the boat and the woman on shore singing. The umiak turned, the crew pretended to harpoon her, then went to sea. She scattered ashes to drive away evil, and returned home. She had to fast until a whale was caught or the crew returned [Curtis in Lantis 1947:41].

Among the Labrador Eskimos a doll fetish was used for deer hunting. "In order to cause the deer to move toward the locality where they may be desired the shaman will erect, on a pole placed in a favorable position, an image of some famous hunter and conjurer. The image will represent the power of the person as conjurer and the various paraphernalia attached to the image assist in controlling the movements of the animals" [L. Turner 1894:196–197].

The following is an account, recorded by William Beynon at Port Simpson, British Co-lumbia, of a Nass River Tsimshian shaman who sought hunting medicine:

> When I was a young man I wanted to be a foremost hunter and to be wealthy, so I trained. I was then able to get many animals during the season when their skins were prime and I became wealthy. I saw shamans hunting when the animals were not prime. I tried it and got only poor skins, but the shamans always brought in fine pelts. I was determined to become a shaman also. I told the foremost shaman on Nass River what I wanted and he agreed to train me. He told me to first go to the Bella Bella chief and ask him to give me dancing power.
>
> In the spring I did as the Nisqa [Tsimshian subdivision] shaman directed. The Bella Bella chief agreed to help me after I had given him a gift of many marmot skins. He sent me to Kitga'ata to get power from a shaman there and then to Kitkatla to see two other men who would give me dance powers. He instructed me to go also to Gitando, Gilutsau and Gitwilgoats. He gave me the names of the men to see at each of these places. I was instructed to tell each of them that the Bella Bella chief had agreed to help me.
>
> I went to the villages and each man sang his shaman power songs over me and put further dance powers into me. Then I went home to the Nass [River], and told the shaman what had happened. He said that I would get power, and instructed me to go to Gitsaxlal where there was a shaman who specialized in making symbols of supernatural power for other shamans.
>
> I told him that I wanted a double-headed, folding knife that I could put into my mouth and it would appear as though I had swallowed it. I gave him presents of marmot skins and he agreed to make it. After many days it was finished. . . .
>
> I went back to the Nass. That spring I became ill and I was still ill when we moved down to the mouth of the river to fish for olachen. The Nisqa shaman knew that I was now possessed by the powers and he instructed me to call all the shamans who had sung their songs over me. They came and gave me more powers. I had visions in which many aides [spirits] came to me.

I was now a medicine man and when I got well I gave my performance [public ritual required for announcing one's powers] and showed my symbol of supernatural powers. I was then as famous as the other shamans, and was able to get prime skins at any time of the year [William Beynon's recorded account in Garfield 1951:47].

Either an individual could obtain a personal hunting medicine or hunters would call upon a shaman. Among the Inuit (Eskimo) at Kotzebue in northern Alaska, for example, "before going fox-hunting, hunters bathed and cleaned their houses and gear thoroughly under the direction of a shaman. After a fox was caught, a feast was held, as for a seal in this region" [Lantis 1947:46]. Here again, the "feast" was a ritual form of offering to the spirits of their hunting medicines, the game taken, or both. Rasmussen [in Lantis 1947:47] noted that after slaying a wolf, "the people [the inland Inuit along the Noatak and Utorqaq Rivers] held a feast, again not for themselves but to provide food for the animal [wolf] on his way home." This "feeding" ritual also often included the ritual disposal of any parts of the game not used.

Among the Monachi (Western Mono) of central California, "Kohomot, a deer shaman [*tasuwadi*], could entice the fawns to him. He had three places to which he sent people to kill deer. He foretold how many they would kill at each place" [Gifford 1932:50]. The Northern Maidu of central California also had a deer-hunting medicine in the form of a quartz crystal charm. When this crystal was "taken out for use, the hunter would blow on it, talk to it, and rub it along the rifle. No one else could go near the charm or touch the rifle without being in considerable danger" [Jewell 1987:147]. Because such charms were dangerous, they were kept buried in the ground outside of the village area when not in use.

Some forms of hunting medicines were designed to work directly on the prey. For instance, among the Nisenan (Southern Maidu) of California, shamans always accompanied a hunting party. They had a medicine (herb) that they placed on a stick before laying this stick in the tracks of a deer. This caused the deer's legs to cramp so that it couldn't get away from the hunters. In addition, when they discovered deer feeding, the shamans had another medicine that kept them from running off [Beals 1933:388].

Among the Shawnee certain "overt acts, accompanied by the proper words, cause a deer to stop so that he may be conveniently shot, make a deer more than normally visible, and make the hunter shoot straight" [Voegelin 1936:17].

One shaman among the Kansa acquired a hunting medicine from the Thunder Beings. When hunting he "had deer killed for him by lightning, and brought them home without a mark on them. He was finally killed by lightning himself" [Skinner 1915c:770].

Among the Assiniboin of the Plains, "the superintendent of the tribal hunt was the one to plant the medicine-pole in the pound, and in order to charm the herd he attached to it a streamer of scarlet cloth, a piece of tobacco, and a buffalo horn. Before the discovery of the game, he beat his drum and chanted every morning, consulting his guardian spirits. The scouts took with them a wakan [holy—see EONAH, pp. 305–306] ball of buffalo hair, which they immediately sent to the director on locating a herd. During the absence of the ball, the master of ceremonies was obliged to fast, and this period of abstention was continued until the close of the hunt, with the limitation that he was permitted to eat animals captured within the pound" [De Smet in Lowie 1909:55]. Also for the Assiniboin, Lowie [1909:47] reported: "Jim Crack, when young, dreamt of a little man, who taught him to prepare medicines and to hunt every kind of game; in consequence, he became a great hunter."

Among the Bungi (Plains Ojibwa) "the elders would sit up all night singing to a rattle accompaniment and in the morning four men would be sent out. Each would infallibly be successful" [Skinner 1914:510].

The Southern Paiute had game shamans who belonged to the class of shamans known as nonosi, or dreamers. They had the power to control the movements of game. "They were known to a number of Southern Paiute groups, at least to those from the Shivwits and Saint George westward, and were particularly well developed among the Las Vegas and Chemehuevi" [Kelly 1939:151].

Sometimes parts of a slain animal would be used as a charm to ensure future success. For example, among the Wadátkuht (Paviotso) a hunter would bury the bladder of a deer at the spot where it was killed in order to be "assured of finding a deer at this same spot when he chose to return" [Riddell 1960:71]. In addition there was a Wadátkuht man who "used to catch owls and eagles by painting his naked body and by singing in front of the birds perched nearby. As he sang he moved slowly toward the bird until he was close enough to grasp it with his hands" [Riddell 1960:71].

One other common form of hunting medicine was divination by a shaman to locate game. Among the Cherokee a shaman made a small, cone-shaped pile of smoldering ashes from a fire and dropped a pinch of cut-up tobacco onto it. "If there is no flare, it is a sign that there is no game in store for them this time and no Cherokee will proceed on the hunt after having received such an answer. The places on the ashes where a particle of tobacco catches fire inform him of the direction of the game. The fraction of time elapsing between the tobacco falling and its catching fire, give him some idea as to the time: whether he will kill the same day, or only the next day, or, maybe immediately. Finally, if the fire answers with a loud burst, this means that the hunter will be so fortunate as to kill big game (bear, deer, e.g.), whereas a faint report indicates the killing of a mere rabbit, pheasant, etc." [Olbrechts 1930:551].

Not only did a shaman divine to locate game, he or she also divined for the amount of game to be had. Again, each shaman had a special, individual ritual for divining such information. Among the Vunta (Crow River Kutchin) one shaman's procedure was as follows: "A large pile of snow was brought together and a fire built a little to one side. The people surrounded the pile and the fire, leaving a space of untrodden snow as a gap in the circle which they formed. The shaman walked around the fire singing and then went up to the pile of snow. He rolled up a sleeve and reached into the snow from which he pulled out a caribou half way. Then he pushed it back in and no sign of it remained. The people were then assured that they could set out on a successful caribou hunt" [Osgood 1936:158–159].

In addition to quests for supernatural aid, a hunter would also perform purification rites for his hunting weapons. Among the Paviotso, "to purify his gun the hunter chopped up wild parsnip, hakínukpa, and poured hot water over it. The hot water and parsnip were used to bathe the gun, which was done over an ant hill. Sometimes a hunter would bind his arm at this time and cut a vein and bleed onto the parsnip which had fallen into the ant hill (but he did not bleed on the gun)" [Riddell 1960:66].

Finally it should be noted that it was common for witches to possess antihunting medicines. For example, among the Alabama of the Southeast area, there was a medicine called impiafotci, meaning "to make him kill nothing" [Swanton 1928:634], which a witch used on a hunter to keep him from killing game.

For other examples of hunting medicines, see *aiyas kumomli, astalax, Black-tailed Deer Dance, cicäwuskw, Eagle-hunting medicine, Ehtskinna, enatcûggedi, hokitta, hoktitasha, ichishatkî, Iniskim, kosksstakjomŏpista, Mahuts, masutïkï, micaduskwe, mishtikuai, mugálu, Pingxangzho, pitowabosons, Pope, Ptitakeoxate, "Red-Stone" Doctor, Returning Hunter, Samaa, sáwanikia, scapulimancy, schucus, Sea Lion, sinkakua, siwín, Slaolhtcu, suin, sxwadach, táhca wicásha wakáng, tuavitok, Wakon Tanga, weather shamans, White Man, Wolf Chief.*

Huuku
Maidu, *California*
The Northern Maidu shamans who are the leaders of their secret medicine society. "They have

in their possession charms known as yo´mepa [elsewhere *yompa*], which cause death to persons if they are touched on the bare skin with these objects. The cure is, as usual, by sucking; and the place sucked is touched and rubbed with the obsidian knife (lomim boso) afterwards" [Dixon 1905:272].

Formerly there was an annual ceremony held in the dance house in which shamans gathered from all over and endeavored to overcome the others by means of their "'poison' or charms" [Dixon 1905:272]. Unlike most power feats (see *power displays/feats* entry) among shamans, this contest began with each shaman trying to eliminate the others by shooting his power into them. This would continue throughout the night until only a few shamans were left. At that point "these remaining dancers would produce in a mysterious manner lizards, mice, small birds, etc., and, after exhibiting them to the spectators, cause them to disappear" [Dixon 1905:273–274].

Huuku shamans have various spirits and receive power from them accordingly. Most of the powerful shamans have many spirits. In one case a shaman "resolved to acquire the spirit of the honey-bee. This he did, and then was able to secure whiskey in unlimited quantities, as the bee could insert its proboscis through the corks of bottles, or through the closed bung-holes of barrels, and suck out the liquor, which it afterward put into other receptacles for the Indians' use. The bee could also enter anywhere, as it could unlock all doors by inserting its proboscis. For a time the shaman was extremely popular, for he was able to substantiate his claims as to the whiskey. His control over the spirit of the bee, however, was suddenly lost" [Dixon 1905:282].

Huviagadi

Kawaiisu, *Peninsula*

Literal translation: "song-possessor" [Zigmond 1977:84]. The term used for a curing shaman [Zigmond 1977:84]. There is no Kawaiisu term for shaman. Instead, each person is recognized by the form of power he or she possesses, expressed through the use of the suffix *-gadi*, meaning "possessor" or "one who has" [Zigmond 1977:84]. In this case the word *huviavi* refers only to songs received through a dream or vision. The last known *huviagadi* was reported to have died around 1930. This shaman had dreamed of singing deer.

At first the novice shaman may not recognize his "doctor's dreams." Once he does recognize them, it might take him four to six years to have a dream strong enough to cure. Moreover, once such a dream comes, it may take the shaman several years before he attempts his first cure through its use.

The *huviagadi* is usually paid in advance for his services. But if the treatment fails or the patient dies, the payment is returned. Shamans are reticent about undertaking cures for patients near death due to possible accusations of witchcraft should the patient die.

Iañi
Keres, *Southwest*
Cochiti Pueblo term for supernatural power [Lange 1959:245].

Iariku
Keres, *Southwest*
Also: *iariko* (EONAH, p. 113). Dialectical variants: *iatiku* (Laguna), *iärriko* (Sia). The eastern Pueblos' term for their corn-ear fetishes used in sacred ceremonies [White 1930:610–611].

Iauni
Wishram, *Plateau*
Making holy. This word is composed of the root *aw* or *awt,* meaning "to be sacred, holy"; *ni,* a qualitative adjectivizer; and *i,* a transitivizing prefix [Boyd 1996:126].

The term *iaulas* roughly means "I was made holy."

Iayulmax
Wishram, *Plateau*
Guardian spirits. This term refers to the guardian spirits of males, while the word *itcayulmax* designates the guardian spirits of females [Spier and Sapir 1930:237]. War shamans usually have sturgeons, rocks, or trees for guardian spirits. Spirits of mountain lizards, snakes, small insects, and small birds gives one "the power to move stealthily, to hide readily, and be hard to shoot" [Spier and Sapir 1930:237], and an individual with a deer spirit becomes a good hunter. A powerful shaman or sorcerer usually has the spirit of the grizzly bear, water monster, mountain lizard, eagle, sturgeon, cougar, or turtle. As always, different guardian spirits bring different supernatural abilities.

Icàma xekwir
Yuma, *Southwest*
Literal translation: "dream wasting" [Manuel Thomas in Forde 1931:187]. Dream poisoning. This is a type of sickness that comes via one's dreams. Symptoms include slight fever with no pain, loss of appetite accompanied by weight loss, weakness, dryness, and the inability to drink anything but water.

"It is one of the worst sicknesses, which is caused by an animal who lives out in the desert. The animal is xumir (chipmunk). . . . This animal appears as a small human being in a dream, to anyone who is going to be afflicted. You always see the desert in your dream before this sickness. The little chipmunk man is walking in the desert. He has a supply of fine ground mesquite flour, damped and made into little balls, which he throws to the dreamer, who cannot resist the temptation and eats one of them. The sweetness goes into the insides and remains there. It slowly dries them all up. On awakening, the dreamer does not want to eat, his insides are all dry and he gets thinner and thinner and will slowly die" [Manuel Thomas in Forde 1931:187].

Other sicknesses in this category include: *icáma hakáp*, literally translated as "dream holes" [Forde 1931:187], which is evidenced by swollen, hard lumps or open sores on the skin, and *icáma yakápet*, which most often afflicts women and is a form of hysteria that includes screaming, wild and rough behavior, not wanting to be touched, etc. Patients suffering from *icáma yakápet* are often so uncontrollable that they are bound with rope before the shaman begins his treatments.

The treatments for all of the above dream-poisoning sicknesses are, for the most part, the same. The shaman begins by inhaling tobacco smoke and filling his mouth with frothed saliva.

> With these he blows a smoky spray on the patient's head. He then sucks on each breast above each nipple and in the middle, a little below the breastbone. . . . He will then massage the stomach with his hands, but this is not considered absolutely necessary. During the treatment a series of songs are sung. This treatment is employed three times a day and three times at night for three days; by this time the patient should show some signs of recovery. The doctor feels the body at each visit. If the body gets cooler he orders a watery mush of green tepary bean. If the temperature remains down, a fire is built and green arrowweeds are placed on top. The patient is bathed in warm water and his body is then smoked over the fire. This is done once a day in

the morning for four days, after which he should be well enough to take a normal diet. The doctor must fast during the cure, eating only a little corn meal without salt. The less he eats the greater his power [Manuel Thomas in Forde 1931:187].

Ichishatkî
Seminole, *Southeast*
Literal translation: "white deer hair" [Sturtevant 1954b:372]. One of several forms of Mikasuki hunting medicine (see entry). This deer hair is kept in medicine bundles and used to magically attract game.

Other Mikasuki hunting medicines include: a willow root medicine that is drunk to ensure success in deer hunting; a dried fungus called *pakpolóhlî* used to fatten up a killed bear; *yatopóskifonî*, or "little people's bones" ("small pieces of material looking like animal bones"); and a *cintlápî*, or "snake horn" ("a spherical black or grayish object about the size of a number eight shot"), used to attract deer [Sturtevant 1954b:372–373].

Ichta
Tlingit, *Northwest Coast*
Also: *ikt* [L. Jones 1914:154]. Shaman. Shamans acquire their powers via solo vision quests in the forest. The novice remains alone, feeding only on the roots of devil's club (*Oplopanax horridum*), until a spirit appears to him. This can take several months.

> When he finally meets the spirit he can count himself among the lucky if he gets a land otter in whose tongue is contained the whole secret of shamanism. The land otter goes directly to the would-be shaman who, as soon as he sees the spirit, stands still and exclaiming four times a loud "oh" in various pitches, kills him. As soon as the land otter hears this sound he falls on his back and dies, with his tongue protruding. The shaman tears the tongue out . . . and putting the tongue in a basket which he has prepared for the purpose, he hides it in an unapproachable place, for if an uninitiated person should find this "kuschtaliute"

(otter's tongue), he would lose his senses. He pulls off the skin carefully and keeps it as a sign of his success while he buries the meat in the ground [Krause 1956:195].

Any helping spirit is called *tu kina-jek*, meaning "his *(tu)* top *(kina)* spirit *(jek)*" [Krause 1956:199–200]. Most shamans acquire additional spirits over time.

During the shaman's ceremonies he most often dons a wooden mask carved in the likeness of his helping spirits. Therefore, shamans often have several masks, any number of which may be used in a ceremony. When not in use these masks are usually kept in a box hidden in the forest, along with the rest of the shaman's paraphernalia. In addition to these masks, the shamans also wear elaborate ceremonial regalia, such as dance aprons made of mountain-goat wool and headgear made from ermine. Sometimes several boxes are needed to contain all of these items. "They always kept the box containing their paraphernalia on top of the house" [Jones 1914:155]. Shamans also have long hair. "The longer and more matted the hair the greater the power of the doctor is supposed to possess. For this reason the hair of an *ikt* was jealously guarded. If shorn of it his power vanished" [Jones 1914:155].

The following is a brief account of a healing ceremony for a young boy that was conducted in September 1882 by a Huna shaman:

A Tlingit shaman's mask.

On a mat beside the fire sat the patient, a five-year-old boy, and at his side was a shaman who looked very old with greying hair that hung in thick strands to his knees. On his head he wore a crown made of wooden sticks, bent to resemble the horns of the mountain goat, which rattled as they struck each other through his movements. Around his neck hung a garland with many decorations. He was naked to the waist, about which was wrapped a brightly colored dancing blanket. Squatting on his haunches he moved the upper part of his body with such convulsive violence that he soon broke out in a great sweat. In his hand he held a wooden rattle in the figure of a crane and he gesticulated with it as he accompanied his song which he often interrupted with wild groaning. He also used a pair of tongs about three diameters [?] long with which he grasped the feet and then the head of the boy. After a while he took the boy's hands and laying them first on his hips and then his abdomen, and calling out the names of various animals, led him around the fire, first in one direction and then in the opposite one. . . . The shaman led the boy around the fire several times more in various directions and after about an hour's work declared that the power of the bad spirits had been broken and the boy was cured [Krause 1956:203].

Each shaman receives a specific power from his helping spirit, and people will call upon the appropriate shaman for their needs. In 1879, when the smelt run was late in coming to the Chilkat, they called for a shaman to bring the needed fish. "So a shaman, after he had fasted for four days, went out to sea in a canoe with all his paraphernalia and let himself be lowered to the bottom on a twenty fathom line. When, after sometime he allowed himself to be raised again, and he appeared with his rattles and bells which he had taken down with him, he announced that the smelt would come the following day. The next morning many seals and killer whales were seen which are certain indications of the arrival of the fish run and when they went to the river they saw the fish in great numbers" [Krause 1956:196–197].

Because of their close association with the ocean, Tlingit shamans often had the power to remain under water for long periods of time. The Russian observer I. Veniaminov reported (circa 1840) on a similar feat by a then-famous Sitka shaman:

With his relatives and friends he went out in a bay on Tschistych Island (at the foot of Mt. Edgecumbe), let himself be wrapped in a mat and tied with a strap of otter, his shamanistic power [animal], and after four loud exclamations was lowered into the sea. The people with him at first had great fear for his life and had first refused to do it. Faster than a stone and faster than a whale which had been shot, he went to the bottom so that the line to which he was fastened could scarcely follow. At the end of this line, his boatmates had tied the bladder of a land otter. After they waited in vain for some time for a sign from him, they went ashore in order to mourn for their friend. The following day they went back to the place without seeing anything unusual. But when they returned on the fourth day they heard a sound like a shaman's drum and as they followed it, they saw the shaman hanging on a steep cliff without being tied down, his face streaming with blood, his head downwards, and small birds swarming around. With difficulty the friends got him into their boat in which he at once regained consciousness and returned home with them [Krause 1956:196].

"The *ikt* was considered not only to be in league and to have influence with evil spirits, but to be a prophet. As such he was often consulted as to weather, the proper time to start on the hunt, whether a certain venture would meet with success or failure and about other such things. He would predict epidemics, deaths and other catastrophes. He was considered also to have the gift of tongues. It was believed, for instance, that a Thlinget shaman could speak the Tsimpshean [Tsimshian] tongue when the Tsimpshean spirit came upon him, but not otherwise" [Jones 1914:159].

Idiagewam

Wishram, *Plateau*

Plural: *itcdagewam* [Sapir 1909:180]. Male sorcerer [Spier and Sapir 1930:244]. This is the masculine form of the word; the feminine form is *itgagewam* [Spier and Sapir 1930:245]. From texts recorded by Sapir, we have the following ac-

count: "He [the *idiagewam*] says: 'Yes! now both of us shall doctor him.' The two of them doctor him, but he has not got well. Now the man dies. Both of the medicine-men are killed, [who] were doctoring him. Those two were wicked, they had 'shot' him" [Sapir 1909:181]. Thus, the Wishram use this term for doctors who are suspected of sorcery. Otherwise, a male shaman who doctors is called *idiaxilalit* (see entry). "Bewitching seems to have been common, or perhaps most serious illnesses and injuries were laid to this. . . . Shamans were not ordinarily killed because they failed of a cure. But they would be if it was thought that they had bewitched the patient in the course of their practise" [Spier and Sapir 1930:247].

I have been curing for more than sixty years and have met all kinds of disease. Some diseases are bad. When a person is bewitched, he will surely die unless the shaman has a much stronger spirit than that killing the patient. When a person dies of witchcraft, the body cracks in many places, although they may appear before he expires. Such cracks are not deep, perhaps only an eighth of an inch, just enough to let the blood run freely. The body turns various colors, especially red and blue stripes lengthwise of the body. This shows that he was bewitched by a strong shaman. A shaman who undertakes to take such a spirit out of the sick must have a stronger spirit himself. If not, even though he draws it out, it will kill the shaman and both will die. In five days the shaman is dead. Some important bone of his body breaks, a leg or his spine. This happens, not from any accident, but while he is lying sick abed. So curing is very dangerous and a shaman must be treated well [eighty-five-year-old shaman named Smith in Spier and Sapir 1930:248].

Idiaxilalit

Wishram, *Plateau*

Male shaman who doctors [Spier and Sapir 1930:244]. Both males and females become shamans, but the Wishram language makes a distinction between medicine men and medicine women. *Idiaxilalit* is the masculine form, and *it-gaxilalit* is the feminine form.

A patient is often treated by two or more shamans. "A shaman always smoked before starting to cure, taking five puffs of his pipe and inhaling the smoke. This made his cure more effective since it made his spirit more active and strong" [Spier and Sapir 1930:246]. The healing ceremony includes the singing of specific sacred songs accompanied by assistants beating loudly with sticks on a long plank spread out before the shaman. No drum or rattle is used. However, "shamans had rattles made of a bunch of dewclaws strung together; we do not know that they were used in curing" [Spier and Sapir 1930:246]. The shaman paints his face in a prescribed manner for the healing ceremony and also wears "a cap bearing eagle feathers" [Spier and Sapir 1930:246]. Cures are effected by removing a disease object from the patient's body. The shaman warms his hands on the fire and then places them on the body of the patient to draw the disease object toward him. He then places his mouth on the patient's body and removes the object by sucking. "Having gotten it into his mouth, he spat it into a vessel of water 'to cool it.' It was then more easily handled. Ordinarily it remained invisible to the laity although other shamans could see it readily enough" [Spier and Sapir 1930:246]. Following a successful healing the shaman is paid for his or her services, usually with a horse, cow, blankets, money (in more recent times), etc.

Igluhuk
Copper Eskimo, *Arctic Coast*
An early-twentieth-century shaman who resided in the area of Bernard Harbour. One of his shamanic performances was witnessed around 1915 by a Mr. Wilkins, who was then the field photographer for anthropologist Diamond Jenness during his 1913–1918 Canadian Arctic Expedition. Wilkins reported that "they had all waited all that day and there had not been a sign of any fish making a run. About nine o'clock at night they thought they should hold a séance to try and induce a few to come along, for although they had a quantity of dried fish they did not care to use that up. A fellow called Igluhuk had arrived at the camp that evening and he had the reputation of being a great shaman. We were all standing about outside watching for signs of a run when one of the men asked me if I would help in a séance to try to make the fish come up the creek. I agreed to do my best, and they all crowded into the largest tent in the village. I was given a seat next to the shaman [seat of honor] which had been reserved for me, although I was almost the last to come in, and there was not room for any others to sit down after and some of them had to lean in and look through the door" [Wilkins in Jenness 1970:201].

Subsequently Igluhuk went into trance and performed for three hours. At the height of his trance, he "began to point to one or the other of the audience and, fluttering his fingers to indicate that the fish were swarming in the river, would prophesy that such and such a person would catch a [certain] number of fish" [Wilkins in Jenness 1970:201–202]. At the conclusion of this ceremony,

one of the men near the door gave a shout and, jumping up, ran for his spear and towards the creek, with the others following as fast as they could. None of them were prepared for fishing in the ordinary way by having taken off some of their clothes or put on long water-boots, and as they ran towards the creek, some of them slipped off what clothes they could, while others rushed for the water in what they were dressed in. It was apparent at first sight that there were a number of fish in the trap, and within a few minutes they had caught sixty, a big haul in ordinary times, and now an extraordinary one for it had seemed that the fish had stopped running the day before. . . . In regards to this séance the interpreter, Patsy—who, by the way, was thoroughly skeptical of all Eskimo shamanism—told me that Igluhuk (or Iglisiak as he should be called) had prophesied that a certain boy

Hogaluk would capture three fish, and that Patsy [Klengenberg] himself would get only two. In both cases his prophesy proved true [Wilkins in Jenness 1970:202].

Ilatsiak
Copper Eskimo, *Arctic Coast*

An early-twentieth-century shaman from Gathurst Inlet whom anthropologist Diamond Jenness hailed as "the greatest of all the shamans among the Copper Eskimos" [Jenness 1970: 209]. In 1916 Jenness met Ilatsiak at Bernhard Harbour. During their time together Jenness recorded on a cylinder phonograph several shamanic performances by Ilatsiak in which the shaman's helping spirits possessed the shaman and spoke through him. Jenness reported that "some of the words are scarcely audible in the record owing to his jumping. As usual too, it is difficult to attach any meaning to them. . . . Ilatsiak gave a gasp at the conclusion and breathed very hard for a moment or two as his familiar [helping spirit] left him, after which he sat down and enquired of the natives what he had said" [Jenness 1970:209].

When Ilatsiak was a boy, he became seriously ill and was left for dead. However, he recovered and became a shaman. His powers were renowned throughout the region.

While he was still but a youth he summoned some white men, who made their appearance in the dance-house before the astonished eyes of all the Eskimos. Maffa, a Tree river native who served us for a year, told us how Ilatsiak once threw a line out into the passage leading into the dance-house and roped in a number of spirits, *tornrait* [see *tornrak*, EONAH, p. 286]. Maffa peered down through the door and saw them all in the passage. Ilatsiak spoke to them, but his language was strange, and all that Maffa could understand was that he was telling them to protect the people and to banish all sickness from their midst.

Ilatsiak's powers were derided by his cousin, who was also a shaman, so Ilatsiak clapped his hands and fire shot up from the floor. His cousin, nothing daunted, went outside and disappeared down a squirrel hole, re-emerging again from the ground a long way off. In the same way, the natives said, Ilatsiak himself once sank down through the snow floor of the dance-house, growing smaller and smaller till he vanished from sight altogether. A few minutes later he came up through the floor of another hut right beside some men who were sitting on the sleeping platform. Uloksak could remember when he was a boy how white men had appeared in the dance-house at Ilatsiak's command. The people sent Uloksak outside, and when he went back again he was amazed to see that Ilatsiak had cut off a leg and an arm [Ilatsiak's own arm and leg] and thrown them to the back of the hut. He was sent out once more, and when he re-entered Ilatsiak was whole again. . . .

On one occasion, his kinsmen told me, he and three other shamans gave a séance together. The four men held their hands behind their backs and stretched out their necks, holding their mouths wide open. Gradually their teeth changed to polar bears' teeth, then as gradually changed back again. On another occasion when two Netsilik shamans were terrifying the people by driving their knives through their stomachs so that the points protruded from their backs, Ilatsiak went into an empty hut alongside, changed himself into a polar bear, and, going back into the dance-house, so frightened the two Netsilik men that they fled from the settlement. On still another occasion Ilatsiak had sunk down through the floor of his hut into the sea below without making even a hole in the ice [Jenness 1970:198–199].

Ilimarneq
East Greenland Eskimo, *Arctic Coast*

Spirit flight (see entry) [Rink in Kroeber 1900:306]. On the other side of the continent, among the Alaskan Inuit, the cognate appears as *ilímarpoq* [Rasmussen in Osterman 1952:130]. This term refers to the spirit flight made by shamans during a ceremony. Among the Alaskan Inuit the shaman often has his hands tied behind his back, his ankles bound, and a heavy stone placed about his neck before making a spirit flight.

Ilisineq

Eskimo, *Arctic Coast*

Also: *Ilisiniq* (EONAH, p. 116). General term for sorcery or witchcraft. Sorcery is practiced by both women and men. A practitioner is generally called an *ilisitsoq*, (plural, *ilisitsut*) or dialectical variants thereof, as, for example, among the West Greenland Eskimo, where they are known as *ilisītoq*; among the East Greenland Eskimo as *iliseetsoq* [Thalbitzer 1931:432]; and among the Iglulik Eskimo as *ilisecut* [Rasmussen 1929:143]. In some cases they are shamans, but in all cases they keep their practice secret. When *ilisineq* is used as a war medicine, "the attempts of the enemy can be warded off, or even pain or disaster brought upon them" [Thalbitzer 1931:432].

To effect the evil medicine the *ilisitsoq* acquires either parts of a dead body, parts of the game killed by his intended victim, or items associated with the victim, such as hair, nails, saliva, etc. These items are then subjected to a prescribed ritual to empower them. Once em-

A nineteenth-century lower Kuskokwim River Eskimo shaman's mask representing the shaman's ability to see into the bodies of others.

powered they are usually touched against the victim or magically sent to him by the witch. In some cases it suffices to merely repeat the name of the victim during the empowerment of the victim's association object. In addition, a witch is capable of stealing a person's soul, thus causing the victim to become ill and eventually die. Among the Iglulik witches this is accomplished by a technique called *supiblungo*, "blowing it out" [Rasmussen 1929:143–144].

Another form of Eskimo sorcery is the use of the *tupilak* (see entry). "According to the missionary Turquetil, the Caribou Inuit, who dwell inland west of Hudson Bay, made a *tupilak* with the head of a bear, the body of a wolf, the wings of birds, the tail of a fish, etc. Life was given to the artificial monster, which was then sent after a victim" [Merkur 1989:15].

"When anyone feels a twinge, he is to grease the place with blubber, for it is a witch who is at work, and everything evil is afraid of blubber. He who finds a round hole in his clothes is also the object of the attack of a witch. He is to cut off the piece around the hole, wave it in the direction against the sun and throw it away. Then the evil falls back upon the witch" [Birket-Smith 1924:456].

Some Eskimos at Christianshaab reported seeing an *ilisītoq* "sitting at the beach, and he had a half sleeve, which he packed with hair, nails, grass and moss, and he furthermore mumbled over it, and when he had gone away, they went there and saw that the half sleeve began to crawl, and when they had run away, out of fright, the Angekok [shaman] came at once saying: 'Go forth and become a Tupiliek i.e. a ghost!' and it immediately jumped into the water; this they thought that he sent out, when he wanted to take the life of someone" [Birket-Smith 1924:456].

In East Greenland a single act of sorcery is known as *kusuineq* [Kroeber 1900:307]. "Virtually every East Greenland adult practiced at least some *kusuineq*, and special shamanic seances were held in which known witches were forced, on pain of death, to confess and thereby to abdicate their powers" [Holm in Merkur 1989:13]. Thus, in this region, only those who habitually practice *kusuineq* are considered witches. Their practice is seen as being in opposition to "legitimate" *angakuneq* (shamanism).

Inernerunashuaq
Netsilik Eskimo, *Arctic Coast*
See *Unaleq.*

Ingukh
West Alaska Eskimo, *Arctic Coast*
Fetish. "Frequently the virtue is inherent in the object, but sometimes is secured by means of a shaman's power or the aid of one who knows" [Nelson 1899:435]. Fetishes come in many different forms and are made of wood, stone, bone, and other such materials. For example, a Malemiut fetish was hung in the kayak of a white-whale hunter. Such hunting fetishes "are supposed to watch for game and, by some clairvoyant power, to see it at a great distance; the hunter is then guided by the influence of the fetich to find it. They are also supposed to guide the spears so that they will be cast straight. Sometimes the influence of the amulet or fetich is supposed to bring the game to the hunter" [Nelson 1899:436–437].

Inipi
Kawaiisu, *Peninsula*
Spirit or ghost of an individual, which is often invisible. Zigmond [1977:64] cited one example: "When you walk through the desert and feel a sudden gust of hot wind 'like a fire,'" this gust is considered to be an *inipi*. Similarly, ringing in one's ears in considered to be an *inipi* calling. At other times one may only hear an *inipi* whistle. "If visible, he may look like a human being and be mistaken for one unless he gives himself away by performing super-human feats like suddenly disappearing, flying off, or being impervious to bullets. Or he may have horns . . . or appear as a skeleton" [Zigmond 1977:64]. Most often it is considered harmful to see an *inipi*. In some cases

the *inipi* is sent to harm an individual under the control of a witch.

In death a person's *inipi* takes on the characteristics of that person. For instance, if the person liked to tease, so would his *inipi* when it came around. "If two people die at about the same time, relatives and friends would be sufficiently familiar with the habits of the deceased to realize whose *inipi* is prowling about" [Zigmond 1977:65].

To chase an *inipi* away, "one places a pinch of tobacco on the back of the hand between thumb and forefinger and blows it in several directions" [Zigmond 1977:67]. The burning of sage or dried wild celery root *(Lomatium californicum kayeeze)* also drives the *inipi* away.

The term *inipi* is also used in referring to shamans as men who are "part *inipi*" or "have become *inipi*." For example, Zigmond [1977:69] reported on one man who had acquired power from "a little insect that jumps," which gave him the power to jump. One time this man was locked up by whites for stealing. "When everyone was asleep, the latter spit on his hands, opened the lock, and walked out. He said 'hello!' and jumped from the door to the top of a mountain. He walked a bit and then jumped to the next mountain" [Zigmond 1977:69]. In another case one such shaman had the power to make herself invisible. "The Yokuts followed her; they wanted to kill her. She had on her basket-hat, and pushed it off the back of her head. Then they couldn't see her. They saw only the hat. . . . She got away" [unidentified informant in Zigmond 1977:69].

Ïnïpic
Paiute, *Basin*
Dialectical variant: *ïnïpi* (singular), *ïnïpiwï* (plural) (Chemehuevi) [Laird 1976:40]; *inïï* (Las Vegas) [Kelly 1939:163]; and *ïnïpit* (Shivwits) [Kelly 1939:153]. The common Southern Paiute term for a ghost or evil spirit, which may assume any form and is more often heard than seen [Kelly 1964:141]. Among the Chemehuevi, whirlwinds are believed to be caused by an *ïnïpi*.

Iniskim

Blackfoot, *Plains*

Buffalo Rock bundle [Wissler 1912a:204]. A medicine bundle that contains a special medicine rock for controlling the movements of the buffalo. The term is also applied to the rock per se. Wissler [1912a:243] noted that "any pebble bearing a special resemblance to an animate object is most certain to be regarded as an iniskim," such that "anyone who chances upon one of these stones may take it and thereafter keep and care for it" [Wissler 1912a:242]. Often a person's *iniskim* would "give birth," and other small stones would appear in the bundle. In former times the *iniskim* was often a large, stationary boulder, which was painted. One informant reported that the *iniskim* was also efficacious in securing horses and for success in war, health, and prosperity [Wissler 1912a:244].

Inkonze

Chipewyan, *Mackenzie-Yukon*

Also: *Eeem cpzzy* (1792 version). Literal translation: "roughly means 'to know something a little'" [D. Smith 1973:8]. *Inkonze* is knowledge derived from a guardian spirit, usually in the form of some animal, through powerful dreams. It is the knowledge that gives one the ability to utilize supernatural powers. D. Smith [1973:8] noted that "the Chipewyan did not have a special status term for individuals with 'usable' *inkonze*. Thus it is inappropriate to refer to them as 'shamans' or by similar standard terminology." However, since some of these individuals operate as curers, diviners, and sorcerers just as shamans do, this must mean that the Chipewyan do not differentiate between someone who only has a small power (for hunting, fishing, etc.) and someone who can heal or foretell the future. As always, shamanism is a matter of degree of personal power, not power per se.

Those individuals who, over time, continue to have strong dreams in which their guardian spirits keep increasing their *inkonze* often became healers. Dreams may direct the novice to certain isolated locations where his or her guardian spirit appears and shows the novice "various herbs and roots good for effecting cures. With this knowledge, the individual could thereafter gather these roots and herbs, storing them in his medicine bag" [Smith 1973:8]. Other instructions cover power songs, symbolic decorations, the use of eagle feathers, etc. Those who perform healings do so only on nonrelatives. Furthermore, the shaman must be requested by the patient or the patient's relatives. Belief in the healer's ability is also necessary "for his powers to be effective" [Smith 1973:10].

The cure begins with the shaman divining the patient's illness. "There were apparently many means of divining illness and forecasting the future" [Smith 1973:12]. The most frequent method is to dream about the case. To accomplish this the shaman places some personal object from the patient under his or her pillow—a hat, shirt, tie, belt, etc. Such dreaming may occur for a week or more. "[Another] technique for predicting whether or not there was a chance to effect a cure was for the adept to chew a piece of tobacco, then place it in the middle of a cup of water. Then he would put his finger in the cup and by running it around the edge, whirl the water. If the tobacco moved, i.e., if it did not stay 'dead-center' in the cup, the adept would say: 'I will try [to help you].' If the tobacco *did* stay dead center as the water in the cup whirled, the medicine man would say (or the equivalent) 'Too late. You should have called me sooner'" [Smith 1973:12]. Once the divination is completed, the shaman follows the instructions given to him or her by the guardian spirit. Often the cure takes the form of removing a disease object from the patient's body. Other cures are psychological in nature—for breaking certain taboos, countering the effects of sorcery, and so forth.

In all cases the advanced dreamer learns to call forth his guardian spirit. That is, "by holding his drum close to his face and singing the chants that he had been taught, the adept could call forth his guardian spirit to, e.g., inform him of the cause of an illness or to tell him (or speak through him at various times while he was singing) of future events. Calling forth the guardian spirit by drumming and singing also allowed one to have other abilities" [Smith 1973:9].

Inkonze could also be used for sorcery. Pierre Squirrel knew a harmful *inkonze*. His technique was described as follows: "He chews medicine root, and blows it out. (Cupping his hand under his mouth and blowing, which sends the magic, often in the form of a fly, to enter the mouth of the victim as he sleeps; a very dangerous condition for the victim)" [Joseph Moose-Sinew in Smith 1973:15–16]. "Aggressive *inkonze* could also be used to make a person's dogs weak ('not lively') or even to kill them" [Smith 1973:17]. "Additionally, there is a story of a young boy with *inkonze* who is compelled to magically kill an old man" [Smith 1973:19].

Inkoze
Slave, *Mackenzie-Yukon*
Also: *inkkon etsi* (early Jesuit), *inkeanzè* (1868) [Honigmann 1946:77]. Shaman. Some indicators suggest that there is no specific term for a shaman among this group and that *inkoze* refers to the shaman's power [Honigmann 1946:77]. That is, a person who can cure or perform other supernatural feats is said to possess *inkoze*.

A boy or girl often obtains a guardian spirit at a very early age, normally around five. It comes either via a dream or in a trance. It is most often an animal spirit, with the Bear, the Eagle, and the Wolf (in that order) being the most powerful guardian spirits. According to one source, an old Slave shaman named Tinite had received his helping spirits at a very young age. "His dead father appeared to him as an angel with wings and carried him in spirit up through a hole in the sky to heaven. He did not dream but was wide-awake all the time; nevertheless he did not eat nor drink for three weeks and his body did not move. In heaven two other angels appeared to him with their names written on their foreheads. These are his guardians and help him to cure, to

prophesy, and to conjure. They gave him the moose, the deer, and the fox. . . . He also gained control over the sun which is the father of all and sees everything, the wind which [is] the spirit of all and pervades everything, and the earth which is the mother of all and touches everything. These are the strongest possible medicines; they obey his behest" [Mason 1946:38]. For each of these last three helpers, Tinite had a calling song. "By singing them he secures their aid in his clairvoyance and prophecies. These songs were taught to him when he went to heaven" [Mason 1946:38].

"Several procedures could be followed in curing. Sometimes the curer gave the patient water across which he had blown his breath; this was always drunk in a 'special cup' wrapped in cloth. Curers also sucked blood and foreign objects from the bodies of patients. . . . While performing, the curer is said to have sung special songs and also to have spoken a great deal, telling what was wrong and how the injury was caused. While the curer was making medicine in this way the sick person and others present were sometimes able to hear the cries of the curer's medicine animal, through whose power he was operating" [Honigmann 1946:78].

In-Lon-Schka
Osage, *Plains*
Literal translation: "playground of the eldest son" [Callahan 1990:19]. A religious ceremony that the Osage obtained from the Kaws and Poncas during the mid-1880s; it originated among the Dhegiha Sioux [Callahan 1990:22]. *In-Lon-Schka* is an annual, four-day Osage ceremony conducted during the month of June. Currently three such ceremonies are conducted, each held on a different June weekend, beginning on a Thursday.

"It is a ceremony in honor of an eldest son in the tribe, who is chosen to be the Drumkeeper for a year, the drum being the sacred instrument in this ceremonial. The Drumkeeper may be as young as a boy or as old as a young man. . . . The

An Osage tribal drum with beaded decoration.

In-Lon-Schka, however, is more than the recognition of an outstanding youth of the tribe. It sets standards of conduct and ways of living for the tribal members; it is religious in context, revealing many of the religious beliefs and ideals of the tribe in the prayer, songs, and ceremonies" [Callahan 1990:19–20]. It is also a celebration of "the season of new growth—of the rebirth of green grass and corn, so equally important to the survival of the tribe. The I'n-Lon-Schka is equally important at the symbolic level as a demonstration that the Osages are in harmony and at peace with one another as well as the universe" [Callahan 1990:135].

"The drum is the center of the ceremony, both literally and symbolically, and respect for the sacredness of that instrument is one of the most important elements in the I'n-Lon-Schka. . . . The drum is the instrument that is used to communicate with the Great Spirit. It contains the thunder and lightning and comes from nature. The Great Mystery—Wah'Kon-Tah—is also the Great Spirit. The drum is the Osages' way of communicating with the Great Spirit. . . . The drum is the center and hub of the people, because the drum carries everything the people have—their songs, their life, their history" [Callahan 1990:21].

The *In-Lon-Schka* also bears a resemblance to the earlier Omaha Grass Dance, which was the early-nineteenth-century form of an even older Pawnee shamanic ceremony known as the *Iruska* (see entry). The Omaha Grass Dance became popular among the Northern Plains tribes, such as the Kaw and Ponca, during the nineteenth century. As a result, over the years the shamanic elements of the *In-Lon-Schka* have been replaced so that the ceremony now serves more as a vehicle for cultural preservation than as a shamanic ritual.

Inorrôrtut
West Greenland Eskimo, *Artic Coast*
Egedesminde Eskimo term for animal spirits that appear to an individual in human guise [Birket-Smith 1924:443].

Inugwak
Labrador Eskimo, *Arctic Coast*
Literal translation: "a little man" [L. Turner 1894: 199]. Wooden doll amulet. The small wooden doll is attached to the belt or other part of a shaman's clothing, such that it always faces outward in order to be on the alert.

Invisibility medicines
There are infrequent accounts of shamans making themselves invisible. Geronimo (see entry), the Chiricahua (Apache) shaman/war leader, had the power to do this, as did Lakota shaman Henry Crow Dog. It is still found among the Lakota in South Dakota. One power associated with this technique and commonly mentioned in the literature is that of shape shifting (see entry and also *transmutation*).

There are also many ceremonies in which the shaman may disappear for a while, particularly among the Eskimos. According to one report from the 1820s, a half-breed who had been raised among whites arranged to enter the ceremonial lodge during a performance of a Cree Shaking Tent Ceremony (EONAH, pp. 246–249). Some time after the shaman entered the lodge, the shaman's voice could be heard rising upward, until it was no longer audible.

> "Well!" said one of the indians [sic] addressing one of the half-breeds, living with the white. "Well! Enter now, and see if he be there: thou art always doubting and denying what we say of these things: enter then and see if he be there, then indeed are our assertions false."
>
> He raised the bottom of the *casement* [material surrounding the lodge poles] and entered, but as he [the shaman] was not below, he rose on his feet and felt for him, but [the conjuror was] not to be found. However he was *paid* [punished by the spirits] for his curiosity: there was a dreadful fluttering within, but especially about his head, his hair flying about in his face as if in a tempest and frequent appearances of small lights before his eyes which ever way he turned: he bawled out and asked those without what was the matter with him: he became afraid and walk'd out as quick as he could" [Nelson in Brown and Brightman 1988:83–84].

Soon thereafter the shaman returned to the lodge.
    See also *inipi, war medicine*

Invulnerability medicines

Shamans have many different forms of invulnerability. In the nineteenth century the most common type was the war medicines (see entry), which included protection against bullets, arrows, etc. Bulletproof medicines (EONAH, pp. 41–42) were also a common aspect of shamanic power feats (see *power displays/feats*). This was particularly true of the powerful Bear shamans, individuals who had acquired some form of bear as their guardian spirit. A Bear shaman among the Kansa "painted his sides black to represent that animal. He would allow other Indians to shoot him and kill him, but after lying dead a little while he would get up whole, even though he had a hole shot through him" [Skinner 1915b:770].

Another large category of invulnerability medicines encompasses the fire-handling medicines (see entry). The ability of shamans to han-dle hot rocks, coals, etc., and even walk or dance on them has been recorded since the first contacts in the sixteenth century. By the early nineteenth century the *Wábano* (see entry) or *Wabeno* fire-handling cult was widespread, and it evolved into the Pawnees' *Iruska* (see entry) and other fire-handling ceremonies.

Shamans are also often called upon to make personal amulets that render their owners invulnerable to the attack of witches (see *witchcraft*). Protection against love charms can also be obtained from a shaman.

Many of the Northwest Coast and Arctic shamans have medicines for invulnerability to drowning and are believed to stay underwater for long periods of time (for example, see *ichta, Red-Stone Doctor,* and *Sea Lion*). Invulnerability to cold weather and water is another known form of this type of medicine power.

See also *Alini, Calf Shirt, Crazy Horse, Matgohari, Paint, Podulte, poigunt, Poor Wolf, Raven, Roman Nose, Shunáwanùh, Takes the Pipe, Tcuiiopi, Wàbik, war medicine, Wegeléyu, Welukúshkush.*

Ipétes
Nez Perce, *Plateau*

Also: *ipätis* [Coale 1958:138]. Sacred bundle. This was a personal power amulet put together by a shaman who had acquired a spirit helper. The contents of one's *ipétes* would be revealed to the shaman during his spirit-dance validation ceremony. Sometimes in addition to providing the neophyte with clues about his *ipétes,* the shaman also "was thought to obtain information about it when in the trance. An alternative method of obtaining the *ipétes* was to inherit it from some ancestor, one informant having called this process *mi´yahánit* [D. Walker 1968:22].

Thus the *ipétes* is different for each individual, and there is a close association between the shaman and his *ipétes* after the sacred bundle is assembled. "A small 'eye' of the *ipétes* customarily was worn on a string around the neck in the form of a feather, a shell, or some other suitably symbolic object. The costume worn at the spirit dances or when entering a risky undertaking requiring supernatural power bore a close relationship to the *ipétes*" [D. Walker 1968:22]. This "eye" was usually a piece of fur from the animal that served as the shaman's helping spirit.

The power of the objects contained in the shaman's sacred bundle is exemplified in the following account: "One time this *tiwé·t* [shaman—see EONAH, p. 282] was trying to kill another one up the river. He got him awful sick, but he couldn't kill him. He knew it was something in his *ipétes,* but he didn't know what it was exactly. He went up to see him and asked the sick *tiwé·t* if he could see his *ipétes.* Ha! Ha! The sick one told his wife to go get it, and she brought it out. The other *tiwé·t* shook his head, and the sick one kept taking things out. Pretty soon he came to a little flint knife. He held it in his hand and pushed it at the other *tiwé·t* and asked him if that was what he was looking for. That other *tiwé·t* kind of shook his head and said he had to go. He got up and walked out. Before he was home, he was dead. That knife had been enough to kill him. He didn't even come close to touching him with it; just pushed it at him" [unidentified informant in D. Walker 1967:72].

Ipnahóywit
Nez Perce, *Plateau*
The process of preparing for a vision quest, which includes "rigorous spiritual and physical cleansing and conditioning" [D. Walker 1967:69].

Iputar
West Alaska Eskimo, *Arctic Coast*
Shaman's drum [Rasmussen 1941:35].

Iron
Blackfoot, *Plains*
A Piegan who founded the Crow-Water Society circa 1860. The native name for this society "seems to signify 'those that own the Crow power of waters,' but is sometimes rendered as 'Crow beaver medicine owners'" [Wissler 1913:436].

Although Iron stated in 1903 that he had learned this religious ceremony from the Crow, there is no similar society to be found among the Crow. Wissler [1913:440] did note certain similarities between the Crow-Water Ceremony and the "tobacco function of a [Crow] beaver bundle owner," but the link was hypothetical.

None of the other Blackfoot bands conducted this ceremony, so it is very likely that Iron was indeed responsible for its origin, as stated. Iron obtained a wealth power via a dream of six dwarfs and then began the Crow-Water Ceremony to empower others. People obtain membership in the society by giving many gifts, such as quilts, horses, etc. Both men or women can join, but married couples must enter the society together. Upon initiation each new member receives a particular animal skin—otter, blackbird, weasel, beaver, mink, muskrat, sparrow, nighthawk, or robin, to name a few—and a power song to go with it. These are kept in a medicine bundle, which may also contain other items, such as a whistle, a wooden hand, etc. All of the power songs, with their associated power objects, are sung in order to bring one prosperity. To this end, "the medicine formula [song] or power may be used as follows:—If a member wishes a horse, he calls in other members and sings the songs and offers prayers. It is believed that one so doing will soon be called upon for some service and receive a horse as a fee. Other wishes may be gratified in the same way. An outsider desiring anything may formally announce that he provides food and presents for a meeting [ceremony]. Then members assemble and hold a meeting" [Wissler 1913:437].

During their ceremonies the women usually do the dancing, while the men sing. Most members "paint their faces yellow, with red bars across the mouth and forehead. A rectangle of red is also made upon the backs of the hands. A few plumes and feathers are worn on the head" [Wissler 1913:437]. The ceremony may be given at any time, but at the turn of the nineteenth century, ceremonies were being held each Sunday and on the new moon. In former times, ceremonies were limited to members only, but they have since become public occasions.

In addition to praying for good fortune, other reasons for prayer also suffice, and thus almost anyone can sponsor a ceremony for any reason. Such ceremonies are often requested for the purpose of healing an individual illness. "Sometimes when a person has made a vow to give a feast because of someone who is sick the members, who are notified, pray for the sick person. As soon as he recovers, the person who made the vow makes a berry soup and goes to one of the members and tells him to have the dance" [Owl Top in Wissler 1913:438].

Iron Maker
Ojibwa, *Canadian Eastern Woodlands*
A well-known shaman during the latter part of the nineteenth century who late in life became a Methodist, although he retained his belief in the spirits. During his youth he had often fasted in order to obtain spirit helpers. As he grew older he obtained more spirit helpers and became more powerful.

Sometime around the fall of 1894, Iron Maker capsized in a boat off Portage Entry and was saved from exposure and drowning by his spirit helpers. As he struggled to the surface of the water,

he thought of the beaver, whereupon the beaver came to him and gave him his body. He swam towards the shore, but before he could reach it, he felt himself losing the power to keep the shape of the beaver. So he thought of the otter. Then the otter gave him his body, and in that form he reached land.

There Iron Maker found himself naked in his own body. It was freezing weather and his camp lay forty miles away on Keweenaw Point. He would have died of the cold but for the help of four other animals which, one after another, lent him their bodies to get home: First the bear, in whose shape he went a good way, then the lynx, then the raccoon, and after that the ox.

When Iron Maker no longer had power to keep the shape of the ox, he was pretty near his lodge. He ran home naked and fell in at the door half dead with cold [Jacques LePique in Bourgeois:1994:69].

Iruska
Pawnee, *Plains*
Dialectical variants: *hethushka* (Omaha), *helocka* (Catlin's *Eh-Ros-Ka*) (Iowa), *helucka* (Kansa), *helocka* (Ponca), *heyoka* (Dakota) [Wissler 1916:859]. Members of the powerful medicine society known as *Pitararis Iruska*, whose shamans handle fire and boiling liquids. *Iruska* performances are designed "to show the power of the members to extinguish the life in the fire, hence the name. Among the Skidí at least, the term iruska has a symbolic or double meaning. The idea is literally 'the fire is in me' and the symbolic meaning is that 'I can extinguish the life in the fire,' or can overcome the powers of other medicines. The members of the society were doctors for they treated burns" [Murie 1914:608].

In more recent times "the well-known Omaha, or grass dance [see entry], is generally known among the Pawnee as a variation of their own iruska, though in its present form it was introduced through Oglala influence" [Murie 1914:624].

Ìsáné
Jicarilla, *Southwest*
Also: *dìghìnkègòsán.* Holiness Rite, formerly called the Bear Dance. Literal translation: *ìsáné* means "the ceremony that exists," and *dìghìnkègòsán* means "the place which exists on holiness" [Opler 1943:3]. Although the term *bear* appears in neither of these translations, this ceremony has been referred to as the Bear Dance by early ethnographers because a bear impersonator appears during the dance. However, because this ceremony has no association with the well-known Ute Bear Dance complex, Opler [1943:3] chose to rename this ceremony as the Holiness Rite. Both of the above Jicarilla terms

refer to this particular ceremony and include the special enclosure in which it is conducted.

The Jicarilla Holiness Rite is a curing ceremony designed to relieve only those illnesses caused by Bear or Snake (accordingly called the Bear sickness and Snake sickness). "A frightening encounter with a bear or a snake or contact of any kind with one of these animals or its skin (including shedded snake skins) is likely to result in sickness for which the Holiness Rite is the appropriate remedy" [Opler 1943:4–5]. However, sickness from certain snakes, such as the water snake, can be cured with different plants, thus avoiding the need for the Holiness Rite. Opler [1943:5] noted that the *ìsáné* is "the most ambitious single ritual of the Jicarilla."

The ritual is expensive, complicated, and dangerous. It is difficult to learn, and if improperly performed, it can cause a person to become sick. For instance, "M. said that he knew the power of the bear and the Holiness Rite. He put a ceremony on. He got very sick and nearly died twice. C. came to him and cured him. C. told him, 'The reason you get sick from it is that you don't know enough about it; you don't know as much as you think you know about it. You have no business putting on that Holiness Rite. Doing it has made you sick. You just make fun of that ceremony [hold it up to ridicule] the way you do it.' M. didn't even know what made him sick until C. told him" [Opler 1943:6–7]. In the early 1940s only eight men knew this ceremony.

The Holiness Rite is never performed for a single patient. Usually the number of patients is three or four, with most practitioners accepting up to twelve patients at a time. To conduct the ceremony a special, round corral is erected from bushes, standing about 5 to 6 feet in height. An opening of about 3 feet is left on the east end for the entrance, and a special tipi is placed on the inside of the corral at the west end.

The Holiness Rite is conducted over a four-night period. In addition to the shamans, singers, and dancers (supernatural impersonators), it includes an impersonator of the Bear, called "he who continually runs out" [Opler 1943:19–20]. On the final night of the ceremony, the shamans, or "wonder workers," and some of the singers and dancers perform power feats. Of this one informant reported:

> The wonder workers are not like this. They pay no attention to what the clowns [some of the dancers] are doing. They are restrained in their dancing and do nothing suggestive of sex [as do the clowns]. They do not speak but are singing softly to themselves. They do all sorts of things before the people to show their great power. They make things appear and disappear. Each shows what he can do.
>
> In the old-time Holiness Rite many wonderful things used to be done. My father saw this; it happened in his time. The wonder worker used to throw an eagle feather into the fire with everyone watching, and run around and have it in his hand again at the other side. . . .
>
> The singers, too, used to do great things this last night. The one from whom J. learned the Holiness Rite used to be able to make corn grow over night. But now these things are not often done. The reason is that in order to have the singer and dancers do things like that, everyone would have to believe, everyone would have to be holy. The men who dance as wonder workers would have to wash themselves and be clean and purified. They would have to keep away from women before the ceremony. But now they are just young fellows who don't care. They do anything.
>
> Yet there is one man here, M., who comes in with a kernel of corn. He shows it to everyone. He asks them, "Is it wet or dry?" "Dry," they say. Then he plants it. In the morning there is a whole corn plant there with full-grown corn on. It grows in one night. This corn he distributes, giving a kernel to all who want it. The kernels are saved and planted in the field, together with a small feather from the back of the turkey, by those who want good crops [unnamed informant in Opler 1943:37–38].

The Holiness Rite closes at sunrise on the fifth morning with a procession moving out from the corral and to the east. The patients are instructed to move their camp to a new location and not to have sexual intercourse for twelve or sometimes twenty-four nights. Some of the other rules for the patients have been reported: "After this ceremony the patient should not go where certain plants (*Coleosanthus brachyphydus*) are thick. He should never eat burned mush or bread turned over in the ashes; the flat bread that is done on top of the fire is all right. He should not lend moccasins to anyone and he should not put moccasins under his pillow. He must not sit on spruce branches and he must not sleep or sit on a string or a rope" [Opler 1943:42].

A diminutive form of the Holiness Rite, called the "Little Holiness Rite" [Opler 1943:43], is also sometimes performed. In this version the corral and the spirit impersonators are left out, although the tipi and singers are used. "For this kind of Holiness Rite, the beads and basket do not have to be given to the singer [shaman]. Those are just given for the big ceremony where a corral is made. But the clay bowl, which has to be made new, the pipe [made from clay], and all the feathers that have to be there for the big ceremony, are given for this one too. They don't have the dancing by the people; they just use the songs. No bear impersonator comes in. This ceremony lasts four days. The singer makes ground drawings for it each day [as done in the big ceremony]. The singer blows on his patients with smoke, on their feet. He presses his own body against the patient's body" [unnamed informant in Opler 1943:43].

In his study of this particular ceremony, Opler [1943:94] concluded that it was most closely related to the Navajo Mountain Top (or Mountain Chant) Way and the Beauty Way ceremonies.

Ishtabe
Chickasaw, *Southeast*
Literal translation: from *ishto*, "big," and *abi*, "to kill" [Swanton 1928:634, n. 17]. An eighteenth-century term given by Adair for witches. The

term *hoollabe*, from *holo*, meaning "what is sacred," is also used.

Issiwun
Cheyenne, *Plains*
Sacred Buffalo Hat. One of the Cheyenne's most sacred objects, sometimes referred to in the literature as the Cheyenne Buffalo Cap or Sacred Hat; it was brought to the Cheyenne by a Suhtai cultural hero/shaman "variously called Rustling Corn Leaf, Listening to the Ground, or Erect Horns" [Grinnell 1923:vol. 2:285]. "The word 'is'siwun' (*esevon*) means a herd of buffalo. However, in the context of the Sacred Hat the term also means a group of female bison. The Buffalo Hat is formed from the horned scalp of a female buffalo" [Powell 1969:4]. The buffalo cow horns have been shaved down, and "the skin of which the hat is composed is covered with large blue beads. No hair is to be seen. The beads do not look as if they were sewed on with sinew, but rather as if they were glued on, and it is said that as one looks at this beaded surface it seems to move" [Grinnell 1910:563–564].

The *Issiwun* "was shown only on the occasion of a great sickness, or when the medicine arrows [see *Mahuts*] were renewed, or when it was taken out to be worn in war. . . . When taken to war, if one or more of the beads stood up above the general surface of the beads, the Cheyenne knew that as many of their people would be killed as there were beads projecting above this surface. After the fight it was always found that all the beads had returned to their places,—that the surface was smooth. If, when a war party was absent, the hat was looked at and some of the beads appeared to be missing, they felt sure that people would be killed, as many as there were beads missing. Afterward, when the war party had returned and they looked at the hat, the beads were all there again, just as if none had been gone" [Grinnell 1910: 563–564]. However, the bundle containing the *Issiwun* is rarely opened.

Traditionally Is'siwun's power guaranteed a plentiful supply of buffalo for the people. In this power to renew the herds the Hat is linked to the Sun Dance and to the Buffalo ceremony. A woman, usually the wife of the pledger of the ceremony, played a vital part in both these ceremonies, for she offered herself in the role of the symbolic reproducer of the tribe, the family, the buffalo, and of creation as a whole.

Consequently, the Sacred Hat is the animate symbol of female renewing power. If the Buffalo Hat is desecrated, there is danger that woman's power will be broken or destroyed [Powell 1969:4–5].

Around 1873 the wife of Broken Dish (then the Suhtai keeper of the *Issiwun*) "in anger and spite, ripped a horn from the Sacred Hat" [Powell 1969:4]. This happened because Broken Dish had been given only temporary care of the *Issiwun* by Half Bear, the former keeper, just prior to his death. Half Bear had instructed Broken Dish to give the *Issiwun* to his son Coal Bear upon the latter's return. But when Coal Bear returned some four years later, Broken Dish refused to turn the *Issiwun* over to him. "While the people were talking about taking the hat away from Broken Dish for Coal Bear, the wife of Broken Dish took one of the horns from the hat. . . . She carried this horn sewed inside the front of her dress, so that it was always on her person" [Grinnell 1910: 566–567]. The horn was eventually returned in 1908. Further desecrations occurred in April 1959 when Ernest American Horse took the *Issiwun* from Lame Deer, Oklahoma, to Sheridan, Wyoming. While it was in his possession, he "sold some of the scalps from the bundle . . . the sacred 'blower' of red catlinite . . . [and] one of the pipes from the Hat bundle" [Powell 1969:399].

Isxíp
Nez Perce, *Plateau*

A particularly powerful form of power acquired by shamans. Shamans who have this power are usually potent doctors. *Isxíp* "was very greedy and required its possessors to cut themselves when participating in the tutelary spirit dance and to give away much wealth during their initiation. Clearly this power was one of the most effective for curing, as well as one of the most dangerous in the practice of sorcery. Persons possessing this power had to exercise great caution lest they hurt innocent bystanders. The power seems to have had a certain volition, bringing about accidental sorcery" [D. Walker 1967:75].

"The making of an *isxí·p* shaman was a long, arduous procedure. Such persons were usually detected as children after they became inexplicably sick and temperamental. A mature *isxí·p* shaman would take charge of the child's development, and as he matured would direct him in the various steps of becoming such a shaman. The process could last ten years according to some informants. . . . During his development as an *isxí·p* shaman, he learned a special *isxí·p* shaman language called *isxí·p tímt*, intelligible only to *isxí·p* shamans. He also learned the distinctive dance of the *isxí·p* shamans occasionally performed at the tutelary spirit ceremony, but which they also danced on other important occasions" [D. Walker 1968:25–26].

"The *isxí·p* concept is present among the neighboring Interior Salish as well as the Coast Salish, and is a strong shaman power in all instances known to me" [D. Walker 1967:75].

Itgagewam
Wishram, *Plateau*
See *idiagewam.*

Itsikawáhidish
Hidatsa, *Plains*
Creator [Pepper and Wilson 1908:320, n. 1].

Iunke warúhawe
Iowa, *Plains*
Fork-Tailed Hawk war bundle. This was a sacred medicine bundle used in warfare. When going

on a war raid, the owner of the bundle would accompany the war party. The bundle "had a song, which, when its owner gave it, could cause a storm to arise and drive back fleeing foemen" [Skinner 1915a:715].

Ivaxi
Tewa, *Southwest*

Hidden Dances. "Hidden dances, directed by the Summer Society [see *xa zhe*], were held by the Summer kachina in late January or early February, on the night of Good Friday, and in late September or early October. In recent years the January-February enactments have been sporadic" [Hill 1982:227]. Such performances are held in the Santa Clara, San Ildefonso, and San Juan Pueblos. These kachina dances stopped at Nambé sometime between 1914 and 1924. "Formerly, unless the rite coincided with a moiety initiation, it was held not in the kiva but in the mountains. The last recorded performance of a 'hidden dance' in the hills, however, was between 1920 and 1925. Essentially the same patterns were followed in all 'hidden dances,' although there were seasonal variations in detail.... The overall purpose of the kachina ceremonies was to promote the general well-being of the village [pueblo], and to insure the continuity of nature. They contained special fertility features applicable to humans, livestock, and crops. There were also rain-bringing rituals and harvest and thanksgiving festivals" [Hill 1982:228]. The ritual takes four days to perform correctly.

Hidden dances include a considerable amount of buffoonery between the audience and the kachinas, who ruthlessly deliver criticisms to named members of the audience. For example, the conversation between two Santa Clara kachinas recorded in 1941 included the following exchange:

> "All these girls (gesturing to include all the girls, but referring specifically to those attending the Santa Fe Indian School) have been having

relations with Navajo boys, elder brother." [The Navajo are despised by Santa Claras, and they are traditional enemies.] "Now that they have come home, and our young men are in training in the army, the older men in the pueblo are getting their share of intercourse."

"Oh yes, younger brother, the two cousins, A and B (naming two girls in the audience), are fighting over a Navajo penis." "Is that so, elder brother!" "Yes; it seems, however, that A won, and now B is brooding over it" [Hill 1982:233].

Nonetheless, these kachina dances were often serious affairs, and any infractions were punished on the spot by the kachina leader. "If an impersonator [kachina] dropped part of his costume or committed an error, that dignitary [kachina leader] whipped the offender and chased him from the kiva" [Hill 1982:240].

Ïwadïmpuaxantï
Paiute, *Basin*

Literal translation: "rain doctor" [Kelly 1939:165]. See *unwadïmbuaxantï*.

Iwenashnawe
Zuni, *Southwest*

One of the orders of the Great Fire Fraternity [Stephen 1936:485] or Big Firebrand Society [Parsons 1939:Table 1, foldout insert between pp. 168 and 169]. The literal translation of this term means "knowledge of sucking" [Stephen 1936:485] and refers to the way shamans treat patients during a performance of this society. Another name for this society is *Onayanakia* (see entry).

Iwilhiltat
Yuki, *California*

Literal translation: "poison giver" [V. Miller 1979:25]. Sorcerer or witch. Yuki sorcerers are always men. They usually receive their training from older shamans. Such training often takes place during the performance of the group's *Hulk-ilal-woknam*, "eye-striped initiation" or "ghost dance," ceremony for boys [Miller 1979:24]. Boys who undergo the training associated with this ceremony learn "poisoning techniques and some became doctors or assistants to *Taikomol-woknam* [lying dance] doctors" [V. Miller 1979:24].

"Great power was attributed to these sorcerers who could cause people to fall ill or die, as well as cure victims of sorcery" [V. Miller 1979:25]. As is often the case, a sorcerer is not seen as an altogether evil person since his powers can also be used against tribal enemies.

The "lying dance doctor," referred to above, is known as *lamshimi* (EONAH, p. 150). Although he dances and sings over a patient during a healing, his cures always include sucking on the patient's "pain" [see *pains*]. Other shamans only sing over the patient and are known as *hilyulit* (EONAH, pp. 106–107), or "singing doctors" [V. Miller 1979:25]. This same term is also used as the name of their healing performance. The *hilyulit* instructions are learned during the *Taiko-mol-woknam*, a four-day training period for boys conducted during the winter.

Iyatiku
Keres, *Southwest*
Dialectical variants: *iärriko* (Sia), *iareko* (Cochiti). The most central of all Laguna spirits. "In the ritual, *iyatik'ü* is the cotton-wrapped ear of corn which is possessed by the *cheani* [shamans] and set out on altars. It is the Zuñi *mi'li* [EONAH, pp. 175–176], although, unlike the *mi'li* the *iyatik'ü* would not be carried in the *k'atsina* dances because, I have heard it said, of its sanctity" [Parsons 1926:95].

Parsons described one of these fetishes as follows: "It was kept together with two stone knives wrapped in buckskin in a niche in the wall in a back storeroom—the third room back on the ground floor. . . . The ear of corn was wrapped thickly with unspun cotton, the butt set in a buckskin cap, the top uncovered. Here in the somewhat hollowed out cob there were seeds, they would be grains of corn, wheat, melon and pumpkin seeds, I have been told. About one inch from the bottom a string of white shell beads, an abalone shell and two olivella shells (*yasi*) encircled the cotton. In use, feathers would have been tied on in a bunch near the top, I was told, not, Zuñi fashion, to envelop the whole cob, nor, Sia fashion, surrounded by what appear to be feather-sticks" [Parsons 1926:96]. "According to one informant, to the four sides of the *iyatik'ü* four arrow points should be attached so that no evil (*tsa-heyasuts* or *naitshgunisha*) may reach it" [Parsons 1926:96, n. 1].

Iyułmax
Wishram, *Plateau*
Upper Chinookan term for guardian spirit [Boyd 1996:116].

Ize
Jicarilla, *Southwest*
Medicine [Goddard 1911:151]. The *ize* is usually some form of amulet that is worn on a person's body for protection. (For additional details see *izzekloth*, EONAH, p. 119.)

Jenness, Diamond

Ethnologist Diamond Jenness was born at Wellington, New Zealand, on February 10, 1886. He attended the University of New Zealand and Oxford University, doing fieldwork in New Guinea in 1911–1912. From 1913 to 1918 he was a member of the Canadian Arctic Expedition directed by Vilhjálmur Stefánsson for the National Museum of Canada, where he worked under the direction of R. M. Anderson. Following service in World War I, he joined the museum staff. By 1926 he had become chief anthropologist at the National Museum of Canada, and he went on to become one of Canada's leading pioneer anthropologists and Arctic scholars. He remained as chief of the anthropological division at the Victoria Memorial (National) Museum until 1946.

During his career he published over 100 papers on ethnology, linguistics, physical anthropology, applied anthropology, and archaeology. His work resulted in five honorary degrees from different universities. In 1929 he was elected to the Royal Society of Canada. His major ethnographic fieldwork was among the Copper Inuit (*The Copper Eskimo,* 1922) in the area of Coronation Bay, Northwest Territories, during the Stefánsson expedition. One of his most popular books, *The People of the Twilight* (1928), recounts his year at Coronation Bay. In 1932 he published his classic *The Indians of Canada,* which has been reissued many times. During 1937 he served as president of the Society for American Archaeology, and during 1939 he was president of the American Anthropological Society. In 1969 he was appointed Companion of the Order of Canada, which is Canada's highest honor. He died near Ottawa on November 29, 1969.

Jesako

Menomini, *Midwest*

Plural: *jesakosûk* [Skinner 1915d:192]. Dialectical variants *djasakid* [Coleman 1937:50], *jessakid* (EONAH, pp. 121–122) (Ojibwa). Shaman. This type of shaman is best known for his use of a conjuring lodge known as a *jesakan.* The ritual use of this lodge is known in the literature as the Shaking Tent Ceremony (EONAH, pp. 246–249) because the lodge begins to shake violently when the spirits enter. This ceremony appears to have originated among the Ojibwa and subsequently spread in various forms to other areas.

135

Among the Menomini

the je'sako begins to pray and sing, meanwhile
shaking a hide-covered circular rattle, resembling
a tiny drum of the tambourine variety. . . . At
last, the wind begins to blow, although it may be
a calm evening. This is regarded as a good sign,
for the breeze heralds the powers. The je'sako
loudly greets each power as it appears, until all
with whom he had dealings are present. It is
thought that most of them seat themselves on
the topmost ring of twigs about the lodge frame,
but a few always are seated on the floor in a
circle. When the gods [helping spirits] are all
thus assembled, they partake of the liquor, in
company with the je'sako himself. The latter is
careful not to become drunk, but only
exhilarated. . . .

   The je'sako talks to the gods through the
medium of the turtle, mikanâ [see *mikenak*], who
speaks Ojibway. The listeners outside can hear the
conversation distinctly. The various powers
mumble and grumble in a way only intelligible to
the turtle, and the conjuror. Often the conjuror is
unable to follow the discourse and is obliged to
fall back on his reptilian interpreter [Skinner
1915d:193–194].

When the *jesakan* is erected for a healing ceremony, the shaman enters the lodge to divine the
cause of the illness and then leaves the lodge

and goes to the place where the sufferer lies.
When in the presence of the sick person he begins
to chant to the time of his skin rattle, and soon,
by gazing at the person lying before him the
doctor is able to locate the trouble. He then
swallows the okanûk bones, kneels beside the
patient, blows on the affected spot, and taps on it
with a bone tube in a fashion similar to that of a
woodpecker rapping on a tree.

   During this performance he sings. At the
conclusion of the song he stoops over, applies the
tube, and sucks out the cause of the trouble. The
evil power concentrated therein may be so strong
that it knocks the performer over flat on his back
and racks his patient with pain [Skinner
1915d:195].

The Shaking Tent Ceremony is also used to locate lost or stolen articles. If an item is stolen, the
jesako never names the thief. Also, "there is a special type of je'sako who only carries medicines
and okanûk bones and does not build a lodge nor
does he always have to swallow bones. Such men
can diagnose a case at once. Such a medicineman
is called, tip'apeo, or, akuhekäo tip'apeo. The
term for the act of blowing on the patient is designated potawananiäo, and akuhuniawäo means,
'he sucked it out'" [Skinner 1915d:196].

   See also *jossokeed*.

Jones, Rock
Havasupai, *Southwest*
An early-twentieth-century weather shaman who
would sing and rattle for four nights. An informant named Sinyella explained

that the flood of August, 1918 was due to Rock
Jones' singing while they were bathing in the
sweatlodge. At the moment these two were alone.
Rock Jones began to sing about great lightning and
rain. Suddenly the storm broke, everyone scattered,
and the two heard the hail pounding on the lodge.

   There is a more extended performance for
producing rain. A ring of brush is made, within
which men sit in a circle with Rock Jones at the
center. At his command they rise (but do not
dance) and sing about the white clouds, the big
black storm clouds, the lightning and thunder,
rain, the wind blowing hard, storm water running
on the ground, the foam on it, and so on. When
they tire he orders them to sit; then they sing
again. This makes rain aplenty (so attests Sinyella,
who has taken part). . . . Rock Jones' hair, face,
and body are painted white; this represents white
clouds. His face and body are also colored black
and red for the storm clouds and the red hue of
the clouds at dawn and sunset. For a robe he
wears a big buckskin tied by its legs over the right
shoulder and hanging under his left arm. He
wears moccasins, leggings, and buckskin pants. An
eagle tail plume is thrust upright in his hair; to the
tip of this the largest, softest down from under
these tail feathers is tied. Two similar plumes are
thrust crosswise through his front hair like horns.

His gourd rattle, a flat one, is painted longitudinally with zigzag stripes of red, white, and black. The other men are stripped to the waist; hair, face, and trunk are painted white. Some also had buckskin for robes [Spier 1928:281–282].

Jossokeed

Ojibwa, *Canadian Eastern Woodlands*
Also: *jessakkid* (EONAH, pp. 121–122). Dialectical variant: *jizikiwinini* (Chippewa) [Ritzenthaler 1953b:198]. Term used by the Ojibwa of Southern Ontario for shaman [Schmalz 1991:7]. The *jossokeed* acquires helping spirits known as *munedoos* (or *manitoos*) via solitary quests. However, "in traditional Ojibwa culture, every person had a guardian manitou who provided protection in battle, success in hunting, and identity within the group. Each person maintained a supernatural relationship without normally consulting religious leaders [shamans] for guidance" [Schmalz 1991:10]. Thus the *jossokeed* is distinguished from the ordinary person by the degree of power obtained.

The following is an account of war medicines used by a nineteenth-century *jossokeed:* "While completely surrounded by the enemy in battle, he was able to change himself and a fellow warrior into 'small turtles,' enabling them to 'creep under a log.' They later escaped to the Sauble River by changing into 'water snakes.' This is not an isolated account. Another Ojibwa tradition tells of an escape by canoe when a group of warriors was pursued by a strong war party. As the enemy were gaining on them, one of the warriors reached in his 'medicine bag' and 'pulled out an old pouch made of the skin of a Saw-bill, a species of duck. This he held by the neck to the water. Immediately the canoe began to glide swiftly at the usual speed of a Saw-bill; and after being propelled for a short time by this wonderful power, they looked back and found they were far beyond the reach of the enemy, who had now given up the chase'" [Schmalz 1991:9].

This type of shaman is best known for his performance of the Shaking Tent Ceremony (EONAH, pp. 246–249) conducted in a newly built conjuring lodge. Among the Wisconsin Chippewa the conjuring lodge poles are often joined at the top to form a dome, although the cylindrical, open-topped lodge is also used. When the *jossokeed* uses this lodge for diagnosing sickness, usually one of five possible causes is given: "sorcery, spirit intrusion, disease-object intrusion, breach of taboo, or soul loss" [Ritzenthaler 1953b:200].

Farther to the north, such as among the Berens River Chippewa in Canada, the percentage of *jossokeed* is much higher.

See also *jesako, King, John.*

Kabítcimalha
Creek, *Southeast*
A shaman whose English name was Laslie Cloud. In 1905 he recorded some of his sacred songs and formulas for anthropologist Frank Speck. The names of some of these songs and their uses follow:

- *Hássi alédja* (Sun the Cause)—sung for headaches caused by the sun.
- *Tcíi alédja* (Snake the Cause)—sung for swollen cheeks or aching teeth and gums caused by the water moccasin.
- *Itcá swalédja* (Beaver the Cause)—sung for constipation and soreness in the abdomen caused by the beaver.
- *Nókusi alédja* (Bear the Cause)—sung for nausea and diarrhea caused by the bear.
- *Wótko alédja* (Raccoon the Cause)—sung for insomnia and melancholy caused by the raccoon.

For more details see Speck 1907:124–133.

Kachina
Pueblo, *Southwest*
See *kopirshtaia, Kotikäne, lhatsina.*

Kahimtcine
Wintun, *California*
Literal translation: "wind bringer" [Du Bois 1935:87]. Wintu wind charm. Two types are known from the Bald Hills area. One was "made of buckeye in the shape of a cross, and then was interwoven diagonally with fine string. The whole object was only three or four inches long" [Du Bois 1935:87]. This was hung from the limb of a tree. The other charm was a stick 3 or 4 feet long with several feathers tied to the end. It was planted on the top of a hill. Such charms were used, for example, by women when winnowing seeds or berries.

Kamanitushit
Montagnais, *Canadian Eastern Woodlands*
Innu term for shaman [Armitage 1991:82].

Kamiokisihkwew
Cree, *Canadian Eastern Woodlands*
A Plains Cree shaman who was born around 1850 and lived to the late 1930s. His English name was (John?)

Fine Day. Although he did not know how to make love medicines or give instructions for using them, he had witnessed their use. He reported:

I have often heard of love medicines, but I saw only one man use them. He had two wives. One was a young girl who did not like him and who kept leaving him. He went to an old man who had that medicine. "I'll have a dog cooked [as an offering] for you to give a feast to your medicine." He also took off his clothes and gave them to the old man.

The owner of the medicine said, "Yes, she'll come back if the medicine is still strong." He spread out the medicine. We boys who were there were told not to look. But I did. The owner cut two figures out of bark, one a man, one a woman. He sang his medicine song. He put some medicine on a little stick and touched it to the heart of the male figure, then to the heart of the female figure. "If the medicine is good, she'll be back tonight. We'll sing a little while tonight." They stopped singing about midnight.

While the girl was sleeping that night she woke up thinking of the man. She had to go to him. She never left him again. Sometimes women bought love medicines also [Fine Day in Mandelbaum 1940:255].

Kamlanie

An anthropological term for a shamanic ceremony. Although not often used by American anthropologists, "this term is extensively used in Russian ethnographical literature on the shamanism of the primitive tribes of Siberia. It is derived from 'Kahm,' medicine man, of the Altaic Turks" [Lopatin 1945:71, n. 1].

Kanatyaiya

Keres, *Southwest*
Also: *kanadyaiya* [White 1930:608], *kanadyeya* (Laguna) [Parsons 1926:118]. Literal translation: "bad people" [Lange 1959:252, 459]. Cochiti Pueblo term for witch or evil spirit. "The sole purpose of these witches seems to be to make Indians sick. . . . They accomplish this in

two ways: they either shoot such things as thorns, pebbles, rags, broken glass, or even a small live snake, into the body of some unlucky person, or, they steal his heart and make off with it" [White 1930:608].

Witches can appear in many different forms, but they usually appear as animals (such as deer, dogs, burros, coyotes, crows, or owls) or as humans. In some cases witches appears as "'fireballs,' 6 to 12 inches in diameter, which consist of a black center with a surrounding surface of fiery, red flames" [Lange 1959:253]. An example of this was described as follows:

One time when I came back from a trip to Santa Fe, I had a little to drink and was sleepy. So I went to bed and was soon sound asleep. The next day my wife told me that she had seen two balls of fire, about eight inches across, come up out of the chimney of a house next to ours—or close to it—and these balls rolled around the edge of the roof. Then they rolled down to the ground and around the plaza. At this point, my wife ran home. I told her she should have awakened me. However, the following night, the same thing happened, and this time I saw them. I wanted to catch them, but my wife and her cousin held me back. Soon the balls of fire turned to ashes, like burned rags. I kicked them and they fell to pieces. The next day, I reported this to Victoriano [Cordero], the cacique [shaman]. He said that I should grab just a piece from these balls of ashes, and then the next day I should look around and if I saw a man with a tear or a hole in his pant, or a woman with a tear or hole in her dress, then I would know who these witches were [unnamed informant in Lange 1959:459].

There are four general types of healing shamans among the Keres (see *Crowi* for details). "The medicine men who are of real consequence in the Keresan pueblos are those organized into societies for curing ailments caused by witches. Curing disease is their major function, but they have others as well" [White 1930:608]. These shamans must remove the witch's object from the patient's body if the patient is to recover. "If the illness is not severe, one medicineman, only, will come. But if the patient is very ill, or wishes to become a member of the curing society, the whole society will come. . . . When a whole society comes, there is an elaborate ceremony in which considerable paraphernalia is used. Usually a society spends four days in its house [kiva] in preparations before visiting the patient. Then, when they go to his house, the medicinemen smoke, sing, and pray over the sick one for three nights and on the fourth have their final curing ritual. But, if the condition of the patient is critical, they will perform the curing ritual at once" [White 1930:608].

Kanochisisin
Blackfoot, *Plains*
All-Smoking Ceremony [Wissler 1913:445]. The powers associated with this religious ceremony are not clearly known. However, some of the general features of the ceremony have been described: "Four undecorated black pipes are used. No metal may be used on the pipes. The man who gives the feast [sponsors the ceremony] fills the pipes while the assistant lights and passes them. Four rattles similar to those in the beaver bundle ceremony are used. The guests sing the songs of the different medicines owned by them. In all each one must sing sixteen songs, four at a time. Anyone who has owned the medicine-pipe may sing four of the medicine-pipe songs; as many of the beaver bundle songs as one wishes to sing may be sung; but of other medicines, only one song may be sung. One song is allowed from each of the societies" [Duvall in Wissler 1913:446].

Káomúčnek
Wappo, *California*
Also: *yomto komutco* (EONAH, pp. 329–330). Sucking doctor. "This doctor uses bleeding among other devices" [Sawyer 1965:31].

Kapina
Keres, *Southwest*
A medicine society at Acoma, Laguna, Santo Domingo, and Zia Pueblos that conducts heal-

ing ceremonies. "At Laguna the *k'api'na* shamans were said to have deposited prayersticks stained red, to allay high winds" [White 1930:615].

Käpin hoi
Keres, *Southwest*
Literal translation: raw person [Bunzel 1932a: 483]. The Zuni phrase for the spiritual essence or consciousness inherent in all objects.

Karuk
Diegueño, *Peninsula*
Cocopa funeral ceremony. This ceremony lasts six days and is usually conducted in the winter. It is held only if the deceased is dreamed of by a relative or if the family's grieving extends over several months. Consequently, it is usually not performed for upward of six months following a person's death. In addition, although the ceremony may be conducted for more than one dead person at a time, it is conducted for any individual only once. In former times, the *karuk* was conducted only for men of repute.

Ceremonial preparations are elaborate and include food and gifts for the visitors and sacrifices to the deceased. Common gifts are beans, maize, tobacco, horses, and clothing, and often the extravagant gift-giving leaves those who sponsor it destitute. The sacrifices include the burning of clothes and food and usually the sacrifice of a horse as well. In addition a special ceremonial house is erected for the ritual.

Although the ceremony is interspersed with gambling (e.g., stick dice games), field sports (e.g., foot and horse races), and feasting, it also has sacred aspects. The shaman is not the official leader of the ceremony but is always present to deal with the spirits of the deceased. For instance, in invoking the spirits of the dead, participants often become sick upon seeing a *loxachak* (the spirit of a deceased person). Therefore, the shaman serves as a ghost shaman and treats such victims on the spot. This is usually done by blowing smoke on the victim, making noises to drive away the *loxachak,* and shaking the victim.

Quite often one or more of the relatives have a vision or dream of the deceased in which the dead person demands that certain sacrifices be brought to the *karuk*. The relatives always obey such demands.

Sometimes the *loxachak* will lead astray the soul of one of the mourners, causing an illness known as *loxachak paya*, "soul taking" [Gifford 1933:297], most often evidenced by the person fainting. In one case the spirit came and said, "'I have a good country for you.' Then mourner fell 'dead.' Shaman blew tobacco smoke toward SE [southeast]. Spirits in Inbawhela [Land of the Dead] saw this, feared lightning, and ghostly kidnapper might leave abducted soul by roadside. Victim's soul returned, [shaman] reanimated body" [Gifford 1933:297].

At the conclusion of the *karuk*, the ceremonial house is burned along with gifts to the deceased. However, the area is still imbued with power, i.e., it remains sacred.Gifford noted that "any man who wished success as orator, shaman, or gambler slept 4 nights in ashes of [the house] center post. Each morning he bathed. He remained continent and fasted from meat, salt, fish, for the period, but he might smoke" [Gifford 1933:298].

Kashim
Alaska Eskimo, *Arctic Coast*
Also: *kazigis* [Lantis 1947:105]. Semisubterranean men's ceremonial house used for holding public and secret rituals. Often in the literature, the *kashim* is referred to as the community "dance house." It also served as a dry-heat sweat house for the men for purification purposes. Most often it was a permanent structure, but in the Point Lay area temporary ones were built from driftwood and caribou skins; at Point Barrows the *kashim* was built from ice blocks [Lantis 1947:105].

Katsina
Pueblo, *Southwest*
See *lhatsina*.

Kaupinauwi
Miami, *Midwest*
Medicine bags [Trowbridge 1938:83].

Kave Na
Tewa, *Southwest*
See *Tong Kegi*.

Kawenho
Arikara, *Plains*
Black Arms Society [Lowie 1915a:651, 668]. This society performs the widespread Hot Dance found in the Plains area, similar to the Pawnee *Iruska* (see entry). In their performances the society members put their arms into a kettle of boiling water to extract pieces of the meat being cooked. The kettle represents their enemies, and the performance as a whole represents a battle with those enemies. A drum and pumpkin-gourd rattle accompany the dancers.

"The performers crouched low and moved round the fire. One man, sitting near a pole, kept the fire alive. He also stirred the water in the kettle until the meat began to boil. Then the singers would say, 'It is about ready.' The fire-tender poked the fire once more, and the Elk actor started up alone, blowing his whistle. Then everyone rose, and followed him round the fire. They approached the fire, but dodged away from it. The leader reached down the kettle with his bare arm and pulled out meat, splashing the others with the water. Everyone had to follow suit. Those last in line had the worst of it, for they were obliged to reach farther down, some even tilting the kettle" [Bear's-Teeth in Lowie 1915a:668–669].

Keeapaait
East Greenland Eskimo, *Arctic Coast*
Ammasalik (or Angmagsalik) wooden mask. These masks are considered to be old, one having been found in an ancient grave in the Ammassalik Fjord. However, by 1906 their ceremonial use was no longer known, and they were employed only as toys "for fooling or frighten-

ing the children, and when they died the masks were thrown into the sea together with their corpses. The masks brought me by Akernilik represented certain deceased persons whose names he gave me" [Thalbitzer 1914:639]. Similar masks, made from both wood and sealskin, are found among the Inuit on Baffin Island.

Keepers

This term is used in anthropology to designate those persons within a Native American culture who are responsible for the care of the group's most sacred items. Among the Gros Ventre there is a Keeper of the Sacred Flat Pipe and also a Keeper of the Feathered Pipe. Among the Cheyenne there is a Keeper of the Sacred Hat and a Keeper of the Sacred Arrows. Among the Lakota there is a Keeper of the Sacred Calf Pipe Bundle. And among the Arapaho there is a Keeper of the Northern Flat Pipe. In addition there is often a cokeeper assigned to these sacred objects.

Such highly sacred objects are generally kept secure in a bundle, which often includes associated objects. For example, the Feathered Pipe bundle of the Gros Ventre contains not only the original pipe itself, a single piece of grayish-brown stone, but also a staff between 3 and 4 feet in length that is completely covered in all kinds of bird feathers and an "image, made of stone and about eight inches long . . . which has the power to change its appearance" [Dusenberry 1961:22].

Annual rites are conducted with these most sacred items, many of which are the original or first sacred pipe, sacred arrow, etc. In most cases the origin of the object is attributed to a spirit being. For example, the Feathered Pipe of the Gros Ventre was given to them by *Bha'a*, the Storm Being. Hence rites with this sacred pipe are given "for rain and for the protection of the people against storms" [Dusenberry 1961:21].

Only those who are highly revered among their people attain the position of keeper, although in some cases the caretaker posts have followed family lineage. Usually the keeper is also a renowned shaman, but that is not a prerequisite for the position in most cases. The first keeper of the Gros Ventre's Feathered Pipe was Whistling Man. "After he had it for four years, the Pipe told him that every Keeper should have custody and care for a period of four years, and then the Pipe would tell the Keeper who should have it next" [Dusenberry 1961:23]. The last great keeper of the Feathered Pipe among the Gros Ventre was Bull Lodge, who died in the 1880s. Eight days prior to his death, Bull Lodge heard the voice of a spirit telling him he had only eight days to live. On the seventh day thereafter the spirit of a former pipe keeper appeared to him and gave him explicit instructions for a ceremony to be performed following his death that would bring about his resurrection.

> That day, Bull Lodge called his family together and told them of his vision and gave them the instructions that he had received. That night, his family was with him. About midnight, he told his family to go to bed—all except his eldest son and his wife. Suddenly, Bull Lodge made a noise like a bear and trembled. When he quit trembling, his son and wife looked at him and realized that he was dead.
>
> The family called the people in the camp together and told them of the prophecy. A great conclave was held to decide whether they should follow the instructions given them. In the end they decided that it was impossible to follow his instructions. The buffalo lodges and robes [part of the paraphernalia required] were gone [Fred Gone in Dusenberry 1961:26].

Kegeior
Yurok, *Oregon Seaboard*
Shaman [Kroeber 1925:66]. See *kegey*, EONAH, pp. 132–133.

Kelizruk
Yuit, *Arctic Coast*
Feathered wands carried by women during their Totem and Comic Dances [Hawkes 1914:16].

Kenaroq

West Alaska Eskimo, *Arctic Coast*
See *kinaroq*.

Keseruk

West Alaska Eskimo, *Arctic Coast*

A late-nineteenth-century Malemiut shaman. In 1940 the oldest man then living at Shungnak, named Pegliruk, recalled the performances of this particular shaman. In the first performance Keseruk would ask the people to make him a birch bow, about 3 feet long, and two arrows. These arrows were then used to seek answers, especially regarding the procurement of game. When the ceremony began,

"Keseruk used stone lamp light at first. He would say, 'Little persons coming now—both have bow and arrow.' Nobody can see them but Keseruk, because *angatkok* has a mind that goes out of the body when another, 'devil' [spirit], mind comes in. When he says those little persons have come, some people put Keseruk on top of a caribou skin, tie his feet together at the ankles, tie his hands tight behind him, tie his knees, and then pull the rope around his neck and under his knees and tie it. He can't move. Now they put the bow on his left side and the arrows on his right. They take charcoal and rub a wide black mark across both eyes.

"By the time Keseruk couldn't move, these people took drums and started to sing. Somebody is ready to put out the lamp. But they never put out the light right away. Keseruk says, 'When the little persons come, they will take my body and use it—when they start to speak, through me, you must put the lamp out.'

"Soon everybody shuts his eyes and sings, and the lamp goes out. Then they can hear Keseruk clapping his hands, and patting his feet on the floor, saying 'ooi, ooi.' Then they hear him let the bowstring go, but that arrow never hits the side of the house. After that Keseruk say, 'Now my arrow has got to the head of that creek over there—now it gets to the Noatak River—now it is some place else—' He follows the arrow like that."

At this point Pegliruk interrupted the narrative to say that people were not supposed to open their eyes during the seance. "Once when Roxie Douglass was about ten years old, Keseruk stopped and said, 'Roxie, don't look!' He knew about this in the dark.

"After those arrows went a long way," continued Pegliruk, "Keseruk would say they were turning around and coming back. 'Now they are back to Noatak River—now to that creek.' Then the people begin to get excited. They are afraid they will be hit. Keseruk says, 'As soon as those arrows come, light the lamp. Now!' he says. They light the lamp. Keseruk is still tied up in the same place, but the bow is under the rope on his back, and an arrow is stuck in each side of his neck, crossed in the middle of his body. The feathers at the ends of the arrows are all that are sticking out. Keseruk has on no clothes—only 'short pants.' Somebody pulls out the arrows. (If the arrowhead is left inside, this means something is wrong.) Then they take the ropes off Keseruk, and he picks up the drums and turns around to the doorway away from the light. When he turns back, the two arrows are on top of the drum. Every person looks at those arrows" [Pegliruk in Giddings 1961:15–16].

The returned arrows were inspected because they gave answers to questions. For example, if Keseruk wanted to know about the availability of caribou over on the Noatak River, the arrows would come back painted with blood and caribou hair if hunting was to be good.

In addition Keseruk had a bead divination ceremony acquired from the Raven spirit. "Another way Keseruk used to do was to ask for Raven. When Raven comes into his body, Keseruk says, 'Raven has my body.' A raven beak comes out of his mouth enough for people to see, and a raven voice says, 'Kahk-kahk-kahk.' After Raven, Keseruk takes his drum and puts a bead on top of the drum. They watch which way the bead rolls. If the bead is working, Keseruk takes the drum handle and throws the bead out through the skylight. Then he dances around the fireplace, singing a song telling where the bead has gone. He tells what he sees when the bead passes by different places. When the bead is coming back, Keseruk gets scared. He runs around the firebox. All at once he catches the bead and falls down. He gets weak—it is hard to breathe—but he has caught the bead. Then he tells what the bead means" [Pegliruk in Giddings 1961:17].

Keskamzit
Micmac, *Canadian Eastern Woodlands*
Power or medicine. *Keskamzit* most often comes suddenly and spontaneously upon an individual, as one source described: "A man acquired *keskamzit* for running. While he was walking, he found tracks, and followed in them. As he went farther, the distance between them gradually increased, until they were very far apart, and he was taking them in immense strides. Thereafter he had *keskamzit* for fast running" [Wallis and Wallis 1955:162–163].

Once a person obtains *keskamzit* he or she must keep secret the means by which it was acquired. If this taboo is broken, the power leaves. Abuse of one's *keskamzit* will also cause it to disappear. "A successful hunter who forgets the fundamental virtue of sharing his game liberally with others will lose his *keskamzit*" [Wallis and Wallis 1955:166]. Even excessive pride in the ownership of *keskamzit* is another form of abuse that will cause it to leave [Wallis and Wallis 1955:302].

Objects can also be imbued with *keskamzit*. Anomalies found in nature often serve as *keskamzit* charms. For example, "A man who was in the woods hunting found a piece of wood resembling a beaver, with eyes, nose, mouth, feet, and tail indicted. After that he had big *keskamzit* for beaver. If you find a stone that resembles a fish, you will have *keskamzit* for fishing. Always secrecy is essential" [Wallis and Wallis 1955:163].

Kethawn
Navajo, *Southwest*
Prayer stick [Sandner 1979:128]. Prayer sticks are a common form of prayer offering in the Southwest area, and different designs are used for different spirits. Most of them are short sticks, sometimes painted, to which certain feathers are attached. In some cases packets of corn pollen, ground cornmeal, etc., are also added.

Each *kethawn* is ritually constructed, accompanied by prayers and songs. It is then placed in an altar display to invoke the intended spirit. When the ceremony is finished, it is usually deposited at a special sacred site.

See *prayer feathers/sticks*.

Kicahoruksu
Pawnee, *Plains*
Evil spirits. This is a class of spirits that are the souls of deceased individuals. Such "ghosts" annoy the living. "Mysterious noises and occurrences, especially such as happen in the night, were attributed to their agency. Sometimes when shooting at an enemy or at game [when] they unaccountably missed, they would say that some of these shades [souls] had mischievously deflected the missile from its course" [Dunbar 1882:736].

Kichil woknam
Yuki, *California*
Literal translation: "obsidian initiation" [Kroeber 1925:191]. This is a special ceremony conducted by the Obsidian shamans of the Tanom (and perhaps the Lilshiknom) branch of Yuki. Kroeber [1925:192] referred to this ceremony as "shamanism partly organized into an approach to a society." Essentially, it was a course of training for future shamans. All children were subjected to a six-day ritual in which they received nothing to eat or drink for the first five days and only water on the sixth day. "On the fourth day there is a special ceremony, to which, besides the conducting [Obsidian] shamans and the children, only those of the people are admitted who have themselves passed through the initiation at some time. To the accompaniment of a particular song, the shamans thrust their sky-obsidians— that is, their long blades—into the children to

their stomachs, it is said, and twist them. Those who bleed at the mouth will be obsidian-doctors themselves; the others can not expect this career. Then, to another song, condor feathers are pushed into the patient youngsters so far that only the butt of the quill projects from their mouths. These are also twisted and signs of blood watched for" [Kroeber 1925:193].

This test only foreshadows a person's career as an Obsidian shaman. Usually such individuals do not become practicing shamans until adulthood.

On the seventh day the children are made to run up a steep hill. Those reaching the top will mature to become courageous and successful in war. Also on this day some of the Obsidian shamans perform power feats. In one scenario the Obsidian shaman "squats before a sky-obsidian [blade] that has been set upright and probes four times in the dry ground with a stick, singing. At the conclusion of his song he draws out the blade and digs the spot where it stood. He digs with his stick perhaps a foot down. Soon the hole fills with water. . . . The shaman is heavily paid for this exhibition" [Kroeber 1925:194]. According to another report "a Pomahanno'm shaman once announced that he had learned from his spirits that young condors were coming from heaven to be among the people. He set up three obsidian blades at equal distances apart and asked the onlookers to watch for the birds and join in his song when they approached. Soon two condors alighted to the north and south of the obsidians, first turned their heads away and then toward each other, and after sitting a short time flew away. This shaman was also well paid for the act" [Kroeber 1925:194].

Kila
Copper Eskimo, *Arctic Coast*
A special term used for a coat that is tied up and used in séances. During the Copper Inuits' shamanic performances a spirit enters the *kila.* Sometimes more than one spirit enters the *kila* over the course of the séance, or two spirits may enter it at the same time. Once the spirit entered

the *kila,* members of the audience put questions to it. The shaman holds the *kila:* If the bundle is heavy, the answer is negative; if it is light, the answer is affirmative. Apparently, anyone's coat may be used. But when a shaman named Higilak borrowed a coat from anthropologist Diamond Jenness to make a *kila,* the answers were reversed, with heavy indicating an affirmative answer, because the coat was from a white man [Jenness 1970:212].

A similar Inuit divination technique, known as *krilaq* (EONAH, p. 139), uses a rope tied about the head or leg of a person; the rope is then lifted by the shaman. Here again, differences in weight indicate either a positive or negative answer. This method "is practiced by the shamans on the plain south of the Yukon [River] mouth. If a man becomes ill they determine the character of his malady by tying a cord attached to the end of a stick to his head or a limb as he lies outstretched, and lifting it by the stick find from the weight of the part the character of the disease. If seriously affected the part is supposed to be very heavy, but becomes lighter or easier to raise as the malady passes away" [Nelson 1899:433].

See also *qilajoq.*

Kiła
Creek, *Southeast*
Literal translation: "knower" [Swanton 1928: 615]. Muskogee term for diviner. A *kiła* was often called upon to diagnose an illness before a shaman doctored the patient. In other cases the shaman performed this function. The *kiła* also functioned as a prophet.

> His diagnosis consisted merely in the examination of an article of clothing belonging to the sick man. From this he claimed to be able to determine the nature of the disorder and he sent back word accordingly. . . . The kiła was something of a clairvoyant and probably a juggler [shaman] also, and about this class many wonderful tales are told. . . . He could foretell death, sickness, or

crime, and in the last case he would sometimes send his dogs to punish the offenders.

It is asserted that a prophet could tell a person where to find a stolen horse; could shorten a road [rope?], making it draw together as if it were made of rubber; could make beads, finger rings, or bullets swim on the surface of the water; could throw a bead into the middle of a stream, make it swim toward shore, and cause another bead to swim out to meet it. He could determine whether a person's life was to be long or short by setting up a stake and making another object move toward it "by his power." If this reached the stake, the person's life would be long; if it fell short of it his life would be short [Swanton 1928:615].

Kilem
Maidu, *California*
See *dudl*.

Kílhlha
Creek, *Southeast*
See *owála*.

Kiluxin
Labrador Eskimo, *Arctic Coast*
Literal translation: "conjuring with a stick" [Hawkes 1916:132]. Divinatory ceremony. This term applies to divinations in which a shaman calls his helping spirit to answer questions put forth by members of the audience via a spirit-calling staff. For example, Tomasuk (see entry), a Southern Labrador shaman around the turn of the twentieth century, was called upon to conjure the spirits of deceased relatives. "He would blindfold the questioner, and rap three times on the ground with a stick. On the third rap, a spirit would come up, of whom he would make the inquiry desired. After the answer had been obtained, the spirit would be sent back by rapping three times on the ground again" [Hawkes 1916:132].

Another form of divining was recorded by Jens Haven, the first of the early Moravian missionaries along the coast of Labrador: "An Es-kimo stretched himself on his back on the floor; one of his bows was laid across his legs and tied fast to his left leg; a woman sat on his right side and laid his right leg over his left, by which the bow and string were moved. The moving of the string was regarded as an affirmative answer" [Haven in Hawkes 1916:133].

Kimauchitlchwe
Hupa, *California*
See *kitetau*.

Kimilue
Diegueño, *Peninsula*
See *echul*.

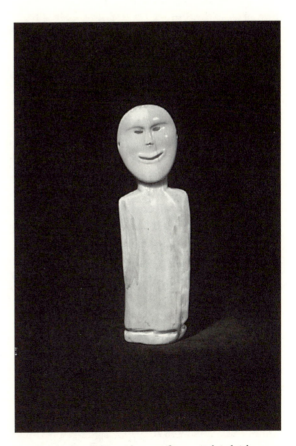

A carved ivory Eskimo shaman figure with inlaid copper eyes, Point Barrow.

Kimucwuminaw

Ottawa, *Canadian Eastern Woodlands*

North Wind [Cooper 1930:515]. If cold weather is desired, a figure of this spirit is made in snow. A similar form of weather medicine has also been noted among the Eastern Cree [Skinner 1911:59].

Kimvuanipinas

Ojibwa, *Canadian Eastern Woodlands*

Rain Thunder [Elizabeth Wasacase in Tarasoff 1980:172] or Rain Thunder Bird [Kimvauni-pinas in Tarasoff 1980:95]. The traditional name of Felix Panipekeesick, a Saulteaux shaman born around 1884. Both his father and grandfather (named Kwewich) were traditional shamans, and both passed their powers on to him. He said that he had spoken to their spirits. "My grandfather said you could talk to a spirit but you can't see him. He said: 'Supposing if I die, well, I'll go someplace. You'll call my name, and I'll want to talk to you myself although I'll be dead. But you won't see me. You'll just see my shadow! . . . When my father died I went out, you know. I went out in the bush [so nobody would see me] and started to talk. All at once I saw a shadow there. That was my father's shadow" [Pa-nipekeesick in Tarasoff 1980:88].

Kimvaunipinas inherited a number of abilities. For one, he owned (inherited or learned) the *Pitalgomik* (see entry) ceremony, although he is more renowned for his performance of the Rain Dance, which is often performed to heal the sick. Kimvaunipinas estimated in 1967 that he had healed around thirty people during his life. Of Salulteaux healing he said: "No matter what sickness you have, they got medicine for that" [Kim-vaunipinas in Tarasoff 1980:110]. Many of his more simple cures, such as those for nosebleeds, toothaches, cuts, and burns, involved the use of medicinal herbs.

The Rain Dance is also performed to produce rain. Of this Kimvaunipinas said, "I remember the dry years of 1938 or 1939, I guess. The local farmers helped me out to make a Rain Dance—so as to make rain. They used to collect money from farmers around here, and would give me $35 or $40 to make a Dance. They used to help me a lot [and] it helped [rain came]. Everytime, you know, when I make a Rain Dance a big rain usually comes in the next day or two" [Kimvau-nipinas in Tarasoff 1980:97–98].

Other powers included the ability to locate lost objects. Of this he said,

A fellow once [circa 1952] came to my place and told me about losing [two weeks prior] a team of horses. I went outside and started to pray. As I prayed, I started to talk, you know—started to know where these things are. I continued to pray—just like a soul—when we were talking about the spirit, you know. And somebody was standing there. But I didn't know who it was, and then he [the spirit] shows me where those horses are—where a lost bag was. So I went back into the house. Next morning this fellow come to me. He lives at Cowessess Reserve [the reserve immediately east of Sakimay]; they call him J. N. Gordan Lerat. That's the one that lost his horses. He came with a truck.

"All right, we'll go," I told him. So we went down. Just other side of Eliceborg [?] in the Valley, the second house—that's where his horses were, in a barn . . . I told him. Yes, I lead him to the place . . . and showed him where to get his horses. We brought his horses home on a truck" [Kimvaunipinas in Tarasoff 1980: 103–104].

On another occasion a man could not locate the farmer to whom he had sold his buckskin coat: "A young fellow once lost his buckskin coat which he sewed himself. He sold that buckskin to a farmer for five dollars. So I told him what place to go—the house and the farmer. He went and got a [his] coat" [Kimvaunipinas in Tarasoff 1980:104].

Kinaroq

North Alaska Eskimo, *Arctic Coast*

Dialectical variants: *kenaroq* (Ungalardlermiut); *kenarqoq* (mainland Alaska); *kenaijoq* (Kangianermuit); *kenaujaq* (Labrador); and *kenagpäk* and *kenarpäk* (Greenland) [Rasmussen 1941:23, 36]. Tikeramiut term for masks. The *kinaroq* is a power mask worn by a shaman during a ceremony. Such a mask is carved secretly in accordance with a shaman's visions. Once carved, the mask is brought to life and thereafter "fed" on a regular basis. When such a mask is worn, the *tunraq* (power) of the mask fills the shaman.

Some examples are the *jûk* (human) mask, which represents a female spirit used for ensuring good weather; the *kaupaq* (walrus mask) used to procure walrus; the *kukil-luneq* (wolf mask), through which the shaman "acquired the powers and abilities of a wolf—quickness, scent, and the *semililiti*: all the arts of the wolf, skill at attacking animals" [Rasmussen in Ostermann 1952:133]; and the *ertjeq* (white-fox mask) used for procuring caribou.

In Greenland, *kenagpäk* literally means "giantface," while the Labrador *kenaujaq* translates as "face-like" and *kenaijoq* translates as "which is a face" [Rasmussen 1941:61].

King, John
Objibwa, *Canadian Eastern Woodlands*

A Chippewa shaking-tent shaman, or *jizikiwinini* (see *jossokeed*), who was from the St. Croix band and lived at Sand Lake. In 1942 anthropologist Robert Ritzenthaler observed one of his performances and reported it in detail. It was held for a twenty-five-year-old male who, several months prior, had been diagnosed with incipient tuberculosis during an army physical. Subsequently, he spent six weeks at the Municipal Sanitorium in Chicago and then returned to his home for treatment by John King. Only because Ritzenthaler had driven the patient and his mother to the ceremony did John King allow him to observe it. Normally, King contended that he could not do his work when white people were around to observe him.

At the beginning of the ceremony, "the wigwam [shaking-tent lodge or *jiziken*] began

shaking very slowly. This seemed to be a signal for Charley [the ceremonial assistant] to start drumming rapidly on the Chief Drum and women to begin shaking their rattles. Soon the ji´zikən began shaking rather violently, and then slowed up again, and shook hard again. This went on for about five minutes (this is when the spirits come into the ji´zikən). Then a disguised voice [spirit] was heard and the drumming and rattling stopped" [Ritzenthaler 1953b:203].

Soon thereafter Mrs. John Butler told the spirit that she had sponsored the ceremony to have her son, Laurence, diagnosed and to find out if the spirit recommended any medicines for him.

The spirit said, "All right, I'll try. I've helped a lot of Indians and I'll see what I can do for this one." The spirit spoke to Laurence and told him to come closer. Laurence moved to a seat about 2 feet from the ji´zikən. The spirit asked Laurence if he could understand Chippewa and Laurence was slightly confused. Mrs. Butler told him to answer the spirit, so Laurence said that he could speak Chippewa (all the talking was, of course, in Chippewa).

The spirit then said, "If you believe in me, I will tell you the truth, but if you don't, I will tell you lies. Come closer and I will look at you." Laurence leaned a little closer, and the spirit said, "That isn't bad. That sickness will leave you." Mrs. King then told Mrs. Butler to ask the spirit to work on him, so Mrs. Butler spoke to the spirit and said, "I would like to have you doctor him and boda´nzik (blow on him) and tell me if there is any medicine that you know will help him."

The spirit said, "Drum for me and I'll see what I can do." So Charley started drumming and the women shook the stick rattles, and the wigwam began to shake hard and every once in a while the sound of blowing was heard. (Whoo', unvoiced. The sickness is supposed to be blown away from the person like this.)

The wigwam shook for a few minutes and then quieted down, the drumming stopped, and the voice of the spirit was heard again. It said, "That isn't a bad sickness and you can get over it by taking medicine." Every so often a spirit would talk in an unintelligible growl, and John King would say ani´ngwənə (all right then), as a sign that he understood what the spirit was saying in that special spirit language [Ritzenthaler 1953b:203–204].

The spirits then gave instructions for Laurence to follow, and the ceremony was brought to a close. "The wigwam began shaking, and when it shakes hard it means that a spirit is leaving. There must have been at least two spirits there, one who talked clear Chippewa and one who talked Chippewa in a growl, that no one could understand except the doctor. No drumming went on while the spirits left, and the wigwam shook hard a few times, then slowed down and stopped. The people got up and started home and Charley took all the blankets off the ji´zikən. John King stayed inside the wigwam in a kneeling position until all the blankets were off, then he crawled out and came over to me. 'Can you do that?' he said, in Chippewa, and I said 'gawi´n—no!' And he laughed" [Ritzenthaler 1953b:204].

Kinqalalala
Tlingit, *Northwest Coast*
Shaman [McDowell 1997:134]. See *ichta*.

Kinubik inäniwûk
Menomini, *Midwest*
Literal translation: "serpent men" [Skinner 1915d:183]. A society of witches. These are men who have obtained power from the mythical horned hairy snakes known as *misi-kinubik*.

Witches meet in secret to perform their rite. "First, the leader opens his medicine bundle containing an owlskin and spreads out its contents before his colleagues. Then he takes a little piece of mä´nätcikwon root and chews it, holding the kon´äpämik shell 'arrow' [a small cowrie shell] in one hand or in his mouth. He ha-

rangues the owlskin, commanding it to come to life, fly to the home of his enemy, and kill him with its magic arrow [the *kon´äpämik* shell], at the same time he motions with his hands in the direction he desires the owl to fly. The owl comes to life, and, imbued with the power of the horned snake, it flies off" [Skinner 1915d:182]. The witches then await the return of the owl, during which time special songs are sung to the owl.

> When the sorcerer has killed his victim, his magic arrows still remain in the body and it is necessary for him to recover them. He waits until the fourth night after the funeral, when, at midnight, he goes to the sepulcher. Here, through the virtue of the horned serpent, he changes himself into a bear and walks four times around the grave. At the fourth circuit, the coffin rises to the surface. The sorcerer orders the coffin to open, the lid comes off, and the corpse revives, shrieking for help. Its remorseless tormentor tears out its vitals, heart, and lungs with his claws. The coffin sinks back into the grave, and the ghoul, transforming himself into a firefly, returns to his lair, where he leaves his ghastly booty till the following day, when he returns. He makes a small fire over which the lungs and heart of his victim are partially roasted, and then devours them, singing songs in behalf of his monstrous patron [Skinner 1915d:183].

Besides changing into the form of various animals, "witches of this sort also travel in the shape of a ball of fire" [Skinner 1915d:185].

Kitdoñxoi
Hupa, *California*
Also: *kitdonghoi*. Witch or sorcerer. Sometimes these witches are referred to as "night runners," and their power is called the "night-runner machine" [Lake 1982:91]. "They are thought to possess some material object which gives them this evil power. There are several kinds of objects which are said to be used. One is said to consist

of a rib from a human being which has been fashioned into a bow. This is provided with a bowstring from the sinews of a human wrist. After repeating the prescribed formula the manipulator is thought to shoot a mystic arrow which causes death. One who possesses such an instrument can turn himself into a bear or a wolf and so pass unknown. He is able to run at great speed by pressing the instrument to his breast. These people are thought to travel at night" [Goddard 1903:64].

The objects used by the *kitdoñxoi* are also called *kitdonoi.* "These devices, or the knowledge of them, were secretly bought by resentful and malicious people from men suspected of possessing the unnatural powers. The *kitdonghoi* might sometimes be seen at night as something rushing about and throwing out sparks" [Kroeber 1925:136].

Kitetau
Hupa, *California*
Also: *kiteau* [Gifford 1940:49]. Chilula sucking shaman. This term is used for shamans who remove "pains" from the patient's body by sucking on the body where the "pain" is located. They are considered to be the most powerful shamans. As is customary, a diagnostic ceremony is held before the actual healing ceremony takes place. In some cases the *kitetau* performs both functions. However, the diagnostic part of the healing is most often done by a "dancing or singing" doctor, known as *tintachinwunawa* [Kroeber 1925:137]. The *tintachinwunawa* diagnoses the patient's illness either through direct clairvoyance or via a dream. He is the one "who determines the disease, its cause, and the steps necessary for recovery" [Goddard 1903:65]. He often uses a rattle made of the hooves of the deer. He is also called upon to locate lost objects "and give other such information" [Goddard 1903:66]. Among the Hupa some of the *tintachinwunawa* never suck disease objects from patients' bodies.

When a shaman acquires a guardian spirit, this spirit is also referred to as a "pain." "The 'doctor pain' is a spiritual power in the form of saliva. It is received by the neophyte as a gift from the spirit world and regurgitated, then reswallowed. The 'doctor spit' is cultivated through spiritual internalization during an altered state of consciousness, and later used as an ally to cure sick people, via healing power in the hands. I suppose it serves to be a liquid conduit [symbol] for the spiritual healing energy to pass from the doctor" [Lake 1982:78].

The shaman must be paid before treating a patient. However, if the patient dies within a year, the fee is returned. During the healing treatment the *kitetau* "applies his lips to the part affected and sucks with great power acquired by practice. After the sucking he vomits, continuing to bring up secretions until he produces the required 'pain' [the disease], probably in the form of coagulated matter" [Goddard 1903:66]. One form of healing treatment is the Brush Dance [Goddard 1903:67].

There are also herbalists, known as *kimauchitlchwe* [Kroeber 1925:137] or *kimautciltcwe* [Goddard 1903:65], who utilize herbs, often accompanied by a sacred chant or prayer, to heal illnesses among the Hupa. These herbalists are most closely associated with the treatment of pregnancy, childbirth, and less serious diseases, such as a chronic cough or annoying headache.

Kiuks
Klamath, *California*
Shaman [Gatschet 1893:112; Spier 1930:107]. Shamans are differentiated from others in that they have acquired more spirit power. All shamanism in this culture is completely individualistic; there are no shamanic societies. Both men and women become shamans, but male shamans outnumber females. Indeed, "women never acquire the prestige of men for they are

rarely credited with such unusual powers as men" [Spier 1930:107].

Among the Klamath, there are no specialized types of shamans as often observed in other cultures. For example, "weather is controlled by the songs of a special group of spirits, but, as elsewhere, this power is exercised by shamans in addition to their usual curative capacity" [Spier 1930:108]. Shamans usually have more than one helping spirit, and they are always seeking additional spirits to add to their powers. Sometimes their power comes in unsolicited dreams rather than through vision quests.

"The shaman's house is always an earthlodge [semisubterranean structure with a conical, earth-covered roof] and practically all performances take place within it. Not only larger than the ordinary dwellings, it differs from them in being decorated" with such items as grass-stuffed skins of various animals, wooden images of spirits, painted posts, etc. [Spier 1930:109]. In addition, the shaman wears a costume when performing. "The shaman's dress includes a band of woodpecker scalps worn on the forehead or around the neck, or a bunch of red-shafted flicker (yellowhammer) feathers attached to the top of the [mink, bear, or weasel skin] hat or worn as a necklace. Shamans alone wear these" [Spier 1930:110]. For certain ceremonies, such as the winter performances, the shaman's body is painted red. At other times his face is painted black. Bear-claw and bear-teeth necklaces are also commonly worn.

"While curing of necessity takes place at any time, shamanistic performances are given at only one time during the year" [Spier 1930:112]. This is at midwinter, around the end of January. Often shamans join together for these performances. Such a performance is called *wahla*, and it is conducted over the course of five days. During the performance of the *wahla*, the shamans display their powers for all to see.

Two tricks, swallowing fire and arrowheads, are part of every shaman's stock in trade. . . . The fire-swallowing trick (ko´pgŭs p'an, torches eating) is performed with the aid of an old lake trout spirit (tcwĭm or me´´yăs), or rather they say the spirit eats the fire. Five men stand in a row each holding a bundle of resinous wood slivers, ten inches long and two inches thick, called ko´pgŭs. The shaman dances in front of them, others dance vigorously with him while they sing. . . . The torches are lighted, the shaman snatches them in quick succession, puts out the fire with a gulp, and flings them aside.

The companion trick is swallowing arrowheads. . . . Perhaps twenty obsidian arrowheads are tied at intervals on a cord, which one man feeds to the shaman as he dances. He swallows these with the aid of certain bird spirits, or rather the spirits eat the blades. . . . A tule mat is arranged like a cape over the shaman who now seats himself. They sing the songs of the bear spirit, now represented in the shaman, to bring back the arrows. Soon they hear him cry out, "ha," as each blade flies back and sticks into the mat. This performance is called stŏpswa´lc. . . . Other shamanistic tricks are of the same order; various objects are swallowed, others are made to appear and vanish, or the stuffed animal skins in the lodge are brought to life. . . .

For the wood-swallowing trick, five, ten, or twenty small flat wooden splints, called wŏkda´lĭs, shaped like arrowheads, are hung from as many strings. A circle of old men dance about the shaman each dangling one of these. The shaman goes to each in turn, swallowing the splint held above his mouth. Another night he brings the splints back as in the arrowhead trick, using a different song. . . . They see the splints stuck into the mat with which is he wrapped. . . .

Shamans also have a trick of drinking huge quantities of water, four or five gallons, without stopping.

Corresponding to the series of swallowing tricks are several in which various things, fish, seeds, frogs, and blood are made to appear in a basket. . . . Throughout the affair the shaman remains on his bed; no one goes near the basket except the man who inspects it each time. . . .

The pond-lily seed trick is similar. . . . The shaman has an old woman half-fill a basket with water and cover it with a smaller one. He lies well back toward the wall during the performance, rising only to smoke. . . . [After singing several songs of the frog spirit] when she looks again the basket is filled with pond-lily seeds. All the old men look at it. When he sings the frog's final song, she finds the seeds gone and a tiny frog in their place. . . .

Pat Kane described a performance which he saw when a little boy at Pelican bay. The shaman held a fire dance during the day. Then he told the people to place various stuffed skins on the floor of the lodge: mink, weasel, a shitepoke (tuwa´), and owl. He sang songs for each of the animals. He first sang one of the shitepoke's songs and told them to watch whether it moved. It did not. He sang its second song and the bird [shitepoke] walked around pecking at the ground. It had been a dried skin for ten years or more. He sang the mink's song three times. The mink moved about holding a little minnow in its teeth. He sang a song of the weasel spirit. The animal rose and danced, holding up his fore paws [Spier 1930:114–118].

"The shaman's art is not confined to these winter performances, but is invoked during the year, not only for curing, but whenever his ability to manipulate conditions and to prophesy is needed. The weather is controlled, fish are made to run, lost articles and thefts discovered, the fate of a war party is foreseen, and the community protected against malignant spirits" [Spier 1930: 118]. Each activity is exercised only through certain spirits. For example, one shaman "could make the weather change. He had two spirits, crow to stop the falling snow and the water snail to bring rain when it grew too cold. While other shamans could make the wind blow, the snow drift, and cause it to thunder [the prairie chicken makes the loudest thunder]" [Spier 1930:119].

Sucking is the most common treatment for illness. Curing is usually conducted at night in the lodge of the shaman, but the ceremony often continues into the next day, during which time the smoke-hole of the lodge is covered to keep out the light.

The patient always lies with his head toward the east, the shaman sits or kneels at his feet, the speaker [who repeats what the spirits are saying] near his shoulders. The singers sit back of the shaman, the prompter near-by. There is no dancing during a cure. . . . The general plan of the performance is first a series of songs to call the sprits to work through the shaman's person; these spirits helpers then tax other spirits with causing the sickness in a second set of songs; finally the shaman tells what he has seen and sucks out the sickness. . . . The shaman begins to suck when he sees with spirit eyes where the sickness is located. . . . Before he sucks, he sticks his finger into water and sucks it. Then he bites the body hard and sucks. . . . When the shaman finally draws the sickness out, his head goes back, his eyes close, and blood streams from his mouth. If they want to know what it is, he lets someone feel it on his tongue or spits it into his own palm. . . . This is always something tiny: a bug, the nail of a frog, or the frog itself, a snake, a rattlesnake fang, or a red-shafted flicker feather. When they have felt it on his tongue, the shaman, representing the spirit, eats it [Spier 1930:124–126].

The shaman is paid only if the cure is successful. See also *spŭtu*.

Klislah
Kwakiutl, *Northwest Coast*

A renowned Kitimat shaman who died around 1895. He was remembered for having walked on fire to demonstrate his powers. A large fire was started, and Klislah "worked himself into a frenzy [trance] until he had reached a state when he was ready to walk in the fire. The people examined his body, especially his feet. This was not difficult, as he had taken off his garments. When the people let him go, with a wild yell he jumped into the fire and walked through it four times. On his coming out of the fire the people again examined his body and saw that he was entirely unharmed" [Christopher Walker in Lopatin 1945:75].

During one performance when Klislah had gone to the Bellabella to doctor a sick woman, he suddenly "grasped two men, stripped them, and placed them by the fire, back to back. They were, as it were, glued to the spot by some invisible force until the shaman had danced round the fire four times. Only after he, on finishing his dance, commanded the two men to separate could they move and again take their seats in the hall" [Christopher Walker in Lopatin 1945:75].

Klo'o
Zuni, *Southwest*
Literal translation: "hard" [Parsons 1956:325]. This term is used to refer to sacred offerings of shell or minerals, such as mica, hematite, turquoise, or abalone. These offerings are made to bless prayers and certain actions, such as killing a deer.

Koca pahtcikan
Cree, *Canadian Eastern Woodlands*
Also: *kosabałcigan* [Cooper 1930:517]. The structure in which the Plains Cree variation of the Ojibwa Shaking Tent Ceremony (EONAH, pp. 246–249) is performed. The lodge is approximately 4 feet in diameter and stands about 5 feet high. It consists of 5-inch-diameter poles about 6 feet long set upright 2 feet into the ground, around which a willow hoop frame is built [Mandelbaum 1940:261]. The structure is then covered with hides. Its main use is in divining answers to questions given to a shaman. Such divinations only take place after dark.

See also *kosabandjigan, Owl Thunder*.

Koitse
Klamath, *California*
Witch or sorcerer [Spier 1930:121]. A sorcerer is usually a powerful male shaman who has as his spirit helper an animal that kills, such as a snake, wolf, coyote, weasel, or golden eagle. Only an equally powerful shaman can catch the spirit sent

by a sorcerer and destroy it. When such an evil spirit is caught, it is held between the palms of the shaman, who then submerges it for a long duration in a basket of water. "Then he exhibits it, a tiny lizard, for example. During all this time blood gushes from his mouth; he can neither sing nor speak. Soon after this some powerful foreign shaman will die, for they have caught his spirit" [Spier 1930:121].

Kokimunyi
Keres, *Southwest*
Magical power [Boas 1928:277]. This is the term used by the Laguna Pueblo people for the supernatural power associated with both spirits and shamans.

Kopati
Maidu, *California*
The term used by the Nisenan (Southern Maidu) for Bear shamans. In earlier times the *kopati* "actually turned into bears and in this form killed people" [Beals 1933:390]. Usually a Bear shaman assumed the form of a grizzly. "With the aid of his supernatural appearance, the bear shaman was in a better position to commit an assassination if he so desired than an ordinary person. The belief in these bear-men must have been very strong, for it survives vividly in the minds of old people from whose memory many other things have faded. And one and all are agreed that many Indians were killed by these creatures. Nearly all had seen them in their youth in human form" [Beals 1933:391]. This transformation was made possible by rubbing the shaman's body with an herb reported to grow in water. To change back to human form, he either jumped into the water or used another herb, which was blown over his body.

The following is an account of a Bear shaman who used rattlesnake medicine to accomplish his transformation. The informant had heard this from Henry Charlton, who died around 1929: "Henry's grandfather had quarrel with wife, who went into hut in rage. Henry followed to door. Took dried rattlesnake, threw on fire, turning over and over until snake became alive. Rubbed snake all over body. Then lay down like bear, got up, walked around like bear, hair grew over body, looked like bear all over except his hands, which remained human. Finally rushed through back of hut, yelling like bear, chased, killed wife, leaving her all torn with marks as though made with awl. Then entered spring, came out like man" [unidentified informant in Beals 1933:391].

In some cases the Bear shaman also became a doctor. In the Nisenan area the Bear shamans in recent times were known to have come from the Auburn area of Placer County. None were reported for Nevada County. Also in more recent times many Bear shamans utilized elaborate bearskin suits, which leads the nonmystical anthropologists to believe that all such transformations were based in costume.

Kopichoki
Hopi, *Southwest*
Cedar-bark fuse—a long, wrapped bundle of shredded cedar bark, about 1 inch in diameter and 8 inches long, that is used during certain ceremonies for lighting ceremonial reed cigarettes *(chonotki)*.

Kopirshtaia
Keres, *Southwest*
Cochiti (Pueblo) general term for *kachinas* (see entry; also *katsinas*—a class of spirits) and sacred fetishes held by their religious societies [Lange 1959:247]. Examples are the *iariko* (EONAH, p. 113), the *mile* (see EONAH, p. 175), and the *yaya* (EONAH, pp. 325–326). The term can also refer to "a deity or supernatural, a ghost, a soul" [Lange 1959:247].

Kosabandjigan
Ojibwa, *Canadian Eastern Woodlands*
Dialectical variants: *kosabatcigan* (Cree) [Cooper 1930:517]; *kocapahtcikan* [Mandelbaum 1940:261] (see entry); *kushapatshikan* (Montaignis) [Armitage 1991:83]. Lodge for the Shaking Tent Ceremony (EONAH, pp. 246–249). This well-known conjuring ritual, held in a cylindrical tent, is found in various forms throughout much of North America. In this region this particular form of divination flourishes side by side with the *Midewiwin* (EONAH, p. 174), known also as the Grand Medicine Society.

Another Ojibwa term used for the cylindrical tent ceremony is *djesikiwin*.

Koshare
Keres, *Southwest*
Also: *kashale, kossa* [Parsons 1939:129]. A clown society. "At San Felipe all of the Flint shamans are *Koshare*" [White 1930:612]. Normally the Flint shamans are members of the Flint society or *Hictiani* (EONAH, pp. 105–106). The Flint society is a curing society and is also responsible for war medicines. However, "the association of the Flint society with the warriors is a primary one and not derived from the Flint-Koshare affiliation" [White 1930:613]. Thus "the War Chiefs and their assistants must always guard the medicinemen at their cures to protect them from witches" [White 1930:613].

Kosksstakjomŏpista
Blackfoot, *Plains*
Beaver medicine bundle [Wissler 1912a:204]. Literal translation: "beaver-bundled-up" [Wissler 1912a:169]. Those who own such a bundle are called Beaver men and also *ijŏxkiniks,* "those having the power of the waters" [Wissler 1912a:169]. These particular bundles are quite possibly the largest medicine bundles found in North America, often with the contents being placed in half a buffalo hide and the entire bundle being contained in an elkskin painted red.

The essential contents for each bundle listed by Wissler [1912a:169] include: "several beaver skins, entire; a pipe; two buffalo ribs; buffalo tail; buffalo hoofs; a digging stick; skins of muskrat, weasel, white gopher, badger, prairie dog, antelope kids, deer kids, mountain goat kids, mountain sheep kids; tail of the lynx or wildcat; scalplocks; skins of loon, yellow-necked blackbird, raven, blackbirds, woodpeckers, sparrows, crow, ducks, and several birds we were unable to identify; buffalo rocks wrapped in wool; wristlets of wildcat claws to be worn by the woman."

The owner of a Beaver medicine bundle has the power to forecast weather. (It is also the duty of the bundle owner to keep a tally of the days, using sets of sticks kept in bags.) The bundle is officially used during the tobacco planting and harvesting rituals, and its use is also connected to the Sun Dance bundle. In addition, the bundle is employed to call buffalo for hunting. In fact, the most powerful songs associated with the Beaver bundle are those used to handle the buffalo [Wissler 1912a:207]. However, any person can call upon the power of this bundle by making a vow, usually only when in dire need, to give a feast to the Beaver men.

Kotikäne
Keres, *Southwest*
Also: *Kotikyanne* [Tedlock 1994:162]. The Zuni *kachina* society to which every adult male belongs. *Koko* (EONAH, p. 137), or *kokko,* is the Zuni term for the standardized Pueblo term *kachina* (or *katsina, katchina, katcina,* etc.). Unlike most other Pueblo people, among whom *kachinam* are found throughout many different medicine societies, the Zuni have concentrated the responsibility for *kachina* performances almost entirely into the hands of the *Kotikäne* [Tedlock 1994:162]. The Zuni are best known for their *kachina* dances, in which each male dons a sacred mask. "The mask is the corporeal substance of the god and in donning it the wearer, through a miracle akin to that of the Mass in Roman Catholic ritual, becomes a god" [Bunzel 1932a:517].

These masks are second in sacredness to the *etowe* of the *Uwanami* (see entry), but the *kachina* dances "have become the most potent of rain-making rites" [Bunzel 1932a:517]. Because these sacred masks are alive, they receive "daily offerings of food from some female member of the household" [Bunzel 1932a:517] in which they are kept.

In rare cases females are initiated into this society as a means of curing them of mental illness caused by contact with supernatural beings. Boys are initiated into this society between the ages of ten and twelve. An interesting aspect of this initiation is the whipping of the boys by the *kachinam.* "The katcinas whip to instill awe for the supernatural, but also to remove sickness and contamination" [Bunzel 1932a:518]. Otherwise, the Zuni hold in contempt and horror the whipping of children for punishment.

The *Koticäne* is organized into six divisions known as *upawe.* Each division meets in a different *kiva* (EONAH, p. 136), and each group dances, both indoors and outside, at least once during the summer, fall, and winter. "At the indoor dances not all participants need be masked, and where no mask is used the same magical power resides in the face and body paint" [Bunzel 1932a:519]. Because of the dire need for rain, the summer *kachina* dances are marked by an air of intense solemnity, while the winter dances are much more lighthearted and amusing. Following the first summer dance, "until rain falls the participants may touch neither food nor drink, nor engage in any unnecessary conversation. They must, of course, observe sexual continence" [Bunzel 1932a:520].

In addition to the *Kotikäne,* the Zuni also have a medicine society of *katchina* priests. "They are the most feared and the most beloved of all Zuñi impersonations. They are possessed of black magic; in their drum they have the wings of black butterflies that can make girls [sexually] 'crazy'" [Bunzel 1932a:521]. The masks of this society derive power from a different order of spirits. In addition to rain-making powers, they also have powers to control the fecundity of their crops.

See also *lhatsina* and *tuviku.*

Kowákocî
Seminole, *Southeast*
See *Coacoochee.*

Kuahu
Hawaiian, *Pacific*
Shaman's altar [Handy 1968:119]. A shaman's altar was usually kept in the *mua,* "men's quarters."

Kue

Tewa, *Southwest*

"Child rock" or "small rock" [Hill 1982:255] of the Santa Clara Pueblo. Small anthropomorphic fetish figures kept along with cornmeal in a wall niche located near the entrance of a house or in one or more inner rooms. The head of a household will get up before sunrise, take a small pinch of cornmeal from this altar niche, go to the doorway, throw the meal toward the east, fold his arms, and say a prayer to the rising sun.

Küïtü

Hopi, *Southwest*

Also: *küïta*, *kütü* [Stephen 1936:1235]. A ceremonial mask of the "pot helmet type" [Stephen 1936:1235], which is cylindrical and covers the face and head [Parsons 1939:339]. "The average size of the küï'tü is 9 in. high, 7½ in. in diameter. When the mask is put over the head the wearer becomes the same as one of the Na´nanivak moñ´mowitü, Chiefs of the Directions, the mask is the same as O´mauwû, Cloud, it is O´mauwû, i.e., the clouds that rest over the heads and upon the shoulders of the Chiefs of the Directions; a man may possess one or more masks, some have three; the masks are personal property, they do not belong to any society; at the death of the owner the mask goes to his son, brother, or nephew" [Stephen 1936:1235].

Kukini

Maidu, *California*

The Northern Maidu term for a helping spirit. It can also mean mysterious powers [Dixon 1905: 265]. The term usually appears as *kakini* (EONAH, p. 129) in other Maidu areas, but Kroeber [1932:379, n. 251] also recorded the use of *gakini* for a helping spirit. The Maidu use *saltu* or *shaltu* (the word is rendered differently by different anthropologists) as well [Kroeber 1932:379], which is the Patwin terms for a helping spirit.

"These beings are regarded as residing at definite spots, to which in particular the sha-mans go to gain power. Every shaman must have one or more of these as his guardian spirit or spirits, and they aid him in all that he does. He also, of course, may have the different animal spirits. Those of the rocks and little lakes are, however, very powerful. At times the shaman calls them to the dance-house; and they are supposed to enter by the smoke-hole, and hang head downward therefrom. They are in appearance like people, but always have the tongue lolling; and, as they hang head downward, the tongue reaches to the ground" [Dixon 1905:265].

Kukini is also used as the term for the spirit impersonators that appear at certain dance rituals.

Kuraurukaru

Pawnee, *Plains*

A secret order of shamans, restricted to those who could achieve some remarkable success with the mystery powers. New members underwent a period of probation and training. "The duration of the pupilage varied according to the candidate's aptitude in mastering the mysteries of the craft. A considerable initiatory fee was demanded, and an additional fee at certain stages of the course" [Dunbar 1880:336].

Shamans of this order were mainly sucking shamans (EONAH, pp. 264–266). The patient's illness was most often diagnosed as some foreign object in his body, which was usually located where the pain was concentrated. The cure was to suck this object from the patient's body. "The doctor would often after long sucking expectorate a pebble, a fragment of bone, or even an arrow-head. . . . Sometimes violent friction, pressure, or a sort of kneading of the ailing parts was tried. At other times they attempted to frighten away the disturbing spirit by noises, as muttering, yelling, barking or growling; or by strange posturing as of a wolf, a buffalo, or bear; or by angry demonstrations, as brandishing a war-club or a tomahawk, and threatening to strike the affected part" [Dunbar 1880:338].

Kusabi
Paiute, *Basin*

The name of a water insect used by the Northern Paiutes for bringing luck in fishing. "These are dried and carried on the person while fishing. This charm only works for fishing. Sometimes some of the dried insects are put on the nets before starting to fish. They are chewed and spat on the fish nets or lines. At the same time the man says, 'this is your own meat. You better come to it and smell it.' It is thought that these insects come from fish" [Park in Fowler 1989:41].

Kushapatshikan
Montagnais, *Canadian Eastern Woodlands*

The Innu term for the Shaking Tent Ceremony (EONAH, pp. 246–249). Innu elder Mathieu André described this ceremony as he witnessed it as a youth:

> The ritual must take place in the darkness, because the shaman is looking for the light in the animal (master's) eyes. As soon as the shaman enters the tent, it starts to shake, the poles bend and flatten on all sides. A whistling sound like a strong wind in the trees can be heard.
>
> Then the buzzing of black flies is heard, and they attack the tent. Once inside, the flies hurl themselves against the walls. They are said to be the spirits of the animals the shaman has killed. The sounds of animals can then be heard, the cries of caribou, geese, (and other birds). You really have the impression you're on a duck hunt.
>
> Next, someone is heard speaking inside the tent, what we call "kainnuaimit," or one who speaks Montagnais or "mishtapeu." He acts as interpreter for the animals, the shaman, and the people asking the questions. Everyone takes part in the rite: children, adults, elders. It lasts several hours [André in Armitage 1991:82].

During the summer the ceremony was conducted in a conical tent made of caribou hides and erected outdoors. In the winter this same shaking tent was set up inside another tent. The ground was covered with freshly picked fir boughs. Only men conducted this ceremony, but women assisted. The power of the shaman to endure this ceremony "could be gained only through hunting. A hunter obtained some spiritual power each time he killed an animal" [Armitage 1991:82].

The last known performance of the *kushapatshikan* was conducted around 1973 by the Innu at Sheshatshit [Armitage 1991:83].

See also *kosabandjigan*.

Kusiut
Bella Coola, *Northwest Coast*

Plural: *kukusiut*. One of two secret societies found in this culture. (The other is the *Sisaok* society.) The term *kusiut* is also applied to a member of the society. The term comes from *siut*, meaning spirit [McIlwraith 1948, vol.2:1]. Membership in the society is based "on the validation of an ancestral *kusiut* name and of the prerogative to perform one of the many *kusiut* dances" [Stoot 1975:27]. "Validation" in this case was accomplished through the distribution of goods. The society usually begins their dances in early November, and they continue until late February or March.

Each *kukusiut* of the society has one or more helping spirits from which he or she receives the powers to perform. Most members have only one spirit, but some have two or three, and one man in the 1920s was known to have six. Most of these spirit powers had been obtained by former relatives who had had direct contact with a spirit being, and the powers thereof were then transferred to subsequent generations. "If an individual inherits prerogatives with the same patron [spirit] from two different relatives, he can merge these to give a composite dance, with consequent additional power" [McIlwraith 1948, vol. 2:21]. However, some powers are the result of a person's own direct contact with a spirit. (In the past, even slaves who had encounters with a spirit were eligible for membership into this society.) In addition, each *kusiut* has a particular power spot somewhere in the vicinity where his or her power had been initially deposited and still resides. Each of these power spots are simultaneously guarded by a supernatural woman named *Anoolikwotsäix* [Stoot 1975:28].

Both males and females are initiated into the society but usually not until they are at least twenty years of age and most often older. During the *kusiut* initiation ceremony neophytes are assisted by a *siki*. These are persons who have "the professional prerogative of acting as healer to every novice" [McIlwraith 1948, vol. 2:34]. Of their performance McIlwraith [1948, vol. 2:34–35] noted:

One of the *siki* contorts himself in an amazing manner, presses his hands against his stomach as if to force something from it, and rolls from side to side on his haunches, until at length he produces, as if from his body, a rock crystal. He waves this to and fro in his hands, then goes through the motion of throwing it to his partner; the crystal disappears! . . . It has entered the other *siki* who falls to the floor as if stricken down by the powerful object given to him. . . . Slowly he pulls himself together, rising at intervals as if crushed beneath a heavy weight, and writhes until he finally produces a rock crystal from his stomach. . . . All this time a *kusiut*, it does not matter who, has been drinking water at intervals and spitting it out over the face of X [the initiate], "to strengthen him." When X has received the stone [crystal], the beating on the floor-boards, stilled during the transference of the crystal, breaks out again with full din. After a short interval the first *siki* stops the noise, goes through the same contortions and produces, apparently from his stomach, another rock crystal, which as before he throws across to his partner who falls down, and later passes it to X. Again the beating on the floor is started. The same ritual is carried out until four, or sometimes only two, rock crystals have been given to X [McIlwraith 1948: vol. 2:34–35].

Following this the *siki* kneads the back of the initiate's neck, drawing out his spirit. The *siki* then takes the spirit "in his cupped hands to the fire where he scoops up some ashes which he puts into his mouth and chews" [McIlwraith 1948: vol. 2:35–36]. In so doing the *siki* alters the spirit of the uninitiated person into that of a *kusiut,* which is then reinserted into the initiate.

During their dance performance *kusiuts* either don beechwood masks or paint their faces to represent their particular helping spirits. In addition each *kusiut* has a whistle, made from two pieces of wood glued together, that is blown to announce the presence of spirits during the ceremony. The most powerful spirit is that of Thunder, and the person who has this power is the senior *kusiut*. The power associated with this person is "the ability to summon all the supernatural beings to witness the dance" [Stoot 1975:83]. During his visit to the Bella Coola in the 1920s, McIlwraith recorded over forty different powers associated with the *kusiut* dancers.

Kúsuineq
West Greenland Eskimo, *Arctic Coast*
Also: *kusuineq* (East Greenland) [Kroeber 1900: 307]. The practice of sorcery [Birket-Smith 1924: 455]. This term is used for a single act of sorcery. The habitual practice of *kusuineq* constitutes *ilisineq* (sorcery—see *witchcraft* entry) [Merkur 1989:12].

Kuwanheptiwa, Jay
Hopi, *Southwest*
A shaman from Second Mesa during the middle of the twentieth century. In the 1930s his practice was based on the fact that he was a twin since the Hopi believe that a "gift for healing but not for shamanistic power was also thought to be possessed by individuals who were twins in embryo" [Levy 1994:319–320]. Later, he became a sucking shaman and extracted disease objects from sick individuals.

Although some authors have reported that the Hopi shamans did not use trance states, anthropologist Jerrold Levy and his family underwent a healing ceremony conducted in 1964 by Kuwanheptiwa in which the shaman did go into a trance state. Levy's account follows:

I, my wife, and our children sat facing Kuwanheptiwa, who, without preliminaries, pressed a black obsidian projectile point against various parts of my body. Returning the point to his bag, an ordinary woman's black purse, he announced that our blood was bad and that he would draw it out. He then produced a projectile point, some three inches long, of milky white quartz with a slight tint of rose at the tip. This he proceeded to press against various parts of my torso. As he did this, the rose color spread and intensified until the whole blade was a deep, rich, rose color. This process was repeated with my wife, who later told me she had also seen the point change color from white to rose. Kuwanheptiwa then sat back, announcing that the bad blood had been removed and that he must determine what had caused it.

Presenting his profile to us, he proceeded to inhale deeply, inducing a trance state by hyperventilating. There was no agitation; all was deliberate and calm. He remained in this state for only a minute. After regaining consciousness, he announced that he had seen the witch, a Navajo who had placed around our home on the Navajo reservation several arrow points, which he proposed to remove. The illness would be dispelled but the witch would not be harmed. Should this strategy prove ineffective it would be necessary for him to turn the evil back on the witch and kill him. Because the second procedure was dangerous, he preferred to use it only as a last resort.

Kuwanheptiwa then instructed one of our relatives to stand by him with paper towels to catch the arrow points he was going to "suck" from our home. Once again, hyperventilation induced a trance. After only a few seconds, he began to regurgitate convulsively into the towels. From where we sat we could not see the five small black arrow points our relative said she caught and disposed of over the western edge of the village [Levy 1994:309–310].

Kwalxqo
Twana, *Northwest Coast*
A form of power. Around 1870 an old man named Sdayaltxw received this power "from an old stump full of water on the top of a hill" [Frank Allen in Elmendorf 1993:188]. The Twana held a special ceremony in which a shaman named Doctor Bob helped bring out this power in Sdayaltxw. The following is an account of how Sdayaltxw displayed this power during his ceremony:

> And then he [Sdayaltxw] stopped [dancing and singing] and said to his daughter, "You get ready for me. Get things ready now." So his daughter got a bucket of water and sdayaltxw took it and drank it down. She got another bucket and he drank that. And another and another. And when he had drunk the fourth bucket his son Bob said, "Don't give him any more! He'll do a bad thing if you give him any more." So they stopped at the fourth bucket. And where was that water? I was there and I saw that old man drink those four buckets of water and his stomach didn't stick out or anything. That water went to his power, to that old kwalxqo stump!
>
> Now when sdayaltxw got on his fifth bucket he would start to piss. The water would run right out of him, and he would fill up the bucket again with the water he pissed out, and drink it again and keep going that way. Over and over again he would drink that bucket down, that's the way he showed his power. But they wouldn't give him more than four buckets this time. So he just got up and sang and danced [Frank Allen in Elmendorf 1993:189].

Kwaneman
Comox, *Northwest Coast*
Clairvoyant. Clairvoyants predict the future. One account described them in some detail: "[They] knew what was going on at distant places and could predict visits, see magic being worked, and so on. When they called upon their spirits (by song) for enlightenment, they shook and gasped in true possessed fashion but with control, just as shamans did. Clairvoyants with power from dead people or owls were thought to be especially qualified to relieve the oppression which settled upon people who were troubled by ghosts in any way [ghost sickness]. Insofar as they attempted

to dispel afflictions of this nature, they were really specialized shamans" [Barnett 1955:150].

Kwere
Tewa, *Southwest*

A generic term used by the residents of the Santa Clara Pueblo for members of their Winter Moiety. The Winter Moiety is in charge of all religious ceremonies from late October or early November until late February or early March. The moiety is divided into three hierarchical groupings, with the *Kwere* being the lowest in rank. The second rank is the *Oxu wa,* the Winter Kachina organization, and the highest ranking group is the *Oyike,* the Winter Managing society [Hill 1982:208].

The *Oxu wa* members are under the direct supervision of two selected members of the *Oyike,* known as the *pa re,* "the elders" or "fathers of the kachina" [Hill 1982:210]. The *Oxa wa* is limited to males, but the *Oyike* has both male and female members. Males, however, cannot become members of the *Oyike* without passing through the *Oxu wa.*

The *Oyike* is basically an esoteric religious society headed by a person known as the *cacique.* He is ceremonially known as *Oyike sendo* [Hill 1982:212]. His is the highest office in the pueblo, and the position is held for life.

A person could choose to join either the Winter or Summer Moiety. However, initially children are dedicated by their parents and initiated into either the Summer or Winter Moiety around the age of six. Ideally these moiety initiations are held about every six or seven years, so ages of the children participating vary accordingly.

See also *xa zhe.*

Kxói
Nootka, *Northwest Coast*

Makah term for medicine. This term refers to power inherent in an object (i.e., a charm, an amulet, etc.). A person who finds such a power object, unlike a shaman on a vision quest, receives no sacred song with the object, but as long as he retains it in his possession, he keeps its power. An individual rarely speaks to others about his or her *kxói,* and the power object is usually kept hidden lest someone steal it and obtain its power. The owner of a *kxói* also has the right to sell it, thus conferring its power to the new owner.

This term is also applied to plants used in healing. However, the power that shamans receive for healing is known as *hitáktákxe* (see entry) versus *kxói.*

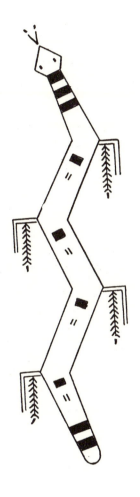

Lahatconos
Wintun, *California*

Wintu ceremonial initiation dance for novice shamans. The name comes from the Wintu stem *laha,* which means to go into trance [Du Bois 1935:94]. Both unmarried men and women can participate, usually when they are between the ages of fourteen and thirty-five. The ceremony is held in an earth lodge and conducted by older shamans.

"The ceremony began in the evening. The shamans and the candidates danced naked [in the earth-lodge] around a manzanita-wood fire and sang to invoke the spirits. Dancing lasted all night. . . . If a spirit found a candidate suitable it entered his body, usually through his ears. Thereupon the behavior of the novice became frenzied. His body jerked convulsively, saliva poured from his lips, and blood might flow from his mouth and nostrils" [Du Bois 1935:89]. "In a moment another whistling may be heard as the spirit touches the house-top and goes in. Another man or woman falls; the spirit has entered that one. The persons into whom spirits have entered know nothing. They become as if crazy, as if they had lost their wits. They try to go to the housetop. Some try to climb the central pole; some want to leave the sweat-house [earth-lodge]; they know nothing for half an hour perhaps" [Curtin 1898:512].

Attending shamans suck on the novices—on forehead, breast, back, arms—to purify the candidates. The shamans then transfer some of their power via a feather. "When they have finished sucking, the doctor sings again, and puts a yellowhammer's feather into each ear of the candidate. The feather may go in [the ear] out of sight, or the doctor puts it on the person's head, and the feather may sink through his skull" [Curtin 1898:511].

Following this acquisition of power, the novice remains under the watch of senior shamans in the lodge for five days. During this time, one report noted, "it seems probable that instruction included methods of sucking out poisons [healing], for which the tongue had to be rolled in a particular fashion. . . . Among the legerdemain (EONAH, p. 151) accomplishments [associated with shamanic powers] were those of extinguishing a lighted brand at a distance, and of sucking coals from the bottom of a basket or sparks from the end of a fire stick used in the roasting of venison. Informants stressed the idea that much power was to be derived from 'eating fire'" [Du Bois 1935:89].

Lahul
Twana, Northwest Coast

Disk-game gambling powers [Elmendorf 1960: 490]. This was a *cshalt* (see entry) power that enabled its owner to win at this game.

Lashowane
Zuni, Southwest

Also: *lashowanne* [Stevenson 1904:517] The hanging feathers from a prayer stick [Parsons 1939:280]. When assembling a prayer stick the feathers attached around the stick are referred to as the dress, mantle, or blanket of the stick, while the hanging feathers are referred to as the hair.

See also *prayer feathers/sticks*.

Laying on of hands
Northwest Coast

This is the main technique of healing in the Indian Shaker Church (EONAH, pp. 245–246), where "healing holds a position of functional primacy in the church, to which worship is second" [Valory 1966:67]. The major difference in using this form of healing is that it is not preceded by a diagnostic ceremony, as usually occurs with shamanic healing. The laying on of hands manifests itself in three main ways: brushing, rubbing, and a push-and-pull motion. In all cases the patient is seated on a stool.

Brushing is the most common technique and is used mainly by women. It comes in two basic forms. "One subtype is a fanning motion of both hands over the surface of the body at a short distance from it, and usually begins at the head or shoulder level and works downward, the healer bending over further and further to cover the patient's entirety. It differs from other techniques mainly in that no physical contact is made with the patient's body. A second subtype is a splashing of light from the candle, either with a plucking and throwing motion which intermittently punctuates the type of brushing described above, or by waving both hands (palms facing the pa-

tient) such that the hand with the candle (from the healer's point of view) goes counterclockwise, the other hand in the opposite direction. During this operation the healer stamps his feet in time to the current song" [Valory 1966:78].

The rubbing mode begins with the shaking (inspired) hand of the healer coming to rest on the patient, often on the exact spot of pain. "After a moment, as 'the Shake' becomes stronger, the hand will move from its resting position and with the other hand will effect a rubbing, cleansing movement, with a firm (but not painful) and usually downward motion (as with fanning or 'brushing'), the hands being pulled over the body with palms down, cupped, until the extremity of a limb is reached. Then the evil or sickness is clenched dramatically in one or both fists and either cast heavenward in a sudden jerky release, or carefully conveyed by the healer to the prayer table and liberated over the candles" [Valory 1966:78–79].

The push-and-pull mode is "considered by Shakers as healing *par excellence*" [Valory 1966:79]. "This technique usually utilizes the downward method of covering an anatomical surface. The motion is firm, more firm than rubbing, and methodic, directed toward an arm, a leg, or merely the waist. It may terminate in a rubbing technique which involves cupping the hands about the heel and dragging the sickness off over the toes" [Valory 1966:79]. The healer will pummel, slap, and yank at fleshy portions and rub on the patient. One variation "is to hold on to both the stomach and back of the patient and shake violently, or push from side to side, sometimes toppling the patient from the stool" [Valory 1966:80].

The Indian Shaker Church of the Puget Sound area on the Northwest Coast should not be confused with the Shakers of the East Coast. The latter were members of the Believers in Christ's Second Coming Church, a Christian sect that originated in England in 1772 and spread to parts of the eastern United States [Waterman 1924:499]. There is no connection between these two groups of Shakers.

See also *Shäpupulema*.

Lehs

Wintun, *California*

Also: *lɛs, läs, loltcit* [Du Bois 1935:77]. Nomlaki and Wintu word for soul. "Lês is in us and is what gives us life. When it is gone, we are gone—it just leaves us like a broken automobile" [Goldschmidt 1951:351]. At death the *lehs* leaves the body and becomes a ghost. It is dangerous to come into contact with a *lehs*.

See also *yapaitu*.

Lehstconos

Wintun, *California*

Wintu Soul Dance. This is a particular type of shamanic healing treatment in which "exorcism is combined with extraction of disease objects" [Du Bois 1935:104]. It is performed by a single shaman, accompanied by singing from the audience. It is considered the most spectacular of the different shamanic healing methods of the Wintu, most likely due to the power performances of the shaman. "In one description, five pitch sticks were lighted and the doctor thrust each in turn into his mouth to extinguish it, smacking his lips as though he were eating something palatable" [Du Bois 1935:105].

Two other healing methods are used by the Wintu. One is disease-object extraction by *winina* (sucking), *sehmin* (massage), or both, and the other is *ehldilna* (soul capture).

The easiest and most common healing method is the *winina*. The spectacular *lehstconos* requires more power. The *ehldilna* is considered the most difficult. It "is employed by the shaman only when a patient is very ill and near death. It may be resorted to after the winina method has proved ineffectual. The supposition is either that the person's soul *(Lɛs)* has already left his body because of the gravity of the illness, or that it has been stolen by a malignant werebeast [spirit]. The doctor's spirits must go in search of the soul. The audience sings while the doctor dances. . . . This treatment for restoration of the soul obviously differs from the others, which are for extraction of disease objects" [Du Bois 1935:105].

Lewekwe

Zuni, *Southwest*

One of the fifteen Zuni rain societies. Sometimes called the Wood Society [Parsons 1933:19]. During January and February members join with the *Makye Lannakwe* (Big Firebrand) society (a division of the Snake Medicine society), which is also a rain society (i.e., a nonmedicine society), to conduct snow-bringing ceremonies during the full moon.

Lhatsina

Tiwa, *Southwest*

The term used at Taos for *kachina* (see entry). Other variations on this term include *katsina* (Hopi), *k'atsi'na* (Keres), *kokko* (Zuni), and *k'at-s'ana* (Towa at Jemez) [Tedlock 1994:162–163].

See also *Kotikäne* and *tuviku*.

Lhulhina

Tiwa, *Southwest*

Literal translation: "old people" [Brandt 1977:23]. The Taos term for those fully initiated into one of their societies. Such a person often serves as a society or kiva leader and, as such, is often a shaman as well.

Lilik

Maidu, *California*

Dialectical variant: *tuyuka* (Northern Maidu) [Gifford 1927:244]. Term used by the Southern Maidu for their shamans' public performances of supernatural powers. During such events different shamans from different districts form competing teams and shoot one another with "poison sticks," called *sila*.

When shooting the shaman makes a hole in the ground with his heel, raising a little mound of earth by turning his heel in the soil. He takes the "poison" [kept in oak balls] between the thumb and finger of his right hand. Then he points at his victim with his left hand, stooping and striking the pile of dust as he throws his poison with an underhand motion of his right arm. Sometimes the intended victim, if he is a good shaman, catches the "poison" as it flies towards him. The "poison sticks" have been dipped into strong "medicine" and they sometimes knock over even a "good doctor."

The visiting shamans, say from Ione, shoot at the party of local shamans, sometimes from a distance of four hundred or five hundred yards. The local shamans dance with chests expanded and arms held back in a nearly horizontal position. When one is struck by a "poison stick" he sometimes falls prone and unconscious to the ground. If he is not attended by his shaman friends within half an hour he will die. The majority of victims get up without aid and spit out the "poison" which is laid on a rock. Sometimes there is an accumulation of "half a panful" of "poison sticks." The Shingle Springs informant claimed to have seen such an accumulation himself.

After shooting away their "poisons" as they approach, the visiting shamans join the host shamans and dance around a fire out-of-doors. This performance is usually on a summer's day. They dance both to the right and to the left. At times people who are not shamans participate in this dance, but they have to be "careful."

Sometimes a stout stick is driven into the ground and shot at with the "poison sticks." A weak shaman will knock only a little off of the top with his "poison," a powerful shaman will break off a good deal or knock the stick over completely [Gifford 1927:244–245].

Liminal states

This term, introduced into anthropology by British anthropologist Victor Turner, refers to transitions in states of being during initiation rituals. "The symbolism attached to and surrounding the liminal *persona* is complex and bizarre. . . . They are at once no longer classified and not yet classified. . . . Their condition is one of ambiguity and paradox, a confusion of all the categories. . . . They are neither one thing nor another; or may be both; or neither here nor there; or may even be nowhere (in terms of any recognized cultural topography), and are at the very least 'betwixt and between' all the recog-

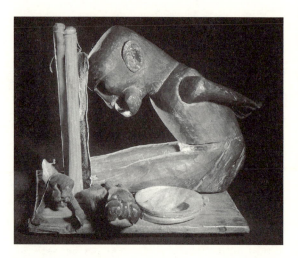

An Alaskan Eskimo carving of a shaman in the middle of a séance and his two helping spirits in the form of animal-like creatures.

nized fixed points in space-time of structural classification" [V. Turner 1967:96–97]. Also, such persons are seen as "unclean" or "polluting."

In recent times anthropologists have begun to refer to the trance states of shamans as liminal states of being. It is in such a state that the shaman then communicates with his or her helping spirit(s).

Among Native Americans, when a person is in deep trance (i.e., when a person loses consciousness), people usually speak of the individual as being "dead." When such persons return to ordinary consciousness, they often have encountered a spirit. For instance, Daniel Lee [in Boyd 1996:119] furnished an account of an early-nineteenth-century incident in which a Chinookan man from The Dalles went into a deep trance, was seen as dead, and upon recovery was renamed *Ukwouianeete,* meaning "heart" or "life."

Among some Native American cultures such "dead" states were induced through the inhalation of native tobacco.

Lit
Yuki, *California*
Any shamanic curing ceremony [Kroeber 1932: 343].

Lo

Yurok, *Oregon Seaboard*

World-renewal formulist shaman. "Individual differences in degrees of knowledge and power are recognized among the formulists and shamans. The effectiveness of the formulist's powers is correlated with the intrinsic strength of his particular formula and with the magnitude of his efforts in attempting to master it by ritual purification" [Posinsky 1965:234]. The *Lo* is therefore only one type among this class of shamans since "formulists are primarily differentiated by the nature of specific formulae which they command. These formulae are private property and may occasionally be purchased, though they are more commonly inherited" [Posinsky 1965:229].

The formulist type of shaman performs rites of passage, birth rituals, death rituals, purification rites, initiation rituals, and so forth but not healings, although he or she may be called upon in serious cases to supplement the efforts of a healing shaman. However, the medicine powers of the formulist type of shaman are not considered inferior to or less supernatural than those of the healer. "The formula which the formulist acquires by inheritance is equally personal and supernatural, and it is equally dangerous to himself and the community if not ritually controlled" [Posinsky 1965:233]. For example, one *Lo* living at Kepel during a world-renewal ceremony "was able easily to move the timber which four men had hardly been able to carry to him" [Posinsky 1965:235]. Among the Yurok, healing shamans are almost always females, while formulist shamans may be either male or female.

See also *Wilohego*.

Loache

Natchez, *Southeast*

An eighteenth-century term for a prophet [Adair in Swanton 1928:628]. See *alexis*.

Loltcit

Wintun, *California*

Ghost. See *yapaitu*.

Long-life ceremonies

Jicarilla, *Southwest*

All ceremonies that have existed "from the beginning" [Opler 1943:9]. These power ceremonies are distinct from shamanic ceremonies. Long-life ceremonies are more elaborate and dramatic than shamanic ceremonies because the latter take form from the shaman's personal supernatural experiences with his helping spirits.

Lost objects

Finding lost items is a common function of shamans throughout North America. The shaman typically gives quite detailed information on locating the missing item, as the following account from among the Canadian Dakota reveals:

A man's horse was stolen. The medicine-woman, after singing, said it would be found about 40 miles to the south. She described the house in which the thief lived, and said he was lame in one leg and had a broken arm. The barn was described as unpainted and other details were given: the door would be fastened with a padlock, and, if this was the place indicated, the horse would neigh when they approached it. We drove about 40 miles south, saw a house like that described, went to it, and found a man lame in one leg and with a broken arm. We asked him whether he had any horses to sell. He said, 'No.' We said that if had any to sell, we should like to see them. He again said he had none to sell. We walked toward the barn. It was as the woman had described it. The door was fastened with a padlock. When we were close to it, the horse, inside, neighed. We employed a detective, who next day went to the place and secured the horse [Wallis 1947:78].

For other examples, see *alini, Brown, Fanny, Charles, Nels, Doctor Black chicken, dodeuks, hanhepi, hasha, horse medicine, jesako, kimuuanipinas, kitetau, kiuks, Mapitcabï, ndishniih, nerfalasoq, Niashaida, Owl Thunder, Pinaeshe Kanas Towagit, wodi.*

Love medicines

One type of sexual sorcery in which individual magical compounds, charms, or incantations (or some combination of all three) are used to cause one person to fall in love with another; philters. Love medicines are widely used throughout North America, and most likely they are found in some form in nearly every culture. Skinner [1915d:189] reported that eighteen different love medicines were known by the Menomini alone in 1913. Most often shamans versus herbalists are called upon for the preparation of a love medicine or charm. Usually this is a mixture of certain herbs, which is worn on the body, ingested, or rubbed on the body, or a combination thereof. In other formulas such preparations must be touched to the body of the victim. Several examples follow.

The contents of a Sac medicine bundle (see entry) (obtained around the turn of the twentieth century and marked Bundle 2/8598 in the Heye Collection) were found to include

> three packages containing love medicine. One of these, a cloth package, has a mixture of three varieties: Wi ko bi jä bi ki, or "sweet root"; A pe nyi gec kik, or "Indian potato"; and Te pi kis ka kik, a weed that grows beside the lakes. The lover puts a little of this mixture into his mouth when he sees the girl he wishes to attract, and takes pains to go around behind her and approach her on the right side. In a red calico package is a piece of blue cloth, in one end of which is tied a sort of powder, Nä thä tci gun, used internally to remove from one's self the evil effects of other medicines. In the other end is a bundle of herb mixture, containing sumach top, We ci hon, painted on the cheeks while courting. The third love medicine is contained in a piece of blue calico, and consists of a lot of scale-like seeds, Mi ca dji a gwi, in which are mixed a few round seeds, I kwä mi ni wä. It is supposed to have the power of attracting women when smoked [M. R. Harrington 1914:221].

Among the Ojibwa of northern Minnesota, a love medicine often "consisted of some powder made of herbs noted for this power, mixed with quicksilver. Frequently, the woman wore a lock of her beloved's hair and made cuts or figurines representing the man she wished to attract. Even today at Red Lake the young women wear these charms to attract the other sex. Medicine was sometimes injected into the heart of a figurine. . . . Round and queer-shaped stones were also carried for love charms" [Coleman 1937:53–54].

Among the Tahitian of the Mackenzie-Yukon area, various love medicines are used. "In one particular variety a white root was obtained from the ground and rolled into pellets. The woman's image was then drawn on a piece of skin and encircled with the pellets. If the charm was to be successful the pellets moved and at the same time the woman found herself attracted to the magician" [Honigmann 1954:112, n. 34].

The Chiricahua (Apache) are known to have love medicines in which either a hummingbird or a butterfly is most often used. "R., they say, knows this [love] ceremony. He got a young woman with it. Everybody knows he influenced her. She chased him all around, day and night, when she was a young girl. He's much older than she is. That girl was very pretty and he was ugly. They think he used butterflies. They say that he has been helping some other people with his power too" [unidentified informant in M. E. Opler 1941:152]. If a love medicine ceremony goes amiss, there is also a ceremony to cure the resulting "love craziness" [M. E. Opler 1941:151].

The Cree in Canada also have love medicines with which "young men so completely and universally succeed with all the women that please them" [Paul in Brown and Brightman 1988:71]. A Plains Cree shaman would often make a figure out of wood, clay, or hide to represent the intended victim of a love spell. In the 1820s Baptiste Paul described his knowledge and use of love medicines. In one instance, Baptiste's preparation was secretly rubbed on the sleeping victims, two married women being pursued by two males who were not their husbands. In each case the medicine was rubbed on the victim's forehead, in an area opposite the heart, on the pit of the stomach, and on the palms of both hands. The men then woke their victims and had intercourse with them. The next day the two men approached the women, who were traveling together, and began talking about their night together. The women "became extremely confused and vexed: a quarrel ensued but my comrades [the two culprits] exultingly told them, 'we can turn and twist you *now* about our fingers as we please.' And they did too. For the women both *giving suck* at that time thought it was their children that were handling them, as they used but *one* finger, and gently" [Paul in Brown and Brightman 1988:70].

Baptiste Paul also told of helping a man whose wife had a secret lover. In this case he told the man to leave his wife for several days after rubbing her with the preparation so that she would suffer for her misdoings. However, she started calling out to her husband shortly after he had finished, and "like a Goose he went immediately" to her. Nelson, who recorded this account from Baptiste, subsequently asked this man if the story was true. The man would not confess to his use of love medicine, but Nelson reported that "from his confusion and precipitancy with which he answered, I believe there is *something* in the business" [Nelson in Brown and Brightman 1988:71].

A Stoney (Assiniboin) procedure for love medicine "probably borrowed from the Cree is for the young man to model an image both of himself and of the woman and to wrap the figures up together with some medicine" [Lowie 1909:47]. The Stoney also use a redolent herb, which is rubbed on the body to attract women, and a philter drunk by a man and then given to his victim to drink.

Among the Shuswap of the Plateau area, "a male and a female cricket are tied together with a hair from the head of the woman or man who is to be charmed. This has the effect of binding their affections together, and is used as a love-charm by persons desiring the affections of parties of the opposite sex" [Teit 1909:619].

The Mikasuki and Cow Creek Seminoles use several different forms of love medicines. In one case a shaman "prepared a medicine by singing to the heart and tongue of the one desired, using his or her name, and the applicant took the medicine home. According to Spoehr, a young Cow Creek man could get the love of a particular girl by singing over bay leaves *(Persea borbonia)* and rubbing them on his body and clothes" [Sturtevant 1954b:400–401]. In addition the Cow Creek Seminole have an antilove medicine: When used by a man "his wife thereupon gets an intense dislike for him and divorces him" [Spoehr in Sturtevant 1954b:401].

Mooney [1891:375–384] listed six love medicine formulas in his study of Cherokee shamanism. According to one Cherokee formula "a man would fast alone in the woods for seven days. His only nourishment came from herbal teas, and hunger pangs were pacified by swallowed saliva. The man took daily baths in a 'branch' and 'put water over his heart.' When he returned to the 'road' (i.e., back to civilization), the desired woman would seek him out, wander after him, and 'crave him.' She wouldn't eat anything. If she got hungry, 'she'd just bend over and eat dirt and think it was bread—she'd really crave that man'" [Natsi in Fogelson 1980:74].

Also in regard to the Southeast area, Swanton [1928:635–636] gave a detailed account of love medicines among the Alabama of Texas:

When a youth fell in love he would sometimes, especially if he were rejected, go to a male or female conjurer for assistance. Then the conjurer would take some tobacco, put it into a small deerskin sack, sing, and repeat the girl's name, and blow into it through a short cane [i.e., empower it]. After doing this four times he would wrap it up in a handkerchief and give it to the young man. The latter would then put on his head band and his other fine clothing, sprinkle some tobacco over his clothes, make a cigarette, and blow the smoke all over himself. Then the girl would fall in love with him. A girl could make a man fall in love with her in precisely the same way. Sometimes, however, this would be tried in vain several times. Then the conjurer would go to a small brook and make a little water hole, perhaps half a foot deep. He would blow into this four times through a cane, repeating the girl's name each time. The youth would then come there, stoop down and drink some of the water, and throw it up again into the pool. He would do this four times. Then he would divide the dam that held the water in this pool and let it all run away. After that he would go to a large creek, remove his clothing, and dive under water four times. Then he would come out and lie in the bushes almost all day (having started out early in the morning) so that no one could see him. About 3 o'clock he started home, avoiding meeting or speaking to anyone. In perhaps a week he would dress himself up as before and go to see the girl he was in love with, who would then fall in love with him. Sometimes, however, the girl's mother would make medicine against him so that he could not succeed in spite of all his efforts.

Among the Oglala Sioux love medicines were prepared by shamans who had dreamed of the elk and were members of the Elk Shamans society. In order to prepare the love medicine, "they may take the white part of the eye of an elk or part of the heart, the inside gristle from the projection of the fetlocks, or the hind feet, and mix it with medicine. The flute and the mirror are regarded as powerful accessories in using such charms" [Wissler 1912b:88].

For other examples see *Billie, Josie, daxw-chaluxw, Kamiokisihkwew, masutïkï, micaduskwe, ntekêllsten, pohagadi, pthlax, Taxtewau, tûkosi-*
wäwûs, ukemauwûsk, Waxablu, wikipinûkûn, and *wodi.*

Low Horn
Blackfoot, *Plains*
See *Ekaskini.*

łqulisxâm
Alsea, *Oregon Seaboard*
Disease object. A patient's illness is frequently diagnosed by a shaman as being caused by the intrusion, most often by a spirit or sorcerer, of a *łqulisxâm* into the patient's body.

> To extract a disease object, the doctor threw himself on the patient either to suck it out or to draw it out with his hands. When he had it firmly, two assistants grasped him by his wide leather belt to draw him back. Such was the power of the malignant particle that it was all two brawny men could do to hold the shaman, once he had it in his grasp. If he had sucked the object out, he spat it into his hands. His helpers seized his arms and by main strength forced them into a basket of water. This weakened the disease object. Then the shaman displayed it—a luminous white thing "like a little worm.". . . They were sometimes, at least, partly identified with spirits, so that when a shaman crushed one of them between his teeth and swallowed it, his powers were increased just as though he had met another guardian [spirit]. At times, the informants spoke of the disease objects as if they had no connection at all with the guardian spirits [Drucker 1939:99–100].

See also *tcuyaliclofor.*

Ma caiyoyo

Keres, *Southwest*

Also: *ma coitcani* [White 1930:609]. A rock crystal used by a shaman for divination. Such crystals are often used to diagnose a patient. "The rock crystal is used to locate objects in the body [of a patient] and to 'see witches'" [White 1930:609].

Madewahin

Malecite, *Canadian Eastern Woodlands*

Also: *medeulin.* Power. "The human possessor of this power can see events happening in a distant place and can perform good deeds" [Wallis and Wallis 1957:31].

Madit

Wintun, *California*

A shaman from the latter part of the nineteenth century who resided at Paskenta. He was best known for his ability to assume various animal forms.

He could make clouds rise over the mountain. He told people he could walk over big, heavy clouds, and then he would go behind the house and soon the people would see him on the mountain. He would go hunting and turn into a buck and get in a deer net and have a great time. They would try to hit him but they couldn't, and finally he would turn back into a man. He could turn into a bear and tear up a net or catch a man. If women were fishing, he would turn into a salmon and come upstream. The women would get clubs and chase him into shallows, and then he would throw water on them. When they got the best of him, he would turn back to a man and just laugh. One day he said to the people to take care of themselves, for he couldn't remain on earth long. A few days later he put some beads around his neck and said, "Now you people watch me; I'm going down by the bank and turn into a rock for the last time." It was in the morning. He laid down on his stomach facing north and he turned into a long rock. He is there today, right across from the Paskenta burial grounds [Freeman in Goldschmidt 1951:354–355].

Madmowun

Potawatomi, *Midwest*

Dream Dance Ceremony or Religion Dance Ceremony [Skinner 1924:222]. This ceremony is also conducted by

171

the Menomini. It is "said to have come from the Ojibway of Minnesota, who in turn obtained it from the Eastern or Santee Dakota dwelling near Devil's Lake, South Dakota" [Skinner 1924:222]. This ceremony was founded in the nineteenth century by an Ojibwa/Sioux girl named Wananikwä [Skinner 1924:223]. In 1923 the Prairie Potawatomi at Mayetta, Kansas, had at least seven active drums, i.e., chapters, of the Dream Dance society.

The ceremony lasts four days, with dancing during the day and feasting during the night. The "chief object of adoration on their part" [Skinner 1924:226] is the large ceremonial drum that is mounted on four supports located in the center of the dance circle. The dance also includes social activities. For example, all men "wishing to divorce their wives throw away blankets during the ceremonies, and whoever picks up one of these assumes the bonds of matrimony with the discarded wife" [Skinner 1924:226]. However, "the original idea of the cult was to worship the Great Spirit through the medium of any attention, so the singers send in one of their number to build minds of the members" [Skinner 1924 226].

Madu

Pomo, *California*

Sucking or dream shaman. Also less often referred to as "maru doctor" [B. Wilson 1968:65]. One of two types of Pomo shamans, the other being the *qoobakiyalxale* (see entry). "These doctors stemmed from the Maru cult, the leaders of which claimed their authority through dreams and sometimes doctored too" [B. Wilson 1968:59].

The main requirement for becoming a *madu* is "to receive from Marumda, the creator, through some mystical experience, power in one's own person to perceive the nature of disease and heal it" [Freeland 1923:58]. Such mystical experiences, or visions, generally come unsolicited, most often during an illness and often not until middle age. During the visionary experience, which usually comes twice, the person receives instructions from a spirit. One report stated, "A Pomo informant told Mr. Gifford of a man who saw fire spouting from the head of a horse. He swooned and remained unconscious several hours. When he awoke it was gone. Through this event, he became a madu" [Freeland 1923:64, n. 5]. Eventually the person told others about his dream, so his or her powers became generally known.

Unlike spirits in most visionary experiences, this spirit does not return to the shaman, and often the spirit has no name but is addressed simply as, for example, "you who taught me to do this thing, to sing this, make this sick man well" [Freeland 1923:64]. The *madu* usually knows only a few songs, has only one herb (angelica root), and uses only a long obsidian knife, called *dupaxaka*. Unlike the *qooxaka* of the *qoobakiyalxale,* this obsidian knife is used just once. Each ceremony performed by the *madu* requires the making of a new blade, usually while being accompanied by special songs.

The *madu* is often called in to diagnose an illness. "Often as soon as he sees the patient he can tell the part affected because a cloud of steam seems to rise from there. If he is in doubt, the madu first sings. Then by feeling, or by sucking on the skin, and tasting, he discovers the nature of the disease. He protects himself by chewing angelica root beforehand and rubbing it on his hands, sometimes on the patient as well. Then if he judges the trouble to be something that bleeding or sucking can help, he goes on with these treatments. The usual fee is eight hundred beads" [Freeland 1923:64]. "The sucking doctors sang, and used herbs to cure their patients, and their method might also include cutting the patient with a sharp flint or piece of glass to let the blood bring the sickness out of the body, sucking the pain out without cutting, or rubbing the afflicted area" [B. Wilson 1968:60].

When sucking is used, the Pomo shaman typically removes a clot of blood through the skin; this contrasts with the more traditional technique of removing disease objects, as practiced by sucking shamans from other cultures. Other *madu* treatments include bloodletting. A typical *madu* treatment that occurred in 1882 was described as follows:

I had the grippe in '82. I was staying near Kelseyville. It came on at night, and in the morning I couldn't get up. They sent for a woman madu who was there. She felt my head and she said, "Your blood is boiling. Turn on your side." Then she cut my cheek right in front of my ear. The blood poured out, and she sucked it. Then she made a fresh cut and sucked some more. She took about a half-gallon milk-pail full. I didn't feel anything until about her third mouthful, then I began to feel better on that side. I turned over and she did the same on the other side. Then she went away. She said, "Don't get up; you might take cold. Eat something tonight if you feel better." At night I ate. Next day I got up. I was all right except for weakness from losing the blood. The madu told me the blood was so hot from the poison in it that it scalded her tongue. She didn't sing at all in this treatment [William Benson (or Ghalganal, "wampum pursuer") in Freeland 1923:67].

Mahuts
Cheyenne, *Plains*
Also: *nimahenan*, "our sacred arrows" [Schlesier 1987:211]. Sacred Arrows. In the distant past four Sacred Arrows were given directly by the Creator to a great prophet/shaman named either Motseyoef, "sweet root standing" [Schlesier 1987: 211], or Motzeyeuff [Dorsey 1905:1]; his English name is usually given as Sweet Medicine.

These arrows possessed magic, and the Great Medicine [Creator] decreed that they should produce effects beyond natural powers. For instance, when this Prophet, or the following Prophets, took the arrows and held the points towards an enemy, or towards any kind of animals, they became confused and unconscious. Two of these arrows possessed power over men, and the other two possessed power over buffalo and other beasts, and so two of them were called "man-arrows" and two of them "buffalo-arrows." . . . If the people were hungry, and had nothing to live on, all they had to do was to find a herd of buffalo and have the keeper of the two buffalo-arrows point them towards the herd. The Cheyenne, who had no horses in those days, could go up to the buffalo and kill all they desired by means of these arrows. When they did this the rule was to take everything except the head, and to leave the horns on, and to leave the backbone attached to the head and the tail. Every animal killed with the medicine-arrows had to be treated in that way. These arrows made the buffalo crazy. They had no will of their own, but would run in a circle until the Cheyenne had killed all they wanted, and then they would dash off. The Cheyenne used these arrows to kill all beasts they desired to eat, but only when they had to do so.

These sacred arrows are somewhat different from ordinary Cheyenne arrows. They are about thirty-six inches long, one-half an inch in diameter, round, very straight, with flintstone points. The points are tied in at the end, and over each of the four arrow points is tied a covering of white, downy eagle feathers. At the other end are whole wing feathers of the eagle, split in two, and tied on each side of the arrows. The shafts are also partly covered with the white, downy feathers of an eagle. All the feathers are painted red. On each of the four arrows are painted figures of the world, the blue paint meaning blue heavens, the sun, moon, stars, the red paint meaning the earth. Buffalo and other animals are also painted [Dorsey 1905:1–2].

"The Sacred Arrows fell into Pawnee hands about 1830, causing the worst spiritual catastrophe ever experienced by the tribe. Mahuts, the four Arrows, are the supremely sacred objects uniting the Cheyenne to Maheo, the All Father Himself. Maheo pours his life into the lives of the people through the Arrows. The Arrows unite the Cheyennes to the All Father and to each other. Without the Arrows, there can be no Cheyenne tribe, no People in any supernatural sense. . . . Two Arrows were regained, and two substitutes later were made by supernatural command and guidance" [Powell 1969:3–4]. In June 1945 the Sacred Arrows were brought north by the Southern Cheyenne in Oklahoma to Bear Butte, for the first time in seventy-five years. There the Sacred Arrow ceremonies were performed by their Arrow priests over a four-day period [Powell 1969:390–391]. Since then the position of Keeper of the Arrows has gone back and forth between the Southern and Northern Cheyenne nations.

There is a power renewal ceremony for the *Mahuts*. Of this ritual Grinnell wrote: "The ceremony did not occur with any regularity. It was not annual like the medicine lodge, but took place when occasion seemed to demand. The arrows might be renewed two or three times within a single year, or a year or more might elapse between the performances of the ceremony. It might take place at the request of a soldier band, or on the advice of priests, but the ceremony might not be performed without the consent of the keeper of the arrows. On one occasion, however, a soldier band, by violence, forced the arrow keeper against his protest to renew the arrows at an inauspicious time. The arrow keeper, White Thunder, prophesied that the next time this soldier band went to war all its members would be killed. The very next spring when this soldier band went to war the party of forty-two was surrounded, and they were killed to a man" [Grinnell 1910:546].

In the renewal ceremony the feathers, the sinews, or both are replaced but not the shafts. The shafts of the man-arrows were originally painted black, while the shafts of the buffalo-arrows were painted red. A Pawnee account of the arrows described them as alternately painted red, white, yellow, and black [Dorsey 1903:646].

Ma-i-yun-a-huh-ta
Cheyenne, *Plains*
Literal translation: "a spirit told me in sleep" [Grinnell 1923:113]. Guardian spirit. When ad-

dressing one's guardian spirit in ritual, one uses the personal name of the spirit rather than this term.

Máke
Pima, *Southwest*
Dialectical variant: *mákai* (EONAH, pp. 159–160) (Papago). Shaman [Grossman 1873:412]. Both the Pima and Papago shamans acquire their power via dreams in a similar manner.

> The Papago [or Pima] dream experience occurred in sleep, like that of the Yumans [see *etsatcev*], but the spirits involved were the animal guardians of the Plains. And the vision was induced. The purposeful motivating of a certain dream is at odds with the modern attitude of scrutinizing dreams as valuable messengers from the subconscious, to be humbly awaited and studied, rather than commanded. But the Papago commanded their dreams—or at least those they remembered. Inquiry has convinced the writer that there were many symbolic expressions of unrecognized desires, like those so much studied today and sometimes spoken of as typical of all dreams. But these, say the Papago, "did not mean anything. We forgot them." Other dreams, however, were motivated by constant thought and desire directed toward one end—say a visit from Coyote—until it must have reflection in dreams. Such a desire was by no means suppressed: these dreams acted as messengers, not from the subconscious to the conscious but in the reverse direction. When a man's subconscious could produce, in sleep, a reflection of the very image toward which his conscious desires and those of his society were bent, he had attained supernatural power [Underhill 1939:173].

However, "the Papago dream brought success only in racing, gambling, war, and curing. Planting was taken care of by communal ritual and office, both ceremonial and secular, descended by heredity, without benefit of vision" [Underhill 1939:174].

An early account of Pima healing reported that "in case of pains in the chest or stomach, they scarify the patients with sharp stones or place burning coals upon the skin, and in rare instances the patient is placed upon the ground, his head to the west, and then the medicine-man gently passes a brush, made of eagle feathers, from his head to his feet; after which he runs several paces, shakes the brush violently, and then returns to the patient to repeat, again and again, the same maneuver. They believe that, by this operation, the sickness is drawn first into the brush and thence shaken to the winds, and bystanders keep a respectful distance for fear of inhaling the disease when it is shaken from the brush" [Grossman 1873:413–414].

Most illness is diagnosed as being caused by a witch, and another shaman must be called in to discover the culprit. "The medicine-man on these occasions masks his face and disguises himself as much as possible. He then swiftly runs around the spot supposed to be infested, widening his circles as he runs, until, at last, he professes to have found the outer limits of the space of ground supposed to be under the influence of the witch. Then he and his assistants (the latter also masked) drive painted stakes into the ground all about the bewitched spot. These sticks, painted with certain colors found in the mountains, are said to possess the power of preventing the escape of the witch. Now begins the search for the witch" [Grossman 1873:413].

Makkortaa

East Greenland Eskimo, *Arctic Coast*
An Ammasalik shaman's spirit-calling instrument [Thalbitzer 1931:434]. See *anaalutaa* for details.

Mamaga

Papago, *Southwest*
An annual ritual performed "to make fresh farm crops safe for eating. The danger that they [the crops] pose is diarrhea, an affliction that is linked to wine drinking and to the ocean" [Underhill et al. 1979:71]. This ritual revolves around hunting and connects "that activity with rain, dryness, farming, and sickness" [Underhill et al. 1979:71]. The *mamaga* (spoken as *ma' m' aga*) is one of several annual ceremonies (e.g., the rabbit hunt or the salt pilgrimage) performed during the fall equinox at the end of the rainy season.

Part of the performance of the *mamaga* consists of a ritualized deer hunt over the course of one day. Although there are no recorded examples, we do know that on the night before the hunt, "songs were sung while medicine men who accompanied the party used their powers to determine the location of the object sought (clouds or deer). Apparently there was no oratory during this phase, only singing" [Underhill et al. 1979:73].

The deer hunt itself differs from other hunts in that the deer are to be killed without shedding their blood. This is usually accomplished by catching the deer in some manner and then strangling them. During the afternoon the hunters return to the village with their butchered deer. The celebration of the return of the hunters begins the next morning. "The meat was cooked without salt by old women. Meanwhile the men cleansed every house in the village. This is the *a'ada* [see entry]" [Underhill et al. 1979:75]. The *a'ada* ritual marked the conclusion of the *mamaga* ceremony.

Mana

An anthropological term used for the very widespread belief in an invisible force pervading the universe that gives rise to all life and forms. The term was taken from the Maori of New Zealand, among whom it means "power, might, authority, influence, sanctification, infused with magic, potency, control, prestige" [Savage 1962:135]. More loose definitions of this term equate it with the modern Western notion of charisma.

More accurately, mana is the inherent power in magic and, as such, is the mystery power wielded by shamans. Therefore, it is known by many different Native American terms, including *ayelkwi* (EONAH, pp. 22–23), *manitowi* (EONAH, p. 164), *natoji* (see entry), *nupeeka* (see entry), *orenda* (EONAH, p. 208), *pokunt* (EONAH, p. 219), *tipni* (see entry), *ulanigvgv*

(EONAH, pp. 297–298), *wakan* (EONAH, pp. 305–306), and *yutir* (see entry), to mention just a few.

Manäo
Ojibwa, *Canadian Eastern Woodlands*
A type of healing shaman who receives his powers from a class of spirits known as *memengwéciwak* [Hallowell 1942:7].

Manetowa
Fox, *Midwest*
Medicine bag [Fisher 1939:92]. Medicine bags contain the religious paraphernalia of shamans. As a rule, they are only unbundled during religious ceremonies. According to the ethnographic literature, these medicine bags are placed into sacred bundles, or "packs," called *mani micami* (EONAH, p. 162), which have specific names, such as "Apenäwänäa pack" [Michelson 1927:97] or "Sagimakwäwa pack" [Michelson 1927:117]. The *manetowa* and associated sacred packs are kept within a family and built up over time. Consequently, there is a historical account surrounding the addition of each item into these sacred bundles.

The term *manetowa* is a cognate of the Algonquian word *manitowi* (EONAH, p. 164).

See also *medicine bundle*.

Manëtu
Delaware, *Northeast*
Plural: *manëtuwák* [Kraft 1986:163]. The Lenape term for the widespread Algonquian term *manitou* (EONAH, p. 164). A shaman's helping spirit, which comes in many different forms. Some examples are: *Gickokwite* (the Sun), *Péthakhuweyok* (Thunder Beings), *Maxackok* (the great Horned Serpent), *Elaunato* (Comet or Shooting Star), and *Ohtas* (Doll Being) [Kraft 1986:164–166].

Mankácutzi warúhawe
Iowa, *Plains*
Red Bean war bundle. This was a sacred medicine bundle used by the Red Bean Society. The bundle "brought success in war, hunting, especially for the buffalo, and in horse racing. Members of the society tied red beans around their belts when they went to war, deeming them a protection against injury. Cedar berries and sagebrush were also used with this medicine. Sage was boiled and used to medicate sweat baths on the war trail" [Skinner 1915a:719].

Mañkanni
Winnebago, *Midwest*
Medicine Dance society [Radin 1911:193]. This is the Winnebago version of the widespread Ojibwa *Midewiwin* (EONAH, p. 174). See *Medicine Dance*.

Mapitcabï
Paiute, *Basin*
Literal translation: "Palm." A Shivwits (Southern Paiute) shaman in the early part of the twentieth century who specialized in locating stolen property. "He concentrated on the quest without singing, while his *ïnïpits* [spirit helper] guided him to the place where the goods were concealed" [Kelly 1939:156].

Mashanyu
Keres, *Southwest*
Literal translation: "great light" [Parsons 1926:119]. The Acoma term for any crystal used for divination purposes during a ceremony.

Mashutkwiunt
Ute, *Basin*
Shaman or medicine man [Fowler and Fowler 1971:180].

Masinisawe
Ojibwa, *Canadian Eastern Woodlands*
Literal translation: "he makes marks with fire" [Cooper 1936:11]. Scapulimancy (see entry). *Masinisawe* is the term used both by the Lake of the Woods and the Rainy Lake (or River) Ojibwa. However, at Rainy Lake, scapulimancy is also referred to as *masinikanasige,* which trans-

lates as "he makes images with fire" [Cooper 1936:26].

In this form of divination, the shoulder blade from any animal (most often the porcupine, marten, lynx, rabbit, beaver, moose, or caribou) is used. The breast bone of the grouse is also used at Lake of the Woods. The bone is held near a fire (never in it) until it has scorch marks on it. These burn marks are then read by the shaman (among a number of other cultures, the fissures on the bones are read instead). Only qualified shamans practice *masinisawe,* and they never do so for fun. This divination technique is often used to find someone who is lost. "In hunting moose or caribou, scapulimancy is resorted to in order to find out where the game is. The diviner can, through the burns on the bone, tell about things and scenes far off" [Cooper 1936:27]. Most often the shaman performs this divination when alone.

Maskakey
Ojibwa, *Canadian Eastern Woodlands*
Saulteaux term for shaman or medicine man [Panipekeesick (see *Kimvaunipinas*) in Tarasoff 1980:108].

Masks
Masks often play an important role in shamanic rituals. They are widely used throughout North America, and they appear in many different forms. Generally the person who dons a mask becomes the spirit represented by the mask's carving (if it is made of wood) or shape (if made of skin or cloth). Masks are often painted and adorned with feathers, hair, cornhusks, fur, etc. Perhaps best known are the masks associated with the Iroquois False-Face societies (EONAH, pp. 79–82) in the Northeast. Masks are also quite prevalent among the cultures of the Northwest Coast and Southwest cultural areas.

Because masks contain a power or spirit, they are generally cared for in a sacred manner. That is, such a mask is kept in a special location or a special container, and regular offerings are made

A Tlingit shaman's face mask.

to the spirit of the mask. For example, among the Zuni, "seeds of all kinds are chewed by the Zuni mask-maker and sprayed over the mask. 'Now I have given you life,' he says. 'I have made you with seeds and given you life. . . . Call the rains for us as long as you live. I have made you into a person'" [Parsons 1939:340].

As one would expect, the complexity seen in sacred ceremonies in these areas is also reflected in mask making. Within the Pueblo area of the Southwest, for example, one overview reported that

masks are of two types, the false face and the
cylinder which covers face and head. The latter, the
"head," is the common type of the forty-six masks
listed for San Felipe, thirty-four are "heads," as are
thirty-seven out of forty-six masks at Santo

A Bella Coola mechanical mask representing a mythical sea monster, in the mouth of which is a human face.

Domingo, and I think this is about the ratio elsewhere. At Zuni all but two of the permanent or chiefly masks are cylindrical. "Heads" are generally flat on top with a superstructure of feathers, unspun cotton, sheepwool for hair, flowers, horns, and wooden slab or tablet, or with side or back slabs or feathers. Ears, gourd or wooden snouts, a tongue flap, bulging eyeballs of buckskin stuffed with cotton, wool, and seeds may be attached. There will be a large collar or ruff of fur or feathers or spruce. The spruce may be tipped with popcorn (Keres, Zuni), sometimes to represent stars (Zuni).

The false face [type] has beard instead of ruff, a long beard, usually of black horsehair, sometimes of yucca fiber dyed red or of leather (San Felipe, Santo Domingo, Zuni) or along which hang feathered strings or bunched feathers. There may be a hair bang, made sometimes from the hair of the owner [taboo at Zuni] or a bang of close-bound willow twigs. Black triangular or rectangular or circular "eyes" and white "teeth" may be painted on, sometimes a nose; a projecting nose is usually a feature only of burlesque false faces. A ring of braided cornhusk may surround eyes or mouth.

Masks are generally made of leather, deerskin or elkskin or buffalo hide or cowhide [also rabbitskin]; a few of gourd or wicker, none of wood; ears or horn may be of wood. Snouts, also horns, may be of gourd neck or ox horn heated and flattened out and reshaped. . . . Koyemshi clown masks are of native cotton cloth (stained

pink with "kachina clay"), except at Acoma where they are leather. These masks have balls on top which give them their name, knobs filled with soil from the footprints of townspeople (Zuni) or with seeds (Hopi, Laguna, also turquoise and shell), and to these potent or sinister knobs prayer-feathers [see *prayer feathers/sticks* entry] are tied [Parsons 1939:339–340].

In the Northwest Coast area, where masks are most often of carved cedar, some of the more elaborate ones have moving parts mounted on hinges [Wherry 1969:58].

See also *Choyo, gagohsa, geestcin, hadui, ichta, keeapaait, kenaroq, kinaroq, kotikäne, küïtü, suglut, tungralik, tuviku, Gaqohsa, Oologogoloq, weather shaman, Windigokan.*

Maskwacimuwin
Cree, *Canadian Eastern Woodlands*
Bear Dance among the Plains Cree [Mandelbaum 1940:278]. Little is known of this religious ceremony because it was no longer being performed by the mid-1930s. Whoever vowed to give the ceremony most likely did so in order to receive supernatural aid. For example, one informant reported: "A person belonged to the [Bear] dance after they had promised to give one or [promised] to give something away at a (Bear) dance for the recovery of a sick relative or for success on the warpath" [Mandelbaum 1940:278].

Mason, Billy
Quinault, *Northwest Coast*
A shaman from around the turn of the twentieth century who, later in his life, became a member of the Shaker religion (EONAH, pp. 245–246). He began his shamanic training when he was about ten years old, under the tutelage of his grandfather, Nicagwats. He reported:

During the time I trained, many men, animals and strange creatures came to me and talked with me. They came to me in my dreams. . . .
Sometimes when I prayed I would see a little man come down and go into me. He was an angel. Perhaps the old guardian spirits were angels too.

When I first started bathing among the snags the sa'xtikulc spirit (which lives on the clouds) came to me. He came to me in the form of a man, but larger than a man. He came up out of the water and I saw that he was Mountain Lion. I saw him at the same place each year for three years. The third time he put me in his small canoe and took me through the air toward the east and landed the canoe on his house. When I came to myself I was inside. He said, "Look now and see where I live. I live in the sun. See where I stand." Then I saw that he was standing on ice. Because he was a strong animal I, too, am strong and a single bullet could not kill me (because it takes more than one shot to kill a mountain lion). . . . .

Soon after I got one of my spirits my nephew came to me and said, "Well, uncle, I don't believe you have that [Shaker] spirit. But if he will shake me I will believe." I said to him, "All right, you come to my house this evening." He came, and I gave him the carved rattle to hold; soon he began to shake and went into a kind of trance. When he came to himself he told us, "A man appeared to me and said, 'Look up there to the north.' Then I closed my eyes and saw a canoe in the air. The bow was carved in the form of a snake's head with the mouth open. Then the spirit said, 'Now look over toward the west—that is where I travel. You can hear my song from afar when I am traveling.'" This was a sign that my nephew would not live long, because the spirit showed him so little and he saw the vision only dimly.

Once my son Harry and I were up the river. He wanted to use my shaman's rattle. The power came to him and shook him. He talked (in the trance), naming all the people of Taholah and how many were away. Then he said, "But one man is soon going to die at the mouth of the river." A few days later Andrew Martin came to our camp, and said he had heard about the message we received. He took the rattle and after his trance said, "Yes, that is true. A fellow will die there." But it was he, though he didn't know it. He was drowned there within two months [Billy Mason in Olson 1936:156–158].

Masutïkï
Paiute, *Basin*
Chemehuevi and Vegas (Southern Paiute) common term for fetish (see entry). Fetishes are most often used by men, but anyone can obtain one. Sometimes they are received as gifts; at other times they may be purchased from a shaman knowledgeable in their use. There are many different types of *masutïkï*. The following are examples of the *masutïkï* for hunting medicine, gambling medicine, and love medicine:

Masu´tïkï for hunting was a small cane filled with honey. A hunter using this bathed early in the morning and abstained from salt and greasy foods for four days before the hunt. The cane he carried stuck in his hair. When he sighted a deer or mountain sheep, he removed the cane and placed it on the track. "This slowed the animal and made it weak in the limbs; in summer its hoofs fell off." Masu´tïkï for gambling worked on the same principle: it "slowed" one's opponent. The gambling charm consisted of various dried plants—which ones the informant refused to specify.

Masu´tïkï for attracting members of the opposite sex proved fatal to the victim within several weeks, and "in ten or twenty years" to the one who exercised the power. The love charm seems to have been used chiefly on women, whence it was called mama´u-masu´tïkï (woman-magic). Its composition could not be determined, but "it was not made of plants." A sorcerer addressed his charm, then established contact with the prospective victim by acquiring some personal possession—a hair, chewing-gum, or the like. Immediately the victim became infatuated, and within several weeks paid with her life. Piïnkwiepu (caterpillar ?), a Ghost-dance singer, is said to have killed many women through masu´tïkï, using a hair of the victim [Kelly 1936:135].

Matak, Tony
Yuki, *California*
A powerful shaman around the turn of the twentieth century who came from the Yuki culture, located above Potter Valley. Raised by a white merchant in Santa Rosa, he was instructed by several different shamans (outfit doctors) from Upper Lake. He doctored among the Pomo both as a *madu* (see entry) and a *qoobakiyalxale* (see

entry). "He never lost a case. . . . He learned eleven hundred songs: five hundred doctor songs and six hundred 'frightening' songs. His outfit was given to him later by an old man" [William Benson (or Ghalganal, "wampum pursuer") in Freeland 1923:68].

Matasukwigadi
Kawaiisu, *Peninsula*
Literal translation: "possessor of medicine" [Zigmond 1977:87]. A herbalist, who may or may not be a shaman.

Matcogahri
Ponca, *Plains*
Bear Dance. Bear shamans are particularly adept at displaying power feats. At the Bear Dance the performers would set up a cedar tree in the center of their ceremonial lodge. "During the dance one of the participators would go up and break off a branch and scrape off the bark. Then he would circle the lodge four times, show it to the members, and announce that he would run it down his throat. He would then thrust it in until the tip barely showed. After a moment he would pull it out, and the blood would gush forth. One shaman had the power of thrusting the cedar through his flesh into his abdomen. After he pulled it out he merely rubbed the wound and it was healed. Still another would swallow a pipe, cause it to pass through his body, and then bring it out and lick it" [Skinner 1915c:792].

In addition, some Bear shamans had a medicine that made them bulletproof. "Big-goose once saw a man, who was performing the bear dance, take a muzzle-loading rifle and charge it in everyone's presence. Another man circled the tent singing, and on the fourth round he was shot by the Indian with the gun; everyone thought he was killed, but he soon sprang up unhurt. Another performer took a buffalo robe, had a third man reload the magic gun, and fired it at the robe. There was no hole visible, but the bullet was found in the center of the robe" [Skinner 1915c:792].

Matinikashauew
Montagnais, *Canadian Eastern Woodlands*
Scapulimancy (see entry).

Matkwisa
Diegueño, *Peninsula*
Cocopa term for soul. This term refers to the soul of a person that leaves the body during dreams *(amuwop)*, as opposed to the *loxachak,* which leaves at the time of death (see *karuk*). Through one's *matkwisa* one can obtain powers via dreams. For example, Gifford [1933:303] wrote of a man who received power as an orator from the spirit of a mockingbird that came to him through his dream. This dream came only once. After receiving it, the man observed the traditional four days of purification, which included daily bathings and abstaining from meat, fish, salt, and sexual intercourse.

Certain types of dreams are known as preludes to certain powers. For instance, dreaming of water causes a warrior to become fearless in battle, while dreaming of successful sexual relations imparts gambling power.

Most often one's *matkwisa* receives information of things to come from dreams. Dreaming of an owl presages death in one's family, dreaming of flying indicates a long life, and dreaming of a bear while sick indicates recovery.

Matoki
Blackfoot, *Plains*
A women's society found among the Blood and North Blackfoot divisions and also the name given to members of the society. The *Matoki* perform only one medicine dance ceremony per year (at the same time as the annual Sun Dance), which lasts for four days. It is conducted in a large wooden structure, built for this purpose, that is similar to the Blackfoot Sun Dance lodge. There are six men attached to the society, but all other members are women, who are divided into four groupings: the snake bonnets, the scabby bulls, the buffalo wool bonnets, and the feather bonnets [Wissler 1913:431]. All of their dances

occur during the daytime. At nightfall the six men are sent home, and the women devote the entire night to hilarity, with jokes and jesting reigning supreme.

"The matoki, like the horns [see *Ehtskinna*], seems to be feared on account of its magical powers" [Wissler 1913:434].

Maxupa mie
Hidatsa, *Plains*
Spirit-woman [Lowie 1913b:339]. *Maxupa* or *maxupá* is generally translated as "medicine" (*xupá*—see EONAH, p. 323).

McKay, Mabel
Pomo, *California*
A world-renowned basket maker and shaman who was born on January 12, 1907, at Nice, California. She was trained in basket making not by her elders but by a spirit [McKay in Sarris 1994:2]. "Her baskets are beautiful, stunning coiled baskets in different shapes and designs: feather baskets, unlike anything seen before, made from the bright yellow feathers of the meadowlark, the metallic green feathers found on a mallard duck's neck, and the orange breast feathers of the robin. And miniature baskets, some no larger than an eraserhead, so small you have to use a magnifying glass to see the intricate design made from the tiniest strips of redbud bark" [Sarris 1994:50].

As a small child she was often sick and had dream visitations by a spirit, sometimes remaining in a dream trance for days. The spirit told her, "You're being fixed to be a doctor" [Sarris 1994:22], though at the time, she didn't even know what a doctor was. There were also other indications of her powers to come. Once, while attending the performance of the *Hesi* Dance, Mabel became afraid when the ceremonial house filled with smoke, and she screamed for her grandmother. She then heard someone repeat her screams, "and when she turned, she saw that it was the *Moki* [ceremonial clown] coming up behind her with a burning ember in his hand.

He forced the hot coal into her shoulder, as if it were a cattle brand, and she screamed with all her might. It was odd. The next day there wasn't a mark on the girl. Nothing" [Sarris 1994:25].

Around the age of fifteen, after years of dreaming and being raised mostly by whites, she was unexpectedly visited by a spirit. She was in an encampment at the time and was returning from the outhouse with her cousin Marie. At one point on the path,

> Marie stopped and said, "Look." Mabel turned and saw in the full moon over the vineyard what looked like a huge bird flying in place. She blinked, focused her eyes. It wasn't a bird, but a man, arms spread out, silhouetted against the massive ball of yellow light, and he wasn't still, situated in place, but hopping up and down, dropping from his place before the moon to the middle of the vineyard, then shooting straight up again. Before Mabel could turn to her cousin, before either of them was able to say a word, the man landed right in front of them. He spoke to Mabel. "Good evening, young lady. How are you this lovely night?" he said, tipping his Stetson hat. He was a heavyset man, but not fat or too old, maybe in his mid-forties. His clothes were clean and pressed, his creased pants held up by fashionable suspenders. He wore a tie.
>
> "Fine," Mabel finally answered, in shock and not knowing what else to say. She turned to Marie, but Marie was frozen. Urine ran down Marie's legs [Sarris 1994:41–42].

Among her medicines was a song for clearing away the fog [Sarris 1994:51]. However, she was best known for her healings, during which she sucked on her patients' bodies. She began her healing work around the age of twenty-one. Her spirit told her to use an elderberry clapper (see *wadada*) and a cocoon rattle (*wayoi*—see *sokut*) when singing her power songs. All of her instructions were sent by the spirit. The spirit told her at one point: "Listen to me now. You make a basket to spit out the sickness you suck with your mouth. Your throat has already been fixed, given. That extra tongue can catch the sickness and stop it. You catch it in your throat, then spit it out. There are many sicknesses. Some move fast, so you have to put them to sleep with certain songs I give you" [Sarris 1994:73].

Mabel McKay passed away on May 31, 1993.

Mecänokw
Fox, *Midwest*

A powerful dreamer shaman around the early 1800s. She received her great powers from "Manito Under Water Animals" [M. R. Harrington 1914:224] during a ten-day vision quest. One of her medicines was known as *Nocäwuskw* [M. R. Harrington 1914:223], which she used in facilitating childbirths. The prescribed use of *Nocäwuskw* was as follows:

> If a woman has a hard time in giving birth to a child, and wishes to try this medicine, she sends tobacco to the woman having the bundle in charge, with a present, such as ponies or goods of some kind. Then, if the practitioner wishes to take the case she accepts the tobacco and throws it into some running stream, praying to the Manito Under Water Animals, and begging them to help the suffering woman. In order to get water for the doctoring, she then dips the shell [*äthi*, "shell"—an accompanying medicine object] into the same stream, dipping with the current, which is supposed to make the discharges run freely from the patient.
>
> Taking the shell to the patient's home, she empties the water from it until it does not come above a natural mark in the shell, then sets it down with point to the east. With the file [*kawipoi*—an ordinary file kept in the medicine bundle] each of the fossil bones [*manito wipits,* "mysterious being's tooth"—a fragment of a mastodon's tooth; *manito hakanun,* "mysterious being's bones"—a bone kept in the medicine bundle] is scratched a few times, beginning with the small black one which is considered the best, and a little pile made of the resulting dust. Using the tip of the small paddle [*puki thahigun*], which thus serves as a measure, a little of the dust is placed gently on the surface of the water at the east end of the shell, then south, then west, then north, after which, beginning at the east, they stir

it four times around clockwise. If the dust sinks they believe the patient cannot live, but if it scatters out over the surface of the water she will recover. Then the patient drinks the preparation. If the dust has sunk, it is given to her but once, for it will do her no good, but if it floats, it is given to her four times, about half an hour or an hour apart [M. R. Harrington 1914:224–225].

The childbirth would then occur at any time during these four ingestions of the medicine. However, if there was no birth after the fourth time, Mecänokw would sing two sacred songs, one in case the baby was a boy and one in case it was a girl.

Mecänokw became a renowned healer and established "a record of one hundred cures" [M. R. Harrington 1914:224]. She was also a high-ranking member of her people's Medicine Lodge Society, and many of the songs sung in this order today still mention her name.

Medicine Boy
Assiniboin, *Plains*

A shaman, interviewed in 1935, who was initiated into this group's Horse society (see *Horse Society Dance*) at the age of three. Of his healing abilities, Rodnick [1938:52] reported: "Black Bull's wife broke her left leg. Medicine Boy was called. He set the bone and within eight days, she was able to walk as well as ever. Headaches were cured by Medicine Boy by scratching the temples with flint, placing some medicine that cannot be named over the scratches and binding it with a piece of cloth. Tuberculosis was cured by him by cutting one of the veins near the elbow. There are two veins here; the one going toward the body is cut. The first blood was black, but as soon as the blood started to run red, the incision was closed and the person soon became well. Sore ears or very bad headaches were cured by opening the vein that led to the head. Sore legs were cured by opening a vein below the ankle. Pneumonia was cured by certain medicines made of the roots that Medicine Boy took out of the ground by a wave of the hand."

By the time of his interview in 1935, the Horse society was extinct and Medicine Boy had lost all of his former powers.

Medicine bundle

Also called medicine pack, medicine bag, sacred bundle, etc. The term *medicine* in this context means those items associated with supernatural power. During the nineteenth century the term *medicine* became synonymous with *mystery* among Native Americans, as explained in the following quote: "The Fur Traders in this country, are nearly all French; and in their language, a doctor or physician, is called *'Medicin.'* The Indian country is full of doctors; and as they are all magicians, and skilled, or profess to be skilled, in many mysteries, the word 'medecin' [sic] has become habitually applied to everything mysterious or unaccountable; and the English and Americans, who are also trading and passing through this country, have easily and familiarly adopted the same word, with a slight alteration, conveying the same meaning; and to be a little more explicit, they have denominated these personages 'medicine-men,' which means something more than merely a doctor or physician" [Catlin 1857:69].

A medicine bundle contains one's personal medicines. Most often these items are wrapped and tied in an animal skin, which then forms the bundle. A medicine bundle can be associated with a particular individual, a particular ceremony, or a particular clan. In some cases, such as the Sacred Calf Pipe bundle of the Lakota, the bundle is associated with the entire culture. Therefore medicine bundles can be either publicly owned or individually owned.

The contents of each bundle differ, but they usually contain the shaman's charms and fetishes (see entries), sacred pipe, body and facial paints, costume regalia, musical instruments, herbs, and other items used in his practice. For example, among the corn-growing Arikara along the Missouri River, ears of corn and a hoe are contained in each medicine bundle [Gilmore 1932:36], and therefore, the Arikara bundles are upward of 4 feet in length and about 20 inches in width [Gilmore 1932:39]. Among the Seminole of Florida, the medicine bundle is also large, occupying an entire deer skin, and can contain up to several hundred items. Normally, however, most medicine bundles are around 18 inches in length. Medicine bundles are used in as many different ways as there are individual bundles.

The medicine bundle has a consciousness of its own, and, therefore, it also functions as a fetish. It often carries a name as well. The bundle is regularly "fed" (through sacred offerings) and handled in a prescribed ritual manner. The opening of a bundle is usually accompanied by a pre-

Menomini quilled otter-skin medicine bags.

scribed ritual, which may involve nothing more than smudging it with sweet grass or sage. The handling and care of the medicine bundle is also ritually defined. Since it contains great power, it is generally regarded with respectful fear. Breaking a taboo associated with a medicine bundle can cause one to lose acquired powers or to be harmed in some way.

Near or after death a person's medicine bundle is usually transferred to some relative. Sometimes it is buried with its owner or destroyed by fire or some other means shortly after the owner's death.

See also *ahalbŏcĭ, bear-knife bundle, chúhari-piru, endóbniwat, Fish, iniskim, ipétes, Iunke Warúhawe, kosksstakjomŏpista, Mankácutzi warúhawe, Medicine Lance bundle, Meshaum, micaduskwe, natoas, nayahtcikan, oskiti, pextcigosan, saam, Tsaidetali, wain waxube, waxobi, wiskwe hpitakan.*

Medicine Dance

In the anthropological literature this term most often refers to variations of the widespread (throughout the Woodland Indians of the Midwest and into the Central Plains) performance of the Grand Medicine Lodge Society, or *Midewiwin* (EONAH, p. 174). This performance "was traditionally the most important religious ceremony of the Woodland Indians, and is still so among the Potawatomi" [Ritzenthaler 1953a: 153]. Central to this performance is the "shooting" of candidates with shells. When "shot," the initiate falls unconscious to the ground.

> The general theory of the Ojibwa-Menominee and of the Winnebago is, that death must thereupon result, but that certain conditions may change this fatal effect into one of temporary unconsciousness. . . . The Ojibwa, Menominee, Winnebago, and Dakota are at one in interpreting the effects of the shooting as the result of the magical powers inherent in the missile [shell] used. Efficiency in shooting, however, depends not merely upon the missile, but also upon the shaman using it. . . . There are indications that this specific efficacy was associated with the general magical power of shamans,—a power that

had been obtained through personal visions, not in any way connected with this society. . . .

> In the Ojibwa-Menominee ceremonies the shooting ritual is always associated with the admission of a new member. . . . Among the Omaha this general shooting is unassociated with initiation, while among the Winnebago it is found associated both with initiation and with the basic ceremony" [Radin 1911:176].

Among the Omaha the Medicine Dance is performed by the Pebble society and the Shell society. In both of their performances, the shooting ritual is not associated with initiation of new members, and only society members are shot.

Among the Winnebago the Medicine Dance society is known as *Mañkanni* [Radin 1911:193], while among the Iowa the Medicine Dance Ceremony is known as *Mankánye waci* (EONAH, p. 165). The ceremony is also found among the Fox, Potawatomi, Ponca, and Kansa. Among the Potawatomi the Medicine Dance society is known as *Midewiwiwat* [Ritzenthaler 1953a:152].

See also *Medicine society, wakan a tcipi, Wolf-Medicine Dance.*

Medicine Lance bundle
Blackfoot, *Plains*

A form of war medicine. Wissler observed one such bundle among the Piegan division around 1910. This particular bundle had a well-known history, and Wissler [1912a:134] noted: "The shaft [of the spear] is something less than three feet in length and carries a long knife-like blade of iron. The bundle is made up by wrapping the shaft, but leaving the blade exposed. In the bundle are bunches of feathers and bells to be tied on the shaft for the demonstration of the ritual. Also, the skin of a small red-winged bird to be worn on the head of the owner when on the warpath and a small pipe for use in the ceremony. Contrary to the usual custom this bundle is kept outside the tipi at all hours and in all weathers, supported on a tipi pole near its middle and parallel to it which leans against the back of the tipi. The point of the lance is upward and kept coated with red paint to symbolize blood."

Concerning the medicine power of this particular lance, Wissler [1912a:135] reported: "This spear was once owned by a small man who went out with a war party against the Crow. At this time the Yellowstone [River] was very high. He asked the tallest man of the party to carry the spear. The current of the stream was so strong that it took them all off their feet. Whenever the spear point touched the water it would get hot and sparks would fly off as it rose from the surface."

Medicine man
See *shamanism.*

Medicine Rock
This is an oracle stone located in the Plains area that was mentioned in the writings of Lewis and Clark, Henry, Catlin, and Maximilian. Ceremonies conducted at this sacred stone would evoke the voice of a spirit. Maximilian, while visiting the home of the Mandans on the Upper Missouri River, wrote of its use as war medicine: "It is situated at two or three days from the village on the edge of the Cannonball River from which it is about one hundred paces. They say it is on the summit of a rather high hill, the top of which is level. It is marked by the footprints of men and other animals, dogs and travois. It is a sort of oracle. They offer it all sorts of valuable articles—knives, pipes, cloth. . . . When going to war they pass near and consult the stone. They approach it, weep, groan, smoke, and retire to a distance where they pass the night. Next day they take down on parchment what the stone shows. This painted parchment is carried to the village where the old men interpret it" [Maximilian in Will and Spinden 1906:138].

Medicine Snake Woman
Piegan, *Plains*
A late-nineteenth-century medicine woman renowned for her clairvoyant medicine powers.

Schaeffer [1969:9] reported an incident involving this woman as witnessed by Jim White Calf following a war raid in the Sweet Grass Hills of Montana: "Six of the raiders failed to return, so a seance was held by the elderly seer. The light was put out in the lodge and her spirit came and left. Upon its return the ghost [spirit] said that the missing party had been located but he was unable to approach it, because of its 'wildness.' A few days later another session was held. Again the ghost went out to search for the missing men. And again he returned, saying that he couldn't get near the group. The third time the spirit succeeded. It was found that all six had been killed and their bodies were to be found on Birch Creek in the Sweet Grass Hills. The following spring a group of Peigan went and searched the area and found the bodies of the missing men."

Because most shamans are experts in handling social crises, it is very possible that Medicine Snake Woman "failed" to locate the missing men on the first two attempts simply because she was not ready to release such bad news to her people.

Medicine societies
In North America, especially among the more sedentary cultures, shamanism is often incorporated into some form of societal organization. Medicine societies, also called dancing societies, ceremonial societies, or sodalities (see entry) in the literature, often evolved into extremely complex ceremonial organizations, with the head "priests" usually being the most powerful elder shamans of the societies. Generally, however, individual shamanism is still practiced within cultures having medicine societies.

Each medicine society has specific functions and duties—some for curing, some for hunting medicines, some for war medicines, some for bringing rain, etc.—although the primary function is curing. The shamans of these societies are very influential. For example, among the Keresan pueblos the shamans of their medicine societies have "supreme political control of the village"

Edward S. Curtis, Medicine Ceremony: The Prayer, *1908. Photogravure.*

[White 1930:604]. Each society has specific rules for entry into the society, coupled with elaborate initiation rituals for new members, all of which differ from culture to culture. Membership is often dependent on one's clan affiliation. Members are most often initiated in secret, and the internal affairs of the society are also kept secret from the other members of the culture. In addition, membership in some societies often means automatic exclusion from other societies within the same culture. The result of this process is that within any culture there usually is a gradation from well-organized, secret medicine societies on one end to individual shamanic practices on the other.

The most complex medicine society ceremonial forms currently appear among the Pueblo people—the Hopi, Zuni, Tanoan (Tiwa, Tewa, and Towa), and Keresan cultures—and the Navajo of the Southwest. For example, some of the Navajo healing ceremonies last more than ten days. The shaman performing only one of them may have to know and sing several hundred songs in a precise order. As such, it is often upward of twenty or thirty years before a Navajo shaman becomes qualified to conduct such a ceremony. Even among these people of the Southwest, the ceremonies often differ, both in existence and in form, among the many different pueblos or village locations. "The 'original' function of the medicine societies was curing diseases. . . . [But] with the growing importance of agriculture, the curing societies undertook ceremonies for rain" [White 1930:618]. "Flint [*Hictiani*—see EONAH, pp. 105–106], Shikame [*Shikani*—see *Shikame* entry, or *Cikame* (White 1930:604)], Giant [*Ckoyo*—see entry], and Fire [*Hakan*—see entry] are the outstanding [medicine] societies of Keres, all organized primarily to control weather and secondarily to cure for witchcraft. There are also Snake, Ant, and Lightning doctors, curing, respectively, for snakebite, for ailments caused by ants in the body such as skin diseases or sore throat, and for lightning shock and broken bones; but these doctors are less well organized; they may be grouped in some other society or may even practice on their own" [Parsons 1939:133]. Membership into these medicine societies is not, in most cases, sought out by individuals but instead results from being cured by that particular society. In fact, among the Zuni "it is very 'dangerous' to join a society except as a result of sickness or mischance" [Parsons 1939:114]. Membership in the Pueblo medicine societies is also based on clan affiliation, as are some of the duties within a society. Among the Zuni, for instance, the medicine water for the altar of the Big Firebrand society "was fetched by a Frog clansman" [Parsons 1939:161]. As for the above-mentioned secrecy of medicine societies, Parsons reported that during her fieldwork at Jemez, a Towa pueblo, she actually "lived in the house of the chief of the Fire society, and but for outside information never would I have learned of his office" [Parsons 1939:151].

The evolution of individual shamanism into more complex forms of social organization is seen by most anthropologists as a natural evolutionary course of cultures. In North America this trend more than likely began among the mound-building cultures of the Midwest and Southeast regions over 2,000 years ago. Although a few early historical observations of some of their ceremonies are recorded, little is really known of their actual breadth and complexity. However, the archaeological recovery of many different ritual objects from the sites of the mound builders clearly points to the performance of very elaborate rituals, including human sacrifice, by these early medicine societies.

Finally, it must be remembered that medicine societies are not the only example of shamans working together. That is, such societies do not need to exist for shamans to cooperate with each other. In regard to severe illnesses, there are many recorded examples of two or more shamans getting together to work on a patient in cultures where there are no medicine societies.

Medicine society

An anthropological term used to refer to the widespread variations of the Ojibwa *Midewiwin* (EONAH, p. 174) ceremony. The Medicine society is of three types: the Central Algonquian type (Fox, Illinois, Kickapoo, Menomini, Miami, Potawatomi, and Sauk), the Omaha/Ponca type, and the Dakota type (e.g., see Gillette 1906) to which belong the Iowa, Oto, Winnebago, and Wahepton Dakota forms. The Dakota type differs from the others in that it lacks progressive degrees, it is not founded on a myth dealing with a culture hero, and the members are divided into four bands with their respective leaders.

These variations also go by other names, such as Medicine Lodge society, Shell society, etc. Among the Omaha the Water Monster society is a "somewhat bastard form of the Midewiwin" [Fortune 1932:88] in which a translucent stone (later on a clear marble) is "shot" by the members versus the shell used in the *Midewiwin*. The Omaha Water Monster society is referred to as the Pebble society or *Inkugthin* by some writers [Fortune 1932:90]. In each case the society is a secret society and primarily concerned with healing; however they also hold public performances.

See also *Medicine Dance, Tatatex Waci.*

Medicine Wheel

On the western side of the Big Horn Mountains in Wyoming is a bald mountain, called Medicine Mountain (latitude 45° 49′ 00.43′′, longitude 107° 54′ 7.67′′), atop of which is an unusually large, circular, stone enclosure known as the Medicine Wheel. "The wheel consists of a wide and somewhat irregular circle of large stones, which has a diameter of from seventy-four to eighty feet. In the center of this circle is an inner circle of large stones—piled up in a wall—about twelve feet in outside diameter and about seven feet inside, and from two and a half to three feet high. From the outer side of the wall of this inner, the central, circle, twenty-eight lines of small stones, set close together, radiate to the border of the outer circle" [Grinnell 1922:300].

The use of the Medicine Wheel is lost to antiquity. Some evidence points to it being Shoshoni in origin, while others speculate that it was made by the early Cheyenne.

The term medicine wheel is also used for other such circles of stones found elsewhere and symbols thereof. For example, see *caugkdeska wakang*.

Megillis Hadjo
Creek, *Southeast*

An early-nineteenth-century weather shaman from Tukabatchi, an Upper Creek settlement on the west bank of the Tallapoosa River opposite Talasse, Alabama. "In the summer of 1840 there was a great drought in the country, threatening the destruction of the crops, and the old man was called upon to make it rain. After performing his ceremony for a time he published that he was about to be successful that the country might be flooded, and he thought it best to desist, which he did. Last winter (1840–1841) was very cold and the old man was requested to moderate the weather; the present winter (1841–1842) is remarkably mild and the old man explains it by saying that he blew off the cold of last winter so far that it had not come back" [Hitchcock in Swanton 1928:630].

Mehtshingweea
Miami, *Midwest*

Shamans. This early-nineteenth-century term appears to have been used for sucking shamans, given the following account of their healing activities: "The doctor examines the patient with the eyes of an eagle, a woodpecker or some other winged fowl which he has borrowed for the occasion, and after repeating some short sentences in a murmur and striking his own breast, he vomits up a small whitish substance which he holds in the palm of his hand and examines at-

tentively. He tells the patient that this will decide his fate. If it works thro' his hand he will die, but if it remains upon the hand he will recover. Then giving him a small supply of roots and encouraging him to have good faith, he leaves him. After a short time he returns to visit his patient and then tells him how he is to fare" [Trowbridge 1938:54–56].

In another scenario the shaman "feels the limbs & body of the patient at the seat of pain, & perhaps squeezes out something from the flesh. He strikes or rubs him upon the breast and the patient vomits. All these things the doctor swallows, and when he has done he takes his present & departs, pronouncing his patient recovered" [Trowbridge 1938:55–56].

Memorate

An anthropological term used for true accounts of personal, supernatural experiences that have, from the perspective of the anthropologist, been "structured and perceived (in the mind of the informant) by a mental set imbued with traditional beliefs" [Barnouw 1977:226].

Meshaum
Fox, *Midwest*

Grand Medicine bag. The sacred bundle that records the religious instructions from the first spirits given to the Fox. These are remembered via knots in strings, stones, hieroglyphic figures, etc., contained within the bundle. Some of the more important things required by the *Meshaum* are to fast every morning during the winter, to give one's belongings to the poor in memory of departed ancestors, to avoid menstruating women, and to be forgiving toward those of one's own nation.

Meta
Kaska, *Mackenzie-Yukon*

Shaman. Both males and females become shamans. Around fourteen to fifteen years of age, boys are encouraged by their fathers to go on a one- or two-day vision quest. Most often the spirit comes to the quester during a dream at this time. "Communications from animals or other symbols constituted the marks of a successful vision quest. . . . Such a dream must never (?) be revealed to another person" [Honigmann 1954:105]. Furthermore, "no formal instruction in shamanism followed the dream quest—'a man taught himself'" [Honigmann 1954:107]. Once successful, the new shaman continues to vision quest in order to obtain additional guardian spirits, with some males remaining alone in the woods for a month or more.

"The successful solicitation of power brought a man into relation with one or more animal helpers upon whose aid he now counted in performing curing and other ceremonies. In addition curers might dream of natural objects (like leaves or bark) that possessed medicinal properties. A shaman collected such materials and kept them in a small pouch" [Honigmann 1954:105]. Shamans who could cure were called *nudita* [Honnigmannn 1954:104].

Clappers, made of two or three pieces of wood, replaced the drum used in accompanying songs during healing ceremonies. A shaman outfitted himself according to instructions received from his helping spirits. "He might represent his power source by donning the skin of a moose, bear, sheep, or other animal" [Honigmann 1954:106]. Among the Dease River Kaska the shaman often uses a rattle during the ceremony, but in other areas its use is unknown. "Sometimes the practitioner 'blew' water from his mouth on the sore part of a patient's anatomy or he might drive the illness into a foreign object, like a rock or a small doll that had been prepared by his wife. He pushed the image into the patient's body, causing it to disappear. Then object as well as illness were extracted and quickly stuffed into the curer's pouch. Sucking blood from the head of an ailing person (never for some reason from the hand or arm) also constituted a recognized pattern of doctoring. Sometimes small gophers or weasels were extracted during sucking and these represented the causes of the particular malady" [Honigmann 1954:111].

One rather unique aspect of Kaska healing ceremonies is that "practitioners [shamans] at work carefully avoided exposing their mouths to women and concealed their features beneath a piece of skin (in post-contact time underneath a handkerchief). The association between the breath and shamanistic efficacy no doubt determined in part such attention to the mouth" [Honigmann 1954:106].

In addition to their healing work shamans are called upon to divine the location of game, diagnose illness, assist war parties, foretell the future, etc. Shamans also hold public power contests. For example, one shaman was able to walk on water "so that everybody could see it," and another was able to make a foot-long, decorated staff disappear [Honigmann 1954:106–107].

Mëteìnu
Delaware, *Northeast*

Lenape term for shaman, usually one with great powers [Kraft 1986:167]. Power is obtained mainly through vision quests at secluded locations in the woods or on a mountaintop. Boys undertake such quests around puberty. However, as Speck [1931:52] noted, "some acquire their personal guardian [spirit] in childhood, some in their youth at the time of the fast-vigil, others in the prime of life." Less often women receive visions and become shamans. Dreams also assist shamans throughout life in supernatural guidance. "In addition to curing, these individuals forecast the weather, performed rainmaking rituals, prepared charms for unlucky hunters, concocted love potions, and performed divinations. *Mëteìnu* also had the power to protect the people in wartime" [Kraft 1986:181].

This same term is also used for wandering spirits or ghosts [Kraft 1986:179].

Metudhauk
Yuma, *Southwest*

Bewitchment. Literal translation: "he is bewitched" [Forde 1931:194]. Sorcery is accomplished only through a very powerful spirit, most often *etsöf*, the hawk. One typical treatment, which occurred in January 1897, was described as follows:

> The witch doctor . . . had red feathers in his hair and the upper half of his face was painted black. He laid the body [of the patient] with its head to the east and as he placed it in position it showed some signs of life and began to twitch all over.
>
> The doctor then stood several yards away to the south of the man. Walking slowly towards him and moving round to his head, he sang his first song. The man now became quite quiet and when he reached the head the doctor leaned over and placed a round mirror on his patient's chest. The mirror was in place of the bowl of water which doctors used in the old days.
>
> The doctor now stood on the north side and began his second song, which he continued while making a complete circle around the patient, going west, south, east and back to north.
>
> He then crouched over the man and sucked blood out of his chest, blew saliva into his ears and eyes, and stood up again ready to sing his third song as he made the same circuit again. Stopping once more at the north he looked into the mirror for a long time and then began singing again as he walked around for the fourth time.
>
> The man was now cured. Although he was very weak he was able to sit up and after four days fasting he was quite well [Miguel in Forde 1931:194].

The Yuma often put to death shamans suspected of sorcery.

Micaduskwe
Fox, *Midwest*

"High-toned or good-will medicine" [M. R. Harrington 1914:211]. This is the name given to a small medicine bundle (see entry) obtained from a man named Mecabekwa, also known as U. S. Grant, around 1910; the bundle is now labeled Bundle 2/5327 of the Heye Collection. The content of this bundle is composed of medicines for war, gambling, and hunting, as well as the "good-will producing" compound, a popular form of medicine [M. R. Harrington 1914:214] that is often used as a love medicine. Thus the bundle is essentially given the same name as that of this particular medicine. The use of *micaduskwe* as a love medicine was described as follows:

> To attract a woman it was only necessary to put a little of the green paint on one's cheeks and chew the medicine that is in the little iron box in the bundle and rub it on the arms and chest, also on one of the eagle down feathers, which should be then fastened in the hair. Thus equipped a man can attract the woman of his choice.
>
> Mecabe′kwa tells that one time he tried to speak to a woman, but she hit him and made his mouth bleed. Angered by such treatment Mecabe′kwa vowed to "get even"; so when he had the opportunity he put on the paint and feather from the bundle. That night she came to his house crying, and told him that she loved him, and even proposed that she lie with him, although his wife was there and she knew it. After a while Mecabe′kwa saddled a horse and took her to her home. On arriving at her place he told her, "Go inside and fix a bed for us while I tie my horse." As soon as she had entered the house he rode away home. But she came back later and bothered him for a long time [M. R. Harrington 1914:214].

The *micaduskwe* is also used by women to attract men, and it is often used by women to bring back a husband gone astray. However, the woman must first send for her husband four times, and if he does not respond, then she may use the *micaduskwe* after completing a preliminary, two-day fast. She must then remain with the bundle for four days, even if her husband returns to her before then.

> Another use for 'Mĭ ca′ dus kwe' is in the "pony smoke" when the tribes visit each other and make presents of ponies. When the Sac and Fox visited another tribe this medicine would make the other Indians give them very good horses as presents.
>
> Or, if one wishes to buy certain horse whose owner does not want to sell, this medicine will make

him change his mind and sell cheap. Sometimes people rub their hands with this medicine just before shaking hands with the person they wish to influence [M. R. Harrington 1914:228–229].

The *micaduskwe* also contains certain feathers from the hawk and eagle and a weasel skin, all of which are used as war medicines. When the owner of such a bundle went to war, "he wore the feathers tied on his scalp lock, the hawk feathers and one bunch of [eagle] down feathers hanging down, the other two bunches of down feathers sticking out crosswise, and these protected him by their power, so that no one could hit him from behind. At such times he used to put red paint on his face from the bundle, four spots on each cheek" [M. R. Harrington 1914:212].

The weasel skin was worn hanging from the neck. "The weasel runs close to the ground, or under it; he is hard to see and harder still to hit. So the man was, when he rode to war with the little weasel hanging from its cord about his neck. The Sioux could not see him—they could only hear his war whoop" [M. R. Harrington 1914:212].

The hunting medicine contents of such bundles are used in the following prescribed manner: "Dipping the bundle four times through the smoke of burning cedar toward the east at sunrise, they opened the bundle and removing certain herbs, macerated them by chewing, and rubbed them upon their bodies, also placing a little of the mixture in their hunting pouches. Each hunter then took a little stick which he dipped in the green paint and applied four times to his cheeks, making two little green spots on each side. As he applied the first spot he might say, 'I will even kill the most difficult animal, the white raccoon'; then as he touched the other cheek, 'the red raccoon.' Or it might be that he would say, 'the white deer' and 'the red deer.' This done, the hunter would start eastward to look for game. If there were as many as four hunters in the party, one would go in each of the four directions" [M. R. Harrington 1914:217]. Two sacred hunting songs are also used with the

hunting medicine, and game acquired via this hunting medicine is ritually processed. For example, blood of the animal is thrown to the four directions, individuals are careful not to break any bones while processing the meat, dogs are not allowed to get any of the meat, bits of the meat are offered in the fire as a sacrifice, etc.

The gambling medicine in this bundle is used primarily for footraces.

In such a case the runner would chew the herbs and rub them on his feet and on the little down feather worn in his hair, in the hopes that this would help him to win. In horse racing they would tie one of the eagle down feathers in the horse's tail, and a little red yarn in the mane, after which a medicine usually kept in the weasel skin in the bundle was chewed to a pulp and placed in the horse's mouth and nostrils, and rubbed on his head, back and legs, and on his hoofs. This was thought not only to give the horse the weasel's power of running swiftly, but to keep rivals off the trail. Other horses, catching the scent of the charmed horse's tracks, would bolt the course and buck off their riders. A feather song similar to the one used in courting was used when preparing a horse for the race, or for that matter when preparing for any sort of gambling. At the end of a race another compound would be given to the horse which would bring him back to his normal condition [M. R. Harrington 1914:219].

Micaduskwe is a powerful and, therefore, potentially dangerous medicine. Its proper uses require the knowledge of sacred songs that go with each of the different applications of the medicine. To ward off any ill effects from its use, another herb, referred to as *Ne the tci gun pa ma dji tci gun,* or "cure for poison," is chewed and rubbed over the body of the user after he is finished with it [M. R. Harrington 1914:229]. Misuse of this medicine can cause insanity.

Mice
Maidu, *California*
The term used by the Nisenan (Southern Maidu) located in the Nevada City area for the shamanic

removal of a "pain" (disease—see *pains*) by sucking [Beals 1933:390]. Only some Nisenan shamans are sucking shamans. All others destroy their *mice* using various rituals.

Mikenak
Ojibwa, *Canadian Eastern Woodlands*
Also: *Michika* [Coleman 1937:51]. Dialectical variant: *mikanâ* (Menomini) [Skinner 1915d:194]. Turtle spirit. Mikenak is the spirit go-between during the Shaking Tent Ceremony (EONAH, pp. 246–249). That is, the shaman, termed *jessakkid* (EONAH, pp. 121–122), first puts questions from the audience to Mikenak. Then Mikenak leaves to obtain the answers. "Upon departure of the turtle, the tent began to shake, swaying from north to south and then from east to west, and did not come to a standstill until the turtle returned to give the answer from the Great Spirit. The approach of the turtle could be heard by a whistling sound as he dropped from the top to the bottom of the tent. Voices could be heard inside the tent, after which the answer was given by the juggler [shaman—see EONAH, pp 124–125]" [Coleman 1937:51]. Although other spirits can be heard during this performance, the voice of Mikenak is easily distinguished by its Donald Duck–like quality.

The *jessakkid* form a distinct class of Ojibwa shamans—namely, seers. "The gift [to foresee the future] is believed to be given by the thunder god, or Animiki´, and then only at long intervals and to a chosen few. The gift is received during youth, when the fast is undertaken and when visions appear to the individual. His renown depends upon his own audacity and the opinion of the tribe. He is said to possess the power to look into futurity; to become acquainted with the affairs and intentions of men; to prognosticate the success or misfortune of hunters and warriors, as well as other affairs of various individuals" [Hoffman 1891:157].

The *jessakkid* is also thought capable of stealing an individual's soul; thus he is somewhat feared.

See also *mishikan, Aperketek* in *tornarsuk* entry.

Millak
Labrador Eskimo, *Arctic Coast*
A female shaman. The following is a brief account of one of her divination ceremonies as recorded by Jens Haven, the first and most famous of the early Moravian missionaries along the Labrador coast: "She began, with deep sighs and groans, to invoke the Torngak [spirit], till at length her loud, shrill voice made the house tremble. After a brief silence she shouted aloud to me and then another what the Torngak had told her in reply to their questions. If the replies were unfavourable, the Torngak was again invoked, until the results were satisfactory" [Haven in Hawkes 1916:130].

Shamans of this region usually acquire only one helping spirit.

Mirarackupe
Hidatsa, *Plains*
A sacred war fetish (see entry) used by members of the Kit-Fox society (*iexoxka* or *ike*) [Lowie 1913b:253]. It consisted of a stick, hooked at the top and approximately 6 feet in height, that was decorated with either wolfskin or otterskin. The wolfskin was wrapped about the stick, and "the upper half of the stick was painted red. The hooked otterskin-stick seems to have been quite similar. . . . The straight staffs are described as long, wrapped with black and red cloth, and decorated at the top with two erect eagle feathers. The otterskin on the staffs represented the otter's activity, and the wolfskin the strength of the wolf as an enemy, the red paint on the stick symbolizing the blood of his prey. Whoever owned this stick had good luck in counting coup on the enemy" [Lowie 1913b:255].

Misatimucimuwin
Cree, *Canadian Eastern Woodlands*
Horse Dance among the Plains Cree. This religious ritual was dedicated to the spirits of Weasel and Horse [Mandelbaum 1940:277]. Whoever pledged to sponsor this ceremony approached a shaman who had the power to perform it and requested that he do so. Some who were able to do

the Horse Dance had been taught by their fathers or other relatives, while others received the power to perform it via a dream. The ceremony lasted for one day.

Mishikan
Ojibwa, *Canadian Eastern Woodlands*
Dialectical variant: *mishtapeu* (Montagnais) [Armitage 1991:82]. The Great Turtle. This spirit acts as a messenger between humans and other spirit beings. He speaks to other spirits in a language not understood by human beings and then translates what is said back into Ojibwa, Menomini, or English. "His talk sounds something like the noise of pulling the fingers over a strip of birch bark. He seems to be under the lodge. He brings the spirit of anybody that you want, so that you can talk to the spirit of a friend. If he is not there at first [during the ceremony], he will always come. You can hear him tumble into the lodge. You hear his voice as soon as he comes. He must have greater power than the other spirits. The lodge shakes when he comes. He makes a good deal of fun and jokes and plays with the other spirits (who) sometimes try to push him out" [Kawbawgam in Bourgeois 1994:51].

See also *Mikenak*.

Mishtikuai
Montagnais, *Canadian Eastern Woodlands*
Highly decorated caribou-hide robes used by Innu (as they call themselves) shamans. Such robes are frequently used by shamans to gain power during a ritual.

When the Innu embarked on a caribou hunt, they looked to a shaman for guidance. By wrapping his body in his caribou robe, the shaman could magically transform himself into a caribou, which allowed him to attract more of his kind. When a herd came close enough to be ambushed by the young hunters, the shaman would remove his robe, transforming himself back into a man.

Less powerful individuals also wore caribou hides. These hides were usually made into coats that were decorated with paints and worn during hunting trips [Armitage 1991:57].

Mitäwape
Menomini, *Midwest*
Shamans who "have the ability to draw or suck out disease sent by sorcerers by means of a bone sucking tube. A member [of their order] is known as mitä´wäpeo akuûhekao [the mitäo who draws out disease]. The function of the association is to combat the activities of the witch society" (see *kinubik inäniwûk*) [Skinner 1915d:197]. Mitäwape are considered to have less power than the *jesako* (see entry).

In a healing ceremony

the mitäwäpeo akuûhekao swallows the four bones, and taking some water in a dish in which he places the sucking tube, and approaching the sick person begins to sing to his guardian [spirit] and rattle his deer hoof rattle. As he sings he begins to see the diseases that trouble the patient. He blows upon one and covering it with his forefinger he gets down on all fours and takes the bone tube which he places over the spot and commences to suck out the trouble. . . .

When he has finished he replaces the tube in the bowl of water and the four bones and all the other things he has swallowed. The trouble that was afflicting the patient will appear in the shape of needles or quills, arrows of some evil sorcerer, or even worms, or frogs, sent there by some witch to torture the sick person. Those are sometimes alive, but are usually dead. When these have been exhibited to the patient and all the bystanders, the doctor takes up the bone tube and sucks back the loathsome mess into his own body. It will have no effect on him, in spite of the evil charms it contains, because the spirit of the mud-turtle (with which all such doctors are endowed, and which lives in their bodies) will take them away to some place where they will never again be heard of. Sometimes, however, the offending "arrow" of the sorcerer is retained and shot back at him [Skinner 1915d:199].

Mittilik
Labrador Eskimo, *Arctic Coast*
Spirits, such as a shaman's helping spirits [Vallee 1966:61].

Mituk

West Alaska Eskimo, *Arctic Coast*

A late-nineteenth-century Malemiut shaman. In 1940 Pegliruk, the oldest male then living at Shungnak, remembered Mituk's performances as follows:

> Mituk was more spiritual than any. When they tied him up, they tied an axe to his feet, using new rawhide to bind him tight. When the lamps were out, the spirit of Mituk left and the devil [spirit] came in. As soon as the lamp is out, an eagle screams. Everybody can hear wings striking the inside of the house. Then, finally, the eagle goes out through the roof, and it can be heard screaming farther and farther away. While the eagle is flying away, a loose dog comes along and curls up in the house. This means bad luck. People can't see the dog, but they know it is there. Then Mituk begins to come flying back, screaming, nearer and nearer. But by the time they hear Mituk land on the roof, the dog has stopped up the hole, and Mituk can't get in. When they light the lamp, the dog is gone, but they find Mituk, still tied up on the roof of the house. They take him in and untie him. They see the axe. It is still tied to Mituk, but it is all bloody—with a person's blood. Mituk has been somewhere and killed somebody" [Pegliruk in Giddings 1961:17–18].

Miwalaqsh

Chumash, *Peninsula*

This term has several uses. It is used, for instance, to refer to both the north direction and Polaris, the North Star. During this group's winter solstice ceremony—the annual *Kakunup-mawa* (also the term used for the sun)—the word *miwalaqsh* refers to a ceremonial sunstaff about 18 inches in height. On the second day of this ceremony, the sunstaff is "erected at the center of the ceremonial ground by a priest and twelve helpers. The perforated stone atop the sunstaff was painted green or blue to resemble a sand dollar. . . . The sunstaff stone was sometimes incised with rays or geometric designs representing the sun and or possibly the cardinal points. To release the power of the sunstaff, the stone was tapped and ceremonial words were spoken by the *puha* (master of ceremonies) and then [the] sun was symbolically pulled in a northward direction" [B. Miller 1988:122]. The ray designs are incised on the top of this stone, and some researchers believe they mark the inclination of the sun and the four cardinal points. We do know that the Chumash "were intensely interested in and aware of the movements of the cosmos" [B. Miller 1988:121].

Miyahánit

Nez Perce, *Plateau*

A shaman whose power comes from having inherited the guardian spirits of a relative [D. Walker 1967:78].

See also *wéyeknin*.

Mohleh

Miwok, *California*

See *hokitta*.

Mole

Miwok, *California*

Generic term for stones that are endowed with power [Gifford n.d. b:39]. Such power stones are known throughout the Miwok region (i.e., northern, central, and southern regions) and among the nearby Yokuts. Finding such a stone will bring its owner some form of good fortune—luck in hunting, an animal spirit protector, and so forth.

"It is believed that a *mole* will jump out at a person that it likes. The person will pick up the stone which thus thrust itself upon him and that person will thereafter be lucky in finding things and be successful in deer hunting" [Gifford n.d. b:39].

Once found the stone indicates its favor by bringing rain shortly thereafter. The possessor of the stone then bathes himself and sings for the stone. Because such stones contain power, others dare not handle an individual's *mole*.

Monday, Johnny
Paviotso, *Basin*

A Wadátkuht shaman who was born around 1850 and died around 1925. He received medicine from the dove that enabled him to be swift-footed. He was able to make the journey from Fort Bidwell to Fort McDermitt, at least 140 miles, in one day on foot [Riddell 1960:71]. (Note: There is a possibility that Johnny Monday was from a neighboring Paiute band instead of the Wadátkuht, for the informant did not specify where he lived.)

Mongkoho
Hopi, *Southwest*

Chief's staff. In certain societies, such as the Agave *(Kwan)* and Horn *(Ahl)* societies, a *mongkoho* is given to each newly initiated member. It is usually made by the sponsor of the initiate. "It is their badge of office, is considered very sacred and is buried with them" [Dorsey and Voth 1901:26, n.*]. When guarding a *kiva* entrance during secret ceremonies, society members on guard duty carry their *mongkoho* in their hands as a sign of their authority.

Mongwikuru
Hopi, *Southwest*

A small ceremonial gourd surrounded by netting; it contains consecrated springwater that is sprinkled and blown on people and altar objects during various parts of a ceremony [Voth 1901:103]. In some cases a little honey is added to the water, rubbed onto the rim of the *mongwikuru,* or both.

Voth [1901:108–109] observed the ritual filling of a *mongwikuru:*

> Arriving at the spring [northeast of Orabi], which is half way down the mesa, he first blew the [eagle] bone whistle four times. Then, after having uttered a short prayer, he deposited four of the eight *nakwakwosis* [see entry] in a rock niche near the spring, then sprinkled sacred meal into the spring from the six ceremonial directions, and

then dipped a little water with the *mongwikuru,* six times, I believe, pouring it on the ground near the spring in order, he said, to induce the clouds to bring more water, and then filled the vessel. Coming up from the spring, he placed the *hikvsi* [see *nakwakwosi*] about six yards from the spring on the trail, and sprinkled a line of meal from the spring over the *hikvsi* toward the village (so that the rain, he said, when coming to the spring, might also go to the village), and then returned to the kiva.

Motsomita
Blackfoot, *Plains*

Brave-Dogs. Members of the Brave-Dog society, sometimes called the Coyote-Brave-Dogs [Wissler 1913:397]. The members of this society are noted for their bravery in war and their strong war medicines. They paint their entire bodies white, except for the lower face (which is painted in red) and don coyote skins. With bulb rattles in hand, to which are attached coyote tails and eagle bone whistles, they dance and sing their medicine songs as they stand fast in front of the enemy during battle. They are renowned for their heroic battle deeds, as depicted in the following example: "Running-buffalo, the father of Elk-horn, was a brave-dog. Once there was a fight between the Blackfoot and the Assiniboine in what is now the southern part of the Montana Reservation. The Assiniboine were in a hole and hard to get at. Running-buffalo rode up, got off his horse, and with his rattle in his hand, singing the brave-dog songs, went directly to the hole and jumped in among the Assiniboine. His war party followed close at his heels and succeeded in routing the enemy. All brave-dogs are believed to have great power. Once Running-buffalo was shot through the abdomen with three or four arrows. He asked that some buffalo intestines be cooked for him, saying that he would use them to replace the injured parts of his body. He ate them and recovered" [unnamed informant in Wissler 1913:398].

This example also indicates that at least some Brave-Dogs carried healing powers as well as war powers.

Mowitihagi
Fox, *Midwest*

Literal translation: "Dirty Little Ani" [Fisher 1939:102]. One of several societies associated with buffalo ceremonies. This society is also sometimes referred to as "Those Who Worship the Spotted Buffalo Calf" [Fisher 1939:100].

Included in the sacred bundle maintained by this society is a small, red-stone buffalo bull, 8 to 10 inches in length and 6 to 7 inches in height. It is brought out twice a year in the sacred feast of the *Mowitihagi* and is considered to be alive and sacred. "It is said that once its neck was broken. The two pieces were put together and the thing placed back into a medicine bag. When this bag was again opened there were no signs of where the break had been. The image was as if whole and unbroken" [Fisher 1939:103]. A prophecy accompanies this stone buffalo: It is said that when the four legs are broken off it, the end of the earth is at hand.

Mugálu
Washo, *Basin*

The name of a specific plant used as a hunting medicine. The shaman dreams of this plant and then uses the root of it in preparing his medicine. "They [shamans] wash and pray before collecting it; afterwards they give pieces of it to friends and relatives. The hunter puts a small piece of the root in a fresh deer track and begins to trail the deer. When he catches up to the deer, he finds it sleeping" [Hank Pete in Freed and Freed 1963:53].

Mukampuaxantï
Paiute, *Basin*

Moapa (Southern Paiute) term for a spider shaman. "From the bite he sucked blood and spat it into his hands. Dreaming of a spider gave power to treat all venomous bites—spider, insect, scorpion, and, upon occasion, snake" [Kelly 1939:160–161].

Mushkiki
Ojibwa, *Canadian Eastern Woodlands*

Chippewa charms and herbal medicines. "Charms, like [herbal] medicine, were usually obtained by purchase from another individual. They were used to bring good fortune in hunting, fishing, trapping, gambling, war, and love; to protect the individual from disease or bodily injury; and for malevolent purposes. The vast majority of charms were concerned with the food quest, with hunting charms being especially numerous. In most instances charms were carried in small buckskin packets on the person, but love or malevolent charms were commonly worked in the home by applying them to clothing, hair, or any personal article of the person they wished to affect" [Ritzenthaler 1953b:209].

Muskekewininee
Miami, *Midwest*

Shaman [Anson 1970:25]. *Muskekewininee* are medical practitioners who primarily use medicinal herbs and therapies rather than appealing to spirit helpers. When these healers fail, the more powerful *meda* (or *meta*) is called in to perform a cure. The *meda* is associated with the Miami Grand Medicine society, the *Medawin* (or *Medewiwin*), and he appeals to the *manito*, which is "the power for good and evil which existed in all things, animate or inanimate, including man" [Anson 1970:24].

Muxuantï
Paiute, *Basin*

Literal translation: "soul" or "mind" [Kelly 1939:164]. Las Vegas (Southern Paiute) term for a shaman who can foretell the future.

Muxu auru xwang
Paiute, *Basin*

Literal translation: "soul gone away" [Kelly 1939:152]. Southern Paiute term for illnesses caused by soul loss. To treat such cases the shaman "pressed his hands on the chest of the patient and dispatched his tutelary [spirit] in search of the missing soul" [Kelly 1939:152].

Naganame wogwum

Micmac, *Canadian Eastern Woodlands*

Literal translation: "sweat wigwam" [Wallis and Wallis 1955:124]. In the seventeenth century, Micmac sweat lodge ceremonies were conducted in a dome-shaped lodge covered with bark, skins, etc. Hot stones were placed in the middle of the lodge, and water was poured over them. After the ceremony was completed, participants would leave the lodge and plunge into a nearby river. This is the typical pattern for most sweat lodge ceremonies. However, by the nineteenth century this basic pattern had become altered. "A fire was made in it [the sweat lodge], and stones were heated in the fire. Everything was then removed except the heated stones. Over them were placed hemlock boughs, whereupon three or four men entered, made the entrance airtight, and remained to have a good sweat. No water was employed. . . . One informant stated that boys used the sweat lodge and, rarely, the women also used it" [Wallis and Wallis 1955:124].

Nagualism

An anthropological term that means having the concept of a guardian spirit, helping spirit, or spirit familiar [Parsons 1939:63]. In Central America the shaman's helping spirit is called *nagual* [Winick 1969:377].

Naha

Hopi, *Southwest*

At Old Oraibi, Powell [in Fowler and Fowler 1971:280] recorded this term for "doctor" in 1870.

Nakadzoq

Iglulik Eskimo, *Arctic Coast*

A phrase meaning "one who drops to the bottom of the sea." Sometimes an Iglulik shaman is asked by an individual to call forth a particular spirit known to the community at large. When the shaman consents and his subsequent *tonrineq* is for the sea spirit *Takánakapsâluk,* the shaman "about to make this journey is said to be nak·a·zɔq" [Rasmussen 1929:124]. This expression is rather remarkable in that it seems to indicate a certain type of trance state is necessary for this particular spirit. However, the use of this phrase may simply be a public recognition of the particular type of ceremony that the

An Eskimo miniature mask dating from around 500 B.C.

shaman is performing. Although it is well known that shamans use different altar displays and ritual paraphernalia for different ceremonies, no research indicates that these different rituals in turn induce different states of consciousness in the shaman.

This particular *tonrineq* begins, once all the oil lamps have been extinguished, by having the shaman sent off to the domain of *Takánakapsâluk*:

The shaman sits for a while in silence, breathing deeply, and then, after some time has elapsed, he begins to call upon his helping spirits, repeating over and over again: . . . "the way is made ready for me; the way opens before me!"

Whereat all present must answer in chorus: . . . "let it be so!"

And when all the helping spirits have arrived, the earth opens under the shaman, but often only to close up again; he has to struggle for a long time with hidden forces, ere he can cry at last: "Now the way is open."

And then all present must answer: "Let the way be open before him; let there be way for him."

And now one hears, at first under the sleeping place: "Halala—he—he—he, halala—he—he—he!" and afterwards under the passage, below the ground, the same cry: "Halele—he!" And the sound can be distinctly heard to recede farther and farther until it is lost altogether. Then all know that he is on his way to the ruler of the sea beasts.

Meanwhile, the members of the household pass the time by singing spirit songs in chorus, and here it may happen that the clothes which the shaman has discarded come alive and fly about round the house, above the heads of the singers, who are sitting with closed eyes. And one may hear deep sighs and the breathing of persons long since dead; these are the souls of the shaman's namesakes [i.e., helping spirits], who have come to help. But as soon as one calls them by name, the sighs cease, and all is silent in the house until another dead person begins to sigh [Rasmussen 1929:124–125].

Nakani
Kutchin, *Mackenzie-Yukon*

Many members of the Northern Athabaskan nations believe in a "bad Indian" known as *Nakani* or by dialectical variations thereof. Among the Vunta people (Crow River Kutchin), he is known as *Nain* [Osgood 1936:157], and among the neighboring Tanaina, he is called *Nándína* [Osgood 1937:171].

The *Nakani* appear as human beings but have supernatural power; they are "said by some to operate through an extensive practice of shamanism" [Osgood 1936:154]. Among the Vunta the *Nakani* "look like men and have bows and arrows. They live underground and are able to do anything that they wish by simply thinking about it. When a Nakani wishes to speak to an Indian, the person falls into a trance and the communication takes place as though it were a dream. Sometimes the Nakani steal men as well as women and make them slaves. In the winter, the Nakani stay underground and bother no one, but in the summer they come out to hunt" [Osgood 1936:157]. Their presence is known by a particular whistling sound heard in the woods.

Nakwakwosi
Hopi, *Southwest*

Prayer offering. The *nakwakwosi* usually consists of a small feather with a short cotton string attached to it [Voth 1901:68]. A similar prayer offering is the *pühtavi* (road marker) or *hikvsi*

[Dorsey and Voth 1901:19] (plural: *hikvspiata* [Dorsey and Voth 1901:15]). The distinction is that the latter one has a long cotton string attached to it.

Another common form of prayer offering is the Hopi *paho* (see entry).

See also *prayer feathers/sticks*.

Nalusaerutut
West Greenland Eskimo, *Arctic Coast*
Literal translation: "those who are not ignorant" [Birket-Smith 1924:450]. These are persons who are trained from childhood to be sensitive to the presence of spirits and other supernatural phenomena. As children, they often spend time in the presence of a shaman during his performances. The *nalusaerutut* were able to recognize the presence of a shaman because "he breathed fire" [Birket-Smith 1924:452].

Naröya
Shoshoni, *Basin*
This is an old dance used for healing. The meaning of the name is no longer known. "Any man might give the dance if some member of his family was smitten with a cold or some more serious disease; to drive this away the performers would shake their blankets at the close of the ceremony. . . . The dance might be performed either in the daytime or at night. . . . In the early days the ceremony lasted five consecutive nights, only the final performance took place in the daytime. Nowadays the Shoshone only dance for one or two days" [Lowie 1915b:817]. There are no musical instruments used during the dance, and upon completion all participants go into the sweat lodge.

Nasosotan
Hopi, *Southwest*
Also: *nasotan* [Stephen 1936:1260]. Stick-Swallowers. From the word *nasosota*, meaning "swallowing." Their ceremony is found throughout the Pueblos. Among the Zuni the stick-swallowing function is performed by the Big Firebrand society, among the Acoma by the Fire society,

and among the Jemez by the Flint society, the latter two being curing societies [Stephen 1936:83, n. 4]. Parsons [1939:79] also mentioned one "Juan Rey, the stick-swallowing shaman who died within the year when he moved to Sandìa, failing to keep his promise to perform his ritual as Isleta."

Among the Hopi the *Nasosotan* perform their stick-swallowing feat during a performance by the *Poswìmka* society, one of the Hopi curing societies (see *Poshwìmkya* in Stephen 1936:1282–1283). In former times the *Agave* (nadir), a war society, had "an affiliated stick-swallowing group" [Parsons 1939:124]. Stephen observed the *Nasosotan* performing "their feats of swallowing sticks" on December 27, 1893 [Stephen 1936:94], but he did not describe it. However, the performance has been observed among the Keres (see *hakan*). "Before stick-swallowing, at Zuni, and probably elsewhere, an emetic is taken" [Parsons 1939:456], and "the stick-swallowers of the Wood society remain continent the night before performing their rite, [otherwise] their throat would become sore" [Parsons 1939:429]. At the Hopi village of Oraibi, "a rough cedar stick is swallowed the first day; and subsequently an ornate swordlike stick; the sticks are swallowed facing the directions; fingers are imbricated; the step is high or prancing; and the body is painted yellow" [Parsons 1939:622].

Swallowing items such as sticks is seen as a power display (see entry), and is not necessarily limited to sticks. For example, Parsons [1939:646] observed Naiuchi, the head shaman of the Zuni War society, holding a live coal in his mouth and swallowing arrows as he danced during a performance by the society.

Natoas
Blackfoot, *Plains*
Sun Dance bundle. According to Wissler [1912a:209] this term comes from *natosiwa*, meaning "sun power," and *mas*, meaning "turnip" (*Lithospermum linearifolium*). The contents of the bundle included items necessary for the performance of the Sun Dance, of which the

most important were the Sun Dance headdress and a digging stick that was painted red and had moose hooves fastened to it. The headdress, called the "holy turnip bonnet" [Wissler 1912a:214], was also referred to by the term *natoas*. The bundle was kept in a cylindrical rawhide case suspended from a tripod.

Natoji
Blackfoot, *Plains*

Power; sunpower [Wissler 1912a:103]. One of many terms found throughout North America for the concept of a force that pervades the entire universe (*mana*—see entry). This force is always seen as being conscious and may therefore manifest through any object, most often an animate one such as an animal. In so doing, this power then communicates directly with a human being. In modern Western culture this force most often manifests itself in the form of "angels." For Native Americans the object becomes, for the time being, "as a person" [Wissler 1912a:103].

Natosiwa, the animate form of this word, means the state of being saturated with medicine power [Wissler 1912a:141, n. 2].

Nátsi
Hopi, *Southwest*

This term refers to two wooden sticks, about 14 inches in length, that are erected outside a *kiva* (EONAH, p. 136) to indicate that a ceremony is taking place. To these poles various items are attached, such as eagle feathers, whips, bows, etc., depending on the society, the ceremony, and the *kiva*. Also, the *kiva* is surrounded with a line of cornmeal to again indicate that a ceremony is in progress [Voth 1903:285].

Nauühic
Paiute, *Basin*

Owens Valley Paiute charm. Most often charms are made according to instructions received from a helping spirit. They are private property and are useful only to the person who has it in his possession. "Some carried rare wood fragments,

quail tufts, and other unusual objects tied up in weasel skins which they sometimes painted, for protection, so that they, like the weasel, might be difficult to capture and kill. . . . Sick people put them under their beds" [Steward 1933:308].

Among the Paiute an eagle feather was also used as a charm. "Women, dreaming of the eagle [as a source of power], had speed; using eagle feathers while pinenutting, they gathered 100 pounds a day while ordinary women gathered 15 pounds" [Steward 1933:309].

Nawuhchingwu
Hopi, *Southwest*

A brief ritual movement made by a shaman for the purposes of purification. Voth called it a "discharming" and described it as follows: "Two priests now entered the kiva and kneeling by the hearth, each took a pinch of ashes between the thumb and forefinger, upon which they spat, twirling the hands in a circular motion, and then cast the ashes up the ladder" [Dorsey and Voth 1902:243].

Naxnox
Tsimshian, *Northwest Coast*

Spirit [Garfield 1939:304] or supernatural [Garfield 1939:299]. Also "unwieldy supernatural power associated with chiefly might, antisocial acts, and distinctive tendencies intended to instill fear into onlookers. . . . *Naxnox* was limited to masked performances and dramatic events held during the winter season" [J. Miller 1984:137].

The supernatural power under the control of shamans is *haleyt* (see entry).

Nayahtcikan
Cree, *Canadian Eastern Woodlands*

The Carried on the Back bundle. Such bundles are sacred family possessions and are carefully tended. At the time of burial, a braid is cut from the deceased's head and hung on a pole at the head of the grave. After four days the braid is removed and ritually incorporated into the family *nayahtcikan,* which contains the braids of other deceased members of the family. Tobacco is also kept in the bundle as an offering to the deceased. In some cases the bundles include the toys or clothing of deceased children [Mandelbaum 1940:250].

During the ceremony for this bundle, the Round Dance (see *wasakamecimuwin*), the soul of a departed ancestor often returns. The bundle is used only in the Round Dance ceremony [Mandelbaum 1940:261].

Ndishniih
Navajo, *Southwest*

To tremble or move the hand about for the purpose of diagnosis [Levy et al. 1987:41]. Among the Navajo some shamans specialize in diagnosing illness, interpreting dreams, and related divinatory activities. One type of diagnostician, known as "men (or women) 'with-motion-in-the-hand'" [Morgan 1931:390], uses this *ndishniih,* "hand-trembling," technique. The spirit guardian of their related power is the Gila Monster. Thus, *ndishniih* refers only to the specific behavior of a shaman when possessed by the Gila Monster. However, hand tremblers "never perform the therapy; they are in a different category than the medicine men and do not enjoy the same status and professional dignity" [Sandner 1979:121]. This type of diagnosing is also the most common form used by the Navajo.

In performing a diagnosis for illness, the shaman sits facing the patient and holds his hand over the patient, arm extended. He then closes his eyes and "thinks of all the possible causes of the illness. When the 'correct' cause 'comes to his mind,' his arm involuntarily shakes" [Morgan 1931:392]. This shaking "may vary from a fine tremor of the hand to rather violent motions of the whole arm, and can become uncontrollable" [Levy et al. 1987:41]. When finished, the shaman not only identifies the illness but also names the chants that must be used to heal the patient and gives the name of the shaman (or shamans) capable of performing the required

ceremony. The ability of the hand trembler comes spontaneously; no learning is involved. "Their rite is very short, lasting less than an hour. They sit beside the patient and go into a trance" [Sandner 1979:121].

One hand trembler reported his technique as follows: "The corn pollen in the hand trembling ceremony is an offering to Gila Monster. I put the pollen down my arm with two branches to the thumb and forefinger like Gila Monster. I start praying, then singing. Then I work my mind very hard. Then I notice shocks running through my fingers. My hand starts shaking and away I go. . . . [It] depends on what sign your hand is making. I wonder what my hand is referring to. It shakes, sometimes at the patient, sometimes at the ground, until I guess the right answer with my mind. When that is done, it stops shaking" [Natani Tso in Sandner 1979:121].

The other two types of Navajo diagnosticians are known as stargazers and listeners, with the latter being the most rare. Another area of divination specialty for the Navajo diagnostic shamans is the finding of lost items— money, horses, sheep, etc. The following is an example: "A child wandered from X and was lost. The advice of a shaman, (N), was sought. His advice was without results. Stargazers, and men with-motion-in-the-hand were asked to advise where the child was. Each day search parties went out as directed. On the seventh day a listener was called. After a preparatory ritual of chants and prayers, he went to the top of a near-by hill. It is uncertain whether he heard voices, or sounds in the air coming from a certain direction. He returned to the hogan, however, and said the child was in a specified canyon one mile from its mouth. A search party failed to find the child, but went again, and this time found [the body of] the child at a distance of about two miles. This eight-day search was remembered by t, who had inspected the spot where the child was found and decided she had been cuffed to death by a bear and cubs" [Morgan 1931:402].

Nechwa
Beothuck, *Canadian Eastern Woodlands*
Tobacco [Winter 1975:154]. The Beothuck, from Newfoundland, became extinct in the first part of the nineteenth century, and nothing is known of their ceremonial use of tobacco.

Nedi
Maidu, *California*
A class of spirits [Gifford 1927:226]. This class is different from ghosts and human spirits. "Each of the *nedi* spirits which was seen by the *temaya* [dance leader] Yoktco [see entry] in his dreams was said to be that of a man who died long ago and for whom one dance was named" [Gifford 1927:226]. The Maidu had eight dances, each named after a different *nedi*. When a dance was performed, the particular *nedi* for which the dance was named was impersonated. "No actual masks were worn, but by means of paint, feathers, ornaments, and grass veils, the participants disguised themselves so as to be unrecognizable in many cases" [Gifford 1927:214–215]. For this reason these *nedi* dances have been assigned to the Kuksu (God-Impersonating) cult (EONAH, p. 140) of central California. Characteristic of the Kuksu cult dances, these Maidu *nedi* dances used a great log foot-drum in the *kum* (ceremonial house) [Gifford 1927:228].

Nemowûk
Menomini, *Midwest*
The society of dreamers. More properly this society is referred to as *nimihétiwinäniwûk*, "dancing men" [Skinner 1915d:173]. The society ranks second in importance to the Menomini Medicine Lodge Society. It is a relatively recent society, having been introduced to the Menomini sometime during the latter part of the nineteenth century. A variant form of the society is also found among the Iowa, Prairie Potawatomi, Ojibwa, Sauk, Fox, and Kickapoo. One of the major differences between these societies is that the Menomini and Winnebago versions "make no use of the cross as a religious symbol, whereas in the dance grounds of the Iowa, Sauk, Fox, Kickapoo, and Ojibway, a large wooden cross is a prominent feature" [Skinner 1915d:175]. The Menomini have three public performances of this dance each year.

In June 1910 anthropologist Alanson Skinner "was, unknown to himself at the time, taken into the association, and from that time forward has had the right to attend and participate in all the ceremonials of the society" [Skinner 1915d:178]. Subsequently, Skinner was able to attend the Dream Dance performances of this society, which are conducted to heal sick individuals. Central to the healing ceremony are large drums; during a ceremony that Skinner observed, "the sound of the drum served to frighten away the evil spirit which troubled the sick child" [Skinner 1915d:176]. These drums are considered also sacred objects. Skinner noted that when a sacred pipe was lighted during the ritual, "the man who held it passed the stem about over the drum in order to permit it to partake also" [Skinner 1915d:177]. Furthermore, "to strike the drum without cause is a grave offense, and can only be atoned for by so costly a gift as a pony, or its equivalent" [Skinner 1915d:178]. On the final day of the Dream Dance, a dog is sacrificed, and a dog soup is prepared and distributed to all present. The highest honor is "an invitation to eat the dog's head" [Skinner 1915d:181].

See also *némoak,* EONAH, p. 193.

Nenuswikatcikäwagi
Literal translation: "they give a sacred feast to the buffalo." Buffalo Feast; "a term used of the gens that is giving a feast to the buffalo" [Fisher 1939:100]. Although the function of such feasts is unknown, there is evidence they are held "for the magical reproduction of the buffalo herds" [Fisher 1939:100].

The complexity of the Fox religion is reflected in the fact that there are many different types of buffalo feasts. For example, anthropologist Truman Michelson has reported (in the Bureau of American Ethnology annual reports and bulletins) on the following buffalo sacred ceremonies: White Buffalo Dance; Worship of the Spotted Buffalo Calf; Buffalo Rite (owned by the Society of Those Named after the Buffalo); Buffalo-Head Dance of the Thunder Gens; Buffalo Dance of the Bear Gens; and Worship of Buffalo and Wapanowi Birds.

During the dance the participants imitate the movement of buffalo in flight, led by a ceremonial leader adorned with a buffalo mane. Food sacrifices to the buffalo always include maple sugar, along with corn and pumpkin if possible.

Neptune, John
Penobscot, *Northeast*

A renowned Abenaki shaman who died in 1865. Among his powers were the ability to scream loud enough to be heard 5 miles away and the ability to talk to others at a distance of 50 miles. "One time in mid-winter his wife had a terrible longing for green corn, and she told him [Neptune]. He went to the fireplace, rolled up some strips of bark, laid them in the ashes, and began to sing a low song. After a while he told her to go and get her corn, and there lay the ears all nicely roasted. He used to make quarters, too. He would cut little round bits of paper, put them to his mouth, breathe upon them, then lay them down and cover them with his hand. By and by he would lift his hand with a silver quarter in it" [Alger in Eckstorm 1945:36]. In another instance Neptune built a small lodge with a fire inside. Then the bystanders heard noises like wings, and one person peeked into the lodge and saw Neptune talking to several salamanders standing on their hind legs. They thought the salamanders had come out of the wood placed on the fire.

Neptune's helping spirit was that of a Snake or Eel, whose form he could take at will. Although Penobscot shamans usually had only one helping spirit, Neptune was reported to have seven spirits (among which were the Wolf, the Beaver, and the Bear) in addition to his main helping spirit, the Eel.

Nerfalasoq
West Greenland Eskimo, *Arctic Coast*

A type of *angákoq* (EONAH, pp. 13–15) who has special powers to find hidden and/or lost objects [Birket-Smith 1924:453]. During his ceremonies he lies on his back; he does not use a drum.

Netdim maidü
Maidu, *California*

Northern Maidu term for a dreamer or seer. These are people "whose abilities are largely those of being able to communicate with the spirits, and with the ghosts of the dead. A man may be a 'dreamer' and not be a shaman, but nearly all shamans are also 'dreamers'" [Dixon 1905:271].

In a typical performance the shaman takes up a position at the main post of the dance house, located behind the fire. He begins to sing while shaking a cocoon rattle, which is also beaten on the post. "The lips are given a peculiar quivering motion, making the voice tremble and quaver" [Dixon 1905:271]. Once the spirit arrives the shaman questions the spirit, and his voice changes in tone as the spirit speaks through him. "At these meetings the ghosts of the dead are often present, and convey their desires to their relatives. They and other spirits give directions as to when feasts are to be held, hunts made, or raids on neighboring villages undertaken. In no case do they attempt to foretell the future. No one but the shaman may interrogate the spirits, or may speak during the ceremonies" [Dixon 1905:272].

Never-Sits-Down shield
Blackfoot, *Plains*

The oldest and most renowned medicine war shield among the Blackfoot. Over the years many of its owners became chiefs through its use. Wissler [1912a:121] reported that this shield originally came from the Northern Blackfoot, was for some time among the Piegan, and, by 1910 had been sold to a Blood man. There are definite rituals prescribed for its use, care, and transference. Of these and its description, Wissler [1912a:119–120] wrote:

> The shield is of two buffalo rawhides, firmly glued together. It is decorated with feathers [hanging around the rim]. The face is not painted but entirely plain. At the center is tied a bunch of many different kinds of feathers; this is to be used in war as a headdress and considered a very powerful medicine. . . . [There is a] hole made by a [rifle] ball that passed through the first layer but not the second and is still in the shield. No one seems to know how or when this was done. There is a single [shield] cover but curiously it bears symbolic decorations on the outside. . . . The cover is of black-tailed deer and across its middle a narrow fringed band of the same. When a cover wears out a new one is made and the old one hung in a tree as an offering to the sun. Over all [the cover] are dots of red representing stars. The tripod [upon which it is held] and the strap are painted red. It is kept in the tipi at night but taken out each morning before sunrise and set up with its tripod on the west of the tipi, so hung that the first rays of the sun will fall upon the painted cover. At noon, again, it is turned more towards the sun and later to face the west. After sunset, it is returned to the tipi by the north side, thus having made a sunwise circuit, and fastened to a tipi pole at the rear.
>
> No dogs must enter the owner's tipi. Should the shield fall down the owner must make a sweat house at once. To this ceremony some old men are invited. The hole in the sweat house is circular. The men enter, but the shield is placed on top. On returning to the tipi these men sing the five songs in the ritual and offer prayers to prevent the ills believed to follow such an event. Should the owner kill a spider, his entire body will be covered with spiders and he [will] be stung to death. He must not put the loop [of the shield] over the head but always draw it up over the feet.
>
> The smudge place [purification altar for the shield] is rectangular, about one foot by two. The grass is cleared off at the natural earth surface and light colored earth spread over all. On the western, or rear, edge of this altar is a row of four buffalo chips and on these some sage grass. The smudge is made with parsnip root at about the center of the altar. The soft earth is kept smooth, but at any time should there appear small horse tracks the owner will soon acquire horses; small human footprints, enemies will be killed.

Nexnôxsesge
Tsimshian, *Northwest Coast*

Mysteries [Boas 1912:221]. This term refers to the power feats of shamans and spirits. It comes from the term *nexnox,* meaning "spirit being." Therefore it is the thing done by spirits.

Néyhommâuog
Mohegan, *Northeast*

Literal translation: "turkey mantle" [Speck 1928:444, n. 2]. Narragansett cloaklike coat made from turkey feathers. Feather mantles, along with other forms of feather artwork, have been reported from this culture in Rhode Island and further south to the Gulf of Mexico and lower Mississippi cultures. Highly developed feather artwork has been reported for the Delaware of New Jersey and Pennsylvania; the Powhatan of Virginia; the Santee, Cusabo, and Catawba of the Carolinas; the Creek and Mobile of Alabama and Georgia; and the Choctaw of Louisiana.

Elaborate feather mantles, neckbands, head-dresses, wands, etc., are used in shamans' costumes throughout this area. In addition to turkey feathers, one finds feathers of the cardinal, flicker, India duck, guinea, shelldrake, loon, heron, swan, and flamingo. The selection of feathers is most often based on their beauty, but with regard to the shaman's regalia, there is no doubt the choice of feathers was also dictated by one's guardian spirit.

In North America such elaborate feather artwork is found only in the above-mentioned areas and among the California and Northwest Coast cultures.

A Tlingit shaman's crown.

Niaqunguaq
Netsilik Eskimo, *Arctic Coast*

A Netsilingmiut shaman interviewed by ethnographer Knud Rasmussen on May 6, 1921. Rasmussen observed him in a trance state, during which *Niaqunguaq* "talked in a squeaky falsetto" voice [Rasmussen 1969:179]. Subsequently, *Niaqunguaq* told Rasmussen that he had about twenty helping spirits, the most important of which was "a lemming with a human face, which could also take the form of an eagle, a dog or a bear" [Rasmussen 1969:179–180].

Nïarï puaxantï
Paiute, *Basin*

Literal translation: "wind doctor" [Kelly 1936:139]. Vegas and Chemehuevi (Southern Paiute) wind shaman. A wind shaman can either bring the wind or cause it to stop blowing. "This they did secretly, so no one knows just how it was done. To bring wind a doctor gathered earth in two small piles, then kicked them. He sang only one song. He dreamed his power, and when he raised his voice in anger, a wind would spring up. He seldom brought wind, and then only for spite" [unnamed informant in Kelly 1936:139].

Among the Chemehuevi the *nïarï puaxantï* is also involved with war medicines, as evidenced by the following account:

Wind doctors were brave men. They had no songs but dreamed that their tobacco smoke became

wind. When scouting, they smoked, so that the wind would cover their tracks in the sand or lash the trees so the enemy would not hear them pass.

When the wind was cold, these scouts would go into the enemy's camp to sleep. They were not recognized in the dark because in those days all wore long hair and the same costume; only the footgear was different. Once a Chemehuevi scout overslept. In the morning he was still in the enemy camp. He pulled his hair over his face and escaped [unnamed informant in Kelly 1936:139].

See also *unwadïmbuaxantï.*

Niashaida
Tsimshian, *Northwest Coast*

A nineteenth-century Kitkatla (also Gitxalha) shaman. Jay Miller [1984:140–141] provided a brief account of one of his divination ceremonies to find some missing boatmen from the Gamayam: "They brought the shaman many gifts, so he took out his best paraphernalia, used only when the fee was large. He filled a bucket with salt water, covered his head, and looked into the water. He said, 'I see they are not dead and will soon arrive home.' He called a man to him and gave him a ceremonial cane, saying, 'Take my cane and place it at the edge of the water on the beach. Do not allow the water to splash on the cane, but when it reaches this mark on the cane, look out toward the point, below the Eagle House, and you will see a canoe, then call out.' The man went out and the shaman began to sing and dance until the man called out and announced the safe arrival of the lost men. The people rushed to the beach to meet them."

Nibawnawbé
Ojibwa, *Canadian Eastern Woodlands*

Spirit beings that are similar to mermaids, with long hair and the lower body of a fish. Reports of their appearance span several centuries. One informant described them by saying, "They had very long hair—one had hair that almost covered her—but in place of legs and feet, each of them had a fish's tail, which I could see like scythes in the water" [Shawonong in Bourgeois 1994:77], while another informant reported, "The first thing I saw was a man in the middle of the breakers, that is, it was a man above the waist but below I could see he had the tail of a fish" [Charlotte Kawbawgam in Bourgeois 1994:77]. Seeing such a spirit is often taken as a sign of bad luck or that someone will soon die.

Another water spirit that is similar in description is known as *memegwessi,* which was translated in the nineteenth century as "siren." Such spirits were mentioned by Father Claude Dablon in a massive publication entitled *The Jesuit Relations and Allied Documents* (originally published between 1896 and 1901 by Burrows Brothers in Cleveland, Ohio) under the term *memogovissionis.* The spirits also had long hair down to their waists and always lived in water. However, one nineteenth-century informant conceived *memegwessiwug* as rock spirits [Jacques LePique in Bourgeois 1994:71].

Niesgane
Tsimshian, *Northwest Coast*
An early-twentieth-century shaman who resided at Port Simpson and was known as a powerful curer among the Nass and Skeena. Due to the influence of Christianity in the area at this time, he was approached only in great secrecy. "One woman he was treating said that he could see through her and would know if she disobeyed him, so she never did anything without his consent. He communicated with the dead who would send messages to their living relatives through him. On occasion, he was called upon to insure success in fishing and other pursuits" [J. Miller 1984:139]. He died in 1935.

Ninampskan
Blackfoot, *Plains*
Medicine-pipe man. A contraction of *ninampskan kweniman* [Wissler 1912a:152]. This is the term used for a man who owns a medicine-pipe bundle. "A pipe-man receives great social, religious, and even political recognition, being regarded as of the first rank and entitled to the first seat in a tipi: i.e., opposite the man of the household" [Wissler 1912a:152].

Ningawbiun
Ojibwa, *Canadian Eastern Woodlands*
A shaman during the first half of the nineteenth century whose power came from a small bird that called upon the Thunderbirds when Ningawbiun needed supernatural help. This power allowed him to find game and fish and to foretell and change the weather. He also performed the Shaking Tent Ceremony [EONAH, pp. 246–249].

One time when the camp was in need of food during the winter, Ningawbiun "led the men onto the ice and said that, through the bird, he could get food for all. Soon he stopped and told them to cut holes in the ice; and in that one place they speared enough sturgeon for the whole camp. I was there as a boy. One of the sturgeon was as black as charcoal, another snow white; but otherwise these two strange sturgeon were just like the rest" [Charles Kawbawgam in Bourgeois 1994:80].

According to another account of his powers, Ningawbiun invited some people to his lodge.

He put the skin of the bird [about an inch in length] beside him and some tobacco in front of him. Then, before the people began to eat, he sang the song of the bird that had come to him when he was a boy, fasting on the mountain.

He said: "Although it is winter, we shall have tomorrow one of the greatest thunder storms ever seen in this country."

It happened as he said. There was tremendous thunder, the snow was half melted, and the ice was overflowed [Charles Kawbawgam in Bourgeois 1994:80].

Nipakwe Cimuwin
Cree, *Canadian Eastern Woodlands*
Dialectical variant: *Nipagwet Cimun* (Bungi band of Plains-Ojibwa) [Skinner 1919a:287].

Literal translation: "Abstaining from Water Dance" or "Thirsting Dance" [Mandelbaum 1940:265]. The Plains Cree Sun Dance. Of all the Cree's religious rituals, this was their most sacred. For the most part their ceremony followed the standard Plains area format for the Sun Dance—dancers were persons who had made Sun Dance vows in return for supernatural aid during the past year; the ceremony lasted for four days, during which the dancers were not allowed to eat or drink; at some point each dancer was skewered to a center Sun Dance pole as a fulfillment of his vow; and the "dance period was one in which the presence of the supernaturals is very close and their imminence keenly felt" [Mandelbaum 1940:270], such that dancers often received revelations.

Although the dancers were not allowed to eat or drink, they were allowed to smoke during this period. Of course, the mystery powers could be used to deviate from any rule. For example, when their dancers were having a particularly difficult time, one of the Sun Dance assistants "might blow water through his whistle or tap the center [Sun Dance] pole for water. The liquids thus produced could be drunk by the dancers" [Mandelbaum 1940:270].

A similar use of medicine powers during a Bungi Sun Dance was noted by anthropologist Alanson Skinner. The dancers told the shaman leading the Sun Dance "that they could not stand it any more without water. He [the shaman] danced up to the center [Sun Dance] pole, blowing his [elongated bone] whistle and holding a kettle. When he reached the pole he thrust his whistle against it, and held it there. Water gushed out of the pole through this improvised spout and he caught it in the kettle and gave it to the others to drink. The water was undoubtedly the gift of the *Inîmikiwûk* (or *Pinäsiwuk*), the thunderers, for this man had power over them and could call them whenever the country needed rain" [Ogimauwinini in Skinner 1919b:314–315].

Nitïna puaxantï
Paiute, *Basin*

Literal translation: "follow doctor" [Kelly 1936:133] (for *puaxantï* see EONAH, p. 222). Chemehuevi (Southern Paiute) evil shaman or sorcerer. Most often a sorcerer harms an individual by having his helping spirit steal the soul *(muxuav)* of his victim or by sending a disease object into the body of his victim. In both cases another shaman must be called in to cure the victim. In the case of soul loss, once the curing shaman

had diagnosed the case, [he] sent his guardian spirit in pursuit, while he himself awaited its return, seated and singing. He sucked, but removed nothing. Upon its return the spirit was met by the shaman, who returned to camp with both the spirit and the missing soul in his mouth. Then with his lips he transferred the two to the patient, either into the mouth or into the afflicted part [of his body]. The spirit then disseminated itself throughout the body, distributing the soul as it went.

Be the illness caused by intrusion [of a disease object] or by soul loss, the tutelary [helping spirit] informed the curing shaman which sorcerer was responsible. The malefactor was summoned. Sometimes he would confess, sometimes not. Then the curing shaman would speak to him privately; "he kept right after him" to retract the evil influence by singing. Sometimes the sorcerer acquiesced and sang, pretending to cure, "and all the time he was killing the person." If such deceit were detected, the perpetrator [sorcerer] would be dispatched promptly, either with a shot or a blow on the head [Kelly 1936:133].

Sorcerers are seen as being forced by their spirit helper to kill and are therefore not held at fault themselves. In some cases the *nitïna puaxantï* is called upon to heal. This is particularly true of the those who have dreamed of Coyote *(sïnab)* [Kelly 1936:134].

Niwaxsax
Blackfoot, *Plains*

Literal translation: "tobacco seed" [Wissler 1912a:201]. Spirits associated with tobacco. This term is applied to "tobacco people," of which there are four, each about a foot in height and appearing as a human being. The Beaver men, those who owned a beaver medicine bundle, propitiated these spirits by leaving small (circa 3-inch) bags of food and 2-inch moccasins outside for them during the night. Only the Beaver men could communicate with the *niwaxsax*. Anyone else who saw one was certain to die.

Nonka
Ponca, *Plains*
Supernatural punishment for deliberate irregular behavior [Fortune 1932:34]. The degree of punishment sent to an individual paralleled the seriousness of the offense. For example, "when at a feast a woman publicly shames herself and her mother-in-law by not giving her mother-in-law any of the food she is dispensing, and is responsible for dispensing, but pointedly gives food to everyone else, *nonka* is expected to follow. In the above case it did. The woman cut her finger with a knife. . . . Thus a man insulting the peace chiefs in a ceremony subsequently ran a rusty nail into his foot and had to have the foot amputated after blood poisoning set in" [Fortune 1932:34–35].

More serious offenses include mishandling a medicine bundle, singing a sacred song when one has no right to do so, and betraying the secrets of one of the secret societies. In the most serious cases death ensues.

Nonzhinzhon
Omaha, *Plains*
Vision quest. "The search for special powers from a Supernatural Patron by solitaries" [Fortune 1932:37]. Boys begin their vision questing around the age of eight or older. One of the most important aspects of their training involves teaching them to stand their ground when a spirit appears rather than running away in fear. "Supernatural beings are like that. If you're not frightened of them the first time they may give you a power. But I ran away and my running

from them hurt them. If you miss out once it's no good trying the same thing a second time. They never come back" [Small Fangs in Fortune 1932:38].

By puberty the training and quest increase in intensity, the latter usually lasting four days. Once a helping spirit is acquired, it often determines which secret society the youth joins. For example, "a Grizzly Bear Society doctor avowed absolutely that his power came from an encounter between him and the Grizzly Bear Supernatural Beings, a Water Monster Society doctor avowed absolutely that his power came from an encounter between him and the Water Monster Supernatural Being" [Fortune 1932:39].

The highest power is the power to heal, but one can also receive a lesser power, such as supernatural help in warfare, hunting, gambling, or racing. However, most of the Omaha secret medicine societies consist only of shamans who have acquired some sort of healing power. These healing powers include personal immunity to sickness. But if an older shaman, near the end of his life, transfers his power to his son, his immunity is often lost in the transfer. The older shaman often dies soon thereafter. This is particularly true with regard to the Water Monster power. However, in most cases an older shaman has several powers and transfers only part of them to his son.

Notwita
Wintun, *California*
A Nomlaki man from the latter part of the nineteenth century who could assume the form of a bear. "My grandfather always told us that he could turn into a bear any time he wanted to. We children always went swimming with him, and he had thick, black hair two inches long all over his body. His fingers were as big around as my wrist. He was a nice man, always full of fun. My uncle is a man who is a clown and doesn't believe in such things, so this fellow turned into a bear and chased him. That was in broad daylight. When he had worn my uncle out, he got

up as a human and laughed" [McGetrick in Goldschmidt 1951:354].

There are many ethnographic accounts, especially in California, of men who could change their form into a bear. Furthermore, this ability was not limited to shamans alone. Another example of a man from the Stonyford area was recounted as follows: "Once my grandfather was down there trading and visiting, and this man asked him if he was going home, and my grandfather said that he was leaving the next morning at sunrise. But grandfather watched the trail very closely the next morning, and soon he saw this bear-man come toward him up the trail. Grandfather had his stick ready and spit on his hand, and when the bear came up he pounded on it. The bear charged him over and over again, but grandfather was getting the best of it when finally it changed back to the man who had asked him about leaving. This bear-man said, 'Don't hurt me; I'm just playing with you.' Grandfather was mad and said that he should have been shot. The bear-man paid grandfather some property and told him not to tell anyone" [Freeman in Goldschmidt 1951:354].

Ntekêllsten
Okanagon, *Plateau*
An unidentified plant "with a strong smell, and from which a kind of steam rises" that is used as a love charm [Teit 1909:619]. "It was used in various ways, i.e., worn as a necklace in the daytime next [to] the body, and put under the pillow at night. Before falling asleep, the person must think of the woman whose love is desired, and next morning early must wash in a creek and pray that by the power of the plant the woman may love him. Other effective ways are to give a woman a present of something scented with it, or to smoke with her, using some of the plant mixed with tobacco. If a man carries this charm and walks up-wind, women will be so attracted that they will follow him" [Teit 1909:619].

Nuchihewe
Delaware, *Northeast*
The Lenape term for witches or sorcerers.

> The *nuchihewe* annoyed people, especially the sick, and sought revenge upon their rivals and enemies through the use of powerful medicines that were kept in pouches or clay pots. It was through the witch's bundle and the parts of the animals or owls it contained, that a witch was able to effect his or her transformation at will, becoming a wolf, an owl, or another creature.
>
> The person possessing the power to bewitch was obliged to take the life of at least one person every year; otherwise, the witch's own medicine would kill him or her [Kraft 1986:185–186].

The harmful substances used by witches are called *mëtakána* [Kraft 1986:186].

Nuhpud
Paviotso, *Basin*
One of three types of shamans found among the Honey Lake area Wadátkuht. To become a *nuhpud* a man or woman must seek power by going to specific power spots in the mountains, such as the cave on *Muhano,* "Moon Turn" (a mountain located about 4 miles out of Dayton, Nevada, on the way to Fort Churchill), or to the sacred pool on *Nabogin,* "Swimming Mountain" (Warren Peak, circa 5 miles north of Eagle Peak in Modoc County) [Riddell 1960:62–63]. These quests are initiated via precognitive dreams occurring over a period of several years that indicate to a person that he or she is to become a shaman. Avoiding this shamanic call (see entry) usually results in sickness. However, such dreams do not usually indicate which type of shamanism a person is to pursue. Therefore, one might try to first become a *numuhgunuhd* (see entry) or a *nutaígut* (see entry). Both of these types of shamans become practitioners through dreams only, rather than by going on a vision quest. However, if the person is not successful at either of these types of shamanism, then a vision is sought through self-isolation in the mountains.

The *nuhpud* is called upon to treat the more serious illnesses, such as sickness caused by witchcraft or soul loss. A formal request for a healing ceremony always takes place early in the morning, before sunrise. At this time the shaman is presented with a gift. Healing ceremonies usually occur in a darkened room and last around three hours. Up to four days of healing are often required for serious cases.

> The patient lay on the floor and the doctor sat beside him and blew smoke into his face (this action was called hái), prayed and then began his song (this last action was called tumanagi). An eagle feather was put upright in a can at the patient's head (this action was called tubihi). This was a specially prepared feather as it had down around its base, and the doctor had a decorated eagle feather in his hair. There was money for the doctor in the can with the eagle feather. Putting the money in the can was called astuwunai. . . .
>
> The shaman had an arrowcane stick, or tube, he put against the patient's body to suck out the sickness, an act he did several times. Sucking out the sickness was called pumu' tumuhamuhn, "something to touch with your lips." The doctor sucked during the period when he sang and prayed. He had to clear his own throat of the "sickness" sucked from the patient and spit it out into a pan. It usually consisted of phlegm and clotted blood, and sometimes a worm. The act of spitting out the "sickness" was called ci'ihn [Riddell 1960:68].

This pan is then taken outside by an assistant, and the contents are buried in a hole in the ground.

At one point in this healing ceremony, the *nuhpud* goes into trance. He remains on the floor, stiff and unconscious, for upward of a half hour. "While the doctor was unconscious and the patient lying ill, everyone watched the eagle feather in the can. If it fluttered the patient would get well, if it dropped he would probably die. The feather usually took either course on the fourth night" [Riddell 1960:69].

Numankmahina
Mandan, *Plains*
Creator [Pepper and Wilson 1908:298, n. 3].

Numina
Paviotso, *Basin*
A spirit [Naches in Fowler and Fowler 1971:212].

Numuhgunuhd
Paviotso, *Basin*
The term used by the Honey Lake area people for one of three types of shamans. Shamans were both males and females. The *numuhgunuhd* is closely related to the *nutaigut,* another type of shaman. Both of these types of shamans cure minor illnesses, such as headaches, mainly through the use of massage techniques, but the *nutaigut* also rubs medicine into the patient's body [Riddell 1960:64].

Both types of shamans receive precognitive dreams over a period of several years, indicating that they are to become shamans. Initially these dreams do not indicate which type of shaman a person is to become. Also, many try to avoid this initial shamanic call (see entry) because of the responsibilities and effort involved in being a shaman and because shamans are always susceptible to accusations of witchcraft.

The third type of shaman is the *nuhpud* (see entry).

(Note: Riddell termed these people the "Honey Lake Paiute," but Murdock's *Ethnographic Bibliography of North America* lists them under Paviotso.)

Numüva vumûn
Paviotso, *Basin*
Sweat lodge. "Usually women do not [go] in the sweat house, but sometimes old women after the period of child bearing go in to obtain luck" [Powell in Fowler and Fowler 1971:244]. The sweat lodge was used as a means of obtaining luck. For success in hunting, one would sweat five times; for success in gambling, one would sweat four times; and for success in war,

one would stay in the lodge for twenty-four hours.

Nunukai
Paviotso, *Basin*

A nineteenth-century Kamötkuht shaman from the Honey Lake area who lived at Secret Valley. He received his powers by vision questing on a mountain called *Nabogin* ("Swimming Mountain"—probably Warren Peak, 5 miles north of Eagle Peak in Modoc County) [Riddell 1960:62]. This mountain contains a pool under the rimrock to which men will go to swim and then seek dreams for power by sleeping on the rimrock above the pool. This spot is also used by the Pit River Achomawi men for power quests.

Nunukai received his initial powers at *Nabogin* and subsequently learned doctoring songs. He was most famous for his ability to "cure smallpox pretty easy," and, thus, he kept his village free of plague [Riddell 1960:63]. Later in life, he lost some of his doctoring powers because he misplaced an ovoid, chipped-stone knife that was one of his power fetishes. His life ended when he was shot while sleeping; immediately thereafter he was cremated on a brushfire for having killed two children through witchcraft [Riddell 1960:66].

(Note: Riddell referred to this Honey Lake group as Paiutes, but Murdock's *Ethnographic Bibliography of North America* lists them as Paviotso.)

Nupeeka
Kutenai, *Plateau*

Mana (see entry) [Malouf in Baker 1955:11]. This is the Kutenai word for an all-pervading power in the universe. This is the power shamans obtain from spirits. As in other Native American cultures, the spirits could take many different forms among the Kutenai, including trees, mountains, birds, rocks, etc. "The original spirits who created things, and who preceded men in the world, possessed this power and gave it to mankind" [Malouf in Baker 1955:11].

Among the Kutenai both women and men become shamans. Shamanic powers are most often obtained via a spirit or solo vision quest at some nearby power location, such as a cave, near a collection of pictographs, or in a rock circle made in the hills. The quest lasts for several days and is always preceded by fasting and other purification rites.

Boas [1918:341] translated *nupeeka* as *manitou* (EONAH, p. 164).

Nupuhawich
Mono, *Basin*

Monachi (Western Mono) term for a shaman who cures by sucking disease-causing objects from a patient's body [Gifford 1932:50]. See *puhake.*

Nutaígut
Paviotso, *Basin*

See *numuhgunuhd.*

Nutlam society
Wishram, *Plateau*

A religious society among the Wasco in which dog-eating was the central ritual [Boyd 1996:138].

In the Northwest Coast, dogs hold a status somewhere between the animals and human beings. Either as a separate society or as a ritual element, dog eating has been reported from virtually every coastal culture between the Tlingits and the southernmost Coast Salish [Drucker 1940:229]. Dog-eating rituals are common in the Plains and Midwest areas also.

Offerings

The symbolic manifestation of individual prayers to the spirits within a culture. Praying is a fundamental social activity in all traditional Native American cultures. The actual time an individual spends in prayer each day of his or her life has been grossly overlooked by anthropologists. For one thing, genuine prayers require a large amount of preparation time in order to be efficacious, a fact that is overlooked in Western culture but well known among all Native American cultures. Aside from these initial preparations, such as fasting, it is not unusual for an individual within any culture to spend several hours a day in some form of prayer activity.

The deeper implications of such social actions are many. For example, the early accounts of the first missionaries often featured complaints of how "lazy" their "savage" converts were. Apparently, it never dawned upon them that because their new religion would free converts from the extensive prayer and ceremonial requirements of their own culture, it would naturally attract "lazy" people. By the turn of the twentieth century, the stereotype of the "lazy, dumb Indian" was accepted by the public at large.

For Native Americans prayers are definitely not seen as merely sincere hopes spoken to the Creator. To them "prayers are acts of personal sincerity that require a great deal of effort and will on the part of an individual. However, prayer is not limited in form to mere recitation. It also comes in the form of song, dance, and bodily actions or postures" [Lyon 1989:38]. This "effort" includes the time spent in making one's prayer offerings. It also includes the time invested in practicing prayer(s) and centering one's focus of attention inward in order to evoke within one's being the virtues necessary to enhance the efficacy of the prayer—humbleness, honesty, sincerity, courage of the heart, endurance, kindness, alertness, etc. [Harrod 1987:91; Bean 1976:412]. This ability to focus attention inward in order to find answers to one's questions is regularly taught to children by their elders [Boatman 1992:2]. In the process one's prayer becomes "strong," which means the prayer becomes an object as opposed to a thought. That is, the prayer becomes a "real" thing. Thus, for Native Americans "prayer is not like you or me. It is like a holy person; it has a personality five times that of ours" [Singer in Gill 1987:113]. This quote

Edward S. Curtis, Offering to the Sun, San Ildefonso-Tewa, *1925. Photogravure.*

from a traditional Navajo named Doc White Singer reveals that not only does prayer become an object, it also becomes a conscious object. At the shamanic level (as opposed to the individual level), all prayers are sufficiently strong to become things unto the shaman. For example, world-famed Lakota shaman "Nick" Black Elk would call forth his spirits by singing: "Behold! A sacred voice is calling you!" [Neihardt 1932:182]. And to him a "sacred voice" was a thing, not a thought, thus his "Behold!" To Black Elk "voices sent" were manifestations of one's power in which words via that power turned into sacred objects.

The initial offerings that precede such prayers come in a multitude of forms throughout North America. In the Southwest area they often take the form of "prayer sticks" (e.g., the Tiwa (Isleta) *nashie* [EONAH, pp. 186–187], also called *shie* [Parsons 1932:274]; see entry *prayer feathers/ sticks*), long sticks to which are attached colored strips of cotton yarn, paints, feathers, and often a "perfect" ear of corn (e.g., the Zuni *yapota*, [EONAH, p. 175]). Sacred cornmeal (e.g., the Hopi *homngumni* [Loftin 1986:185]), pollens, and prayer feathers not attached to sticks are also used. In the Plains area prayer offerings often take the form of "tobacco ties" (e.g., the Lakota *canli wapahta* [EONAH, p. 46]), small squares of colored cotton cloth into which pinches of tobacco are placed as individuals say a prayer. The pieces are then tied onto a single cotton string. In whatever form a prayer offering comes within any culture, its primary purpose is to increase the efficacy of one's subsequent opportunity to pray. Afterward the offerings are placed in a sacred spot, burned in a ceremonial fire, buried, or disposed of in some other ritually prescribed (sacred) manner.

Also see *hatawe*, *kaetcine* (EONAH, p. 127), *oneane*, *prayer feathers/sticks*, *shkalina*, *talasi*, *telikinane*.

Ogichidanimidiwin

Ojibwa, *Canadian Eastern Woodlands*

Dialectical variant: *ogichidawigauen* (Potawatomi) [Ritzenthaler 1953a:153]. The Chippewa Chief Dance. This ceremony is performed "if a person is sick, or if someone dreams that sickness is about to invade the community, and the main function of the ceremony is to enlist the aid of the guardian spirits of a group of people in the curing of the sick person, or in warding off the impending sickness" [Ritzenthaler 1953b:186].

In the nineteenth century this particular dance was a war ritual performed before a war party was sent out on a raid; thus, on some reservations (such as the Lac du Flambeau and the Lac Vieux Desert) and among the Potawatomi, this ceremony is referred to as the War Dance.

Ohgiwe

Iroquois, *Northeast*

Feast of the Dead or Ghost Dance [Fenton and Kurath 1951:143] or Death Feast [Kurath 1954:88]. "The Iroquois who follow the Longhouse way believe that although the main soul goes the long trail to the land of the dead beyond the setting sun, the ghost spirit hangs around the reserves" [Fenton and Kurath 1951:144–145]. On the fourth day after the death of an individual, which is the day after burial, a special ceremony that translates as "Fourth Night Departure Singing" [Kurath 1954:87], a spirit release ceremony, is conducted. "That night they will share a last meal with the spirit which has hovered on earth till now. The specially invited singers will free the spirit to follow the path to the abode of the dead. Otherwise the ghost would continue to wander among the living and cause sickness" [Kurath 1954:87–88]. This ceremony is one of three major rites of the *diehoono* or Tutelo [Kurath 1954:87].

Sometimes a person is possessed by a ghost and can "be cured only by the *ohgiwe*" [Kurath 1954:88]. This is a semiannual ceremony held in the spring and fall. The major purpose of this all-night ritual is to appease the ancestral spirits, but it also functions as "a private healing ceremony to cure ghost sickness and [is] held usually half the night in a private dwelling of the patient and sponsor; a renewal of a former cure held briefly at the Midwinter Festival" [Fenton and Kurath 1951:145].

Oiaron
Iroquois, *Northeast*
A term used by early Jesuit missionaries for a shaman's helping spirit or medicine powers. "By means of the *oiaron,* he [the shaman] could transform himself, transport himself and do what he pleased" [Mavor and Dix 1989:145].

Ojonimigijihg
Ojibwa, *Canadian Eastern Woodlands*
Literal translation: "Busy Sky" [Densmore 1949:26]. An elderly Chippewa shaman in 1945 who was then the leader of his people's Grand Medicine society. He was from the Lac Vieux Desert band living in the vicinity of Keweenaw Bay in Michigan. His English name was John Pete.

John Pete also treated patients on his own, as is often the custom of *mide* (EONAH, p. 173) shamans. He was well known in the community for his effectiveness in obtaining a cure. During his healing ceremonies he sang over his patients while shaking a rattle. In curing the patient he employed the bone-swallowing technique common to shamans of this region. He would swallow one or two tubular, smoothed bones. (They are usually around 2 ½ inches long and about ½ inch in diameter [Densmore 1910:120].) Concerning the actual use of such bones, Densmore [1929:46] reported: "Small sections of tube-like bones were swallowed and regurgitated according to the custom of the djasakid [EONAH, p. 64]. He [the shaman] then placed one of these bones against her [the patient's] congested throat and blew through it repeatedly and with such violence that the congestion 'broke internally,' the poisonous matter issuing freely from her mouth. This relieved her distress and she recovered rapidly. . . . A man who treats the sick by this method frequently wears one of the bones attached to his hat, with the feather of an eagle or hawk in it. This is worn as an evidence or badge of his profession." After being swallowed these bones become empowered by the shaman's helping spirits and are then used to effect a cure.

See also *wikwajigewinini.*

Oka wafe
Tewa, *Southwest*
The name of a plant used at Santa Clara as a protective amulet (see entry). The root of this plant is "carried in the pocket, purse, or belt, especially by school children. It also protected a person from robbery or losing money" [Hill 1982:315].

Oldest Whose Ears Hang Backwards
Hidatsa, *Plains*
Also: *Oldest Grows His Ears Backward* [Pepper and Wilson 1908:314]. A sacred buffalo skull that is part of a particular medicine bundle. This skull is used when there is little food to be had. "When the people starved and brought presents to the Eagle-man [holder of the medicine bundle] to bring buffalo, he would take down the buffalo-skull, place it before the shrine, take the medicine-pipe and anoint it, hold it in incense [cedar], sing a mystery song, and then lay the pipe before the nose of the buffalo-skull" [Pepper and Wilson 1908:298]. According to Wolf Chief (see entry), "the skull hears all over the world" [Wolf Chief in Pepper and Wilson 1908:314]. This ritual was performed only in times of great need, and after each performance the buffalo would soon be spotted.

Old Sam
Carrier, *Mackenzie-Yukon*
An early-twentieth-century shaman who lived on the Carrier Indian Reservation at Hagwilgate, 4 miles from Hazelton, British Columbia. During the 1930s anthropologist Diamond Jenness attended a healing ceremony conducted by Old Sam to heal his wife of a sickness brought on by the *Kyan,* a dreaded mountain spirit. The ceremony was conducted at Old Sam's house in the evening, and he was assisted by three persons.

Two 7-foot planks on which sticks were beaten and a tambourine accompanied the singing.

The ceremony began with the shrill sound of a whistle.

> It was blown by Old Sam, though none of us saw it. To the Indians it blew *kyan* into the room, the mystic mountain force that drives them insane. The Chinaman's wife [also a patient, suffering from land-otter dream sickness] flung her head to the floor with a shriek and beat a wild tattoo with her hands on the bare boards, while her two companions sighed loudly *hoo, hoo, hoo,* and swayed their bodies up and down and from side to side. Old Sam from his chair began to shout his medicine-song, and his assistants joined in, beating the tambourine and pounding the planks. The three women in the middle were seized with violent dementia, evidently possessed by *kyan;* their eyes were staring and dilated, their bodies swayed, their hands quivered as with a palsy. . . . The song, repeated over and over again, louder and with more frantic drum-beats and pounding of sticks whenever the women's frenzy threatened to break out into greater violence, lasted some fifteen minutes [Jenness 1933:15–16].

At the conclusion of the third song, Old Sam went to each patient and said, *"hoo"* into their ears. This was to expel the *Kyan* spirit, which the shaman then drove into a pan of water. At the end of the ceremony, "Old Sam hastened over to *hoo* into their ears, and to beat them upwards on chest and back with a bundle of eagle feathers in order to expel any *kyan* that still remained in their bodies. Each woman gave a loud-breathed *hoo* as it left her and Old Sam blew it away from the crown of the head" [Jenness 1933:18]. The ceremony lasted two hours.

Jenness also notes that Old Sam "adopts a treatment for hysteria that might be beneficial to many patients of European descent. . . . [In the treatment] the hysteria is forced to express itself in slow rhythmic movements until the patient becomes physically exhausted and her mind clears" [Jenness 1933:18, 20].

Old Tom Mouse
Quinault, *Northwest Coast*

A weather shaman during the first part of the twentieth century. Given the large amount of annual rainfall in this region, the main duty of the weather shaman was to cause the rain to cease. With respect to Old Tom Mouse, it was reported that "after a storm of several days he would call the people together and say, 'I'm getting tired of this weather. I am going to stop it.' Then he would place a mat on the middle of the floor, sit down on it, and start his songs. The onlookers helped in the singing. His spirit would say, 'The sun is shining on the middle of my (spirit) canoe. You will soon see the sun low over the horizon.' After about an hour the shaman would send a man out to see if the sun were breaking through the clouds. If it was not they continued singing. But before the day was done the sun was sure to appear" [Olson 1936:150].

See also *Atámántán.*

Omawtapi
Hopi, *Southwest*

"Cloud blower" [Dorsey and Voth 1901:22]. One of several types of ceremonial pipes. It is tubular in shape and larger than most ceremonial pipes used by the Hopi, being about 2 inches in diameter. As a rule, only native (wild) tobacco *(Nicotina attenuata Tow)* is used in this pipe [Voth 1901:75]. It is used for "blowing cloud on the altar" [Voth 1901:68]. In general among the Hopi, tobacco smoke is associated with clouds. Thus tobacco smoke not only carries one's prayers to the spirits, it also has the power to bring rain.

Omaya
Maidu, *California*

Also: *omeya* [Dixon 1905:268]. The Northern Maidu term for power [Jewell 1987:146]. Maidu shamans receive power in the form of "pains" (see entry). That is, a spirit power received on a vision quest is referred to as a "pain." Furthermore, the disease object in a patient's body, known as *itu* [Dixon 1905:280] by the mountain Maidu and *kumi* by the Concow Maidu [Jewell 1987:148], can also be referred to as a "pain." This is because the shaman often swallows the disease object in order to increase his or her own powers. The swallowing demonstrates the shaman's ability to control the "pain" and thus benefit from its power. Consequently, *omaya* may be substituted for *itu* or *kumi* when referring to a disease object. As Dixon [1905:268] wrote: "Immediately on getting the o'meya out of the body of the patient, the shaman falls to the ground insensible. He revives after a while, and spits the o'meya out." It is then buried in the ground or swallowed by the shaman. In fact, Kroeber [1925:422] stated that "the 'pain' is called *omeya*" among the valley Maidu.

Omehwílĭš
Wappo, *California*
Dancing or singing doctor. "The dancing doctor may be either a man or a woman, although usually a woman; this doctor is the dance leader and an adviser for the group" [Sawyer 1965:31].

Onawabano
Menomini, *Midwest*
A shaman of the Jessakkid (EONAH, pp. 121–122) class during the latter part of the nineteenth century. An Ojibwa named Kawbawgam once attended a Shaking Tent Ceremony (EONAH, pp. 246–249) conducted by Onawabano for his sick stepmother, Iquewagun. In attendance was Iquewagun's son Mukkudde Wikanawe:

> He asked the spirit who could now be heard talking [from the shaking tent], to fly to the Carp [River] and see if his mother was still alive. The spirit was absent about five minutes. He told Muk-kud-de Wi-kan-a-we that his mother was better; she had already taken the broth of a grey duck and that she was going to recover. These spirits seem to be obliged to answer any question.

When the lodge was shaking the hardest, the spirit said: "Is that all you want to ask?" Nin-gaw-bi-nu [another Ojibwa in attendance who took them to Onawabano—a two-day journey] said: "Wait! Here is some tobacco for you to smoke. As we came by Pine River, we set two traps. Go now and see if there are any beavers in the traps."

The spirit was gone a few minutes. When he came back, he said: "There is a beaver in the upper trap belonging to the young man who came with you [i.e., Kawbawgam]. . . ."

When they got to Pine River, about half way between Lake Michigan and Lake Superior, they found a beaver in my trap [Kawbawgam in Bourgeois 1994:49].

Following this ceremony Onawabano returned to the mouth of the Carp River with the Ojibwa to conduct a Shaking Tent Ceremony there. Of this ceremony Kawbawgam said, "Of all of the medicine lodges I ever saw none shook so hard as this, and none came so many spirits, all singing and shouting" [Kawbawgam in Bourgeois 1994:49].

During this particular performance Onawabano located, via his spirits, a keg of whiskey that had been buried and hidden by Black Cloud, husband to Iquewagun, and Kawabawgam's father. "When the performance was over, they went with torches and found that some of the whiskey was gone from the keg. [The spirits had claimed they had drunk of it.] Black Cloud asked the medicine man to forgive him for not offering him some of the whiskey before, and presented him with the keg. The spirit said that O-na-wa-ban-o must take care of the squaw [Iquewagun] for four days. By that time, I-que-wa-gun was cured and they made a feast for four days. When the whiskey was gone the old medicine man returned to Lake Michigan. I-que-wa-gun lived for many years and at last died of old age" [Kawbawgam in Bourgeois 1994:50].

Onayanakia
Zuni, *Southwest*
One of three orders of the Great Fire (termed "Big Firebrand" by Parsons [1939:196]) society that

Stevenson [1904:485] called the "Mystery medicine" society. The other two orders of this healing society are called, by Stevenson [1904:485], the "Great god order" and the "Great Fire order," with the latter having five subdivisions.

The *Onayanakia* ceremony is basically a four-day healing ceremony marked by shamanic feats of fire handling and sword swallowing. On November 11–14, 1891, Stevenson observed a four-day initiation/healing ritual for this society. Of activities on the second night, she reported that: "a guest from the pueblo of Sia, who belongs to the Fire fraternity of that pueblo, goes to the fireplace and stamps in the fire and literally bathes himself in the live coals. He then takes a large coal in his right hand, and after rubbing his throat and breast with it he places it in his mouth. Others of the Fire fraternity also play with the coals, rubbing them over one another's backs" [Stevenson 1904:495]. The handling of coals was repeated on the third night. On the fourth night, "after some minutes he [the shaman] runs into the back of his belt the two eagle-wing plumes he carries, and dashing forward to the fireplace takes a large coal and, dancing about with it first in one hand and then in the other a moment or two, puts it into his mouth, where it remains thirty seconds, during which time he indulges in extravaganza. He is soon joined by other men and by women. . . . Their eyes almost as bright as the coals in their mouths, which scintillate with every breath. . . . The longest time a coal is held in the mouth is one minute; the shortest, thirty seconds. . . . Again the theurgists [see entry] come forward two or three at a time and pelt the members of the choir with live coals, and then lighting large bunches of corn husks, shower the choir with the sparks, and each one runs the burning mass into his mouth" [Stevenson 1904:503]. Following this handling of coals and fire, a young man belonging to the *Piännithle* (Sword) order (a suborder of the Great Fire order) enters, and after dancing for a short time, "he secures a sword of his order from behind the altar, and, dancing before the altar and facing it, he gracefully throws his body forward, twisting and turning. . . . After a time he turns and faces the east, and dropping on one knee swallows the sword. When this rite has been repeated three times he places the sword by the altar" [Stevenson 1904:503].

Healing is conducted on anyone who needs it during this ceremony. Most often the shaman resorts to sucking on the patient, with the subsequent removal of disease-causing objects. However, extraction is also done with eagle feathers [Stevenson 1904:497, 501]. Stevenson reported: "Most of the extracting of disease is done by sucking, but in some instances the plumes only are used to draw disease to the surface, when the material [extracted] is caught with the hand. . . . Stones varying in size from minute to that of a pigeon's egg, bits of old cloth, and strings of various kinds are exhibited by the theurgists. The men always show what they . . . have extracted. . . . Usually each theurgist waves the hand containing the extracted material before the altar previous to depositing it in the large bowl provided for the purpose. . . . The first time he usually throws it [the extracted material] into the fire; then he takes a pinch of meal from the basket before the altar and leaves the [kiva] chamber to sprinkle it outside with a prayer" [Stevenson 1904:501].

During one performance of the *Onayanakia,* Stevenson observed, on the fourth night, a shaman approach a human figure on the ceremonial altar. She reported: "He moves his eagle plumes over the human image with queer incantations until it is supposed to catch the tips of a plume with each hand, when the juggler [shaman] elevates it [the human figure], apparently by having the image hold the tips of the plumes. The illusion is perfect" [Stevenson 1904:525]. Two other shamanic feats were also observed. "A yucca rope apparently passes through the body of another, the rope being held by a man at each end. The illusion is perfect. Another trick is the changing of a basket tray of balls of blue mush. The writer, taking one, finds it to be as pliable as firm mush. The tray, with the balls of mush, is afterward raised high and waved to the six regions [directions] with prayers for snow, when it is again passed and the balls are found to be as hard as stones. A third time the basket is passed, after prayers have been offered, and the balls are in the same condition as when first examined" [Stevenson 1904:526–527].

Oneane
Zuni, *Southwest*
Corn pollen [Parsons 1939:296, n.†]. The offering of corn pollen is a common ritual procedure in the Southwest area. Corn pollen is offered at certain points of a ceremony, when saying individual prayers, and in "feeding" sacred objects. In fact, anything that needs to be blessed can be sprinkled with corn pollen. For example, when a deer is killed the hunter performs a ritual over the slain deer to assure luck in future deer hunting. This involves digging a hole where the deer is killed, blessing the hole with a sprinkling of *oneane* and *klo'o* (see entry), and then placing the deer over the hole.

See also *hatawe, talasi.*

One Spot
Blackfoot, *Plains*
A noted nineteenth-century warrior from the Blood division. His great deeds were attributed directly to a personal war medicine charm he carried. This particular charm "was very much desired by others but the owner always refused to transfer it. It is in the form of a scarf, a broad strip of yellow dog skin from the nose to the tail tip, mounted on red flannel. To the eye holes are attached beaded discs bearing brass buttons; and over the ears are what may be the symbols of feet on quill-covered strips of buffalo hide. At various points are feathers of owls, hawk, eagle, and prairie chicken, together with strips of weasel skin. Two bells adorn the tail piece. This, like others of its kind, is based upon a dream experience and bears a formula with songs [to activate its use]. In singing, the tail piece is held in the

hand and a bell accompaniment given" [Wissler 1912a:96].

Onotcikewinini
Ojibwa, *Canadian Eastern Woodlands*
Literal translation: "foretelling man" [Cooper 1936:9]. This term is used by the Lake of the Woods Ojibwa for shamans who employ their powers to foretell coming events, such as the imminent arrival of travelers to the camp, the coming of rain, etc. In their divining the shamans use no special paraphernalia.

Among the Rainy Lake Ojibwa this term is also used to designate the shaman who performs the Shaking Tent Ceremony (EONAH, pp. 246–249). The shaking tent shaman is also called *tcisakiwinini* [Cooper 1936:25]. However, among the Lake of the Woods Ojibwa, the shaking tent shaman is known as *djesikiwinini* (EONAH, p. 64), meaning "*djesikon* man" [Cooper 1936:9].

Oosimch
Nootka, *Northwest Coast*
Ahousaht purification rite. This is a spiritual purification rite that is passed down through a family lineage. It is performed for all important undertakings. It consists "of bathing in the sea, scrubbing the body afterwards with tree branches and singing songs of prayer in our native language. Each family had its own Oo-simch. Some carried out the ceremony for a few hours each day for a period of time; others for a continuous period of as long as 8 days" [Chief Peter Webster in Kirk 1986:86].

Opi
Keres, *Southwest*
Also: *upi.*
Laguna war priest [Parsons 1926:109]. The term also was used for warriors who had slain an enemy. "Before the [scalp] dance the scalp was taken around to the houses of the *opi,* as the killers were called, and food and other things were requisitioned for the scalp. The *opi* (*u'pi*) had to keep a piece of the victim, a piece of skin

or something else *(koimata)* wrapped around their feet until the end of the dance. For twelve days after the kill the *opi* might not have sexual intercourse. Scalps were kept in jars in a cave to the north. The *opi* took care of this cave and from this function were called *dyinidit^ykaiame* (north cave)" [Parsons 1920:122].

Oshadageaa
Iroquois, *Northeast*
Literal translation: "cloud dwellers" [Fenton 1942:29]. The Seneca term for a particular type of giant spirit eagle known as the Dew Eagle. Among the Cayuga and Onondaga it is called *haguks*. This particular spirit is the patron spirit of the Iroquois Eagle society, and Dew Eagles have the "powers of restoring life to wilting things and to human beings on the very brink of the grave" [Fenton 1942:29]. The Eagle society performs the Eagle Dance (also called the Striking Dance) to evoke shamanic healing on serious cases of illness.

In this healing ceremony they use a special song called *gane ondaadon* ("shaking a fan") in Seneca and *ganegwae gaena* ("striking a fan song") in Onondaga [Fenton 1942:29] to evoke their healing powers. The dance that accompanies this song "appears to be a survival of the ancient calumet dance with which Father Marquette was first welcomed among the tribes living south of the western Great Lakes. The Iroquois acquired a variant of the calumet ceremony during the eighteenth century, and the Eagle Dance is its descendant" [Fenton 1942:29]. In contemporary performances of this ceremony, the dancers hold "a small gourd rattle in the right hand and a feather calumet fan in the left hand" [Fenton 1942:29], while singing to the accompaniment of a water drum and cylindrical horn rattles called *onōkae kastáwēshae* ("cowhorn rattle") [Conklin and Sturtevant 1953:280].

Oshkosh
Menomini, *Midwest*
A famous chief/shaman from the early part of the nineteenth century who founded the Menomini semiannual (spring and fall) Buffalo Dance, called *picäkiwi siûkwûn*, "cooking for the buffalo" [Skinner 1915d:201]. Oshkosh received powers from the buffalo during a vision quest. "They gave him two buffalo heads as talisman to carry into battle, and they taught him all the sacred medicines, roots, and herbs that are of use in war, or in the healing of diseases and how to manipulate them. They told him when and how to give feasts and ceremonies in their honor" [Neopit in Skinner 1915d:204].

Neopit, Oshkosh's son who died in 1912, gave the following account of the use of this buffalo medicine on Oshkosh himself:

> When Oshkosh was dwelling on Lake Poygan in 1830 or '40 he went on a hunting trip and on his return was taken sick at Cattle Lake, near Portage, Wisconsin. After a day or two he died and was prepared for burial. A favorite aunt came to see him as he lay in state, and wept over his corpse, repeating the words of the buffalo that he had received in his sacred dream. Although he was cold and stiff the words had so much power that they caused him to open his eyes. Noticing this, the aunt directed that the buffalo heads and tails be brought to the place at once, and as soon as this was done she took some sacred herbs that Oshkosh had kept in or near them, pulverized them, and dissolved them in a bowl. She dipped up some of the brew in a tiny wooden spoon and forced it into his mouth, at the same time taking some more in her own mouth and spraying it over his face and body, rubbing it in at the same time with her hands and reciting the buffalo formula. Then she took a buffalo tail and dipped it into the liquid and shook it on Oshkosh's face, and brought him back to life. Others saw this, and said it was the power of the buffalo that brought him back to life [Neopit in Skinner 1915d:205].

Oskaskogi waski
Cree, *Canadian Eastern Woodlands*
Literal translation: "Green Grass World" [Mandelbaum 1940:251]. The is the Plains Cree term for the Land of the Dead. After death one's soul wandered about for four days and then traveled

to the Green Grass World, where it led a carefree life.

Oskitci
Cree, *Canadian Eastern Woodlands*
Pipestem bundle of the Plains Cree. Medicine bundles are most often personal items, but the *oskitci* is a tribal bundle that had "been given by Great *Manito* to Earth Man, the first human being" [Mandelbaum 1940:259]. The band council would choose the keeper of this particular bundle since it was not for sale, as were the personal bundles.

The bundle contains an elaborately decorated pipestem about 3 feet long with no bowl. In addition the *oskitci* contains some sweet grass, tobacco, and a decorated pipe tamper. The stem is not used for smoking but for mediating differences. The owner of the bundle is obligated to intervene in any tribal disputes. "No intemperate action could occur in the presence of the Pipestem and in this quality lay its peculiar potency. If two men were engaged in a quarrel, no matter how serious, they were bound to desist when the *oskitci* was presented to them. A man bent on avenging the death of a relative could not continue in his purpose if confronted with this Pipestem. When peace was to be made with a hostile tribe, the Pipestem Bearer led the way. When the enemy saw the pipe [stem], they recognized it and respected its sanctity" [Mandelbaum 1940:259].

Otgun
Iroquois, *Northeast*
Also: *utgon* [Fogelson 1977:185]; *otkon* [Hewitt in Hodge 1910:164 (Part 2)]. Dialectical variant: *okki* (Huron) [Mavor and Dix 1989:145] or *oki* (EONAH, p. 201). Power that is used in a malevolent way. Also, "it is the name in common use for all ferocious and monstrous beings, animals, and persons" [Hewitt in Hodge 1907:164 (Part 2)]. Among the Iroquois *orenda* (see *mana*), or power, is seen as neutral. The use of *orenda* for evil purposes results in *otgun*.

Other sources have reported that *otgun* is a spirit that becomes attached to a shaman. The *otgun* is symbolized "by some material object which brought him good luck or otherwise affected his life. This object was held as dear as life itself" [Mavor and Dix 1989:145]. This same concept appears among the Algonquian, where it is known as *manitou* (EONAH, p. 164).

Otterskin war medicine
Blackfoot, *Plains*
A personal charm used by a nineteenth-century Piegan warrior. This complicated charm was accumulated over the years by transfers and individual experiences.

It is an otterskin. The skin has been removed from the animal in one piece, split down the belly from the nose to the tip of the tail. In the holes where the legs were, pieces of leather, wrapped with flannel and beads with feathers are inserted, bells and weasel skins hang from the ends. The tail is tipped in a similar fashion. A slit is cut in the top of the head and neck pieces. Across the top is the bill of a white swan with the skin of the neck attached. This is to give the owner general powers in life and war: the song for this expresses the idea, "Alone I (swan) walk (fly); it is medicine." To the bill of the swan are hung duck feathers to give the power of swiftness: the song, "The lake is my lodge." At the end of the swan skin the wing of an owl is hung to give power in the night so that the horses of the enemy may be taken: the song, "The night is my medicine; I hoot." To the skin of the swan are attached two metal discs; the large one represents the morningstar, the small one the "smoking star," or "daystar." The songs are: "I am the morningstar," and "The daystar, he hears me; he is my medicine." The bells represent the power of the sun; the song, "These medicines are powerful." The entire skin of a jay bird, found in the mountains, is tied to the back of the skin and this is said to give power to treat disease as well as secure success in war: the song, "The mountains are my lodge: the woods are my medicine." A number of feathers are arranged in groups on the specimen and refer to birds in general as the song is, "All flying beings are sun-powerful; they hear me." There is one song for the otter: "I am swinging around in the water." The bells are shaken as an accompaniment to this. . . .

Two face paintings are associated with the formula [of the charm]. The jaybird bore a formula useful in treating disease for which the face was painted yellow with blue on the forehead. When on the warpath, the face was painted yellow and dotted over with blue to represent the owl; for this there is a song, "I (the owl) am looking for something to eat (an enemy or a horse)" [Wissler 1912a:97–98].

Oüahich

Micmac, *Canadian Eastern Woodlands*
Also: *aouten.* Gaspe shaman's helping spirit [Wallis and Wallis 1955:146].

Owála

Creek, *Southeast*
Shaman, doctor [Speck 1907:121]. This is the term used by the Taskigi division, who call themselves the Maskogalgi [Speck 1907:106]. Most shamans use their power for healing. In so doing the first step is to diagnosis the patient. All illnesses are seen as being caused by some foreign object or matter in the body, placed there either by an animal spirit or an evil shaman. The method of individual diagnosis is a secret, but Speck [1907:121] reported that some shamans "can tell a patient's ailment by examining his shirt, for which a charge of twenty-five cents or its equivalent in tobacco is made."

In treating patients prescribed formulas (obtained from animal spirits) are followed. A formula usually includes invoking the spirit of the animal that caused the disease to induce it to release its power over the patient. Formulas also often include the use of certain medicinal herbs. The herbs are steeped in a pot, and the liquid is strengthened by the shaman blowing into the pot through a tube. When the medicine has reached its full potential, the shaman administers it to the patient, who drinks it while the shaman also applies the liquid externally. "In some such

way as the animal invoked in the formula is believed to withdraw his cause [of the disease], so the spirit of the plants used are invoked to aid in driving the trouble out" [Speck 1907:123]. During the ceremony the shaman catches the disease and throws it into an animal but not the one that caused the illness.

Another type of shaman was the *hobáya* (see entry).

A similar term, *owǎlî* (pl. *owǎlálî*), appears among the Seminole; Sturtevant [1954b:155, 169, 368–369] translated it as "prophet," "wiseman," or "magician." The Creek equivalent in this case is *kílhlha,* translated as "knower" [Sturtevant 1954b:369]. The *owǎlálî* are no longer known among the Seminole. "Such people had many powers. They were doctors who not only could cure serious illness (even reviving the dead), but discovered new medicines (songs and plants) by supernatural means. . . . They could predict the future, tell what was happening at a distance, control the weather, and perhaps find lost objects. They protected themselves and their people during wartime by their knowledge of magic" [Sturtevant 1954b:369].

Owl Thunder

Cree, *Canadian Eastern Woodlands*
A Plains Cree shaman around the turn of the twentieth century who was capable of performing their form of the Ojibwa Shaking Tent Ceremony (EONAH, pp. 246–249). The following is an account of one of his performances conducted in 1903:

Two men tied Owl-thunder outside the tipi. After they tied him, they ran back into the tipi, a distance of about ten yards, but Owl-thunder was in the booth before they entered. Soon the ropes [which had bound him] were thrown out at the top. I saw that the knots had not been untied. It was as if he had slipped right out of the bonds. The booth shook. There were bells on it somewhere and they rang. We could hear all kinds of animals and birds—and also Old Woman spirit power. Then Thunder spirit power was asked, "Why is this man sick, Thunder?" (The reply was), "He had many horses. He refused to lend one to *kumustusumit,* Cattle Owner, and that man sent a *pitcitcihtcikan* (an intrusive object) into him."

Many other questions were asked. White-calf had lost two horses. He asked where they were. "Directly south of your house there is a small slough with willows all around it. They are feeding there now. In the morning they will be a little west of there." The next morning I myself went there to look. There were the two horses that had been lost for a week. White-calf later promised to give a cloth to Owl-thunder (as an offering to Owl-thunder's spirit helpers).

Another man had married a young girl and he asked if the child she bore were his. The answer was, "Yes (you are right) that is not your child; it is the child of your testes." We all laughed.

Then we saw sparks fly upward. It was the spirit powers leaving. Owl-thunder came out and the fire was built up [Baptiste Pooyak in Mandelbaum 1940:261–262].

Ozunya cin nupa
Teton, *Plains*

"A kind of war shaman wolf cult" among the Oglala [Wissler 1912b:91]. A shaman who has acquired the Wolf spirit is the leader of this society, which is closely associated with warfare. Members of this society are known for being fleet of foot like a wolf and are used as scouts on war raids. As the war party approaches the camp of the enemy, "the shaman takes the black pipe and the medicine on the back of the wolf hide and holding the pipe chews some of the medicine and blows it out into the air to make it misty and dense (a wolf's day). Thus, they approach the enemy unseen and take the horses away" [Wissler 1912b:91].

When performing ceremonies the Wolf shaman displays his powers. "The shaman chooses four men who are instructed to go out, each kill a wolf and have the skin tanned by some virgin. When this is done they bring them to the tipi. Some medicines are fastened to the whistle and some on the skins, also four crow feathers and one eagle feather. Below the eyes the skins are painted red and the ends of each foot have a piece of buckskin painted red attached. The back end is strewn with wild sage while the front end is just scraped off. He sings, whistles are heard to make a noise without being blown, the wolf hides move about, and wolf tracks can be seen" [Wissler 1912b:91].

Pabuaxantï

Paiute, *Basin*

Literal translation: "water doctor" [Kelly 1939:159]. See *unwadïmbuaxantï*.

Pâdoyum

Kiowa, *Plains*

Plural: *pâdoyuwi*. Buffalo doctor. Shaman who receives his power from the Buffalo spirit. For a healing ceremony a "buffalo doctor uses a rattle of buffalo hoofs, with beard of buffalo, and painted with red clay to represent blood. The doctor fasts for four days" [Parsons 1929:117]. In more recent times some *pâdoyuwi* have become peyote users.

Pagitsh

Ute, *Basin*

A Northern Ute shaman who was interviewed by anthropologist Francis Densmore around 1917. His power came from a little green man (a class of spirits called *pitukupi* [A. Smith 1974:155]). Pagitsh's specialty "was the treatment of acute pain, and he said that he could cure pain in any part of the body" [Densmore 1922:129].

Persons who approached Pagitsh for a healing "brought with them a stick about 18 inches long, painted green and forked at the end. This was his particular token" [Densmore 1922:128]. During his healing rituals he used no paraphernalia such as drums or rattles; he simply sang a series of healing songs. Densmore recorded nine of his songs, all of which he sang during a treatment. He doctored only at night. "Pa´gitš said that throughout his treatments the little green man stayed outside the tent, and he could see him and hear what he said, every phase of the treatment being according to his direction" [Densmore 1922:129]. His treatment consisted of removing a disease object from the patient's body via sucking. When the object was removed, the shaman would take it from his mouth and display it to the audience. "As soon as this substance was removed from the patient's body he began to recover. Sometimes this substance is one of the little green man's arrows which he has shot into the person's body. In shape this 'strange something' was said to be 'like a carrot' and 1 or 2 inches in length. In color it was red, like blood, and in texture it was not unlike a fingernail. The 'arrows' were always of the same kind, differing only in size"

[Densmore 1922:129]. Pagitsh reported that he usually had to sing five times before removing the disease object.

Paho

Hopi, *Southwest*

Also: *paaho, baho* [Dorsey and Voth 1902:173]. Plural: *paavaho* [Loftin 1986:188]. Prayer stick [Parsons 1939:270]. "Different prayer sticks are made by different Hopi at different times for different purposes, though all *paavaho* embody a prayer for moisture" [Loftin 1986:188]. With reference to the ceremonial prayer sticks, only persons with the prerequisite power and authority are allowed to assemble them. Many different types of *pahos* are used by the Hopi. Generally they consist of a ritual arrangement of specific bird feathers, attached to certain types of sticks with handspun cotton twine. Most often one flat stick or two round sticks are used. The sticks are around 5 inches in length and about ½ inch in diameter. They are often painted green, black, or brown. Sometimes a face, called *taiwa*, is faceted in the *paho* stick [Voth 1901:68]. This "face" is actually a notch carved into the upper end of the stick, which is painted light brown. In other cases 2-foot-long willow branches are used, and cornhusk packets (*möciata*) [Voth 1901:97] containing cornmeal or honey. Other such offerings may be tied to it. Herbs are also attached to the *paho*—most frequently mountain sagebrush, called *kunya* (*Artemisia frigida*) [Whiting 1939:94], and snakeweed, called *maövi* (*Gutierrezia euthamiae*) [Voth 1901:68].

The *pahos* are consecrated by blowing smoke onto them, sprinkling cornmeal on them, spitting honey on them, or some combination of these three techniques [Dorsey and Voth 1901:21].

Once completed, the *pahos* are usually deposited or stuck into the ground at designated locations. It is not uncommon to see several hundred *pahos* at such sites.

Among the different types of *pahos* are: the *nölöshoya*, the first *paho* made for a boy by his father, asking for a long and happy life; the *makpaho*, a hunting *paho* that is "a wish or prayer for good

luck in the chase" [Dorsey and Voth 1901:57]; and "the short double *bahos* (double green, double black or green and black)," which "are said to be made for the dead in general, who are believed to reciprocate the kindness by sending the Hopi good crops of corn, watermelons, squashes, etc." [Dorsey and Voth 1901:57] (these double *pahos* are sometimes call *kaö* [corn ears] [Voth 1901:76].) This last type is the most common.

In addition to these general forms of *pahos*, the Hopi also have many very specific types used in their different ceremonial altar displays. For example, in the *Powamu* Ceremony there is a particular form of *paho* called the *taka paho* (man paho) [Voth 1901:77]. This *paho* is always made by a warrior chief (*kalehtakmongwi*). It is made from the stem of the Rocky Mountain beeweed, called *tumi* (*Cleome integrifolia*, Nutt; *C. serrulata*, Pursh) [Voth 1901:77; Whiting 1939:77]. (Note: Voth gave this Hopi term as *duma*.) The stick is short, pointed at both ends, and painted. Four of them are used on the altar display, each placed in a *paho* stand located in the middle along each side of the altar edge. "This stick is colored yellow in the stand on the north side, green on the west, red on the south and white on the east stand. To this stick is fastened a *yahpa* feather (identity uncertain)" [Voth 1901:77]. When in place on the altar, each of these *pahos* "represent[s] a *kalehtaka* (warrior) standing at the end of the baho stand, keeping watch over and protecting the various objects on the baho stand" [Voth 1901:77].

The ritual of making *pahos* is termed *paholawu* [Voth 1901:67] and is usually conducted in a kiva.

Another form of Hopi prayer offerings is the *nakwakwosi* (see entry).

Since the success of a ceremony is based on the prayers given to these offerings as they are made, the actual rite of *paho* making is a sacred undertaking. Persons assembling them must keep their minds focused on the ceremony at hand and be filled with pure thoughts. "We all undressed except for the loincloth or, in some cases kilts, arranged ourselves in rows in the lower section of the kiva, and began making pahos with feathers, native string [woven cotton], herbs, and willow sticks. I had never done this work before, and had to be instructed by my ceremonial father, who spoke in a whisper because of the presence of ancestral spirits. I made first the prayer arrow, then soft prayer feathers for my Guardian Spirit . . . and for all the other spirits I could remember. I also made them for all the members of my family, my special friends, the livestock, dogs, cats, houses, trees, and other objects of value. I thought about each god, spirit, person, or object while I made a paho for him. I learned that this is the most important work in the world" [Sun Chief in Simmons 1942:169].

See *offerings, prayer feathers/sticks.*

Pahokataua
Pawnee, *Plains*

Literal translation: "Kneeprint by the Water." A great war chief who was killed during battle; his body was never recovered. Thereafter his spirit returned to the Pawnee and aided them by "exerting himself incessantly in their behalf, advising measures, and forwarding designs against their hereditary enemies [the Dakotas], foretelling how many they should kill and how many they should themselves lose. His method of communicating intelligence was by dreams. This is the only instance I ever discovered in their [religious] system of any thing like apotheosis [deification]" [Dunbar 1882:736].

Pains
California

Throughout much of north-central and northern coastal California, disease-causing agents are called "pains" in the anthropological literature. "These pains are variously described, frequently as being sharp at both ends and clear as ice. They possessed the power of moving even after extracted [from the body of the victim], and were able to fly through the air to the intended victim at the command of the person who had sent them" [Kroeber 1907:333]. This particular view of illnesses as "pains" found in this area of California is unique to North America.

The shaman must locate the pain in the patient's body and then suck it out by some means. However, unlike the disease objects so well known elsewhere, the pain is "not an ordinary physical object working mischief by its mere presence in the body or by the supernatural properties with which the shaman or his spirits had endowed it, but an object itself supernatural" [Kroeber 1907:333]. Thus the extracted pain is seen as a source of power for the shaman. "The pain is not a spirit, but yet possesses power of itself, and is at the same time the cause of the disease" [Drucker 1937:257]. Because this type of pain carries a power, a novice shaman often "may receive her first pain in a dream" [Drucker 1937:257].

In fact, gaining such pains through dancing and fasting at isolated spots is the first step to becoming a shaman in this area. Once the pains are acquired, the novice must learn to control them. This is evidenced when the shaman can vomit up the pain at will, display it for all to see, and then swallow it again. Therefore, when extracting a pain a shaman either destroys it, which is the most common method of disposing of disease objects in other cultures, or keeps it for his own use. Such a pain is stored in the shaman's body. "In Northwestern California he sometimes swallowed it, the degree of his power being thought to be dependent upon the number of pains he kept in his body" [Kroeber 1907:333]. In either case, the shaman almost always displays the pain to the ceremonial participants after it has been extracted from the patient. Once he has acquired power over it, he is able to vomit it up at will and display it.

Given this concept of illness, in this particular area of California the nearly pan–North American concept of a guardian spirit "is weak or entirely lacking. . . . I could discover no trace of the concept among the Tolowa" [Drucker 1937:257]. In this area women most often become shamans through dreams of pains. These dreams are symbolic in nature. "One dreamt 'about the mountains' [since the pains come from the mountains], or 'about the sunrise' [whose color indicates the color of pain the dreamer will obtain]. There is no hint of a personal supernatural benefactor"

[Drucker 1937:257]. Therefore, shamans in this area receive their healing powers through the control of pains, and the most powerful shamans have many pains under their control.

Among the Hill (or Northern) Maidu a pain is called *itu* [Dixon 1905:280], while the Valley Maidu use the word for power, *omeya* (see *omaya*), for a pain [Kroeber 1925:422]. The Wiyot term is *silak* (see entry); the Shasta term is *aheki* (see entry); the Wintu is *dokos* (see entry); the Tolowa is *sisene* (see entry); the Yurok is *telogetl* (see entry) [Posinsky 1965:236]; and the Yuki is *tihil* (see entry). Although mainly found in the above-mentioned regions of California, the notion of pain as a disease object and source of disease extends to the Southern Paiutes of Nevada where they are termed *pakankii* (see entry).

See also *Brown, Fanny.*

Paint
Arikara, *Plains*

A powerful shaman during the latter part of the nineteenth century. He was most renowned for his bulletproof medicine, which he often displayed. "He would wrap himself completely in a large buffalo robe, placing a piece of eagle down at the armpit. He would then stand in the corner of the covered entrance or vestibule of the medicine lodge. Another member of the band would stand out before the entrance at a few paces distance with his rifle, powder horn, and bullets. He would hold out the powder and the bullet for the audience to examine as he slowly loaded the gun and rammed down the charge. He would then shoot directly at Paint who would apparently drop, severely wounded while the blood flowed. As usual he was carried out, surrounded by the band which would perform certain mysteries over him, after which he would walk out from the midst of the band quite uninjured" [Will 1934:46].

See also *Bear's Belly, invulnerability medicines, Running Wolf, Shunáwanùh.*

Paitâpeki
Kiowa, *Plains*

Witch or sorcerer [Parsons 1929:137, n. 2].

Pakahkus
Cree, *Canadian Eastern Woodlands*

A spirit known as "Bony Specter" [Bloomfield 1934:204] among the Plains Cree. This spirit was honored in an annual Give Away Dance [Mandelbaum 1940:275] that was conducted in the fall or early winter. This was a religious ceremony conducted in a ceremonial tipi during the night. Couples danced facing each other, giving away and receiving gifts; during the event, a great deal of wealth was exchanged. Those who were generous were blessed by *Pakahkus,* while those who were stingy usually suffered ill fortune. One participant reported: "I was cheated [in the giveaway] like that once. But I didn't mind, even though afterward I didn't even have a horse with which to hunt buffalo. The one who cheated me got a fast horse, but couldn't make the use of it because he [the man] grew blind soon after. The old people said, 'He got blind because he cheated you.' *Pakahkus* has strong power" [Fine Day in Mandelbaum 1940:276].

Pakankii
Paiute, *Basin*

Dialectical variant: *paxanxi* (Las Vegas) [Kelly 1939:162]. Pain (see *pains*). Shivwits (Southern Paiute) term for a disease object. "The pain, resembling a small stick covered with 'light-colored blood,' could be sucked out by a shaman. Although invisible to a 'common man,' it was exhibited before being held up and blown away" [Kelly 1939:154]. However, among the Las Vegas the pain was not displayed by the shaman after extraction because that was considered showing off.

Palladium

Plural: palladia. In standard usage this term means anything believed to provide protection or safety. Since such "safety guards" are really a form of amulet, the term is infrequently used in the anthropological literature to refer to tribal medicines, shamanic-made amulets, ceremonial stone fetishes, or the like.

Parsons, Elsie Clews

Elsie Clews was born on November 27, 1875, in New York City. She was the only daughter of Henry Clews, a wealthy, upper-class banker who married Lucy Madison Worthington, a descendant of President James Madison. She received her Ph.D. in sociology in 1899, and in 1900 she married Herbert Parsons, a Republican New York lawyer who later (1905–1911) served in Congress. While a young woman, Parsons gained a reputation as a radical feminist and pacifist—a reputation that would remain with her throughout her life. During the early 1900s she met anthropologists Alfred Kroeber, Franz Boas, Pliny Goddard, and Robert Lowie, but her real interests in anthropology began after a trip to the Southwest in 1910. Subsequently she became the first woman trained in anthropology by Franz Boas (at Columbia University). Throughout the remainder of her life, she was a patron of anthropology. She occasionally taught at Columbia University and the New School for Social Research, but after 1905 she "chose to carry on independent research" [Hieb 1993:64]. Beginning in 1916, she devoted twenty-five years to field research among the Pueblo.

Parsons was a prolific writer, and between 1916 and 1918 alone she "produced 75 publications, including 28 on Zuni, Laguna, and Acoma" [Hieb 1993:67]. Between 1920 and 1924 she worked among the Hopi, and eventually she purchased from Stewart Culin the Hopi field notes of Alexander MacGregor Stephen, which she edited and published in 1936 (*The Hopi Journal of Alexander M. Stephen*). This major contribution and her two-volume work entitled *Pueblo Indian Religion*, published in 1939, constitute her most important works. Over the years her work and reputation became so great that in 1941 she was the first woman ever to be elected as president of the American Anthropological Association. However, "just eight days before she was to officiate as president at the annual meeting of the American Anthropological Association, she died in New York City of complications following an appendectomy" [Hieb 1993:75].

Patash

Wishram, *Plateau*

Dialectical variant: *patish* (Yakima). Literally "large branch" [Boyd 1996:123]. Images, usually wooden, carved in the likeness of spirit helpers that were used by shamans in their winter ceremonies. Two common carving motifs are "the skeletal rib cage and the owl-like eyes" [Boyd 1996:126]. The term also includes "power sticks [see *askwitit*], power boards, medicine bundles, and talismans" [Boyd 1996:122].

Such images have also been noted among the Upper Chinookans, appearing in the rear of a chief's lodge next to his bed and at gravesites.

Among the neighboring Lower Chinooks, such as the Kathlamet, these wooden images have also been noted. For example, Boas mentioned a Chinook shaman who shook a figure, made of cedar bark, that guided him to the land of the dead to recover lost souls [Boas 1894:206] (see *qlaqewam*).

Among the Yakima *patash* could also refer to "visible representations of the *'tah-ma'* [power]" [Perkins in Boyd 1996:125]. This is more akin to the practice of the Plains cultures, whereby the vision quester often received such power objects from his helping spirit. These objects were imbued with power from the spirit and treated as sacred objects. Most often these objects were physical aspects of the shaman's helping spirit, such as an eagle claw for an Eagle spirit, a bear canine tooth for a Bear spirit, a wolf tail for a Wolf spirit, and so forth. However, they could also be as simple as a small stone.

Patashe

Yakima, *Plateau*

Plume [Boyd 1996:125]. This term refers to a feather wand (feathers attached to a stick) that is used for ritual cleansing.

Pauborong

Paiute, *Basin*

Dialectical variant: *poro* or *pooro* (Chemehuevi) [Laird 1976:31]. Paranigat (Southern Paiute) term for a shaman's doctoring cane. The cane "was made from a length of serviceberry, knobbed on the end, which he [the shaman] heated, straightened, and decorated with feathers. Magical powers were ascribed to this staff, which 'was a doctor itself. It stood up and talked, but only the doctor could hear it. It was put on top or underneath a patient to take the sickness away'" [Kelly 1939:158]. Most often eagle feathers were attached to the top of the staff.

Among the Chemehuevi the cane is reported to be "shaped like a shepherd's crook" [Laird 1976:31]. "This cane is said to have 'talked just like the spirit, only not very much. It told where the pain was and how to cure it.' The communication was audible to the shaman alone, but he might relay the message. A really good shaman was able to tell, by means of his cane, whether the patient would recover. At the conclusion of the séance, he stuck the staff into the ground at the head of the sick person. If it would not sink its full length the patient was doomed" [Kelly 1936:132].

Such staffs are also used by shamans from the Kaibab, Gunlock, Moapa, Las Vegas, and Shivwits bands of Southern Paiutes. This staff also serves as a badge of office for the shaman.

Pawágan
Ojibwa, *Canadian Eastern Woodlands*

Plural: *pawáganak*. Dialectical variant: *pawakan* (EONAH, pp. 214–215). Literal translation: "dream visitor" [Hallowell 1992:87]. Spirit. A common term for a spirit or for spirit powers obtained through dreams. Children, especially males, are encouraged to seek power dreams from the age of six onward. Between ten and fourteen years of age, most boys are sent into the woods, usually in the spring, on a vision quest lasting upward of a week or more. At a selected site a platform, called *wázisan,* literally "nest" [Hallowell 1992:88], is built in a tree for the boy. There he remains until his quest is completed. The content of any dreams acquired is not divulged by the quester lest it cancel the powers he has received. The spirits, when they appear, usually come in human form to the quester.

The powers one receives are "always contingent upon the fulfillment of obligations that took a variety of forms. In cases where the 'owners' of animal species dispensed benefits, there was often a food taboo. One man was forbidden to kill or eat porcupine by the 'owner' of the porcupines. In another case a man was commanded [by his *pawágan*] to wear the kind of headgear attributed to a character in mythology who had blessed him in a dream. Another man was forbidden to speak to or to have sexual intercourse with his wife for a defined period after marriage. . . . Consequently, the observance of the personal taboos imposed by other than human persons [spirits] often requires the firmest self-discipline, especially when it means behaving in ways that are not always intelligible to others yet cannot be explained to them" [Hallowell 1992:92]. The breaking of such taboos not only causes the shaman to lose his powers, it can also bring sickness to him or to his family.

Some of the men who receive powers become proficient at performing the Shaking Tent Ceremony (EONAH, pp. 246–249). Hallowell [1992:85] reported one interesting performance in which the shaman called the spirit of another shaman, from Lac Seul in this case, into the ceremony: "The conjurer said, 'I'm calling for the man from Lac Seul.' Shortly afterwards there was a thump indicating a new arrival in the tent, followed by a strange voice saying, 'I was sleeping, but I heard you calling me.' This was the soul of a noted Lac Seul conjurer. People in the audience asked for news and received replies to questions. Then the visiting conjurer sang a song and departed for his home 200 miles away."

Spirit beings are also respectfully called "grandfather" [Hallowell 1942:7].

Peace Pipe Dance
This is a Plains area, four-day ritual that is "practiced by the Omaha, Kaw, Osage, Pawnee, Dakota, Iowa, Ponca and Oto. . . . In general the ceremony represented the ceremonial capture, adoption and return of the hungga 'beloved child.' This ceremony honored the father of the child and the child

itself" [Whitman 1937:121]. However, because gift giving was associated with this ceremony, the ritual also served to distribute wealth.

In the 1930s the Ponca had only two sacred pipes in their possession, one with a red stem and one with a blue stem. Attached to the red stem were seven golden eagle feathers and feathers from the timber hoot owl, while the blue stem had the head of an ivory-billed woodpecker and feathers from the black eagle tied to it. "In place of the pipe bowl, (the pipes could not be smoked,) the Ponca set the head of a duck. . . . These pipes, which could only be made by men with appropriate holy knowledge were not, strictly speaking, the property of any special person or class. It was said that any one who had the sacred pipes presented to him four times might present them in his turn to another. A man who wished to present the pipes [the initial prelude to the subsequent performance of the Peace Pipe Dance] would go to those individuals who had the pipes and by making suitable presents obtain possession of them [for use in the Peace Pipe Dance]" [Whitman 1937:122].

When not in use these two Ponca sacred pipes "were bound together in a lynx hide. . . . The rest of the paraphernalia [in the pipe bundle] consisted of a forked stick painted red on which the pipes rested, a gourd [rattle], and a whistle made from an eagle wing [bone]" [Whitman 1937:122].

Pedro
Yuma, *Southwest*
A shaman who was also the leader of the Yuma village located near Pilot Knob (Algodones) in the latter part of the eighteenth century. One rare, albeit brief, account of a shamanic healing, observed in 1775, follows: "Last night I heard this fellow [Pedro] chanting a canticle very deliberately and melancholic, having a sick man in his house to whom he gives such rubbings of the belly with sand that only a brute would be able to stand it. He blows on him many times and then blows against the wind making many passes as he blows. They say that in order to perform his of-

fice properly he bathes himself very carefully early in the morning" [Eixarch in Forde 1931:181].

Peh
Tewa, *Southwest*
Also: *pe* [Douglass 1917:350]. Generic term for prayer stick [Parsons 1939:270]. There are many varieties of prayer sticks among the Tewa. Some primary ones include: the *oupe,* the single rain-cloud, male prayer stick [Fewkes in Douglass 1917:350]; the *wege,* the double rain-cloud prayer stick [Douglass 1917:350]; the *mawake,* the sun prayer stick [Douglass 1917:351]; the *wadape,* the chief's prayer stick [Douglass 1917:352]; and the *gowane,* the warrior's prayer stick. On male prayer sticks the faces are painted turquoise, while on female ones the faces are painted yellow [Parsons 1939:279]. Secondary prayer sticks include the *mawape, wewawive, atikani,* and *awape.*

See also *offerings, prayer feathers/sticks.*

Pekitwewin
Potawatomi, *Midwest*
Lacrosse. Among the Potawatomi the three most important games—lacrosse, double-ball *(peskowewin),* and dice *(kwezagewin)*—"were played in honor of the guardian spirit of the sponsor of a game, with tobacco and food dedicated to the spirit. It was believed that if a person did not sponsor a game once or twice a year he might fall into ill favor with his spirit, and even become sick" [Ritzenthaler 1953a:163].

Perkitigsak
East Greenland Eskimo, *Arctic Coast*
An Ammasalik (Angmagsalik) *angakok* (shaman, see *angatkok,* EONAH, p. 15) who lived around the turn of the twentieth century. He was their most skillful hunter at the time. Eventually he was accused of being an *ilisitsok* (sorcerer) after becoming ill with fever. The delirium associated with his fever was seen as an indicator that he had gone mad, which happens to sorcerers as a result of their practice. In such cases the person must confess his crimes or be subjected to a confession ordeal in which he "is bound with his

hands and feet stretched out on the platform or on the floor, and is gagged. He gets neither food nor drink, and sometimes heavy stones are lain on his chest. He is left in this position till he dies. . . . The only way in which the [delerious] patient can escape this treatment, is for him to confess that he is an *ilisitsok* and to name all the crimes, real or imaginary, which he has on his conscience" [Holm in Thalbitzer 1914:102]. Perkitigsak confessed to having sent out four *tupileks* (see *tupilaks* entry), but such confessions are often falsely made in order to avoid the treatment described above.

Perkitigsak did make a *tupilek* against a fellow hunter who had harpooned a walrus that he himself was about to harpoon. He made it from walrus skin, and it resembled a walrus wearing women's drawers. "He created and made it grow in the usual way, after which he sent it forth to kill the man who had taken the walrus from him. One day after this he saw a walrus at *Ikerasar-suak,* and was just about to harpoon it, when he discovered that it was the *tupilek* [he had made]. It made for the shore and went on land, where it turned into a human being. Some time after it killed the man against whom it was sent" [Holm in Thalbitzer 1914:102].

Petcuduthe utakohi
Iowa, *Plains*
Fire or Hot Dance Ceremony. During their performances "the members danced up to the kettles and plunged their naked arms into the boiling broth and drew forth collops of meat which they handed the spectators. The food was so hot that uninitiates could not take it even then, but often dropped it, whereas the society members were hardly troubled, the only effect noticed being a slight reddening of their arms" [Skinner 1915a:702–703].

See also *iruska.*

Pextcigosan
Potawatomi, *Midwest*
The general Mascouten (Prairie Potawatomi) name for the sacred bundles belonging to each clan. The sacred bundles are, as a rule, large and contain many different items. They "are used for war, naming of children, doctoring the sick, hunting, and general good luck. . . . They also call by the same name the small packets containing nothing but a single wooden guardian doll, and the minor bundles of fetishes sacred to individuals through revelation by their dream guardians" [Skinner 1924:55].

Each spring a watch is kept, day and night, by men looking to the west. The first lightning spotted is their signal to begin anew for the year by ceremonially opening each of the clan bundles. If the lightning is spotted in the middle of the night, everyone is awakened to start the ritual. They begin by putting out all of their fires and re-lighting them from a new pure fire that is started from a bow drill. That morning (or the following morning if the rites begin in the night), they perform the "Opening Up the Bundle" rite, known as *äpaxkumikäk* [Skinner 1924:55]. Each year the tribal chief selects a different bundle owner to take the lead for the season. The person whose bundle is used becomes, ipso facto, the master of ceremonies for the year. The actual opening of this bundle begins "with four ceremonials, a prayer, the feast, another prayer, and the passing of the pipe. . . . At noon there are more rites of song and prayer, but no dancing. These are repeated at two, and again at four in the afternoon. At the conclusion of the last ceremonial the leader dismisses the people, and announces that it is now in order for the other clans and bundles to give their spring feasts in any order that may seem best to them, but he usually decides on who is to start first" [Skinner 1924:55].

Philter
Also: *philtre.* A potion or charm used to make a person fall in love. See *love medicines.*

Piännithle
Zuni, *Southwest*
One of the suborders of the Great Fire fraternity or Big Firebrand society. According to Stevenson

[1904:485] the Great Fire fraternity has three orders: Great God; Mystery Medicine (also called *Iwenashnawe*, "knowledge of sucking"); and Great Fire orders. The Great Fire order, in turn, has five suborders: Sword, Spruce, Arrow, Navajo Dance, and the *Posikishid* (commonly interpreted as "spruce tree"). The *Piännithle* from the Sword suborder are known for their sword-swallowing feats (see *Onayanakia*). During the 1890s Stevenson witnessed a five-day initiation ceremony performed by this society. She reported:

> At the close of the prayer the swords are reversed with the same precision, and the ʿHlĕmʾmosona steps before the boxes and swallows his sword. Again they move on for a moment or two, when all turn and face the center; then the others in turn leave the circles in groups and swallow the swords.
>
> As soon as one group returns to the circle others step out, some swallowing two swords at once, one man swallowing three. . . . The Great Mother of the fraternity swallows two swords at once. It is noticed that many of this fraternity run the sword through the mouth to moisten it before swallowing it [Stevenson 1904:510].

She also described this activity among the *Posikishid*, the Spruce Tree society [Stevenson 1904:485]: "The swords are made on the fourth morning. The novice, who is instructed by his fraternity father, makes his own sword. When a woman is initiated her sword is made by her fraternity father. The swords are fashioned like those of the Sword order, at the butt of the tree, the trunk being slender. . . . The swords are afterward rubbed with cougar grease and red hematite. . . . [Stone knives] are used to polish the swords. When the sword is completed the maker attaches a laʾshowanne [see entry] of a turkey feather to the top of the tree from which his sword is fashioned, and the tree is deposited in the east end of the room, with the sword pointing east" [Stevenson 1904:517].

Pichimu

Paiute, *Basin*

Owen Valley Paiute term for pipes [Steward 1933:319]. Pipes were tubular in shape and made from pottery. "Doctors sometimes smoked while curing. Others 'blew out smoke to blow away disease'" [Steward 1933:320].

Among the Mono Lake Paiutes the term for pipes is *odoic*.

Pihtwowikamik

Cree, *Canadian Eastern Woodlands*

The Smoking Tipi Ceremony among the Plains Cree (see also *Pitalgomik*). The ceremony is second in rank to their Sun Dance. Like the Sun Dance, it is given to fulfill a pledge made to the spirits. It is usually held in the spring in a large tipi. The ceremony lasts one entire night and mainly involves the ritualized manipulations of sacred pipes and rattles, accompanied by singing. As is to be expected, some details of the ceremony differ from area to area, for example, between the River People band on the Battleford Reservation and those on the Peepeekisis Reservation [Mandelbaum 1940:274].

Piikati

Ute, *Basin*

Literal translation: "man with power" [A. Smith 1974:152]. Northern Ute term for shaman. Both males and female become shamans, but "only men shamans could control weather, and only certain shamans could cure illness caused by ghosts" [A. Smith 1974:154]. Power is obtained through a series of dreams, both involuntary ones experienced at home and others sought out in isolation. Usually the dreams are auditory ones in which the spirit teaches "the dreamer the songs to use in curing, the paraphernalia he should acquire and use, various details of the ritual that should be followed in curing, and sometimes what the payment for services should be" [A. Smith 1974:154]. Power usually comes from a particular animal spirit and carries a specific cure. For example, from the Kingfisher spirit comes healing powers for venereal disease and hemorrhages, and from the Badger spirit come healing powers for foot troubles. However, the most powerful spirit comes from the *pitukupi*, a class of 2-foot-tall dwarfs, usually dressed in green. "Anyone having the *[pitukupi]* as a source of power could cure any illness, including those exhibiting soul loss and those caused by ghosts" [A. Smith 1974:155]. Shamanism often runs in family lineages.

The primary role of the shaman is that of healer. Healing ceremonies are conducted after dark. The shaman uses a drum and rattle to accompany his songs, which are without words [A. Smith 1974:158]. Once the audience members catch the tune, they join in. The shaman enters a trance to locate the "pain" (see *pains*) and then removes it by pressing the top of his head on the patient's body at the spot where the "pain" resides. As one patient described it: "He put the top of his head to the place where the rheumatism was and he pressed hard. It hurt so, I screamed and hollered. I could feel the pain going around inside. Then he took his head away and it stopped hurting. He spit out a little something; that was the pain. He didn't put his mouth to where the pain was, just the top of his head" [unidentified informant in A. Smith 1974:159]. In difficult cases when the "pain" is too strong, the shaman "has to rest and have another smoke. He uses cigarets, a mixture of Durham and larb [a plant that grows in the mountains]. . . . Then he cures again and draws out the sickness" [unidentified informant in A. Smith 1974:160]. An earlier form of treatment involved the shaman lying flat on his back and the patient lying atop the shaman, also on his back. In this case the shaman used his hand to remove the "pain."

Densmore [1922:127] reported that herbalists also use songs in administering their herbs; however, unlike shamans, they sell their songs. "A good remedy was worth a horse, this price including the herb, the history of its medicinal use, and the song without which it would not be effective" [Densmore 1922:127].

Pilhashiwanni
Zuni, *Southwest*
Bow-priest [Parsons 1933:85].

Pilsi
Delaware, *Northeast*
The term for the state of spiritual purification necessary for acquiring a guardian spirit. "To be pi´łsi is to have gone through all the native teachings. And to live with a guileless character, child-like, is sufficient to entitle a man or woman (irrespective of marriage or celibacy) to be referred to as . . . 'pure, clean, man,' or . . . 'pure, clean, woman'"[Speck 1931:51].

Pinaeshe Kanas Towagit
Ojibwa, *Canadian Eastern Woodlands*
Thunder Born. A Saulteaux shaman whose English name was Peter George. He was born in 1888 on the Sakimay Reserve, north of Broadview, Saskatchewan. He knew the Rain Dance Ceremony (used for healing as well as rain) and used different roots in his cures, along with medicine songs. He began performing the Rain Dance in the 1930s and by the mid-1960s had done twelve dances. During his seventies he was considered one of the most powerful shamans on the reservation. "In fact, some Indians from other reserves periodically visit him and seek a medicine to cure their maladies" [Tarasoff 1980:10].

He was interviewed in 1967 and recalled the following ceremony conducted during the early nineteenth century to find a lost sacred pipe: "Well, he lost that pipe. All right. The old man [shaman] was sitting and facing northwest. It was night. 'I'm gonna sing twice,' he says. 'When I finish, you will hear the coyote howl.' So he started to sing. In front of him lay a coyote skin with head on one side. When he was about to finish there was a 'swish' through the air. The old man told that man who lost his pipe to look under the coyote hide. He did—and there was the pipe that he lost about 60 miles away. The coyote had brought it back. You couldn't see him, only hear him. You see. Some of them couldn't believe it, but I believe it" [George in Tarasoff 1980:185–186].

Pingxangzho

Tewa, *Southwest*

Literal translation: "mountain lion man" [Hill 1982:343]. At Santa Clara this term is used for the head of the Hunt Society. "The Hunt Society organized, directed, and was in overall charge of all ritual hunts, such as the rabbit hunt which preceded a kachina dance in the hills. . . . The society was also in charge of all communal hunts and fishing ventures" [Hill 1982:344]. Individuals or small groups going on a hunt always requested prayers from this society. "The leader or other society members 'worked' and deposited prayer plumes and [corn]meal at various shrines to insure the success of the venture" [Hill 1982:344]. In addition, the society was responsible for the maintenance of the various hunting shrines located in their vicinity. Members were not allowed to cut their hair and had to wear buckskin clothing.

Pisausut

West Greenland Eskimo, *Arctic Coast*

Kangatsiak term for life force. This is the force that gives vitality to an animal, human, etc. [Birket-Smith 1924:439]. This force manifests from the *inua* (EONAH, pp. 117–118), the soul of any object, animate or inanimate. In recovering individual lost souls the shaman restores a person's *pisausut* when his or her *inua* is returned to the body of the patient by the shaman.

See also *mana*.

Pitalgomik

Ojibwa, *Canadian Eastern Woodlands*

Smoking Tipi Ceremony. Saulteaux term for this particular regional ceremony (see also *Pihtwowikamik*). The ceremony lasts one night. There is no dancing, and no drums are used. Preliminary preparations include the erection of a special tipi in which, among other things, cloth offerings are made, items to be used in the ceremony are smudged with sweet grass, and the sa-

cred songs that go with this ritual are rehearsed. Following this there is an afternoon sweat lodge, followed by a feast. Also during the afternoon four women erect the enlarged sacred tipi in which the ceremony will begin around sunset. The door of the tipi is on the east side.

A Smoking Tipi Ceremony was observed in June 1966 on the Sakimay Reserve in southern Saskatchewan. Although this was the group's first Smoking Tipi Ceremony in forty years, it was conducted by an eighty-year-old shaman named Kimvuanipinas (see entry) whose father had regularly conducted the ceremony and then passed it to his son. The altar was displayed in the center of the tipi and faced west. Its main contents included a buffalo skull, four directional sticks each tipped with an eagle feather, and four sacred pipes. In the center of the altar was a fire from which coals were used to light sweet grass throughout the ceremony. Throughout the night-long ceremony sacred songs were sung, accompanied by rattles. During singing intervals the pipes were smoked, prayers were offered, offerings were given, and so forth.

Kimvuanipinas also recalled attending his father's "Smoke Tepee" in the nineteenth century: "My father made a Smoke Tepee [and] the people gathered and sang all night. There were big clouds and then a thunderstorm. This took place about a half-mile south from where my house is today, by an old road. Many people, including [shaman] Peter George's daddy came to the Smoking Tepee there. You know that night the Thunderbird must have laid on the grass, for there were his burnt marks on the ground. It was just like a bird, you know. . . . I saw the burnt grass where the Thunderbird landed—just like when you make a prairie fire, you know. The marks on the ground were 15 to 16 feet across" [Kimvuanipinas in Tarasoff 1980:91].

Pitowabosons

Ojibwa, *Canadian Eastern Woodlands*

Dialectical variants: *pitowabucwan* (Cree), *katciabucuc* (Montagnais) [Cooper 1930:514]. This term refers to the fetus taken from a slain rabbit and used in hunting medicine.

The use of animal fetuses in hunting medicine is comparatively rare. We know that the Huron and Wyandot used deer fetuses, and the Beaver used moose fetuses. The use of otter, marten, lynx, and bear fetuses has also been recorded. The fetus is ritually prepared and dried, and even the handling of the fetus is done in a prescribed manner. For instance, when taking a rabbit fetus, the Cree would pass it through the snare in which it was caught [Copper 1930:514].

Pizikiwûs

Ojibwa, *Canadian Eastern Woodlands*

Dialectical variant: *picäkiwûs* (Menomini). A Bungi (Plains-Ojibwa) medicine obtained from the buffalo that this group used in their Buffalo Dance, "a variant of a widely spread custom found among the central Algonkin, the Iroquois, and the Plains tribes" [Skinner 1914:507]. Among the Bungi this dance "was held to heal the sick and to bring the buffalo in times of scarcity" [Skinner 1914:507].

When the *pizikiwûs* "is given to a patient it would make him vomit blood caused by internal bleeding, and then recover" [Skinner 1914:507].

Poawi

Ute, *basin*

To practice sorcery [Fowler and Fowler 1971:178].

Poboctü

Hopi, *Southwest*

Literal translation: "eye-seekers" [Stephen 1894:212]. Originally the *poboctü* were probably the same as the *powaka* (see entry), but "the eye-seekers are now wholly beneficent, and devoted to counteracting the evil of the malignant sorcerers. In some unaccountable way the society has been allowed to die out almost completely, for as near as I can ascertain there are only three surviving members" [Stephen 1894:212].

Pocwimi

Hopi, *Southwest*

See *poswimkya*.

Podulte

Kiowa, *Plains*

Literal translation: "Eagle Skin Bag" [Parsons 1929:116]. A nineteenth-century shaman who received his powers from the Snapping Turtle spirit. He trained other novice shamans and was known to have upward of ten assistants at a time. His medicine powers included invulnerability to arrows and the ability to materialize things. For example: "Podulte was doctoring a woman. He asked her what sort of root food would she like to have. He rolled up his sleeve, hit the ground, his arm penetrated and he brought up the root she had asked for. . . . Another time when Podulte was in his tipi he said, 'I am going hungry for canned goods, go and get some cans.' They brought in four empty cans. He put a black kerchief over the cans; he puffed smoke from a cigarette over the kerchief. He took away the kerchief. He told his wife to open the cans. She opened them. In the first were peaches, in the next two apples, in the next, cherries" [Kumole in Parsons 1929:116].

Pofkadjuli

Creek, *Southeast*

A powerful Creek mulatto shaman around the turn of the twentieth century. The following is an account of one of his power display (see entry) contests with an Osage shaman, which took place near Bird Creek, north of Tulsa, Oklahoma:

> In the morning they began. The Osage shaman did a trick. He danced and mumbled and performed a wonderful exploit. But when Pofkadjuli got up on the space where the contest was taking place, he did one just as good as the Osage's. Then the Osage did another. Pofkadjuli equaled him. The Osage did another, but Pofkadjuli equaled him again. And so it

continued. Now, the Osage kept performing better ones all the time, and the Creeks began to think that Pofkadjuli was going to lose after all. At last the Osage made medicine and performed a feat that could not be excelled. Then it was Pofkadjuli's turn. He went out to the plot in the center and began dancing all around the Osage, singing and enchanting, and all the time closing in on the Osage shaman. Suddenly, just as he was in front of the latter, he jerked up his blanket from behind and swung his back around toward the Osage. Immediately a swarm of bumblebees poured from beneath the blanket and crowded about the Osage's head, driving him headlong from the field [Speck 1907:133].

Pogok
North Alaska Eskimo, *Arctic Coast*
Tikerarmuit carved fetishes. These fetishes are carved from wood and are usually burned after being used in a ceremony. They represent "seals, polar bears, caribou, whales, walrus, birds, or mythical animals; others were human figures" [Rainey 1947:248]. The *pogok* is used in a fashion similar to their *qologogoloq* (see entry), but the latter are permanent sacred figures. When the *pogok* is burned, its spirit is released or "allowed to go to the sea" [Rainey 1947:252]. The *pogok* was hung in the ceremonial dance house, and those who desired good luck in hunting came early each morning to touch it [Rainey 1947:249]. To find twenty such figures in a ceremonial dance house would not be unusual.

Pohagadi
Kawaiisu, *Peninsula*
Witch or sorcerer. Little is known of the training of such individuals, for it is always conducted in the strictest secrecy. However, "one element in this training is to toughen the skin by walking nude through a stand of nettles" [Zigmond 1977:63]. In some cases dreams sent by a *pohagadi* might cause the victim to also become a *pohagadi*.

In harming people the *pohagadi* often use an unidentified poisonous powdered substance known as *puyumaaku*. "If placed anywhere on the skin, [it] will sting like the bite of a red ant—and cause death.... It makes dead worms come to life and can grow flesh on bare bones" [Zigmond 1977:83]. This powder is also used as a love potion. "If the substance is kept in the house, a couple cannot stay apart. They will spend their time making love" [Zigmond 1977:83].

Pohagam cuzita
Paviotso, *Basin*
Medicine bag [Fowler and Fowler 1971:234].

Pohaghani
Gosiute, *Basin*
Power spot [Malouf 1951:53]. The power spot is a particular location imbued with supernatural power to which a novice shaman (*pohaghant*) goes to seek power. It is usually either a cave or rock outcroppings associated with pictographs. Ritual preparations for the quest include bathing and painting the body white.

Poigunt
Gosiute, *Basin*
Shaman. Shamans are named according to their powers. For example, a shaman with bulletproof medicine is called *navagunt poigunt,* while a shaman who has acquired arrowproof medicine is called *upahai poigunt* [Powell in Fowler and Fowler 1971:253].

Poje
Tewa, *Southwest*
Meeting of Waters Ceremony at Santa Clara Pueblo. This four-day ceremony is a purification rite that is occasionally held just prior to a "large treatment" (see *Wanke*). The final night is conducted in a *kiva* (EONAH, p. 136). At the foot of the *kiva* ladder, members step into a hoop that is raised and lowered several times. During the ceremony all of the participants have crosses drawn in black earth (obtained from the bottom of a swamp) on the backs and palms of their

hands, on the tops and soles of their feet, and on their shoulders by Bear society members.

Pokidjida obánga

Creek, *Southeast*

Taskigi Ball-Game Dance. This medicine dance was performed to secure supernatural aid for the players in a ball game [Speck 1907:136].

Poku

Tewa, *Southwest*

Water Immersion Ceremony [Hill 1982:213]. This is the name of the initiation ceremony for boys and girls of the Santa Clara Pueblo Summer and Winter societies (see *kwere* and *xa zhe*). The moiety initiation ceremony encompasses twelve days, with the actual rite itself lasting ten days. Initiations into the Summer society are conducted in September or October, while those for the Winter society are held in November or December. Initiations are held every five to seven years.

Both initiation rituals follow the same general pattern, although variations do exist. For example, each novice in the Summer society has two sponsors to assist him, while those in the Winter society have only one. The first four days of the ritual involve the purification of the participants and initiates, the preparation and deposit of prayer plumes, and the making of articles for the altar displays used in the ritual. For the Winter society initiation the candidates also plant sacred corn, the sprouts of which are used on the final night.

During the initiation ritual, which is conducted in a *kiva* (EONAH, p. 136), each sponsor takes water from the sacred water bowl and asperses the water into the mouth of the pledge. "Following the aspersing, a scratching stick was tied with a string around the neck of the initiates, and feathers from a yellow warbler and a roadrunner were placed in their hair. Finally a prayer was said, and a new name was bestowed on the initiate. . . . It was believed that a person who failed to use the scratching stick would suf-

fer a cut or broken finger. Scratching sticks were used only by the Summer Moiety, not by the Winter" [Hill 1982:215].

The initiation also includes, among other activities, crop fertility dances, kachina dances, sacred songs, ritual whipping (four blows) of the boys by a kachina, periods of instruction for the initiates, ethical discourses, food taboos, and, in the case of the Summer Society, a river immersion for the initiates. Gift giving and feasting come near the end of the ceremony. Following the ritual whipping the kachina "told the novice to stand erect [he is leaning forward], and the kachina leader reenacted the pantomime [ritual] of deriving and bestowing power, 'wisdom,' this time with the initiate" [Hill 1982:219]. This is a shamanic empowerment procedure that enables the initiates to handle power, and it is a common element in most Native American power initiation rituals.

Most initiates are either infants or young boys and girls. However, membership to a society is also gained via cures. When a person is ill, someone will petition either the Winter or Summer society *cacique* (head of the society) on behalf of the patient for a healing by the society. Part of the cure usually involves the patient becoming a member of the society once the cure has been effected.

Pokwia

Yavapai, *Southwest*

"Black stone, supernatural power, medicine power, also term applied to shamans" [Gifford 1936:307]. However, shamans are often designated according to type. For instance, among the northeastern Yavapai a curing shaman is called *basemacha* (see entry), an arrow-wound shaman is *bahasumacha*, a Rattlesnake shaman is *ilui sumacha*, a Bear shaman is *mawhata sumacha*, a Deer shaman is *akwaka sware*, a singing shaman is *kitiye sware*, and a weather shaman is *ikwivchisiwe* [Gifford 1936:310].

Among the western Yavapai the *kisiye* is called for curing afflictions caused by dreaming of a ghost. He treats the patient by singing. The Rattlesnake shaman is called *iluikisima* (*ilui,* snake; *iluihana,* rattlesnake) [Gifford 1936:316]. His treatment for snakebites is also done by singing; he does not suck on the wound. For diagnosing an illness the *miye kisima,* ghost specialist, is called "to learn from ghost if person with serious illness would recover" [Gifford 1936:316]. During this performance the shaman remains within the ceremony house and posts a "fearless man with big heart" outside to question the ghost when it approaches. "Shaman summoned ghost by singing. Frightened audience heard its approach. Questioner made inquiries, ghost replied. Ghost not of definite person. If wrong kind of ghost came (i.e., Walapai or Mohave, or one making sound like roadrunner, etc.), person sitting in house threw dust out into darkness and ghost left" [Gifford 1936:316].

Pónlhĭkî

Seminole, *Southeast*

Sometimes translated as "poisoning" [Sturtevant 1954b:383]. Mikasuki term for witchcraft (see entry). Most suspect are shamans who are known to have healing powers because such persons are also capable of knowing how to harm people with their powers. Therefore, a shaman who loses a patient is bound to come under suspicion of witchcraft. This is most often an older man or woman. Also suspect are shamans who attended a Mikasuki shaman's training school (see *ayikcmífosî*) for a long period of time.

In the case of murder, the witch or sorcerer is sometimes punished. "But because a sorcerer usually knows magical techniques for protecting himself from injury, it was necessary more often than with ordinary murders to execute another member of the same sib, rather than the murderer himself (although, traditionally, a closely rather than distantly related sib member was preferred). It is said that if the victim belonged to the same sib as the sorcerer, the latter went unpunished, presumably because the sib was reluctant to lose still another member" [Sturtevant 1954b:386–387].

The most frequent form of witchcraft involves the poisoning of food or drink, such as liquor, which is accomplished by the shaman singing special songs over it. "In addition to the songs which contaminate the material, the practitioner must sing (after administering the liquor to his victim?) a song to keep the poison from 'turning back on' himself and killing him instead of the victim. . . . Some people know how to make the poison leave liquor, by singing a certain song and knocking the bottom of the bottle with the palm of the hand" [Sturtevant 1954b:390]. However, the widespread technique of a witch "shooting" an object into the victim has not been reported in more recent times among the Mikasuki [Sturtevant 1954b:398].

A less frequent form of witchcraft is the capture of a person's soul or spirit. "To perform this it is only necessary that the sorcerer know his or her victim's name; distance is not a factor, as this conjuring is effective at any distance" [Sturtevant 1954b:393]. In order to effect this spell, the witch "gets four splinters of wood six or eight inches long from a lightning-struck tree, and makes a doll-like model of the right sex to represent his victim. He builds a fire and stays awake until midnight, when by using the proper songs and his victim's name he calls to him his soul. . . . He then sticks the four splinters into the doll's belly and puts it into the fire, thereby burning the soul. The victim awakes in the morning with a fever and thirst, and unless cured will die in the number of days set by the sorcerer" [Sturtevant 1954b:394].

Poor Wolf

Gros Ventre, *Plains*

Poor Wolf was born in 1840 near the mouth of the Knife River. At the age of seventeen, he recovered from smallpox when a bear came into his lodge and doctored him. At nineteen or twenty years of age, he undertook a twenty-day fast. In subsequent years he was ritually tattooed to increase his power. He reported: "I was tattooed on my arms and neck and other places on my body. This was done with great ceremony. Song was used in the performance. . . . It was thought that the tattooing would give courage and afford protection; one would not be struck by bullets. . . . I have an eagle claw tattooed on my right hand. My uncle put it on so that I could grab a Sioux [in warfare]" [Poor Wolf in Hall 1906:441–442].

Eventually Poor Wolf acquired and used seven different medicines: a dried turtle shell, a muskrat skin, a mink skin, red muscles, a crane's head, an otter skin, and herbs. He became a skilled eagle catcher (see Wilson 1928 for details of this art). He also demonstrated an immunity to bullets and became a war shaman/leader. However in May 1893 he was baptized into Christianity and abandoned his shamanic ceremonies [Hall 1906:442].

Pope
Quinault, *Northwest Coast*

A powerful shaman around the turn of the twentieth century who acquired many different helping spirits during his life. One of his spirits, known as *Sligwilamicelos,* meaning "among the humans" [Olson 1936:147], was used for finding the lost soul of a young person. However this spirit could only travel in the world of humans and could not access the land of the dead. He had two other spirits called *djilotsoomic,* meaning "along the beach" [Olson 1936:148], that were used to find lost souls that had taken the beach trail, called the "upper trail," to the land of the dead.

His best hunting medicine came from the Thunderbird or Thunder spirit. "For years he bathed in the ocean and in the lakes and creeks, trying to get this power. Finally it came to him in a form like a huge eagle, yet like a man, dressed in bearskin, and taught him how to hunt. The spirit had a huge knife which he told Pope to use in case he wanted to kill someone. Pope was told to carve an elbow pipe out of a hard clay with an eel in the angle. (In some way the eel was regarded as the spirit also.) This pipe could travel

about, for somehow it partook of the nature of a spirit. The power of this spirit was such that many times Pope was able to kill elk without shooting them!" [Olson 1936:148].

Pope
Tewa, *Southwest*

A seventeenth-century Taos shaman who led the Pueblo Revolt of 1680, assisted by the Picuris and Achos Apaches [Tiller 1983:447]. Three spirits appeared to Pope in a *kiva,* emitting "fire from all the extremities of their bodies" [Naranjo in Nabokov 1978:66]. These spirits instructed Pope to send a knotted cord among the various pueblos indicating the number of days until an attack was to be launched.

The revolt was launched on August 10, 1680, three days earlier than planned due to leaks of the revolt. In the attack 400 Spanish colonists were killed, including 21 priests [Hewitt in Hodge 1910:281]. Pope's vision was to return to the old ways by destroying everything associated with the Spanish. He died around 1690.

Porcupine
Cheyenne, *Plains*

A renowned shaman, born around 1848, who became more influential "than the official medicine chief, the Keeper of the Sacred Tepee" [Marquis 1978:124]. His father was Sioux and his mother Cheyenne. He grew up among the Sioux but married a Cheyenne woman and then permanently joined the Cheyenne.

"When he spoke, all other listened, for his mind was stored to fullness with wisdom appertaining to old time Indian social relations and spiritual lore" [Marquis 1978:124]. In addition to possessing sacred knowledge, he was also a chief and spokesman for his people. He was spokesman in four treaty counsels and even met President Harrison on a trip to Washington, D.C.

In November 1889 Porcupine made his way to the Paiutes in Nevada, where he spent the winter learning the Ghost Dance from its founder, Wovoka (EONAH, pp. 319–320). Of

Edward S. Curtis, Porcupine—Cheyenne, *1910. Photogravure.*

this experience he reported: "I and my people have been living in ignorance until I went and found out the truth [from Wovoka]. All the whites and Indians are brothers, I was told there. I never knew this before" [Porcupine in Mooney 1896:794]. In the spring he returned to the Tongue River Reservation. There he began to teach the Cheyenne this ritual, the basic function of which was to call upon the spirits to eradicate whites on their land.

During the last forty years of his life, he lived in a log hut in the upper Rosebud Valley. He died in 1929.

Poswimkya

Hopi, *Southwest*

Also: *Pocwimi* [Titiev 1972:69]. One of two Hopi curing societies. By the 1890s this society of sucking shamans was inactive, although the group's fetishes were still kept at Walpi. By 1906 the last member of the society was dead. Of the last members Dotuka (Kokop) was said to be "the oldest and smartest" [Titiev 1972:69]. The Badger was the tutelary spirit of this society, but its members also used Bear medicines and prayers. Other tutelary spirits included Porcupine, Horned Toad, and the star Aldebaran.

This was "the only society specializing in the sucking cure, and . . . only members of this society could use datura [Jimson weed] to induce trances or as a medicine" [Levy 1994:315].

The other Hopi curing society is the *Yayatü society* (see entry).

Shamans who heal but do not belong to a medicine society are called *tuuhikya* (EONAH, p. 296).

Pota

Hopi, *Southwest*

A ceremonial object used in the Powamû society initiation ceremony, consisting "of round discs, each of which is made of two sticks bent into a semicircle and over which is stretched a piece of *owa*, a native material resembling canvas. These discs are sewn together in the middle

in such a manner that they can be opened and closed like a book, the segments or semicircles forming the leaves" [Voth 1901:89]. Different drawings are painted on each of these semicircles. Also, a strip of rabbit skin is attached to each disc along the circular edge of the semicircle. The straight edge of the disc is about a foot in length.

At one point during the *Powamû* initiation ceremony, a *Chowilawu kachina* (or *katcina*) "dances around the mosaic [sand painting on floor] in a sinistral circuit four times, constantly waving the *pota* in such a manner that the different segments or leaves would open and close at different places" [Voth 1901:92].

In the Hopi villages on the second mesa, this term is also used for woven basket trays or plaques [Voth 1901:89, n.*].

Powa

Hopi, *Southwest*

Dialectical variants: *poha* (Shoshone), *puha* (Paiute/Comanche—see EONAH, p. 223). Supernatural power [Levy 1994:320]. From this term comes *powata*, meaning to cure, to make whole or perfect; *powaka*, meaning to use the power for sorcery; *powalawu*, meaning ritual; and *powatawi*, meaning song [Levy 1994:320–321].

Powa is neither good nor evil. It is the shaman's use thereof that determines this factor. Among the Hopi the healing and purifying aspects of *powa* are controlled by the priests of their societies via annual ceremonies. The use of *powa* "for good purposes, however, is completely in the hands of the priests and is denied to the shamans. . . . The individual Hopi shaman was called a *tuuhikya* [EONAH, p. 296 and entry *tuuhisa*] and did not control *powa* for healing purposes" [Levy 1994:321–322].

Powaka

Hopi, *Southwest*

Witch or sorcerer. A male witch is called *powak taka*, "witch man," and a female witch is called *powak wuqti*, "witch woman" [Stephen 1936:276].

A Tlingit raven rattle. A shaman lies on the back of the rattle, his tongue extended to the mouth of the raven.

Powamû

Hopi, *Southwest*

An exorcism ceremony [Stephen 1936:1283]. This particular ceremony is performed by the *Powamwïmkya* (Powamû society) [Stephen 1936:539]. Members of this society are versed in purification rituals, called *powatañwû* or *navochiwa* [Stephen 1936:494].

Power displays/feats

A display of supernatural feats by a shaman using one or more of his medicine powers. This area of anthropological inquiry has received very little attention. The primary reason for this is that, historically, most anthropologists have chosen to believe that shamans have no inherent supernatural abilities. In addition there have been few opportunities to witness such performances in the field. Nevertheless, they have been well documented since the seventeenth century. In fact, there is reason to believe that in former times, Native American supernatural abilities were far greater. There appears to be a direct correlation between strength in one's personal belief in spirits and the manifestation of medicine powers. For this reason those who have a shadow of a doubt in their minds are quite often asked to leave a shamanic ceremony before it begins. Fur-

thermore, it stands to reason that as these people were converted to Christianity, their belief in the spirits would be undermined, and this condition, in turn, would weaken the ability of any shaman in any culture to display his medicine powers.

This trend is also documented in the ethnographic data. For example, the Shaking Tent Ceremony (EONAH, pp. 246–249) among the Cree and Ojibwa was well noted by the end of the seventeenth century. Not only were there more shamans around who could perform this ceremony but their associated power displays were also far more powerful than those we read about from the last half of the nineteenth century and later. During the 1820s George Nelson, a fur-trade clerk for the Hudson's Bay Company, observed several Shaking Tent Ceremonies. He wrote that the shaman was "bound hand and foot" and "barricaded and cross-corded" with rope until he was bound "as a Criminal" and "crumpled into a heap" [Nelson in Brown and Brightman 1988:39]. Furthermore, some shamans were so powerful that they required a double ceremonial lodge, "that is two rows of Setts of Poles one on the outside (of) the other; and each row fastened with good strong hoops well tied, after which the outer and inner row are fastened—thus arranged, they seem to be beyond the Power of any 3 or 4 men to move, yet when the Spirits enter it sets a-going with a motion equal to that of a single pole indifferently stuck in the Ground and violently moved by a man" [Nelson in Brown and Brightman 1988:43]. (Note: After one ceremony Nelson shook a lodge pole with both hands and all his strength, "but the motion was nothing like that of the Conjurors" [Nelson in Brown and Brightman 1988:44].) In some cases of the spirits subsequently unbinding the shaman during the ceremony (which always occurs), "all of a Sudden, either from the top or below, away flies the cords by which the indian [sic] was tied *into the lap of he who tied him* [Nelson in Brown and Brightman 1988:39]. Finally, "some of them to shew their Power have had small sticks of the hardest wood . . . about the size of a man's finger, made as sharp pointed as possible, and dried, when they become in consequence nearly as dangerous as iron or bayonets. Some have 18, 24, more or less, tho' seldom less than 18, planted in the bottom of their hut [the Shaking Tent lodge]—they are about 12–14 ins. out of the Ground. On the Points of these Sticks is the conjuror placed [naked except for 'his Cloute'], sometimes on his bottom, at others on his knees and elbows . . . and when he comes off no marks of injury appear" [Nelson in Brown and Brightman 1988:44].

In 1708 le Sieur de Dièreville reported observing shamanic feats among the Micmacs as follows:

They chew a piece of flintstone in their mouths, and grind it up like Gravel; they spit it out into their hands, to show it to you, and afterwards they swallow it to the last grain. . . . When the flintstone, ground to gravel, is in their stomachs, they take a little stick about a foot long and very smooth; they smoke, and offer it the fumes of the Tobacco, mumbling some words from the Black Book; then they thrust it down their throats, their faces become completely livid and it seems as though they were about to choke; they rummage, so to speak, with the stick, and, after a few grimaces, they draw it out with the flintstone whole at the end of it. . . . The skin of an Otter

which had been flayed, perhaps six months before is made to walk, and this is how they go about it. After spreading it on its belly, they bring the head toward the hinder part by means of folds, made in such a way that it appears to be all in one piece.

A little tin mirror is placed on the right of the head, at a distance of four or five feet. . . . It is only with great difficulty that it [the otterskin] moves at first, but, little by little, it stretches out and drags itself as far as the Mirror where it stops [Dièreville 1933:183–184].

In Native America shamanic success is based on one's ability to handle medicine powers. For that reason in many Native American cultures shamans gathered together to give public demonstrations of their personal powers. These special medicine power performances, for which there is no term in anthropology, would serve to rank the shamans within their particular geographical areas. As such, they were a form of public competition between existing shamans, with each one trying to outdo his opponents, and they represent some of the most spectacular feats ever recorded. In the older literature these events were often referred to as public exhibitions of "feats of legerdemain." By the 1920s few remained.

One of the most well-known occurrences of power feats is associated with performances of the widespread Medicine Lodge (Medicine Dance, Grand Medicine, and so forth) society, all originally derived from the Ojibwa *Midewiwin* (EONAH, p. 174). Best known is their "shooting" of the candidates with small shells (for example, see *wakan a tcipi*), but the event was also an occasion for older shamans to demonstrate their powers. For example, among the Canadian Santee, it was reported, "Joseph Goodwill told of a magical performance by a Medicine Dance member. Pointing to the stone in the center of the lodge, he boasted that he would magically shoot a bear claw through it. He charged toward the stone as if it were the candidate in the shooting rite, extended his medicine bag, and stamped his foot. Spectators saw a spurt of dust from behind the stone and retrieved the bear claw. Then they examined the stone and found a small opening from which blood was slowly oozing" [Howard 1984:136–137].

The following is an account of power performances among the Pawnee:

> At those entertainments, usually given in the open air, they [shamans] appeared entirely divested of garments except the indispensable breech-cloth, and with no elaborate paraphernalia, thus reducing the possibility of delusion to a minimum. They swallowed arrows head downward till the point had apparently reached the region of the stomach, and in this condition, with the feather end protruding from the mouth, turned somersaults and executed various acrobatic movements involving violent contortions of the body. Instead of arrows, long-bladed knives or pieces of nicely dressed board about two feet long and two inches wide were used at the pleasure of the performer. Sometimes they appeared to drive these objects, particularly the boards, down the throat by beating heavily upon the exposed end with one hand, blood meanwhile flowing copiously from the mouth. . . . There were also more difficult feats, as apparently cutting their own throats; shooting each other with arrows, the arrow still sticking from the body of the apparently dead performer; and taking out and replacing the vitals of such seemingly dead persons. The following will answer as an example of their bolder feats:
>
> Two performers, during a pause in one of the exhibitions, led from a neighboring lodge a small boy stripped naked. After laying him upon his back on the ground, one of them held the boy's hands extended above his head; the other seated himself astride the child's body, seemed to cut into his chest, to insert two fingers and draw out one lobe of the liver, from which a part was cut and eaten by the two men. The mutilated liver was then crowded back, the opening closed, and the boy borne away. Soon after he was about again as usual [Dunbar 1882:748].

The Omaha are also known to have conducted power tests between shamans. "One form of test consisted in trying to jump or fly over one another; the one who succeeded in so doing was regarded not only as possessing greater magic but as controlling the one defeated" [Fletcher and La Flesche 1911:583].

The foothill Maidu shamans of central California perform public power displays.

> They gather in the dance house from long distances. Each doctor, having previously fasted and prepared, dances for himself. The clown is the leader of the dance. Any touching of a competitor, either with the body or with a held object, is debarred. Power is exerted by a supernatural shooting or transmission. The hands are held against the breast and then thrown forcibly forward as if warding off or sending out mysterious influences. After a time the weaker contestants begin to be taken with seizures and pains, some bleeding from the nose, some rolling on the floor. Others follow, and such as have recovered from the first shock busy themselves sucking out the cause of the later victim's succumbing. As the number of competitors decreases and the survivors are those of the intensest power, the excitement and the imaginative faculties of the audience as well as the participants increase. Flames and light are seen about the few who are still contending, and they, to demonstrate their strength, cause lizards or mice to appear and disappear. Finally the contest narrows to a pair, and when one of these yields the lone survivor is victor of the occasion. It is said that women have been known to win, although as a rule their milder powers cause them to be among the first to be taken ill [Kroeber 1925:424].

Among the Monachi (Western Mono), also from central California, "there were performances by shamans (puhake) in which their abilities were displayed. . . . At the dance place at Soyakanim a shaman caused a coyote to come down from the sky during a dance. He also caused it to disappear again into the sky" [Gifford 1932:50].

Another central California culture, the Wintu (Northern Wintun), also had shamans' contests.

One informant had watched his aunt perform against another shaman: "I saw her doctor against another woman. They put five pitch knots about as far off as that tree (ca. fifteen feet), and lighted them. Then by clapping her hands she put them out. It was the kind of spirit she had. It made her strong to do things like that. I heard it was a thunder or lightning spirit that gave her this power" [Nels Charles in Du Bois 1935:103].

In another Wintun example a Patwin (Southern Wintun) shaman "leaned a stick against the center post of the house, then made it move, and finally travel in a circle. The other [shaman] made a stone leap from the floor. Then, as he sang, he made his standing opponent jump. When the other sang, he made all the seated spectators jump off the floor. Some of the people became scared and left the house" [Kroeber 1932:360, n. 211].

A power contest between the Las Vegas (Southern Paiute) and the Cahuilla has been recorded. In this case the Las Vegas journeyed to the Cahuilla country. When they arrived,

> they were the last to come and everyone was waiting. After sundown a fire was built and each doctor showed his powers. Some competed in smoking, making pipe, smoke, and all come out of their toes. Others brought black "stink bugs" out of their ears and toes. Certain mountain-sheep doctors took pieces of sheep fat or meat from their clothing and threw them on the coals; the pieces looked like fresh kill.
>
> They could not decide who was the winner; the Paiute could equal the tricks of all the others. They sang all night, in turn. Toward morning the [Las Vegas] boy who had burned himself said, "Make a hot fire; use mesquite wood." At daylight the fire turned to red coals. The Paiute boy came close and threw himself in the center. Everyone was surprised. The Cahuilla said, "What are we doing? We have lost a man!" Then at sunrise, when there were only ashes left, they saw the doctor who had been burned walk toward them, smiling [Kelly 1939:164].

The Las Vegas won the contest.

Shamans of the Northwest Coast area often perform power feats. For example, shamans in the area of the Copper River Delta (Ahtena?) were visited in the early 1880s, and it was reported that "the shaman goes on making all kinds of tricks to astonish his audience. One of his most enjoyable bravado pieces consists of asking two pairs of men to stand opposite each other across the fire and hold heavy tow cords down close to the fire. The shaman lies or hangs on these and the men swing him to and fro. Often the cords catch on fire, and then the men let him out. Another trick is that the shaman eats a long bone in the sight of the public, and to their astonishment pulls it out of his throat again in one piece. The magician also takes a red-hot knife in his hands and licks the blade without any sign of pain. Some shamans also practice ventriloquism. In the middle of a song there is often a pause and the shaman bends over towards the ground and seems to answer an evil spirit that lives deep below the surface" [Jacobsen 1977:209]. It should be noted that Jacobsen had no faith in shamans, and he did not see any of these performances. This information came from native informants.

The Halkomelem (Cowichan) along the Fraser River in Puget Sound also conducted shamanic contests. Examples from the Kwantlen tribe follow:

> A certain shaman invited several others of his class to his house, and then called upon them to show their thaumaturgical powers. The first to respond to the invitation began in the usual way with his dance and seuwe´n [dance songs]. After a while he showed them a peculiar stone and bade them note it. He then cast it into the fire, and a moment afterwards it was heard to fall upon the roof. Another then began his dance and seuwe´n. Presently he showed them two stuffed mice. These he cast into the fire, and two live mice were seen to come out of a hole in the ground close by. A third then exhibited his "medicine." This man commenced his dance with a large feather in his hand. After he had been dancing a while he threw

the feather into the fire, and a moment later it came up from a hole in the ground and stood up and danced. The last to perform was an old man. He begged someone to do his dancing for him; but no one complying, he cast into the fire some native fish-hooks he had in his hand, whereupon they flew hither and thither and fixed themselves in the lips and mouths of the bystanders, from which they could not remove them till he himself did so. . . .

The following account of some shamanistic feats was given me by an old settler who has lived among the Kwa´ntlen people for a great many years and has an Indian wife. He relates that at a shamanistic performance at which he was present he saw a shaman take a feather and stick it apparently into a piece of rock. The stone then began to roll about, but the feather remained in it. Another wore in his cap a number of dried birds' heads. He took these out of the hat and threw them into the air, whereupon each became a living bird and flew about the shaman. Another took a bucketful of water and danced round it for a while. Presently a little fir-tree was seen to grow out of it, each branch of which was tipped with feathers. Another, to show his powers, sat with his feet and lower limbs in an oven. Presently water began to run out of the oven and put the fire out; but when he withdrew his legs and feet the water disappeared and the fire came again [Hill-Tout 1903:413–414].

Shamanic contests have also been reported for the Lummi of northwest Washington.

To test their power over spirits, medicine men engage in tournaments. In the course of their travels, two medicine men may meet in some remote place and challenge each other to a test of strength. They may measure their skill in drawing sickness out of the body of a patient with their cupped hands, by trying to pull a knot out of a green piece of wood, or from a tree. They sing their spirit songs and placing their hands upon the projecting knot they seek to extract it from the wood without using physical methods, relying entirely upon their spirit power. If one medicine man is successful in extracting the knot, his opponent endeavors to pull another knot. In these contests, medicine men take stones in their cupped hands and while singing their spirit songs cause the stones to become invisible and to skim over the water. On one occasion one of the medicine men instead of causing a stone to disappear as his opponent had done picked up a snake by the head and with one stroke stripped off all the flesh, leaving the backbone and ribs bare, but the head intact. After doing this, he held the skeleton of the snake in his hand and said to his opponent, "It is easy enough to cause things to disappear, but now watch this." He then caused the skeleton to swim up the stream as if it were alive [Stern 1934:78].

For the Thompson of the Plateau area, it has been reported that "often contests occurred among shamans, where the one having the most cunning or powerful spirit conquered the others, resulting in their death, or in leaving the marks of his victory in the shape of distorted faces or crippled bodies" [Teit 1900:363].

North of the Plateau area in the Mackenzie-Yukon region, the Slave, Dogrib, and Beaver all had shamanic power performances. "It is related that the best of them would hold a file in his hands until it melted and then return it to its original condition. Others would swallow a red-hot iron and spit flames and smoke and then re-move the iron unhurt. Many of the rivals were killed in endeavoring to imitate them" [Mason 1946:40].

Any shaman who felt his power was not being recognized by the community at large could per-form a power feat. The following is an example from an Ingalik shaman from the Arctic Coast region:

The local shaman who had lost some respect, so he felt, showed the men in the kashim [house] a sample of his own power. Taking his tambourine drum by the handle, he swept it through the air in front of him four times. When he had finished there was a noise as though someone had thrown a little stick at the drum. He stepped up on the cover boards of the fire hole and held the drum up against the light of the smoke hole asking those who wished, to look. In the center of the drum cover there appeared a tiny thing about the size of a red currant. Then the shaman put the drum over his hand and the "spirit," for such it was, disappeared in his palm. Then he threw the "spirit" up in the air, showing everyone that his hand was empty. Then he reached out and caught it again. He held out his hand and the "spirit" was in it. He blew on it once. It could be seen moving—a little man no bigger than a berry. Then he let it go, for it was the spirit of a living person" [Osgood 1958:58].

Among the Canadian Dakota it was reported that "old man Pashee once heard a medicine-man tell some people he could swallow a knife. They said they did not believe it. He thrust a large one, about the size of a butcher's knife, blade first, down his throat. The people stood around watching, and a little later they saw him pull it out of his anus" [Wallis 1947:81]. Further to the south the Crow shamans perform power displays during their Bear Song Dance. "In the Bear Song dance all those individuals who had in their bodies such animals as bears, eagles, horses, and the like, would come together and display the supernatural presence within them, which was made to protrude part of its body from the performer's mouth. This ceremony resembled the dream cult performances of the Dakota inasmuch as all who had had a similar religious experience joined in a demonstration of their mystic relationships" [Lowie 1913b:150].

Cushing noted that the Zuni also annually perform power displays. The members of the Cactus society "and their brother orders give public exhibitions of their various powers—sometimes, as is the case with the slat swallowers (or "Bearers of the Wand") [for an example see *Onayanakia*], producing injuries for life, or even suffering death; but, nevertheless unflinchingly, year after year, performing their excruciating rites" [Cushing in Green 1979:104]. Throughout this Pueblo region many of the medicine societies incorporate power feats in their ceremonies. Some of these feats include "making corn or wheat plants grow under

your eyes, drawing grain from wall pictures or from corn-ear fetishes, getting spruce from a distant mountain within a few minutes, producing a live animal (rabbit or deer), making feathers or other objects levitate, tarnishing silver, or shriveling leather. Sia shamans, reports a townsman, 'can make a bowl dance on the floor, with nobody near it. They can call clouds and make it rain in their room. If they ask Boshaianyi for corn, it will fall from the ceiling. They can call in different kinds of animals, and their fur will fall from the ceiling'" [Parsons 1939:440].

Power feats were also well known among the cultures of the Southeast.

> Upon one occasion a [Creek] doctor showed his power by throwing his handkerchief at a tree up which it ran like a squirrel. His opponent then produced a number of centipedes which ran about everywhere but hurt no one. The first then began to try to reach his antagonist in the shapes of various animals, sometimes burrowing under the earth to get at him. Finally, however, the other created a centipede which bit him in the hand and killed him. . . .
>
> Shawnee doctors were in particular esteem among the Creeks, an esteem shared by all other peoples in contact with them. Even the Texas Alabama know the reputed powers of Shawnee doctors well and told me the following story regarding the accomplishments of one of them.
>
> Some Alabama were once traveling along with this doctor. One night they heard what sounded like the whinnying of horses. The Shawnee told them, however, that it was produced by some Comanches Indians, and when day came they discovered four of these Indians in a tree. By his medicine he caused these persons to fall asleep and then tumble to the ground without waking up. In a river bend near by was a great crowd of Comanche, but the Shawnee rendered himself and his companions invisible, so that the Comanche did not see them, and they passed safely on [Swanton 1928:626–627].

A rather humorous form of power display was reported for the Mikasuki Seminole. The informant said that he "once saw a relative of his whom he believes to possess curing and witchcraft powers, chew up a beer bottle after challenging the white man who had given him the beer, 'I bet you can't do whatever I do'" [Sturtevant 1954b:406].

In addition to these special group or individual performances, shamans also often include such power feats at the onset of their rituals. These feats are used to gain the confidence of the participating audience with regard to the shaman's power and his or her ability to effect a successful cure. Many people do not understand that a single doubter in the audience can indeed cause a ceremony to fail. Therefore the shaman's power feats work to rid the audience of any doubters.

While some anthropologists suggest that the shaman is using a hypnotic technique to influence the audience (e.g., Kroeber 1925:194–195), it is more likely that a trance-induction technique is being used, both for the shaman and for advanced members of the audience. As is well known, suggestibility with regard to a cure is directly linked to the eventual success of the cure, and this fact is appreciated by shamans, who use it to the patient's advantage.

For other examples see *angalkuk, angaxkox, bear medicine/possession, Bear's Belly, Beautiful Feathers, Big Bill, Blue Bird, chayan, fire-handling medicine, Hadihiduus, Horse Society Dance, huuku, Ilatsiak, Ìsáné, Kichil woknam, kiuks, kusiut, Kwalxqo, lilik, Matcogahri, meta, nasosotau, Neptune, John, Onayanakia, ozunya cinnupa, Pofkadjuli, qwazq, Running Wolf, shinka, Shunáwanùh, tamanowash sticks, Tatatex Waci, Tawaru Kutchu, Tcéthinjiwagre Wasi, Tcuiiopi, Tenektaide, tsanati, Tsikomó, Turiyo, Wàbik, wagiksuyabi, Wäkatishkwä, Witaltal, Yanpavinuk, Yayatü society.*

Powha
Gosiute, *Basin*

Spirit or ghost [Powell in Fowler and Fowler 1971:254].

Prayer
See *offerings.*

Prayer feathers/sticks
Pueblo, *Southwest*

Prayer offerings. The use of feathers alone and feathers attached to sticks as sacred offerings is found in all religious ceremonies throughout the Southwest region except at Taos, where there are no prayer sticks [Parsons 1939:270, n.*], and in some ceremonies among the Tiwa and Tewa [Parsons 1939:270]. Prayer sticks may also be made for individual use. They may be made for someone about to undertake an important journey or for someone who has just died, or they may be planted in one's field to bring rain. Most often, however, they are displayed on an altar during a ceremony. Sometimes they are bound together in bundles for ceremonial use. In all cases they are constructed according to sacred prescriptions before being used in rituals. When not used in ceremony, they are "buried in field or riverbank or riverbed; cast under shrub or tree or into pits; sunk in water, in springs, pools, lakes, river, or irrigation ditch; carried long distances to mountaintops; immured in house or kiva wall or closed-up niche; set under the floor or in the rafters, in cave or boulder or rock-built shrine [or] held in hand during ceremonial or cherished at home for a stated period or for life" [Parsons 1939:270].

The terms used for such offerings differ from pueblo to pueblo. They include: "Zuni, *telikyanane*; Hopi, *paho* [see entry]; Keresan, *hadjamuni* [see entry], *hächamoni* [see EONAH, p. 97], *hachaminyi*; Tewa (First Mesa), *odupeh*; Northern Tewa, *peh* [see entry]; Isleta, *to'ai* or *shii'*; Jemez, *wotaki*" [Parsons 1939: 270, n.*]. Among the Navajo they are known as *kethawn* (see entry).

See also *nakwakwosi, offerings, lashowane, Tong Kegi.*

Pretty Louse
Crow, *Plains*

A female shaman during the latter part of the nineteenth century. Pretty Louse was not only a healer but also, at that time, the group's official "weather-prophet" [Marquis 1928:188]. Thomas Leforge, a white man who lived among the Crow, reported that she had cured him of an ear-ache and deafness by making an herbal tea and pouring it into his ears.

Pretty Louse was a trance clairvoyant and much sought out by her people. "She received high fees and always had a herd of about a hundred horses. Often it would occur that some one would give her a complete buffalo-skin lodge, so she owned extra lodges. These she would trade off for horses. She was liberal, and she gave away lots of presents to needy Indians. The white people called her 'the princess'" [Marquis 1928:188].

Priests

Within the context of Native American sacred ceremonies, the use of the term *priest* often leads to confusion. The "priesthoods" of Native America are very different from those of Western Christianity. In most cases Native American "priests" are actually shamans. That is, it is most often the shamans who lead complex religious societies and ceremonies. However, among the more sedentary cultures—especially those in central California, along the Northwest Coast, in the Southwest, among the Algonquian in the Northeast, and among the Mound Builders of the Southeast—ceremonial structures evolved into elaborate and complex medicine societies. Within these societies there are different offices, some held by shamans and others held by those less adapt at handling supernatural power. Nevertheless, the anthropologist often assigns the term *priest* to such offices.

Quite often the assumption of an office in a medicine society is dependent on a person's demonstrated abilities at handling the uses of power for which that particular medicine society is organized. This may or may not involve the use of a guardian spirit. Thus the religious organization of Native America is much more concerned with utilizing the demonstrated powers of shamans than with merely filling offices. Conse-

quently, assigning the term *priest* to each of the offices in any medicine society may result in a failure to distinguish between those who are shamans and those who are not. Furthermore, these societies keep their affairs quite secret, so we have very little knowledge of how their shamans are trained or about the qualifications needed to assume their different offices.

The root of this problem lies in the way in which early anthropologists first approached the study of Native American spirituality, beginning in the nineteenth century. These anthropologists were looking for Native Americans' "religion," when in fact their religions were, and still are, more a matter of a way of life. That is, their "religion" centered around the use of supernatural powers, and the ability to handle these powers was very dependent on the way they lived their lives. This was a very foreign concept to early anthropologists, who really had no idea of how to deal with "medicine powers." Furthermore, those anthropologists were highly influenced by the science of the times, which was then in the throes of Darwinism. Therefore the tendency was to see cultures throughout the world in terms of various evolutionary stages, going from very simple cultures to highly complex ones. In this context "priests" were seen as an evolutionary stage above the shaman. In other words it was considered the natural destiny of the shaman to be replaced by the priest over time in any culture.

As an example of this, consider anthropologist Edwin Loeb's analysis of the Kuksu Cult (EONAH, p. 140) in California: "North Central California has for its typical religion the Kuksu Cult. This cult was probably in its original form merely an association of shamans [Kuksu was a renowned shaman of earlier times], with initiations for the purpose of instruction in the shamanistic arts, and god impersonations [more likely trance possessions] for the sole purpose of curing. Later, the society commenced giving four day cycles of esoteric dances with increasing complexity of god impersonations, and the original shamanistic ideas became almost extinguished in ceremonial display. In the meantime the original shamans developed into a hierarchy of priests, having a secret language, mythology, and system of crude astronomical knowledge. The head priest now had sole charge of the sacred dances. Curing was almost entirely delegated to non-initiated members of the tribe" [Loeb 1926:469].

In this example Loeb's assertion that "curing was almost entirely delegated to non-initiated members of the tribe" was merely speculation on his part. The fact remains, as evidenced in his own work on the Kuksu Cult, that this society also conduced a four-day healing ceremony via the Kuksui Dance [Loeb 1932, 1933]. Furthermore, the Kuksu Cult held various rituals in which trance possession more than likely played a significant role. For example, in describing their Bear Ceremony (betilkal xe), Loeb [1932:130] wrote: "The candidates got into a frenzy and bled from their mouths (as though possessed by spirits)." It is significant that in this region of California, spirit possession is evidenced by the shaman bleeding from the mouth. Therefore, here again, Lowe's parenthetical claim, "as though possessed by spirits," was merely speculation on his part.

In some cases one finds the term *priest* used inappropriately. For example, W. Thalbitzer, in writing of the shamans of East Greenland, chose to call them priests simply because "they are to be regarded as mediators between common mortals and the supernatural powers of the universe" [Thalbitzer 1931:430]. This, however, really describes a shaman. In other cases, the Native Americans themselves use the term differently. The term for *priest* among the Zuni, for instance, "seems to be applied to anyone endowed with the means of securing or bestowing blessings, regardless of whether they are human or immortal" [Bunzel 1932c:808, n. 68]. Therefore, among the Zuni, *priest* also refers to a spirit.

In summary, although the term *priest* is frequently used in the literature, it has inherent weaknesses when applied to Native American spirituality.

See also *shamanism*.

Pte watci
Ponca, *Plains*
Buffalo Dance [Skinner 1915c:792]. Buffalo shamans were powerful doctors who treated war wounds. With the end of warfare, this society became obsolete during the latter part of the nineteenth century.
See also *love medicines*.

Pthlax
Twana, *Northwest Coast*
Love charms. These are usually herbal recipes, prepared most often by women who have inherited the secret formulas. They are then worn around the neck "to compel passionate attachment of the 'victim' to the charm [wearer]" [Elmendorf 1960:527]. These charms do not use power obtained from a helping spirit. Both males and females use *pthlax*. For an example see *Waxablu*.
See also *love medicines*.

Ptitakeoxate
Mandan, Hidatsa, *Plains*
The White Buffalo Cow Women's society. This is the most sacred of the women's societies. The medicine powers of this society are used to attract buffalo. "The object of the[ir] ceremony was to lure the buffalo near the fireplace. Once, when the performance took place in a clearing in the woods, one buffalo came directly to the doorway [of the ceremonial lodge], and was killed on the spot. During the same season a great abundance of buffalo were found in the timber. Apparently, anyone who was desirous of making the buffalo come could take the initiative and ask the society to undertake the performance" [Lowie 1913b:351].

Puagunt
Paiute, *Basin*
The Kaivavwit term for "one who exorcises" [Fowler and Fowler 1971:144]. This word is a

dialectical variant of *poagunt,* the common word for shaman or medicine man. Among the Owens Valley Paiutes the shaman is called *puhaga* (EONAH, p. 224).

Puhagüm
Paviotso, *Basin*
Also: *puhagai.* Term used by the Gidütikadü of Surprise Valley, California, for shaman. As is usual, different shamans have different abilities. For example, the *düna puhagüm,* Antelope shaman, heads the ceremonial hunts [Kelly 1932:189]. Other shamans find lost objects, prophesy, control the weather, heal, and so on. Power is acquired through both dreams and vision questing at power spots, where there is usually a pool of water that the novice bathes in to acquire a guardian spirit. Most often this spirit comes in some animal form and gives the novice power in the form of a song to be used to evoke the spirit.

In healing ceremonies the shaman diagnoses the patient's illness through a divination with beads. A stone pipe is filled and smoked before the shaman sings his power songs. During the healing the shaman often doctors with an eagle feather, either letting the patient hold the feather or placing it on the seat of the patient's "pain." The most powerful shamans are sucking doctors. As is common in this area, the shaman swallows the disease object ("pain") once he has removed it, thus increasing his own power over the disease. Other shamans merely sing and rattle. They use a deer-hoof rattle, which is used only by shamans [Kelly 1932:191]. Drums are not used. "If very ill, the patient was doctored during the day. When a shaman doubted his ability to cure, he put an arrowpoint on the coals and blew on it until it was red hot. He then took it in his hand, placed it to his mouth, and swallowed it" [Kelly 1932:192].

See also *puhágam,* EONAH, pp. 224–226.

Puhake
Mono, *Basin*
Plural: *puguhanewa* [Gifford 1932:49]. Monachi (Western Mono) term for shaman. "A puhake

was characterized as one who received a visitation from an animal spirit (either mammal or bird) during a dream or when he went into the forest to sing and dance" [Gifford 1932:49]. This is the generic term for shaman. However, shamans are also named according to their particular powers. For example, a sucking shaman is called *nupuhawich,* a shaman who can call forth deer is called *tasuwadi,* and a shaman who uses his powers to harm others (a sorcerer) is called *kapuhat.* "There were also weather shamans who by singing could raise a rain or windstorm" [Gifford 1932:50].

The *soahubiere,* "talker," is a singing shaman who is called upon to drive away the evil effects of ghost visitations via dreams. "Certain songs were sung by the soahubiere or talker to cure illness thus caused. Tugayau, who was such a shaman, possessed many songs for curing. The afflicted person informed the shaman of his dreams. The shaman talked to the guilty spirit at night outdoors, asking the spirit to cease making the person sick. Sometimes this effected a cure. In one instance the practitioner acquired his knowledge from an older soahubiere, who was not his father" [Gifford 1932:51]. Before going out to consult with this exorcised evil spirit, the shaman would "sing before the patient and shake the cocoon rattle" and upon return he would "put ashes on the head of the patient, blow them from him, and announce a cure" [Gifford 1932:51].

In all cases the making of a shaman is dependent on the individual acquiring a guardian spirit. However, shamanism also tends to run in certain family lineages. That is, a particular spirit continues to pass on the powers to subsequent members of the same family. The principle implement of the *puguhanewa* is the *sanadj,* or cocoon rattle (see *sokut*).

Pühüwanpi
Hopi, *Southwest*
Literal translation: "soothing implement" [Voth 1903:285, n. 2]. Ceremonial whip. This term

comes "from pühüwanta, to soften, make pliable—for instance, a hide; or to soothe, make gentle—for instance, a child, animal, etc." [Voth 1903:285, n. 2].

The *pühüwanpi* is used in various ways. For example, it is the whip employed in hunting snakes for the group's summer Snake Ceremony, where the whips are referred to as *tcá wuwahpis* (rattlesnake whips) [Voth 1903:285].

Puhwagantï

Paiute, *Basin*

Literal translation: *puhwa,* "power to heal or harm," and *gantï,* "having" [Laird 1976:31]. Chemehuevis (Southern Paiute) term for shaman. See *puaxantï,* EONAH, pp. 222–223.

Puplem

Luiseño, *California Peninsula*

Shamans [Boscana 1969:311]. In 1846 Father Geronimo Boscana reported his observations of the Luiseño culture associated with the San Juan Mission at Capistrano Beach, California. This mission was founded in 1776, and by the time of Boscana's observations, their shamanic ceremonies were still imbued "with an air of great mystery" [Boscana 1969:311].

Shamanic healing involves curing mostly by means of sucking a disease object from the patient's body, i.e., the use of a sucking shaman. As with most Native American shamanic healing ceremonies, the shamans always begin by conducting a diagnostic ceremony in which "divers [patient] infirmities were explained, and their causes" [Boscana 1969:311]. During these diagnostic ceremonies the shaman touched every part of the patient's body in order to "find" the hidden disease object.

Although Boscana believed the Luiseño shamans were "impostors," he did report a successful shamanic healing that he had observed at the Mission of La Purissima in 1809:

A young woman of eighteen years of age, had been sick for nearly a year, suffering from the effects of dysentery and fever, so that she had wasted away almost to a skeleton, and was to all appearances dying; having received the holy sacrament preparatory to her supposed departure [i.e., Extreme Unction]. One morning, whilst walking in the garden of the mission, I saw her sitting with other females performing the task of clearing the grass; surprised at beholding her there, when I supposed her dying, I asked her how she felt? Her mother, who was at her side, replied to the question, and said that she was well, because such a one (naming one of the sorcerers) had taken from her some bear's hairs, which were the cause of her illness, and, immediately, she was restored. I inquired how they were introduced into her stomach, and how long she had had them? She replied, that when in childhood, and about eight or nine years old, one night, whilst asleep with other children in a room by themselves, a bear came and placed some of his hairs in her stomach. How he came there, or how the hairs got into her stomach, she could not explain; for all that she knew about it, had been stated to her by the sorcerer. This was all deception, of course, but still it happened from that day, that the girl improved in health, and, in a short time, was as robust and hearty as any one!" [Boscana 1969:313].

Boscana also witnessed the actions of spirits but attributed what he saw to the work of the devil. In one instance, which occurred at the Mission of St. Luis Rey in 1813, he was alerted to the fact that the ghost of a recently deceased Luiseño man had returned to his garden at night. The deceased was seen moving about the garden and touching his plants, such that "in the course of one night, nearly all [the plants] were destroyed as if consumed by fire" [Boscana 1969:323]. Interested in this report, Boscana went to the garden to see for himself and found "the greater part of the plants dead, or in a perishing state; some, however were still flourishing. These I took particular notice of, and on the following day I returned, and found seven of them, consisting of corn, pumpkins and watermelons, dried up, and consumed to their roots. In this way the whole [garden] was destroyed. . . . But that which has caused me some difficulty to explain is, why the plants were thus decayed. It was not from want of care, or from disease received from insects, or animals either, because, if so, there would have appeared spots about them, and they would not have been diseased to their very roots" [Boscana 1969:324].

Purification rites

Purification rites take many different forms and range from short acts of smudging (see entry) with a burning piece of sage, cedar, or some other plant to very intense, ten-day-long rituals. In addition to smudging, the rite may include a simple spoken formula, singing a sacred song, taking an emetic, participation in a sweat lodge ceremony, abstaining from sexual intercourse, fasting, diet restrictions, or other such acts. Taboo violations also cause one to need to undertake purification rites. In fact, every undertaking involving the use of medicine powers is preceded by some form of purification on the part of the participants. Hence, it is one of the most frequent ritual actions observed among Native Americans.

Purification rites are designed to cleanse one's body, mind, and spirit of contaminating factors that would otherwise be disruptive to the acquisition of power or even harmful to the person coming in contact with power. On a deeper level purification is a preliminary action designed to prepare one for an encounter with medicine power. As such, purification serves to focus one's consciousness inward and to remove worldly thoughts and concerns. It also causes one's thoughts to stay focused on what one is trying to accomplish. Like prayer, purification rites and rituals help one assume the proper spirit of the occasion and to fortify one's convictions of success. In this sense they serve as the preliminary step from the secular world into the world of power.

In another sense purification rites are used to induce individual sincerity. That is, ritual efficacy is dependent on sincere prayers, and purification rites are designed to bring forth this necessary sincerity in a person.

See also *nawuhchingwu, oosimch, pilsi, poje, smudging rites, Sori wokang, vomiting, Wanke.*

Qanimasoq

West Greenland Eskimo, *Arctic Coast*

Literal translation: "one who shivers with fever" [Birket-Smith 1924:453]. A sorcerer. A shaman who practices sorcery via spells is called a *serrasoq*.

Qaqu

Achomawi, *California*

Doctoring Feather bundle. This bundle, similar in appearance to a small feather duster, is used by Achomawi and Hat Creek shamans in doctoring patients. Shortly after a shaman acquires power, he goes into the woods to find a *qaqu* (as a rule, shamans are men, although woman can become shamans, too). "They are found growing singly in remote spots. When the novice finds a 'QaQu,' he endeavors to pick it, but cannot pull it up, as when he pulls, the whole earth comes up with the 'QaQu.' He leaves this, and looks for another, which he succeeds in pulling up. When uprooted, the 'QaQu' drips blood continually" [Dixon 1904:24–25].

In doctoring a patient, if the case be serious, the shaman goes out and finds a "QaQu" and holds it while dancing near the patient, also using it as an aspergill, to sprinkle the sufferer with water. The "QaQu" talk to the doctors, and tell them in what part of the body the "pain" [disease-causing object] is. When he knows this, the doctor sucks out the "pain." The "pain" is a small black thing, like a bit of horse-hair. When removed, the doctor shows the "pain" to the patient and to others, then he chews it up, and swallows it, or else spits it out into a small hole dug in the ground, which is then filled up again, and stamped down hard. The "pains" were obtained from the "QaQu" by doctors who wished to injure any one, and were then snapped toward the victim. The "pain" flew very fast toward the person, who, when the "pain" struck him, felt as if a wood-tick had bitten him on the back of the neck. The "pain" always struck at that spot, it is said, and then crawled up under the hair to the crown of the head, and there bided its time, till the period set by the doctor had elapsed. Then the "pain" entered the man's head, and traveled to the portion of the body to which the doctor had sent it. The doctor who sends a "pain" knows when the victim dies. As soon as this takes place, he goes at once into the woods, finds an old stump, and places on this a skin and a cap, and addresses it as a person. He then begins to talk to the "pain," now free from its victim, and

255

returning to him who sent it. He soothes and pacifies the "pain," for, after killing a person a "pain" is always very bloodthirsty. The "pain" returns flying rapidly through the air, and strikes the stump which has been dressed up, thinking it is the doctor, for the "pain" always tries to kill the doctor who sent it, when it returns. Once the "pain" has struck the stump, the doctor catches it, and quiets and soothes it. It is only by these means that the doctor escapes being killed by the returning "pain." Sometimes the doctor who extracts a "pain" from a patient gives it back to the one who sent it. The latter then thanks him, and keeps the "pain" carefully in a hollow bone, stuffed with yellowhammer feathers [Dixon 1904:25].

Qetwíyewet
Nez Perce, *Plateau*
Literal translation: "the one who wishes the accident" [D. Walker 1967:67]. Sorcerer. The act of "shooting" a victim with one's power is called *qetíwit,* meaning "to sorcerize" [D. Walker 1967:74].

Qilaain
East Greenland Eskimo, *Arctic Coast*
Dialectical variants: *qilaun* (Kangianermiut and Ungalardlermiut); *qilaut* (Labrador); and *qitlaun* (mainland Alaska) [Rasmussen 1941:23, 35]. Ammasalik drum [Thalbitzer 1914:641]. Drums are made by stretching a piece of skin, the most preferred being the stomach skin (peritoneum) of a polar bear, over a wooden hoop, also called the *qilaain,* that is about 18 inches in diameter. The drum is the only instrument used by the shaman. In playing the *qilaain* the drumstick (*kättiwa*) is struck against the lower border of the wooden hoop rather than striking the skin cover as is done in most cultures.

When used in shamanic rituals the *qilaain* is usually played by the shaman's assistant, while the shaman keeps time with his *anaalutaa* (see entry). Often a shaman will add an amulet (see entry) to his drum to improve his voice in singing. One such amulet among the Ammasalik "consists of the 'whiskers' of a raven (stiff feathers near the root of the beak) and is inserted under the lashing *[kilikirpia],* by means of which the handle [*kattälua* or *kalilua*] of the drum is fastened to the wooden rim" [Thalbitzer 1914:629].

Qilajoq
Iglulik Eskimo, *Arctic Coast*
Plural: *qilajut* [Rasmussen 1929:141]. An Aivilingmiut shaman who can perform the *qilaneq* conjuring ceremony, the most common form of questioning a shaman's helping spirits. In fact, this particular form of conjuring is widespread throughout the Arctic Coast area (see *qilalik,* EONAH, p. 229). The Aivilingmiut have two forms of conjuring, the *qilajut* type and the *sakajut* type [Rasmussen 1929:132]. In the latter the shaman sits behind a curtain of skins on the sleeping place in the house.

Although the *qilajoq* was not always necessarily a shaman, "the one who is to consult the spirits, lays a person down on the floor, or on the sleeping place, face upwards, the operator's waist-belt being often fastened round the subject's head. Various questions are now put to . . . the person through whose head the spirits are to answer. While asking the questions, the operator endeavours to raise the person's head by means of the belt, calling upon the spirit, which is supposed to enter on the scene immediately below the body of the qilanga [patient]. When the latter's head grows heavy, so heavy that the operator, despite all his efforts, cannot move it in the slightest degree, this means that the spirits are present and answer in the affirmative. If, on the other hand, the head is normal and easily moved, this constitutes a negative answer to the question put" [Rasmussen 1929:141].

See also *kila.*

Qivigtoq
West Greenland Eskimo, *Arctic Coast*
Plural: *qivigtut* [Birket-Smith 1924:451]. Persons who live isolated from society and have powers. They are said to have a burning thirst for

revenge and are often associated with evil and thus feared. When the *qivigtoq* receives power, he also receives a special *qivigtoq* sound from the first animal he eats thereafter.

The following is an account of a man from Aulatsivik who happened across the home of two *qivigtut:* "During a deer hunt in the interior of the country a man caught sight of a house with a crooked house passage. He became frightened, for from the smell he understood at once that it was a *qivigtoq* house, but nevertheless he entered. There was someone who at once covered his eyes with his hands, saying: 'Let me cover your eyes; otherwise you will be frightened.' However, the man peeped out between the fingers, and then saw a *qivigtoq* whose eyes were hanging out of their sockets. In his fright, he turned towards the entrance, but was stopped by someone saying: 'Only stay! There is nothing to be afraid of.' When he turned his head in the direction of the sound, he discovered another *qivigtoq* with his cheek bones laid bare. . . . Full of horror the man fled to his home and never more dared to go deer hunting" [Birket-Smith 1924:29].

Qlaqewam

Chinook, *Northwest Coast*

Shaman [Boas 1894:202]. One informant described the Spirit-Canoe (healing) Ceremony used by shamans to retrieve lost souls:

> The seers [shamans] go to the ghosts (the souls of the deceased). When three go, one having a strong guardian spirit is placed first [in the spirit canoe], another one last. One having a less powerful guardian spirit is placed in the middle. When four seers go, the two lesser ones are placed in the middle. A strong seer goes in front, another one behind. They pursue the soul of a sick chief. When the trail (which they follow) begins to be dangerous, the one in front sings his song. When a danger approaches from the rear, the one behind sings his song. In the evening when it begins to grow dark they commence the cure of the sick person. When the morning star rises they reach his soul. They take it, and the guardian spirits of

the seers return. Sometimes they stay away one night, sometimes two. Then they give the sick person his soul and he recovers. . . .

> When a seer wants to shake his manikin (a figure made of cedar bark) he gives it to somebody who has no guardian spirit. Now they go to the ghosts. He [the manikin] helps him. Now this person sees everything in the country of the ghosts. The manikin carries him there.

> When only one soul leaves the body of the sick person, when it remains in the country of the Indians and it is taken, then the sick person recovers at once. When the lesser soul of a person is caught in the country of the Indians and is given back to the person, he recovers after a short time. A soul is in the country of the ghosts; the spirits of the seers pursue it and reach it when it arrives at the ghosts. They bring it back, return it to the sick person, and he recovers. . . .

> When they try to take the soul of a sick person and sparks fall down, he will die. It seems just like a firebrand. They try to gather the sparks up. Then the shaman says: "Behold, I shall not cure him." . . .

> When a shaman tries his power, he sends disease to the bark of a tree. The bark bursts at once and falls down. Then he thinks: "Indeed, I have the powers of a shaman." When an eagle sits on top of a spruce tree, the shaman sends disease against him. He falls down at once, his mouth full of blood. Then he thinks: "Indeed, I have the powers of a shaman."

> When the weather is bad, the people ask a good person who has a guardian spirit of the sea to sing for good weather. He says: "When the sun stands there and there, it will clear up" [unidentified informant in Boas 1894:205–209].

Qologogoloq

North Alaska Eskimo, *Arctic Coast*

Tikerarmiut charm. Charms of this type are carved from wood in the form of different figures or objects, such as a mask, whale, canoe, or bird. They are used in various ceremonial ways. For instance, they are sometimes hung from the ceiling of a ceremonial house, where "all the men who desired good luck in hunting took their turn in washing the figures in urine" [Rainey

1947:248]. Similar fetishes that are destroyed after ceremonial use are called *pogok* (see entry).

Qoobakiyalxale
Pomo, *California*
Also: *koobakiyalhale* [Kroeber 1925:259, n. 1]. Literal translation: "performer for somebody poisoned" [Freeland 1923:57]. Outfit doctor or singing doctor. Sometimes called a "rattle doctor" [B. Wilson 1968:57]. One of two types of healing shamans found among the Pomo. "Becoming a q'ɔ'ɔbakiya'lxalɛ depended on one's family or connections, and practicing as one depended on the possession of the proper equipment and knowledge of its use" [Freeland 1923:57]. "The power and right to practice as a singing doctor was handed down in hereditary lines from generation to generation. A great deal of time had to be devoted to the learning of the profession; one informant said that it took four years" [B. Wilson 1968:58].

Outfit doctors begin their training in early childhood. Over time they learn the proper sacred songs and the location and preparation of various herbs, and they act as an assistant to their mentors. Some singing doctors have been reported to know as many as 1,100 songs. The older shaman transfers his outfit to the novice when the latter is deemed proficient. The ability of the shaman rests in his outfit. Most often such transfers follow hereditary lines; at the least the outfit is transferred to a son-in-law.

The ceremonial items used by the shaman are kept in a bag made from the whole skin of a deer and tied together with a rope. The contents of the bag usually include:

1. The wayɔ'i *[wayoi]*, or cocoon rattle, for beating time in singing. [Also see *sokut.*]
2. q'ɔ'ɔxaka *[qooxaka]*, obsidian blade three or four inches long like a spear head but without the heel. These are rubbed with herbs,—different ones according to the illness—heated, and pressed upon the painful parts while the doctor sings.

3. q'ɔ'ɔxabɛ *[qooxabe]*, rocks of strange shapes taken from mineral springs. These are heated, rubbed with herbs on one end, and used for pressing the patient.
4. ɣanɔ' *(pin) [ghano]*, a sharpened stick, usually mountain manzanita wood, one and a half to two feet long, and flat like a bow, covered with rattlesnake skin. This is used to pin the feather hats to the head net, but during his singing the doctor may take it and press his patient with the points. The pin is also described as being made of a sort of stone found in Robinson Creek, looking like granite but softer. This pin is worked down until it is only an inch in diameter and pointed at both ends. Tail feathers of the "emerald bird" are fastened on a string, drawn through a hole near one end of the pin and looped up with a little hoop of dogwood or oak to form a loose cluster, called bitɛ'rk (feather hat). In this form the ɣanɔ' is not worn but heated, rubbed with herbs, and used for pressing.
5. bɔ'lmaki *[bolmaki]*, the head net.
6. bitɛrk *[biterk]*, the feather hat. These feather hats were of many kinds, and used in ceremonial costumes as well as by the shamans. Several might be pinned on at once to give an especially startling effect. Matsi'gini bitɛrk, a big one of owl feathers; qiya bitɛrk, a big one of yellow hawk feathers; gaci'ltcia, one made of emerald bird feathers. This type was used to wipe the hands when handling herbs, and, gaining in this way a value in healing, was also used to press upon a patient.
7. behɛ'p'tsqwam *[beheptsqwam]*, breech clout of braided pepperwood (laurel). The strong odor is considered beneficial.
8. q'ɔ'ɔ'daqɔn *[qoodaqon]*, the stone pestle.
9. xabɛ'carɛ *[xabecare]*, the stone mortar or bowl, used to grind up paints, or herbs and other medicines which the sick man will then drink directly from the bowl [Freeland 1923:59–60].

In addition this bag also contains the various herbs, seeds, roots, greases, paints, etc., that are used in various ceremonies. For example, a person whose illness is caused by being haunted by a ghost undergoes the "frightening" cure. In this case the shaman paints his face and sings his "frightening" songs. (Sometimes he is assisted by singers.) These bags also often contain such items as "eggs of the turtle not yet laid . . . cooked with herbs and then chewed before using," as well as "bulb of a kind of wild onion . . . seeds of a small red pine . . . pine sugar . . . rattlesnake grease . . . fragments from the hill of a certain ant . . . powdered elk horn . . . powdered whalebone [and] human bone left from the cremation of a person dead by violence" [Freeland 1923:60–61].

Members of this class of shamans are called upon to treat any type of illness. However, they are most skilled at removing poisons that have been shot into the victim's body by an evil shaman or sorcerer. Such poisons come in all forms: plants, herbs, mushrooms, rattlesnake juice, blood of a waterdog, coyote paw, oak blossoms, snake blood, etc. [B. Wilson 1968:54]. Only a shaman can remove such poisons.

The shaman's healing ceremonies are most often conducted in the house of the patient, and they usually last four days. "All his songs were sung in a series of four songs. . . . The doctor sang the same song four times" [T. L. M. in B. Wilson 1968:56]. Upon the shaman's arrival the family of the patient erects a pole, around which is placed the shaman's payment. At the turn of the twentieth century, this usually amounted to goods (wampum, furs, etc.) worth from $50 to $200, depending on the seriousness of the cure. This payment remains untouched by the shaman until his work is completed. In more serious cases the shaman may occasionally take some beads or other such items from his payment, which he then uses as offerings, "throwing them south, east, north, and west" [Freeland 1923:62] as he recites his sacred prayers in a secret language.

Four days is typical for the shaman's visit. For most illnesses the treatment involves the application of various herbal mixtures to the patient's skin, either rubbing it onto the skin with a heated obsidian blade or stick or inserting the mixture into a small slit made in the skin. When the shaman leaves, his outfit is usually left behind to aid in the recovery of the patient. Then, usually in eight days, the shaman returns and either continues his treatment or, if the patient is well, retrieves his outfit and payment.

If the patient fails to recover after several visits and treatments from the shaman, the shaman begins to doubt his diagnosis and suspect the haunting of a spirit. In such cases the shaman "consults with the family to discover what the man had been doing at the time he first fell sick, whether he had been out at night when he might have seen a ghost, or whether he had visited the shore or perhaps some spring in the woods. So they form a guess as to the probable nature of the spirit. The doctor then prepares to test the patient by reproducing the vision as closely as he can. He may himself dress as a ghost, or may construct a model of a monster, the bagi′l, combining perhaps the traits of several animals that frequent such spots as the sick man has visited, sea-bird and snake, or beaver and lizard. A realistic setting for the bagi′l is devised as well, and the scene is suddenly revealed to the patient. If he reacts strongly, struggling and then fainting, the doctor regards his hypothesis as verified" [Freeland 1923:63]. The shaman then revives the patient and either destroys the *bagi′l* or removes his ghost outfit before the eyes of the patient in order to relieve his fear. Usually a rapid recovery is then made.

These shamans use many other forms of treatment. The sick person may be sweated on a bed of moist grass atop hot manzanita wood coals, or the shaman may give his patients preparations of various herbal teas. Shamans also treat broken bones.

The other type of Pomo shaman is the *madu* (see entry), who is a dream or sucking doctor and is considered less powerful. However, "sucking doctors were also reputed to be able to cure sickness caused by poisoning" [B. Wilson 1968:61].

Qoogauk
Pomo, *California*
Literal translation: "poison man" [Freeland 1923:69]. Sorcerer or witch, usually called a "poisoner" in English. A poisoner could be either male or female. Sorcery is rarely practiced, so the Pomo shamans, both the *madu* and the *qoobakiyalxale* (see entries), are not held in fear. If a patient dies under treatment, the shaman is never suspected of sorcery, but his reputation as a healer suffers. In fact, the shaman is still offered his doctoring fees in such cases, though he often declines them. However, Wilson [1968:53] reported that "many informants remembered the time when everyone believed in poisoning, and in 1940 the older and middle-aged Indians, especially women, still believed, although some were not sure. Those who believed feared strangers and insisted one should only visit among relatives. They said one should be wary of accepting food or drink from anyone who did not first take some himself."

Medicines for poisoning a person are extremely difficult to make, although not as technical or powerful as healing medicines. An old man once told a fellow Pomo that he had made poison only twice in his entire life. Subsequently the recipient of this information reported:

He said it was not easy to make poison. "Don't let any one tell you it's easy to make poison," he said, "it's very hard; it takes a long time." He told me how he had made poison the second time, the last time he made it. Somebody had poisoned his daughter. Now he made up his mind that he would take his revenge. He thought he knew what man had poisoned her and he made up his mind that he would make poison. "It takes a long time," he told me. "It takes a whole spring. You have to gather a great many plants. You know they don't all bloom at once; they come at different times. And it's just some part of the plant that's good for poison; maybe the leaf, maybe the flower, maybe

the seed, and there's a certain time when that part of the plant is just right to make poison and you've got to get it just at that time. Then you must collect a lot of bugs, all sorts of poisonous bugs, scorpions, and stings from bees, snakes, too. All the animals that have got poison and all the plants that have got poison. And it's hard because all this time you must eat very little and not go near women, especially women that have their menses. That is so you will be pure, you know!"

Then when he had everything ready he made poison with all that. You must use it pretty soon while it's still strong. So he took the poison and touched that man with it. But you can't stop then. A man must help the poison, he told me. He has to keep it up. For one thing, you can make an arrow of poison oak and a bow of poison oak, too, and in the morning you go and shoot the arrow over the man's house. And if the arrow sticks in the roof, all the better. Well, that man began to get sick. He got sicker and sicker.

But you must keep up helping the poison. So he makes another arrow of poison oak and when he goes by the house he kind of slips it under the house, or in the grass in front of the door where the fellow is sure to step over it. That man got more and more sick all the time. He couldn't leave his bed. Well, he died.

So then the poisoner was through. He went to the river and washed himself carefully. He rubbed his arms and his chest, all his body he rubbed over with different herbs so as to be all rid of the poison.

Well, now he was satisfied. Now he ate [unidentified informant in Freeland 1923:71].

Sometimes the *qoogauk,* once he has gathered the necessary ingredients, takes several other men with him into the woods to prepare the poison medicine. Such preparations are long and difficult, and they require knowledge of the songs and prayers that go with each item used. Often "a little forked stick, a model of a man is made. Something of the victim should be built into it: a hair, nailparing, perhaps a bit of dance costume. Sometimes such a scrap is included in the poison, too. Then the figure is touched with some of the new-made poison and the men enact the death. They dig a grave, cremate the figure, bury its ashes, and hold a crying" [Freeland 1923:70].

Upon completion of this preparation ceremony, these men return to the village and attempt to touch the victim. A man who has been so prepared must take care that one of his friends does not touch him while he is in this "poisoning" state of being. Usually a simple hint, such as, "Don't touch me, I'm all fixed for gambling," suffices [Freeland 1923:71].

Qorit
Wintun, *California*

A Wintu sucking-doctor shaman who died in the fall of 1937. There are some indications in the ethnographic literature that a shaman who heals a person must pay for saving this person's life by giving up some of his own life to his helping spirits. In the following account, given a few months before his death, Qorit hinted at this possibility:

> When I sorrowed for my son, through that I received command of a spirit power. North uphill, I think, I travelled to Mount Shasta, seen by no one; I must have done so, as it was my intention to act thus. Two weeks I travelled around Mount Shasta, seen by no one. I sang, I sang, I remained a number of days, I reason. Then, I reason, I went west downhill to the ocean. And there I remained, I reason, one summer: I must have done so for the reason that I was receiving command of a spirit power. Then I recollected myself and came (I know this through direct sensual evidence) homeward.
>
> I received command of a spirit power when I was on the west coast. I deduce this from the fact that I command a spirit power which comes from over there. But I did not know [did not recognize] him whom I command; for this reason, that I must have got a *yoh* [see *nomyoh*—EONAH, p. 196] for my spirit power.
>
> Though all was well with me when I returned, now I do not feel well. The beings who dwell there came here and took me over there. I reason that it is they who are killing me now. A doctor, I

reason, is never very full of health [Sadie Marsh quoting Qorit in Lee 1941:408].

Qwaxq
Twana, *Northwest Coast*

Also: *qoxq* [Waterman 1930:553]. Ceremonial power. This *cshalt* (see entry) power is "a thing that travels in the air and it can be anywhere you are and it speaks to you out of the air when you get it. Then you see it, but only in your vision" [Frank Allen in Elmendorf 1993:186].

The following is a short account of a Skokomish woman named Jane Henry who inherited *qwaxq* from her mother:

> When my aunt [Jane Henry] started and sung for qwaxq everybody with that power started and joined in, everybody singing their own song. And the same way when any other qwaxq person started a qwaxq song.
>
> And after a while my aunt gets up to sing again. Her poles want to play now. And Big John and Bob Burns, Skokomish men, held the poles. And my aunt went up to her poles and hollered "co'co'co'co" at them. . . . And when those two men got tired, two others hold the poles.
>
> And for three of four days they kept on like that. Singing and eating, night and day [Frank Allen in Elmendorf 1993:187–188].

The poles mentioned in this account were special ceremonial poles with figures carved on their tops showing the belly and head. During the ceremony these poles became animated and moved about on their own accord. In fact, *qwaxq* most often manifested as "levitation or animation of paraphernalia at ceremonies" [Elmendorf 1960:490].

Specific guardian spirits of the *qwaxq* power were also used in the Skokomish eating contests. These contests were held between different villages, mostly with non-Twana peoples to the south such as the Satsop and southwestern Puget Sound groups. "The visiting community on its journey to the host community might test the consumption powers of its members by attempting to drink up small streams or ponds on the way. These feats were made possible by the spirit powers of certain individuals but were performed by the community personnel in unison. . . . Certain individuals, village eating champions with specially potent guardian spirits, might perform prodigies such as draining an entire small canoe full of boiled salmon eggs without removing mouth from the vessel. In theory, the extra quantity eaten on this occasion was absorbed by the eater's q'ᵂa'Xq power" [Elmendorf 1960:140].

These eating contests were both social and religious in nature. The religious aspect entailed "exhibiting a specific skill empowered by a certain kind of guardian-spirit power" [Elmendorf 1960:141]. Following the contest, members of the host village would journey to the challenging village within several weeks in order to outdo their former guests' performance.

Rain-making ceremonies

Many Native American cultures have shamans who specialize in or have the power to control the weather. Many have heard of the Native American "rain dance." However, bringing rain is usually only one aspect of this particular power. The power to disperse rains, storms, hurricanes, etc., is also included in this type of shamanism. As such, the weather shaman (see entry) would also bring high winds to confuse his group's enemy in battle and demonstrate other such power feats.

There are many recorded accounts of this type of activity among shamans. During the early part of the eighteenth century Heckewelder [1819:236–238] commented disbelievingly on Native American rain-producing shamans:

There are juggelers [EONAH, pp. 124–125] of another kind, in general old men and women, who although not classed among doctors or physicians, yet get their living by pretending supernatural knowledge. Some pretend that they can bring down rain in dry weather when wanted. . . .

In the summer of the year 1799, a most uncommon drouth happened in the Muskingum country, so that every thing growing, even the grass and the leaves of the trees, appeared perishing; an old man named *Chenos,* who was born on the river Delaware, was applied to by the women to bring down rain, and was well feed for the purpose. . . .

He had [by the time Heckewelder observed his ceremony] encompassed a square of about five feet each way, with stakes and barks so that it might resemble a pig pen of about three feet in height, and now, with his face uplifted and turned towards the north, he muttered something, then closely shutting up with bark the opening which had been left on the north side, he turned in the same manner, still muttering some words, towards the South, as if invoking some superior being, and having cut through the bark on the southwest corner, so as to make an opening of two feet, he said: "Now we shall have rain enough!" . . .

I thought it impossible that we should have rain, while the sky was so clear as it then was and had been for near five weeks together, without its being previously announced by some signs or change in the atmosphere. But the chief answered: "*Chenos* knows very well what he is about; he can predict what the weather will be; he takes his observations morning and evening from the river or something in it." On my return from this place after three

Navajo shaman Gray Squirrel ritually blends the sand of a sand painting as part of a four-day ritual to bring rain.

great haste to make it rain. The tops of wigwams were soon crowded. In the mystery lodge a fire was kindled, around which the rain makers, burning sweet-smelling herbs, smoking the medicine pipe, and calling on the Great Spirit to open the door of the skies to let out the rain. At last one of the rain makers came out of the mystery lodge and stood on the top of it with a spear in his hand, which he brandished about in a commanding and threatening manner, lifting it up as though he were about to hurl it at the heavens. He talked loud of the power of his medicine, holding up his medicine bag in one hand and his spear in the other; but it was of no use, and he came down in disgrace. For several days the same ceremony continued, until a rain maker with a headdress of the skins of birds ascended the top of the mystery lodge, with a bow in his hand and a quiver at his back. He made a long speech, for the sky was growing dark, and it required no great knowledge of the weather to foretell rain. He shot arrows to the sunrise and sundown points of the heavens and also to the north and south, in honor of the Great Spirit, who could send rain from all parts of the sky. A fifth arrow he retained until it was almost certain that rain was at hand. Then sending up the shaft from his bow with all his might to make a hole in the dark cloud over his head, he cried aloud for the waters to pour down at his bidding and to drench him to the skin. He was brandishing his bow in one hand and his medicine in the other, when the rain came down in torrents [Frost 1845:109].

o'clock in the afternoon, the sky still continued the same until about four o'clock, when all at once the horizon became overcast, and without any thunder or wind, it began to rain, and continued so for several hours together, until the ground became thoroughly soaked.

Another early account was provided by someone unfamiliar with Native American shamanism, who did not understand that it sometimes takes many days to produce rain:

It was in a time of great drought that I once arrived at the Mandan village on the Upper Missouri. The young and the old were crying out that they should have no green corn. After a day or two the sky grew a little cloudy in the west, when the medicine men assembled together in

The following account regarding wind control is from an 1844 book entitled *The Fourteen Ioway Indians*: "A packet ship with Indians on board, was becalmed for several days near the English coast. It was decided to call upon the medicine man to try the efficacy of his magical powers with the endeavor to raise the wind. After the usual ceremony of a mystery feast, and various invocations to the spirit of the wind and ocean, both were conciliated by the sacrifice of many plugs of tobacco thrown into the sea, and in a little time the wind began to blow, the sails filled, and the vessel soon wafted into port" [Harrington 1896:253].

Raven
Kutenai, *Plateau*

A shaman from the nineteenth century who had bulletproof medicine. According to one report, as Raven was leading the Kutenai into battle he "left his group and encircled the enemy. They kept shooting at him but the bullets did not penetrate his body. When he returned to his men, he shook his garments and the bullets fell to the ground. The men gathered up the bullets, loaded their guns with them and fired them at the enemy. The chief [Raven] did this several times in order to get ammunition for his men" [Baker 1955:13].

Red Road

This term is widely used in Native American discourse to refer to the following of traditional ways, especially with regard to supernatural powers and spirit guardians. It is also sometimes known as the Good Red Road. Among the Canadian Santee it is known as *cangkú dúta,* literally "road red" (the noun is always followed by adjective in Sioux) [Howard 1984:137]. Naturally, the exact tenets of the Red Road differ from culture to culture.

Red-Stone Doctor
Ingalik, *Mackenzie-Yukon*

The name given to a powerful shaman who lived at "Red-Stone" in the Anvik area. (It was common to name individuals according to locations associated with them.) The Red-Stone Doctor lived around the turn of the twentieth century and was esteemed for his great powers. Osgood [1958:59] noted that "everyone agrees that none has more power than the 'Red-stone' doctor." His main power came from a "little owl with . . . black-and-white spotted back feathers" [Osgood 1958:56], the skin of which he kept tied to a post in the rear of his house. This owl skin would "give an alarm and break loose from the post if

danger threatens the village" [Osgood 1958:56]. The Red-Stone Doctor also had a Mink spirit and a Rabbit spirit.

One year the fish did not arrive as anticipated, and all of the people became worried. They called upon the Red-Stone Doctor to help them. He told them that he knew something about the cause of their problem and began a ceremony in which the people helped him drum and sing.

> Then on the third evening [of drumming and singing] the shaman said to the people, "Let me try anyway and if I do not come back it is all right." He told them to prepare a stick several feet long like a broom handle with a loon's head carved on the end. When this was done, a few stripes of red paint and some feathers were added to make it look right [i.e., be properly prepared]. Then the "Red-stone" doctor put on a new muskrat parka and, taking the stick, went down to the edge of the pier. There men lashed two canoes parallel and about four feet apart with poles between for the shaman to sit on. Just before the shaman climbed onto the platform, he told one man that when morning came he was to go periodically to the river and listen, and he also warned that while he was gone, no one was to lie down, not even the babies. Then he got on the platform and while beating his drum and singing his songs, two men paddled him out into the river. When the canoes had stopped in the center of the stream, the shaman, making the cry of some water animal, stepped down into the water still holding onto the poles connecting the canoes. Curiously the canoes acted as though anchored. The shaman faced down river holding his stick and wherever he stepped the water did not touch him. Shaking himself and singing, the shaman went lower and lower, the water disappearing from beneath his feet but surrounding him as in a whirlpool. Lower and lower he went until the water was even with his head. Then as he disappeared altogether, some loon cried out.
>
> The two men in the canoes paddled back to shore for the canoes began to drift as soon as the shaman was gone. They joined the others in the

kashim [house], all the men and women as well, some holding up their sleeping babies. There the men sang and drummed all during the night.

Toward morning, the fellow who was asked by the shaman, went out to the river once in a while to listen. As the light in the sky appeared, he ran back to the kashim and said, "I heard loons on the water." Then the black-and-white spotted owl [skin] fastened to the shaman's post at the back of the kashim began to make a noise as though it were crying. The people kept up their singing and drumming. It was not long before the shaman came in through the door, but he had shrunk to about four feet in height. His clothes were perfectly dry, but his stick was gone. He walked around the kashim four times making medicine, going down on one foot by bending his knees and then on the other, with his hands behind his back but not singing or speaking. As he did this he began to grow to his full height again. Then the shaman went to each corner and made more medicine. He made a cry like a loon, bowing his head low toward the corner. After turning toward the center of the room, he blew from his mouth four times. Then he stopped and someone asked, "How are those people?" referring to the loons. . . .

After this exchange, the doctor went to his place on the bench and started drumming with his own drum, telling the people, "Don't pay any attention to me, just get your nets ready." The people went off to prepare their nets. The shaman drummed and made medicine all day, but in the evening he stopped.

The next morning every man went out in a canoe. Whenever anyone caught a fish, that person made a noise like a loon. Some fish had feathers in their mouths. Then someone caught a fish with a piece of the shaman's stick between its teeth [Osgood 1958:59–60].

Reincarnation

Although reports of reincarnation are rare among shamans, they have been recorded. One old Eskimo shaman from Selawik lake, near Kotzebue Sound, told Nelson [1899:433] "that once he himself had died and gone to the land of shades [dead], remaining there until he became tired, when he returned to the earth and entering the body of an unborn child, was born again." In some cultures a young person with graying hair was said to be an old one who had reincarnated.

See also *Ekaskini, Thunder Cloud.*

Returning Hunter
Assiniboin, *Plains*

In 1935 this man was reputed to be the best hunter among the Fort Belknap Assiniboin in Montana. When he was young he paid a shaman to make him a hunting charm, for which he paid the shaman a horse. The shaman made a charm from the claws of a chickadee and tied it to Returning Hunter's whistle.

"By whistling I could now put all the game that I hunted to sleep. After I received these chickadee claws I decided to try them out to see if they would work. I then went hunting on the north bank of the Missouri, southeast of the reservation. Looking off in the distance I saw a black-tailed buck lying in the open. I had a spy glass with me that I had received from a trader. Looking into it I saw two chickadees resting on some timber near the deer. Soon they left that place and came to rest on the horns of the deer and it wasn't long before the deer was fast asleep. I ran the distance to the deer and shot and killed him before he could awake. My charm had worked" [Returning Hunter in Rodnick 1938:26].

Subsequently, Returning Hunter received additional hunting power via a dream visitation by the Hawk spirit. "Thereafter, many were the times that the hawk spirit aided him in killing deer and other game" [Rodnick 1938:26].

Roman Nose
Cheyenne, *Plains*

A nineteenth-century warrior whose war bonnet gave him the power of being invulnerable to bullets.

With this war bonnet went the tabu that he could eat no food taken from the pot with a pointed, iron utensil. The psychological association is clear. As the pointed implement pierces the food, so will a pointed metal bullet pierce the flesh. Just before the big fight with Colonel Forsythe's command at Beecher Island in 1868, Roman Nose had been entertained in the Sioux camp. Ignorant of his guest's tabus, his host served him fried bread taken from the pan with a fork. A Dog Soldier noticed it and told Roman Nose. The fight with the Americans began before Roman Nose was able to go through his long purificatory rite, so, like Achilles, he stayed in his tent while the battle dragged on. Finally, he gave in to the pleas that he come forth to lead his men. He put on his war bonnet, and while riding up to the battlefield, he was shot and mortally wounded. He did not even get into the fight [Grinnell in Hoebel 1960:76].

Running Wolf
Arikara, *Plains*
An early-twentieth-century shaman who was a member of the Buffalo Medicine society. He was a leader of their Medicine Lodge Ceremonies and is remembered for his power feats. He "used to stand in the center of the medicine lodge and allow another medicine man to cut off his arm. He would then pick up the arm from the place where it had been dropped and hold it up for all to see, when it would appear as the foreleg of a buffalo. After displaying it in every direction, it would be replaced against his shoulder, when it would assume its normal appearance and no sign of the cut would remain" [Will 1934:46].

The Arikara had several variations of this particular feat. "One man used to withdraw behind the [medicine] lodge and cut off his own arm. He would then throw it out before the entrance where it would appear as the leg of a buffalo. He would then replace it, when it would resume its normal shape. Still another man would go through the same performance, but his severed arm would appear as the forepaw of a bear" [Will 1934:46].

See also *Bear's Belly, Shunáwanùh.*

Saam
Blackfoot, *Plains*

Medicine bundles, or medicines [Wissler 1912a:69]. "Bundles and their contents as well as rituals are designated by this term" [Wissler 1912a:141, n. 2]. Blackfoot medicine bundles are individually owned, and, therefore, the ceremonies that go with each bundle are also individually owned. Most men own some kind of bundle, however small it may be. Also, it is possible to transfer bundles, and by such transfers, "a kind of purchase, a medicineman may acquire the visions and supernormal experiences of others" [Wissler 1912a:72]. Each bundle contains one or more medicines. "The power of these medicines is specific in that each particular medicine has power only over a definite thing. The Blackfoot regard them with fear and consider them very dangerous to handle or use. Those who do make use of them must pray continually and exercise great care to carry out all the directions and requirements. They must be used secretly and are first held over a smudge of sweetgrass while praying to them. The bag is then opened and the medicine used according to directions" [Wissler 1912a:87–88].

Sacred Arrows
Cheyenne, *Plains*

See *Mahuts.*

Sacred bundle/pack
See *medicine bundle.*

Sacred language
In anthropology this refers to any special language, usually unintelligible to others, used by shamans to communicate with their helping spirit(s). The fact that spirits often use a special language is so well known in Native North America that there is often a distinct word within the language that refers to this special form of communication. For example, in Lakota it is called *hanbloglagia.* "*Hanbloglagia* is our sacred language. It is a language of tones and frequencies and is taught to a very small number of persons" [Charlotte Black Elk in Doll 1994:156].

Quite often the shaman's sacred language is composed of old cognate words and, as such, is partially intelligible to the ceremonial audience. At other times only the shaman can understand what is being said, and in these cases one of the shaman's assistants often serves as translator.

Among the Inuit (Eskimo) the situation is even more complex. Here the shaman uses a special spirit to interpret to the shaman himself what his helping spirit is saying. The same is true for the Ojibwa Shaking Tent Ceremony (EONAH, pp. 246–249), where the spirit *Mikenak* (see entry) serves as a go-between.

Sadada

Twana, *Northwest Coast*

Messenger power. A form of Skokomish *cshalt* (see entry) used to treat illnesses due to soul loss [Elmendorf 1993:221]. Insanity is often diagnosed as soul loss, and the little-earths (spirit dwarfs) are usually the culprits. Sometimes when using *sadada* to retrieve the patient's lost soul, the shaman will bring back the wrong soul and, therefore, not cure the patient [Elmendorf 1993:222]. It is also true that once a person's soul leaves the body, the shaman has only so long to bring it back. After a certain point the soul will jump out of the person's body no matter how many times it is put back in by a shaman.

Samaa

Havasupai, *Southwest*

Spirit. Many individuals acquire minor powers via a spirit, mainly through dreams, but are not classed by the Havasupai as true shamans who cure, called *githiye* (EONAH, p. 89). The former are referred to by the name of their type of power followed by the classificatory term *gĭsámá*. For example: *ágwágá gĭsámá* is a deer doctor, *gwetávŏg gĭsámá* a doctor for sickness, *pakaúa gĭsámá* a doctor for fractures, *nahámĭ´dvĭdjá gĭsámá* a doctor for wounds, *nunálaídjĭ gásámává* a doctor for stomach trouble, and *ăluwí sámá gá* a doctor for snakebites [Spier 1928:282].

Game "doctors" can only lure certain species, namely, those seen in dreams. "Before extended hunting forays, the shaman would sing special songs calculated to quiet deer and prevent them from running when hunters approached. These were sung at night and repeated four times. Content involved not only information about the habits of the animal, but also that the hunters were sorry for killing the game they needed to assuage their hunger. Locations the hunters intended to visit were also mentioned" [Smithson and Euler 1964:11].

In addition, game shamans are called upon to treat diarrhea, for which they have special songs. "During these songs the shaman (or, in the case of a baby, its father) would gently massage the patient's abdomen in an attempt to locate flatulent areas. The singer also would take ashes from the fire, rub them between his palms, and blow them to the east, exhaling audibly as he did so. This action was thought to remove any accompanying pain" [Smithson and Euler 1964:11].

An account of a Snake shaman follows: "Descumalaua's father was a snake doctor. A man who had been struck in the calf by a rattler came to his house. He immediately made short incisions all about the puncture, tied a ligature about it, and sucked out the blood. At night he sang just as a shaman does, waving a feather (the longest from the eagle's wing, covered with white gypsum) over the wound. A ring of sagebrush (*Artemisia ludoviciana*) is put around the limb to draw out the poison, not the blood, on the ground that the snake may know and use this plant" [Spier 1928:283].

The term *samaa* is also used for "medicine" [Spier 1928:282].

Samahiye

Keres, *Southwest*

Acoma stone fetish (see entry) used in altar displays. These are natural formations that are rounded on one end and flat on the other. During rituals they are dressed with feathers on the back and encircled with beads, and a face is painted on the front in turquoise and yellow. When the fetishes are not in use, they are wrapped in cornhusks after the dressings are removed.

"Similar stones and somewhat similarly decorated, called likewise *tcamahia* are found on Hopi altars. They figure also on Zuñi altars" [Parsons 1926:118, n. 4].

Samhalait

Tsimshian, *Northwest Coast*

Literal translation: "real power" [J. Miller 1984:139]. This term is used to refer to the power of a shaman acquired through a vision quest. This power is most often evidenced by the novice's long period of sickness after the quest, during which he or she undergoes treatment by advanced shamans who doctor the power-associated affliction. "The father of the patient would gather in all the shamans, who would (each in turn) take the same rattle and begin the cure by singing a song that belonged to a former shaman of this house. Night after night they would continue to sing in order to strengthen the supernatural power of the patient-cum-shaman. . . . Eventually the cure progressed to the point where the patient began to sing his or her own personal curing song. At this juncture, the initiate would be exhibited before his or her tribe" [J. Miller 1984:139]. Although both males and females may receive *samhalait,* most often it is received by men.

The term comes from the stem *halait* (EONAH, pp. 99–101), meaning "shaman."

See also *haleyt.*

Sanadj

Mono, *Basin*

Monachi (Western Mono) term for the cocoon rattle used by shamans throughout central California [Gifford 1932:50]. For its use see *puhake;* for cocoon rattles see *sokut.*

Sauel

Wintun, *California*

Also: *sauäl.* Wintu power spots that are visited by shamans or novices (usually male) to acquire guardian spirits. Quite often the *sauel* is a pool. In such cases the shaman dives into the pool in an attempt to reach the bottom; this is known as *memtuli sauel,* "water-swimming sacred-places" [Du Bois 1935:81]. Sometimes a shaman finds a charm stone at the bottom of the pool. Most often the guardian spirit comes to the shaman at the *sauel* via dreaming.

Frequently a *sauel* is associated with a particular animal spirit, such as Deer, Wolf, or Grizzly Bear. One type, the Coyote *sauel,* is visited only by female shamans or novices [Du Bois 1935:81]. *Sauel* visitations are also made by nonshamans to acquire powers for gambling, basket making, witchcraft, or other skills. "Frequently young men who were just beginning to hunt used them to assure themselves of skill in the future. A young man, however, was often discouraged from this by his elders, who feared he might acquire an undue amount of supernatural power and thereafter be set off from other young men by a variety of taboos on food and sexual intercourse" [Du Bois 1935:81].

Sacred pools are also places where shamanic regalia and paraphernalia are properly disposed of [Du Bois 1935:82].

The Nomlaki name for such power spots is *sawal* (see entry).

Sauhino

Maidu, *California*

A Nisenan (Southern Maidu) shaman who resided at Auburn during the latter part of the nineteenth century and was famous for his spirit séances. He was fatally wounded in a quarrel but "before dying apparently conveyed [his séance] technique to relative, Oite (Captain John), next to last chief at Auburn" [unidentified informant in Beals 1933:392]. His séances were often conducted every night for a period of six days. A typical account of one follows: "During seances, bunch of feathers placed on ceremonial post where spirits come first. Pan or cover placed over fire, making house dark. Shaman sings at bottom of post, using cocoon rattle [*sokot*—see entry]. Soon wind comes, house creaks, sometimes noise like thunder. Rattle seems to travel up post, rattles all time spirit talking. When spirit goes away, rattle drops to ground, shaman picks up, sings again. Some spirits cry, others sing, some say nothing. Occasionally coyote spirit comes. Hear howling far off. Then everyone sings, shouts to scare away. At intervals during night, cover taken off fire, audience smokes, talks" [unidentified informant in Beals 1933:392].

During such séances the spirits speak in a special sacred language (see entry) that is often not understood by members of the audience. In such cases, the shaman, after the spirit has left, interprets what was said.

Sauyit
Yuit, *Arctic Coast*
Dialectical variant: *tcauyak* (South Alaska Eskimos) [Hawkes 1914:19]. Drum [Hawkes 1914:15]. The drum forms the core of the Yuit sacred ceremonies; indeed it is the only instrument they use. Their drum is an 18-inch, circular hoop with a walrus or seal bladder stretched over it. The bladder cover is held in place by a rawhide cord *(oklinok)*. When played the drum is held aloft and beaten around the rim with a small stick *(mumwa)*, which is sometimes adorned with a piece of white ermine. At other times the drummer simply uses a fox tail. In most cases, an assistant plays the *sauyit* while the shaman sings and accompanies him by beating the floor (in "a continuous tattoo" [Hawkes 1914:15]) with a small baton.

Among the South Alaska Eskimo the winter season is a time of mirth, songs, and dance festivals, all designed to empower the religious feeling of the people. This time is known as *Tcauyavik,* stemming from the word *tcauyak,* mentioned above. This is another indicator of the important role drumming plays in their sacred ceremonies.

Sawal
Wintun, *California*
Nomlaki power spot. These are springs inhabited by one or more spirits. Different springs contain different kinds of power. These springs are vis-

ited, usually in the spring, by people wanting to gain power. The more powerful *sawal* is used only by a shaman; others are not allowed to go there. However, anyone can go to a less powerful *sawal* to obtain medicine for gambling, hunting, warfare, etc. Visitors usually leave offerings there to the spirits. The afterbirth and the navel cord of a newborn is often buried at the hunting *sawal* [Goldschmidt 1951:352].

"They have a name for every spring, good and bad. In the old days you couldn't drink out of every spring. Sawal is a bad spring (i.e., has magical potency). . . . If you drink the water from one of them in Dry Creek, it will kill you. The water doesn't hurt you, but something in there does. If you stoop down, something that lives there faces you, and you are done for. The animal or the man or woman that is in the spring is called *pômpuri*" [McGetrick in Goldschmidt 1951:353].

The Wintu name for such power spots is *sauel* (see entry).

Sáwanikia
Zuni, *Southwest*
"Magic medicine of destruction" [Cushing in Green 1979:199]. In this form of hunting medicine, the hunter makes the "roar or cry of a beast of prey . . . which, heard by the game animals, is fatal to them, because it charms their senses" [Cushing in Green 1979:199]. In addition the Zuni hunters also use their breaths, "derived from their hearts, and breathed upon their prey, whether near or far, [and their magical breaths] never fail to overcome them, piercing their hearts and causing their limbs to stiffen, and the animals themselves to lose their strength" [Cushing in Green 1979:199]. This magical breath "derived from the heart" is the Zuni *Haianpinanne,* the "Breath of Life," a term synonymous with "soul" [Cushing in Green 1979:199].

Sbetedaq
Snuqualmi, *Northwest Coast*
Dialectical variant: *sbatatdaq* (Snohomish) (EONAH, pp. 243–244); *smatnatc* (Lummi)

[Stern 1934:80]; *sbatadaq, bitidaqw, spɬdaqw* [Waterman 1930:129]. The Duwamish (or Dwamish) Spirit Canoe Ceremony. This is a ceremony performed for a person who is ill due to soul loss. This particular healing ceremony is "one of the few institutions which the Puget Sound people developed along special and peculiar lines" [Waterman 1930:131]. "The general background of the ceremony is a belief (which is by no means unique) that the people in the Land of the Dead steal souls from people in this world, or their 'medicines' (spirit-helpers), and take them away to Dead-land. The person whose spirit-part or spirit-helper is gone, languishes, becomes weak, loses his property, and finally dies" [Waterman 1930:131]. For example, among the neighboring Twana, *sbatadaq* is a special form of power used to travel to the land of the dead to recover lost souls. This soul-recovery power is granted to individual Twana by "blowfly, graveyard post *[sqa'lax^w təd]*, and a number of named earth-dwarf spirits *[təbta'bax^w]*" [Elmendorf 1960:490]. *Sbatadaq* is a form of *cshalt* (see entry).

For the Coast Salish *sbatadaq* is a twofold power that allows a person to open the way to the land of the dead and then to travel there. "Sbətəda'q men can take anybody along [to the land of the dead] if they have some kind of power, any tamánamis [see entry]. But the real sbətəda'q people have little-earth [spirit dwarfs] power *[təbta'bax^w]*. . . . [Two shamans] had that little-earth power, and after they had thrown down that rock, and opened the way to the ghost land, they could take anybody along who had any kind of tamánamis" [Frank Allen in Elmendorf 1993:223].

The Skokomish performance of this ceremony is known as *scab,* meaning "holding a group soul recovery ceremony" [Elmendorf 1993:224].

The Spirit Canoe Ceremony is held within a house and lasts up to four days. For an example of it, see *touchtd.* For details on this ceremony, see Haeberlin 1918.

See also *shcub.*

Scapulimancy

A form of divination (see entry) in which future events are determined by reading the bones of an animal, most often the scapula, or shoulder blade. In North America this form of divination is, for the most part, limited to the areas of Labrador and Quebec; it is considered to be of Asian origin [Eliade 1964:164, n. 97]. Scapulimancy has also been reported for the Kaska of the Mackenzie-Yukon area [Honigmann 1954:110, 114].

Among the Innu (Montagnais-Naskapi) it is known as *matinikashauew* and is used, among other things, as a hunting medicine. "To use this method of foretelling the future, an elderly Innu man holds the shoulder blade of a porcupine or caribou over the flame from a stove or candle until it is charred and cracked. The scorch marks and cracks are then studied like a map to determine the possible location of game" [Armitage 1991:81].

Among the Ojibwa of Lake of the Woods, it is known as *masinisawe* (see entry).

Sccuctab

Twana, *Northwest Coast*

Spirit Dance. This is a religious dance ceremony sponsored by a single individual during the winter that finalizes his control over his helping spirit. This ceremony often takes place many years after one's initial spirit acquisition via a vision, sometimes upward of twenty years. The dance "consisted essentially of a display or demonstration of the sponsor's individual spirit power" [Elmendorf 1960:496]. An older shaman initially assists the sponsor, and often during the ceremony some of the sponsor's guests become possessed by their own helping spirits.

This ceremony is required only of the *cshalt* (see entry) powers, not of the *swadash* (see entry) powers.

Schalaq

Twana, *Northwest Coast*

Also: *schálaq.* War powers [Elmendorf 1960: 488]. These powers, a form of *cshalt* (see entry), enabled their owners to be successful in warfare. Most often these powers came from some animal spirit, such as the Black or Grizzly Bear, the Wolf, the Cougar, the Eagle, and particularly the Hummingbird [Elmendorf 1984:290]. However, other sources also existed. For example, another form of war power was known as *sthlqet* (see entry), "dawn light" [Elmendorf 1960:489].

Schucus
Twana, *Northwest Coast*
Sea-mammal hunting medicine [Elmendorf 1960:490]. This was a *cshalt* (see entry) power that enabled its owner to be successful in hunting sea mammals.

Scrying
Any form of divination (see entry) in which the shaman uses a crystal or a container of water to peer into when searching for answers; this practice is widespread in North America. For example, scrying in blood and water has been found as far north as north Alaska [Lantis 1947:90], and it extends intermittently down to the Southwest area. Quite frequently the shaman covers his or her head when peering into the container of water (e.g., the Nunivak Eskimos [Lantis 1946:203]; see *Niashaida*).

Among the Ojibwa of Lake of the Woods, scrying is generally done by looking into a cup of water, but mirrors are also used. "Andrew Flett had heard of a man from the Lake St. Joseph region who used to carry a mirror on a string at his breast and who could through the mirror see when people were coming to camp, even when they were still far off" [Cooper 1936:11].

See also *metudhauk, tarrarsortoq, wapi munipi.*

Sdanc gohat
Arikara, *Plains*
Goose society. This is a woman's society that functions to ensure the growth of corn and other vegetables. An account from the latter part of the nineteenth century told of one woman who remained in her field overnight and was blessed by the Corn spirit. She joined the Goose society and would manifest corn during society performances. As Bear's Teeth reported: "She stepped out from the ring [of dancers] into the center, and closed her eyes tight. Suddenly some corn seeds came out of the corner of her eyes. Two old men singers laid down their things and approached the performer. They placed some sage on coals and smoked it. Then one of the old men smoked [smudged] his hands and placed them on the woman's eyes, thus making the corn seeds recede again" [Lowie 1915a:677]. Eventually this woman became blind, and as she neared the end of her life, "a cornstalk about eight inches long came out of her mouth. It was pretty well withered. The reason for its coming out was that the woman was approaching death. As soon as it came out entirely, she died" [Lowie 1915a:677–678].

Sea Lion
Haida, *Northwest Coast*
A late-nineteenth-century shaman who lived at Dorsal-Fin Town. He was a member of the Rear Town family, which was scattered over the north end of Grahm Island and is a part of the Raven clan [Swanton 1908:490, n. 6]. A detailed account has been given of Sea Lion's efforts to save his village from starvation. He undertook a ten-day purification ritual before divining whether his spirit would help the villagers. At the height of his divination, while still in trance, he said "'My servants, they are going to give you food.' He said so, because he saw the soul of a whale in the water. Then he sat down. After the supernatural being had gone out of him, he dipped a cup in [sea water and drank it]" [Swanton 1908:581].

At the conclusion of his divination, Sea Lion said,

"Tomorrow morning, when I go out, look at me. Do not let the women look at me." The day after, he went out early. He directed them: "In the morning, let all come in front of my house." So they did. And they brought the shaman's box to him. Then he took the cover off of it. And they put a dancing-apron around him. He said, "Tomorrow the sea will be calm." It was calm, as he had said.

Then they put a dancing-hat upon his head. When he was ready, he said, "Now look at me." He said, "Do not enter the houses. As long as I am away, watch the place whither I go." It was low tide. Then he went seaward.

They thought that he would stand near the shore. When he came near the shore, he walked upon the sea. Sä′lgᵘtclao spoke through him. This was a reef. Then they watched him. When he came to Tclao-qāLas (reef), he went down under the waves. They looked at him for a while when he vanished underneath. They watched for him.

As he had said, after a while there came a sound like the noise of a cannon. Then the tide was rising. While they watched, a whale's tail came out. And he came out by the side of it, as it lay half in the sea. Then he came away upon the sea. But when he came up, he threw something upon them. "All of you take it," he said to them. He said to them, "Sit in a straight line" (i.e., one behind another). So they sat in a straight line. After he had thrown something upon them, they all seized it. He said to them, "Do as I do." And they drew it towards themselves.

While they were doing as Sea-Lion did, the whale went down. And then it floated upon the sea. Then he danced still more. After they had pulled thus for a while, the whale came ashore in front of the town, at the ebb of the tide. They did not see the thing he threw to them. They did not see the rope that the shaman had fastened to it. They pulled it with empty hands. Only the shaman saw it. They did not know what he did. And it (the whale) was left by the tide in front of the town. . . . This town was saved [Swanton 1908:582–584].

Seer

Shamans throughout North America who are called upon to see what is going on at a distance. The power to do this is used to locate game, to warn of the approach of the enemy, to find lost objects, to inquire of missing persons, and so forth.

One seer among the Flathead "was a constant source of entertainment to his friends, being a veritable mine of reservation gossip. He would lie on his floor and delight everyone with what was going on, even events of a most intimate nature. One night he turned on his elbow and told one of his guests that a friend was enjoying his wife. The cuckold rushed home and saw enough to justify manhandling the false friend almost to the point of death. This shaman would consistently lie on his side and tell the room just who was approaching, how far away he was, just which horse he was riding, just when he would arrive, etc. Even the skeptical younger men say that he never made a mistake" [Turney-High 1937:29–30]. This shaman died in the 1920s.

See also *divination*.

Sehrsartoq

West Greenland Eskimo, *Arctic Coast*

Egedesminde Eskimo bullroarer (EONAH, p. 42) that shamans used during their healing ceremonies. Birket-Smith [1924:424] reported that a *sehrsartoq* "was placed close to the head of the patient, in order to drive away the disease." However, shamanic healing was extinct among these people by the end of the nineteenth century due to missionary efforts, and no record was ever made of the actual use of the *sehrsartoq*, which eventually became only a toy for children. Given that disease was often believed to be caused by the presence of an evil spirit, it is most likely that the *sehrsartoq* was sounded during the group's ceremonies, with the resultant noise driving away the harmful spirit.

Serrat

West Greenland Eskimo, *Arctic Coast*

Plural: *serratit* [Birket-Smith 1924:445]. Spell. Spells usually come in the form of inherited sayings that carry a magical influence. Some spells are addressed to an individual owner, while others are general in nature. One ethnographer noted at least twenty-five kinds of spells used by these Eskimos. However, little is know of them because it is difficult to induce the Eskimos to speak about them. Telling someone about a *serrat* may diminish its powers.

Shaltu
Wintun, *California*

Also: *saltu* (EONAH, p. 240). The Patwin term for a guardian spirit [Kroeber 1932:379]. This term is also applied to spirit impersonators who appear during dance rituals.

Shamanism
Shamanism is what shamans do with regard to supernatural power. In this context Kroeber [1907:331] observed early on that shamanism throughout North America "centers about disease and death." Within his work the terms *medicine man* and *shaman* were used interchangeably. However, some anthropologists, such as Wissler [1912b:82], prefer to reserve the term *medicine man* for the herbalists. However, this has not been a consistent practice in anthropology, and

A Tlingit shaman's face mask.

most often the terms are not differentiated in the ethnographic literature. In this encyclopedia, *shaman* is used interchangeably with both *medicine man* and *doctor* (or *physician*).

Shamanism per se is a process in which an individual develops the ability to tap into a "holy" source of power within his or her own being. Humans are known to be created "in the image" of the Creator. However, unlike most of Western civilization, the Native American cultures have for untold centuries known of the deeper profundities of this most fundamental understanding of human existence. To them this "image" within has always been a human reality that they actively encourage each other to seek out and explore. Those who do discover it return with "grace" in hand, that is, "medicine powers."

That this "holy" center exists within every human being is not a new message. Socrates admonished each individual to "know thyself," and Jesus proclaimed that "The Kingdom of Heaven is within." In fact, this is a pan-cultural message that has been repeated in a multitude of forms throughout all ages. The essence of these various messages has always been: "That which you are looking for is within you."

In order to realize the deeper reality of this center "within," Native Americans have established, throughout time, many individual (holy) rituals designed to focus one's attention on this point "within" rather than on the external world. The most common example of this is the vision quest ritual that appears in many different forms throughout North America. Those who succeed in realizing this center "within" return to the space-time world with "holy gifts" in their possession, gifts that they call "medicine powers"—"medicine" in the sense that they are for the health and help of people and "powers" in the sense that they are capable of bringing about directed change in our reality, what we often call "magic."

From this understanding of shamanism, it becomes obvious that anyone who acquires a spirit helper in any form is a shaman. In addition, the

George Catlin, Medicine Man Performing His Mysteries over a Dying Man, *1832.*

form of one's medicine power also determines one's role in the society. For example, a warrior who goes on a vision quest and acquires a bulletproof medicine (see *war medicine*) would more than likely become the leader of one of the culture's various warrior societies. Another person might acquire the ability to foretell the future and become a diviner within the society. In addition, a person might acquire a singular, small power, such as the ability to be successful in hunting, fishing, or gathering acorns (see *alini*). For that reason shamans are quite often classified within a culture according to their different shamanic abilities rather than by a singular term for shamans. That is, a culture might have twenty or thirty different words designating a shaman. When a specific cultural term does exist for shaman, it is quite probable that the term is applied only to those individuals, male or female, who have acquired a prestigious amount of shamanic power. In other words, a person who has the ability to heal illnesses through shamanic ritual will definitely be called a shaman, while a person who has a "small" helping spirit that gives her luck in finding acorns will more than likely *not* be called a shaman by members of that society. From this perspective, shamanism then becomes a matter of degree in one's power abilities (for example, see *suin*). This is the most likely scenario for most Native American cultures.

Traditionally, anthropologists have remained rather smug about the issue of the shaman's powers or magic, preferring to make it taboo for field anthropologists to "go native" on the matter. However, within the last decade, that has changed. Younger anthropologists, hoping to break new ground, and even established anthropologists such as Edith Turner have realized that by "going native" one achieved "a breakthrough to an altogether different world view, foreign to academia, by means of which certain material was chronicled that could have been gathered in no other way" [E. Turner 1997:22]. Given this "new" academic understanding, one can only deduce that "real" anthropological studies of shamanism are merely in their infancy at this time.

Those trappers, missionaries, explorers, and others who did spend time around Native American shamans in years past were all well aware of the magical abilities of these individuals, and much has been recorded in this regard. For example, the Jesuit missionaries of the sixteenth century in the Northeast cited many instances of the shaman's "work of the devil."

Perhaps most interesting is the fact that shamanism remains fundamentally a mystery not only to the public at large but also to the shamans themselves. Shamans are simply given instructions by their spirit guides, and when these instructions are carefully followed, their desired results are brought about. But just how this magic works remains a mystery even to them.

Given this understanding, shamanism can also be seen as the act of calling forth one's "medicine," but it remains fundamentally an ongoing process in which individual medicine powers come and go in varying degrees over time throughout the shaman's life.

"The word 'Shaman' is considered by some to be a corruption of the Sanskrit *Shramana*, Pali, *samana*, an ascetic, which, indicating a disciple of Buddha, became among the Mongolians synonymous with the magician. But the most acceptable explanation of the word is derived from the Manchu *saman*, pronounced *shaman*, the fundamental meaning of which is 'one who is excited, moved, raised,' thus answering to the principle characteristics of the shaman. The name shaman is only found among the Tunguse, Buryats, and Yakuts, but it is only among the Tunguse that it is the native name, the Buryats and the Mongols calling their shaman *bo* or *boe*, and the female shaman *odegon* or *utygan*. Among the Yakuts the shaman is called *oyum*, a female shaman, *udagan*, among the Ostyaks, *senin*, female, *senim*. The Samoyeds call their shaman *tadebei*, while the Altaians use the term *kam*" [Casanowicz 1925:419].

For those more disposed toward the Sanskrit origin of the term *shaman, shramana* is derived from the root *shram,* which means "'to be (become) weary, to exert one's self (especially in performing acts of austerity).' Thus the original meaning of *ēramana* is 'making effort, toiling'" [Mironov and Shirokogoroff 1924:107]. Later the meaning changed to "ascetic" among the Buddhist, explaining its association with shamanism. This means that *shramana* is a pre-Buddhistic word. In going from Sanskrit to Dhauli, Jaugada, and Khalsi, the *shramana* changed form to *samana.* This theory holds that in then going to Tungusian, the form became *saman, shaman,* and *xaman* [Laufer in Mironov and Shirokogoroff 1924:110]. Other theorists contend that the Tungus terms were derived from the Turkish via their *kam, xam,* and *kamna* variants [Mironov and Shirokogoroff 1924:111]. Finally, as stated above, the term is most often described in the literature as having developed spontaneously among the Tungus.

See also *spirits.*

Shaman's call

This metaphor is used by anthropologists to refer to cases in which the acquisition of medicine powers comes by means of the spirits seeking out the novice shaman. In Native America shamans most often seek medicine powers via vision quests or dreams. However, in some cases, men or women are born to inherit these power from the spirits, and thus they are sought out by spirits. This is usually indicated to the elders by the child's behavior at a very early age; for example, the child may prefer to be with elders in ceremony rather than playing with other children. A prolonged sickness is also a common manifestation of the shaman's call and usually must be treated by other shamans.

Because anyone can be subject to the shaman's call, there are many accounts in the literature of people who did not want to become shamans. Most often such individuals are unsuccessful at avoiding the call, but some do prevail. However, more often than not, it does come as a surprise to them that they have been chosen.

Shape shifting

The ability of shamans to transform themselves into other shapes, particularly those of animals. This phenomenon is widespread in North America. In fact, "transformation into animals and getting power from animals—these are the double aspects" of a culture's belief in spirits [Parsons 1939:63]. Bear shamans in particular are renowned for this ability, and witches/sorcerers are also frequently described as being able to change form, most often assuming the shape of the owl.

A Kwakiutl potlach transformation mask representing a wolf.

Of course, shamans are not limited to animals in their shape shifting. Geronimo (see entry) could change into a doorway, and Dekanawida (see entry), the famous Iroquois prophet/shaman of the fifteenth century, would change himself into a tree to escape detection by his enemies. Shape shifting is often associated with war medicines (see entry).

See *transmutation* for details.

Shäpupulema
Yakima, *Plateau*
Blowers [Waterman 1924:504]. A sect of the Indian Shaker Church (see *Shakers*—EONAH, pp.

245–246) whose members had formerly "practiced shamanic 'medicine' in the Medicine Valley of the Yakama Reservation. . . . They used an expiratory procedure to cure, and they blew on other Shakers when they met them" [Ruby and Brown 1996:75].

Healings are performed by Shakers. "Those with the spirit to heal claim to see the sin of the illness or the problem as a shadow. Shakers may also burn the sin or pain [disease] out by passing a burning candle along the sufferer's limbs. . . . In Shaker healings, such sin is believed to be in the air where it can pervade a room" [Ruby and Brown 1996:74].

The following is one account of a Shaker healing. "On the Skokomish Reservation during the 1940s, Joe Dan's daughter, Irene, reportedly went out of her head after a man had become angry at being asked to give up his seat in church to some visiting Shakers. After several shakings over her, the faithful effected a cure when the visiting Rev. William Hall of the Jamestown Shaker church brushed out the malevolent intrusion. To dispose of it, he buried it in a baking powder can. A day or so later, the man who had become angry was caught digging down to recover the intrusion, which he claimed was his power, but he reportedly died on reaching the receptacle" [Ruby and Brown 1996:74–75].

Most Shaker healing involves brushing and blowing on the patient, combined with the use of fire. In addition, the "Jamestown Shakers used a handkerchief to catch a 'bad ghost' that they then blew away after emerging from their church house. The Quinaults used a can with a lighted candle on its top to hold sin. Taken to the forest, the can and candle gave the purveyors time to escape the malevolence of the sin" [Ruby and Brown 1996:75].

See also *laying on of hands.*

Shcub

Twana, *Northwest Coast*

Soul-Recovery Ceremony. This is a complex curing ritual that involves the use of *bas-*

batadaq, "soul-recovery curers, having special lay-spirit power for recovery of souls from the first land of the dead" [Elmendorf 1960:521]. This religious ceremony was most often conducted during the winter months. It entailed a mimetic voyage by the *basbatadaq* in a canoe to the land of the dead. This very elaborate, dramatic, and spectacular ritual is peculiar to the Puget Sound area.

See also *sbetedaq, touchtd.*

Shii

Tiwa, *Southwest*

A term used at Isleta for a prayer stick; another term for prayer stick at Isleta is *taai* [Parsons 1939:270, n.*]. See *offerings, prayer feathers/sticks.*

Shikame

Keres, *Southwest*

Also: *Shikani* (Laguna) [Parsons 1926:109] *Cikamɛ* [White 1930:604]. This medicine society is primarily concerned with healing. It appears in all of the Keresan pueblos except Acoma, where by 1930 it was extinct [White 1930:612]. "At Chochiti the *Ci'k'amɛ* society was also the hunter's society. . . . The Flint [and *Ci'k'amɛ*] society of Laguna participated in the scalp dance" [White 1930:612–613].

At Laguna "the Shikani is differentiated into a curing and rain-making society" [Parsons 1939:132]. Members of the *Kurena,* one of the clown societies of the Keres, handle the weather control functions, while the *Shikani cheani* (shamans) handle the curing. Also, the *shikani-kurena cheani* was once designated as the *hanigye* (topmost) *cheani* at Laguna, where the *shikani cheani* were in general charge of all *cheani* [Parsons 1926:109].

When summoned for a healing, the *Shikani cheani,* like all shamans, is invited by being given a package of meals by a relative of the patient. "The *cheani* gives the meal to his *iyatik'ŭ* [see entry], asking for help. He visits the patient for four days before the ceremony. *Kuati,* 'going after' i.e., of the heart of the patient, the ceremony is called. The heart is believed to have been carried off by *kanadyeya* (witch, evil spirit), the witch taking animal form" [Parsons 1926:118].

During the healing ceremony the *Shikani cheani* wears only a breechcloth. "He has across his nose two lines of red paint *(hakacha)* [red ocher] and two lines across his lips. There are four lines on each side of his face" [Parsons 1926:119]. Sometimes another shaman assists. A crystal is used in the beginning to locate the stolen "heart."

[The] *Shikani cheani* proceeds to suck places on the body of the patient. Then having rubbed ashes on his body as a prophylactic against witches and on the calves of his legs so as not to get tired, with his bear paw in his left hand, a flint knife in his right, he rushes outdoors, slashing the air with the flint. Two "war captains" with bow and arrows and a blood relative of the *cheani* with a gun follow the *cheani* as he goes forth, running so fast that it is with difficulty his companions keep up with him. He may go to the river for the heart (it is usually found in the river bank) or he may dig somewhere with his bear claw. . . .

Returning to the house of the patient, *shikani cheani* creeps in on hands and knees, clasping in the bear's paw the "heart." The "war captains" take the "heart," from him, and so violent is his behavior, that the "war captains" have to hold him down. He stiffens into a kind of spasm, and his female relatives have to massage him back to consciousness. They rub him with ashes. Restored, he is given warm water to drink, and he goes out and vomits. Returning, he takes from the altar the *hishami* of four eagle feathers and with them rolls up to the patient the "heart," three or four grains of corn wrapped one by one in red cloth, bound with cotton. He undoes the tangle, searching out the thickly wrapped grains. If there are three grains only, the patient will die, if four, the patient will recover. . . . He places the four grains on the palm of his right hand and blows as if blowing them back into the body of the patient. He blows towards the left arm of the patient, then towards the right arm, then towards the left knee and the right knee. After this, in a shell, he gives the patient the four grains of corn to swallow together

with the medicine *(wawa)* from the medicine bowl from the altar. In conclusion, the relatives of the *cheani* wash the heads of the relatives of the patient [Parsons 1926:121–122].

Shila
Maidu, *California*
Term used for poison by the Nisenan (Southern Maidu) of the Placerville area. This term encompasses a variety of different poisons used by sorcerers. For example, the ground bones of the dead added to one's food was "a deadly slow poison" [Andrew Jackson in Beals 1933:389].

The act of shooting a poison into someone is known as *shilamu* [Beals 1933:390].

Shinka
South Alaska Eskimo, *Arctic Coast*
A Chugach shaman from the village of Chenega who lived during the late nineteenth century. Among his powers was the ability to cause the earth to shake. He would sing his medicine songs, fall on his back in trance, and then get up to see how close he was coming to "the pole of the earth." Once he arrived, after falling several times, he would grab the "pole" and shake it. "Then there came a noise and the earth would shake. A white man named King, who was skeptical when he witnessed the performance, did not believe that the shaking was a real earthquake. Therefore he sent someone to all the houses in the village, and everywhere the earthquake had been noticed" [Birket-Smith 1953:129].

Shi′wanakwe
Zuni, *Southwest*
Also: *Shi′wannakwe* [Parsons 1933:80]. Rain society. This society is also a healing society and is "the oldest of curing societies and Zuni-born" [Parsons 1939:134].

Shiwanna
Keres, *Southwest*
Thundercloud society [White 1930:607]. Sometimes also given as Storm Cloud society [Parsons

1926:95] or Rain Cloud society [Parsons 1926: 91]. This is the society of the Lightning shamans, one of four general types of medicine men found among the Keres (see *Crowi* for details). These shaman mainly treat people who have been struck or shocked by lightning, have broken bones, or have "bad smells in the stomach" [stomach disorders] [White 1930:607]. "At times when the Fire and Flint societies are having a communal curing ceremony, the *Shiwanna* society prays and sings for rain and for crops" [White 1930:607].

"At Santo Domingo, the *Shiwanna* medicinemen are included within the Giant [*ckoyo*—see entry] society" [White 1930:607]. At Acoma and Cochiti there is a *Shiwanna* society, with the society at the Cochiti consisting only of women. "At Laguna, the *Shiwanna* medicinemen were those persons who had survived a shock of lightning and who wished to become *Shiwanna* shamans" [White 1930:607].

Shkalina
Keres, *Southwest*
The Cochití Pueblo term for cornmeal. Offerings of cornmeal, particularly blue cornmeal, play a significant role in both ceremonial and everyday life. In former times a man or woman who wanted to ask for someone's assistance with any task would offer that person some cornmeal when making the request. If the person accepted, he or she took the offered cornmeal and threw it toward the sun.

In rituals *shkalina* offerings are made for prayers, blessings, summoned spirits, etc. Such an offering "invokes supernatural assistance in the matter at hand; it bestows religious sanction upon the proposed activity" [Lange 1959:231–232].

Shljam schoa
South Alaska Eskimo, *Arctic Coast*
Kodiak spirit. This term was misunderstood and translated by missionaries as the "heavenly divinity" [Birket-Smith 1924:434] but should be considered as a cognate of the term *silap-inua*.

Shotikianna
Zuni, *Southwest*
The Arrow society, a division of the Great Fire society (also called the Big Firebrand society). "Only men belong to this order. The ceremonial occurs every fourth year in February, in connection either with the *po'sikishi* (Spruce Tree) ceremony or with the *pa'et'towe* (Navaho Dance). The arrow swallowing is always combined with sword swallowing" [Stevenson 1904:511]. This ceremony is very similar to the performances of the *Piännithle* (see entry; also *Onayanakia*— EONAH, pp. 204–205) society. In February 1891 Stevenson observed a performance of the Arrow society in connection with the Navajo Dance. At one point during the performance,

> a new song is begun, when the 'Hlĕm'mosona [ceremonial leader] advances to the novice [being initiated into the order] and, facing east, swallows the arrow. After the arrow swallowing is repeated by all, the fraternity father draws his arrow before the shoulders, mouth, and over the head of the novice. The novice makes four unsuccessful efforts to swallow the arrow. . . . [Later] the arrow director steps before the boxes and, facing them [the other participants in the ceremony], waves his arrow gracefully from right to left over them, then waving it in a circle, he turns from right to left and swallows the arrow, facing east. Both the swords and the arrows are held horizontally and placed to the mouth while the head is erect, then the head is moved gradually backward as the instrument is pushed down the throat. Great care is observed in the feat, only three men venturing to dance while swallowing the arrow. One man gives three quite violent pressures to the shaft after the arrow is down the throat. Each one in turn steps before the boxes, faces east, and swallows his arrow. . . . [Then] the arrow dance is repeated three times in the plaza [Stevenson 1904:513].

Parsons [1939:646] also noted arrow swallowing and the handling of live coals by Naiuchi, head shaman of the War society during a performance of the Zuni *Owinahaiye*.

Shúhat

Columbia, *Plateau*

Contemporary Columbia Sahaptin word for guardian spirit [Boyd 1996:116]. In this area guardian spirits are acquired mainly via vision questing. The power obtained by the new shaman from the guardian spirit is not revealed until the winter ceremonies, at which time it is expressed through song and pantomime.

Shula

Twana, *Northwest Coast*

Literal translation: "health, vitality" [Elmendorf 1960:512]. Soul [Elmendorf 1993:200]. The loss of one's *shula* was often diagnosed as a cause of illness, especially illnesses that involved irrational behavior. Among the Twana each individual possessed two souls. The *shula* was the life soul and was seen as "a miniature image of its owner, about the length of a finger, and of fog-like consistency" [Elmendorf 1960:513]. The *shula* was visible to shamans only when it appeared in the world of the living as a ghost. When in the form of a ghost, it is known as *thlkwadathl* [Elmendorf 1960:513]. It was the *shula* that went to the Land of the Dead after death.

The other soul was known as *yidwas* (see entry).

Shumakwe

Zuni, *Southwest*

One of twelve curing societies. This is the only curing society that also operates as an *Ashiwanni* (or rain, see entry) society (there are fifteen *Ashiwanni* among the Zuni). When the *Shumakwe* conducts a rain-making ceremony rather than a healing ceremony, only the chiefs of the society are allowed to participate: In other words, "the Shuma'kwe functions through its chiefs as a rain society" [Parsons 1933:16].

The societal rain ceremony is known as *Yaya* (Keresan for "mother"), and it is performed in spring or summer but not necessarily every year.

Shunáwanùh

Arikara, *Plains*

Literal translation: "Magical Performance" [Howard 1974:247]. The annual fall performance held jointly by the eight medicine societies of the Arikara: the Ghost; Buffalo; Owl or Moon; Bear; Deer or Elk; Duck or Big-Foot; *Kohnít* (Edward S. Curtis) [Howard 1974:254], variously translated as Cormorant, Bald Eagle, and Crane; and "Sioux" [Howard 1954:169; Howard 1974:270, n. 1]. "This last is the same as [Edward S.] Curtis's Mother Night or Young Dog, and [George F.] Will's Rabbit and Dakota band. It has also been called the Blackbird or Grass society. It would appear to be the old Prairie-Plains 'Hot Dance' or Grass dance society which, with the Arikara, was grafted onto the medicine fraternity system in spite of its warrior-dancing society origin" [Howard 1974:270, n. 1].

The ceremony is commonly referred to in the literature as the Medicine Lodge Ceremony, mainly because the members of the various medicine societies remained in their ceremonial lodge throughout the duration of the *Shunáwanùh*. These ritual performances are not to be confused with the widespread Medicine Lodge Ceremonies that originated among the Ojibwa. Sometimes the *Shunáwanùh* ritual is referred to as the Holy Lodge [Will 1930:251].

The *Shunáwanùh* began in September and "lasted for a couple of months or more, with public performances every evening, and closed with an especially spectacular day and evening" [Will 1934:39]. During their night performances the eight medicine societies took turns demonstrating their various medicine powers. In addition, "on the closing day of the Medicine Lodge each band [medicine society] erected a small tent for itself in the plaza before the Sacred Lodge. Most of the feats were performed in the plaza itself, each band vying with the others in the power of their own tent to perform these miraculous cures" [Will 1934:41].

Edward S. Curtis, Arikara Medicine Ceremony: The Ducks, *1908. Photogravure.*

The first Westerner to witness these performances and report on them was Pierre A. Tabeau, around 1804. He wrote:

I saw a man, named *Scarinau,* absolutely naked, his hands empty, the lodge well lighted, show to me, nearby, a leather garter and, after having rolled it in his hands, throw it on the ground, changed into a living adder. He took it up and showed it to me again, a garter. He repeated the same trick ten times without giving the least hint as to the means that he employed.

A man all in black comes stealthily behind one of the actors and, with all his force, deals him a blow with a hatchet upon his head. The sound of the blow leaves no doubt that he really received it. All the spectators and the medicine men yell horribly; but, after many contortions, one of them undertakes to cure him and the dead is brought to life.

Another shoots a gun through the body of his companion who falls down upon his back, dead. The blood gushes forth from two openings, showing that the bullet has gone through the body; but, after a great many grimaces and lamentations, he is also mysteriously healed.

Some thrust a knife blade through the hand, pierce the arms, the thighs, the tongue, and all these wounds, so apparent, merely result in making the power of the doctors shine.

Finally, to crown the work, an elderly man, showing all the symptoms of despair and transported by rage, plunges a barbed arrow into his heart. He falls weltering in his blood. The actors, not being able to withdraw the arrow without leaving the barb in the body, seize the point to make it pass through. The spectator really believes that he sees the feathers gradually enter and the arrow, all bloody, come out on the other side under the shoulder blade [Tabeau in Howard 1974:248].

In the summer of 1831, a fur trader named D. D. Mitchell and party became stranded near the largest Arikara settlement after losing their horses while crossing the Missouri River and took shelter therein. That evening they were invited to attend a power performance of the Bear shamans of the Bear society.

[The shamans] were painted in the most grotesque manner imaginable, blending so completely the ludicrous and frightful in their appearance, that the spectator might be said to be somewhat undecided whether to laugh or to shudder. After sitting for some time in a kind of mournful silence, one of the jugglers [shamans] desired a youth, who was near him, to bring some stiff clay from a certain place, which he named, on the river bank. This we understood from an old Canadian, named Garrow (well known on the Missouri), who was present and acted as our interpreter. The young man soon returned with the clay, and each of these human bears immediately commenced the process of molding a number of images exactly resembling buffaloes, men and horses, bows, arrows, etc. When they had completed nine of each variety, the miniature buffaloes were all placed together in a line, and the little clay hunters mounted on their horses, and holding their bows and arrows in their hands, were stationed about three feet from them in a parallel line. I must confess that at this part of the ceremony I felt very much inclined to be merry, especially when I observed what appeared to me the ludicrous solemnity with which it was performed. But my ridicule was changed into astonishment, and even into *awe,* by what speedily followed.

When the buffaloes and horsemen were properly arranged, one of the jugglers thus addressed the little clay men.

"My children, I know you are hungry; it has been a long time since you have been out hunting. Exert yourselves today. Try and kill as many as you can. Here are white people present who will laugh at you if you don't kill. Go! Don't you see the buffaloes have already started?"

Conceive, if possible, our amazement, when the speaker's last words escaped his lips, at seeing the little images start off at full speed, followed by the Lilliputian horsemen, who with their bows of clay and arrows of straw, actually pierced the sides of the flying buffaloes at the distance of three feet. Several of the little animals soon fell, apparently dead; but two of them ran around the circumference of the circle (a distance of fifteen or twenty feet), and before they finally fell, one had three and the other five arrows transfixed in his side. When the buffaloes were all dead, the man who first addressed (the) hunters spoke to them again, and ordered them to ride into the fire, (a small one having been previously kindled in the centre of the apartment) and on receiving this cruel order, the gallant horsemen, without exhibiting the least symptoms of fear or reluctance, rode forward at a brisk trot until they had reached the fire. The horses here stopped and drew back, when the Indian cried in an angry tone, "Why don't you ride in?" The riders now commenced beating their horses with their bows, and soon succeeded in urging them into the flames, where horses and riders both tumbled down, and for a time lay baking on the coals. The medicine man gathered up the dead buffaloes and laid them also on the fire, and when all were completely dried they were taken out and pounded into dust. After a long speech from one of the party . . . the dust was carried to the top of the lodge and scattered to the winds.

I paid the strictest attention during the whole ceremony, in order to discover, if possible, the mode by which this extraordinary deception was practiced; but all my vigilance was of no avail. The jugglers themselves sat motionless during the performance, and the nearest was not within six feet. I failed altogether to detect the mysterious agency by which inanimate images of clay were, to all appearances, suddenly endowed with the action, energy, and feeling of living beings [Mitchell 1962:311–312].

During the early 1830s Prince Maximilian observed similar feats. He wrote of one: "On another occasion a man's head is cut off with a saber and carried out. The body remains bleeding, without the head, and this headless trunk dances merrily about. The head is then replaced but with the face to the back. The man continues to dance but the head is seen in the right position and the man who was beheaded dances as if nothing had happened to him. The bleeding wound is rubbed with the hand, it disappears, and all is in order again" [Maximilian in Howard 1974:249].

In the 1840s Father De Smet reported: "They pretend to have communication with the spirit of darkness. They will fearlessly plunge their arm in boiling water, having previously rubbed it with a certain root; they also swallow without ill effect, substance of fire, as well as shoot arrows against themselves" [De Smet in Howard 1974:249]. This ability to place one's arm in boiling water and the ability to swallow live coals "are both associated with the 'Sioux' medicine society of the Arikara, also known as Mother Night, Young Dog, Rabbit, Dakota, Blackbird, and Grass" [Howard 1974:249].

In 1867 General Phillippe de Trobriand (then the commander of Fort Stevenson) observed the *Shunáwanùh*. He reported: "One of them advanced holding an ear of maize in his hand; he held it by the butt against the pit of his stomach and pretended with a great show of strength to bury it in his flesh. When at length he ceased his efforts the ear remained sticking horizontally, fastened to his skin. . . . The third band [Buffalo society] poured a bowl of maize on a buffalo robe, and made the robe eat it; that is to say, that the grain disappeared. . . . A little doll fastened to the floor seized with both hands the stem of a pipe which was presented to it to smoke [Deer or Elk society]; a heavy necklace placed flat on the breast of a squaw wrapped in a buffalo robe remained there without anything apparent to keep it from falling to the floor" [Trobriand in Howard 1974:251].

In 1884 anthropologist W. J. Hoffman reported witnessing this same performance.

One now observed on the ground a small doll dressed as a warrior, about five or six inches high, made of wood and rags, but well painted and ornamented with feathers. When the music had ended, one of the principal dancers continued to dance alone, quietly before this small image, begging it in various ways to join in the festivities, imploring the *spirit* of the warrior, which it was supposed to represent, to affirm its presence and show that it approved of the ceremony by dancing. And, little by little, one observed the doll keeping time, finally following the choreography of the dancers which surrounded it. One could not see the finest thread attached to the doll, and this act was admittedly done well. . . .

The principal performance took place at the end of the ceremony. A shaman presented himself to the crowd and announced to the assembly that he would be shot in the head by another Indian but would catch the musket ball in his mouth. The musket was loaded publicly, but I was not able to satisfy myself as to whether the ball was really placed in the barrel or if it was composed of some soft material, nor was I able to ascertain whether the shot was truly aimed at the shaman's head, but the Indian certainly appeared to aim at the open mouth of that worthy and, immediately afterwards, the shaman showed a musket ball which he held between his teeth [Hoffman in Howard 1974:252–254].

Beginning in the 1920s George F. Will collected additional information concerning these performances as remembered by elders. The battle between shamans in the Medicine Lodge, they recalled, often resulted in a shaman being mutilated.

One of my informants states that a brother of the late chief, Sitting Bear, was thus carried out of the lodge on one occasion. His skin and flesh appeared to be cut to ribbons, his ribs showed through the flesh in places and his liver and other organs seemed to be protruding from rents in the abdominal walls. The Bears took him in hand and he was soon entirely recovered. . . . Another member of the Bear band [Medicine Society] would dress himself in the skin of a bear and amble around the fireplace imitating a bear in his actions. A second member would take up a rifle and shoot him, often several times. The first man would drop, roll about on the floor, and would bleed profusely. The medicine men would then surround him. Soon he would stand up, cough, and spit the bullets out into his hand, when he would be as well as ever.

Another man would stick his tongue out, thrust a wooden skewer through it, seize his knife and cut the tongue off. The blood would pour from his mouth and in his hand he would appear to be holding the tongue of a buffalo. He would then replace it, when it would assume its normal appearance, and grow in place again.

Another medicine man would thrust a long knife far down his throat; he would then turn a back somersault and break off the hilt against the ground. The blood would gush from his mouth and he would writhe about the floor apparently in great agony. A fellow medicine man would rush up, pick up the broken hilt, and insert it into the injured man's mouth. The knife would become whole again and would be withdrawn. After certain mysteries were performed, he would be perfectly well again.

Another performance of a different character represents a whole group which were the special province of certain particularly endowed individuals. In this case the performer would stand up at his full height and beat his sides a few times with his hands. Soon a miniature jack rabbit would leap from his mouth into his hand" [Will 1928:62–64].

During the nineteenth century the *Shunáwanùh* became well known for its demonstrations of a wide variety of medicine powers. "Edward Hall, a resident on the reservation since 1869, says that the medicine lodge was known to the people at the various trading stores as 'the Opera,' and they frequently attended the performance in the evening, much as they might go to the theatre. Each band [medicine society] had its special type of sleight of hand which had a connection with the type of cures in which it specialized" [Will 1928:56]. By 1885 the government had banned these performances. "The medicines societies, however, have continued, mostly as religious organizations, with sometimes a minor curing function as well" [Howard 1954:171].

See also *Bear's Belly, Blue Bird, Paint, Running Wolf*.

Shwomtan
Comox, *Northwest Coast*
The term used by the Squamish division for shaman [Barnett 1955:148]. See *siaiuklw* and *snäem*.

Siaiuklw
Comox, *Northwest Coast*

The term used by the Sechelt division for shaman [Barnett 1955:148]. "Shamans' dances, as was usual on this side of the [Georgia] strait, were spectacular, awful, and miraculous. One involved the handling of coals and hot rocks, and the eating of fire. Another was the thigh-slashing performance" [Barnett 1955:307]. Such power displays were also seen among the Squamish. However, among the southern divisions—the Maskwiam, Sanetch, Cowichan, and Nanaimo—the shamans "danced like other people, and, although their powers were believed to be stronger, they never gave terrifying or miraculous performances. It was known that such performances took place elsewhere, but these southern groups did not like to see them. Some years before . . . a Slaïäman visitor had put on his winter dance at Nanaimo. It involved, first, a slashing of his arms and thighs with a butcher knife. After this phase of the performance, the dancer sat down in full view of the audience and scraped the blood from his body with his hands and licked them. The wounds were then revealed to be miraculously healed. The dance revolted the Nanaimo and several of them waited upon the man to ask him not to give it again" [Barnett 1955:276].

See also *snäem*.

Siawa
Comox, *Northwest Coast*

The term used by the Sanetch division for a clairvoyant [Barnett 1955:150]. See *kwaneman*.

Sii
Keres, *Southwest*

Ant society [White 1930:604]. The Ant medicine men are one of four general types found among the Keres (see *Crowi* for details). "The 'Ant School' of medicinemen is based upon the notion that ants cause ailments, such as sore throat, skin troubles, etc. They enter the body, usually when one is urinating on an ant hill, and then affect the throat or skin. Cures are effected by drawing the ants to the surface of the body with prayer and song and then wiping them off with broom straws" [White 1930:607].

Sikyahonauûh
Hopi, *Southwest*

A sucking shaman who treated Alexander M. Stephen (a field ethnographer hired by J. Walter Fewkes) on February 6, 1894. Although Stephen was "in a listless, half torpid condition, not at all in good plight for observing with accuracy" [Stephen 1936:859], he did provide a brief description of his healing. The shaman used a crystal to locate the disease object in Stephen's right breast area and then proceeded to cut a small slit in his skin at the identified location with a "pretty green knife . . . just enough to draw blood" [Stephen 1936:862]. Then Sikyahonauûh bent over Stephen, who was sitting on a pallet facing the shaman, and,

> placing his lips against the wound, he exhaled twice upon it, and the effect was to send an icy chill through me from head to foot. (My ill condition prevented me from exercising any very nice discernment, but the occurrence impressed me vividly, and it is that I seek to note as precisely as may be.) After each of the exhalations he raised himself on his knees and breathed ostentatiously away from me; he again bent over me and, placing his lips again on the wound, he inhaled twice, no marked sensation following these inhalations. But after the second time he carried my left hand to his mouth and spat into my palm an abominable looking, arrow shaped, headless sort of centipede. It was about an inch and a quarter long; it was of a dark brown colour and seemed to be covered with a viscid substance; it had no head that I could make out, but its legs certainly moved, and it seemed to be a living insect. . . . Sikya'honauûh only permitted me to look at it briefly. . . . At any rate the pains in my chest ceased from that day [Stephen 1936:862–863].

Sila
Maidu, *California*

Power objects used to test novice shamans. During the training of a novice, "the older doctors gradually test the young man by throwing into him, or inserting into his nose, magical objects called *sila*. If the candidate bleeds or can not extract the *sila* he will not be a successful shaman" [Kroeber 1925:423].

For the Eskimo meaning of this term, see EONAH, pp. 250–251.

Silak
Wiyot, *Oregon Seaboard*

Pain (see *pains*). Disease "pains," the disease-causing objects found in the cultures of this particular area of California, are often described as being "minute, wormlike, self-moving, soft, and transparent" [Kroeber 1925:117]. For a cure to be successful, the shaman removes the "pain" from his patient by sucking on the body at the location or seat of the "pain." The Wiyot shaman sometimes sucks through his tubular tobacco pipe when removing the "pain." However, Kroeber [1907:348] noted that the shaman has one pipe for smoking and another for sucking.

Siluthaup
Yuma, *Southwest*

A weather shaman who died in 1893. The following is an account of his rain-making powers:

I remember a time when there was no rain for two years and the [annual spring] flood was very low. There was very little overflow. Everybody got very worried and all the men got together. They decided to send for this old man who was living out to the west at the foot of the mesa. He sent a message telling them to place four bamboo tubes filled with tobacco in the middle of the big shelter where the meeting was held; to build a fire close by them and let it die away into embers.

When he came to the place hundreds of people had gathered around. He picked up the tubes one at a time and smoked them very quickly. He made a short speech, saying that it was the spirit Turtle *(kupet)* that had given him the power on the mountain amyxape (to the west of Pilot Knob). The spirit had shown him exactly what to do and had told him to think of the Turtle and name him when he performed the ritual. He commanded the people to follow him out of the shelter and run in a body towards the north, raising as much dust as possible. This they did and the old man went off home. Before he had gone very far there were patches of cloud all over the sky and rain had fallen in several places. In less than an hour a heavy downpour had begun which lasted about four days [Miguel Thomas in Forde 1931:197].

Weather shamans can prevent as well as cause rainfall. They also have the power to control the force and direction of the wind. Most often they use their powers to bring rain for the winter season crops and to confuse their enemies.

See also *weather shamans*.

Sinel
Yokuts, *California*

A shaman from the Tachi branch of the Yokuts near the north shore of Tulare Lake who specialized in rain making. He lived during the late nineteenth and early twentieth centuries, southeast of Lemoore, California, and was known to the local inhabitants as "Indian Bob, the Rain Dancer." He used special charm stones commonly referred to as plummets or plumb bobs due to their shape, along with special medicine songs to bring about "anything from a sprinkle to a cloudburst" [Latta 1949: 200]. Like most shamans he also wore an elaborate costume during his rain-making ceremony, consisting of feathers from the magpie, crow, eagle, sparrow hawk, red-tailed hawk, and flicker.

See also *weather shamans*.

Sing
Navajo, *Southwest*
See *hatáál*.

Sinkakua

Kalispel, *Plateau*

A nocturnal hunting dance or ceremonial used to produce hunting medicine. During this rite, a drum made of a stiff rawhide is placed on the ground, and men beat on it with sticks. Both men and women participate in the ceremony, with the women standing behind the men and also singing. Included in the ceremony is the singing of personal power songs.

"Their most important hunts were directed by male shamans who used spirit powers to find animals, incantations and dances for success, and spirit songs, paints, rattles, and other charms to divine the conduct of the hunt" [Fahey 1986:35].

Sisene

Tolowa, *Oregon Seaboard*

Also: *sisenä.* Pains (see entry) [Drucker 1937:258]. Among the Tolowa, these disease-causing agents are removed by a sucking shaman, called *tinun.* Most often these are women who have had dreams of certain "pains," usually beginning in childhood, and have subsequently undergone a course of shamanic training, typically administered by a male relative. The training period is long and rigorous, and most novices do not become shamans until after they have matured. One aspect of the training is a dance held by the novice in an isolated spot. The novice fasts and dances for five days. Often during such dances the "novice might hear cry of yellowhammer, or see flicker of light. Pain approached until she could seize it, throwing it into mouth. She usually fell unconscious, assistants revived her, took to sweat house where male kin and hired singers waited" [Drucker 1937:258]. There the novice remained another ten nights for doctoring and learning to control her newly acquired pain. During the internment "when especially powerful song sung, 'she danced just like wild'; often entered trancelike state, ran to another sweat house, even to another town; men there had to sing for her. No

harm could befall her while in this state. Danced until able to vomit pain into acorn-soup basket, which she held before her; swallowed pain again, repeating until she could bring up easily, thus gaining control of pain, the object of dance" [Drucker 1937:258].

Once such pains are controllable, the novice begins to practice on patients who need pains removed. Such cases are most often diagnosed by a shaman who has clairvoyant powers but no power to remove pains. Then the *titun* "sucked it out through pipe, or by applying mouth directly; she usually fell back unconscious, 'the pain was so strong.' When recovered, danced, vomited pain into hands, displayed it; then danced until it disappeared" [Drucker 1937:258].

For less serious ailments a "talking" or "singing" shaman, called *tcäcä,* is called in. This is a member of a different class of shamans who use herbs and special formulas that are inherited or bought to treat illnesses. The treatments usually involve the *tcäcä* blowing an infusion of herbs over the patient while reciting special incantations. However, sometimes a *tcäcä* receives power songs via dreams. In this case the *tcäcä* sings her songs and smokes her pipe during her healing ceremony.

Siwad

Twana, *Northwest Coast*

A formal, intercommunity give-away ceremony. Although this was primarily a social ceremony in which gifts were graded and given according to social rank in order to validate one's social standing, it contained a final religious ritual. "Following formal distribution of gifts the give-away sponsor sang his wealth-power song as the terminating act of the gift-distribution ceremony. . . . This was in fact the way in which its owner publicly exhibited a s'iya´lt [see entry] power, the give-away substituting for the spirit dance in the case of this special class of spirit powers" [Elmendorf 1960:342–343].

The *siwad* and the *sxädab* (see entry) were the two most complex ceremonies of the Twana.

Siwín

Klallam/Comox, *Northwest Coast*

The term used by several Coast Salish cultures for magical spells. These spells are essentially an appeal for supernatural power and are most often evoked during life-crises ceremonies. They can be used for individuals or the community at large. *Siwín* can be possessed by anyone and are therefore not limited to shamans. A person using these spells acts as "an intermediary between the layman and certain supernatural forces over which the layman had no control" [Barnett 1955:129]. *Siwín* can manifest as hunting medicines, fishing medicines, love medicines, etc. The use of such spells seems to have been much more important in the Halkomelem-speaking area on Vancouver Island and along the Lower Fraser River.

"Siwín utilized a varied assortment of traditionally determined word formulas, gestures, acts, and objects (principally eagle down and red ocher). The knowledge of it was jealously guarded; the magical utterances especially were kept a secret. Sons inherited siwín secrets from fathers and daughters from mothers. The distinctive attributes of siwín were its association with family lines, its formalism, its antiquity, and its learned character. In all of these respects, it is to be distinguished from the prescriptions and behaviors enjoined by individual guardian spirits. At the same time it should be pointed out that the validity of siwín rested on its supernatural sanction. Presumably all forms of it were originally acquired in dreams, but one supernatural contact was sufficient; thereafter it was passed on by precept" [Barnett 1955:129]. In each of these spells, special names for the objects or persons to be influenced were recited.

Some forms of *siwín* found among the Nooksack "could numb the elk so it could not run from the hunter, paralyze the enemy so he would be powerless against the warrior, and deaden the feet of a rival in a foot race (and in modern times even the legs of a rival race horse)" [Amoss 1978:16]. Among the Maskwiam the family of

Chief Jack owned a rattle containing *siwín* that manifested as hunting medicine. "When the owner of the rattle shook it at a grizzly bear and sang a certain song, the animal was made dizzy, confused, and powerless" [Barnett 1955:54]. Among the Nanaimo one family owned *siwín* to call salmon. Their ritual was performed near Jack's Point, using a large rock upon which figures of different fish were incised. "When the salmon run was late, the ritualist painted over these figures with red ocher; at the same time he also painted bits of four different substances, including goat wool and a grass, and burned them at the foot of the rock" [Barnett 1955:89].

Sixwilexken

Shuswap, *Plateau*

A nineteenth-century shaman whose father was also shaman. His father's guardian spirits were Fire, Water, the Owl, and the Coyote, of which only the Water spirit was later acquired by Sixwilexken during his training. One time "Sixwi'lexken got very sick, and thought he would die. Then his guardian power appeared to him in a dream, and told him that if he cut his hair and made an offering of it to the sickness, he would recover. The next day he had his hair cut, and burned it in the fire, at the same time praying to the sickness. . . . After this he soon became well. In this way his guardian spirit saved his life twice" [Teit 1909:607].

In another incident Sixwilexken was called upon to treat a shaman who had gone insane.

An old shaman belonging to Clinton once lost his soul. He sang, and blood came from his mouth. He was wearing a marmot-skin robe fastened around the middle with a belt, and tied on his left shoulder. After singing, he went outside and gathered frozen excrements of the people, with which he filled the front part of his robe above the belt. Returning, he held up each piece before the people and ate them one after another. When he had finished, he sang again, and then went outside looking very wild. The people said, "His soul has gone from his body." When he came in again, he walked around, talking foolishly and looking wild. Then Sixwi´lexken—a shaman whose guardians were all helpful [i.e., the shaman was not a sorcerer]—asked him to sit down and smoke with him. Sixwi´lexken took his pipe out of his medicine-bag, and, filling it with tobacco, he lighted it with a stick at the fire. After taking a few puffs, he handed the pipe to the insane shaman. The latter took four puffs, and then cried like his guardian the fox. Sixwe´lexken put some water on the crown of the shaman's head and blew on it. Then, relighting the pipe, he took a few puffs and handed it back to the old man. The latter took a few puffs, and then fell down as if in a swoon. Very soon he arose and crawled over to his bed, where he lay down and fell fast asleep. When he awoke, Sixwe´lexken invited him to smoke again. He was now in his right mind, and smoked quietly, as was his wont. He conversed properly, and seemed to have no recollection of what he had done. When the people told him of it, he would not believe them [Teit 1909:614–615].

Siyalt

Twana, *Northwest Coast*

Wealth power [Elmendorf 1993:178]. A form of spirit power (*cshalt*—see entry) that is considered good *tamánanis* (see entry). *Siyalt* manifested in many different ways. For instance, it might come as the ability to bring a certain type of fish or animal, to win at certain gambling games, etc. It was the only form of *cshalt* in this culture that did not require performance of the *sccuctab* (see entry) [Elmendorf 1960:497]. Instead the owner of *siyalt* would have his wealth spirit's sacred song sung by the sponsor of a *siwad* (see entry), a giveaway ceremony.

Skaiyu

Snuqualmi, *Northwest Coast*

Plural: *skaikaiyu* [Waterman 1930:137]. Duwamish (or Dwamish) spirit of the dead, or ghost, that dwells in the Land of the Dead below and across a great river. During their Spirit Canoe (soul loss) Ceremony (see *sbetedaq* and *touchtd*), shamans must question such ghosts in

order to find the patient's lost soul. "A ghost acts differently from an ordinary man. He walks with his head thrown far back and his eyes closed. Moreover, he 'weaves' back and forth as he walks; that is with his right foot he steps far over to the left, and with his left foot he steps every time far over toward the right" [Waterman 1930:138].

Skelaletut

Salish, *Northwest Coast*

See *cshalt*.

Skep

Wishram, *Plateau*

Also: *skaiep.* Dialectical variants: *sxáyp* (Umatilla); *isxíp* (see entry) (Nez Perce). Spirit-ghost. The *skep* (pronounced scape) is the disembodied spirit of a deceased person. Coming into contact with a *skep* "may cause a wasting illness or death, on the one hand, or produce moodiness, uncontrollable behavior, or insanity on the other" [Boyd 1996:135]. Contact could be as slight as hearing the spirit's voice in a dream.

Shamans often acquire a *skep,* which confers curing power and powers of clairvoyance. Among the Coast Salish this spirit is associated with strength and war power. It is often depicted as a skeleton and thus is sometimes referred to as "skeleton power."

Sketotsut

Sanpoil, *Plateau*

A term used by the Colville branch for their special "to be cut in two" power ceremony, conducted only once each year by powerful *cpepqolitc* shamans. *Cpepqolitc* is a special kind of spirit-fish that is needed to perform this feat.

This spirit-fish came to the seance from the distant ocean and would not attend unless the shaman cut himself in two. It was the "boss" of all the other spirits that came to the seance and the most potent . . .

Before the people began to dance, three or four shamans hung up within the house a large mat, partitioning off a small space against the wall. A special door for the spirits opened into this compartment from the outside of the house. Nothing in the compartment was visible to the audience while the mat hung in place. The mat had been specially made before the dance and painted with human figures. Only the shamans handled it.

The seance was held after the people had danced for two or three nights. In preparation, the *cpEpqōlītc* shaman bound his waist tightly with a rope. His thumbs were tied behind him, and his big toes were also tied together, so that the animals could carry him conveniently by their tump-line. The other shamans then threw him under the mat partition into the sanctum. The congregation, having stopped dancing, sang his [the shaman's] power song. When they heard the toot of a little whistle from behind the mat, a whistle which the shamans had placed there or had tied to the top of the mat, they knew that the performer had been cut in two by the rope around his waist. They heard *cpEpqōlītc* come into the compartment and take him away, but they continued to sing his song. With the spirit of the 'big ling fish' [as it was translated] entered those of other fish, animals, and so on. The people could not see these, and with the exception of *cpEpqōlītc* the spirits did not address them, but could be heard "thumping around." The ling fish, whom the congregation called by name, responded in a thick muffled voice, like that of a toothless old man, and answered their inquiries with regard to lost articles, lost relatives, or the prospects for the immediate future, such as success in a war expedition. After about an hour of this, he told them that he had to hurry away to a seance at another Indian village. . . . The spirits who had carried the shaman away to the mountains returned him to the house after four or five hours, and threw him under the mat into the public room. He lay there unconscious, but the people restored him to his senses. . . . He then resumed his singing and dancing [Cline 1938:152–153].

Skinner, Alanson Buck

Anthropologist Alanson Skinner was born in Buffalo, New York, on September 7, 1886. He grew up on Staten Island, where he began to collect Native American artifacts. At the age of sixteen, he spent the summer working for the American Museum of Natural History excavating a shell mound on Long Island (near Shinnecock Hills). Two years later, in 1904, he went to western New York with an expedition from the Peabody Museum of Harvard to visit a reservation.

By 1907 he was taking courses at both Columbia and Harvard, and soon thereafter, in 1908, he led an expedition to study the Cree of the Hudson Bay area. This was followed in 1909 with an expedition to Wisconsin. By 1913 he had also visited the Seminole in Florida and made a detailed study of Algonquian archaeological sites in New York.

In 1916 he led an archaeological expedition to Costa Rica for the Museum of the American Indian, Heye Foundation. In 1918 he left the Heye Foundation to become the curator of anthropology at the Public Museum of Milwaukee. However, by 1924 he had returned to the Museum of the American Indian, where he remained until his untimely death on August 17, 1925, in an automobile accident near Tokio, North Dakota.

Skinner was remembered as a good-natured, friendly person who easily gained the confidence of his Native American informants. His wife, Dorothy Preston, was part Wyandotte. In addition to his early fieldwork among the Cree, he subsequently worked among the Northern Saulteaux, the Menomini, the Ioway, and the Mascouten (Prairie Potawatomi).

Skokum

Wishram, *Plateau*

Also: *skookum.* Term used by the Rev. Alvan Waller in 1845 to refer to the disease-causing object removed from a patient's body by a sucking shaman [Boyd 1996:121].

Skookum is also a term in Chinook jargon for "ghost or evil spirit"; it means "strong," as well [Boyd 1996:221].

Skukum

Quinault, *Northwest Coast*

A general class of guardian spirits whose name is often translated as "monsters" because of the general danger they pose to humans. "It was dangerous for two men to see a skukum monster, or even an animal guardian spirit [another class of spirits]. The skukum would not kill a man alone but would shout at and kill a group of persons" [Olson 1936:147].

"There was no sharp distinction between the 'real skuku′ms,' who were cannibal women named oε′h and those called skuku′m ma′ɬikulc or heca′itomixw (devil of the forest), who live in the high hills and mountains. . . . Most old people had one spirit of this type. For some reason it was known as an elk spirit. Some of the skukums were in the form of men. Lizzie Copalis lived for a time at Copalis beach. Many times a skukum came to her and talked. He told her never to marry, for he was her husband. He wore a blanket of elk skin with the hoofs attached. She kept these visitations secret until just before she died. Some skukums were said to be 'long, black and tall, with a human face.' They disappear at the approach of humans" [Olson 1936:146].

Skuykwi

Twana, *Northwest Coast*

Mountain whistler. The Skokomish name given to power obtained from the mountain marmot. The following is an account of its use by a shaman named Tyee Charley in curing an illness due to soul loss, some time around 1840:

> They put the sick man on a mat in the middle of the house and Tyee Charley came to him with a basket of water. And he began to sing. . . . And now Tyee Charley said, "That's my business; sickness is my business. And now my doctor power says he is going to cure this man." And now he sang his skuykwi song again. And he stopped. "Oh, this man was fishing way down the canal, north of here. And the little-earths [dwarf spirits] got him, they got him there, they took his shula [soul], and that's what makes him act crazy

and talk as if he was out of his head. And now I'm going to go down there and get him back from those little-earths."

And now he sang again and sent his skuykwi down the canal to get this sick man's soul back from the little-earths. And Tyee Charley just sat and sang while skuykwi was going after that man. And all the people there helped him sing.

And now skuykwi came back with that sick man's shula, and Tyee Charley stopped singing. And he told the people that his power had brought the man back all right. And he reached out in the air and took that man's shula from his power and held it in his cupped hands and then he put it on the man's head and stroked it in, without touching him. And he passed his hands up and down that man's body and pulled off a few little-earths he found sticking to him and bothering him. And now that man stopped raving and talking wild, and he sat up and looked around him. And that man told the people, "I don't know what I was doing. Where was I?" And he was all well now [Frank Allen in Elmendorf 1993:213].

Slahal

Twana, *Northwest Coast*

Also: *slahál.* Hand game, stick game, or bone game [Elmendorf 1960:239–240]; the gaming sticks (bones); also hand-game gambling powers [Elmendorf 1960:242, 490]. The game is played with two short bones or sticks held in one person's hands. The "ace" stick ("male *slahal*") is unmarked, and the other stick ("female *slahal*") has three bands of black thread around its middle third. The opponent must guess in which hand the "ace" is held in order to win. Since the mid-nineteenth century the game has been played with two people on a team holding a set of bones. The individuals manipulating the bones are called the bone shakers (*yadaxadab,* "works the arms" [Elmendorf 1960:242]), and their team leader is a person who has obtained special helping-spirit power for the game in the form of songs. "The bone shakers, while manipulating the bones, and their team mates, led by the team leader, sang as long as the bones were kept in motion. The singing stopped when the opponent leader pointed" [Elmendorf 1960:243]. These power songs were sung both to gain gambling power and to confuse the opposing leader.

Slahal power was a form of *cshalt* (see entry). "You have to get a special vision for slaha'l. The gambler may see the slaha'l bones in his vision. My cousin Solomon Balch, a Klallam who lived at Lummi, was hop picking at Puyallup. He had no luck in the gambling at the hop picking. He lost everything and had to walk home. On the way he lay down by the road to sleep, and he got a slaha'l song from a hazel bush there. My brother has his own slaha'l song, from loon spirit. He used to be head man on the Skokomish team (in intertribal gambling)" [Henry Allen in Elmendorf 1960:244].

Slahul

Twana, *Northwest Coast*
Dialectical variant: *luhalub*—Puget Sound [Elmendorf 1960:235]. Name of the disk gambling game and also of the "ace" black-edged disk. The game consists of a person guessing in which hand the ace disk has been hidden by his opponent. During the game players sing special *qwaxq* (see entry) power songs obtained from their guardian spirits in order to make the proper guess.

Slaolhtcu

Quinault, *Northwest Coast*
Also: *Slào'ltcà* [Olson 1936:145]. Literal translation: "in the west" [Olson 1936:154]. This phrase is used to refer to the whale guardian spirit, called the "western" spirit. Whale hunters need the help of some spirit to be successful in hunting, and this is the "ultimate" spirit for whalers. Use of this spirit is a form of individual hunting medicine. The following is an account of one man who acquired *Slaolhtcu:*

Hoh's grandfather achieved the ultimate in supernatural aid by acquiring the whale guardian spirit, which is called slào'ltcu (in the west). His

brother had died and as the surviving brother he went every day to a rocky island to mourn, and to bathe in a small creek. One day he noticed something at sea moving toward him. As it approached he saw that it was a beautiful woman with flowing hair and feet shaped like the tail of a whale. He fell unconscious and was placed in a whale-shaped canoe by the woman. They traveled to the other side of the ocean, passed through a narrows to another ocean, and turned into a bay. They went into a house where the sena'xos and whale spirits lived. (They are brothers and the woman was their sister.) They showed him the lines, harpoons, floats, etc., to use in whaling, and gave him the lightning power which is used in whaling. (That is why there is thunder and lightning when a man harpoons a whale. The whaler calls for his helper, who gives him superhuman strength. Without such help no one could kill a whale.)

When he returned to his home he fell ill from an over-abundance of power. He lay at the point of death for two months. He could neither eat nor drink, and could not speak above a whisper. His relatives hired famous shamans to cure him but they could do nothing. Finally a woman shaman came. She told what he had seen in his vision and said that he was ill because his soul had remained at the spirit village. She got a man helper to hold her rattle, sprinkled eagle and seagull down about, and the two went [in trance] to the spirit village. Within a day they had brought the soul back [i.e., the shaman's soul-retrieval ceremony lasted one day]. In a few days he was able to take a little food. He drank only water from a special spring, as the spirit had ordered. Every day he sang the songs the spirits had given him. When his strength had returned he went out in his canoe to hunt. His power was so great that porpoises and other animals died before he could hurl his harpoon. Later he speared whale. He would talk to his guardian spirit and a fair wind would come which enabled them to raise the sail and tow the whale home. During his life he speared 77 whales. . . . In potlatches he used to sing his paddling, harpooning, and fair wind [power] songs. He used to drink gallons of whale oil at a single draught, then spew it on the fire, making

Edward S. Curtis, The Whaler—Makah, *1915. Photogravure.*

the flames roar up to the smokehole" [S.H. in Olson 1936:154–155].

Small Ankle
Hidatsa, *Plains*

A shaman from the Midipadi band who died in 1888. One of his medicines was known as bear-claws medicine. He had obtained this when he was about thirty years old, following a buffalo hunt in which a bear was killed. The bear was skinned, leaving the skull and paws intact.

> He [Small Ankle] then took off his clothes. He then pierced the dead bear's nose with his knife and put a rope through the hole. He then had a man pierce the muscles of his back in two places; he thrust a stick between and fastened a rope to the stick so that my father might drag the bear's head and skin.
>
> All day until evening my father dragged the bear-skin in a lonely place. At evening he came toward camp. Something caught as if the bear-skin had been snagged on something. At the same time he heard a sound like a live bear, *Sh-sh-sh-sh!* He looked back and the bear-skin had stretched out its legs as it lay on the ground, as if it were alive. He then came back to the camp, and then the other men released him from the bear-skin.
>
> That night he dreamed the bear showed him how to cure sick people. He was to sing a mystery song, which the bear taught him, and to take the piece of buffalo-felt and hold it out toward the sick man, when the sick man would recover. . . .
>
> When my father awoke he lost no time in getting the piece of felt. . . .
>
> After that when men were sick they sent for my father, who cured them, and he was paid many horses (Wolf Chief in Pepper and Wilson 1908:305).

This bear-claws medicine consisted of two bear's claws, a bear's tooth, and a lock of Small Ankle's hair wrapped up in buffalo felt (buffalo hair that is shed in mats during the summer).

Subsequently, Small Ankle passed his medicines over to his son, Wolf Chief (see entry).

Smohalla
Wallawalla, *Plateau*

Literal translation: "a Sahaptin term meaning dreamer" [Du Bois 1938:5]. A renowned Wanapam shaman/prophet of the nineteenth century who was "just one prophet in a whole series of Washani [see entry] dreamers" [Du Bois 1938:5]. He was the founder of the Smohalla cult of the Middle Columbia River area, of which Chief Joseph of the Nez Perces was "among the most devoted believers" [Mooney in Hodge 1910:603]. "He belonged to the Sokulk, a small tribe cognate to the Nez Percés and centering about Priest rapids on the Columbia in eastern Washington. He was born around 1815 or 1820 . . . and began to preach around the year 1850" [Mooney in Hodge 1910:602–603]. Eventually "all the river tribes went to the Walula meeting. There were Umatilla, Walla Walla, Nez Percé, Cayuse, Yakima and Warm Springs people there—all the people from the Snake and Columbia Rivers" [Martin Spidish (Wishram) in Du Bois 1938:12]. However, the Wasco did not join this cult because a drum was used in their meetings.

Smoking Star
Blackfoot, *Plains*

A nineteenth-century shaman. When anthropologist Clark Wissler first met Smoking Star, the shaman was over ninety years old and "was regarded as by far the oldest living Blackfoot" [Wissler 1922:45]. As a youth he offered a pipe to an old shaman named Medicine Bear and asked the shaman to train him for a vision quest. Medicine Bear undertook the training, and subsequently the youth received a vision from the Smoking Star (Mars), which told him to take the star's name and said that he would have powers.

Thereafter Smoking Star became a successful war leader and scout, but later in life his interests turned toward conducting ritual via sacred societies. He spent years learning the medicine of the beaver bundle and eventually became the leader of the Beaver society.

An undated woodcut of Smohalla and his priests.

Smoking Star told Wissler: "In the course of time everyone came to look upon me as a shaman. No one will now walk before me as I sit in a tepee [a common taboo regarding shamans]. In my presence all are dignified and orderly and avoid frivolous talk. Four times in my life the Smoking-Star has stood before me. All visions are sacred, as are some dreams, but when a vision appears the fourth time, it is very holy. Even a shaman may not speak of it freely. Many times have I gone to lonely places and cried out to the powers of the air, the earth, and the waters to help me understand their ways. Sometimes they have answered me, but all the truly great mysteries are beyond understanding" [Smoking Star in Wissler 1922:61].

Smudging rites

The act of purifying a ritual object, person, or ceremony with the smoke from a burning plant. The plants most frequently used in North America are sweet grass *(Savastana odorata)*, wormwood *(Artemesia spp.)*, tobacco, and different varieties of sage/sagebrush and cedar/juniper. The smoke is used to drive off evil spirits and influences. Nearly all Native American sacred ceremonies integrate some form of smudging.

See also *purification rites*

Snäem

Coast Salish, *Northwest Coast*

The term used by the Sanetch division for the "spirits of shamans or doctors" [Barnett 1955:

148]. Most shamans are males, but females may also obtain shamanic powers. "Young men striving to become shamans were expected to get most of their powers before marriage. Typically, their attempts to acquire spirit helpers rendered them unconscious at the moment of contact and caused them to have hemorrhages [in the nose]. Their favorite method of hastening spirit contact was to dive into lakes and remain submerged until consciousness was lost. Sometimes a heavy rock was carried into deep water. Sexually weak or inverted individuals were not likely to become shamans" [Barnett 1955:149].

Most shamans seek to acquire more than one spirit helper. Certain animals confer specific powers. For example, the spirit of the Woodpecker aids one in canoe making, the spirit of the Yellow Jacket aids one in fighting, and the spirit of the Owl confers the power of clairvoyance. Once powers are obtained, it is up to the shaman to decide when he will begin his practice. "The 'good' shaman very often began his career with four attempts at curing without accepting any pay" [Barnett 1955:149].

It is common for a shaman to attempt to transfer some of his power to one of his sons, but in such cases the spirit itself was not passed on. "Spirit power manifested itself as a rodlike thing welling up in the throat and chest. After the shaman had worked himself into the proper state, he clutched his power and made motions of thrusting it into his son; then he blew on the boy's chest and smoothed the power down with his hands. But passive participation in this 'transfer' ritual was only a preliminary preparation for the boy. He still had to go through the same training as other boys and was required to have his own personal spirit encounter" [Barnett 1955:149].

See also *siaiuklw.*

Snake Dance
Hopi, *Southwest*
See *Chüawimkya.*

Snam
Thompson, *Plateau*
Spirit helper. This is the term used by the Nkamtcinemux division located on the upper part of the Thompson River and by the Nlakapamuxoe division located around the confluence of the Thompson and Fraser Rivers in British Columbia. Teit [1898:53] referred to *snam* as a "protecting spirit," and in his footnote 167 [p. 111] it is equated with the Algonquian term *manitou* (EONAH, p. 164).

Almost everyone has some form of guardian spirit, which is most often acquired during puberty ceremonials. The Thompson are most unusual in that their guardian spirit may be a part of something else, such as bird's down, a tree stump, the top of a mountain, the feet of a man, or pine cones [Teit 1900:354–355].

See also *haxa.*

Soahubiere
Mono, *Basin*
Literal translation: "talker" [Gifford 1932:51]. Monachi (Western Mono) term for a singing shaman [Gifford 1932:51]. See *puhake.*

Sodality
An anthropological term referring to "an association based on voluntary or involuntary membership. Sodalities are often religious societies limited to a single objective" [Winick 1968:493]. For an example see *medicine societies.*

Sokăpofkĭkî
Seminole, *Southeast*
Literal translation: "to blow into liquid" [Sturtevant 1954b:172]. A Mikasuki term for a medicine tube used by shamans. The tubes are usually from 10 to 18 inches in length and made from a reed, vine, or sawgrass. Some tubes are more than 1/2 inch in diameter, but none are decorated. These tubes are filled with plant medicines mixed in water, which are blown over the patient or into a bowl of prepared medicine.

The use of such medicine tubes is also known among the Creek, Yuchi, Catawba, and Cherokee, where their tubes often reach 2 feet in length and are made from cattails.

Another term for the medicine tube among the Mikasuki is *iskăpofkĭkĭ,* meaning "to blow in liquid with" [Sturtevant 1954b:172].

Sokot
Maidu, *California*

Dialectical variants: *sol* (Nevada County Nisenan); *soloya* (Northern Maidu) [Dixon 1905:268]; *sokoti* (Concow Maidu) [Jewell 1987:149]; *sohkosa, sokossa* (Central Miwok) [Gifford n.d. a:19]. Term used by the Placer County Nisenan (Southern Maidu) for a particular type of shaman's rattle, made by attaching several cocoons to a stick [Beals 1933:398]. Such cocoon rattles are used by shamans throughout central California and extending into the Basin area. In most cases the cocoons from the genus *Attacus* are used [Kroeber 1925:419]; they are filled with pebbles before being attached to the stick.

Another term given for the cocoon rattle among the Southern Maidu is *wososo* [Gifford 1927:241]. Among the Pomo the cocoon rattle is known as *wayoi* [Freeland 1923:59], among the Miwok as *sokossa* or *sohkosa* (see *alini*), and among the Monachi (Western or Northfolk Mono) as *sanadj* [Gifford 1932:50].

Throughout central California the cocoon rattle is one of the major implements used by shamans and thus is also a sign of his office. Jewell [1987:149] reported that during a healing ceremony, "the rattle would be taken by a spirit from the doctor's hand and would fly about, rattling." Anthropologist Bertha Parker Thurston was, in the early 1930s, a patient of a Maidu shaman named Jim Stevens. During the healing ceremony conducted on her, "Jim called the wind from the north, and it suddenly started blowing very hard, making the canvas slap. . . . The rattle would leave his hand and travel all around the tent. . . . A strange bluish light started to play around the top of the tent. . . .

The stove lids kept up an incessant rattle" [Thurston in Jewell 1987:151].

Solhằtłiu
Alsea, *Oregon Seaboard*

Guardian spirit [Drucker 1939:98]. Although it is possible to acquire minor powers from a chance encounter with a spirit, the more powerful guardian spirits must be acquired via a solitary quest in the woods.

There were a variety of supernatural beings which one might meet. Many kinds of birds and animals and a few natural phenomena (sun, moon, comet, thunder, west wind) were potential guardian spirits. There were also beings, such as a long-haired female woods sprite (osun), who gave power. A person might have several subsidiary spirits besides the main one: in fact, the more powerful shamans usually had a number of spirits. Laymen knew about the spirits only in a general way; people who had them were secretive about their experiences with the supernatural. Apparently the being appeared in a dream after the seeker had fasted, bathed, and remained alone long enough. In this dream or vision, the guardian told his protégé how and when to train, visiting him in dreams from time to time to instruct him in the shamanistic arts. Songs, special regalia and paints, and similar tokens, would be "given" to the novice in this fashion. The latter continued his training in secret for a fairly long time, often until after he had reached maturity [Drucker 1939:98].

Solia
Cowichan, *Northwest Coast*

A dialectical variant of the Coast Salish *sulia* (EONAH, p. 266) used by the Tcileqeuk division of the Halkomelem and, in this case, meaning a person's guardian spirit. "Not only the shamans, but every other Indian, had one or more guiding or protecting 'spirits.' . . . There was a vital need of a protecting 'influence' or 'spirit' in their lives. This 'guide,' 'protector,' 'influence,' 'power,' 'charm'—for it partakes of the character of all these—the Tcil'Qē´uk call by the name of *su'lĩa* or *so'lĩa*. This is the abstract or nominal form of the verb *u'lĩa,* 'to dream'" [Hill-Tout 1903:361–362]. The *solia* comes to an individual through either a dream or a vision.

See also *sqelam.*

Songs

From a Native American perspective songs imbue one's voice with power. For this reason shamans regularly address their helping spirits via songs. During the aspiring shamans' vision quests, a spirit, if it appears, almost always reveals powers to the shaman in the form of sacred songs, which the novices must learn in order to recall the revealed power. The power inherent in song is recognized by all Native American people, not just shamans. But the power is not inherent in the words themselves because "Indian song texts largely do not say anything that one can translate into ordinary speech" [Fenton 1942:3]. As Reichard [1950: 279–280, 282] stated: "Songs among the Navaho, as among other Indian tribes, may be distinguished by syllables, which on the surface seem to have no meaning. Furthermore, syllables that have meaning may be separated by syllables whose chief function is to fit the word to the music: that is, words and sentences are lengthened by the addition of syllables, either by insertion or by increment. . . . Navaho ritual contains many onomatopoeic elements which may exist independently without 'word content' or may be stems, parts of words depending upon grammatical forms. For this reason, and because other unusual devices are incorporated in the ritual, it seems quite possible that the nonsense syllables may have a meaning to one who understands the

A group of Native Americans beats a drum and sings at a powwow in Wisconsin in 1992.

full context of a rite, even if they never became linguistic forms."

"Song was not simply self-expression. It was a magic which called upon the powers of Nature and constrained them to man's will. People sang in trouble, in danger, to cure the sick, to confound their enemies, and to make the crops grow. . . . The power of song was an honor to be earned; it could not be assumed lightly at the mere whim of an individual. The describing of a desired event in the magic of beautiful speech was to them the means by which to make that event take place. All their songs describe such desired events, and besides the songs there are stately ritual orations intended for the same purpose. . . . Magic will be worked if the description is vivid and if the singing or the recitation is done, as it should be, at the right time and with the right behavior, on behalf of all the people" [Underhill 1938:5–6].

The relationship between song and power is clearly evidenced in the Iroquois term *orenda* (EONAH, p. 208), which, among other things, refers to the shaman's power via his or her helping spirit(s). *Orenda* is glossed as "song." Furthermore, the current idiom for *sing* "originally meant 'stand up (raise) supernatural power'" [Chafe in Isaacs 1977:169].

Power songs are among a person's most precious possessions, and no one has the right to sing another person's song. In order to obtain that right, one typically must pay the owner for its use. Even prayers were most often delivered via a chant in some form. As a Netsilik shaman told Rasmussen: "Songs are thoughts, sung out with the breath when people are moved by great forces and ordinary speech no longer suffices" [Rasmussen in Merkur 1991:54].

More extensive in number than the power songs of individual shamans are the sacred songs used in the lengthy, complex rituals of those cultures containing organized religious societies. For instance, Reichard [1950:286] reported that "the number of Navaho songs is incalculable." One of her informants knew 447 songs for the Hail Chant alone. It is not unusual for certain members of such cultures to be selected as "keepers" of such songs. These individuals are remarkable for their ability to hold in memory a great number of songs. For example, among the Seneca at Coldspring during the 1930s, John Johnny Channey was the leading song master. Then a singer of fifty years, it was reported that his "knowledge must approach a thousand verses of two score ceremonies" [Fenton 1942:5].

See also *Matak, Tony, sumesh, swis̆, torniwoq.*

Sorcery
See *witchcraft.*

Sore-Eye Bill
Twana, *Northwest Coast*

A man who received, circa 1860, a hunting power that enabled him to spear many porpoises. An account of his power follows:

> Sore-eye Bill's father was a gambler. One time when he was gambling, and losing, [Sore-Eye Bill] happened to be looking on, with a blanket around him. And when his father had lost everything he turned to Bill, took the blanket off his back, bet it, and lost that too.
>
> This was such shame to [Sore-Eye Bill] that he went up to . . . Tekiu Point, a point about nine miles north of Dewatto, intending either to get power or commit suicide. He went out on the point and into the water, and then dived, holding on to some rocks wrapped up in cedar bark.
>
> When he reached the bottom somebody opened a door for him and he saw a beautiful land, filled with sunlight. The next he knew, he was in a canoe and the waves were rolling and rocking him. He saw a porpoise on either side of the canoe. This meant that he would have power to be *sča'c'us* (porpoise hunter) and spear many porpoises. Then he came to and found himself on the beach . . .
>
> [But Sore-Eye Bill] never made much use of his *siyalt* power. He showed his power and sang it, but it never did much for him [Henry Allen in Elmendorf 1993:166–167].

Sori wokang
Tewa, *Southwest*

Literal translation: "large treatment" [Hill 1982:330]. This is an annual purification ceremony conduced at Santa Clara Pueblo. (Many other pueblos hold a similar ceremony.) The purpose of the ritual is "to cleanse the tribal territory and everything it contained of witches and their malignant influences" [Hill 1982:330–331]. Four days are needed to perform this ceremony, which is usually conducted by members of the Bear societies (see *Wanke*) in March or April.

Sometimes the performance of the *Sori wokang* is preceded by another purification ceremony known as *Poje,* or Meeting of Waters [Hill 1982:336]. In this ceremony the villagers, assembled in a *kiva* (EONAH, p. 136), have crosses drawn on their hands, on the tops and soles of their feet, and on their shoulders with black earth obtained from the bottom of a swamp. The *Poje* is performed only in conjunction with the *Sori wokang.*

Spirit flight

This term refers to the shaman's ability to relocate his consciousness to any point in space. This is usually done with the assistance of the shaman's helping spirit. Thus, the shaman is said to ride on the back of his helping spirit or be taken by the hand by his spirit, etc., to the desired location. Shamans make such journeys to find out what is going on at other locations. Spirit flights are used to find missing persons, to locate lost objects (see entry), to find the whereabouts of one's enemy, to locate game, to retrieve lost or straying souls, etc.

Spirit flights are a common element in vision quests. Quite frequently, when a helping spirit appears to the novice shaman, he takes the novice to another location to teach him and impart powers to him. It is not uncommon for such flights to extend to the moon or even to distant stars because the shaman's consciousness in this state of being is no longer bound by the parameters of space and time. Consequently, very long spaces can be covered in a very short period of time.

An Alaskan Eskimo mask probably representing a shaman's spirit flight, with the face in the center representing the shaman's soul.

Less frequently the shaman's body also relocates in space.

For examples see *angalkuk, Asetcuk, bear medicine/possession, hmuga, Ilimarneq, inipi, mituk, nakadzoq, pawágan, sqelam, tornarsuk, tuavitok, Yayatü Society.*

Spirit intrusion

A form of spirit possession (EONAH, pp. 261–262) in which some form of evil spirit enters the body of a victim, causing that person to become ill. As such, spirit intrusion is often diagnosed as a cause of disease in Native North America. The removal of the disease-causing spirit usually requires the aid of a shaman, and the cure most often utilizes some form of frightening the intruding spirit away.

A shaman's face mask, probably representing the spirit of the devilfish.

Spirits

The notion that what is termed *spirits* are a reality is a relatively recent and increasingly popular concept among anthropologists. For the most part anthropologists throughout history have avoided the issue of spirits and have been satisfied merely to classify them in some manner. In fact, many anthropologists have tried to ensure that they disassociate themselves from any belief in spirits. In their ethnographic reports, this attitude is expressed through the use of personal qualifiers, such as "it is believed," "it is said," "it is supposed," "they have the notion," etc. This approach serves only to clutter the literature with personal, ethnocentric misconceptions regarding shamanism.

However, "a field of study is beginning to develop in the anthropology of consciousness and the anthropology of religion, in which researchers do experience what their field people experience. They take their experience seriously and record them in the spirit of the natural historian. . . . Ritual experience proves itself to be true and valid *in use,* not as a preordained system of structure. In exactly this way, the Iñupiat's [i.e., formerly Eskimo] spirit-related life has validity in use. Ritual is a matter of process; symbols live when in use" [E. Turner 1996:231]. In the United States this trend has manifested itself in the recent formation of the Society for the Anthropology of Consciousness. The basic premise of this organization is that spirits do have a reality and can no longer be perceived as simply the workings of a primitive imagination or a disturbed mind. That is, we can no longer remain ethnocentric with regard to our own concepts of reality when dealing with the spirit phenomena associated with shamanism.

I, myself, am a member of this anthropological society, and like many of the members, I have had numerous direct experiences of spirit manifestations during my two decades of fieldwork among Lakota shamans. As Turner has noted, these spirit perceptions and spirit experiences come in flashes. "This 'flash' characteristic shows the elusiveness of the subject matter and teaches the need for the utmost caution in the matter of ethnographic documentation. No dogmatic statements can be made" [E. Turner 1996:230]. Furthermore, it must be acknowledged that when it comes to the matter of spirits, it is a philosophic "need to know that we know" that seems to drive the Western mind to present a "rational" view of spirits.

For the shamans this is not the case. Spirits, for the most part, remain a "mystery" to them, with no uneasiness about that on their part. When it comes to the use of spirit powers, their attitude is more one of "whatever works"; they do not try to understand how the spirits work. What is known is that "the ability to have these experiences is like the use of a faculty, eyesight for instance, something one uses continually" [E. Turner 1996:224].

This ability derives from the fact that, as contemporary physics has shown, the universe at the deepest level is completely interconnected. The human ability to directly sense this reality, when developed, gives rise to the reality of spirits. That is, one experiences spirit powers when one is attuned to the inner connectedness of everything. This connectedness is "the Kingdom of Heaven," and it is to be found within one's being, as Socrates long ago admonished in his "know thyself" statement. As Turner [1996:232] concluded, "We may have to come to terms with the fact that we are not the only souls occupying this earth, that there are indeed other entities, and that the sense needed to communicate with them requires a little care to develop. . . . Put one's hands in it, and it flows off like water. But the hands feel it."

Spŭtu
Klamath, *California*
Vision quest [Spier 1930:94]. It is common for a man to seek supernatural power at the birth of a first child, although such quests can be undertaken at any time. In many cases the quest is for a specific power—for gambling, hunting, wealth, etc. "The experience does not ordinarily include a vision, but is made manifest in a song heard in a dream. In some instances where a vision is had, a dream song follows, but it is clear that the latter is the essential experience" [Spier 1930:94].

"Power is sought in lonely spots on the mountains, in mountain pools, in eddies in the rivers, in all places where spirits are known to dwell" [Spier 1930:94–95]. Such known locations of spirit power are called *spŭtuks* [Spier 1930:98]. "The formula prescribes fasting for a number of nights on the mountains, continually running about and piling up rocks, combined with diving into lonely pools, or following the latter plan alone by diving beneath whirlpools in the river or lakes which spirits are known to haunt. The supplicant loses consciousness and wakes to find himself on the shore bleeding profusely from the mouth and nose. He does not ordinarily have a vision, but success is manifested in a song heard in a dream on a night soon following" [Spier 1930:239]. "Power may be sought at any time during the year, but they do not dive for it until

the first willow buds appear (in the seventh month, March or April)" [Spier 1930:96]. When so done, "the spirit appears standing in the water and then disappears, or it drags the swimmer below the water for the purpose of devouring him" [Spier 1930:95]. "Such persons only who have been trained during five years for the profession of conjurers can see these spirits, but by them they are seen as clearly as we see the objects around us" [Gatschet in Spier 1930:104]. Spirits of this type come in many different forms—animals, dwarfs, reptiles (especially frogs), mythical beings such as a horned water snake, clouds, thunder, lightning, rainbow, etc. "The number of spirits is indefinitely large" [Spier 1930:103].

See also *kiuks, swiĭs.*

Sqelam
Cowichan, *Northwest Coast*
Dialectical variant: *sqenäm* (Kwantlen) [Hill-Tout 1903:413]. Literal translation: "to heal or make well" [Hill-Tout 1903:361]. The term used by the Tcileqeuk for a shaman. The Tcileqeuk and the Kwantlen are two of about fourteen separate bands located along the Fraser River that are collectively referred to as the Halkomelen (or Henkomenem) [Hill-Tout 1903:355], a division of the Cowichan. In addition to the *sqelam,* there are also *olia* and *yeuwa.*

The *olia,* derived from *ulia,* meaning "to dream" [Hill-Tout 1903:361], is a shaman who uses his (or her) power to cure wounds and other bodily injuries. "His chief function, however, was to interpret dreams and visions, as his name indicates. He was specially skilled in the reading of omens and portents. Other of his functions were to take charge of the bodies of the dead and prepare them for burial, and protect the people from the evil influence of the *palakoe'tsa,* or ghosts of the dead. . . . The O'lia figured also in the puberty and other social customs of the tribe" [Hill-Tout 1903:364].

The *yeuwa,* derived from *yeuwa,* meaning "to bewitch or enchant" [Hill-Tout 1903:361], is a sorcerer or witch. These shamans are the "last in rank" and deal "in *seu'wa,* or witchcraft" [Hill-Tout 1903:364]. Among the Kwantlen the term *seuwa* is used for a sorcerer [Hill-Tout 1903:413].

The function of the *sqelam* is

> to restore health and vigour to the body when prostrate or suffering from some inward sickness or malady, as when under the . . . influence of some spell or enchantment. He was pre-eminently the "pathologist" of the tribe. . . . He alone had the power to restore a lost soul or spirit . . . or drive out a disease caused by a magic spell or by witchcraft. To effect the former he would go apart by himself, crouch down, and cover his head and shoulders with a mat, and permit himself to pass into a trance state, when his soul . . . would leave his body and go in search of that of the patient. . . . To effect the latter he beats a stick or board, and sings and dances round the patient. To acquire these powers he usually underwent a long and secluded training in some lonely spot in the forest or on the margin of some lake. This training consisted in prolonged fasts, trances, body washings and exercises, accompanied by invocations of the Mysteries. His "medicine," or "power" . . . was bestowed upon him by his guiding spirit or spirits, who appear to him and instruct him in dreams and visions. Another of his functions was to conduct the mortuary sacrifices. He is, *par excellence,* the "Master of the 'Mysteries'" [Hill-Tout 1903:361].

See also *solia.*

Sqenäm
Cowichan, *Northwest Coast*
Also: *seuwen; seuwa.* The term used by the Kwantlen division for shaman [Hill-Tout 1902: 413]. Barnett [1955:148, n. 2] equates this term with the Sanetch term *snäem* (see entry).

Sqeqet
Shuswap, *Plateau*
Literal translation: "Spider" [Teit 1909:614]. A nineteenth-century shaman who lived at Soda Creek. The following is an account of a cere-

mony that he conducted to rid his village of an impending epidemic, which the villagers called the "mystery sickness":

> He and three other shamans cut four sticks, and, sharpening the points, stuck them into the ground. Then putting on their mat masks, their souls went to search for the sickness. It was very hot weather, and the people squatted on the ground near by, watching them. The shamans called out, "We need to go far. See, it is coming here, we will meet it!" They ordered the people away some distance. At last they said, "It has arrived." Now they told the sickness or mystery to leave, or to return whence it came, but it would not go back, and the shamans could not make it return. Neither could it pass them. Then the shamans took their sticks and dug a hole in the ground. Now the mystery tried to pass the shamans; and when it came to the mysterious powers [their guardian spirits] with which they intercepted it, the combat was so violent that the earth shook as with an earthquake, and the people's dogs, which were tied, broke their halters and ran away, yelping with fear. The children also began to cry. Then the shamans seized the sickness, and with much exertion pushed it into the hole they had dug. It got out several times, but they rolled it back again with their sticks, and at last covered it with some earth. They said to it, "You must go away beyond the habitations of people, and must not come out of the earth this side of Fort George, for beyond that place there are no people." At last the mystery left, and, traveling underground, came out beyond Fort George in the shape of a gale of wind, which blew northward so violently that it devastated the country, in some places overturning all the trees. No other Shuswap shamans were able to master "mystery sickness" like those of Soda Creek [Teit 1909:614].

Sqwacathl
Twana, *Northwest Coast*
Skokomish squirrel power. This was one form of *swadash* (see entry). A shaman named Squaxon Bill, who lived during the mid-nineteenth century at North Bay in Squaxon country, was

known to have used squirrel power to harm people. "That's a pretty clever little power. . . . Now when he [Squaxon Bill] got mad, other doctors could find his squirrel power anywhere. They couldn't track him, couldn't kill him. When Squaxon Bill was mad at a person he'd . . . shoot his power into them, and the other doctors could never find it. . . . That was all his power was good for, to shoot people with, he never used it in curing . . . but they could never get at that squirrel of his. And no one ever heard his song, he never doctored with it" [Frank Allen in Elmendorf 1993:216].

Stephen, Alexander M.

Alexander M. Stephen was born in Scotland. After graduating from the University of Edinburgh, he immigrated to the United States and served for three years with Company A, 92nd New York Infantry, during the Civil War. Eventually he traveled to the Southwest, where he befriended Navajo trader Tom Keam (at Keam's Canyon, Arizona) and learned to speak Navajo.

By 1882 he was assisting Victor Mindeleff in his study of Hopi architecture. Eventually Stephen lived in both a Tewa and a Hopi household. Initially he communicated with the Hopi in Navajo, but he went on to learn the Hopi language itself, although subsequent scholars have realized that he never became fluent in it. In 1890 J. Walter Fewkes (see entry) realized Stephen's unique position among the Hopi and hired him as part of the Hemenway Southwest Expedition. Fewkes hired Stephen to live among the Hopi mainly to gain insight into their religious life. Stephen was most successful at this effort, having already been adopted by the Hopi and initiated into three of their religious societies. Most of his work was done on First Mesa. He continued taking notes on the Hopi from 1891 until his death from tuberculosis in April 1894. At the time of his death, Stephen was under treatment from a traditional Hopi shaman named Yellow Bear (see entry).

Eventually his detailed notes were edited, beginning in 1922, by Elsie Clews Parsons (see entry), and they were published in 1936 by Columbia University Press in a massive, two-volume work. Of Stephen's notes Parsons commented:

The notebooks are written in pencil so clearly that seldom is a word illegible. Even the notes made in the obscurity of a kiva or outdoors under stress of weather are usable. . . . There are undoubtedly many errors in these linguistic notes due both to the recorder and to the editor, nevertheless they may prove useful to the student of Hopi language, particularly in a study of ritual terminology which consists of obsolete terms and in itself tends to become obsolete. . . . Stephen was learning to speak Hopi. Had his accomplishment in the language continued, he would have been distinguished in interpreting the ceremonials as well as in recording them. As it is, as far as he goes, and he goes farther than Voth, his only rival in the field, his understanding is reliable. He had opportunities for observation that, one fears, will never again be afforded [Stephen 1936:xxi].

Stevenson, Matilda Coxe

Matilda ("Tilly") Coxe Evans was born in Texas on May 12, 1849, and moved with her family to Washington, D.C. In 1868 she studied chemistry and geology at the Army Medical School in Washington, D.C., although women at that time were not given degrees. She married Col. James Stevenson, a self-taught geologist, naturalist, and anthropologist from Kentucky, in April 1872. During the 1870s she accompanied her husband on federal geological field expeditions to the Southwest, where she first became acquainted with the Zuni. In 1879 her husband was appointed director of the first collecting and research expedition to the Southwest, then sponsored by the newly formed Bureau of Ethnology (later called Bureau of American Ethnology). John Wesley Powell, a friend of Stevenson's, was the new director of the bureau, and Tilly was allowed to go along on her husband's expedition as the official "volunteer co-adjutor in ethnology" [Parezo 1993:40] of the expedition. Joining the expedition were photographer John K. Hillers and ethnologist Frank Hamilton Cushing. Cushing trained Tilly in ethnographic technique, and she began her fieldwork by learning the Zuni language. Thereafter, the focus of her fieldwork was on the role of women in Zuni society.

By the 1880s she was one of the first woman anthropologists in the field (e.g., see Hewitt). Thus Tilly was able to access information (on such topics as pregnancy, childbirth, sex, infant care, and women's roles) that was absolutely inaccessible to male researchers [Parezo 1993:40]. This caused Margaret Mead and Ruth Bunzel to subsequently write that "Matilda Coxe Stevenson was the first American ethnologist to consider children and women worthy of notice" [Parezo 1993:41]. However, it was Cushing who recognized this hole in his ethnographic work, and he therefore trained Matilda to do fieldwork in exactly those areas that were not accessible to male anthropologists.

In 1888 Matilda's husband died of heart failure brought on by Rocky Mountain tick fever. Two years later, Matilda became the first (and only) woman ever to receive a permanent appointment with the Bureau of Ethnography. Her fieldwork extended to other pueblos such as Jemez, Sia, and the Hopi. Her work at Sia was published in 1894. By then her fieldwork also focused on religious ceremonies, particularly among the Zuni, all of which resulted in her classic manuscript entitled "The Zuni Indians: Their Mythology, Esoteric Fraternities, and Ceremonies"; it was published in 1904 in the *23rd Annual Report of the Bureau of American Ethnology*. Like Cushing, Matilda also adopted the field technique of "participant observation" among the Zuni "by adopting their dress, painting her face, and witnessing all their secret rites" [Stevenson in Parezo 1993:41]. However, she was not as well accepted by the Zuni as was Cushing, most likely because of her condescending attitude toward Native Americans, whom

she regarded as "superstitious" and "barbarous people" [Parezo 1993:48].

Matilda remained employed by the bureau until her death on June 24, 1915. Like most women at that time, she was undersalaried. She began in 1890 at an annual salary of $1,500 (her husband's salary in 1888 was $3,000), which was raised to $1,800 in 1907. In 1905 she began a comparative study of Pueblo religions, which was never completed primarily because of her inability to elicit secret information from field informants. However, she did manage to publish several articles on the Tewa of San Ildefonso, among whom she lived during the last years of her career. She remained influential in Washington and lobbied for the right of Native Americans to practice their own religions, even as such practices were being declared illegal by reservation agents (the Sun Dance, for instance, had already been abolished).

Sthlkeyin
Klallam, Northwest Coast
See *cshalt.*

Sthlqet
Twana, *Northwest Coast*
Literal translation: "early daylight" [Elmendorf 1960:488]. A spirit who grants war power (called *schalaq*—see entry). This is one of the few instances among the Twana in which a natural phenomenon, in this case the light at sunrise, acts as a helping spirit to an individual.

Stick swallowing
Pueblo, *Southwest*
See *Hakan, Nasosotan, Onayanakia, Piännithle, Shotikianna.*

Stlalcop-schudoptch
Snuqualmi, *Northwest Coast*
The Duwamish (or Dwamish) carved and painted cedar slabs that are used to form the "spirit-canoe" in the performance of the Spirit-Canoe Ceremony, known as *sbetedaq* (see entry).

The slabs are usually carved from "rough-hewn cedar planks averaging seven feet in height, sixteen to twenty inches in width at their widest part, and about one and a half inches in thickness. The base of these slabs is, to the extent of about twenty inches, so shaped that they may be readily set upright in the earth. This portion of the slab is not painted" [Dorsey 1902:228].

See *touchtd* for details of this ceremony.

Strength medicine

There are many examples in the literature concerning great feats of physical strength performed by shamans in their use of supernatural power. The following is an example from the Owens Valley Paiute near Lake Mono in Utah: "J. McB. told of five powerful doctors who killed mountain sheep in Tioga pass. In Leevining canyon, near the highway, they argued about whose power was greatest, and shot arrows into the horns of the large sheep to settle it. Each had three shots, and the winner was to receive five arrows from each loser. The first doctor glanced his arrows off the tough horns; the second and third failed; the fourth's stuck but were easily pulled out. H. T.'s great-grandfather said, 'I am going to try something new.' 'Any way you like,' they said. He blew in his hands [empowered them], seized one horn with each, tore them from the skull and threw them completely into a near-by tree, and thus won all the arrows. Today the horn tips just project from this tree trunk" [Steward 1933:311].

See also *Big Bill, Lo, slaolhtcu*.

Stsuq

Thompson, *Plateau*

Mark or picture of any kind, including the white man's writing, pictures, and papers. When such drawings were made by a shaman, they had supernatural powers. "Some rock paintings are also 'mystery,' and have not been made in any ordinary way. Some of them have not been made by the hand of man" [Teit 1898: 118, n. 283].

Stuyichad

Twana, *Northwest Coast*

"Boss of the salmon" [Elmendorf 1960:531]. This term was applied to the leading fish in each salmon run. Among the Twana five different species of salmon were taken from their rivers, and the "leader of the dog-salmon run was the crooked-jawed salmon yəbuʹs, 'something wrong with face'" [Elmendorf 1960:118].

A first-salmon ceremony was conducted each year for the first *yabus* to be caught each season. "When caught the crooked-jawed dog salmon was carried from the river to the village by two elderly persons, its head kept always pointing upstream. It was prepared by roasting, and all in the community partook, including children. All of the salmon except the bones had to be eaten. The meal was followed by dancing. Many persons, especially all children older than infancy, plunged in the river following the feast. . . . Children held the cross spits which had held the salmon open during cooking between their teeth and dashed into the river with them and after splashing about threw the spits in a downstream direction, while thanking the salmon leader and inviting him to come again" [Elmendorf 1960:118].

The first-salmon ceremony was a religious event conducted annually to ensure good salmon runs in the future. It was done only once each year and for only one crooked-jawed dog salmon. Each community conducted this ritual individually; two or more communities never performed the ritual jointly.

Suglut

North Alaska Eskimo, *Arctic Coast*

Tikerarmiut ceremonial masks. These are actually half-masks made from tanned white caribou skin. "They are tied over the forehead so that a fringe or caribou hair attached to the lower edge hangs down over the face" [Rainey 1947:249]. Some of these masks are painted with representations of hunting, such as attacking a whale.

Suin
Klallam, *Northwest Coast*
Lummi term for medicine power. The use of *suin* "is not confined to medicine men although they are adept in it, but is known also by others among both men and women. Its use is always surrounded with great secrecy and mystery" [Stern 1934:83]. As such *suin* is also used by sorcerers seeking to kill someone, by the makers of love medicines, in the painting of protective symbols for warfare, in making hunting medicines, to hypnotize or cast spells, and so forth. For example, "if a person who knows *suin* wants a boy to win a foot-race, he stands in a position where he can get full view of the runners. With the object in mind of interfering with the efforts of the opponents of his favorite he pronounces the secret name used in *suin* for thigh. Concentrating all his powers on the thigh of the best of the rival runners, he deprives the runner of the full support of his limbs and his choice wins the race. In telling of such an experience, the people say, 'He named his legs for him'" [Stern 1934:84].

The following account describes the use of *suin* in hunting deer: "Early in the morning as the sun is rising a person understanding *suin* talks as if addressing someone who knows his plans. He names the places where he intends to hunt and then says, 'I suppose our grandchild is wandering along the shores about this time. Her limbs are strong and she trusts them to escape us, but let them become numb when we see her.' With these words, the hunter starts on the hunt. When he approaches the deer, it does not seem to notice him but appears busy or hypnotized, and he easily shoots it with his bow and arrow" [Stern 1934:84].

According to Stern a man experienced in halibut *suin* addresses his fishing hook by saying, "How nice it will be when the halibut will try to find his way to you. I suppose he is waiting for us to come" [Stern 1934:84]. Then, "while doing this the man names the halibut by its secret *suin* name. When the hook is set in the water, the hal-ibut as if hypnotized does all in its power to get in a position to bite the hook and get caught, even fighting with others to get at the hook" [Stern 1934:85].

Knowing *suin* also means knowing the secret names for animals, fishes, trees, etc., that are used in manifesting a particular medicine power. "*Suin* can be bought, sold or transferred from one person to another. Parents who know it teach it to their favorites among their children" [Stern 1934:85].

Sukwiya
Diegueño, *Peninsula*
Cocopa generic term for shaman [Gifford 1933: 309]. Both males and females become shamans, but males usually outnumber the females. Female shamans typically treat "childbirth, children's diseases, eye trouble, stomach trouble, diarrhoea, arrow and gunshot wounds, bone fractures, injuries from falls" [Gifford 1933:310]. Shamans receive their powers via dreams, most often from an animal spirit that appears in human guise. Following a power dream the novice shaman undertakes a four-day purification period, which includes abstaining from meat, salt, and sex. In addition he bathes himself daily. After the shaman's initial dream the spirit occasionally returns to him to impart more instructions. This period of instruction usually lasts from two to three years before the shaman begins to practice.

The type of animal that appears to the shaman often determines what types of power he receives from this spirit. If it is some form of doctoring power, the spirit often takes the novice to a sacred mountain or some other spot and has the novice perform a doctoring treatment. What he learns in this dream then becomes the method he uses for future cures. For instance, "whoever dreamed of Roadrunner could treat snake bite. Roadrunner in human form took dreamer up in air to listen [learn]. Novice heard people talking and treating sick. Roadrunner took novice to Feather mt., his [the spirit's] home. Sick person in his house. Every doctor tried, but none cured invalid, neophyte told. First, Roadrunner treated sick man; then neophyte treated him. Treatment: singing 4 songs, rubbing, blowing, blowing smoke on invalid. Then patient got up. Neophyte should treat in same way any sick person in actual life. Fox, in dreams, gave certain women shamans power to cure eye trouble" [Gifford 1933:309–310]. These women place their tongues on the afflicted eye as the means to cure. Coyote also brings healing powers.

Most Cocopa shamans acquire some form of healing power. A shaman who is proficient at healing is called *kusiya paxwe*, "good doctor" [Gifford 1933:309]. Shamans who use their powers maliciously (that is, sorcerers) are called *kusiya sinyapis*. They usually obtain their powers from the Vulture, Hawk, or Rattlesnake. Shamans who specialize in illness caused by soul loss are called *loxachakiapas*. Shamans who specialize in the treatment of arrow wounds are called *ipayapas*. Shamans who treat burns have the ability to sit "unharmed in fire" [Gifford 1933:310]. Whatever his power is, the shaman normally declines from speaking about it because that may cause his power to fail.

During a healing the shaman usually dreams. If he has a good dream, such as a dream of his helping spirit, this is an indication the patient will recover; bad dreams indicate the opposite. Cures usually entail the shaman blowing tobacco smoke over the patient, singing his power songs, and rubbing the patient. Sucking is also used, often preceded by making a small incision in the patient's skin. In some healing ceremonies the shaman also makes a rudimentary sand painting on the ground outside the patient's house (or wherever the sick person is being treated) in order to bring dreams.

If a shaman loses several patients he is usually accused of sorcery and clubbed to death. As such, shamans are often reluctant to undertake healings for people who are very sick.

Sulíxw

Twana, *Northwest Coast*

"The experience of encountering or getting power, in a vision granted by a guardian spirit to one seeking such power" [Elmendorf 1984:284]. Such power may either be *swadash* (see entry) or *cshalt* (see entry).

Sumesh

Kalispel, Flathead, *Plateau*

Power songs or incantations received from a helping spirit during a vision quest [Fahey 1986:36]. Both males and females seek spirit powers via such quests. Males venture alone into the mountains, while females are watched over during their quests "so they would not be harmed" [Fahey 1986:36].

For the neighboring Flathead Turney-High [1937:27] used this term for a shaman's guardian spirit but also equated it with the term *medicine*. "Most commonly the *sumesh* appears to the individuals in theriomorphic [see entry] form, the rattlesnake and bear being the most usual. Anthropomorphic guardians also occur; the dwarfs, as mentioned, being especially powerful. Peripatetic decomposed corpses and skeletons are also encountered. A common guardian is the spirit of some ancestor, or rarely of some famous person to whom the seeker is not related. . . . The guardian then tells the seeker how to call upon him. It teaches him at least one song, at times even more, and rehearses him until he can sing it. Ordinarily the seeker has never heard the song before" [Turney-High 1937:27].

When a person is ill due to soul loss, the Flathead shaman and participants enter a darkened lodge. "A small hole is then made in the roof, through which the conjuror [shaman], with a bunch of feathers, brushes in the spirits, in the shape of small bits of bone and similar substances which he receives on a piece of matting. A fire is then lighted, and the conjuror proceeds to select out from the spirits such as belong to persons already deceased, of which there are usually several; and should one of them be assigned by mistake to a living person, he would instantly die. He next selects the particular spirit belonging to each person, and causing all the men to sit down before him, he takes the spirit of one (i.e., the splinter of bone, shell, or wood, representing it), and placing it on the owner's head, pats it, with many contortions and invocations, till it descends into the heart, and resumes its proper place" [Hale 1846:208–209].

Sun Dance

This is perhaps the most famous religious ceremony of the Plains area. It is a widespread ritual that has many variations from culture to culture. In former times a person pledged to perform the Sun Dance upon requesting supernatural power under dire circumstances. In more modern times the dance serves to reconfirm Native American identity, and participants dance for varying reasons. "During the 1880's the government was trying to suppress the old religion as another step in civilizing the Indians. The Sun dance was forbidden by the Department of the Interior in 1882 and by 1890 the old ceremonies were no more" [J. Smith 1967:9]. Those who did conduct a Sun Dance thereafter did so in secret. However, since the 1940s the Sun Dance has been reinstated by many different nations, and today it has spread to areas where it had not been performed in the past, such as Big Mountain on the Hopi Reservation.

Quite frequently healing is an aspect of the Sun Dance. For example, with regard to the

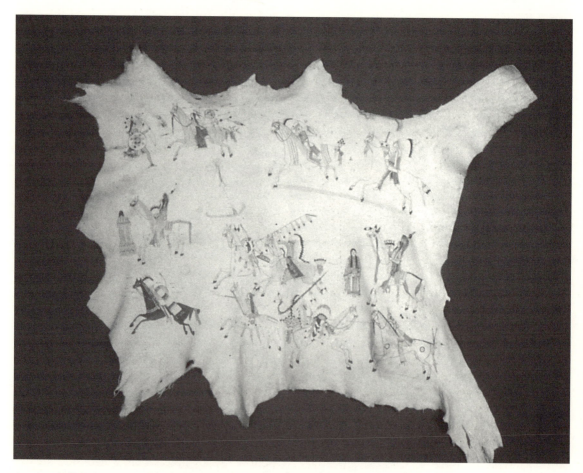

A painted elk hide depicting the Sun Dance. Painting by George Washakie (Shoshone).

Sun Dance of the Ponca Indians, Arizona, *photograph circa 1890.*

Northern Ute Sun Dance on the Wind River Reservation, where it is known as *tavukai*, "thirst dance" [Jorgensen 1972:280], it is reported:"It is the special powers of the dancers, as opposed to the skills of white physicians, which adds an important dimension of meaning to the dance and helps validate and perpetuate the ritual. We have made it clear that a basic intention of dancers and spectators is to receive supernatural power which will cure the ailing and allow a functionary to effect cures. Stories about how dancers have effected cures unattainable by white doctors, much to the latter's puzzlement, are legion at Sun dance time. Many Utes and Shoshones are ill periodically and remain ill after visiting Public Health Service doctors and other white physicians. After undergoing Sun dance treat-ments, however, they get better" [Jorgensen 1972:274].

Although the dance is not designed to be a vision quest, frequently dancers are blessed by visions while performing.

Sunusa
Wintun, *California*
Literal translation: "Full-of-Straw" [Lee 1941: 411]. A powerful Wintu healing shaman during the 1930s. Sunusa was a great medicine man and had been called upon to doctor a woman who had been doctored by many shamans for a week. Sunusa told them, "Tomorrow when the sun is barely risen, she will go onward, I sense [i.e., he heard this from his spirit helper]. . . . Already her spirit stands a short distance behind her, I sense"

[Sunusa in Lee 1941:411]. Early the next morning, just before sunrise, the woman died. It was common for shamans to diagnose an illness as too advanced to be cured, just as Sunusa did in this case.

Sutkwi towats
Ute, *Basin*

Also: *sutkwi tauats* [Fowler and Fowler 1971: 168]. Literal translation: "medicine man" [Powell in Folwer and Folwer 1971:53]. Around 1870, while doing fieldwork among the Northern Utes, John Wesley Powell reported that this term was being used for a shaman who heals. Powell observed several healing ceremonies during the course of his fieldwork between 1868 and 1880. In some cases the shamans used obsidian knives, called *topi,* to make small incisions in the patient's skin for extracting a disease object. In other treatments, he noted, "live coals are placed upon the flesh, and the Medicine Man keeps them aglow by fanning them with his breath until a fearful sore is made, and then new coals are placed in a fresh place until quite a number of blisters have been formed. Usually these sores are made from the neck down the central line of the back for the whole length of the body, and ten or twenty such blisters are formed" [Powell in Fowler and Fowler 1971:57]. In more serious cases, additional burning is done along the arms and legs. The term *tauwai* means "to sear for purpose of driving out evil spirit" [Fowler and Fowler 1971:178].

In December 1868 Powell attended a sucking ceremony at the White River camp (of "Tabuats" Northern Ute) in northwestern Colorado, which he recorded in some detail. The ceremony consisted of a series of four rounds of pipe smoking, followed by several suction treatments. Of this latter part Powell wrote:

> Then he [the *sutkwi towats*] stretched his patient out upon the ground once more at full length, and going to the back of his head, parted his hair and sucked at the skull as if he expected to extract

something from the man's head. When this was done he arose, walked to the door of the tent, and extending his hands a little way outside, seemed to blow a something from the palm of his hand which he had previously taken from his own mouth. Then he returned to the tent, walking backwards, but with averted head, and making motions with his hand, the palm turned away from him as if he was forbidding some one to enter, and occasionally turning his face again to the door, shutting his eyes and blowing something back. At the same time all those [ceremonial supporters] who were in the circle waved back some imaginary being as if to prevent them from coming into the tent and they also would blow. In like manner he sucked at each of the patient's heels and after apparently extracting something there-from (went) through the same performance. . . . On returning to the tent the third time he filled his mouth with water and set up a gurgling sort of howl, most terrific, swaying his body back and forth and to and fro, leaping into the air, tumbling onto the ground until he seemed to be in a state of utter frenzy. All this time the circle kept up the chant. Then once more he knelt beside the patient, and commenced a process of extracting by suction an evil spirit from the man's navel. Finally he seemed to have it—to have got it into his mouth, and this time he spit it into his hand and carried it out of the tent, his head averted again, and with the other hand dug a little hole in the ground in which he placed the evil spirit and covered it with dirt. This time on returning he exhibited signs of great rejoicing. It was very evident that he had now succeeded in extracting the *U-nu'-pits* [evil spirit—see entry]. The general blowing of the mouth and waving back with the hand was taken up by all the people in the tent for a short time [Powell in Fowler and Fowler 1971:59].

Suwi
Diegueño, *Peninsula*

English name: Sam Clam. A Cocopa ghost doctor during the early part of the twentieth century. (The Cocopa are from the central division located along the lower Colorado River.) He received his first power dream at the age of ten, but at the time, he didn't understand that he was to become a shaman. Within the next year he dreamed of the Horned Owl, Turtle, Spider, *Kamuyum* ("hairy person"), *Sumalitup* (chief of winds and clouds), and *Mistau,* all of whom taught him power songs. At first he told no one of his powers, and then, after several years, he began to treat members of his family.

In diagnosing an illness Suwi laid the palm of his left hand on the area of the patient's body where the pain resided. If there was motion in the outer joint of his little finger, he knew that a cure was possible; in addition his mouth would water. However, if his mouth became dry, he would tell the patient to call in another doctor.

Suwi was particularly adept at treating illnesses caused by soul loss. In fact, he was known to be able to cure such cases within a matter of hours. He would send his own soul ahead of the soul of the patient on the road to the other world. "Although Suwi sent [his] own soul with smoke, he continued conscious and active" [Gifford 1933:314]. He would blow tobacco smoke in the direction the lost soul had taken, which was always to the southeast toward *Inbawhela* (the Land of the Dead). This caused the fire burning within the healing room to spring up toward the southeast, which in turn caused the ghost who had stolen the soul to release it. Suwi would then revive the patient by blowing tobacco over his body, especially around the ears.

Suwi also used Jimson weed to obtain gambling medicine for his people's stick-guessing game known as *peon.* He would ingest Jimson weed about six hours before the gambling started. During the game the spirit of Jimson weed, in human form, would stand behind his opponent and tell him how many sticks were being held [Gifford 1933:306]. However, when conducting a healing ceremony Suwi never used Jimson weed.

Suwi was capable of attaining states of consciousness that would allow him to "see everything that happened, even what other shamans

[were] doing. [What] ordinary mortals could not see" [Gifford 1933:314].

Swadash

Twana, *Northwest Coast*

Dialectical variants: *sxwnam* (Straits Salish) (Klallam); *sxwdab* (Puget Sound) [Elmendorf 1960:487]. Skokomish medicine power [Elmendorf 1993:190]; doctor power [Elmendorf 1993: 191]; shaman powers [Elmendorf 1960:499]. This power is a form of *tamánamis* (see entry) that is used mainly for healing. Available to both males and females, it is the power of shamans, acquired from helping spirits. This power can come to a person either through a revelatory vision or through inheritance. "So if your mother or grandmother had lots of visions in her time, you can inherit them. If you get ailing the doctor diagnoses and says, 'Your mother's vision wants you and I'll bring it to you'" [Henry Allen in Elmendorf 1993:191]. In such cases, the shamans would always assist in bestowing this power upon the person. However, sometimes "they did drive away a power from the dead, rather than bring it to the person it wanted to come to. The doctor would get it and throw it away or waft it away, and by doing this make it let the [sick] patient alone. . . . Driving it away sometimes caused the death of the person it wished to come to" [Henry Allen in Elmendorf 1993:191].

Swadash power was differentiated from *cshalt* (any other kind of power—see entry) in that *swadash* power resides in one's body at all times. That is, *swadash* is available at any time to the shaman, but the same does not hold true for an owner of *cshalt.* Furthermore, with the *swadash* power, "you can take it out of your body and show it and play with it" [Frank Allen in Elmendorf 1993:199].

Most novice shamans train under a person who has already obtained *swadash.* This training begins early, around the age of five or six. The training centers mainly on effecting a successful vision quest later in life. The training involves purification procedures such as cold-water bathing and hard scrubbing with conifer boughs, fasting, periods of isolation at designated power spots, and, to a lesser extent, sweating. Intensive questing is usually conducted between the ages of eight and fourteen. Such systematic questing usually ends for both sexes with marriage.

A person's first successful vision quest, in which he or she establishes a personal relationship with a helping spirit, is known as *sulixw.* Such encounters determine the shaman's powers and abilities via the sacred songs and instructions given to him or her by the spirit. Most often, this is some form of power to heal certain sicknesses. Such powers differ from individual to individual, and the highest powers are known as *swǝlu'saɬwa'daš,* "chief doctor powers" [Elmendorf 1960:500]. One unusual aspect of the acquisition of *swadash* is that "shaman spirits which conferred curing power on their human owners always accompanied this grant with subsidiary powers termed *kǝda'bǝlǝs,* 'weapons,' that could be used to cause illness but not to cure it" [Elmendorf 1960:500]. Thus every healer is also potentially a sorcerer.

The possession of *swadash* is usually evidenced by the shaman going into a true trance, called *ɬa'padbǝt,* "losing consciousness" [Elmendorf 1960:494]. Once power is obtained, it often takes the shaman several years to bring his power under control (see *chidid*). In fact, the "normal sequence pattern of activities followed in acquiring power from a shamanistic guardian spirit differed considerably" [Elmendorf 1960:501] from the pattern followed in acquiring *cshalt* powers. Once they obtain their doctoring power, most shamans begin by curing members of their own family for free as a means of establishing their reputation beyond the immediate community.

"Spiritual power and secrecy are closely associated everywhere among the Coast Salish. Aboriginally, the whole topic was shrouded in secrecy. It still is. Others know about an individual's power only through cryptic communications from the owner, and, most importantly, they infer the presence of power from the individual's demonstrated competence. . . . People still look for successful performance as proof of supernatural connections" [Amoss 1977:134].

Most Skokomish doctors use a sucking procedure in healing patients. "Some suck blood and matter through their two fists, held like a tube, and some suck by putting their mouth directly on the sick man's skin. No Skokomish doctors used a pipe in sucking" [Frank Allen in Elmendorf 1993:199]. However, this form of healing is seen as a "low-class" power from the Wolf, Cougar, or Loon. The more advanced shamans have "chief doctor powers," such as *ayahos* and *stadukwa* [Elmendorf 1993:199]—both "mythical monsters of extraordinary potency" [Elmendorf 1960:500]— that granted wealth acquisition power in addition to curing power. Such shamans "just pull sickness out of you by hand and then 'bale' matter and slime out of you. The doctor does it by hand" [Frank Allen in Elmendorf 1993:199]. The following is an example of the use of *stadukwa* by a shaman named Kwaqs circa 1830:

So kʷ'a'qs came to where the sick man was.

And people came in to help the doctor sing. And kʷ'a'qs kneeled down by the sick man and sang. . . . And now he stopped and laughed. "Oh, people, you don't have to sing. I want to look to see what sickness this man has. And now I see that sickness." And he told them, "Get me a basket full of water."' So they brought a basket of water. And kʷ'a'qs pulled a long string of slime out of that man's side, he just pulled it right out of him with his fingers and held it up for the people to see. And then he put that stuff in the water. First he held it on the palm of one hand and hit it with the other hand, and then he dumped it in the water. kʷ'a'qs would kill that sickness that way. And he kept on pulling matter and blood out of that man, just bailing it out of his stomach with his hands, after he had killed that sickness. He didn't use his mouth for that, some do if they have a little power for sucking, but kʷ'a'qs didn't need to.

And pretty soon that sick man stirred and looked around, and then he got up. He wasn't sick any more [Frank Allen in Elmendorf 1993:206].

Shamanic healing among the Skokomish operates in a group context that includes the shaman, his assistants, singers, and drummers. "You see, a doctor is no good without qʷaqʷaʼwʼqīd (audience help). His power will refuse to work [and] the audience gets behind the doctor and makes more noise in the singing and helps him" [Henry Allen in Elmendorf 1993:221].

A shaman would often first make a person sick and then get paid to cure him. Frank Allen reported: "All doctors did that at times, they'd pick on someone and pester his tamánamis [see entry] or tie it up so he'd get sick. And then that man might come and ask that same doctor to doctor him and pay him to do that. It was a way of getting business, and all doctors did it. And they didn't tell on each other usually, unless it was a case of a bad doctor really trying to kill somebody" [Frank Allen in Elmendorf 1993:211].

From *swadash* comes the Twana term for shaman known as *bəswaʼdaš*, meaning "one having shaman-spirit power" [Elmendorf 1960: 501]. Because *swadash* also carries with it the power of sorcery, there is always the "fair likelihood of a shaman's meeting with a premature and violent end" [Elmendorf 1960:509]. For example, Elmendorf [1960:510] noted that "the malignant functions of some shaman spirits . . . grew progressively stronger and more dominant as the shaman grew older, until at last he might be unable to summon the spirit for curing purposes but be continually plagued by it to use it in magical 'shooting' or other victimizing practices." This condition sometimes causes mentors in the helping-spirit-quest training to advise their young relatives to refuse a shaman spirit when it appears.

For other examples of *swadash*, see *cixax*, *sqwacathl*.

Swiïs
Klamath, *California*

Song, spirit [Spier 1930:95]. All songs are called *swiïs*. However, because a guardian spirit only manifests in the form of a song heard in a dream, this term is also used for spirit. "When it is said that a man has a Coyote swiʼïs, for example, it means that he has the appropriate song or songs and that this animal is his supernatural helper" [Spier 1930:95]. See also *kiuks*, *sputu*.

Sword swallowing
Pueblo, *Southwest*

See *Onayanakia*, *Piännithle*, *Shotikianna*.

Sxädab
Twana, *Northwest Coast*

"Growling one" [Elmendorf 1960:483]; also the secret-society initiation ceremony [Elmendorf 1960:551] and the name given to a special spirit power that did not act as one's helping spirit. This particular spirit possessed groups of initiates during the secret-society ritual and also endowed them with supernatural aid in acquiring a helping spirit in subsequent spirit quests [Elmendorf 1960:483]. During the secret-society initiation ritual, one of the most complex rituals among the Twana, proficient shamans would also use *sxädab* to reinforce their own helping-spirit power [Elmendorf 1960:523].

Sxwadach
Twana, *Northwest Coast*

Stop-game spirit power. This was a special form of hunting medicine used by a specialist to slow down hunted mammals. The Skokomish held an annual public ceremony—the First-Elk Ceremony—for the first elk killed each year. The ceremony was designed in part to "feed" this particular spirit power. The main purpose of the ritual, however, was to appease the "father of elk"; "[when] so treated this prototypal elk would assure the Skokomish, or other community holding the ceremony, an abundance of elk for the next season" [Elmendorf 1960:117].

This was a religious ceremony that occurred in the fall. "Everyone present, normally the entire village community, ate of the first elk [killed], and its edible portions had to be entirely consumed" [Elmendorf 1960:117] during the ritual. The hide of the elk was used as a kettle, termed *stlab,* into which hot stones were placed to boil the meat. "This was the only occasion on which an animal hide was used for stone boiling" [Elmendorf 1960:117].

Sxwdach
Twana, *Northwest Coast*
A ritually prepared object, usually a sharpened bone or stick, that a sorcerer "shoots" into the body of his victim. The process of magically shooting such an item is known as *cixax* [Elmendorf 1960:508]. The *sxwdach,* once empowered, is held in the hand of the shaman and thrown toward the victim, at which point it disappears, entering the victim's body magically.

This technique is not often used because the shaman treating the victim can, with relative ease, extract the *sxwdach* and throw it back to the sender, thus injuring the sorcerer. However, it was used frequently by the Skokomish "in the mid-nineteenth century to weaken their opponents' horses in intertribal horse racing" [Elmendorf 1960:525].

Taartaa

East Greenland Eskimo, *Arctic Coast*

Also: *taarteq* (EONAH, p. 275). Literal translation: "successors" [Thalbitzer 1931:435]. Ammasalik shaman's helping spirit. These spirits reside below the ground and possess the body of the shaman during his performances. Thus, during a shamanic ceremony, "the angakok's [see *angakoq*, EONAH, pp. 13–15] soul, not his body sinks below the ground. This takes place gradually, and his spirit (taartaa) rises up and enters into him through his anus. It makes its exit afterwards by the same way. His body is thus like a house which changes tenants" [Ajukudooq in Thalbitzer 1931:435].

Taáxtoyx

Nez Perce, *Plateau*

A "bloody item" that certain sorcerers have in their body, which serves as a source of evil power for them [D. Walker 1967:74]. The *taáxtoyx* can be removed.

Taboo

Also: tabu. A prohibition, which, if violated, leads to an automatic penalty inflicted by magic or religion [Winick 1968:522]. The breaking of religious/spirit-sent taboos is seen in most Native American cultures as one of the primary sources of human illness. In most healing ceremonies the shaman not only attempts to effect a cure but also informs the patient what future actions he or she must do to prevent the illness from recurring.

The following breaches of taboo for the Santa Clara Pueblo are typical examples: "sacrilegious thoughts; lack of attention to religious instructions, which might result in ritual mistakes; violation of food tabus or continence while engaged in ceremonial activity; failure to perform in ceremonial activity when requested; failure to live up to religious standards as outlined in the kachina initiation. . . . and practicing witchcraft" [Hill 1982:310].

Taboo restrictions are most rigorously enforced on shamans and on those who have been initiated into a religious society. Because the uninitiated adults and children do not know the difference between good and evil, they are not held as socially accountable as those who do know the "right" way to live. Nonetheless, most adults are very aware of the dangers that arise from breaches of taboo, which is evidenced by the great number of daily prayers and actions they perform to avoid such dangers.

The handling of power by shamans has many taboos associated with it. Basically, all shamanic power is seen as dangerous. "You may get power, but it may endanger you, shorten your life" [unidentified informant in Hill 1982:313]. Power acquired from a helping spirit almost always comes with associated taboos. Most often the shaman is prohibited from eating the flesh of the animal from which the power comes. However, the taboo may take any form, and there are many variations cited in the literature.

If the shaman breaks such a taboo at any time during his or her life, the power is lost. In fact, taboo violation is the most frequent reason given by shamans themselves for losing powers. Indeed, power is so dangerous that even if the shaman unwittingly breaks a taboo, it is lost (for example, see *Takes the Pipe*).

Given the inherent dangers, many people are inclined to avoid the acquisition of power. To this end there are many recorded accounts of the various means people have used to avoid the shaman's call (see entry).

See also *aglirktok*.

Tah
Yakima, *Plateau*

Plural: *tahmas*. Northwest Sahaptin term for guardian spirit [Boyd 1996:116]. The term can also refer to the supernatural power that comes from a guardian spirit [Schuster 1975:114] or a specific manifestation of that power in any form or shape.

The term *tahinsh* means "one who possesses a guardian spirit" [Curtis in Boyd 1996:116]. See *tahmahnawis* for details.

Táhca Wicásha Wakáng
Teton, *Plains*

Literal translation: "Deer Holy Men" (class of shamans) [Howard 1984:138]. Term used by the Canadian Santee for a Deer shaman. "One time an old shaman of this type spread loose dirt on the ground and smoothed it. He then announced that he was going to do something miraculous. He walked through this loose dirt and left four deer hoofprints. This same man could accurately predict through his deer power the coming of winter and of spring. He also had the power to call the deer to the hunters with a sacred song" [Charles Padani in Howard 1984:138].

Tahmahnawis
Yakima, *Plateau*

Also: *tamanowash* [Hines 1993:26–27]. Dialectical variant: *tamánamis* (Twana) (see entry). A general term for an invisible force and the supernatural power received by a shaman from a guardian spirit. Both males and females seek *tahmahnawis*, usually between the ages of seven to twelve, via vision questing alone at isolated spots. To the fortunate candidates a *tah* [spirit] appears. "While he remains in a trance-like condition, the wonderful apparition speaks to him in a dream, telling him what to do. He is commissioned to heal, destroy [witchcraft] or prophesy. When he comes out of his trance, the strange being is gone; and he is alone in silence and darkness" [Hines 1993:29].

The type of animal or object that appears determines the shaman's future abilities. For example, "a doctor receiving his *tamanowash* from the *tlchachie* (ghosts) can handle corpses or go into the 'dead-house' or graves, and can communicate with the dead" [Hines 1993:31]. Once the *tahmahnawis* is acquired, it often takes several years, sometimes a decade or more, before the shaman learns to control and use it. "This *tah*, or *tahmahnawis* is a very dangerous element, which may get the upperhand of the one possessing it, making him subservient to a bad purpose even against his will. His *tah* may become a 'killing' *tah*, in which case the man cannot help killing people" [Hines 1993:168].

Once the shaman feels confident, he formally announces that he has acquired a *tah* during the winter dances. This formal announcement takes the form of a potlatch giveaway. After the event the shaman becomes recognized as a *tahmah-nawis* man or *tawati* (see entry). "The more expended in gifts . . . the greater will be the medicine man's control over his *tahmahnawis* power" [McWhorter in Hines 1993:164]. One shaman, "who has been more or less successful in the profession of a medicine man, when entering on his career as such, made a five days' and five nights' festival, where a wagon-load of blankets and calicoes were distributed. . . . In addition to the dry goods given away, the gifts included many articles of Indian manufacture and five head of horses" [McWhorter in Hines 1993:164].

When used, the emanation of this power that comes from the shaman is called *towtenook,* or "medicine" [Hines 1993:33]. It is employed in many different ways. For example, one "young man 'shot' his *tahmahnawis* at the eagle [far up in the skies], which immediately came tumbling down through the air, falling dead near the camp" [Hines 1993:170].

Tahmahnawis can also be inherited, as one individual reported: "My father told me his power before he died, and he gave me his power. It is strong. I wear the wings of the 'rock hawk' tied to my hair on back of my head when in war, and nothing can hurt me" [Histo in Hines 1993:147].

Taiwetälem

Cowichan, *Northwest Coast*

The Kwantlen (Halkomelem division) Fire Dance. This is a shamanic ceremony in which the shaman

would handle fire, place hot coals in his mouth, and dance upon hot stones. . . . Eye-witnesses of them, both native and white, are unanimous in declaring that these fire-shamans could handle fire and burning objects and dance upon scorching hot stones without apparently burning or otherwise harming themselves. The late Bishop Durieu, who spent over forty years among the Indians of this district, once told me himself, in a conversation on this subject, that he had seen a

shaman handle burning brands without apparent hurt to his hands. He said he had been preaching to the tribe of the power of the Christian's God, and had observed an Indian squatting apart by himself in a far corner of the house. When he had finished his discourse this man came forward, and made some remarks to the effect that it was all very well to talk, but the proof of the pudding was in the eating. Could the white medicine-man give them an example of his "power"? and he thereupon challenged the Bishop to a contest with himself. Said the Bishop: "He seized from the midst of the fire, in his naked hand, a fiery burning brand, and held it there for some time, and then offered it to me. I declined, and was straightway scoffed at by him and his friends; but eventually I turned the tables upon him by declaring that his power came from the Wicked One, with whom I could have no dealings, and not from the true God" [Hill-Trout 1903:412].

Tak

Quinault, *Northwest Coast*

A female shaman around the turn of the twentieth century from the Queets division of the Quinault.

[Tak] lived at the village of na′ukałxw (big village) at the mouth of the Clearwater. Her guardian spirit was a dwarf. When it came to her it said, "I heard that you are a poor woman and that the people make fun of you because you have no property. I am going to help you." It gave her a carved rattle wrapped with cedar bark and with dentalia shells lashed to it. Her song ran heiiya, heiiya kȧtcaadjitȧn sklo′inatcowco, making fun of me (because) I have no dentalium (i.e., Some people used to make fun of me because I was poor). She had the power to foretell when visitors were coming. When the ducks flew past the village she could interpret their quackings. (Flying up and down the river they knew of all canoes on the way.) They would tell her who the people were, and how many.

Hers was a powerful spirit who could go far along the road to the land of the dead to find lost souls. Once a man was spearing salmon in the riffles. When he had speared several he noticed fog drifting toward him. He suspected it was a ghost so he paddled home. As soon as he was inside his house he fell in a faint and his legs twitched as if he were running. They sent for the old woman. She and her guardian [spirit] took after the ghost, who had run far along the trail. The faster they traveled the faster the ghost ran, but at last her guardian spirit caught the ghost and took away from it the man's soul. On the way back the old woman saw that the elderberry bushes were loaded with berries. The spirit picked some. "There will be a big crop of elderberries next year, because it is bringing some back," she said. She returned the soul to the sick man, who shortly recovered [Olson 1936:152–153].

Takes the Pipe
Crow, *Plains*

Nineteenth-century warrior who acquired a great war medicine and subsequently lost it due to breaking a spirit taboo. Robert Lowie gave a detailed account of this warrior's life in which Takes the Pipe sought a vision that would give him the power to become a great chief. He was so intent on success that during his vision quest he cut off the end of one of his fingers as a sacrifice to the spirits. He lost consciousness and awoke that night with great pain in his hand and suffering from the cold. Soon a spirit approached, saying, "The one whom you wanted to come has arrived" [Lowie 1922:26]. He bestowed a medicine power on Takes the Pipe, saying, "Though you fight all the people of the world, dress as I do and you need have no fear of death before you are a chief. . . . As I am, so shall you be; arrows will not hurt you, bullets you can laugh at. You shall be like a rock. But one thing you must not do: never eat of any animal's kidneys" [Lowie 1922:27].

Subsequently, after succeeding as a warrior but before he became a chief, Takes the Pipe unwittingly ate some kidney meat at a feast and was wounded in his first battle thereafter. He went on four vision quests over time, but though a different spirit appeared to him in each quest, none could restore his medicine. After these four fail-

ures he sought his own death in a foolish, single-handed charge on a party of Dakota warriors.

Ta konyondai
Kutchin, *Mackenzie-Yukon*

Literal translation: "he sees things" [Osgood 1936:156]. Tatlit (Peel River Kutchin) phrase used to refer to a shaman. Most shamans are males, but some women also become shamans. "Shamans acquire power through dreams, generally at the early age of six or seven" [Osgood 1936:156], usually from some animal spirit. Sometimes, however, as among the Vunta (Crow River Kutchin), power is acquired "even before birth" [Osgood 1936:158]. Shamans use their power to help people as well as to see into the future or at a distance. "Spirits of shamans can travel great distances while the body sleeps" [Osgood 1936:158].

They also give public demonstrations of their power abilities, which vary from shaman to shaman. One shaman "took a marten skin which was hanging on the wall of a lodge and put it down on the floor in the middle of a group of people. Immediately it began to run around like a live animal, jumping all over everyone and causing all the excitement which might be expected under the circumstances. Then the shaman picked it up again and hung it on the wall. It was [then again] only a tanned skin" [Osgood 1936:157].

Another source noted that "a shaman who has a wolf as his medicine animal has an advantage in catching caribou for he can acquire the ability of the wolf. Shamans can also kill animals of the same species as their medicine, and do this easily" [Osgood 1936:158].

In their healing ceremonies Kutchin shamans remove the disease-causing object or "evil" symptom "either by sucking it out or cutting the individual open and literally extracting the disease by hand. The physical results of at least the latter procedure are miraculous, for no indications of the dissection remain" [Osgood 1936:156]. As he conducts his power procedures, the shaman sings his power songs and drums. In addition to a tambourine drum, the shaman also uses "a special stick called t'c' made from a root, sometimes with an animal head carved on top" [Osgood 1936:156]. Some Kutchin shamans, including the Vunta (Crow River Kutchin), use rattles made from dried skin filled with pebbles instead of drums. "Some [of their rattles] look like miniature double-faced tambourines with handles such as are found among the Naskapi of Labrador" [Osgood 1936:158].

A specific example of the above-mentioned "psychic surgery" follows: "One man had something wrong with his stomach so the shaman had a special wooden knife made. He opened up the breast of the sufferer and took the end of the esophagus in his mouth and extracted the disease. Then he washed out the stomach and the esophagus snapped back into place. The skin which had been cut, he folded back and rubbed until it appeared whole, without a trace of a scar" [Osgood 1936:159].

Talasi

Hopi, *Southwest*

Corn pollen. Sacred corn pollen and sacred cornmeal *(homngumni)* are commonly used in Hopi rituals for blessings. The pollen is sprinkled on sacred paraphernalia and on individuals as a prayer offering. It is also sometimes used for altar displays. For example, the altar display of the Flute society has a "yellow zone" marked out in *talasi* on the floor [Stephen 1936:791]. "Formerly it was customary at childbirth, immediately after a child was born and washed, and before it was given any suck, for the mother, or her mother, to take a feather, any feather, and place on it a little corn pollen moistened with water and lay a little of it on the child's tongue with the feather. This insured the child to be swift and tireless. Sometimes this is yet done" [Stephen 1936:1299].

Talasi is gathered annually during August and September by holding basket trays under the blossoms and tapping on the stalks of the corn.

In some cases flower petals are ground and added to the *talasi* [Stephen 1936:154]; on other occasions the *talasi* is mixed with other kinds of pollen, such as larkspur, rose, campion, and tulip pollen. In the latter case the mixture becomes known as *shidosi* (or less properly as *shoyohim talasi,* meaning "all kinds of pollen" [Stephen 1936:512]).

For other examples of corn pollen use in the Southwest area, see *oneane, hatawe.*

Talbixw

Twana, *Northwest Coast*

Good luck amulets. These are usually strange-shaped objects found by individuals, who then either wear them as amulets or wrap them up in cedar bark and keep them in a safe place in their homes. They include such items as oddly shaped stones, tiny arrowheads, and pieces of fungus shaped like faces. One informant spoke of a *talbixw* that he had found on the beach, which he described as "a piece of leaf with animal hair on both sides" [Elmendorf 1960:527].

Talisman

A charm (see entry) that carries good fortune for its owner. "Sometimes the special qualities of the talisman are absorbed by its owner, even in the absence of the object. A talisman may also guard against evil" [Winick 1968:524].

A charm that has a protective function and is worn by its owner is known as an amulet (see entry).

See also *atikomaskiki.*

Talisóhkocî

Seminole, *Southeast*

The Mikasuki name for a small medicine stone used as a war medicine. "This stone was used to ward off bullets" [Sturtevant 1954a:36]. "When soldiers came, the medicine man placed this rock in front of his people and sang [walking] around it four times with a rattle. The rock grew high, but not very broad, so that if people stayed behind it the soldiers' bul-

Waldo Mootzka (Hopi), Corn Prayer, *circa 1910–1938.*

lets glanced off harmlessly, but if they got frightened and ran out from behind they got hurt" [Sturtevant 1954b:378].

Tamánamis
Twana, *Northwest Coast*
Dialectical variant: *tahmahnawis* (Yakima) (see entry). The general term for power. Power comes to individuals through many different animate and inanimate forms known as *siyalt,* or spirit helpers. *Tiyuɬbax tamánamis* is the "biggest *s'iya'lt* power" [Elmendorf 1993:166]; the following account from the latter half of the eighteenth century describes one man's experience in obtaining it:

> That man [a Chehalis man at Westport, on Grays Harbor] would send his son up to a big bluff near Aberdeen . . . and make him take a big rock in his hands and dive down off the bluff into the water to look for this tamánamis. Now after a while this young fellow discovered tiyu'ɬbax there, in a big house under the water. The tiyu'ɬbax asked, "Is it from high-priced people you come?" The young man said, "Yes." So the tiyu'ɬbax said, "All right, open the door!" And the tiyu'ɬbax opened the door and put the young fellow in. He says, "You see all these women and all these slaves in the other end of the house? I'll give that to you, young man. It will be all yours!"
>
> Well, the young fellow woke up, lying on the beach. Then he braced himself and went home to Westport. When he got home all his relatives asked him, "Have you got it?" He says, "Yes."
>
> After a while people from all over hear about it, that this fellow has got a big tiyu'ɬbax now. So they go to this young fellow to play disk game, bet him slaves, women, everything. And this young man plays and wins. It's just as if tiyu'ɬbax has given him all these things" [Frank Allen in Elmendorf 1993:167].

Some people have a powerful *tamánamis;* others may have only a simple one. Those who have a simple one usually do not show it until later in life, when they are around forty or older, but those who acquire a strong *tamánamis* usually show it at an early age. When a *tamánamis* wants to come to a person, the person usually becomes sick. A shaman who diagnoses the sickness as such will help bring this power to the ailing individual. Henry Allen reported: "When a person dies his power does not go with him to the country of the dead. It has always followed him around like a dog, and after he dies it is just like a lost dog. Sometimes the power will just forget its dead owner, but sometimes it wants to belong to someone and it comes and hangs around a relative or a descendant of its dead owner. This makes the person it chooses sick, until a doctor can treat him and find out what is the matter and bring the power to him. Then he has to show that power at scc'u'ctəb [power dance]" [Henry Allen in Elmendorf 1993:191].

Elmendorf [1960:485] noted that the "guardian-spirit concept was the most highly elaborated body of Twana religious beliefs."

For other examples of *tamánamis,* see *cshalt* and *swadash.*

Tamanoas water
Klallam, *Northwest Coast*
Medicine water. *Tamanoas* (power—see EONAH, pp. 276–277) comes in many forms. Among the Klallam people who resided at Elkwa during the first part of the nineteenth century, a source of *tamanoas* water was known. "Far up in the mountains at the head of the Elkwa River are basins in the rocks; one of these is nearly full of black water and it is always as full whether the weather is wet or dry. In this water, which is thought to be tamanous [earlier spelling of term], the Elkwa Indians washed their hands and arms and thus, it was believed, gained their dreaded power" [Eells 1889:673].

This "dreaded power" consisted of remarkable abilities. For instance, "if they wished to call a person a long distance off, 20, 30, or 50 miles away, they simply, talking low, called him and he came; that if they talked thus about a person, his heart was in a complete whirl, and that if they talked ill and wished to do evil to any one thus, distant, his eyes were made to whirl and the evil wish came to pass" [Eells 1889:673].

Tamanowash sticks
Umatilla, *Plateau*

Dialectical variant: *tamanoas* sticks (Klallam); *tamahnous* sticks (Chinook jargon). Power sticks used by shamans. The following is an account, circa the 1880s, of the use of these items at the Cascades:

> An old doctor who became quite famous for his exploits in making sticks dance used to keep five "Tamanowash sticks" for his seances. They are from one inch and a half to two and a half inches in diameter and from two to three feet or more long. All gathered into the lodge. . . . After the old doctor had sung four times then any person present was invited to take hold of one of the sticks as the old man sung and kept time with his hands the person was jumped about by the stick which began hopping up and down.
>
> As the old tamanowash man warmed up and sung louder and faster, the stick danced more vehemently and the party holding it was instructed to keep it from moving and hold it still. The more strenuously he tried to resist the dancing the more violently it hopped up and down and around the lodge. Finally the stick raised up and jerked up violently the uplifted arms of the one who was trying to hold it. At last being overcome he fell over in a cataleptic state holding on to the stick with a death grip.
>
> The old tamaowash man then stopped his singing and went to the one who had fallen over and stroked him or made some passes over his head when the rigidity relaxed and the man or woman wakened up as from sleep and was soon all right again.
>
> Indians familiar with the performance have described the sensations they felt on taking hold of the Tamanowash sticks to be almost exactly the same as that experienced when holding the electrodes of a magnetic battery. They say their muscles are thrown into a state of powerful contraction so that they cannot let go their hold by any effort of the will [Kuykendall in Boyd 1996:123–124].

See also *wakckwitit.*

Tänagi
Tolowa, *Oregon Seaboard*

Literal translation: "at night travels (?)" [Drucker 1937:259]. Sorcerers. Among the Tolowa, sorcerers are usually men, while shamans are usually women. Most *tänagi* (or *tɛnagi*) operate with a set of ten small, animate objects called *tcäsä,* each of which carries a different harmful power [Drucker 1937:259]. These powers range from causing headaches to causing sudden death. "For safety reasons two sorcerers often combined forces, each using a little poison from his set" [Drucker 1937:260]. The sorcerer selects the desired poison and then sends it rapidly to his victim, "like a bullet," by reciting the proper formula [Drucker 1937:259].

In addition the *tcäsä* gave the sorcerer other powers, such as the ability to assume an animal form or to travel rapidly over great distances. Because *tcäsä* are purchased, a sorcerer usually hides his set somewhere in the woods, in a tree, in a cave, etc. Fasting, continence, and the use of certain formulas are necessary in order to handle *tcäsä;* if not handled properly, they will turn on the sorcerer or some member of his family. The sorcerer must also guard against anyone seeing the occasional flashes of light that are emitted by his *tcäsä* when sorcery is being practiced.

Tanyuwish
Yokuts, *California*

This term comes from *tanai,* the Yokuts word for Jimson weed *(Datura meteloides* or *stramonium)* and refers to their Jimson weed, puberty-initiation ceremony for young men [Kroeber 1925:502]. The candidates usually fast for six days prior to the ceremony. The effects of the drug, once taken, can last more than six days. "The Jimson weed would give them health, long life, ability to dodge arrows in battle, and general prosperity. . . . The drinking took place in the sweat house and was followed, before the intoxication took effect, by a brief dance of the participants. Men would experience or obtain what they saw in their visions; the sight of beads would make the dreamer wealthy" [Kroeber 1925:504].

Ta raris
Pawnee, *Plains*

Deer society. This society is found in all branches of the Pawnee division, "but its ritual seems to be in keeping of the Skidí organizations. The fundamental elements of the ritual seem to be based upon the mescal bean, for this society teaches that all animal powers were learned through the power of the mescal bean" [Murie 1914:605].

The shamans of this society "are able to cure all suffering from snake bites" [Murie 1914:608]. If anyone brings in a new red blanket during the shaman's performance, he or she is required to magically produce mescal beans. "The performing members then rise and dance, presently shaking mescal beans from bunches of sage and other unexpected places. The leader does not dance but industriously sweeps up beans from the bare ground. At the end all the beans magically produced are placed in a pile and later given to the donor of the blanket. Other shamanistic feats may occur, but seem to be individual and entirely optional" [Murie 1914:605–606].

The Comanche also have a Deer Dance in which the dancers "swallow red beans and then draw them out through the breast" [Clark in Lowie 1915b:809].

Tarrarsortoq
West Greenland Eskimo, *Arctic Coast*

Term used for an *angákoq* (shaman—see EONAH, pp. 13–15) who has the power to tell the future by peering into a tub of water [Birket-Smith 1924:453].

Tartaq
East Greenland Eskimo, *Artic Coast*

Also: *tartok; târtâ* (Eskimos of the southeast coast of Greenland) [Birket-Smith 1924:441]. Ammasalik name for a shaman's helping spirit [Kroeber 1900:304]. The term is derived from *tarne,* meaning "soul," and *taq,* meaning "human being." According to Birket-Smith [1924:441],

tartaq literally means "its human being." In accordance with this concept, a shaman's helping spirit often appears to him in human guise.

Ta Sunka Witko
Teton, *Plains*

Crazy Horse (see entry).

Tatatex Waci
Iowa, *Plains*

Bone Shooting Dance, which was no longer performed by the turn of the twentieth century. In earlier times "the members were stripped to the clout. They divided into two companies, danced up to each other, blew on their clenched hands after striking them on their left breasts, and thrust them at the opposing party, at the same time flinging their palms open. Magic bones which were then plucked from the flesh of their breasts were 'shot' right into the flesh of their opponents.... Bystanders who ridiculed the performance were liable to be shot with the bones by members, and such a proceeding was extremely painful. The bone could only be removed by the shooter, who had to be handsomely fed for his pains. He then removed the magic bone by rubbing one hand over the wound. The dancers would even shoot their mysterious bones into the drum and knock the sound out of it so that it could no longer be beaten" [Skinner 1915a:717–718].

According to one account a disbeliever was challenged by a member to "'wrap up your blanket and put it over in one corner and I'll send two bones into it.' This was done, and sure enough the member shot the strange bones from his hand into the blanket, and sent a third into the cheek of the non-believer. The pain was so great that the victim cried aloud. He found two holes through his blanket, and the bones lying in the center. The member, having proved his power, then drew the bones back into his breast" [Skinner 1915a:718].

Tawaru Kutchu
Pawnee, *Plains*

"Big Sleight-of-Hand" Ceremony [Murie 1914: 602]. This is the twenty-day, Grand Medicine

Ceremony that is conducted annually by each of the four tribal divisions of the Pawnee. They also call it the Twenty-Day Ceremony, but in fact this event often lasts up to "thirty days and was an intense affair" [Murie 1914:601–602]. "It is found among all the divisions, but seems to have originated with the Squash Vine village, to whose medicinemen alone certain parts of the ritual were known. From the originators it passed to the Skidí and then to the other divisions. The twenty-day ceremony proper is given in the early autumn after all the bundle ceremonies have been performed, the corn harvested, etc." [Murie 1914:602].

Within the ceremonial lodge each shaman builds a booth of green willows. At the proper time during the ceremonial period, these shamans are called upon to demonstrate their medicine powers. "This is the time when remarkable feats of juggling [shamanism] were performed; thus it is told that stalks of corn were made to grow up and mature in a moment, likewise plums and cherries, the bear men tore out a man's liver and ate it, after which he rose unharmed, and so on, in bewildering variety" [Murie 1914:603].

Tawati
Yakima, *Plateau*

Shamans who have the "big medicine" [Kuykendall in Hines 1993:50]. The Yakima have many different types of shamans, whose varying powers are determined by the nature of the *tahmahnawis* (see entry) they have acquired from their *tah* (guardian spirit). Those shamans possessing the *wahkpuch* (rattlesnake) *tahmahnawis* have the power to heal snakebites; they also know the movements and locations of the rattlesnakes in the vicinity and are immune to their bite. The *nchee twatima* (big doctors) "profess to be equal to almost any emergency, and often were reported to have resuscitated dead persons" [Kuykendall in Hines 1993:37]. "The *pamiss pamiss itta* has the ability to cast a spell or charm over the minds of others so as to soften anger, change purposes or will, or even compel a certain course of action. . . . Their power was invoked to charm away the spirits that linger about and poison the food of those in mourning" [Kuykendall in Hines 1993:37]. However, the *pamiss pamiss itta* is mainly a diviner who prophesies the outcome of hunts, war raids, healings, etc.

There are also the less powerful *wootkt twati* (half doctors), *ixpix twati* (small doctors), or *ixsix tawati* (little doctors), as they are variously called. One particular form of these is the *meanus ashuquat* (baby understander), who is "able to understand all the thoughts and feelings of a baby" [Kuykendall in Hines 1993:38]. Another related form is the *koosi koosi ashuquat* (dog understander), who can communicate with dogs.

Shamans are recognized by a special *tahmahnawis* hat worn during their performances. In addition, they often use *tahmahnawis* sticks (see *tamanowash sticks*), which are about 2 inches in diameter and about 3 feet long. During a ceremony the shaman animates the stick that is being held by an assistant.

Tawi
Klamath, *California*

Spirit poisoning or bewitching [Spier 1930:121].

Taxtewau
Omaha, *Plains*

Deer Woman [Fortune 1932:167]. A vision of *Taxtewau* brings the possibility of acquiring love medicine. However, only those who are not seduced by her will receive such power. The medicine is a preparation of certain roots.

Love medicine is not attached to any of the Omaha secret medicine societies but is practiced by individuals. However, such practice is considered improper.

Tcäcä
Tolowa, *Oregon Seaboard*

See *sisene*.

Tcaianyi
Keres, *Southwest*

Shaman among the Laguna Pueblo people [Boas 1928:291]. Novice shamans are trained by older shamans, and all of the novices' relatives help pay for this service. Eventually a shaman becomes a member of one or more of the Laguna medicine societies. In 1920 and 1922 Boas [1928:291] found several groups of shamans: *cïts tcaianyi* (called by Boas "raw shamans"), *saiyap tcaianyi,* and *hakanyi* (fire) and *hictcianyi* (flint) *tcaianyi.*

The *cïts tcaianyi* dance kachina dances and "together with the Antelope and Badger clans and the war captains look after the kachina" [Boas 1928:291]. The *saiyap tcaianyi* do not sing but dance while others sing for them. During their dance a piñon tree is placed in the plaza, and they dance about it. The third group participates in a solstice ceremonial, during which they swallow sticks as part of their power display. "The members of these societies are allowed to impersonate kachinas" [Boas 1928:291].

Tcainte
Beaver, *Mackenzie-Yukon*

Supernatural power [Goddard 1917:348] or supernatural doings [Goddard 1917:426].

Tcanunba wakan
Assiniboin, *Plains*

Sacred pipe [Lowie 1909:51]. A sacred pipe is a person's most prized possession. Lowie [1909:51] gave an account of a battle between the Assiniboin and Bloods in which the Assiniboin killed a Blood warrior and took his sacred pipe. Although the Bloods were winning the battle, they ceased their efforts and told the Assiniboin they would be spared if they returned the pipe, which they did.

Tcäsä
Tolowa, *Oregon Seaboard*

See *tänagi.*

Tcaúiyuk
South Alaska Eskimo, *Arctic Coast*

Bladder Feast [Hawkes 1914:26]. This is a four-day, hunting medicine ceremony conducted just prior to the full moon of December. Throughout the year each hunter saves the bladder from each animal he has taken. These bladders retain the *inua* (spirit) of the slain animal and are offered up by the hunters during this ceremony. Even the women bring the bladders of small animals slain by children, such as mice and ground squirrels, which have also been saved throughout the year.

The ceremony is conducted both to appease the spirits of these animals and to ensure good luck in hunting for the coming year. After the bladders are consecrated and the ceremony is complete, the hunters await the full moon. On the morning thereafter they go to an appointed hole made in the ice, and each hunter returns his pile of bladders to the sea, thus releasing their spirits. A leading *tungralik* (shaman) is also present at this hole, and he divines, according to the floating and sinking of these bladders, each hunter's luck in the forthcoming year.

Tcauyak
South Alaska Eskimo, *Arctic Coast*

Drum. See *sauyit.*

Tcéthinjiwagre Waci
Iowa, *Plains*

Buffalo Tail Dance. "This is a sort of shamanistic society that closely resembles the hawk bundle group" [Skinner 1915a:713]. During their performances a shaman would use the buffalo tail medicine to show his powers. "The host [shaman] then produces two little dolls, three or four inches high, made of basswood, and makes them dance by reason of his magic power" [Skinner 1915a:713].

Tcev
Yuma, *Southwest*

Healing shaman (suffix). This term appears in Yuma only as a suffix to a noun that indicates the exact type of doctoring done by a shaman. Some examples are: *avetcev*, snake(bite) shaman; *ipatcev*, arrow wound shaman; *xwemanatcev*, stunned curer; *alyecatcev*, fracture shaman; and *metudhavàtcev*, witch shaman (curer of bewitchment) [Forde 1931:183]. See *etsatcev*, *metudhauk*, and *xelyatsxamcàma* for details.

Tce Waci
Iowa, *Plains*

Buffalo Dance. The dance is led by shamans who have received healing powers from the Buffalo or the Bear and are effective at doctoring wounds and broken bones. "Buffalo doctors stay with their patients for periods of four days, keeping the bandages they use saturated with medicated water" [Skinner 1915a:712].

During the latter part of the nineteenth century, a shaman named Iwatcexga (Little-Rock) received healing powers from the Bear and formed a branch of this society. The spirits "gave him a bearskin hat . . . and told him that if he had a patient who was suffering from the hot weather he could take this cap and sprinkle water on it and it would be foggy, rainy, and cool for four days. If it was placed under the head of a very sick man it would watch his spirit and prevent it from getting away" [Skinner 1915a:712–713].

In earlier times the Buffalo Dance was performed prior to going on a buffalo hunt.

Tchúpash
Klamath, *California*

A special medicine arrow used only in healing ceremonies. See *hänäsish* for details.

Tciniki, Ben
Assiniboin, *Plains*

A Stoney weather shaman. Lowie [1909:46] gave an account of this shaman's use of weather medicine to assist in raiding horses from the Blackfoot: "A member of his party filled a pipe for him, which Tci´niki extended, saying . . . 'Let

bad winds come!' It became cloudy and began to rain. All the Blackfoot stayed within their lodges. The Stoneys approached unseen, stole horses, and made their escape. When at a safe distance, Tci´niki said . . . 'This is enough,' and the weather cleared" [Lowie 1989:46].

Tcipinini
Menomini, *Midwest*

Plural: *tcipininiwûk*. A class of healing shamans "who receive their power from Naxpatäo, the guardian of the dead. They act as mediums, and receive aid for the sick from the ghosts" [Skinner 1915d:200]. These shamans are called upon to treat illnesses due to soul loss. "The [wandering] spirit is coaxed back and put into the head of the sick person where it belongs. For this purpose a reed whistle is usually used to call back the soul, which wanders near until sucked into the tube. Cat-tail down is then used to close the ends of the tube, which the tcipinini keeps four days before he is able to put it back" [Skinner 1915d:200]. These shamans are considered less powerful than the *jesako* (see entry).

Tcota
Klamath, *California*

See *heswombli*.

Tcuiiopi
Dakota, *Plains*

Literal translation: "Shot-Through-the-Side" [Wallis 1947:79]. A nineteenth-century (?) shaman who received his power from the Thunderers. His name derived from the fact that he had been shot through the body by the Chippewa, although he was not injured. In one of his power performances,

> he had them make a grass tipi and said he wished a young man to shoot him with bow and arrow. A young man proffered his services. He entered the grass tipi [which was made for the occasion].

The fish [jack fish which he also requested] lay in the center. A small birchbark bowl, filled with water, was near the fish; near the bowl was a stone. Medicinemen were dancing outside the larger long tipi. The man stripped; he painted a red spot over his heart. When the time came to shoot the arrow, he emerged, went to the grass tipi, and walked around it. The marksman, using an arrowshaft, half of which was painted red, shot the arrow into the red spot on the man's body. The medicineman attempted to pull it out. The shaft came out, but the arrowhead remained embedded in his side. He went into the tipi. He dug with his hand into the ground, and took a handfull of earth, which he put into his mouth, where it turned blue. He rubbed this over the wound. He drank some water from the bowl near the stone, replaced the bowl, knelt, and leaned over it. He sang, slapped both sides smartly, and spat out all of the blood that normally would have come from his side, as well as the arrowhead that had been embedded in his flesh [Wallis 1947:78–79].

Tcuyaliclofor

Alsea, *Oregon Seaboard*

Shaman. Shamans acquired helping spirits via solitary quests in the woods. Once a spirit was acquired, it would train the shaman via dreams. The paraphernalia he was to use, his costume and body painting, and his songs were all given to him by the spirit. This training was conducted in secret. Once completed, the novice announced his powers via the *phkilhit* dance.

The most powerful shamans are healers. Fees are offered to the shaman, most often by a relative of the patient, before he begins the cure. Unlike many healing ceremonies, there is no preliminary smoking. The shaman simply begins to sing his spirit-calling song(s). "As he sang, 'his power came closer to him.' Finally he began to dance. If his guardian spirit had granted him power to work minor miracles—such tricks [power feats], for example, as fire eating, plung-

ing the hands in boiling water, sprinkling the patient with water which turned to blood—he displayed them" [Drucker 1939:99].

In trance the shaman, with his clairvoyant powers, diagnoses the patient. Most often the diagnosis is soul loss, object intrusion, or breach of taboo. "To recover a vagrant soul the shaman sang, sending his familiar [helping spirit]. He did not go himself, either in person or in spirit" [Drucker 1939:99]. If the diagnosis is object intrusion, the shaman will suck the disease-causing object (called *łqulisxàm*—see entry) from the patient's body.

Sometimes the shaman determines that he cannot cure the patient, and in such cases he will most often recommend another doctor. Should a shaman not succeed in curing the patient, he forfeits his fee.

The shaman's other major responsibilities include ensuring a good salmon run, preventing famine, and bathing "mourners after the burial of a kinsman" [Drucker 1939:100].

Another less powerful class of shamans among the Alsea is the *tumsa* (see entry).

Tdiyĭn

Coyukon, *Mackenzie-Yukon*

Tena term for shaman [Chapman 1914:159]. The Tena reside in Anvik, Alaska. Shamans in this culture had the ability to assume the form of animals, such as otters or hawks.

Téchuge ke

Tewa, *Southwest*

The Tesuque Bear society at Santa Clara Pueblo. See *Wanke* for details.

Teish

Yokuts, *California*

Also: *tesh* [Kroeber 1925:511]. The Chukchansi term for shaman. Among the neighboring Tachi, the phrase *teshich gonom* is used for "rain doctors" or weather shamans.

See *antu*.

Teladasit

Micmac, *Canadian Eastern Woodlands*
A bad wish. Evil-minded shamans are capable of striking an individual with a *teladasit,* which is recognized by the victim as a quivering of the heart or flesh in some part of the body [Wallis and Wallis 1955:156].

Telikinane

Keres, *Southwest*
Also: *telikyanane* [Parsons 1939:270, n.*]. Zuni prayer stick [Bunzel 1932b:549]. Prayer offerings (see entry) in the form of feathers attached to a stick. These offerings accompany sacred ceremonies as well as individual prayers. Different ceremonies require different forms of prayer sticks. The offerings are made in a prescribed and sacred manner by qualified individuals.

See also *prayer feathers/sticks.*

Telogetl

Yurok, *Oregon Seaboard*
Also: *teilogitl* [Kroeber 1925:63]. Pain (see *pains*). Among the Yurok, where nearly all doctoring shamans are females, "pains" are the form in which power first comes to the shaman. Through a series of dreams, a spirit visits her and places the "pain," which is a material object, into her body. Likewise, once she gains control over this "pain," she then has the ability to cure—i.e., remove such disease-causing "pains" in her patients. "These 'pains' do not differ from those of the laity; but their presence within her permits her clairvoyantly to diagnose them and to remove them from her patients by sucking. She precedes each treatment by a solo dance which, though it may bring her to the point of collapse, heightens both her clairvoyance and her interactions with the patient. After sucking out a patient's 'pain' she vomits it up and exhibits it" [Posinsky 1965:239].

There is a remarkable if inverted similarity between the dentalia shells (the aboriginal money

of the Yurok) and the *telogetl* or "pains" which are the primary cause of illness among them. These "pains"—which are finger-like in shape and covered with blood or slime when extracted and [sometimes animate when] exhibited by the shaman—are similar in appearance to dentalia, except that the *telogetl* are maleficent rather than beneficent. Since Yurok values and morality are couched in financial terms, virtue and asceticism are expected to result inevitably in dentalia (wealth), whereas violations of morality and taboo produce the maleficent dentalia (*telogetl* or "pains") in the patient's body.

Whether solicited by the shaman or not, these "pains" are the source of her therapeutic powers; and they are also a life-long source of discomfort to her" [Posinsky 1965:236].

During shamanic performances the shaman often vomits up her "pains" and displays them for all to see, whereupon she reingests them. "Pains" extracted from patients can be either destroyed or swallowed by the shaman to increase her powers, given that the more "pains" a shaman is able to control, the more efficacious she becomes with regard to cures. "Pains" sent by a sorcerer are often "shot" back by the doctor, sometimes resulting in the sorcerer's death.

Tenektaide

Kiowa, *Plains*
A shaman during the middle part of the nineteenth century. In 1927 Tsâlpa, at the age of eighty-four, described a ceremony performed by Tenektaide around 1873 while they were both prisoners in St. Augustine, Florida. Tenektaide proposed to call forth a particular sacred fetish in the form of Gâdombisohi (Underground Old Woman) [Parsons 1929:112] that was kept by the Kiowas back in Oklahoma. "He said he was going to ask Underground Old Woman to come over to them. I did not believe she could come, it was too far. We were sitting on a cement platform. Then Tenektaide called all the prisoners, Kiowa and Cheyenne, to come to where they were to see the image. It was moonlight. Tenektaide commenced

to sing. He sang the song four times. After he sang the fourth song, they saw the image coming up through the platform [Gâdombisohi lives underground]. It was the length of the hand and had a feather erect at the back of the head. Tenektaide sang another song, and the image danced around in a circle (motions clockwise). Then all the Indians began to pray and Tenektaide gave a shout. . . . There are two other Kiowa still living who saw that image dancing around. It kept on dancing, then it disappeared" [Tsâlpa in Parsons 1929:113].

Thaumaturgist

Miracle worker or magician. This term is sometimes found in the older literature to refer to a shaman. For example, Gillette [1906:461] noted that "the medicine man among the Dakotas is both thaumaturgist and physician." The shaman's medicine powers are also sometimes referred to as "thaumaturgical powers" [Hill-Tout 1903:413].

Theehone

Beothuck, *Canadian Eastern Woodlands*
Heaven [Winter 1975:156]. This Newfoundland culture became extinct in the first part of the nineteenth century, and the origin of this term is unknown. Most likely it was a term retranslated by missionaries.

Thekenendatetco

Sekani, *Mackenzie-Yukon*
A shaman who was the most famous prophet in the area of the Great Slave Lake in the 1940s. "His spirit is said to visit the sky nearly every night where it learns everything transpiring. When his spirit returns at noon the following day, his drum on the wall first commences to beat untouched, his singing is heard afar off, and soon his body gets up and dances about six inches above the ground without touching it. Then he awakens and relates his experiences. . . . His wonderful deeds are manifold. He is very old, but will never die; he hears and knows everything that passes and all Indians must obey his will" [Mason 1946:39–40].

Theriomorphic

A term used earlier in anthropology to refer "to beings, especially gods, who resemble animals" [Winick 1968:535].

Theurgist

A person who practices theurgy (magic). This term was originally applied to shamanic Neoplatonists who worked miracles through the use of helping spirits. In some of the older ethnographic literature (e.g., Stevenson 1904), it was used to refer to shamans or priests.

Thomas, Albert

Achomawi, *California*
A shaman of wide repute throughout northern California around the turn of the twentieth century. Thomas was half Wintu and half Achomawi. He was raised among the Achomawi, but, as a healing shaman, he traveled widely among the Wintu, with whom he conversed in English. He became a shaman later in life, after he had married and had three children. He regularly sought guardian spirits by swimming at power pools (see *sauel*), "even when it was icy cold" [Sarah Fan in Du Bois 1935:92]. One of his assistants during the early part of his career reported: "We stayed together two months that summer. I used to go around and interpret for him [i.e., tell the audience what Thomas was saying during trance]. I went as far south as Vina. The first time that the lizard spirit came to him I couldn't understand very well what he said, so he told me to call the 'old white man' spirit. Then a white man's spirit came to him and he began talking in English. That summer, I used to see Thomas draw fire with his hands from a lamp and light his pipe with it. I saw him do it often. He said it was electricity which drew fire. Once I saw him lift a blazing piece of live oak. He didn't even scorch his shirt or hair. He does this best when he has the lizard spirit. But he can do it only when he is in a trance" [Wash Fan in Du Bois 1935:92].

Thunder Cloud
Winnebago, *Midwest*

A remarkable late-nineteenth-century shaman who related his life story to anthropologist Paul Radin. Thunder Cloud told Radin that this was his second incarnation, as he remembered his death on the battlefield in his last life. Before his second reincarnation as a human, he had been a fish, a bird, and finally a buffalo. In the fourth incarnation he came back a human and did not lose consciousness at birth. Furthermore, he said, before the fourth reincarnation the spirits endowed him with powers—that is, he was born with his shamanic powers. The spirits placed before him a black stone. "Four times I breathed upon that stone and finally I made a hole right through the stone by the force of my breathing. So now, whoever has a pain, if he permits me to blow upon him, then I can blow his pain away for him. It makes no difference what kind of pain it is, for my breath has been made holy. They, the spirits, made my breath holy and strong" [Thunder Cloud in Radin 1922:77].

He also received a power from the spirits that involved asperating water. "This power of spitting upon people, of squirting water upon people, I received from an eel. . . . Therefore it is that I can use water and that the water I possess is inexhaustible" [Thunder Cloud in Radin 1922:77].

While growing up he fasted, "and then again all those who had blessed me before sent their blessings to me once more. It is for that reason that I am the dictator over all these spirits. Whatever I say will be so" [Thunder Cloud in Radin 1922:77–78]. Accordingly he received powers from Tobacco, Fire, Buffalo, Grizzly Bear, Eel, Turtle, Rattlesnake, Night Spirits, Disease-Giver, Thunderbird, Sun, Moon, and Earth.

Tihil
Yuki, *California*

The disease object removed from the body of a patient by a sucking shaman. "When he [the shaman] has sucked the pain [disease object] out, he coughs it into his hand, sings, slaps it onto his head or body. It enters him (and leaves him again?); he wipes his hands, it is gone. Sometimes he will shove it into the ashes of the fireplace. An ordinary pain-object is not shown after extraction because it might bring on blindness; though it might be exhibited to a persistent disbeliever. Only actual arrowheads shot in warfare, and the pain-objects injected by rattlesnakes and black spiders, are shown" [Kroeber 1932:372].

See also *pains.*

Tihu
Hopi, *Southwest*

Doll. This term is used for the different forms of charm dolls used in various ceremonies. They are small, carved wooden figures that are painted, clothed, or both. Often the doll represents some particular Hopi *katcina* (or *kachina*).

One unique form of *tihu,* known as *Powamu-Wuhti-Tiata,* are used by the Powamu society. During their ceremonies "certain men are dressed up as decrepit women. These wear masks which represent wrinkled, ugly faces of old hags. They carry little doll babies, which are generally partly hidden in large pine branches. . . . Some represent little boys, some girls. They are made in many different styles. Women who are sterile, and also others, throw pinches of corn-meal to these dolls as prayers that they may bear children. The meal is thrown towards the male doll if a boy, to the female doll if a girl baby is desired" [Voth 1901:121].

Tintachinwunawa
Hupa, *California*

See *kitetau.*

Tinun
Tolowa, *Oregon Seaboard*

See *sisene.*

Tipapeo
Menomini, *Midwest*

A special type of shaman. See *jesako* for details.

Tipni
Yokuts, *California*

The Yokuts term for *mana* (see entry), the power of a shaman. For example, a Bear shaman, "through his *tipni* or *mana,* turns his own person into a bear's body" [Kroeber 1925:259].

Tiponi
Hopi, *Southwest*

A specially selected ear of corn that is decorated in a specific manner and used as a ritual fetish. Similar corn fetishes appear among the Pueblo, called *yaya* (EONAH, pp. 325–326), and among the Zuni, called *mili* or *mile* (EONAH, pp. 175–176). When the *tiponi* is used in a ceremonial altar display, other ears of corn are usually placed next to it, as is a hollow cane stick, to one end of which some feathers are bound by winding the cane with twine. These latter objects are called *nákwa mókiata* and referred to as "the husbands" of the corn ears [Parsons 1933:65]. (Among the Zuni they are known as *ettowe* or *etowe* and filled with seeds.) They act as the receptacles for prayers.

The *tiponi* is associated with the curing societies, and it is in the care of the chief of each curing society. When a new leader is installed in a curing society, a new *tiponi* is made or at least the old one is remade. In some Hopi societies, such as the Wöwöchim and Singers Societies, the *tiponi* consists of an ear of corn and a hollow cane [Parsons 1933:65, n. 256].

Titsïpuaxantï
Paiute, *Basin*

Dialectical variant: *ibibuaxantï* (Las Vegas) [Kelly 1939:162] and *iwipuaxantï* (Saint George) [Kelly 1939:156]. Literal translation: "evil doctor." Paranigat (Southern Paiute) term for a sorcerer or witch [Kelly 1939:159].

Tiwét
Nez Perce, *Plateau*

Shaman. This term is generally applied both to shamans who can cure and to sorcerers, who are called *peléyc tiwét,* "hidden shamans" [D. Walker 1968:25]. Less powerful possessors of spirit powers are called *wéyeknin,* from the word *wéyekin* (helping spirit—EONAH, p. 315). From this term comes *tiwetunéwit,* meaning shamanism [Walker 1968:26].

Once a helping spirit is acquired, there are four basic methods by which the shaman can increase his or her power: stealing another shaman's power; adding more helping spirits through repeated vision quests; gaining more control over already possessed spirits; and ritually transferring power during a spirit dance [D. Walker 1968:24].

The power given by one's helping spirit is often designated by a specialist's title; for example, a hunting or game shaman is called *wáptipa.* However, the shaman might also be regarded as simply a very powerful *wéyeknin* [D. Walker 1968:25]. The most important type of shaman was the *isxip* (see entry) [D. Walker 1968:25].

Whatever form of spirit appeared to the neophyte, the powers therefrom had to be validated through a tutelary spirit dance. "This was an annual affair, usually given in late winter. It was under the control of a given shaman or group of shamans and usually sponsored by a prominent headman or chief. . . . It provided opportunities for validation of the tutelary spirit power of the aspiring *wéyeknin,* as well as for the power demonstrations and competitions so characteristic of the system. Tutelary spirit power was increased, curing took place, and on occasion tutelary spirits were bequeathed through a formal ceremony. The tutelary spirit dance, therefore, was essential to the perpetuation of the tutelary spirit system, demonstrating its efficacy and serving as a means of acquiring, practicing, and bequeathing power" [D. Walker 1968:28].

Tlahit
Wintun, *California*

Nomlaki seer. The *tlahit* has the ability to go into trance and see what is going on in the area or look into the immediate future. Usually such individuals lie on the ground and smoke during their trance inductions. Once in trance they speak in a "secret" language, and an interpreter tells the people what is being said. These shamans do not have healing power. They are most often called upon to assist in warfare or to locate lost persons and objects.

"These men can lie down and smoke and tell how many soldiers are coming and where they are, and in this way their side gets an advantage. They can tell what is happening somewhere, also what will happen in the future" [Jones in Goldschmidt 1951:363].

Toai

Tiwa, *Southwest*
One of two terms used at Isleta Pueblo for a prayer stick; the other term is *shii* [Parsons 1939: 270, n.*]. See *offerings, prayer feathers/sticks.*

Tobacco

Of all the sacred plants used by Native Americans in North America, none is more widely used in ritual than tobacco. In fact, "tobacco was cultivated more widely than any other North American plant" [Driver and Massey 1957:262]. As such, it is difficult to imagine a shaman who does not in some way incorporate its use in ceremony. "Clearly tobacco was a plant of enormous ritual potency and enormously variable use, but behind all the variety of uses was the idea that tobacco had the power to put one into a spiritually exalted state which was necessary even for secular enterprises. Because of this power, it made a particularly appropriate gift to the spirits and means of addressing them" [Springer 1981:219]. It is a common practice to "feed" one's spirits with tobacco offerings.

Several species of *Nicotiana* grow in North America. The most widespread species, found throughout the eastern half of the United States, is *Nicotiana rustica.* It is a cultivated "hybrid, having been derived from two wild species growing on the west side of the Andes near the border of Ecuador and Peru. . . . Probably the next most widely distributed species is *Nicotiana attenuata,* which grows wild in the Great Basin, the Oasis,

and the southern Plains. It was used by Indians in these areas, both as a wild plant and as a cultivated one, and extended north as a cultivated plant into western Canada" [Driver and Massey 1957:261–262]. Tobacco was even cultivated by some cultures that were never agriculturalists, such as the Crow.

"Tobacco was smoked everywhere it was known except on the northern Northwest Coast, where it was only chewed with lime" [Driver and Massey 1957:262]. Tobacco may be smoked by wrapping it in its own leaves (cigar), wrapping it in a burnable material such as cornhusks (cigarette), or in pipes of various forms made of either wood, clay, or stone. The preferred stone is catlinite (see *sacred pipe,* EONAH, pp. 238–240).

Many rituals surround the use of tobacco. For instance, a ceremony may be held when the first tobacco of the season is gathered and smoked for the first time. Among the Thompson of the Plateau area an elder would lead this ceremony. After gathering the participants in a circle,

he sat or stood in the middle of the circle himself. Sometimes he addressed the people at some length, but as a rule simply said, "Be it known to you that we will cut up the chief (tobacco)." Then he cut up some of the tobacco, and after mixing it with roasted bearberry-leaves, he filled a large pipe, lighted it, and handed it to each of the individuals, following the sun's course. The people each took one whiff, and holding up their hands, the palms close together, the tips of the middle fingers level with the mouth, blew the smoke downward between their fingers, and over their breast; and as the smoke descended, they crossed their hands on their breast, and rubbing their chest and shoulders with both hands, as if rubbing the smoke in, they prayed, "Lengthen my breath, chief (tobacco), so that I may never be sick, and so that I may not die for a long time to come." After every one had had a whiff, some of the tobacco was cut up in small portions, and a piece given to each individual. . . . Smoking was considered the privilege of people possessed of mysterious

A medicine bundle belonging to the Weasel chapter of the Crow Tobacco society.

powers, such as shamans and others [Teit 1900:349–350].

Tohópko
Hopi, *Southwest*
A stone fetish representing the puma that is used in various altar displays, such as those of the Snake society [Voth 1903:287].

Toka
Maidu, *California*
The Southern Maidu term for a ceremonial whistle that is "made of *antai,* a red-barked shrub which grows near creeks, [and] was used in the *yohohanup* dance. It is about fifteen inches long with a hole in the side. It is blown from the end" [Gifford 1927:241].

Tomasuk
Labrador Eskimo, *Arctic Coast*
A shaman around the end of the nineteenth century who resided in southern Labrador near Sandwich Bay. E. W. Hawkes [1916:132] reported that by this time, "the old angekok [shamans] have degenerated into mere conjurers," and he offered Tomasuk as an example.

See also *kiluxin.*

Toner
Nunivagmiut, *West Alaska Eskimo*
Shaman's helping spirit [Rasmussen 1941:35]. (See *torngak,* EONAH, p. 285; *tornrak,* EONAH, p. 286; and *tunraq,* EONAH, pp. 295–296.)

Tong Kegi
Tewa, *Southwest*
"Edge of Spring" Ceremony [Hill 1982:247]. This religious ceremony is conducted by the Summer society (see *xa zhe*) at Santa Clara Pueblo in late January, and a corresponding ritual, called *Kave Na,* is simultaneously performed by their Winter society (see *kwere*). It takes four days to properly conduct the ritual. The purpose of the ritual is to "wake up the Earth-mother" [Jeançon in Hill 1982:248], but in former times the major purpose was to transfer religious authority from the Winter society to the Summer society.

The ceremony requires the construction of many different types of prayer plumes, which are then empowered during the ceremony. There are prayer plumes for Sun, Moon, Mother Earth, Big Snake, Evening Star, and the twelve Ancestors of the War Captain. One account of such a ceremony noted that "the man who was charged with constructing the offering associated with Mother Earth wrapped his plume with an unusually long cord. 'A string long enough to reach around the entire room. This was so the coming year, the summer, might be a long one'" [Hill 1982:249]. In addition, prayer plumes are made for the participants of the *ange share,* "slow dance" [Hill 1982:249], to be worn later in the year. "The final set of plumes was constructed by all those owning livestock. These sets consisted of bundles of turkey breast feathers and warbler tail and breast feathers. The number of plumes made depended on the needs of each individual" [Hill 1982:249]. Once empowered, the livestock plumes are tied to the tails of their horses, cattle, burros, etc.

Tornarsuk
East Greenland Eskimo, *Arctic Coast*
Literal translation: "peculiar, separate *tornaq*" [Kleinschmidt in Kroeber 1900:304]. Ammasalik shaman's helping spirit [Holm in Thalbitzer 1914:80]. This is a special spirit that answers questions put to it when summoned by the shaman. Another spirit, the *Aperketek,* acts as a mediator between the shaman and his *Tornarsuk* during the questioning sessions. A shaman's *Tornarsuk* is particularly dangerous because it takes other people's soul, causing them to become dull, heavy, and eventually ill.

Among the Eskimos of Smith Sound (Aleut), *Tornarsuk* appears to be a more general term for a shaman's helping spirit (see *angakussarfiks*). Among the Central Eskimos and the Mackenzie nations, the word *Tornarsuk* is unknown [Boas in Kroeber 1900:304; Petitot in Kroeber 1900:305].

The more general term for a shaman's helping spirit among the East Greenland Eskimo is *tornguang.* "The angakoq [shaman—see EONAH, pp. 13–15] uses his tornguang as an instrument for almost every purpose, and it is in possessing a tornguang that all his angakoq power seems, directly or indirectly, to lie. By means of his tornguang he discovers whether a sick person will recover; by it or on it he can fly to the moon and back; to it he prays and sings" [Kroeber 1900: 305]. In obtaining a *tornguang* the shaman depends on a spirit named Torngaxssung. "Torngaxssung instructs the angakoq, asking him what sort of tornguang he wants, giving it to him and telling him how to use it. For one night he keeps the angakoq, who must then go. He is now a complete angakoq" [Kroeber 1900:304].

The exact relationship of Torngaxssung to the *tornguang* is far from clear. For example, Torngaxssung is variously described as the oldest *tornguang*, as a powerful *angakoq*, as a ghost of a dead person, as a great bear, as having no shape, etc. Regardless of these vague and differing descriptions, Torngaxssung is always conceived of as an individual. For example, dogs see Torngaxssung and bark at him, driving him away. There is one report of "a woman who had died [and] could not be lifted from the ground . . . this was caused by torngaxssuin" [Kroeber 1900:305].

Torngaxssung

East Greenland Eskimo, *Arctic Coast*
See *Tornarsuk*.

Torngraq

Iglulik Eskimo, *Arctic Coast*
Plural: *torngrät* [Rasmussen 1929:113]. Dialectical variants: *tôrnaq* (singular), *tôrnat* (plural) (West Greenland) [Birket-Smith 1924:453]; *torngak* (singular—see EONAH, p. 285), *tornait* (plural) (Labrador). Spirit, usually a shaman's helping spirit. The shaman's spirits are his primary instructors. Little training is received from older shamans beyond instructions on their sacred language and a preliminary *angakua* (see *anakua*, EONAH, p. 13, and *qaumaneq*, EONAH, p. 229) initiation, in which the novice receives his "lighting" or "enlightenment" and light fills his body. Furthermore, any power derived with the assistance of older shamans can only be maintained through the subsequent acquisition and use of helping spirits.

But before a shaman attains the stage at which any helping spirit would think it worth while to come to him, he must, by struggle and toil and concentration of thought, acquire for himself yet another [in addition to the *angakua*] great and inexplicable power: *he must be able to see himself as a skeleton.* Though no shaman can explain to himself how and why, he can, by the power his brain derives from the supernatural, as it were by thought alone, divest his body of its flesh and blood, so that nothing remains but his bones. And

he must then name all the parts of his body, mention every single bone by name; and in so doing, he must not use ordinary human speech, but only the special and sacred shaman's language which he has learned from his instructor. By thus seeing himself naked, altogether freed from the perishable and transient flesh and blood, he consecrates himself, in the sacred tongue of the shamans, to his great task, through that part of his body which will longest withstand the actions of sun, wind and weather, after he is dead [Rasmussen 1929:114].

In acquiring a helping spirit the shaman, going alone into "the great solitude," wishes for one of the more powerful animal spirits, such as Fox, Owl, Bear, Dog, or Shark, which most often appear to him in human form. However, the novice has no choice over which spirits will eventually come to him, provided his solitary vision quest is successful. So seriously are all the shaman's preparations considered "that some parents, even before the birth of the shaman-to-be, set all things in order for him beforehand by laying upon themselves a specially strict and onerous taboo" [Rasmussen 1929:116].

The psychological relationship between a helping spirit and the shaman runs extremely deep among the Iglulik Inuit shamans. The joy that a shaman experiences in obtaining a helping spirit and the depression he knows when his helping spirit abandons him are all eloquently expressed in the story that Aua, an Iglulik shaman, told to anthropologist Knud Rasmussen [1929:116–120] in the early 1920s. The formula is simple: Once the shaman is approached by a spirit and taught its powers, the "shaman has his own particular song, which he sings [i.e., trance-induction technique] when calling up his helping spirits; they must sing when the helping spirits enter into their bodies, and speak with the voice of the helping spirits themselves" [Rasmussen 1929:122].

Tornguang

East Greenland Eskimo, *Arctic Coast*
See *Tornarsuk*.

Torniwoq
East Greenland Eskimo, *Arctic Coast*
The performance of an Ammasalik shaman in which he calls upon his guardian spirits. "There are four main occasions in which the services of an angakok [see *angatkok,* EONAH, pp. 15–16] at Ammasalik will be called in request, and when he must summon his spirits to a meeting under the floor of the huts: dearth of sea animals in the sea; snow-masses blocking the ways to the hunting-places (on the land or on the fjord ice); a man's loss of soul (illness); a married woman's barrenness. Any one of these circumstances is sufficient reason for him to summon a meeting of the spirits, when the inhabitants of the place or even people from a distance so demand" [Thalbitzer 1931:433].

In such performances the shaman is "tightly bound behind his back, being lashed from the hands to the elbows with a long thong which is tied in knots" [Thalbitzer 1931:434]. During his performance the shaman is freed from these bindings by his guardian spirits.

"A diligent angakok torniwoqs almost every night the whole winter through. No singing is so lovely as the singing of the spirits; the singing of mortals is nothing to it" [unidentified shaman in Thalbitzer 1931:436].

Tosanawïn
Paiute, *Basin*
Literal translation: White Tip [Kelly 1936: 132]. A Vegas shaman from Cottonwood Island who lived in the latter part of the eighteenth century. Both the Basin and Southwest areas have a long ethnographic record of sorcery and witchcraft. Only powerful shamans have the ability to ward off their illness-producing attacks, and only such men or women are called upon to heal a victim of sorcery. However, detailed accounts of such instances are rarely seen in the ethnographic literature. In regard to Tosanawïn we find one of the better examples available:

Tosanawïn was on a trip to the northeast. "He was somewhere north of Shivwits country [branch of Pauite Nation], where they understood his language [Vegas, the Nevada division of the Southern Paiute]. A doctor there asked him and three others to smoke with him. The Cottonwood island man was suspicious. He went to one side and called his guardian spirit and asked it to sit in his throat. Then he smoked without difficulty. The other doctor had planned to kill him.

Before he left the Cottonwood island man decided to kill the one who had tried to murder him. He had the power of knowing where another person was and where his head lay in sleep. For a spirit helper he had a spotted cat (?) (paru´-kumumunts, water-lion) and this he sent to kill the other doctor as he slept. The cat traveled underground so it could not be seen, and clawed the man to death as he slept. The next morning the Cottonwood island doctor left very early. About midday he fell asleep on the trail. His spirit helper came to him and said, "I have killed the one who tried to kill you," and he showed him a bloody arrow.

After this the man did not dream of his spirit for a year and a half. This was because it had plenty of flesh (of the victim) on which to feed. And for a year and a half the doctor himself dreamed of feasting on the meat. It was always so when a doctor killed a person. The Cottonwood island doctor told us this when he was old and did not care if people knew [unidentified informant in Kelly 1936:132–133].

Tötöeqpi
Hopi, *Southwest*
A ceremonial eagle-bone whistle [Voth 1901:68].

Touchtd
Snuqualmi, *Northwest Coast*
Also: *techted.* Canoe pole. This is the Duwamish (or Dwamish) term for the pole used to propel a canoe upstream. It is also the term applied to the canoe poles used in the *Sptdaqw* (EONAH, p. 263) or *Sbetedaq* (see entry)—the Spirit Canoe Ceremony [Dorsey 1902:234] among the Coast Salish. In ceremonial use these poles, from 4 to 8

feet in length, are pointed on one end and blunt on the other. Toward the upper end there is usually a slightly constricted area, about which is tied a string of cedar bark. In addition, sometimes the poles are painted.

The Spirit Canoe Ceremony was conducted mainly for patients whose illness had been diagnosed as soul loss. The shamans then journeyed to the Land of the Dead to recover the lost soul. The following is a brief account of a four-day Spirit Canoe Ceremony:

Toward the afternoon the sick man was carried into the house and placed on a pallet in the corner. The invited guests and friends from the nearby settlements gathered around the sides of the long house and the four doctors took their places in the "canoe," each armed with a long pole *[touchtd]*. The ceremony began at sundown about the middle of January, as nearly as I could learn. The doctors began by singing, which was accompanied by the beating of rattles and drums by the friends of the invalid. At the same time the shamans began movements with the poles, as though they were propelling the boat. This kept up all night and by noon of the next day they were supposed to have entered the under-world, where the struggle for the possession of the spirit of the sick man began. Dr. Jack was very emphatic in his declaration that to compel the return of the spirit when once it became accustomed to the under-world was a very difficult matter; and that without the assistance of the small effigies or tahmanaous [power] figures which accompanied them, it would be an impossibility. He admitted that the desire of his own spirit and those of his fellow-doctors to remain in the under-world was very great; but he explained that a man, to be a doctor, must possess an unusually strong will; otherwise, on his first attempt to rescue the spirit of the sick man in the under-world, he would not only be unsuccessful and consequently permit the sick man to die, but would die himself. . . .

The struggle in the other world, so it was said, in this particular dance, lasted about a day and a half, at the end of which time they began the return journey, having been successful in their

quest. At the end of the fourth day one of them signified to the spectators and friends of the sick man that they had been successful, when the sick man was lifted from his pallet and placed within the line formed by the upright slabs, that is, within the boat. The combined strength of the four doctors was then required to lift the spirit and place it on his body, where they finally forced it back into place. I was informed that the patient, from this time on, mended speedily and soon was restored to perfect health [Dorsey 1902:236–237].

In this journey the shamans encounter at least nine familiar locations along the trail to the Land of the Dead, some of which are dangerous. For example, there is a wide lake (called *Taxwatab*) that has to be crossed. "If anyone has a 'power' which is weak, however, he is likely to be lost here" [Waterman 1930:139]. Then there is the Mosquito-Place (called *Obstetcaks*), where the mosquitoes are as large as birds. "If a shaman is bitten by one of them, his whole body swells, and he dies" [Waterman 1930:140]. The final and most difficult point is the crossing of a torrential river, whose banks are continually caving in and in which giant boulders are being tossed downstream. "In our world above the shaman plants his pole *[touchtd]* in the small circle and vaults out through space, landing on a specified spot. If one of the war-party [those in the spirit canoe] should fall into the stream, the corresponding shaman up in our world would die, right while he was dancing. The slightest slip or misstep on the part of the dancer was interpreted to mean that his supernatural power had failed him" [Waterman 1930:142].

In his work on the Spirit Canoe Ceremony, Dorsey [1902:231] also used the term *techted* to refer to the "long cane or dancing wand" used by shamans.

See also *stlalcop-schudoptch*.

Toxobuaxantï
Paiute, *Basin*
Dialectical variants: *toxoabuaxantï* (Saint George) [Kelly 1939:157]; *toxwabuaxantï* (Paranigat)

[Kelly 1939:159]; *kwiabpuaxantï* (Moapa) [Kelly 1939:160]; *kwiyavuwagantï* (Chemehuevi) [Laird 1976:35]; and *kwiabuaxantï* (Las Vegas) [Kelly 1939:164]. Kaibab (Southern Paiute) term for a Rattlesnake shaman. These are shamans who receive their medicine powers from dreams of Rattlesnake. They are called upon to treat snakebite victims. In a typical shamanic treatment the "snake shaman touched his cane to the breast of a [snakebite] victim, and upon removing it, displayed a small rattlesnake on the tip. This he deposited on a near-by stone, from which it soon disappeared. With the removal of the snake, the swelling began to subside. The doctor then sucked, not from the bite but from the chest and stomach, either blood or yellow-green matter. This he sometimes swallowed, sometimes spat out" [Kelly 1939:153].

Among the Las Vegas the snake shaman "treated any venomous wounds—snake, tarantula, or spider. The treatment lasted four or five days and consisted of singing, dancing, and sucking. By means of the latter, 'poison' was removed from the wound, but never a miniature snake or other visible object" [Kelly 1939:165].

The Chemehuevi had a snake doctor who could also cure a toothache. "If a person had been bitten by a rattlesnake on the hand or foot and had recovered, he [the snake shaman] could take away the pain of toothache by laying the hand or foot, as the case might be, against the afflicted cheek" [Laird 1976:35].

Toyaqca
Nez Perce, *Plateau*
A shaman's trance [D. Walker 1967:71].

Tozriki
Hopi, *Southwest*
Bandolier. This term can refer to the bandolier worn by a warrior [Stephen 1936:44], which is properly termed *kale'takto'zrikiata* [Stephen 1936:1308]. The *tozriki* is a form of war medicine that "prevents a warrior from having any fear of an enemy" [Stephen 1936:98]. Each time an enemy is slain, his Hopi slayer makes a new bandolier from the dead man's clothing. Therefore, "some famous warriors had a bandoleer as thick as one's arm. Some had two bandoleers worn cross belt fashion. A warrior with one, wears it across his right shoulder" [Stephen 1936:98].

Medicines in the form of powdered roots are placed in small, white clay pellets, which are then attached to the *tozriki;* other possible forms include mouth hairs from the wildcat, mountain lion, and bear and a "miniature bow and arrow a span long" [Stephen 1936:98]. Particularly powerful is the *hohoyaüh* (see entry), which is also placed into the clay pellets.

Other forms of the *tozriki* include the *lepostozriki* [Stephen 1936:477], or juniper seed bandolier, worn by Zuni *kachina* dancers and the *nütkya tozriki* [Stephen 1936:370], or journey food bandolier, used by the Squatting society clowns.

Transmutation
The ability of shamans to transform objects into other substances or forms is mentioned frequently in the ethnographic data on Native American shamanism. This includes the ability of shamans (and also witches) to transform their own forms into other shapes (see *war medicine*). Quite often transmutations involve animating an animal skin or object; in other cases substances are changed into different forms.

The Canadian Dakota had a medicine man who, when he wanted tobacco, used a special stone to assist him in transforming leaves from a bush into tobacco. When the leaves were dry, "he rubbed them between his hands. Now and then he smelled them and tasted them, while he sang. While he was doing this, there lay beside him a certain stone, which he had asked to aid him in transforming the leaves into tobacco. He continually tasted and smelled the leaves. Finally, they tasted like tobacco, and, indeed, became tobacco" [Wallis 1947:79].

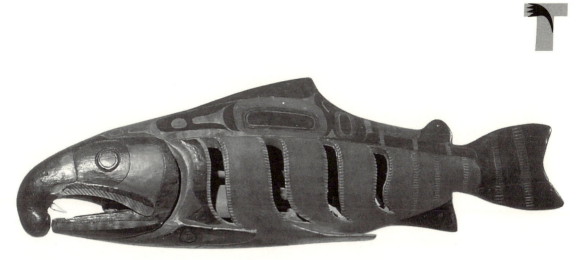

A Tlingit rattle in the form of a salmon containing an effigy figure of a shaman.

Another Dakota shaman, while sitting in a specially constructed ceremonial tipi with a black-painted stone placed in the center of it, "pulled out the longest feathers from the tip of an eagle wing and placed them near the stone. After showing the people the feathers, he sang. While he was singing, he picked up a feather and using it like a spear thrust it through the stone. He had caused the feather to turn into a knife, with which he pierced the stone. When he pulled it out, warm blood came from the hole which it left. He then exhibited the feather, which was as limber and as soft as any other feather, and allowed them to test it with their hands" [Wallis 1947:83].

A final example from the Canadian Dakota involves a shaman who was accused of using his powers to murder a man. Those wanting to convict the shaman told the judge (Indian agent) of the shaman's potential powers, declaring that this shaman could sing to stones, causing them to roll on the ground to him.

The Indian Agent was skeptical and told the culprit that if he could cause stones to come to him by singing, the Agent would dismiss him. For a long time the accused man did not reply. Finally he agreed to sing. He bade the Agent secure a certain young man, to assist with the singing, and also a drum and a flute. About 10 o'clock in the evening, he began to sing. Many of the people were watching the large stone known as Standing Rock (in North Dakota). After a while they heard him play the flute. He blew it four times, then beat the drum, sang, and signaled the assistants to join in the singing. They watched this stone closely. No one saw it start from its place, but they all saw it moving on the ground toward the drum; it was then about a quarter of a mile away. It moved slowly, shoving along, to the place where the man was singing. When he stopped singing, the Agent went to him and told him that the stone had not come into the tipi. The man replied that it was ashamed to do so, because it was blind and had no legs on which to walk; but he had done his utmost; the stone was shy because of the people present, and therefore would not go into the tipi. The Agent dismissed the man and placed the stone in his own house; next morning, however, it was back on the hill where it belonged. Afterward they would not allow him to perform any of these feats. He did not wish to be called "the devil." This is a true story [Wallis 1947:102].

Among the Copper Eskimos at Coronation Gulf, a female shaman named Mittik was observed to change form. During a séance she "walked away towards the sun up the side of a ridge. Suddenly she disappeared into the ground, and a moment afterwards a dog sprang out from the same spot; then the dog disappeared and the woman took its place again. This occurred three or four times in the sight of all the people, then finally Mittik walked back to the camp in her human form, but with her faculties impaired. Other shamans laid hands on her, and with the aid of their familiars [helping spirits] restored her to her senses" [Jenness 1970:192].

In fact, such transmutations are common among the Copper Eskimos.

> A shaman will often change his form and take on that of the animal by which he is possessed, or will assume at least some of its characteristics. This metamorphosis may even take place in the presence of spectators, though sometimes it can occur only when the shaman is alone. Thus Ilatsiak [see entry] said that when his grandmother was a child there was a shaman named Makettak who could change into a polar bear. He would bend down to the floor of the dance-house, resting his hands on the ground. Slowly his hands would change into polar bear's feet, then his arms become legs, and finally his whole body and head would assume the shape of the bear. In this state he would go out of the dance-house and visit the neighboring houses. . . . Higilak's father could change into a polar bear, but only when he was alone. Uloksak claimed the power of transforming himself into a white or a brown bear, a wolf and a white man. Ilatsiak's wife, who was a shaman like her husband, put her fingers into her mouth on one occasion; gradually her hands became the feet of a wolf, then her head and body began to change and finally only her legs remained human [Jenness 1970:193].

A Copper Eskimo shaman named Pannaktok, who lived at Bathurst Inlet,

> took off one of his mittens and laid it on the floor; presently it stood up on end and changed to a tiny man, who turned around and gazed on all the audience. Pannaktok stooped down and picked it up, and it changed to a mitten again. Then he laid both his mittens on the palms of his hands and held them out toward the spectators. First they changed to polar bear's claws, then two tiny bears jumped down and began to scratch on the floor; again they changed to mittens when he picked them up.
>
> This same Pannaktok, according to native accounts, told a man to stand upright against the wall of the dance-house, then drove his seal-spear right through his chest and threw the weapon to

the back of the hut. The natives had to hold the man up to keep him from falling. The shaman then made the spear return through his chest, leaving the man whole and unharmed [Jenness 1970:199].

One of Pannaktok helping spirits was *Ukumaura* (see entry) [Jenness 1970:211].

See also *arnagtoq, Asetcuk, bear medicine/ possession, Coacoochee, Daganawidah, Geronimo, Hadihiduus, hmuga, hunting medicine, Ilatsiak, Iron Maker, jossokeed, kanatyaiya, kinubik inäniwûk, kitdoñxoi, kopati, Madit, mishtikuai, Neptune, John, Notwita, nuchihewe, tdiyĭn, tipui, tsanati, tuuhisa, Unaleq, ünü, Wakiasua, Wapakiniwap, White Bear, wyagaw, Yayatü society.*

Tsaidetali
Kiowa, *Plains*

Literal translation: "Split Boy" [Parsons 1929: 110]. The name of a spirit, which also refers to a type of medicine bundle, sometimes known in the literature as a "shield," that was associated with war medicines. Part of the war medicine involved attaching scalps to this bundle. The *tsaidetali* was also used in healing ceremonies.

Such a bundle was kept in a special location and carried with it specific handling instructions—for example: Before touching a *tsaidetali*, one had to make an offering to it; the bundle was not to come into contact with a bearskin; dogs were not to come near it; and vulgar language was not to be spoken in its presence.

Tsakorankura
Paiute, *Basin*

Literal translation: "wild-geese-neck" [Kelly 1936:129]. A Chemehuevi shaman during the first part of the twentieth century. His guardian spirits were Ocean-Woman, Bat, and Mouse. "These he sometimes exhibited publicly, in the form of white balls 'like an egg or a snowball'" [Kelly 1936:129]. When Ocean-Woman, called *Xutsimamapïts*—"'just a name; not a woman and not in the ocean' . . . arrived, one could hear him 'grinding corn on a metate, and the grinding sounded like the beating of a heart'" [Kelly 1936:129].

He was his people's most renowned shaman and considered more powerful than all others at the time. His uncle, Enemy Head (Tuxuantto-tots), was also a powerful shaman and had the identical three helping spirits. When Enemy Head died his powers were first passed to his daughter and then later to her younger brother. However, during this time Tsakorankure also began to dream of these spirits (the main method of obtaining their powers), and after the children of Enemy Head died, these powers transferred to Tsakorankure. This notion of passing one's shamanic powers to others is found only among the Southern Pauite, in particular the Las Vegas and the Chemehuevi, but not among the other Pauite divisions [Kelly 1936:131].

During a healing ceremony, Tsakorankure would suck a disease object from the patient's body. This would usually occur near dawn when his helping spirit arrived from the north, following an all-night ceremony. "Toward morning the guardian spirit arrived. The shaman advanced to meet it, taking it between his palms and placing it in his mouth. He returned to camp and blew it directly from his lips into the seat of the ailment. The length of time the spirit remained within the patient was a gauge of the shaman's ability. . . . With Tsakorankura it took no time at all" [Kelly 1936:131–132]. In most cases the disease object is removed prior to the insertion of the helping spirit.

As part of his doctoring paraphernalia Tsako-rankure used a cats-claw staff that was hooked at one end. This cane would talk to Tsakorankure during his healings, telling him the location of the disease object within the patient's body. "A really good shaman was able to tell, by means of his cane, whether the patient would recover. At the conclusion of the séance, he stuck the staff into the ground at the head of the sick person. If it would not sink its full length the patient was doomed" [Kelly 1936:132].

Tsanati
Jicarilla, *Southwest*

Painted dancers. The following is a brief account of a corn-growing medicine ceremony conducted around the turn of the twentieth century on the west side of the Rio Grande, opposite Taos:

I was a spectator. The two old men conducted the ceremony for two persons. They put corn in a deep hole and made it grow. . . . The ts'anati had mullers in their hands. They gave each of the ts'anati and the tc'actcini four ears of corn. Then a large fire was built. The enclosure [for the ceremony] had been built near the river. They put the musk stirrers in the pot.

When the dancers came in here by the door, they put the corn which they had in their hands in the pot. They put the pot some way from the fire where it did not get hot. They poked in the pot with a stick and there was a crackling noise inside, and smoke came out of it. They danced around the fire four times. The pot was filled with corn. They stood in a row and began to dance. The ts'anati stood in front holding the mullers. Corn commenced to grow and put out leaves. When they stopped dancing they held up the mullers to the east, south, west, and north. They broke a muller in two and made it just like one again. They took corn out too. They danced on both sides, carrying the stones.

Then they carried the pot which was filled with corn behind them. They made the people stand in a line and threw the corn to them. . . . It was not cooked. . . . They made good medicine for all. That way they made the corn grow up [unnamed informant in Goddard 1911:264–265].

Tshapuya
Miwok, *California*

Central Miwok sweat house [Gifford n.d. a:40].

Tsik
Tsimshian, *Northwest Coast*

Dialectical variants: *tsayeq* (Nootka); *tsaeqa* (Kwakiutl) [Garfield 1939:298, n. 8]. An untranslatable term referring to a ceremony for children in which power was initially conveyed to them. "The supernatural power received by children was that of the chief who conveyed it. He, being strong, could cope with a spirit that would have destroyed the weaker child, hence he regulated and controlled the influence through him. This first ceremony prepared the child for seeking a supernatural power through his own efforts and gave him the necessary strength for coping with it when he did receive one by himself" [Garfield 1939:299].

Tsikomó
Tewa, *Southwest*
Literal translation: "the place of much rock" (believed to be the true meaning); "the place up high"; "the place of worship" [Douglass 1917:345]. Referred to in English as the World-Center Shrine, this is a rock enclosure atop an 11,400-foot mountain of the Jemez Range. It is oval in shape and about 15 feet by 11 feet. "From the crest of the high peak, some ten miles distant, it overlooks one of the most remarkable centralizations of prehistoric habitations to be found within the United States" [Douglass 1917:354]. Its use dates to prehistoric times and is unknown, but it was obviously a site of elaborate ceremonies. Some scholars believe that the paths leading from the oval point toward specific pueblos, thus indicating its overall importance to this region.

For another example see *Medicine Wheel.*

Tsitsika
Kwakiutl, *Northwest Coast*
Literal translation: "everything is not real" [Nowell in Ford 1967:198]. The annual Winter Ceremony in which shamans demonstrate their supernatural powers. This is a series of performances that go on "for many days and many nights, sometimes right along during the winter. Every time there is nobody else [who] gives a feast, the Kweka chief gives a feast, and any time nobody else gives a dance, he gives a dance" [Nowell in Ford 1967:202].

"The recipients of the various dance privileges were said to be motivated by the supernatural beings whose original contact with the dancers' ancestors began the tradition. The dances were dramatic reenactments of the ancestors' adventures or demonstrations of the power or characteristic actions given them by supernatural beings" [Holm 1990:379].

One informant, named Charlie Nowell, recalled from his youth a "good dance" known as the *Towidi:*

A woman that comes around the [ceremonial] house slowly, and when she gets up to the front of the singers, she stands up and face[s] the fire while all the people are sitting down and says, "Will some of you bring me a knife?"—that is to cut her head off. Nobody brings her one, and then she turns and says, "Bring me a hammer to crush in my head." Each time she says that she always turns around and face[s] the singers, and the people ask each other who has the hammer, and nobody has it. Then she says, "Bring me a paddle to chop my head in two." And nobody has a paddle. Old ones but not new enough. And then she says: "Bring me a box, one of the Indian boxes [cedar chest], and put me inside it. Put the cover on and put the box and me into the fire and burn me up." They all try to find a box big enough, but none is big enough. And then the chief says to the singers, "Beat your board with your sticks, and let us see what she will do." And she go from one end of the house to the other pretending to try to catch something that she alone can see. When she catches it the chief says, "Stop beating that board." The chief listens but she don't say nothing so they beat it again. She does the same thing four times. Then when she catches something it whistles when she moves her hand and she throws it among the singers, and there at once there is a lot of whistling among the singers and then a big snake will come out that reaches to both sides of the house, and she come along with a wood made like a sword and there is a man on the centre of this serpent—a man's face. And she comes there and strikes the man's head with it and it splits and the two sides of the serpent spread apart, and then it comes together again and begins to go down and is supposed to go under the ground. Then the people begin to sing her song, and she goes around the house and back behind the screen and stays there. She does this only one night [Nowell in Ford 1967:205–206].

Tsityu
Keres, *Southwest*
Sacred [Parsons 1926:95].

Tuavitok
Labrador Eskimo, *Arctic Coast*
A personal hunting fetish (see entry) that is made from "a semicircular piece of wood ornamented with strings of beads. . . . The hunter holds it in his hand when he sights the game, and the tighter he grasps it the faster he is supposed to get over the ground. It is supposed that by the use of this one may be able to travel faster than the wind and not even touch the earth over which he passes with such incredible speed that he overtakes the deer in a moment" [L. Turner 1894:198].

Tûkosiwäwûs
Menomini, *Midwest*
Literal translation: "roots drawing each other" [Skinner 1915d:189]. This is a love medicine made from the roots of a particular plant. "The roots are thought to be of both sexes, so the shaman finds a 'male' and a 'female' plant and traces a line in the ground from one to the other. Tobacco is offered to them and the male root is told to visit the female. If the right songs have been sung and the proper incantation made, the two roots will come together over night. They are gathered next day, dried, and ground together" [Skinner 1915d:189].

This powder is then placed in a little bag and set between two wooden dolls, *musininisê*,

carved to represent the user and the object of his or her affections, and named for them. A hair, a paring, or a bit of cloth from the garment of the one desired is placed in the little bag, and the whole tied up. The tighter they are tied, the more powerful is the charm. Sometimes it is too strong

and the string has to be loosened or the victim will go crazy or die. The affair can be ended by untying the bag and taking out the hair, but as this is apt to cause so violent a revulsion that the victim will become demented, it is best to do so gradually.

In manipulating this charm the two dolls named are set up facing each other about three feet apart, while the roots are being pulverized, and the songs sung. The dolls will come together during the song" [Skinner 1915d:189].

Tukyaini
Hopi, *Southwest*
A sorcerer's arrow [Stephen 1936:863]. The disease object that a shaman sucks from the body of his patient during a healing ceremony. It is also called *powaka hoadta*, "sorcerer his arrow" [Stephen 1936:863].

Tumánog
Paviotso, *Basin*
Wadátkuht term for doctoring [Riddell 1960:67]. See *nuhpud*.

Tumsa
Alsea, *Oregon Seaboard*
Shaman. This term is applied to a class of shamans who are less powerful than the *tcuyaliclofor* (see entry). These shamans cure minor ills, usually by singing. "The source of their power was not clear to the informants, who surmised that it may have been derived from guardian spirits" [Drucker 1939:100]. They are not capable of sucking out disease objects or retrieving lost souls.

A *tumsa* is not always publicly known, and therefore many people feel "he more often 'poisoned' than cured" [Drucker 1939:101].

Tumsowit
Wishram, *Plateau*
Also: Tomsowit. The principal Wascopam shaman during the late 1830s. He was converted to Christianity during the Wascopam Revival of

1839–1840 [Boyd 1996:342] but soon thereafter returned to his traditional ways. The following is an account of one of his healing ceremonies observed by Dr. George Suckley and Lt. Archibald Graci, circa 1853 (and related to George Gibbs); on that occasion they witnessed the rarely reported "back dancing" of shamans in this area, a form of power transference:

> An Indian named Tomasowit, a great medicine man at The Dalles, was the operator. The patient was a young girl who had a spinal affection [sic]. The Wascoes had a dance which lasted five days, and the whole band were assembled in a lodge, at one end of which there was a board platform somewhat raised. Tomasowit stood upon this, dancing, swinging and shouting, and tearing off, as his excitement increased, one article after another of his clothing, until he stood perfectly naked. At length he exclaimed, "I feel a wind coming which will make me strong enough to put her to sleep." And becoming apparently exhausted or weak from his exercise, he grasped the pole, which supported the roof, at the same time stooping so as to bring his back into a horizontal position. His knees shook under him and his voice subsided into a low, monotonous song. The girl was then brought in and laid upon him, with her back to his, her head lying over his shoulder and kept in her position by a couple of squaws who held her legs. She had on only a shift. Meantime the people present kept on singing and pounding upon boards, and the m[e]n continued dancing and singing. In a short time, perhaps ten or fifteen minutes, the girl went to sleep [i.e., entered trance]. She was then laid on the floor, and the Doctor kneeling by her commenced a low, wailing cry. The Indians stated that no one but he could awaken her. As the slumber passed off, she commenced crying, then singing louder and clearer and finally got up and danced with all her strength [Clark 1956:135–136].

Tunax
West Alaska Eskimo, *Arctic Coast*
Plural: *tunaxăt* [Lantis 1946:197]. Nunivak word for a shaman's helping spirit. This is a gen-

eral term for any kind of spirit—an animal spirit, a dwarf spirit, or any other form of spirit. The Nunivak also use the term *kala* to refer to any spirit [Lantis 1946:197]. *Kala* is used on the nearby mainland, while *tunax* is used on Nunivak Island.

In a similar manner the term for shaman on Nunivak Island is *tunagalix,* while on the mainland it is *kalalix* [Lantis 1946:197, n. 81]. In the Unalit dialect the shaman is called *tunghalik* (EONAH, p. 295), while on nearby Kodiak Island the word for shaman is *kalalik* (EONAH, p. 129).

There are many different types of spirits.

> There were half-people, with one eye, half a mouth, one leg, and half a body. There were half-birds, too, with one wing, one foot, and so on. There were animals that walked on air. There were delightful small harmless dwarfs, some of whom lived on land, some in the sea. . . . They were quick. If a person tried to hit one, even when very close and very fast, the dwarf would dodge. Yet they were astonishingly strong. If one took hold of a man's wrist, it was impossible to get away unless the dwarf voluntarily let go. There were bigger dwarfs who were more dangerous. . . . Shamans sometimes used this kind as a spirit helper and carved masks to resemble it. Giants were not so common. . . . The most numerous species of spirits, aside from animal spirits, were the i´xcit. The two sides of the face were different: one side awry, the other ordinary human, or one half like an animal's face and quivery, the other half human. Some had an entirely human face but an animal body [Lantis 1946:198].

There are many other types of spirits as well, and "almost all spirits could take human form" [Lantis 1946:199]. However, the most important of all are the animal spirits.

Tungat
Labrador Eskimo, *Arctic Coast*
Ungava term for a helping spirit [Hawkes 1916:127]. This is the form of the word used in

southern Labrador. In northern Labrador and on Baffin Island, the cognate appears as *torngak* (see EONAH, p. 285).

Tunghât
West Alaska Eskimo, *Arctic Coast*

Plural: *tunghät* [Nelson 1899:427]. Unalit term for a shaman's helping spirit. From this term also comes the Unalit word for shaman, *tunghalik,* meaning one who controls or owns a *tunghât.* "Some of these *tunghät* are more powerful than others.... These beings possess supernatural power, and the more of them the shaman subjects to his will the more powerful he becomes.... They have various strange forms, usually manlike, with grotesque or monstrous faces, such as are shown on many of the masks obtained in this region. They have the power of changing their form; in many instances becoming animals or assuming very terrifying shapes. At such times if they render themselves visible to ordinary people the latter may be killed merely by the sight of them" [Nelson 1899:428].

"The Unalit told me of a shaman who once lived among them and was aided by his dog, with whom he could talk, the dog being a *tunghât* which had taken that form. A common form of *tunghât* is the *yu-ă,* or spirit of the elements, places and things" [Nelson 1899:429].

Shamans are greatly feared for their powers. However, consistent failure on their part can result in their being put to death for telling too many lies. "On the Yukon they [shamans] claim to climb up to the moon, but at the head of Norton sound an old man told me that he used to fly up to the sky like a bird. In all this region the shamans claim to possess the power of visiting the moon.... On the lower Yukon and southward they say that there are other ways of getting to the moon, one of which is for a man to put a slip noose about his neck and have the people drag him about the interior of the kashim [ceremony house] until he is dead" [Nelson 1899:430].

Tungralik
South Alaska Eskimo, *Arctic Coast*

The term for shaman in the Yukon dialect [Hawkes 1914:17, n. 1]. The cognate of this word among the West Alaska Eskimo (the Kinugumiut) is *tungalik* or *tunghalik* (EONAH, p. 295). A *tungralik* is a person who possesses a *tungraniyak,* or spirit, most often an animal spirit. The dialectical variant of the word for *spirit* among the West Alaska Eskimo is *tunghat* (see entry) or *tungat* (EONAH, p. 294).

Alaska Eskimo shamans don wooden masks in their ceremonies. Among the North Alaska Eskimo these masks are so large that they are suspended by a rawhide cord from the ceiling of the ceremonial house *(kasgi)* while the dancer performs behind them. Among the West Alaska Eskimo these masks have become complete figures of their totems, although shamans there still wear masks as well. Once such a mask is put on, the spirit associated with it possesses the shaman. Shamans usually have several helping spirits.

Tupilak
Inuit, *Arctic Coast*

Also: *tupilek* (among the Copper Inuit this term and the term *tornrak* are both used for a shaman's helping spirit [Jenness 1970:191]). Plural: *tupilat* [Merkur 1989:14]. A widespread term for an animal image used in sorcery. A sorcerer will most often make the image of a particular animal (or sometimes a human figure) and then imbue this effigy with power through a magical spell such that it seeks out and harms or kills the sorcerer's victim. Among the Iglulik, on the western shores of Hudson Bay, a "*tupilak* could not come into existence on its own, but it could instead be created by a shaman. A *tupilak* could cause game to vanish in the district, and anyone other than a shaman who saw one would die" [Merkur 1989:15].

To be effective the *tupilak* need only be a part of the animal, such as the head; sometime various animal parts are used. In turn, the *tupilak,* once empowered, can assume the shape of any of its components [Rink in Merkur 1989:16]. Among the Polar Inuit, in northwestern Greenland, "a witch made a *tupilak* out of the bones of various animals, which were covered with turf and clots of blood and brought to life by means of a magic song. A *tupilak* would attack the witch's enemy while the latter was at sea, either by capsizing his kayak or by allowing itself to be harpooned and killed. A person [other than a shaman] who killed a *tupilak* would lose his strength and become a cripple" [Merkur 1989: 16]. Merkur [1989:18] noted that when several animal parts are used, the *tupilak* "binds together, as a single being, the spirits of a variety of different animals that would otherwise not cooperate with each other. I suggest that the physical binding of the bodily parts is a ritual precondition for the metaphysical binding of the spirits."

Sometimes the *tupilak* is as simple as an empowered strip of seal skin that is placed under the foot of the intended victim. However, if the sorcerer makes any mistake in the construction and empowerment of the *tupilak,* the power will turn back on him. The same is true if the victim possesses a particularly powerful *ârnuaq* (see entry).

Most often the *tupilak* must contain something taken from the person against whom it will be used. This can be something as simple as a piece of meat from an animal the intended victim has killed. The completed *tupilak* is brought to life by the shaman through ritual. Once alive, "in order that the *tupilek* may grow, the ilisitsok [sorcerer] makes it suckle himself between his legs. . . . He sits on a heap of stones close to where a river discharges itself into the sea and makes the *tupilek* suckle. When the latter has grown big, it glides down into the water and disappears. It is to bring death or misfortune to the man for whom it is destined. If it fails in this object, it turns against its master" [Holm in Thalbitzer 1914:100].

Once a *tupilak* has been brought to life, it is often seen to move of its own accord. Mitsuarni-anga had such a *tupilak* in 1910. It "consisted of the body of a dog with the legs of a fox and a human head. It had originally been made by a man called Pikinak who had been dead for several years when Mitsuarnianga and his companion Perqilaak suddenly one day caught sight of the tupilak while they were rowing along the foot of the Angeen mountain in Sermilik. The tupilak was then on the point of creeping on shore dragging behind it two inflated sealing bladders, which were made fast on its back by means of long lines, because it had once been harpooned, unknown by whom" [Thalbitzer 1914:644].

In order to negate the power of a *tupilak,* an *angakok* [shaman] must call it forth and do battle with it. "The angakok usually stabs it to death in the passage [of the ceremonial house], and next morning people can see the stain of blood on the spot where the tupilek was killed. The angakok does not tell the ilisitsok [sorcerer] who has made the tupilek that he has killed it, in order not to disconcert him" [Holm in Thalbitzer 1914:101]. However, shamans generally avoid any battle with a *tupilak* because they are not easily killed.

Tupitkaq
North Alaska Eskimo, *Arctic Coast*
Tikerarmiut amulet [Rainey 1947:272]. See *angoak.*

Tuponot
Yokuts, *California*
The Tachi term for shaman [Kroeber 1925:511]. See *antu.*

Turiyo
Luiseño, *California*
A renowned shaman during the latter part of the nineteenth century who was able to perform many public power displays. One of his more famous feats involved taking a feather headdress and throwing it into a fire for all to see as it burned. Then he would restore the headdress and replace it on his head.

Tutuvï

Paiute, *Basin*

Dialectical variants: *tutuxuas* or *utuxuxuang* (Kaibab) [Kelly 1939:152]; *tuxubï* (Saint George and Gunlock) [Kelly 1939:156, 158]; *tutuxubï* (Las Vegas) [Kelly 1939:163]; and *tugubï* (Paranigat) [Kelly 1939:156, 158]. The Chemehuevi (Southern Paiute) term for a shaman's helping spirit or power [Kelly 1936:129]. Laird [1976:33] used the term *tutuguuviwï* (plural) for animal spirit helpers.

The shaman receives his power via dreams of a guardian spirit. For a healing shaman "the mouse and the packrat were especially desirable as familiars because they were able to 'steal the disease away'" [Laird 1976:32]. "In his dreams a doctor talked with his spirit helper. It told him what to do and how to do it. It gave him a song, told him how to suck, and how to dance. And when he treated someone, it told him just what to do and whom to blame (i.e., named the sorcerer). During a [healing] treatment the spirit stayed far to the north until just at daybreak, when it came to the doctor" [Kelly 1936:129–130]. At the time of this morning arrival, "the shaman advanced to meet it, taking it between his palms and placing it in his mouth. He returned to camp and blew it directly from his lips into the seat of the ailment. The length of time the spirit remained within the patient was a gauge of the shaman's ability" [Kelly 1936:131–132]. The less time the spirit remained, the more powerful it was. "The tutelary [spirit] traveled through the body of the patient, emerged of its own accord with the sickness, and departed for the north, accompanied by the disease" [Kelly 1936:132]. This form of treatment is used for the most serious cases. In illnesses caused by disease-object intrusion, the shaman first sucks the object from the patient's body; if this does not result in a cure, then the shaman's helping spirit is inserted into the patient.

Most often the shaman's helping spirit comes in unsolicited dreams. In other cases the novice shaman seeks power at a known power spot, such as *Puarïnkan* (Doctor-Cave) in the Vegas area [Kelly 1936:129]. In addition, a shaman can pass his power on to a younger member of the family. "'Certain families had certain songs that came to them from way back.' It is said that the same curing song and the same guardian spirit might pass to a person even though he had never heard the song nor seen the relative who last possessed the power" [Kelly 1936:130]. However, the inheritance of shamanic power "is a notion quite foreign to the Southern Paiute at large; it was encountered only among the two westernmost groups, the Las Vegas and the Chemehuevi" [Kelly 1936:131].

For illnesses caused either by disease-object intrusion or by soul loss, "the tutelary informed the curing shaman which sorcerer was responsible" [Kelly 1936:133].

Tuuhisa

Hopi, *Southwest*

Also: *duhisa* [Titiev 1943:549]. Supernatural power. The Hopi differentiate between the power of a *tuuhikya* (shaman—see EONAH, p. 296) and the power, called *powa* (see entry), of the priests of their ceremonial societies. Furthermore, Titiev [1943:549] reported that *tuuhisa* refers to the power, i.e., "black magic," a witch receives from his animal spirit.

The division of supernatural power into two categories is uncommon in Native North America. This has led some scholars to infer that the *tuuhikya* is "a survival of a pre-Pueblo type of curer common to Great Basin and Southern California Shoshoneans, and that, as the ceremonial sodalities [i.e., medicine societies] of the agriculturalist period developed, the *tuuhikya* was relegated to a subordinate position and the change of status reflected in the use of *powa* by the priests and *tuuhisa* by the individual shamans. . . . Trance states and visions came to be disvalued and the *tuuhikya* became a healer who, although frequently called upon, did not have the power or respect accorded the priests of the rainmaking societies who also had the power to heal. The earlier symbols of shamanism, those of the prey animals, were absorbed into the priestly rituals, while ideas of soul loss and the ability of the shaman to send one of his hearts to the spirit world were lost, remaining only vestigially as attributes of witches" [Levy 1994:322, 324]. Therefore, this differentiation is not based on the nature of power per se but rather on who is wielding that power.

The manifestation of supernatural power comes in many different forms among the Hopi. A Zuni shaman reported: "Once, when a friend and I were visiting Walpi, a member of the order of Jugglery of the Snake fraternity called to us to give him a head-kerchief. My friend handed his to the man, who first held it at diagonal corners; then he pulled it, first through one hand and then through the other, beginning each time midway of the head-kerchief, on the bias. He then pressed it to his breast and presently threw down two snakes, which at once moved about. The head-kerchief was nowhere to be seen. He secured the snakes, and, pressing them to his breast, the head-kerchief soon reappeared" [unidentified informant in Stevenson 1904:568].

Tuviku
Hopi, *Southwest*
Mask. This refers to a mask worn by a *kachina* (also: *katsina, katchina*) performer. However, the Hopi themselves rarely use this term, preferring instead to refer to a mask as *kwaatsi,* "friend," or masks as *itaakwatsim,* "our friends" [Hieb 1994:25].

Masked *kachinam* (plural form) play an integral role in many different rituals throughout the Pueblo area of the Southwest. The *tuviku* is worn only during the public aspects of rituals [Hieb 1994:27]. During a performance the mask transforms the wearer into the embodiment of the spirit represented by the mask. "The *tuviku,* the mask, is what defines the *katsina,* [it] is the essence of this 'person'" [Hieb 1994:27].

Such masks are considered to be sacred objects and are treated accordingly. "A mask is made of leather but it is believed to be alive. Therefore it must be kept fed and hidden when stored, just like other animate ritual objects" [Geertz in Hieb 1994:28]. It is conjectured that the use of such masks spread to the Southwest from northern Mexico during the thirteenth century [Adams 1994:45]. By the late 1200s masked figures began to appear on Pueblo pottery, and by the mid-1300s masked figures were a widespread phenomenon on their pottery [Hays 1994:47].

See also *Kotikäne, lhatsina, masks.*

Tuyuku
Miwok, *California*
Also: *tooyugoo.* Dialectical variant: *koiahpe* (Tuolumne Muwah) [Merriam 1955:69]. Central Miwok "poisoner" or sorcerer [Gifford n.d. a:introductory notes]. A sorcerer "poisons" an individual by shooting something into the victim's body—a mole, a special rock from the ocean, a porcupine quill, or whatever object the sorcerer chooses. Often the effect is instantaneous, causing the victim to die within minutes; other victims may linger for several weeks, slowly wasting away because they are unable to eat.

The shaman receives his power of sorcery mainly through dreams. He stores some of his poison medicines at home near his fire to keep them strong, but the more dangerous poisons that are a threat to his family members are kept in nearby hills wrapped in bird feathers under a stone at some hidden location. Poison feathers are wrapped in deer hide.

In shooting his victim the sorcerer holds the poison in his right hand between his middle finger and thumb. With his palm held up and close to the ground, the shaman then swings his hand forward, releasing the poison as his hand strikes a small pile of dirt, scattering some of it. "Sometimes if poisoner doctor hates person very bad he heats up a glass like rock very hot and holds it in his left hand. With his right hand he keeps shooting poison. The hot rock in the bare hand makes the poison he shoots that much stronger. This sort of poisoning kills a person in spite of his doctor" [John Kelly translating for Tom Williams in Gifford n.d. a:5]. Over time the sorcerer's hand becomes afflicted from too much shooting: It grows stiff, his joints enlarge, and his fingers bend in toward his palm.

In shooting the poison the shaman usually calls out the name of the victim in order to direct the poison to its selected target. If the victim lives at a distance, the shaman procures some item belonging to the victim, such as a piece of hair, some spit, excrement, etc., and then shoots at that. If the shaman wants to shoot an entire family, he uses a piece of a board from their house or a similar item.

A particularly dangerous poison medicine is the *wanawana*. This is a soft red stone, about ¼ inch in diameter and 4 inches long, that is touched to the foot of a sleeping victim. "Person does not wake up, he merely starts in sleep. The poison gradually eats flesh down to bone, then up bones into body. Person suffers fearfully, can't sleep, finally dies. Doctors can't cure. Pukano it is called. This same stone can be used on spit, in which case person's mouth is place where disease starts. If used on urine, the disease starts on penis; if on excrement it starts on anus" [John Kelly translating for Tom Williams in Gifford n.d. a:7].

Many other types of poison exist, among them: toad poison *(olasaiyi)*, which causes the body to swell and the intestines to burst and cannot be cured by doctors; rattlesnake poison *(wakali)*, which causes the victim to die from a ratttlesnake bite; and bear poison, which causes the victim to be killed by a bear while hunting.

Miwok sorcerers are also known for their ability to handle red-hot rocks and put hot coals in their mouth. "The fire-eating is done out in hills away from village. It is done in daytime" [John Kelly translating for Tom Williams in Gifford n.d. a:42]. The heat is used to increase the potency of their poisons.

If a sorcerer is identified, he will likely be put to death, often by another shaman hired by the victim's relatives.

Among the Tuolumne Muwah band of Miwok, the term *tuyuka* is used for their dance doctor, who "heals by dancing and does not give medicine or suck out the evil. But he has the power and may poison or kill at a distance" [Merriam 1955:70].

Tuzinobi
Paiute, *Basin*

Literal translation: *tuzi,* "small," and *nobi,* "house" [Park in Folwler 1989:96]. The Northern Paiute term at Pyramid Lake for a sweat lodge. "The sweat house came from some Indians up north, in California or Oregon. The Paiutes got the sweat house around 1880. The people came from around Susanville and Surprise Valley. They took sweat baths and the people at Pyramid Lake learned to take a sweat bath from them" [Joe Green in Fowler 1989:95].

This culture's sweat lodge is a small, dome-shaped structure made from willows. In part, it is used for healing to remove sickness. The sweat bath ceremony is called *tupinabagia,* from *tupi,* "rock," and *nabagia,* "swim" or "bath" [Billy Roberts in Fowler 1989:96]. It is also called *udutnabagia* (hot bath), while the sweat lodge structure is called *udutnabagino* [Joe Green in Fowler 1989:96]. The Walker River Paiutes call the sweat house *namosain* [Tom Mitchell in Fowler 1989:96].

For details see Sweat Lodge Ceremony, EONAH, pp. 269–270.

Two Wolves
Arikara, *Plains*

An early-nineteenth-century shaman who was famous for his medicine powers to foretell coming events and find out information. He received the power to speak with Thunder, via a Prairie-Chicken spirit.

The following is an account of a ceremony performed by Two Wolves at the request of Roving Coyote, who wanted to find out who had killed one of his horses. Prior to conducting the ceremony, Two Wolves sent the camp crier around to announce that the culprit who killed Roving Coyote's horse was to report to his lodge:

> The crier repeated this over and over. When all had heard he went into the lodge again. While the ceremony had been going on black clouds rose in the west, and "Ah ho! Ah ho!" was repeatedly said by Two-Wolves. "Now my father is coming." He called again for the man [culprit] to hurry, saying there was no use of secrecy and that he should know. Another call was given, and the Thunder was heard in the distance. Two-Bears [the culprit] did not believe that Two-Wolves could learn anything from Thunder, and so would not come. Thunder told Two-Wolves that Two-Bears was the man who had killed the horse. When Two-Bears did not come, Two-Wolves sent his servant [i.e., ceremonial assistant] to tell him to come right away. When he had come he was greeted heartily by Two-Wolves and placed beside him. "I am glad you have come. Now I want to say that my father [Thunder] says you are the man that killed Roving-Coyote's horse." "Yes," said Two-Bears, "I know now that you are a wonderful [i.e., powerful] man. I did what you have accused me of. Ah! my friend," said he to Roving-Coyote, "you know how trying your horses are sometimes, and we lose our temper and are sorry for it afterwards. I did kill your horse with a picket pin, but I did not think you would find it out. I have nice ponies, and you may have your choice for my deed." . . . Two-Wolves lived a long time, doing good work, discovering thieves, and prophesying many wonderful things [Strike Enemy in Dorsey 1904:157–159].

Ubuaxantï

Paiute, *Basin*

Also: *huvwuwagantï* (Chemehuevis) [Laird 1976:35]. Southern Paiute term for an arrow shaman, sometimes rendered as "wound doctor." This shaman was a specialist at treating arrow wounds, gun wounds, broken bones, and club blows received during warfare. In his treatments, he would suck on the wound, sing his sacred songs, blow upon the patient, and press on the patient's body. An arrow shaman "cured more rapidly than a regular shaman. He had no guardian spirit: 'he did not need one for he had a cool breath and a good hand'" [Kelly 1936:137]. However, Laird [1976:35] conjectured that "it must be that snake doctors and wound doctors have familiars, but they do not summon them when treating because time is of the essence."

The Paiute had many arrow shamans. The following is a brief account of the cure given by two of them: "Once two Yuma were hurt in a Cocopa-Yuma battle. Two Chemehuevi arrow doctors were visiting the Yuma and were asked to treat the boys. They had the people cut down three or four willows and build a shade. In the evening one doctor attended one patient, the other [doctor], the other patient. They placed the boys with their heads to the east. Then each doctor kicked the sand at the foot of his patient, then at the head. They started to sing and to blow upon the boys. They had finished four parts of the song and were blowing, when the boys opened their eyes. Each stood up, as though he had been asleep. The Yumas gave the doctors beads and other things in payment" [unnamed informant in Kelly 1936:138].

Uhane

Hawaiian, *Pacific*

A person's spirit. Helping spirits most often come to individuals via dreams, *na moe* (sleep) *uhane*. "In olden days dreams were taught by dream interpreters and their teachings spread everywhere even to this day. . . . Their meanings were memorized like a catechism learned by memory in childhood. . . . There were two important kinds of dreams as regards the dreamer, unpremeditated dreams and those which were the result of premeditation on the part of the dreamer. Of all dreams the most significant ones were those which came when one was startled in a very deep sleep or just as the eye-lashes closed together when falling into a doze. These were true dreams" [Kepelino in Handy 1968:119].

Ukemauwûsk
Potawatomi, *Midwest*
Dialectical variant: *ukemauwas* (Menomini) [Skinner 1915d:190]. Literal translation: "chief" [Skinner 1924:207] or for the Menominni "kingly medicine" [Skinner 1915d:190]. This term refers to one of two roots used in love medicine; the other is *ukemaukwäwûsk,* or "chieftain-ess" [Skinner 1924:207]. These roots are also known by the same name among the Sauk, Fox, Menomini, Kickapoo, and Plains-Ojibwa.

> One or both of these [roots] is mixed fine, vermilion and pounded mica is added, and the juice of beaver castor. This is placed in a little deerskin bag, and a tiny bow and arrow is made, the arrow being tied up with its point in the mixture.
>
> A figure of the person desired is now drawn on the earth with a stick, or on a piece of bark with charcoal or a leaden bullet. The tiny arrow is withdrawn from the medicine, and shot into the heart of the picture of the intended victim, who is named aloud. The arrow is allowed to remain there for four days, and is then taken out, and the user takes it and uses it to apply a small spot of the medicine paint to each cheek, and to the palm of the right hand. He endeavors to shake hands with his enamorata and thus get some of the paint on her. He also takes care to get on the windward side of her, so that the breeze will blow the magic of his charm on her [Skinner 1924:207].

Love medicine is often carried in thimbles on necklaces worn about the neck.

The only cure for this love medicine is the use of another medicine called *sûmo.* "The shaman demands a bit of the hair, a nail paring, or even a piece of the clothing of the first operator. This he ties up with the medicine and attaches it by a cord to a twig, stick, or tree, so that it will twirl

in the breeze. This causes the action of the first [love] medicine to be reversed, and the user becomes crazy, while the victim recovers" [Skinner 1924:207].

Among the Menomini *ukemauwas* also gives the user "second sight and the ability to read minds. It brings gifts and fortune, secures credit at stores and luck in gambling and games" [Skinner 1915d:190].

Ukumaura
Copper Eskimo, *Arctic Coast*
Literal translation: "The Heavy One" [Jenness 1970:211]. Also called the "Big Island," this term refers to a widely known spirit power that manifests in the form of a large stone. "Occasionally a shaman will summon it to come and have a feast; then it falls unseen from the sky and kills many people with rocks, and other shamans have to drive it back again. A shaman too will sometimes make it drop on an approaching kayaker and kill him, though it is sometimes affirmed that the magic stone uses a small spear to kill its victims. The stone can sing like a man, and the shamans have a special incantation or invocation, *akeun,* for it, but my informants did not know the words" [Jenness 1970:211].

Ukyahana
Zuni, *Southwest*
This term refers to the downy eagle feathers worn by males during certain sacred ceremonies [Parsons 1933:94].

Ulixw
Twana, *Northwest Coast*
Skokomish term for the process of getting power; vision questing [Frank Allen in Elmendorf 1993:214].

Ulunsata
Cherokee, *Southeast*
Also: *ulonsudon.* Literal translation: "it is transparent" [Olbrechts 1930:549]. Sacred quartz crystal used by shamans for divination and also

to diagnose illness. These special crystals come from the head of the Cherokee's Horned Serpent. *Ulunsata* is also "used when describing a beam of sunlight before it strikes a surface" [Olbrechts 1930:549]. "The diviner gazed at the stone fixedly for a few minutes, after which he saw it filled with a streak of whitish, milky fluid, or else with a vein of blood, the latter proclaiming the imminent death of the client. This mode of divination was extensively practised before parties set out on the warpath and the very human course was followed of keeping at home those whose death was prophesied by the crystal" [Olbrechts 1930:549–550]. However, one Cherokee informant reported "that they [shamans] owned a crystal on which they would place a drop of blood . . . in which they could see faces and the whole of a person's future life including marriage, number of children, length of life and many other things" [Dasi in Fogelson 1980:76].

Because it was alive, "the crystal had to be periodically fed drops of animal or human blood, as befits its origin, or it would cause great misfortune to its caretaker. This powerful object is also regarded as a person" [Fogelson 1977:190].

Umeleyek

Yurok, *Oregon Seaboard*
See Brush Dance.

Unaleq

Netsilik Eskimo, *Arctic Coast*
A Cree shaman from the vicinity of Pelly Bay who had lived among the Netsilik for twenty years; by the early 1920s he was an elderly man. His real name was Inernerunashuaq, but he preferred to be called Unaleq [Rasmussen 1929:37]. He had ten helping spirits, the most powerful of which was *Nanoq Tulorialik,* "The Bear with the Fangs" [Rasmussen 1929:38]. The others included the spirits (ghosts) of four deceased Netsiliks (two males and two females), two Chipewyan ghosts, one ghost from the Tuneq ("the people that inhabited the country before the present Eskimos made their way to the coasts" [Rasmussen 1929:38]), and "two mysterious mountain spirits of those which are called Norjutilik" [Rasmussen 1929:38].

When Unaleq called upon *Tulorialik* (his giant Bear), the spirit would possess him, upon which Unaleq was able to "transform himself into a bear or walrus at will, and was able to render great service to his fellow men by virtue of the powers thus acquired" [Rasmussen 1929:38].

In March 1921 Knud Rasmussen first met Unaleq. Shortly thereafter the shaman conducted a séance to ask his spirits about Rasmussen's impending journey. Unaleq then questioned Rasmussen concerning his ability to handle spirits. Rasmussen toyed with Unaleq, all in the name of science (i.e., he was studying the Eskimo mind), and told Unaleq that he himself was a shaman. Subsequently, all of Unaleq's failures through the following winter were blamed upon Rasmussen, for Unaleq claimed Rasmussen had stolen his spirits and said that, under great protest, he had drawn pictures of them and named them for Rasmussen. Learning of this, Rasmussen went back to Unaleq the following year and publicly announced that he had returned the shaman's spirits and forbidden them to ever come to him again. Only then was Unaleq freed from the fear that had plagued him for a year.

Ünü

Paiute, *Basin*
Owens Valley Paiute term for the transformed shape of a bear shaman. Ordinary bears are called *pahvitci;* a bear shaman transformed into the shape of a bear is called *ünü* [Steward 1933:309, n. 180]. The ability of shamans who received their power from the Bear to transform themselves into the shape of a bear is well known throughout Native North America (see *bear ceremonialism*). Among the Owens Valley Paiute the Bear shamans imitated the actions of a bear during their ceremonies, and the more powerful bear shamans "could transform themselves into bears" [Steward 1933:309].

A man who was attacked by an *ünü* would sometimes know of the deception and would then use his power against the Bear shaman in the ensuing battle. The following offers an example: "Another hunter ambushed bears coming for acorns. A bear shaman, to stop this, transformed himself and went after him, was shot with an arrow, then chased the hunter, who disappeared in a crack in the earth [using his power]. The obsidian arrowpoint grew in the bear's stomach; he could not vomit it [a shamanic technique]; it grew, cutting him so that he died. Transformed back into a human, the shaman lost his power. Later, burning the bear remains, he found a pile of obsidian arrowpoints inside. The hunter had greater power than he. Later, the shaman said to the hunter, watching a hoop and pole game, 'Hello, boy. I tried to get this fellow and he certainly was a great man [i.e., a powerful shaman]. He jumped and ran everywhere. I tried to get him but couldn't. You certainly are great, aren't you?' The hunter was frightened, knowing what had happened" [Steward 1933:310].

Unupits

Paviotso and Paiute, *Basin*

Plural: *unupin* [Powell in Fowler and Fowler 1971:59]. Witch [Powell in Fowler and Fowler 1971:61].

Powell gave this same term for an evil spirit [Powell in Fowler and Fowler 1971:61], which he described as "a little being or pygmy. There are supposed to be vast numbers of these everywhere and many things are attributed to them. The whirlwind is said to be made by an angry *u-nu´-pits*. Any strange noise in the forest or among the rocks is at once referred to as an *u-nu´-pits*. When gas from a burning stick of wood bursts out in a little stream of flame they say an *u-ni´-pits* is lighting a brand. If any article is mysteriously lost they say an *u-ni´-pits* has stolen it. It is enjoined upon children not to whistle at night lest an *u-ni´-pits* should fly into their mouth. Many headaches, pains in the stomach, rheumatic pains, and other transient troubles are blamed to these beings" [Powell in Fowler and Fowler 1971:66].

See also *sutkwi towats*.

Unwadïmbuaxantï

Paiute, *Basin*

Dialectical variants (among the Southern Paiutes): *unadïmpïpuaxantï* (Shivwits), "rain doctor" [Kelly 1939:156]; *uadïpuaxantï* (Paranigat), "rain doctor" [Kelly 1939:159]; and *ïwadïmpuaxantï* (Las Vegas), "rain doctor" [Kelly 1939:165]. Chemehuevi (Southern Paiute) weather shaman. Such shamans usually dream of rain, lightning, thunder, and, to a lesser extent, ripe fruit. In performing a rain-making ceremony the shaman sings and, in many cases, whirls a bullroarer (EONAH, p. 42) made from the horn of a mountain sheep. "The horn was boiled until soft, then, with a stone knife, was notched its full length. The tip was perforated for the attachment of a light wand handle" [Kelly 1936:138].

In addition to making rain, a weather shaman also has the power to send away rain that he sees coming or to direct oncoming rain to a particular location. The main purpose of rain making is "to make the grass grow on the desert; to make the deer fat; and to provide drinking water during the fall harvest of yucca fruit and pine nuts" [unnamed informant in Kelly 1936:138].

Among the Paranigat the weather shaman is also called *pabuaxantï* (see entry), "water doctor" [Kelly 1939:159]. One informant recalled the use of such a shaman: "We were thirsty and asked an old weather doctor to make rain. He held his bow and arrows [said to have been part of his power] in his hand and pointed to a small cloud. He sang. . . . He was asking the clouds to move into the valley. The rain came. There was so much that everything washed away, even the pine nuts that were in baskets. The people asked him to stop the rain, so he said, 'That is enough.' He held up his arms and blew; then it cleared" [unidentified informant in Kelly 1939:159]. In addition the Paranigat have a wind shaman known as *nïarï puaxantï* (see entry).

Weather shamans among the other Southern Paiute bands often use crystals in their rain-making ceremonies.

See also *Avenarï.*

Utuxuxuang
Paiute, *Basin*
See *tutuxuas.*

Uupuhagadi
Kawaiisu, *Peninsula*
The term used for shamans who could control the weather. "There was a Kawaiisu rain shaman at Tejon who had not made it rain for a long time. The creeks were almost dry. Some Kawaiisu people and a non-Indian cattleman visited him and gave him money to make rain. He sang and danced all night. In the morning he told the people to look at the sky. They saw a huge black cloud. Soon it rained very hard" [Zigmond 1977:88].

Weather shamans are very secretive about their work, and little is known of their exact procedures. In some cases they use a tree lichen *(Ramalina menziesii),* which they place in cold water. However, the effect of this lichen is unpredictable: Although it might bring rain, it might also bring "cold, sleet, snow, and high winds" [Zigmond 1977:89].

Uvineq
West Greenland Eskimo, *Arctic Coast*
The name of a shaman during the latter part of the nineteenth century. On one occasion he performed a ceremony in a darkened room to find the cause of a very loud noise emanating from the spot where a woman had placed a *tupilak* (see entry) the previous year (not long before her death): "His [the shaman's] first word was 'Sun!' and at that very moment a mosquito was heard humming at the backwall of the house. It was one of the assisting spirits. Then there was a loud outcry in a foreign language. This was his *qavdlunâsartartoq* (a spirit speaking the white men's language). After that the first spirit ceased; but from the ceiling came now the third *tôrnaq*

[spirit], his *tûlerut,* an animal resembling a human being with his palm turned upwards, the touch of which causes death. He turned all the skins of the sleeping platforms [in the house], and all the inhabitants of the house were stricken with horror. Finally, the conjurer explained that the son of the [deceased] woman, who had neglected the deceased in the division of a skin, was to walk with a stick, as his legs would otherwise rot" [Birket-Smith 1924:455].

Uwanami
Keres, *Southwest*
Rain makers. The Zuni term for water spirits. There are many elaborate rituals directed to *Uwanami.* During the 1920s twelve priesthoods conducted such rituals, each having from two to six members. The power of each shaman rested in their *etowe* (EONAH, p. 71), small stone fetishes kept in sealed jars. Also used in their altar displays were black paint, "thunder stones," obsidian knives, and other objects. All of these sacred items were brought from the lower world at the time of the Zuni's emergence into this world. The *käetowe* (*kä* means "water") is used for the *Uwanami* ceremony, which is always conducted in secret in the house where the shaman's *etowe* are kept. (The *tcuetowe,* whereas *tcu* means "corn," is used for crop-growing medicine.)

"In addition to the objects on the altar of their retreat, the chief priesthood is said to maintain a permanent altar in the fourth underground room of their house. In addition to the usual objects on priestly altars, this altar contains two columns of rock, one of crystal and one of turquoise, a heart-shaped rock which is 'the heart of the world,' with arteries reaching to the four cardinal points, and various prayer sticks, including two, male and female, which are 'the life of the people.' All objects on the altar, including the etowe, are said to be petrified. This altar is the center of the world, the spot beneath the heart of känastepa when he stretched out his arms. Only the high priest himself has access to this chamber" [Bunzel 1932a:514].

Throughout July and August *Uwanami* ceremonies are constantly in session to ensure rain. "The four chief priesthoods, associated with the north, east, south, and west, go in for eight days each. They are followed late in July by the pekwin and the Bow Priest, who go in for four days each, and later by the minor priesthoods ('darkness priests'), who also go in for four days. . . . Should the days of any group fail to be blessed with rain it receives the censure of the community, and one of its members will surely be suspected of laxness in the observance of his duties" [Bunzel 1932a:515].

Also associated with rain-making medicine is *Kolowisi,* "the horned water serpent who inhabits springs and underground waters. . . . Kolowisi is the guardian of sacred springs and punishes trespassers, especially women" [Bunzel 1932a:515]. The effigy of Kolowisi used in the *Uwanami* ceremonies "is kept by the *Kolowisi* priesthood, a group belonging to the Corn clan" [Bunzel 1932a:516].

Vision quest

A ritual process in which an individual, male or female, attempts to acquire a helping spirit. Native American vision questing is the primary means used in North America for "catching" a spirit. (Dream acquisition is the second most common means.) Vision questing is found in many different forms throughout North America and is very prevalent among the Plains cultures, where there is "an inordinate pursuit of the vision" [Benedict 1922:1]. Therefore it is one of the most well-documented shamanic rituals. Of course, not all vision questing is done for the purpose of becoming a shaman. In many cultures all young adults are encouraged to acquire helping spirits. That is, everyone is socially encouraged to obtain some form of medicine power, be it for fishing, hunting, basket making, canoe carving, gambling, or whatever. For example, among the Comox of the Northwest, one person's encounter with a helping spirit yielded a medicine that enabled him to call forth the salmon if they were late in arriving. Subsequently, this fish medicine was passed down through his family for generations, and evidence of the site where the ceremony was conducted still existed in 1935 [Barnett 1955:89, 129] (see *siwin*). In other words, if one person acquires just one type of medicine power, the benefits thereof may be retained within that family for a very long time. Consequently, Native Americans basically believe that a little magic is worth obtaining in one's life.

In this sense shamanism may be broadly construed as a matter of the strength and extent of one's personal medicine powers, with the term *shaman* being reserved for those individuals who are deemed to have "great" power.

Vision questing, the most commonly used method in North America to obtain such levels of power, fundamentally entails a person going to an isolated spot and remaining there for some period of time. The ritual procedures involved in doing this are extremely varied and greatly dependent on the shaman who is conducting the novice's training. One might well say that every vision quest is different in form but not intent.

Anthropologists have spent a great deal of energy recording these various forms of vision questing, but the underlying meaning has yet to be fully grasped. Clearly the length of the vision quest is not directly related to obtaining a helping spirit. In most cases the quest itself lasts

Edward S. Curtis, Hastobiga—Navajo Medicine Man, *1904. Photogravure.*

from one to four days coupled with more than ten days without food or water. Furthermore, this length of time is certainly not a dictate: Nelson [Brown and Brightman 1988:34] reported that one Cree vision quester "remained 30 days without eating or drinking, such was the delight he received from his Dreams [visions]!"

We do know that shamans usually undergo a lengthy training period for vision questing, often beginning in childhood. Frequently a boy is sent out to spend the night alone in the woods as early as six or seven years of age in order to begin his conditioning. Lakota shaman Wallace Black Elk reported that he began his training when he was five years old [Black Elk and Lyon 1990:3]. In early adolescence, around twelve to seventeen years of age, most novices undertake their first vision-quest ritual. Yet even with their extensive training, most do not "catch" a spirit on their first vision quest. That is why the Native American terms for *vision questing* often literally translate into English as "crying for a vision." It is known to be a difficult undertaking.

Most often the vision quester remains humble and seeks any spirit, but vision quests are also made for specific medicine powers. This is especially the case with advanced shamans who seek to acquire many medicine powers. When a spirit does consent to appear, it can come to the quester in virtually any form, but most commonly it manifests as a voice. That is, the quester receives instructions directly from a spirit voice. Instructions typically include an explanation of the medicine power(s) granted and one or more sacred songs to recall the spirit power and to be sung when the medicine is used. Instructions can also cover the use of ritual paraphernalia (such as drums or rattles), altar displays, objects received on the vision quest, etc.

It is commonly agreed that during the actual "vision," the quester is in a transcendental state of consciousness [Lyon 1984:141]. This is the sense in which Eliade [1964] described shamanism as "techniques of ecstasy." The state of being comes upon the quester suddenly and without

warning, and often the shaman reports being transported to another location in such states of ecstasy. Lakota shaman Pete Catches (EONAH, p. 46) reported that "it's like this: it isn't a dream. . . . It's like looking out in space and suddenly somebody shows you a picture" [Pete Catches in Powers 1977:137].

When a helping spirit actually appears to a vision quester, it is most often in the form of some animal, but it can also be something as simple as a stone. When animals appear, the shaman usually acquires the skills attributed to that particular animal—slyness for the Fox or Coyote spirit, great strength for the Bear spirit, keen sight for the Eagle spirit, swiftness for the Deer spirit, etc. Quite often the spirit first appears in an animal form and then changes into a more human guise. Usually there is a one-way conversation, with the quester remaining silent; if the quester does say something, it is normally just a simple "thank you" uttered every now and then. Above all, the quester must not question the spirit—even if the instructions given by the spirit do not make sense to him. The duration of the contact is usually brief, sometimes a matter of minutes, and it most often results in the quester being overjoyed.

What happens after a new shaman returns with a medicine power varies from culture to culture. For example, among the shamans of the Northwest, usually nothing is revealed for some time, often upward of several years, while the shaman learns to "control" his newly acquired power. Among the Plains cultures, by contrast, the shaman usually recounts his vision in its entirety within the confines of a sweat lodge immediately upon returning [Lyon 1987:276]. In other areas, such as the Basin, the shaman might spend several years gathering the paraphernalia his helping spirit told him to acquire before he can begin his practice.

Vomiting

Many Native American cultures recognized induced vomiting as a means of ritual purification (see entry). That is, vomiting was used to help induce altered states of consciousness.

Most well known is the use of the leaves and twigs of the Yaupon holly *(Ilex vomitoria Ait.)* to make the "black drink" (called *cassina*) known among the cultures of the southeastern United States and extending into eastern Texas (among the Tawakoni, Tonkawa, Hasinai, Karankawa, and Atakapa). Yaupon holly is the only North American plant known to contain caffeine. This caffeine-rich brew was ritually consumed from cups made of conch shells. Of its use Hudson [1979:3] noted: "Perhaps it is enough to say that the southeastern Indians went to great lengths to keep themselves in a ritually pure condition. This was particularly true of men. Ritual purity depended in part on the careful observance of certain rules. . . . It is likely that their drinking it [black drink] before meeting in council with other men served to separate them ritually from women. And it is likely that they induced vomiting to rid themselves of any possible contamination by impure [mystically contaminated by witches] food."

However, ritual vomiting was not limited to the southeastern area. For instance, it was noted among the Nez Perce around 1840 by Asa Bowen Smith: "A few days ago I witnessed a practice among the Indians which they perform at this season preparatory to hunting deer. They run small sticks down their throats into their stomachs to cause themselves to vomit. The sticks are small timber osiers. Four are usually taken at a time & passed down more than a foot in length & held there til he commences vomiting. Soon four more are taken in the same way & this is repeated 8 or 10 times during the same morning. The rest of the day is spent in washing the surface of the body in water heated by hot stones dug for the purpose at the margin of the water. . . . They have an idea if they do not vomit themselves and wash they will not be skillful in killing game" [A. Smith in Drury 1958:122–123].

When liquids are drunk to induce vomiting they are referred to as *emetics* in the anthropological literature. Their known use is widespread. There are scattered reports of their use in the northeastern area from Maine down to Virginia; many reports of their use in the southern United States extend as far west as the Zuni and northwest to the Coast Salish of British Columbia.

Waarïvpuaxantï

Paiute, *Basin*

Las Vegas (Southern Paiute) term for a Horse shaman. These shamans, who treat injuries caused by horses, obtained their power through dreams of the Horse.

In their treatments "they neither sucked nor used a staff; but they had one song, and stroked and blew upon the victim" [Kelly 1939:165]. One account of this treatment was recorded as follows: "Once a man at Cottonwood Island fell from a horse; he was unconscious. A horse doctor was nearly two miles distant but he knew of the accident. He made sand into a small mound; it became hard, like a rock, from which he knew that no bones were broken. He came to treat the man. He tapped him with a small stick, after which he became conscious. The doctor stroked the man's body, blew upon him, and he recovered" [unidentified informant in Kelly 1939:165].

Wábano

Menomini, *Midwest*

Also: *wabeno* (EONAH, pp. 303–304), *wabano*. Plural: *wabánowûk* [Skinner 1915d:191]. This is a class of shamans who have received power via dreams of *wapanänä,* the Morningstar. These shamans are also found among the Potawatomi, Ottawa, Ojibwa, and Plains Cree. "The wabánowûk are the best seers and clairvoyants known to the Indians" [Skinner 1915d:191]. The *Wábano,* "like the Siouan heyoka [EONAH, pp. 104–105], performs the hot dance, eats fire, swallows sticks, and is adept at all manner of juggling [shamanic feats]" [Skinner 1914:505].

"The best known functions of the wabano are, however, entirely of a spectacular nature. At intervals it is customary to give a public performance and exhibition of their power. At such times the wabano provides a feast of deer or bear meat for his guests, and, after the proper ceremony and songs, he chews up certain medicines and sprays them on his hands and arms. He then has ability to handle fire, or plunge his naked arms into boiling water or maple syrup. He will hold up one finger, and, as he dances in a circle it will appear to blaze. He is also said to be able to eat fire and to blow it from his mouth. Sometimes a wabano will spray his whole body with morningstar medicine and then apparently setting himself on fire, dances about blazing; yet he is never burnt. Often a wabano will hold a glowing brand in each hand, and never be scorched" [Skinner 1915d:191–192].

Wâbik
Micmac, *Canadian Eastern Woodlands*
The most famous shaman among the Micmac of Nova Scotia. Although there are no direct accounts of him, he probably lived during the late 1700s. His power was such that he could kill merely by pointing his finger directly at the victim. Many power feats are attributed to him. For example, he would sit on the beach and make eel spears, throwing them into the water as fast as he made them. When these spears were collected, each one had an eel on it—he never missed a shot. He was also able to stop bullets and cannonballs with his chest and "had control of the elements so that he could raise terrible storms whenever he wished" [Johnson 1943:78].

Wacickathe
Omaha, *Plains*
Shell society. One of the names given for the Omaha variation of the *Midewiwin* (EONAH, p. 174) society [Fortune 1932:90].

Wadada
Maidu, *California*
Term used by the Placer area Nisenan (Southern Maidu) for a split-stick clapper device that served as a rattle to accompany singing. The stick was usually around 12 to 14 inches in length and under 1 inch in diameter. The stick was peeled and split to within 2 to 3 inches of the end and then hollowed out in the center. In some cases a spiral design was burned into the stick [Beals 1933:397]. When used "it was either quivered or beaten against the palm of the hand" [Kroeber 1925:419].

This particular form of rattle is known throughout central California, where it is most often associated with the ceremonies of the Kuksu cult (EONAH, p. 140).

Wae
Tewa, *Southwest*
General term for spirits at the Santa Clara Pueblo [Hill 1982:256].

Wagiksuyabi
Assiniboin, *Plains*
Also: *waka' xambi* [Lowie 1909:45]. Public performances used to demonstrate the supernatural powers of shamans. Such shamanistic exhibitions are no longer held, but during the nineteenth century such performances regularly took place in large lodges, created by joining several smaller ones. The participants ate a feast exclusively of berries. Each shaman performed his own particular power display. For instance, one shaman "was dressed in a buffalo robe, and held two arrows in his hands. He sang several songs, then he announced that he could not do much, nevertheless he did not like the other shamans to laugh at him for not doing anything. He asked two men to step up to him. Singing, he told these men to push the arrows through his body from side to side. They followed his directions until the arrows crossed. He showed them to the spectators, then he sang again, and the men pulled out the arrows. The blood came spurting out of his body. He simply rubbed fire over the wound and effaced every trace of it" [Lowie 1909:46].

See also *power displays/feats*.

Wahwun
Winnebago, *Midwest*
A late-eighteenth-century shaman who was called upon by a government agent to divine the whereabouts of three lost men in 1804. The agent paid Wahwun a quarter pound of tobacco and 2 yards of ribbon to perform the ceremony. In addition, the agent told Wahwun that if the facts the shaman divined turned out to be true, he would add a bottle of rum to his payment. The morning after the nighttime ceremony, the agent went to see him. Wahwun told him:

I went to smoke the pipe with your men last night, and found them cooking some elk meat which they got from an Ottawa Indian. On leaving this place they took the wrong road on the top of the hill; they traveled hard on and did not know for two days that they were lost. When they discovered their situation they were much alarmed, and, having nothing more to eat, were afraid they would starve to death. They walked on without knowing which way they were going until the seventh day, when they were met near the Illinois River by the Ottawa before named, who was out hunting. He took them to his lodge, fed them well, and wanted to detain them some days until they had recovered their strength; but they would not stay. He then gave them some elk meat for their journey home, and sent his son to put them into the right road. They will go to Lagothenes for the flour you sent them [for], and will be home in three days [P. Jones 1861:148].

The agent then asked Wahwun to describe the encampment he had visited, and the shaman replied, "They had made a shelter by the side of a large oak tree that had been torn up by the roots, and which had fallen with the head towards the rising sun" [P. Jones 1861:148]. The three men returned on the third day and confirmed all that Wahwun had divined.

Wain waxube
Omaha, *Plains*

Medicine bundle. Also known as *xube* (EONAH, p. 323) pack. The bundle contains the power objects that a shaman has received from his helping spirit for use in his work. The objects are most often parts of the animal from which the shaman derives his power, and the contents in the bundle determine the powers of the shaman who possesses it.

Each medicine bundle has a specific ritual treatment ascribed to it. For example, in ritually opening a bundle, the names of the previous owners may be recited. Moreover, "the doctoring owner of a medicine bundle believes that he must keep his reservoir in his possession and deal with it in certain ritual ways in order to keep his powers of curing patients. But he also believes that if he makes a slip in the correct ritual in so doing, or fails in any one of the precautions incident to keeping a medicine bundle in his tipi, lodge or frame house, then he will be stricken by an 'influence' from the medicine bundle. This influence is termed *bathon* [see entry]" [Fortune 1932:30].

Waionewaci
Iowa, *Plains*

Calumet or Pipe Dance. This ceremony "is one of, if not the most elaborate of all Iowa dances or ceremonies except perhaps the medicine dance. . . . It is a form of the well-known and very widely disseminated calumet dance, found in some form among the Omaha, Pawnee, Oto, Kansa, Osage, Plains-Cree, and probably other tribes" [Skinner 1915a:706]. The ceremony functions primarily to establish new "relatives," maintain social relationships, and honor brave warriors.

Wakan
Omaha, *Plains*

Gambling [Fortune 1932:168]. Little is known of Omaha gambling medicine. However, anthropologist R. F. Fortune reported the following incident concerning its use: "An Iowa Indian visiting C. W. said to the latter as he made ready to go out. 'Where are you going?' 'I'm going gambling.' 'I have a root. Stay awhile.' The Iowa smoked C. W. all over with smoke from the burning root. C. W. won a hundred dollars in two nights. He gave forty dollars to the Iowa and the Iowa thereupon showed C. W. and his wife the plant from which the root was to be obtained" [Fortune 1932:168].

Among the Lakota *wakan* refers to the mystery power of shamans and is usually translated as "holy" (see EONAH, pp. 305–306).

Wakan a tcipi
Dakota, *Plains*

Also: *wakán wacípi* (American Dakota) [Howard 1953:608]; *wakan watcipi* (Santee, Sisseton, and

Wahpeton) [Lowie 1913a:137]. Dialectical variant: *wakáng wacípi* (Canadian Santee) [Howard 1984:131]. Literal translation: "Holy Dance" [Wallis 1947:69]. The Canadian Dakota name of the Medicine Lodge society (or Holy Dance society), a variant of the widespread Ojibwa *Midewiwin* (EONAH, p. 174), sometimes referred to only as the Medicine Dance, but more often as Holy Dance. Central to the society's performances is the magical shooting of shells with their medicine bags—the *Wahmnoohah,* or "shell in the throat" medicine [Neill in Wallis 1947:76]. During initiations the shaman shoots the *Wahmnoohah* into the novice, then "pats upon the breast of the novice, till the latter, in agonizing throes, heaves up the Wahmnoohah or shell, which falls from his mouth. . . . With the mysterious shell in his open hand, the new made member passes around and exhibits it to all the members and to the wondering bystanders" [Neill (1872) in Wallis 1947:76].

Howard [1984:131] noted that "the Medicine Dance seems to have disappeared by the 1860s among the Santees in the United States, but it persisted for at least seventy years longer among the Canadian Sioux." Of the famous "shooting" connected with this society, Howard reported that "each shooter held his animal skin bag extended head first toward the candidate, then stopped a short distance away and shook the animal skin in the candidate's direction, uttering the sacred cry. This was supposed to propel the 'medicine arrow' (a small shell) from the bag into the candidate's body. If allowed to remain, he would supposedly sicken and die. The candidate, however, would retch violently and bring up the shell. Then the whole process would be repeated. During the medicine shooting each group shot in turn. When all had shot the candidate there was a general shooting, the initiate joining the more experienced members of the order. According to Arthur Young, some people with great power simply staggered a bit when shot. Others fell as if dead and required 'doctoring' to remove the magical projectile" [Howard 1984:134–135].

The format of a healing ceremony can be, in part, determined by the patient himself. For example, Wallis [1947:70] gave an account of a sick man who, though not a member of this society, sponsored one of their healing ceremonies. Shortly before the healing he had a dream in which a man appeared. "This person said I need have no fear of dying; all of the powers had sent him to tell me to get 12 pots, kill a cow, cut it up, and cook it in these 12 pots. That was all this person told me in the dream" [unidentified informant in Wallis 1947:70]. He subsequently followed these instructions in his healing ceremony.

Wäkatcihagi
Fox, *Midwest*

Society of sorcerers. It is reported that the ceremonies of this society were similar to those of the *Midewiwin* (EONAH, p. 174) but "the difference being in the throwing of charcoal at one another instead of shooting each other with the otterskin pouches. The charcoal was thrown with the hand. A newly elected member when shot would fall more readily than an older member" [Fisher 1939:105]. See *wakan a tcipi* for details.

Wäkatishkwä
Potawatomi, *Midwest*

Throwing-Out-Medicine Ceremony [Skinner 1924:231]. An obsolete healing ritual, performed by members of the Eagle and Bald Eagle clans, in which participating shamans partook of a brew of red mescal beans before conducting their cure. One man, Wapûkä (see entry), recalled attending such a ceremony as a child and witnessing four shamans treat a man for blindness throughout the night until dawn:

One of the leaders danced around the fire and suddenly blew on the sick man. Fire issued from his mouth and flickered all over the patient's body and face. The song was then changed, and a second shaman went over to the patient and scraped his face, rising with a double handful of downy feathers which he displayed, dancing before the assembly with them in his cupped hand. . . . It was difficult for Wa´pûkä to see where he could have concealed these feathers if he did not indeed get them from the patient's face, as he and the other performers were naked and painted.

Then the second shaman walked around the lodge pounding on his abdomen and groaning. Suddenly he paused and blew very hard, expelling a great cloud of eagle plumes from his mouth. The air seemed full of them, and they fell in a shower around the patient. He sang a song and picked them up, and behold, there were only four plumes after all. These he laid beside the patient.

A third shaman, with long flowing hair, now arose, went to the patient, raised his arms, trembled, groaned, and cried out that someone had shot medicine into his stomach. He danced like a madman, and then seemed to pull his belly open and tear out several large black silk scarfs. He placed these over the sick man and passed them around. Then he laid them beside the patient.

The fourth shaman sprang up and ran on all fours around the fire. . . . He rose on his knees and growled like a grizzly bear, produced two butcher knives, and thrust them into his abdomen. When he drew them out blood gushed forth. He patted his wounds, wiped them with a black silk scarf, feathers, and down, and then exhibited himself to everyone, completely whole, only scars remaining.

By this time the patient was sitting up, and the shaman shouted to him . . . "Can you see?" The patient replied in the affirmative, and the shaman went across the lodge and tested him out by holding up his fingers. . . .

The shamans also swallowed knives, sticks, and feathers, all performing at once after the supposed cure had been accomplished. None of the audience was allowed to leave before daylight [Skinner 1924:231–232].

Wakaxambi
Assiniboin, *Plains*
See *wagiksuyabi.*

Wakckwitit
Wishram, *Plateau*
Short billets of wood, approximately the length and thickness of the forearm, that are thumped vertically on a long, horizontal wood plank to keep time with ceremonial singing. Wishram shamans and other shamans throughout the Northwest Coast and Plateau areas often sing their spirit power into the *wakckwitit,* and the individual who bears the *wakckwitit* can then not release it and is dragged around the room by it. The following is a short account of such a "dance with the thumping sticks," performed by a Wishram shaman named Salmin: "He [Salmin] stood before the five [assistants with *wakckwitit* sticks] throwing (duck?) feathers into the air. One of the boys' sticks began to sway, pulling him about. He could not let go. It pulled him to his feet; he had a little spirit power. The shaman told some strong men to watch the boy, to grasp him from behind by the blanket which was firmly tied about him. They were to hold him back and make him stay in his place. The boy lay stiff and lifeless but still held the stick upright on his chest, clenched in his hands. Two or four boys lay thus. Then someone with a little power blew on the boy's stick to loosen his grip, so that the spirit would not draw his hands tight and kill him" [Spier and Sapir 1930:243].

See also *tamanowash sticks.*

Wakiasua
Dakota, *Plains*
A nineteenth-century (?) shaman among the Canadian Dakota. According to one account he used his medicine powers to find a missing wife, who had run off with another man. "While he was asleep, he learned where she had gone. Next morning he sang. He went around the tipi [his own] four times, changed into a buffalo, and tracked the eloping couple. On the following morning he went into another camp. Here the tracks were so numerous that he could no longer follow them. He went around the camp four times. He then learned that they had not gone

into the camp, but instead had made a detour around it. He went past this camp, into the bush, across a valley, and tracked the two up a hill, to a small patch of bushes. He changed himself into a man. Because of the medicine he had used on them, they neither heard nor saw him. He went close to them, shot the man, and cut off his head. He brought his wife home to the large camp and told her father all that she had done" [Wallis 1947:105].

Wakon Tanga
Assiniboin, *Plains*

Great Power, Creator. An ineffable supernatural being that sometimes appeared to humans in the guise of a man and from which all manifested. "It was the abstraction of the universe and its power could be enlisted to aid one were the proper compulsives of ceremony, sacrifice and fasting engaged in" [Rodnick 1938:45]. The following is an example of hunting power obtained through such prayer:

> Hunting was difficult in the 'eighties [1880s]. The buffalo was gone and the few deer and antelope that remained were hard to get. It was only with the aid of the Great Spirit that I was able to keep my family from starving to death.
>
> One day, the results of my hunting were meager. Towards afternoon, I saw an antelope with her young one standing in the center of a level plain. I tried to get close to them; but found it impossible. I followed a coulee that led to this level ground, but even then I couldn't get near enough to shoot. I became desperate, for I needed that food for my family. I cried and prayed to the spirits of the Thunderbird, the eagle and the bullet-hawk, for they had often come to me in dreams. I begged them to help me.
>
> The Great Spirit heard my prayer and as I looked at the game that I could not shoot, I suddenly noticed a huge eagle swoop from the sky. The antelope and her young one ran in all directions, but in vain, for the bird soon had its claws in the antelope's ribs. It was the prettiest sight that I had seen, for the antelope appeared to be winged and about to fly. The antelope

staggered along a few feet and then dropped. And as soon as the eagle appeared certain of the antelope's death, it loosened its hold and flew to a nearby hill, to wait while I claimed my meat. I shouted to the eagle, "You eat first. I'll get my meat later." The eagle quickly understood, for it flew to the fallen antelope and busied itself for a few minutes tearing out the liver as its payment and then flew back to the hilltop to eat its meat there. I thanked it and after I had cut up and skinned the antelope and packed the meat on my back, I looked back and there was the eagle still eating its meat. My heart was glad [unidentified informant in Rodnick 1938:46].

Wallace, Emma
Wintun, *California*

A Wintu shaman during the early part of the twentieth century. She was renowned for her clairvoyant abilities and often consulted by others.

A shaman, Tilly Griffen, while in a trance prophesied that Mrs. Fan would soon receive bad news in a letter. Mrs. Fan felt that her son had died, and she therefore went to another shaman, Emma Wallace, to learn what she could. Emma Wallace was informed by her father's Lεs, which was her guardian spirit, that the spirit of Mrs. Fan's son was olεl (meaning "above," generally rendered into English as in heaven). He had said that he was sorry not to have died at home, to have left his body behind, but that his body would be sent back to his home. The next night Emma Wallace was asked what the white people would do about sending the body back to Bald Hills. She said: "The white people have turned his face this way. They are sending him back. He is in a good box, in an awfully pretty house (coffin). They are talking a lot. Some want to send him back. Some want to leave him there." Three days later the same shaman said that the next morning the body would arrive. So complete was the faith in her prophecy that a grave was dug and preparations made for a funeral. The next morning they all went to Anderson and found that a truck bearing the coffin had arrived [Du Bois 1935:77].

Wananikwä
Ojibwa/Dakota, *Midwest*
See *Madmowun*.

Wanaxirï
Paiute, *Basin*
A Chemehuevi *tïmpi buaxantï* (rock shaman) during the first part of the twentieth century. He had the power to climb high cliffs in order to steal baby eagles from their nest. He also cured injuries received in falls. When treating fractures he would sing, suck on the patient, and set the fractures with splints. Although he did not have a helping spirit per se, he had "good dreams of rocks" [Kelly 1936:137].

Wanke
Tewa, *Southwest*
The Jemez Bear society at Santa Clara Pueblo. This is one of two Bear medicine societies at this pueblo; the other is called the *Téchugeke,* or Tesuque Bear [Hill 1982:319]. In former times there was a third Bear society known as *Temake,* or Cochiti Bear [Hill 1982:318]. In more recent times all members of both societies have come from the Summer Moiety at Santa Clara. In addition, both societies, as their membership dwindles, have been coming together to form a single unit when villagewide ceremonies are performed. This has led some ethnographers, such as Elsie Parsons and Jean Jeançon, to state that there is only one medicine society at Santa Clara. The primary function of both societies is healing, although they perform other functions (such as purification rites) at the annual irrigation ditch opening. Curative rites performed by the Bear societies are called *pivah,* while the preventive (i.e., purification) rites are called *fehreh* [Hill 1982:321].

Wanke society members undergo a period of training usually lasting three to four months, followed by a final initiation at Jemez. Both males and females join the society, but males occupy the dominant roles. A similar procedure is followed by *Téchugeke* members at Tesuque. The altar displays and songs differ between the two societies, with the *Wanke* songs being sung in Towa rather than Tewa. During their healing ceremonies the Jemez Bears paint their faces red and dance, while the Tesuque Bears do neither. Finally, the Tesuque Bears insist "that for four days after a cure, the patient be accompanied at all times by a relative; no such instructions were given by the Jemez [Bears]" [Hill 1982:320].

Both the *pivah* and the *fehreh* rites vary, ranging from performances by a single Bear society member for an individual to combined society rites for the entire pueblo. Distinctions between the various rites are "made on the basis of the number of participants and the amount of territory encompassed. Thus the rites were categorized as a 'treatment, or cure, with food or meal' (hu cong wogi wokang); 'treatment, or cure, with house'; 'treatment, or cure, with yard'; and 'large treatment' (sori wokang)" [Hill 1982:321]. All these performances entail payment, in cornmeal, to the Bear society participants.

The "treatment, or cure, with food or meal" is the simplest healing ceremony. It is conducted by one to three members of a Bear society on an individual suffering from a stomach disorder, fever, fright, witchcraft, etc. For example, a Tesuque Bear often treats a patient suffering from shock or fright by giving him a *kaji* (sacred stone) wrapped in a cloth, which is secured about the waist of the patient for four days (or longer if the cure is slow in coming). "During this period the patient was accompanied at all times; this precaution was taken in case the illness stemmed from sorcery. No witch would approach a person so guarded in an attempt to 're-infect him'" [Hill 1982:323]. In more serious cases of shock or fright, the patient is first purified before wearing the *kaji*. In these cases the patient kneels over a bowl of coals onto which either bear or mountain lion hairs have been placed, and a blanket is laid over him to let the hair smoke permeate his entire being, while the Tesuque Bear says a prayer. "When the prayer was completed, the blanket was removed, and the coals taken from the container. The ash remaining from the hair was placed in another bowl, and water was added. The Bear member asperged some of this solution on the patient's head and on his hands and feet, which were placed together. The patient then drank the remaining liquid from the bowl" [Hill 1982:324]. Following this purification the patient is then given the *kaji* to wear about his waist. The technique of sucking an intrusive disease-object from the patient is not employed in any of the "treatment, or cure, with food or meal" healing rituals. The actual ritual rarely lasts more than one night for treatment.

A "treatment, or cure, with house" ceremony is a one-night ritual. Such a ceremony usually requires the services of several members, if not the entire society, and is held in a kiva if the patient can be moved there. During the cure Bear members cough and growl like bears and howl like wolves. One report described such a ceremony:

> Bear members with stone fetishes made gestures of embracing evil and blowing it away. Some took a fetish in one hand, placed a gauntlet on the other, dipped it in the sacred water, went to the patient, placed both the fetish and gauntlet on the person's head, drew out the evil, and dispelled it. Others practiced the laying of hands, "felt the patient with their hands or bear-paws." Still others massaged and rubbed the patient's arms, legs, and various parts of the body, concentrated the evil in one spot, and then sucked it out through their cupped hands or gauntlets and swallowed it. "One had a special trick; he would place his foot on the patient, draw the object out with his toes, and exhibit it."
>
> When a member swallowed evil, he arose and came to the altar and walked back and forth in front of it, staggering as if he were drunk, and attempted to vomit the disease cause. The noises he made were very realistic. Finally he vomited it beside the altar. If it was a particularly large object, it might be dragging along the floor behind him and coming out his mouth at the same time. The things extracted included long rags, lengths of yucca tied together, rocks, down

feathers, broken glass, sticks, cattail fuzz, etc. [Hill 1982:327].

Once finished with the patient, the Bear society members would then purify the entire house.

A "treatment, or cure, with yard" is like the "treatment, or cure, with house" except that it includes "a purification of the corrals, livestock, crops, and landholdings of the household group, as well as of the house and kin group" [Hill 1982:330].

The "large treatment," or *sori wokang,* is an annual ritual conducted in March or April. The purpose of the ceremony is "to cleanse the tribal territory and everything it contained of witches and their malignant influences" [Hill 1982:330]. However, in more recent times it has not been held every year. The ceremony takes four days to conduct. On the first three nights of the ceremony, six sacred shrines are visited and purified each night, beginning with those that are farthest from the village and ending with those that are the closest. On the fourth night the ceremony is conducted in a *kiva* and concentrates on the members of the pueblo. During this time the Bear society members approach all the people present and remove evil from them in the same manner as in the "treatment, or cure, with house" ceremony.

Wanoxiswehi
Oto, *Plains*
Clairvoyant Doctors' society [Whitman 1937: 120]. The shamans in this society specialize in curing spasms, among other things.

Wapakiniwap
Cree, *Canadian Eastern Woodlands*
Literal translation: "White Flower." A Plains Cree shaman who was living near Cowessess Reserve north of Broadview, Saskatchewan, when he was around the age of ninety in the early part of the twentieth century. He is reported to have been a small but powerful man. He was renowned for his healing of difficult cases, such as venereal disease and pleurisy. During his healing

ceremonies he would use a sacred pipe, administer herbal medicines while singing the proper medicine songs accompanied by a rattle and drum, and say the appropriate prayers.

His spirit helper was the Rattlesnake. "He used to have a rattlesnake skin which he placed beside whoever he was doctoring, whether on the floor or on the ground in a tepee in summertime. Well, he'd ask this patient to lay down and he'd sing to this rattlesnake. This rattlesnake was [then] just like it was alive; he had no head, only a tail. And he'd start crawling. If he'd crawl over this person that's being doctored, this meant the patient would get well. He knew how to cure them. That really happened, all right—right here west of Cowessess" [Alec Tanner in Tarasoff 1980:136].

Wapi munipi
Cree, *Canadian Eastern Woodlands*
Literal translation: "Mirror Water" [Mandelbaum 1940:262]. A water scrying (see entry) technique among the Plains Cree. Fine Day reported of this technique: "The Plains Cree did tell the future by looking into water. On the warpath each man would carry a cup (for drinking). On one trip the leader filled his cup half full of water. Then he talked to *Manito* [Creator]. The men built a big fire. The leader kneeled, pulled a robe over his head, grasped it on both sides so as to shade his eyes. He peered at the water intently—gazing from different angles continually. He asked, 'Does the fire shine brightly on the water?' The men answered, 'Yes.' When the fire died down he told them to build it up again. Finally he said, 'Tomorrow, the enemy will discover you while you are hunting buffalo.' What he said came true. I never saw this done except in war but it may have been done for the hunt, too. . . . It sometimes didn't turn out as the seer had predicted, but pretty often it did" [Fine Day in Mandelbaum 1940:262].

Waptashi
Klikitat, *Northwest*
Literal translation: "feather" [Du Bois 1938:5]. The Sahaptin term for the Feather cult. It is also known by the Sahaptin term *waskliki,* meaning "spin." The cult became established by around 1904. "In English, Feather cultists are generally referred to as the bum-bum or pom-pom Shakers" [Du Bois 1938:5].

This religious movement was started around 1898 by a Klikitat dreamer named Jake Hunt, who lived at Nakrepunk (now Husum), 7 miles north of the Columbia River along the east banks of the White Salmon River. As the cult founder and leader he adopted the name Earth Thunderer [Du Bois 1938:25]. At one point he also converted to the Shaker (EONAH, pp. 245–246) religion.

As a shaman, Jake Hunt was renowned. "He was believed capable of anticipating the arrival of an unannounced visitor. He could divine illness even when the patient was not present. He could read people's thoughts and gauge their moral character at a glance. On Umatilla Reservation, he knew of a secret murder and secured a confession from the culprit. If intoxicants were brought into his encampment, he knew it without seeing them and could find them wherever they might be concealed. In one case of this sort, he returned with some whiskey, whereupon the malefactor's hands became rigid in an attitude of prayer until Jake released him by pouring the liquor on the fire. The colored flames resulting from this act were considered further proof of his miraculous powers. . . . Among his supernatural gifts was his power of locating objects with his eyes closed" [Du Bois 1938:24].

"Jake had two pairs and many single tamanos [see *tamanoas*—EONAH, pp. 276–277] which just gave him songs. One pair was eagle and grizzly bear; the other was chinook salmon and raccoon. The grizzly bear is one of the most powerful and dangerous familiars [spirits]. One of his single powers was the wind which made you spin when he blew on you. The power of the wind was in the feather he made you hold in your hand. The eagle spoke to him and told him to do this feather work" [Jo Hunt (Klikitat) in Du Bois 1938:25]. He also had a Thunderbird spirit.

In his Eagle vision he was told to take his teaching to seven nations. Between 1905 and 1907 he visited the Yakima, Warm Springs, and Umatilla Reservations. Later on his teaching spread as far as the Paviotso in Nevada and the Klamath Reservation in Oregon. "Although the ceremonial procedure of the Feather cult strongly resembles that of the Washani [see entry], two features differentiate it sharply from the older religion. The initiation with its spinning and vomiting features is one marked innovation. . . . Curing is another. Whereas the spinning and vomiting aspects of the initiation seem to be completely original with Jake Hunt, the curative functions of the cult may well be a direct borrowing from the Shaker religion" [Du Bois 1938:33]. A typical healing session lasts for three nights. During the healing ceremony the shaman calls forth his spirit power. "The power which enters him from prayers and drumming leads the outer edges of his hands to the pain [disease object causing the sickness—see *pains*]. Then his assistants [in a group healing] also place their hands on the same spot. 'When they have a good grip on the sickness,' they all slowly raise their hands to draw out the illness. Then all let go at once and the illness is dissipated into the air. It is not returned to the mountains like the older shamanistic 'pains.' But it is obviously similar to the Shakers who brush or draw off illness with their hands" [Du Bois 1938:34].

Jake Hunt died in 1917. Around 1919 his body was exhumed for re-dressing. "Reports say that no decay had taken place and that the corpse appeared as natural as in life" [Du Bois 1938:21].

Wáptipas
Nez Perce, *Plateau*

Shamans who have tutelary spirits, such as Elk, Deer, Wolf, and Cougar. "Persons possessing these powers were known for their ability in handling fire, which they frequently demonstrated, and for their ability in locating and attracting game. Theoretically, any song in this complex of tutelary spirits and powers was capable of producing the legitimizing trance in individuals who had received their power from any other member of the complex" [D. Walker 1968:21].

Wapûkä
Potawatomi, *Midwest*

Literal translation: "Watching" [Skinner 1924: 12]. A leader of the Native American Church (Peyote cult) who belonged to the Wabash band of the Prairie Potawatomi at Mayetta, Kansas. His English name was Samuel Derosier or "Sam Bosley" [Skinner 1924:12]. Having converted to peyotism later in life, Wapûkä felt the old ceremonies (many of which were extinct by then) were of little value, and in 1923 he gave some of the most complete descriptions of them ever rendered to anthropologist Alanson B. Skinner. Subsequently, Skinner wrote that Wapûkä "was intensely religious, and in 'seeking the right way to live' he joined every organization in his power, and attended every clan ceremony. . . . His knowledge is quite comprehensive. His memory is abnormally developed. . . . [He] was a great devotee of this cult [the Dream Dance society]" [Skinner 1924:12, 226]. On March 8, 1924, Wapûkä died at McLoud, Oklahoma, where he had gone to live among the Kickapoo. (Note: For more on the Dream Dance society, see *Madmowun.*)

War bridle charm
Blackfoot, *Plains*

A horse medicine (see entry) charm literally known as "a thing to tie on the halter" [Wissler 1912a:107]. It was used to provide protection and power against the enemy in battle. Many bags containing war bridle charms were used among the Blackfoot, who hung them under their horses' bits. One such charm obtained from the Blood division included a special form of quirt that went with its use. "The feathers are the secondary part of the bundle, the vital element being found in seven small bags tied at intervals in the fringe. . . . These bags contain earth from where horses had pawed at the margin of a certain lake, taken as directed in the initial dream conferring the formula" [Wissler 1912a:107]. When this charm was used, several special power songs were also sung (recorded for the American Museum of Natural History, as phonograph records 437–41).

Such charms were also used to increase the speed and sure-footedness of one's horse during a buffalo hunt.

War medicine

Any use of supernatural powers to bring success in warfare. War medicines came in many different forms throughout North America, and "any big war party will have a shaman along to tell them how to get success" [unidentified informant in Opler 1941a:344]. Although the literature on Native American warfare seldom mentions the use of war medicines, it is difficult to imagine any warfare being conducted without their use. However, these medicines were employed in a religious context: A war raid per se took on the air of a religious ceremony in that it was accompanied by a prescribed set of ritual actions and by certain taboos. For example, there were elaborate ritual procedures for preparing for war, for approaching the enemy, for handling the scalp of a slain enemy, and so forth. It was within these actions that war medicines were applied.

Some war medicines were as simple as the wearing of an amulet (see entry) that had been empowered by a shaman. At the other end of the continuum, war medicines consisted of complex rituals that were to be performed prior to undertaking a battle, during the battle, and afterward. Among the Plains area cultures at least nine different types of personal war medicines were observed: (1) designs, (2) animal parts, (3) inanimate objects, (4) plants, (5) sounds, (6) clothing, (7) war paraphernalia, (8) horse charms, and (9) complex-combination bundles [Aquila 1974: 24]. All warriors knew of the existence of such medicine powers, and most were inclined to pursue war medicines in some form.

The Plains-Ojibwa used many different forms of war charms. Most often the way in which such charms were to be made was revealed to the warrior by a guardian spirit during a dream. Warriors "also carried medicines in which they

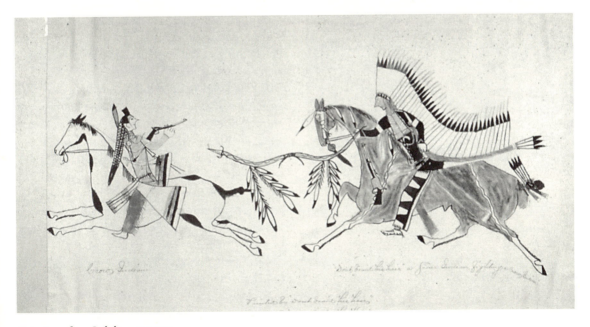

Painting of an Oglala war party.

An eagle talon medicine charm, possibly of the Crow, worn as an ornament by a warrior to ensure the presence of a "sacred helper" when used in conjunction with body paint and song.

steeped their bullets to make them fatal" [Skinner 1914:493].

Wissler [1907] studied the protective designs used by the Dakota on their bodies and war shields, war shirts, and other paraphernalia. Shield designs were revealed only via dreams or visions "and were painted by the person experiencing them, who prayed and sang over his work to give the shield power. Usually but four shields could be made from a single dream: to make a great number was sacrilege" [Wissler 1907:30]. However, in painting a shield a warrior would draw his design "in conformity with the conventional modes of representative art practised by his tribe" [Wissler 1907:23]. "In many cases the designs were painted upon the rawhide itself, and protected by a buckskin cover; while in other cases the designs were painted upon the cover" [Wissler 1907:22]. In addition, various objects, such as feathers, were also often attached to the shield. With the advent of firearms, these shields, being good targets, were, for the most part, abandoned.

In addition to designs, songs and herbs were used as Oglala war medicines. "In a battle some must sing to encourage the others. Each [Oglala *Cante Tinza* warrior society] member carries a bit of calamus root as medicine which he chews and spits over himself to induce courage, etc. If in a fight a member becomes confused or panicky, the others spit this root over him. There is no definite form of painting for ceremonies, but when going to war two black marks are made diagonally across the face" [Wissler 1912b:26–27]. The *Iku Sapa* (Black Chins) warrior society also used the calamus root, but "they painted their chins black from the mouth down on each side. . . . When mounted, their horses are painted red. The power of their regalia and medicine was so great that they were seldom wounded" [Wissler 1912b:28–29].

One of the most sacred war medicines among the Dakota was their medicine bow. "It consisted of a bow of plain wood, of the usual length, to the end of which was attached a spear-head. Fastened to the bow was a stick somewhat longer, sharpened at one end, and decorated with feathers and other symbolic objects. The purpose of the stick was to support the bow, since all such

Edward S. Curtis, The Oath, *1908. Photogravure.*

sacred objects would lose their power if allowed
to touch the ground. The bow was not used as a
weapon, but was carried as a standard, because of
its supposed magical power over the enemy"
[Wissler 1907:50]. A warrior who carried a medicine bow also had to have his body elaborately
painted.

Eaglebone whistles were used in warfare, as
well as in the Sun Dance and other ceremonies.
"The Sioux used these in battle or at crucial
times to call upon the power of the thunder. . . .
The Cheyenne made war whistles from the wing
bone of cranes, as well as eagles" [Aquila
1974:27]. Hats, capes, coats, necklaces, sacred
stones, scarfs, and other items were also worn as
war medicines. The Contraries, warriors who
had dreamed of the Thunderbird and had to do
everything backwards (e.g., the Lakota *heyóka*—
see EONAH, pp. 104–105), carried a special
lance in war, known as a thunderbow, which was
only used to count coup on (strike) the enemy
and not as a weapon.

On the Iowa war parties "a seer or prophet was
taken along to insure success, and warn them of
impending triumph or disaster" [Skinner
1915a:687]. In addition, prior to going into battle, the warriors "painted and rubbed themselves
with the sacred bundle medicine intended to de-
flect the arrows and weapons of the foe, armed
themselves, and prepared. There was generally,
and should always have been, a buffalo shaman
present with his sacred bundle, its flutes, buffalo
hoof rattles, buffalo tails, and medicines calculated
to heal wounds, and cause clotted blood to be cast
out or drained away. . . . During the fight, the
bundle owner stayed behind and sang and rattled
to help his men" [Skinner 1915a:687–688].

Boas [1922:994] reported the use of war medicines among the Pueblo cultures of the Southwest area:

If a person wants to become a brave warrior he
must bring many sacrifices at midnight to a place
on the Rio Grande called Muskrat House. He
must take off all his clothing and throw down

sacred cornmeal. He must go into the water and
sit in it so that the water reaches up to his neck.
Then he will feel that somebody is pulling him.
After sitting in the water for some time, he dresses
again and goes home. He is not allowed to look
backward, and may not run, but he walks home
very slowly. Then he will feel that somebody is
pulling him and trying to induce him to look
back. If he should be frightened and look back on
the way, he loses his life, or at least he will not be
successful in his endeavors. If he is not afraid, he
will become a great warrior.

People also go to a short, deep canyon in the
Peralta. It is a short, deep canyon which runs
northward and is called Ga´ectaya, that is, Windy.
Four days before starting, the man must purify
himself by taking cedar emetics. He must go to
the place at midnight. When they arrive there,
they must sacrifice cornmeal to the Supernatural
Beings. Finally, they arrive at a waterfall. There he
must take off his clothing and stand there looking
northward. He sacrifices again and prays to the
Supernatural Being (Mai´-mai) who lives in the
canyon. He also sacrifices turkey feathers (*yectde*).
He asks to be made brave and to be able to
withstand the Apache and Navaho (in battle).
After praying, he draws in his breath four times,
holding his hand in front of his mouth, and goes
back. As soon as he turns, terrific noises are heard
as though rocks are falling down. He feels as if
people are pulling him, and a tornado is rushing
through the canyon. He must go out slowly
without looking back. If he goes out slowly, the
noise finally ceases as soon as he leaves the canyon.
As soon as he leaves the canyon, he has to turn
back and draw in the breath four times through
his hands and then he prays. [See also *Hotshanyi*.]

The nearby Papago shamans also performed
war medicines against their enemies, most often
the Apache.

Each village if possible brought a shaman to "see"
the enemy and to recite spells to disable him.
These shamans were of a particular class, the "owl
meeters," who had owls for their guardian spirits.
The dead are supposed to fly back from the east,
where they live, in the form of owls. Dead Papago

warriors, in owl form, haunted the enemy country where they died and with these the shaman communed.

The parties from the partner villages met at night at the rendezvous and went through a series of ceremonies. During these, it was the duty of the shaman to retire and to practise divination which would tell where the enemy might be encountered. If there were several shamans, they all worked together [Underhill 1939:132].

Stephen mentioned that the Hopi warriors of the Warrior society never danced in public because their medicine powers "would cause gales of cold wind and evil disturbance in the air" [Stephen 1936:95].

Shamans were also very much involved in the use of their powers to aid in warfare. For example, weather shamans (see entry) were called upon to bring bad weather if the enemy was known to be planning an attack. In the heat of battle, a weather shaman might be called upon to produce a thick fog so they could make their escape.

Powerful shamans were able to command bulletproof medicines (EONAH, pp. 41–42), and there are many examples of this in the literature. The following is an example from the Owens Valley Paiute near Mono Lake in Utah: "A. G. described a 'doctor' from the south [with] proof against arrows and bullets. He made a handful of bullets disappear by rubbing his hand when dancing. E. L. mentioned a doctor proving his power to doubters by folding his hands over his breast and being shot with a 'six shooter' from a few paces. He handed them the bullet which passed through only one hand, showing the bloodless bullet hole" [Steward 1933:310]. However, such performances could result in the death of the shaman (e.g., see Lowie 1913a:139).

Other forms of war medicine from these Paiutes have also been described:

Some Indians trapped on Baker creek by soldiers said, "What powers have we that will help us out of this?" One claimed the gray haze [weather shaman?] which would hide them; another had the mirage which would make bushes and grass look tall like men, and one man running like many. They escaped, assisted by the haze, mirage, and individual powers. The last, looking back [a taboo], was wounded and fell, but hid under a bush, made invisible to the searching soldiers by his power, and escaped.

The power of another warrior made him suddenly stop running in bushes when bullets fell ahead which would have killed him. He ran on, shot at, but escaping unhurt. His body was black and blue from bullets which his power had prevented from penetrating his skin [Steward 1933:310].

Another example of bulletproof medicine was given in the following account of an Ingalik shaman:

There was a shaman at Shageluk who demonstrated his power by remaining uninjured when shot at. Taking his gun he would start in the corner of the kashim [house] at the left of the door and reach for an imaginary gun rod. Then in the second corner he put in imaginary powder, in the third, the wadding, and in the last, he primed the gun. Then he gave the weapon to a man who was present, and the shaman told him to aim it at him and pull the trigger, warning, however, that the man doing the shooting must have faith or the shaman would be hurt. Then at the signal, which was the cry of the shaman's "spirit-animal," the man shot the gun which went off with a loud noise. The shaman staggered backward, people grabbing him to prevent his falling over. As he staggered, smoke began to merge from his mouth and he spat up bullets. Some men did not believe that he had been shot, however, so he challenged anyone to bring his own gun and load it. When one man did so, the gun was given to the first shooter who had the necessary faith in the shaman. The same thing happened all over and the people said nothing more [Osgood 1958:58–59].

Among the Tanaina of southern Alaska, it was reported that "a common performance is for a shaman to give a man a loaded gun and tell him to shoot him through the chest. The man with the gun is afraid of killing the shaman, of course, and the emotions of the spectators rise as he is being persuaded. When he finally fires the shot, blood spurts all around the shaman but the bullet flattens against his chest without leaving a trace of a wound. Then everyone tries shooting the shaman but with the same result" [Osgood 1937:180].

In the nearby Mackenzie-Yukon area the Chipewyan also used war medicines in their battles with the Dogrib and Caribou Eaters. "The old men, about fifty years old, no good to fight, but they are good for medicine lots of times. They dream that the enemy is close and they want to fight. . . . The medicine man could sing and make the others lose their brains like the enemies. They go crazy, get lost" [D. Smith 1973:19].

One shaman among the Flathead was reported to be such an expert seer "that no Blackfoot scout ever dared sit on the hills and spy out the camp to which this man was attached. During his lifetime the enemy feared to attack this band. They believed that he actually knew just what was taking place in a Blackfoot council as if 'he had a radio there.' Seers could tell where there were herds of bison, could foretell the results of battles and campaigns" [Turney-High 1937:29].

The Chiricahua (Apache) of the Southwest also possessed a bulletproof medicine. Geronimo (see entry) and some of his warriors used it. "Old Man S. was with Geronimo's bunch all through the war. . . . He has power from the gun, they say. They say he used to get out on the bank; all the soldiers shot at him and couldn't hit him. One who went to shoot him might fall down or drop his gun; then S. would kill him instead. Another man told me he knows a gun ceremony. He, too, went through all the wars safely. Geronimo is said to have known this ceremony. He never got hurt either. Something always happens to your gun when you try to shoot at such a fel-

low. Your gun jams, for instance. The one who knows this ceremony can fix it for someone else so that, when he is shot at, he will be missed" [unidentified informant in Opler 1941a:310].

In addition many shamans had "power of weapons" [Opler 1941a:341], by which they used their war medicine to make protective shirts, hats, lances, shields, etc., for the warriors. Chiricahua warriors often paid a shaman to make a protective shield. "The shield is always ceremonial and belongs to this kind of power. When you see a man with a shield, you know it was made for him by a ceremonial man in connection with a war ceremony. It's not like a bow or a sling. It's not just a weapon. Anyone couldn't have this. The shield is called 'that which I hold up' in a ceremonial way. It is the same with the lance. You could only get it from a man [shaman] who has the right to make it. . . . The shamans of the war ceremonies made hats. [Most of the time the hat was just rolled up and tied to the quiver.] These went with the shields; they were made by the same men" [unidentified informant in Opler 1941a:311].

In former times the Seminole had powerful shamans "who did not bleed when shot, and could walk long distances after being wounded. Others seemed to be very broad in the chest (three or four feet) but were actually only two or three inches wide, so that soldiers missed them when they shot at them. . . . Other owǎ:lá:łi [see *owála*] could make themselves invulnerable by causing bullets to swerve around them, or could 'fix' dogs so that they could no longer smell a trail they were following. . . . Some could change themselves into bears in order to travel faster. . . . Some knew how to make themselves invisible by singing a song, lying down in the grass, and putting a blade of grass on top of themselves; the soldiers could then not see them" [Sturtevant 1954b:376–377]. The "thunder missile" or "thunder bullet" *(tonohkahcíłakî)* was the white, fused-glass stone found where lightning strikes the ground. These stones were used to frighten or confuse the enemy. A silvery powder called *sápiyî* ("sickness") was used in warfare to put soldiers to sleep. Seminole shamans also used a "living medicine" *(ayikcfîsahkî).* "During wartime, the medicine man stayed awake all one night and used this medicine to capture the souls . . . of the sleeping soldiers, which made them easier to kill in the morning" [Sturtevant 1954b:380].

Among the Cow Creek Seminole, powerful shamans "sometime carried a 'lightning ball' on their shoulders which protected them from bullets and arrows and could also be shot at game or at people" [Spoehr in Sturtevant 1954b:396].

The Hupa also had a war medicine that caused their enemies to sleep. They would use certain songs "to put the enemy into sound slumber when a night attack was to be made" [Goddard 1903:63].

Among the Klamath of California, the shaman predicted who would "be killed or wounded, and how the enemy [would] suffer. He [saw] them bleeding. . . . For example, while a mixed group of Klamath and Modoc were encamped on the way to Pit river, a Modoc shaman predicted, 'If you are to be shot, then your bowstrings will snap,' and the strings of two did snap. Shamans [accompanied] war parties, not only to fight, but to watch over them and cure the wounded" [Spier 1930:122].

One of the more interesting forms of war medicine is the ability to disguise oneself by transforming one's shape. For instance, Geronimo (see entry) was able to make himself invisible. Deganawidah (see entry) also had the power to transform his shape into that of a tree. One branch of the Tiger band of the Mikasuki Seminole was reported to have a medicine that turned them "into some kind of plants . . . so that when the following enemies touched them, they were not distinguishable from bushes" [Sturtevant 1954b:27]. The Assiniboin had a shaman during the nineteenth century who had received power from the Buffalo that enabled him to transform. "In battle, such a man might turn into a buffalo. When the enemy retreated, he would follow, hooking and killing them with his horns. An aged informant

spoke of a man who had killed thirty hostile Indians in this manner" [Lowie 1909:47].

Warriors changing forms was widely known. In the following account of a mistaken transformation, given by a Sioux Valley informant among the Santee (Canadian Sioux in this case), the use of medicine powers was indicted: "One time a party of Dakota attacked an enemy war party. The enemy were outnumbered pretty badly and the Dakota succeeded in killing all of the enemy except for one man. This man had a medicine bundle on his back which seemed to protect him from their arrows. This man took refuge in a thicket of chokecherry bushes. In this thicket he found another occupant, for a grizzly bear had made its den there. Somehow the bear accepted the man with the bundle and let him into his den. When the Dakota warriors would approach the bear's den the bear would charge out and in this way the bear killed several men and horses. The Dakota thought it was the enemy who had changed himself into a grizzly" [Eli Taylor in Howard 1984:110].

Ritual thanksgiving ceremonies following successful war raids were another typical form of war medicine. These rituals ranged from the elaborate "scalp dances" of the Plains area to very simple individual rituals, such as smoking one's sacred pipe. Most often these thanksgiving rituals involved some form of sacrifice made to one's helping spirit(s). For instance, among the Inuit [Eskimo] on Little Diomede Island, the warriors, following a war raid, "would sacrifice to this spirit [the Moon Spirit] a small portion of every plundered article, for example a little corner cut off each piece of fur clothing" [Weyer in Lantis 1947:35].

For other examples see *Ahayuta tikä, Akikita, axwecama,* bear-knife bundle, *Crazy Horse, Ekaskini, Geronimo, gidahim, hobáya, hohoyaüh, hopini, invulnerablility medicines, Iunke warúhawe, mankácutzi warúhawe, Medicine Lance bundle, micacluskwe, mirarackupe, Motsomita, One Spot, Otterskin war medicine, ozunya cin nupa, Poor Wolf, Roman Nose, schalaq, talisóhkocî, tozriki, waxobi, weasel-tail suit, weather shamans, White Crane Dance, Wolf Chief, Wolf-Medicine Dance, wotawe.*

Wasakamecimuwin
Cree, *Canadian Eastern Woodlands*
Also: *nanapawnikamowikamik.* Literal translations: *wasakamecimuwin,* "dancing around;" *nanapawnikamowikamik,* "night singing tipi" [Mandelbaum 1940:278]. Round Dance among the Plains Cree. This is a religious ceremony given for the souls of the dead that lasts one night. The sacred family bundles, called *nayahtcikan* (see entry), in which braids of hair from deceased relatives are kept, play a central role in this religious ceremony.

Wasê
Winnebago, *Midwest*
The magical aspect of medicine, as opposed to its medicinal aspect, which is known as *mañkan* [Radin 1911:193].

Washani
Northwest Coast
Also: *washat.* Dialectical variants: *walashine, walashat* (Umatilla). Literal translations: *washani* means "dancers," and *washat* means "dance" [Du Bois 1938:5]. This is a Sahaptin term, which is also known and used by the Upper Chinookan–speaking cultures, for one of the major religions in the region of the upper Columbia River. The term "includes both the early Christianized Prophet dance of Spier [1935] and what has come to be known as the Smohalla (see entry) cult" [Du Bois 1938:5]. It is also related to the Feather cult (see *waptashi*) of this region.

Wäsiu
Potawatomi, *Midwest*
The ceremonial name used for dogs that are sacrificed for all sacred bundle feasts and other similar rites. The common name for dog is *anämush,* but the term *wäsiu* addresses "the purity of the animal" [Skinner 1924:53].

Dog sacrifices are a common ceremonial requirement among the Plains and Midwest cultures. In former times these dogs were highly regarded. Among the Potawatomi, the "dogs used for this purpose are raised with especial care, and are of selected stock. They are regarded as members of the family in which they are brought up, have their own beds in the lodge, are addressed by familiar terms of relationship, fed choice food, and under no circumstances beaten or abused. They are kept away from the polluting contact of other dogs" [Skinner 1924:53].

Wasna
Teton, *Plains*
The Lakota term for pemmican (which is an Algonquian term) [Powers 1990:69]. It is made by mixing dried, powdered buffalo meat with lard and chokecherries. Formerly it was a traditional food carried by hunters, warriors, and others on a journey, but today it is only used for the feast that occurs at the conclusion of most sacred rituals. In a traditional sacred feast there are four basic items—water, corn, berries, and meat. Chokecherries are the preferred berries and *wasna* the preferred form of meat, although substitutes are often resorted to if the need arises.

Wawa
Ponca, *Plains*
Sacred pipe [Whitman 1937:121]. (For the Keres meaning of this term, see EONAH, p. 312.)

Wawaskeciwcimuwin
Cree, *Canadian Eastern Woodlands*
Elk Dance among the Plains Cree [Mandelbaum 1940:277]. This is a religious ritual that is pledged mostly by women. In fact, it is one of the few religious ceremonies that women participate in. Informants recall that it was held in former times to ensure that young people would grow old. The dance lasted an entire day.

Waxablu
Twana, *Northwest Coast*
A Skokomish woman during the mid-nineteenth century who was known to have a love medicine

(*pthlax*—see entry). Her love medicine power was known as *słqet,* "first sunrise" [Elmendorf 1993:250]. "She had a song to get a man . . . and she'd sing that for a certain man, and in a day or two he'd be crazy to get at her. She had thousands of husbands, they say, got any man she wanted. . . . She received power at sunrise, and that early sunrise was her power to get men. . . . All the people laughed and said, 'That's penis tamánamis [see entry].' And that's what it got her, that power" [Frank Henry in Elmendorf 1993:250].

Waxobi

Ponca, *Plains*

Dialectical variant: *waxobe* (Kansa) [Skinner 1915b:747]. Medicine bundle. Medicine bundles are left in the hands of individual keepers, and quite often they are passed down from generation to generation. Some bundles contain medicines for individuals, while others are used within extended families or larger social groupings. Each clan has one individual who holds its war medicine bundle. "These men acquired the privilege through fasting and prayer which brought them the proper vision. After this had been obtained they sought out an old bundle owner and paid him to teach them how to make and use a clan bundle; henceforward, the new bundle owner was a potential war chief and might be called upon at any time to lead a war party" [Skinner 1915b:748]. "In addition to being a war talisman this bundle was looked upon as a watcher of the lodge and a guardian of health" [Skinner 1915b:748].

The term *waxobi* is also used as an adjective to indicate that something is sacred or imbued with supernatural power, i.e., powerful [Skinner 1915b:783].

Wáyatin

Nez Perce, *Plateau*

Vision quest. Both boys and girls underwent vision quests, beginning between the ages of five and ten.

Rigorous spiritual and physical conditioning usually preceded the quest and was considered essential to the proper training and education of the child. . . . Aboriginally a formal quest for a tutelary spirit could be undertaken at any time during the year, but seems to have occurred more often in the warmer months. The isolation of the neophyte usually was directed by a responsible older relative or shaman. A shaman was thought to watch the progress of the quest magically and to take action should anything untoward occur. The period of isolation might last up to a week. . . .

After a day or two of fasting and concentration on the quest, most individuals were visited by a tutelary spirit. Its appearance was signaled by a song the neophyte usually heard before actually sighting the spirit. The spirit continued singing the song and eventually explained its meaning and the power it conferred [D. Walker 1968:18–19].

Following the quest a child often forgot about his experience, "and the song or spirit usually did not reappear to him until he was at a tutelary spirit dance, often years later. At such ceremonies when someone sang his or a related song, the neophyte again went into a trance in which he revisited his tutelary spirit and received a clearer idea of the dress, song, power, and other accoutrements of his *wéyekin*" (EONAH, p. 315) [D. Walker 1968:20]. It was the spirit dances that solidified the relationship between the shaman and his helping spirit.

"Those who knowingly obtained weak, useless, or evil spirits sometimes had them removed by shamans or at least had them ritually deactivated and were careful not to let them come out at the spirit dances. Should their power become fixed at a spirit dance, individuals were thought to be permanently subject to the same undesirable tendencies attributed to the given tutelary spirit. For example, it was thought that individuals who had power from Crow fixed in this manner were likely to become thieves and steal from their relatives" [D. Walker 1968:20].

Wayucid
Twana, *Northwest Coast*

The process of a person's spirit power becoming manifest, i.e., entering the owner's body; the first public showing of one's spirit power [Elmendorf 1993:199].

Weasel-tail suit
Blackfoot, *Plains*

A form of war medicine. Weasel tails were attached to the shirt and leggings of a man's suit by a shaman, and the suit was considered to be a medicine bundle. The shaman would then sell the bundle to a purchaser via a transference ritual. Of this ritual Wissler [1912a:111–112] wrote: "The entire body of the purchaser is painted yellow and a red band marked across the eyes and mouth. A smudge of sweetgrass is made and the suit passed through the smoke. The purchaser puts it on. Then he dances with the seller on three bunches of sage grass, to the northeast, the southeast, and the southwest of the fire, moving around to the south and dancing the fourth time at the starting point. This practically ends the ceremony. From four to seven [war] songs may be sung at this time."

Weather shamans

Many shamans have the ability to control rain, wind, fog, and other elements associated with the weather. Among the Lakota it is known that if the proper power song is sung, a sacred pipe can be used to "split the clouds" of an oncoming storm so that it will bypass one's area. In the Northwest Coast region weather shamans are called upon to stop the rain, while in the Southwest area they are used to bring rain. Weather shamans also used their power during warfare, for example, to bring in a fog so that people could escape from their enemies (see *war medicine*). They also used their power for hunting (see *hunting medicine*); the nineteenth-century Kutchin shamans from the Mackenzie-Yukon area, for instance, "made wind in order to hunt moose" [Krech 1981:82]. A Gidütikadü (Paviotso/Paiute) female shaman

from Surprise Valley, California, was known for her snow melting (known as *tüsaibidun* [Joshua Brown in Kelly 1932:202]). She "cried like a stallion, took a firebrand of sagebrush, and pointed it toward the south, saying, 'Come on rain; come on, rain!' She did not dance. The wind blew, the rain came, and the snow began to melt" (Piudy in Kelly 1932:201].

The following is an account of a Vunta (Crow River Kutchin) shaman who brought a whirlwind to save a drowning man:

> A man was paddling across a river to look at his fish net. When he was in the middle of the stream, he decided to change his position because his legs were cramped. In doing so, he put his hands on the side of the canoe, but he slipped, precipitating himself into the water. He managed to grab the canoe after it had rolled over several times and began to float helplessly down the river as he could not swim. The people who had observed the accident from the shore likewise could do nothing as there were no more canoes at hand. They went shouting along the shore, preventing each other from going into the water in desperation. The situation was particularly trying because the girl whom the young man was soon to marry was also a witness to the accident. So was her father and his nephew, a shaman. On realizing the hopelessness of the situation, the girl's father addressed the shaman, "Our brother-in-law-to-be is about to drown—where is your power?" Then the shaman spoke out loudly so that everyone heard him, "Where is that of which I have dreamed?" This shaman had a double medicine relationship and was very powerful. When he spoke, the people could see that trees were being disturbed by a whirlwind across the river. As it traveled over the river, the shaman shouted, "Hold on, grandson!" The whirlwind blew the young man and his canoe straight to the shore and safety, carrying him on the crest of a whirlpool so strong that it raised him half out of the water. Up and down the stream all was calm [Old Charlie (a witness) in Osgood 1936:159].

The Mikasuki Seminole shamans have a jug-like object called the "Twins' Plaything" that is used in making rain. "The object is a hard, rock-like spheroid, about one and one-half inches long, and colored red, brown, green and yellow. In war it is used . . . to ward off bullets" [Sturtevant 1954a:36]. When used for rain making, "the object is fastened to one end of a stick about four inches long which is stuck in the bottom of a stream or the swamp until the water barely touches the bottom of the 'jug,' and left there until rain comes. The user must fast for four days before placing the object in the water. Not only will it cause rain, but perhaps also whirlwinds, and it is used to change the course of an approaching hurricane" [Sturtevant 1954b:403]. The neighboring Cow Creek Seminole also have a similar ceremony in which a special pot is put into the ground, filled with water, and sung over by the shaman, who also blows his breath on the pot. "Then the rain is called through chants. One must not eat all day long till the rain comes. To make the rain stop it is merely necessary to light tobacco pipes and blow smoke against the rain for ten or twenty minutes" [Greenlee in Sturtevant 1954b:403].

In a similar fashion the Iroquois shamans use certain masks to control the weather. For example, the Wind mask is used to placate violent storms and to invoke the aid of the wind to bring gentle rains. In addition, during their New Year's Festival, "the Wind mask just at dawn [is] called upon to invoke the breezes to fructify the earth by dispersing the pollen and seed of all the useful plants" [Keppler 1941:34].

In the Southeast area among the Texas Alabama, there was a shaman "who stopped rain by fasting and putting medicine on the water of a creek. Another stopped a storm which was brought on when his companion shot a buzzard, mistaking it for a turkey. On another occasion some people were in the middle of a lake and were surrounded on all sides by enemies who had lighted fires all about on the banks so that they could not escape during the night. However, a prophet among the people on the water made it rain, thereby putting out the fires, and enabling

them to get through the lines of their enemy. Still another prophet brought on rain in the following manner. He sent a boy out to catch fish, and when they were brought he dived with them to the bottom of a creek and gave them to certain long, horned snakes living there which go under both the water and the land. . . . Then these snakes made the rain fall" [Swanton 1928:616].

Among the Shawnee "an intricate string figure, symbolically 'tying up a star,' is talked to and untied in order to secure cool weather; a buffalo tail is carried to a spring by a calm man, and shaken very gently in order to secure rain" [Voegelin 1936:17].

Swanton reported Adair's observation of a Creek rain maker

who was shot because the river overflowed the fields to a great height in the middle of August. These men had a transparent stone "of supposed great power in assisting to bring down the rain, when it is put in a basin of water," and this power was supposed to have been passed down to this one from a stone to which the power had originally been committed. As usual, this stone could not be exposed to the gaze of the vulgar [impure] without losing mightily in efficacy. The control of the rain maker extended only to the summer rains and not to those which fell in winter, and it was believed that this was also of supernatural ordination. . . .

There were others who claimed they could make the waters in swollen streams subside, and still another class of dew makers, who could also prevent the dew from falling. . . . It is said that such a man could not assist anyone, even though he desired to do so, unless he were formally invited. . . .

According to early writers some doctors claimed to be able to control the thunder and lightning [Swanton 1928:630–631].

The Thompson of the Plateau area use the following technique for ending a period of heavy rain:

The supplicant held in the fire for a short time a stick about three feet long and two inches in diameter, then described a circle with it, commencing near the east, and following the sun's course until it reached the east again, toward which quarter he held the stick, and addressed the Rain as follows: "Now then, you must quit raining, the people are miserable. Ye mountains, become clear." The stick was again placed in the fire, and then a circle was described with it in the same manner, commencing in the east, and following the sun's course around to the east again, and stopping in the south, to which quarter the stick was pointed, and the previous address repeated. The stick was again passed through the flames, and other circles were described, stopping at the west and then at the north, each quarter being addressed as before. The stick was then thrown into the fire, and the supplicant sat down or smoked [Teit 1900:345].

It is interesting to note that among the nearby Seri (on Tiburon Island in the Gulf of California), although this is not a North American culture per se, "rain making seems to be by amulet rather than by direct shamanistic power" [Kroeber 1931:14]. In this case a white powdered substance was kept in "a two inch length of cane, with a wooden stopper. . . . A little of this powder put into fresh water, brings dew; into salt water, rain" [Kroeber 1931:15]. In another instance the cane amulet was seen to contain a "blue sand" [Coolidge and Coolidge 1939:245].

A rather unique form of weather control has been recorded for a Klamath shaman from the California region. "The shaman kiu´ksmag (Shaman Man) went to Ashland [Oregon] in the autumn to trade but he could not return because of deep snow on the Cascade range: He was challenged to make it rain. He melted a strip of lead in a frying pan and had someone pour it down his gullet. They could hear it hiss. In the middle of the night it rained so hard that the snow melted away" [Spier 1930:119].

For other examples of weather shamans or weather control, see *Ansote, Atámántán, Avenarï,*

Big Cloud, Big Ike, Buffalo Doctors, chikauvasi, Chüawimkya, Crowi, Enatcûggedi, Gabe, Charlie, Horqarnaq, Jones, Rock, Kimucwuminaw, Kimvuanipinus, kiuks, Lewekwe, Megillis Hadjo, nïarï puaxantï, Ningawbiun, Nipakwe Cimuwin, Old Tom Mouse, pabuaxantï, rain-making ceremonies, Shumakwe, Siluthaup, Sinel, Tce Waci, Tciniki, Ben, umwadïmbuaxantï, uupuhagadi, Uwanami, Wâbik, Wolf Chief.

Weekwetset
Nez Perce, *Plateau*

Literal translation: "dance of the dream faith" [Spinden 1964:262]. Guardian Spirit Dance, Ghost Dance. Possibly the most religious ceremony of the Nez Perce, this dance was performed during the winter and in many places. It was not associated with the widespread Ghost Dance religion of the nineteenth century.

Both men and women participated in the ceremony. The songs that were sung had been obtained from a helping spirit, either by an ancestor or by a living person. Those who had not obtained such a song were not allowed to sing individually but could join in during the chorus. Those with helping spirits usually painted their bodies accordingly, most often as some form of animal.

The ceremony had many different purposes due to the many different powers of its members. It was sometimes performed to bring changes in the weather, while at other times it was used to make hunting more successful.

Wegeléyu
Washo, *Basin*

"The Washo call both the sources of power and the power itself *wegeléyu,* and the term also denotes the implements used by a shaman in the curing ceremony" [Freed and Freed 1963:42]. Such supernatural power comes unsolicited to a person via dreams. "'The *wegeléyu* picks the man.' Power can neither be bought, inherited, nor acquired. . . . When this happens, a person either learns to use the power and becomes a shaman or else he hires a shaman to rid him of the power, for to have power and no knowledge of its control results in illness" [Freed and Freed 1963:42].

Power usually comes from some animal, such as a rattlesnake, bear, eagle, lizard, or magpie. It can also come as blood, "water-babies," storm, and other such forms. Some powers confer special abilities. For example, the Deer *wegeléyu* gives the person the ability to control the weather. Rattlesnake and Blood *wegeléyu* are often the power of a sorcerer. "People with power from the water-baby walk into springs and can stay under water for long periods" [Freed and Freed 1963:43].

Welukúshkush
Washo, *Basin*
A nineteenth-century shaman who had a water-baby for his helping spirit. He also had a young boy who traveled with him as an assistant. "One day the boy had a fit and became unconscious on the shore of Lake Tahoe. His parents sent for Welukúshkush who they blamed for the boy's condition; they wanted to kill Welukúshkush. Welukúshkush said that the boy's soul had been taken by the water-baby and that he could bring back the boy. Welukúshkush had the water-baby for his *wegeléyu* [see entry]. Welukúshkush began to shake his rattle and pray. He walked into the water and stayed underneath for 10 minutes. . . . He walked around the boy four times and had the boy's mother call his name four times. The boy began to revive; his nose bled and blood covered his chest. Welukúshkush faced the boy toward the lake and gave him his rattle to shake. Then Welukúshkush walked the boy around in a circle four times. The boy acted as if he had been asleep. After this experience, the boy became a shaman" [Hank Pete in Freed and Freed 1963:44].

Weni
Maidu, *California*
The Nisenan (Southern Maidu) term for medicines used by shamans [Beals 1933:385]. *Weni,* when properly administered, effects a cure. "If a man could discover the secret of a shaman's medicine for any particular disease, i.e., the herbs he used and the way of compounding them, he could then cure that disease himself. The learning of these medicines was the most important part of a shaman's training and it was only in this rigorous course of training and the learning of 'medicines' which had a supernatural effect that the ordinary shaman differed from the person who might have a knowledge of herbs for curing ordinary ailments" [Beals 1933:385].

To designate specific medicines, a noun is added to the term *weni*. For example, *weni otatai,* which means "medicine steaming," is the term used by the Nisenan for their sweat lodge, where healing often takes places. In some cases the medicine is mixed with water and poured over the hot rocks, and the patient inhales the steam containing the medicine through his mouth. Afterward the patient is washed in cold water, wrapped in a rabbitskin blanket, and given more medicine to drink from a bowl [Beals 1933:387]. This treatment was for chills or fever. In curing sprained muscles the person's afflicted area would be covered with hot mud, and then he would remain throughout the night in the sweat lodge [Beals 1933:389].

Wepelét
Nez Perce, *Plateau*
The disease object a shaman removes from the patient; in most cases it is something "shot" by a witch.

Infrequently this object is also called a *taáxtoyx.* "Terms equivalent to *ta?áxtoyx* are present among related Sahaptian-speaking groups, where they seem to appear more frequently than among the Nez Perce" [D. Walker 1967:83].

Wéyeknin
Nez Perce, *Plateau*
Shaman. "Power is defined by the Nez Perces essentially as supernaturally sanctioned ability. It is called *wéyekin,* a term referring either to the tutelary spirit or to the ability derived from such a spirit through either the vision quest or inheritance" [D. Walker 1967:67]. A person having *wéyekin* is referred to as *wéyeknin.*

Another Nez Perce term for shaman is *tiwét* (EONAH, p. 282).

White Bear
Arikara, *Plains*

A shaman around the turn of the nineteenth century who had the spirit of Bear and was a prominent member of the Bear society. His father, Strike Enemy, was also a member of the Bear society and had often taken White Bear to the society's ceremonies when he was a child. In his youth White Bear had a vision of Bear while in the medicine men's lodge and experienced many powerful things there. "I used to stay in the medicine-men's lodge and inside of the Bear's lodge. I learned many things about the mysteries of the Bear Society. My father gave me a bear skin that was stuffed, so that it was like a bear. When we had a Bear dance my little bear used to be placed on the south side of the lodge and I would be placed opposite. When the singing for dancing was begun I danced, and as I danced I would notice my little bear doing the same thing that I was doing. If I moved my head sidewise, it would do the same thing. If I raised up my arms towards the sky, the little bear would do the same. People saw it. I kept the bear a long time" [White Bear in Dorsey 1904:175].

White Buffalo Calf Woman
Teton, *Plains*

See *Wohpe*.

White Crane Dance
Assiniboin, *Plains*

This was a special ceremony conducted by a shaman for all young men who wanted to acquire war medicine. The dance was not part of any regular Assiniboin society and therefore was rarely conducted. Although only men danced, women would join in singing the sacred ceremonial songs [Rodnick 1938:40].

During the ceremony, warriors acquired personal war medicines prior to embarking on a war party, and offerings and prayers would be given to the war spirits. "The spirits of war were the wolves and to these the war party leaders sacrificed scarlet cloth and tobacco. If the war parties were to be successful, the wolves would howl at the giving of sacrifices to them, if unsuccessful, the wolves would be quiet" [Rodnick 1938:42].

White Man
Blackfoot, *Plains*

A shaman who was still alive at the turn of the twentieth century and was remembered for his ownership of a Horse medicine (see entry). The following account describes how he used the Horse medicine power to cripple a buffalo:

> White-man and another man were running buffalo and as their horses were too slow to overtake the buffalo they were unable to get within shooting range of them. White-man thought of the horse medicine which he had the power to use. He told the man with him to ride off to one side of him as he was going to use the medicine. First he sang the horse song; then he put some prairie turnip in his mouth and spat on his whip. Following the tracks of the buffalo he crossed them three or four times and whipped them. As the herd of buffalo went out of sight into a coulée they followed them. When they came in sight of them at the foot of the coulée they saw a buffalo cow with a broken back trying to move away while dragging her hind part. They killed the cow and had some meat to take home. This was the result of the use of the horse medicine" [Red Plume in Wissler 1912a:111].

Widaldal
Tsimshian, *Northwest Coast*

A nineteenth-century Gitsamgelon shaman who lived along the Nass River. Jay Miller [1984:140] provided a brief account of one of Widaldal's divinations to determine the fish run for that year:

> The gifts [of payment] were brought and placed before the shaman, who filled two vessels with water drawn from the Nass River. One bowl he placed at the entrance and the other at the back of

the house, then he took a dried eulachon and cut it in two so there was a piece in each vessel, and finally he said to those watching, "When I start to dance around the house watch these vessels. As soon as any fish come to life call out." He danced three times around the house and called out, "If the fish do not come to life, then there will be no eulachon and the people will starve." Before he was half way around for the fourth time, one of the watchers called out, "The fish has come to life." The shaman then said to the Gilutsau people [who had hired the shaman], "Get your eulachon nets and set them tomorrow, as there will be many eulachon," and there were!

Wihtikokancimuwin

Cree, Canadian Eastern Woodlands
Literal translation: "*wihtiko*-like-dance" [Mandelbaum 1940:274]. A sacred dance often performed during the Plains Cree Sun Dance period. *Wihtiko* (also *witiko* [see entry], *wetigo*, *wiihtikow*) literally means "heart of ice" and is most often rendered as a cannibalistic spirit that lives in the forested areas. However, "the *wiihtikow* was not simply a cannibal . . . but a more general condition or quality, 'a capacity for doing damaging or anti-human behavior'" [Long 1989:4–5].

The dancers wore masks cut from tipi material, dressed oddly in bits of mismatched old clothes, and enacted the sacred clown or contrary roll. In so doing, the dancers made light of all that is serious, and the people would harry the dancers. The obvious role of this ceremony was to relieve social tension.

See also *Windigokan*.

Wikipinûkûn

Menomini, Midwest
Literal translation: "tied up in it" [Skinner 1915d:189]. This is a love medicine made from "blood drawn from the vulva of an amorous woman. This is added to a certain variety of root, pulverized, and is given in food. It steals a man's mind away so that he will follow the woman who drugs him as a dog follows its master. This medicine is used only by a woman. It may not be kept with other medicines and must be used at once after making" [Skinner 1915d:189].

Wikwajigewinini

Ojibwa, Canadian Eastern Woodlands
Chippewa sucking shaman [Ritzenthaler 1953b:198]. In removing a disease object from a patient, this shaman uses a hollow bone tube about 3 inches in length and about ¾ of an inch in diameter. During a typical healing ceremony "the spirit enters the body of the doctor. One of the tubes is 'swallowed' and regurgitated by the doctor who kneels over the patient, locates the origin of the sickness, sucks it out through the tube, and spits it into the shallow dish along with the tube" [Ritzenthaler 1953b:206].

A healing ceremony observed in 1941 was presided over by "a man over ninety, also a mide´ priest, and the most feared and respected man on the reservation" [Ritzenthaler 1953b:207]. On the first night

two bone tubes had been put in a pie tin partially filled with salt water and covered with a handkerchief. The doctor swallowed one of the tubes after bending over the patient who was lying on a blanket on his back. He sucked several times near the navel and once on the groin, sometimes regurgitating the tube and sometimes not. Spat out the saliva after each sucking as a rule, and finally spat out tube, the drumming stopped, and the first attempt was over. After a song and another series of sucking he spat out a small piece of white stuff which we all examined with a flashlight. The doctor said he thought he could get the rest of it out the next evening. The assistant carried the pan outside and threw it into the brush. . . . The same people were present the second evening, and the doctor spoke saying he was going to use a stronger spirit tonight. The patient laid on his back on the blanket with his torso bare. After another long speech and song the treatment began. He swallowed the bone, gagged until we became worried, but finally coughed it up. He sucked on the same part of the body as before, with the bone well into his mouth and his lips touching the body of the patient. On the second attempt he had one of the women insert the bone in his mouth, and had another lady shake his rattle. After several suckings he asked his assistant to get a larger bone tube hidden under the bed. He unwrapped it, swallowed it and on the first sucking attempt got three or four pieces of white stuff which were spat into the pan. He sucked several times more and stopped. We inspected the contents of the pan which were again thrown outside by the assistant. The doctor said he got it all out [Ritzenthaler 1953b:208].

Slight variations on this theme do occur. For example, often the removed disease-object is thrown instead into a fire. In one instance a shaman used empty, 2-inch, .45-caliber shells (from which the ends had been removed) instead of bones for sucking on the patient.

Wílanta
Pima, *Southwest*
This is a recent ritual derived from Christianity. The term comes from the Spanish *vela,* or "household prayer vigil" [Bahr 1977:39]. When used for a healing, prayers are addressed before the house altar by several old women. The songs sung during this ritual are Spanish hymns. However, unlike other Pima curing ceremonies, there is no sucking on the patient's body in this ritual. "At the end of the rite, the patient comes to the altar and inhales from the same holy object that the singers had addressed their songs to" [Bahr 1977:40].

Wilohego
Yurok, *Oregon Seaboard*
Literal translation: "that-one-dam-he-makes" [Waterman and Kroeber 1938:52]. The title of the shaman who heads the Yuroks' annual, ritual construction of a fish weir across the Klamath River. He is also called *wokowis-hego* ("stake-maker"), but most often he is referred to simply as *"Lo"* (see entry).

The construction ceremony is "one of the greater rituals of native northwest California;

perhaps the greatest. At any rate it [is] the most elaborate, possessed [of] many peculiar local features" [Waterman and Kroeber 1938:49]. It takes ten days to build the dam, which is done in a ritually prescribed manner. The ceremony begins with all of the participants going into the sweat lodge. Thereafter the *Wilohego* directs the gathering and carving of the stakes and their ultimate placement. From the second through the sixth day, the "lo and his assistant remain in the sweat house. They never come out or walk about" [Waterman and Kroeber 1938:55]. Also, once the stakes are carved "they had been 'talked to' and were 'medicine'" [Waterman and Kroeber 1938:57]. Once completed, the weir is then left in use for the next ten days and thereafter immediately dismantled.

Wimesin Shkibijigen
Ojibwa, *Canadian Eastern Woodlands*
Literal translation: "we are going to make an image" [Ritzenthaler 1953b:213]. A Chippewa ceremony in which a straw-man fetish is made and then destroyed as a means of warding off impending sickness. When the ceremony begins,

[the] Dreamer then tells the people his dream and why they are going to do this. The food is laid out on the floor, tobacco is passed around and smoked, and the Dreamer gets up and dedicates the food and tobacco to the ma´nidog (spirits) and asks their help in doing this thing. The people then eat, it being believed that the food and tobacco are really offerings which go to the ma´nidog. After the f[e]ast the men take their guns and the women and children their clubs, knives, and axes, go outside and cautiously approach the straw man which has been set a short distance away from the house by the runner. The figure is made of straw or hay (to be inflammable) varying in height from about two to four feet, and dressed in a miniature man's costume. It is either made by the runner the night before, or by the women just before the ceremony begins. . . .

As the people approach the straw man, the Dreamer gives the signal to the men to shoot it with their shotguns, he joining them. The women and children then rush up to club it, cut it, and chop it to bits. The remains are gathered up by the people or runner, placed in a pile, and burned. They may return to the house where the Dreamer thanks them for their assistance [Ritzenthaler in Ritzenthaler 1953b:213].

Wimi

Hopi, *Southwest*

Plural: *wiwimi* [Stephen 1936:1318]. In the singular form this is the general term for ceremony. In the plural form it also denotes all of the altar objects used in a ceremony.

Wincasta wakon

Assiniboin, *Plains*

Also: *wintca'cta wakan* (EONAH, p. 316). Literal translation: "holy man" [Rodnick 1938:53]. Term used by the Fort Belknap division for shaman. The *wincasta wakon* is a person who has received his spirit helper(s) via a vision, while the *pejuda wincasta* (or *peju'da wintca'cta* [Lowie 1909:42]) is the herb doctor. Each *wincasta wakon* specializes in one or more areas, such as curing, leading war raids, weather control, etc. That is, "it depended solely on the nature of the communication [with the spirits] whether they became founders of dancing-societies, wakan practitioners, owners of painted lodges, fabricators of war shirts, or prophets. In every case, implicit obedience to the directions received was obligatory" [Lowie 1909:47]. In addition, "women received dreams, without fasting, in which they received powers to cure the sicknesses occurring only in women and to act as midwives" [Rodnick 1938:54].

The *wincasta wakon* is called in to treat the more serious cases of illness. The first step is to diagnose the patient. "By means of his spiritual advisers he is to decide as to the adequacy of ordinary doctoring or the necessity for wakan practices" [Lowie 1909:43].

According to Rodnick [1938:53], by 1918 there were no more *wincasta wakon* among the Fort Belknap Assiniboin.

Windigokan

Ojibwa, *Canadian Eastern Woodlands*

Dialectical variant: *wetigokanûk* (Plains Cree) [Skinner 1914:528]. Bungi (Plains Ojibwa) Cannibal Dancers society. This was a society of men who had dreamed of a skeleton spirit known as *pägûk* [Skinner 1914:500] (also known as *paxkax* among the Menomini [Skinner 1914:533, n. 2] and *pahgat* among the Plains Cree). During their dances the members wore "a costume of rags with a hideous mask, having an enormous crooked beaklike nose, the whole being daubed with paint. . . . The functions of the cannibal dancers were of two sorts, for the healing of the sick and exorcising the demons of disease, much as was done by the false face [EONAH, pp. 79–82] dancers of the Iroquois. When a sick person's case had been diagnosed by the doctor or seer as one of infection by disease demons, word was sent to the leader of the windigokan who brought his troop into the patient's lodge where they danced before the invalid, pounding their rattles on the ground, singing, whistling, and dancing. They approached, looked at the sufferer, started back, ran away, and reapproached with all manner of grotesque and fantastic actions, until the demons of ill health had been frightened away" [Skinner 1914:500–501].

The members of this society use inverted speech (saying the opposite of what they mean), similar to that of the Sioux *heyóka* (EONAH, pp. 104–105), and as a result are also referred to as "clowns." In fact, "the heyoka society of the Eastern Dakota also bears many points of resemblance to the cannibal society of the Bûngi" [Skinner 1914:505].

Among the Plains Cree, shamans who dreamed of *pahgat* are "adept at all weather practise" [Jefferson in Skinner 1914:533].

See also *Wihtikokancimuwin.*

Wintgopax Wacipi

Assiniboin, *Plains*

An annual hunting ceremonial dance that became extinct around the turn of the twentieth century. Translates as "Fool's Dance" [Rodnick 1938:41]. Although primarily conducted to recount successes in hunting and warfare, it was also a healing ceremony designed "to cure all diseases of the eyes after the dance was over" [Rodnick 1938:41].

Wioha
Assiniboin, *Plains*
Painted lodge. The *wioha* is used by shamans who have had a vision in which a spirit gives them power to heal. For their *wioha* they use a tipi that is painted in a manner prescribed by the spirit. The following account begins with the instructions received from the spirit, called "the old man":

"Near the fireplace plant one end of a tree-trunk not stripped of its foliage, and stick the other end into the flap-holes; get three or four dressed buffalo skins, and construct a little booth. Allow yourself to be tied hand and foot with buckskin thongs, then have tanned robes wrapped about you and tied from the outside. Have a rock put near the fireplace. It should be painted red and ought to rest on a clean piece of calico. Have a little dog suckling cooked and set near the fireplace. Two or three drummers are to sit on the right-hand side of the entrance; no one else must be admitted. Suspend a bell from the trunk."

Next the old man taught me a song. He told me that one drum should lie by the painted rock. The two drummers were to begin singing, then I was to join in the chant. When they began singing the second time, another man was to ladle out the pup-meat into a pan and deposit it on the right side of the rock. In the interval between the third and fourth songs a spirit would call, ring the bell, and speak plainly, so that all the people could understand. A noise would be heard in the skies. The visitant was not to be seen, but only to be heard. He would ask what was the matter. "Then you must ask him for aid. He will first eat the pup. Then he will tell you whether the patient can be cured, and, if so, how soon. If a cure is impossible, he will say so. He will disappear, but first he will free you in the twinkle of an eye, and

hang all your bonds on the tops of the tipi-poles. This is the way to doctor in a painted lodge" [unidentified informant in Lowie 1909:49].

Wiskwe hpita kan
Cree, *Canadian Eastern Woodlands*
The generic name for the medicine bundles of the Plains Cree. Literal translation: "kept in a clean place" [Mandelbaum 1940:258]. These bundles were used to house an individual's personal medicine, and each bundle was given a specific name. The power objects therein were usually obtained from a shaman or gathered together after the person had dreamed of them. In addition, the bundles often contained sweet grass, tobacco, and small charms.

The power objects were most often associated with war medicines and rarely with hunting medicines, which the people seemed to use infrequently. The objects were also taken out for certain ceremonies. The bundles were, however, never used for healing ceremonies.

If the contents of a bundle proved efficacious for its user, the bundle's value would rise. Since bundles could be transferred to other individuals, valuable bundles were often sought after. In the transfer the new owner would be taught all the medicine songs that went with the bundle and how to properly use its contents. Each bundle had its own songs and its own procedures for use. Usually the transfer involved smoking the sacred pipe and the giving of gifts to the former owner by the new owner.

Witaltal
Tsimshian, *Northwest Coast*
An eighteenth-century Kitselas shaman renowned for his contests with other shamans.

Especially was he always competing with Nisatneats of the Ginaxangik. He would sit and meditate in his home at Kitselas during the winter saying, "Oh! I wish my brother Nisatneats would think of me and send me some cockles." Now these two people were very far apart [circa 80 miles]. . . . Not long afterwards, Nisatneats also sitting by his fire in his Metlakatla house, felt that someone was whispering into his ear. At once he recognized the voice of Witaltal at Kitselas asking for cockles. This was how these two great shamans made their thoughts known to each other. One day Witaltal said to attendants, "Make ready, as my brother on the saltwater is sending me some cockles." He had no sooner spoken, when down through the smoke hole of his home came down a huge quantity of cockles. There were at once gathered up and fed to all the people who marvelled at this.

Another time Nisatneats was sitting by his fire at Metlakatla and the snow was on the ground. He spoke more to himself saying, "I wish my brother would send me some fresh tamit." At the same time Witaltal, sitting by his fire, felt that someone was communicating with him and he recognized the wish of his brother on the sea coast. He said to his aides, "Gather some fresh tamit, I want to send it to my brother at Ginaxangik." Nisatneats was sitting by the fire, when he suddenly said, "Get ready, my brother at Kitselas is sending me some tamit." He had scarcely spoken when a great box of tamit came down through the smoke hole. These he fed to the people in his house. They marvelled at what these great shamans had done [Harriet Hudson in Cove and MacDonald 1987:135].

A Quinault shaman's carved guardian spirit/fetish.

Witchcraft

Although some anthropologists choose to differentiate between witchcraft and sorcery (e.g., Middleton and Winter 1963:3–4; Saler 1964: 320–321), the twentieth-century anthropological literature on Native North America has, for the most part, used the terms interchangeably. Therefore, within the context of this work, that practice is maintained, especially since much of the material herein consists of quotes.

To understand witchcraft as it operates in Native North America, one must first understand that in most cultures, its use is ordained, especially against outside enemies. This was especially true in the nineteenth century with regard to war medicines (see entry). There are many accounts of shamans confusing or harming the

A Haida shaman's charm (soul catcher) used by a Queen Charlotte Island shaman to capture the soul of an ailing patient.

enemy in battle. This means that witchcraft was seen more in terms of doing something that was unnatural rather than evil. That is, the relationship between humans and the Creator was one in which supernatural power was bestowed by the Creator (via helping spirits) upon specially endowed humans for their welfare. To use this power to bring harm to others was contrary to the nature of things.

Therefore, witchcraft is best considered as something that is innately disruptive to the order of things. That is, it is "unholy" but not necessarily "evil." In this context any person who uses an evil spell against someone they wish to harm is not necessarily labeled a "witch." Witches are persons who do such things consistently, and this title draws the boundary line, pushing the practice into the antisocial realm.

For this reason Native American witches are extremely secretive about their affairs. In former times witches were often put to death, most often by the relatives of their victims. This procedure was socially sanctioned, so no one was punished for killing an exposed witch.

Accusations of witchcraft are most often associated with illness because illness is frequently diagnosed as being caused by witchcraft. That is, witchcraft manifests most often in the form of the victim becoming ill in some manner. Shamans who are unsuccessful in healing a patient are also often accused of witchcraft. In fact, most people fear the more powerful shamans because of their ever-present potential to turn to witchcraft.

The body of evidence seems to indicate that powers used by shamans are no less dangerous than powers used by witches—another important aspect in understanding witchcraft. The fundamental difference is that the evil medicine sent out by a witch can be turned back on him or her by a powerful shaman, causing the witch to come to harm or be killed. At the same time, shamans who fail to cure their patients never have power turned back on them. Usually they are simply seen as not being powerful enough to control their helping spirits; in some cases the explanation is that the helping spirits lack the power to cure the illness at hand.

Within this context witchcraft in Native North America appears more as an extension of shamanism into antisocial activities.

As is to be expected, witchcraft comes in many different ritual forms. Most often the witch pro-

jects, by magical means, some poisonous substance or object into the victim's body. It is the task of the shaman to find and remove this poison in order to effect a cure. Here again, many different techniques are used to attain such ends. In other cases the witch may use magical means to steal a victim's soul or spirit. The shaman must locate the wandering soul and return it to the patient. Together, these two forms of witchcraft constitute one of the most frequently diagnosed causes for human illness to be found in Native America. This diagnosis appears most frequently among the cultures of the Southwest area, but in no region of North America is it absent. Where there are shamans, there are also bound to be witches.

One of the more characteristic capabilities of witches is their ability to transform into other shapes (see *transmutation*). This is an oft-repeated theme in the literature on witchcraft among Native Americans. For instance, among the Mikasuki Seminole a witch most often took "the form of a horned-owl. . . . Some may perhaps have become other animals such as bears or bison. A witch of this type is not satisfied by the meat which ordinary people eat, but requires human blood" [Sturtevant 1954b:397].

Also see *haldaugit, idiagewam, ilisineq, kinubik-inäniwûk, kitdoñxoi, metudhauk, Pónlhikî, qoogauk, Tosanawïn, transmutation.*

Withaiyowe

Oto, *Plains*
Sacred pipe [Whitman 1937:121]. See *Peace Pipe Dance.*

Witiko

Cree, *Canadian Eastern Woodlands*
Also: *wihtiko, wetigo, wiihtikow.* Dialectical variant: *windigo* (Ojibwa). A giant spirit "who has a heart of ice or who vomits ice" [Cooper 1933:20]. Possession by this spirit produces the illness known as *witiko* psychosis, a form of hysteria in which the patient has unnatural cravings for human flesh. "The craving for human flesh appears pretty clearly to be derived *directly* from

prevalent environmental and cultural conditions. The transformation into an ice-hearted Witiko seems to be derived indirectly, through the Witiko folk-lore concept, from the same conditions" [Cooper 1933:24].

See also *Wihtikokancimuwin, Windigokan.*

Wochangi
Teton, *Plains*

Power received by a Lakota shaman from a spirit; spiritual power [Brown 1964:17]. Famed shaman Nicholas Black Elk explained *wochangi* as follows: "We regard all created beings as sacred and important, for everything has a *wochangi* or influence which can be given to us, through which we may gain a little more understanding if we are attentive" [Black Elk in Brown 1953:59].

In his use of *wochangi*, Black Elk included any instructions given to him by a spirit. For istance, he noted: "Crying [vision questing], I returned to the center [of the sacred place], and then when I went towards the place which we always face, I saw a red-breasted woodpecker standing on the offering pole. I believe he may have given to me something of his *wochangi*, for I heard him say to me very faintly yet distinctly: 'Be attentive! *(wachin ksapa yo!)* and have no fear; but pay no attention to any bad thing that may come and talk to you!'" [Black Elk in Brown 1953:62].

Wodi
Cherokee, *Southeast*

Literal translation: "reddish brown." Red ocher or hematite. *Wodi* is not only used to paint warriors, it is also used by shamans for divinations and in the making of love medicine. For love medicines the shaman takes a small fragment, about the size of a small grape, and ties it "to some string or thread, usually of white color, and 25 to 30 cm. long. The free end of this string is held between the thumb and the index finger of the right hand, while the left hand with the fingers extended is held—apparently in quite an innocent way—in front of the right one" [Olbrechts 1930:547].

For divination purposes the same string is held by the shaman when looking for lost items, and "the stone, dangling from the end of the string starts a pendulum-like motion, almost imperceptible in the beginning, but gradually gaining momentum. The direction in which the soothsaying stone sways most violently—other informants say: the direction in which is *starts* swinging—indicates the direction in which the search has to be started" [Olbrechts 1930:547–548]. The search is then started in the given direction, and the shaman proceeds along the designated course, stopping intermittently to repeat this procedure to finely tune his course of direction until the lost item is found.

When using the *wodi* string to find a lost person, the procedure is as follows: "A handkerchief or a piece of calico is folded so as to cover a space of about 10 cm. by 10 cm. It is put on the ground, in front of the diviner, and at the far end, away from him, a small lump of bread is placed on the cloth; on his near side, a piece of charcoal, taken from the fire. The piece of ocher, fastened to a thread as already explained, is put down exactly between the two, and after a formula has been recited, the hematite is suddenly lifted by the free end: the direction it first swings in when raised, indicates the fate of the subject of the ceremony; the bread symbolizes his being alive, the charcoal his (mostly tragical) death" [Olbrechts 1930:548].

A similar Cherokee procedure involves placing two forked sticks into the ground, with a crossbar set between the forks. Then "an 'arrow rock' (flint) is suspended from a cross-bar. The suspended flint will point the direction of the searched object, after proper ceremony and fasting. The device is carried by the searching party and set up every so often to check directions" [Dasi in Folgeson 1980:76].

Cherokee shamans also use the following procedure to locate lost objects or animals: "Two or four stalks of grass . . . about 7 to 8 cm. long, or the same number of tiny twigs of the same dimensions, are stuck upright between the thumb and index finger of the extended hand; immediately after the recitation of the formula [spell] they are seen to quiver and to reel; the direction in which they droop, again indicates the whereabouts of the lost article" [Olbrechts 1930:548].

Wohpe
Teton, *Plains*

The Lakota term for the White Buffalo Calf Maiden. Wohpe first brought the Sacred Calf Pipe bundle (EONAH, pp. 237–238) to the Sioux [J. Walker 1980:109]. She gave the bundle to Standing Buffalo (or Buffalo Stands Upright), who was then the chief of the Red Water subdivision of the Sans Arc band of the Teton Dakota [J. Smith 1967:2]. Smith [1967:6], comparing different Dakota *waniyetu wowapi* ("winter counts"), estimated that this exchange occurred between 1785 and 1800, although some winter counts indicated an earlier date, such as High Hawk's with a date of 1540. From this initial sacred pipe (EONAH, pp. 238–240), all other subsequent sacred pipes have been generated. As such, this particular bundle is the most sacred object known to the Sioux. The present keeper of this original pipe, made from the leg bone of a buffalo calf and kept in the original bundle, is Arval Looking Horse.

Woina
Paiute, *Basin*

Owens Valley Paiute flute. Wooden flutes, most often carved from elderberry and about 8 to 9 inches in length, are often used by a shaman (*puhaga*—see EONAH, p. 224) in his healing ceremonies. For example, circa 1927 to 1928, anthropologist Julian Steward noted: "B. T. is a very famous doctor and much-liked man. His grandfather was a doctor. His power is Mount Dana in the Sierra Nevada mountains. To cure he sucks the ailing place and plays an elderberry flute. One song says, in effect: 'This is my flute which sings in the split rock.' He doctored a man shot by three bullets, two of which a white surgeon had extracted. He sang, waved his flute over

him, and sucked out the third bullet" [Steward 1933:316].

Wolf Chief
Hidatsa, *Plains*

A shaman around the turn of the twentieth century. He had acquired most of his medicines from his father, Small Ankle (see entry), who died in 1888. Small Ankle had received them from a shaman named Missouri River. Some of Wolf Chief's medicines included, among other things, a medicine pipe, two human skulls, a buffalo skull, and a turtle shell.

The medicine pipe was 19 inches in length and made of hickory. One power the pipe contained was a war medicine. When an enemy approached, the pipe was taken out and rolled on the ground toward the enemy while a specific medicine song was sung. This procedure would cause the enemy to be overcome and flee.

The two human skulls contained various medicines. During a drought the skulls would be placed on a bed of pennyroyal, and water would be sprinkled on them and songs would be sung in order to bring rain. Pennyroyal was also placed in water before the skulls and then rubbed on an ailing person to heal him. When the Hidatsa could not find buffalo, the medicine pipe was filled and rubbed with buffalo fat. It was then placed before the skulls, and a sacred song was sung to bring the buffalo. Wolf Chief, around the age of seventeen, had seen his father perform this latter ceremony:

When the men [making the request] had gone away, my father took down the two skulls and placed them on a cloth; he then took out the medicine-pipe, anointed it with buffalo-fat, laid it on top of the skulls, and sang a mystery song. When he sang he covered himself with the buffalo-robe that had covered the skulls. Thus he did all night. In the morning he sent me out to call the chiefs and head-men together. They all came, and he said to them, "Yesterday you came and gave many things to my gods [spirits]; so I prayed, and my gods answered me. I had a vision that in four days many buffalo would come. So I now tell you."

After two days some men shouted from the house-top, "Buffalo come from the hills! The buffalo come toward the village!" This was the Fort Berthold village, and the buffalo were in the hills about five miles away [Wolf Chief in Pepper and Wilson 1908:295].

On another occasion Wolf Chief also saw his father use the skulls to bring rain:

That summer our gardens grew until the corn was about three feet tall, but there was no rain. So the people collected things, piled them up before the medicines, and asked my father to pray for rain. . . .

He prayed and sent me for aromatic weed (pennyroyal), and I went to a wet place in the timber to get it. He put this on the ground and on it laid the skulls. About noon, while the people sat there, I went out and made a fire outside and cooked dinner. But my father sat with the buffalo-robe—hairy-side out—over him, and sang and prayed for rain.

At dinner all ate. Then some old men went out and came back saying, "Black clouds gather. We see them."

My father got up, took water and threw it over the skulls, and walked around them.

In the afternoon clouds came over the village. At night rain fell. The clouds hung overhead until midnight. Then fell a gentle shower, then harder and harder the rain came until the afternoon of the next day [Wolf Chief in Pepper and Wilson 1908:296].

Wolf-Medicine Dance
Hidatsa, *Plains*

An annual initiation ceremony held each summer to impart Wolf medicine, which was used for power against enemies during warfare. It consisted of a wolfskin painted with white clay, a coyote skin, a scalp, and a small pipe with a black bowl. "When one who owned these medicines went on a war expedition he would lay the skins and scalp down and pray to them. Often he took the two skins and the scalp along with him on the war-trail, and when the party came to camp they untied the [Wolf-medicine] bundle, took the medicines out, and prayed for help to kill many enemies and capture many horses. The leader, in going to battle, often wore the white wolf-skin thrown over one shoulder and brought head and tail together under the opposite arm, or else a slit was cut in the wolf-skin in the neck and the man's head thrust through, the tail hanging down the man's back" [Pepper and Wilson 1908:322–323]. The war leader would also carry the small black-bowl pipe and smoke it just before attacking the enemy. If a warrior's Wolf medicine failed him he would return it to the leaders of the Wolf-Medicine Dance for renewal.

Worero
Yurok, *Oregon Seaboard*
See Brush Dance.

Wososo
Maidu, *California*
Cocoon rattle [Gifford 1927:241]. See *sokot*.

Wotawe
Assiniboin, *Plains*
Dialectical variant: *wotawi* (Oglala Sioux), "war medicines" [Wissler 1912b:90]. War charms or medicines. Warriors obtained, through payment, special medicine charms from shamans. Once a charm was made, the owner was not to give it away or sell it lest he suffer for doing so. "Each Assiniboine carried different war charms with him. Thus, one of Lowie's informants used the dried and fleshed skin of a blue bird, with jackrabbit ears sewn to its neck, the whole attached to a piece of rawhide painted red on the opposite side. During a fight the head of the bird was fastened with string, or cord, to a lock of the owner's hair. Another individual noticed by Lowie had for his Wo'tawE a large knife with a handle made of a bear's jawbone, to which was tied little bells and a feather" [Rodnick 1938:44].

See also *war medicine*.

Wotijaxa
Assiniboin, *Plains*

Home-Building Dance [Rodnick 1938:48]. This is the Assiniboin form of the widespread Sun Dance ceremony. Several accounts of this ceremony through time indicate that their Sun Dance was preceded and followed by various other dances, which were often confused by the early observers to form part of the Sun Dance complex. Like many other Sun Dances, the Home-Building Dance was performed in late June (on the first full moon after the sun had reached its most southerly course) by individuals who had sought, during the previous year, supernatural aid by vowing to perform the Sun Dance. Generally, the first person since the last Sun Dance to declare his vow was also the leader of the Sun Dance.

Prior to conducting the dance, the gathered bands would undergo four nights of purification, with the last night's activities lasting until dawn. These ceremonies were conducted in a tent, which was occupied by the dancers, singers, and drummers for the four-day period.

Following the period of purification, the Sun Dance was conducted in a conical-shaped lodge built especially for this purpose. The south side of the lodge was left open, and it was from here that spectators were allowed to watch. The top part of the lodge was left open for the sun.

In former times the dancers danced for three days and two nights without food, drink, or sleep. Each dancer decorated himself to represent his personal helping spirit and wore only a breechclout. Body painting was changed morning, afternoon, and evening. During the second day of the dance, those who had vowed to torture themselves were pierced above the nipple with skewers, and a rope was tied from these skewers to the cottonwood tree that had been erected in the middle of the lodge. Once the dancer's helping spirit appeared to him, he would then attempt to break free from his bindings.

Wyagaw
Ojibwa, *Canadian Eastern Woodlands*

A chief of one of the Ojibwa bands on Lake Superior during the mid-nineteenth century and a shaman well known for his powers, which came from Thunder. He had the power to control the weather as well as cause himself and others to assume various animal forms.

Once while accompanying a war raid against the Fox, Wyagaw's party was surrounded on an island by the enemy. "But when Wyagaw saw that they were hemmed in, he called a thick fog and turned himself and his men into saw-billed ducks. In that form they made a dash to get through the enemy in the fog; and when the ducks could not take them fast enough under pursuit, he turned himself and his men into muskalonge. In that form they all reached the mainland; but Wyagaw and one of his men who was lame, were captured, while the rest escaped" [Charles Kawbawgam in Bourgeois 1994:126].

Wyagaw was then taken back to the enemy's camp, where he refused to reveal his medicine power songs to the Fox (who were aware of his shamanic abilities). The Fox then decided to burn Wyagaw on a scaffold, as was their custom in treating prisoners of war.

Before putting Wyagaw on the scaffold, they offered him the [Wyagaw's] medicine rattle once more. Suddenly he made up his mind to take it . . . and he began to sing his [medicine] song. When he had thus got his power into his hands, he climbed the scaffold. All at once the sky turned black; it was so dark the people looking on could hardly see each other. The scaffold broke down with a crash. Rain fell in torrents, the lightning flashed, and it thundered terribly. The Fox were filled with dread and begged Wyagaw to calm the storm. After a while it began to clear and slowly became fine again.

The Fox decided to send Wyagaw homeward with an escort of ten or twelve men. . . . After that the Fox troubled him no more [Charles Kawbawgam in Bourgeois 1994:127].

Xa zhe

Tewa, *Southwest*

A generic term used by the residents of the Santa Clara Pueblo for all members of their Summer moiety. The Summer moiety assumes jurisdiction over all religious ceremonies in the pueblo from late February or early March until late October or early November. The moiety is divided into three hierarchical groups, with the *Xa zhe* being the lowest ranking. Next in rank is the *Oxu wa,* the summer *kachina* (see *lhatsina*) organization, and the highest ranking group is the *Payojke,* the Summer Managing society [Hill 1982:208].

The members of the *Oxu wa* are under the direct supervision of two selected members of the *Payojke,* known as the *sen su,* "fathers of the kachina" [Hill 1982:210]. In former times "all males of the pueblo inevitably became members of the Summer or Winter kachina organizations. . . . Undergoing the moiety 'water immersion' (po ku) was prerequisite to becoming associated with a kachina organization. . . . Novices were placed in limited seclusion. Food tabus and continence were enforced. . . . During the [initiation] ceremony boys were whipped, purified, and supernatural power, 'wisdom,' was bestowed upon them" [Hill 1982:209]. Women were not initiated into the *kachina* cult, while males usually entered between the ages of twelve and fifteen.

The *Payojke* is essentially an esoteric religious society headed by a person known as the *cacique.* The head of the managing society of the Winter moiety is also known by this name. The *cacique* is the highest office in the pueblo, and the position is held for life. The pueblo always has two *caciques.* The screening of potential candidates for this office usually begins many years before a vacancy exists. Because deliberations over who should fill this office are often quite lengthy, a temporary replacement, known as the *interino,* is appointed. A *cacique* would often indicate before his death who he wished for *interino.* "Only those who exhibited intense preoccupation with religion and who participated extensively in religious rites over a long period could hope to be considered" [Hill 1982:184] for the office of *cacique.*

Individuals in the pueblo can choose which moiety, Summer or Winter, they want to join, based on which they feel best suited them. However, it is not unusual for a person to switch moieties. For example, after marriage women will often join the moiety of their husband if they belong to different moieties.

See also *Kwere*.

Xaca

Kwakiutl, *Northwest Coast*
See *hasha*.

Xaha

Thompson, *Plateau*
See *haxa*.

Xahluigax xaikilgaiagiba

Pomo, *California*
The Eastern Pomo "Ghost" or "Devil" Ceremony [Barrett 1917:401], one of the most important sacred ceremonies conducted by the Pomo. It is performed as an atonement for offenses against the dead. The ceremony lasts for four days and is most often held in the spring. Only initiated men participate in the ceremony. Women and children are never allowed to attend, and uninitiated persons stay clear of the ceremony, fearing that serious illness will occur if they approach too closely.

The ceremony is held in a special dance house built for this particular ritual. In earlier times a new house was built for each dance, but in the twentieth century houses were sometimes reused.

Two classes of dancers participate. One type is the ordinary ghost-dancer or "devil," and the other is the "ash-devil," who performs fire-eating power feats. The "ash-devils," called *katsa'tala*, never actually dance during the ceremony but act more as messengers and clowns. The *katsa'tala* often do strange things to provoke laughter among the participants—making distorted faces, throwing objects at participants, etc. However, if anyone loses control and laughs, he is fined or punished.

Xanełné

Navajo, *Southwest*
Also: *Haneełnehee* [Frisbie 1987:466] and *xahnełnéhe* [Wyman and Bailey 1943:5]. Up-

ward-Reaching Way (formerly rendered as Moving Up Way) Chant. Evilway chant ceremonies are used by the Navajo specifically to ward off the influences of ghosts of their deceased relatives. Such ceremonies may be conducted for the prevention and treatment of diseases and misfortunes. Therefore each Evilway ceremony is called a "ghostway." *Xanełné* is the most fundamental "ghostway" ceremony, so much so that it "is the one meant when a native informant refers to a chant as 'Evilway' *[Hochoiji]* without further qualification" [Wyman and Bailey 1943:5].

Xawôk

Chinook, *Northwest Coast*
A shaman's guardian spirit [Boas 1894:197].

Xelyatsxamcàma

Yuma, *Southwest*
Also: *xelyatsxamcáma,* [Forde 1931:183]. Ghost dreamer, spirit dreamer [Forde 1931:183, 192]. A special class of shamans called upon to treat *ipa,* coma, and *halyatsxamn huthao,* ghost taking. "The task is more severe than ordinary curing, since in severe cases the soul no longer hovers round the body and has to be brought back from the land of the dead" [Forde 1931:192–193]. Because of this the name for these shamans does not end with the traditional suffix *tcev* (see entry).

These shamans also accompany war parties to treat *xweman,* club wounds, and *hataolyuk,* knife or spear wounds. Before leaving the camp the shaman

> collects young willow plants about three feet high, cuts them at the ground, peels them, and coils the bark into little balls. He generally makes four of these, one from each plant. Before beginning to cure a man, he puts one in his mouth, this draws out the saliva and makes it sharp and cold when it leaves the mouth, so that when he blows froth in the cure it drives away faintness and prevents coma. . . .
>
> If the cure is going to work, the doctor has a creeping feeling which starts in the feet and rises

over the body. If this stops at the knees or the waist he knows he cannot do much good, but if it goes on rising he knows the patient is getting along, and when the tingling gets right up to the top of his head something goes out of the doctor into the sick man and he knows he has made a cure [Manuel Thomas in Forde 1931:192].

Xosi
Wintun, *California*
Wintu charm. Most often such charms take the form of strangely shaped stones. For example, ammonites are commonly kept as a *tlak xosi,* rattlesnake charm, and deer enteroliths as a *nop xosi,* deer charm [Du Bois 1935:82]. Other types of charms include rattlesnake skins and tamarack seeds. The latter are strung about the neck to procure luck in fishing [Du Bois 1935:84].

Women are not supposed to see charms, let alone keep them. However, in practice this is not the case. "Charm stones had to be wrapped in grass or hide and buried or in some way secreted at a distance from dwellings. When the owner desired luck he went secretly to their hiding place, blew smoke on them, spat acorn meal over them, and prayed to them for success. Visits to charms had to be spaced from one to three months apart" [Du Bois 1935:83]. In addition, certain taboos were associated with the charm. For instance, it was never to be brought into a dwelling. If any taboo was broken, the charm would disappear or, worse yet, cause its owner to become ill. However, if the charm was fond of its owner, it would multiply itself. "The possessor would find two or three identical stones where he had left only one" [Du Bois 1935:84].

Xunxanital
Klallam, *Northwest Coast*
A Lummi secret society of shamans that functions to restrain "the medicine men and the men and women skilled in *suin* [see entry] from using their arts too frequently to injure others. The members of the society act in the role of vigilantes and execute those who are considered

harmful to the tribe because of the misuse of their power. The mode of punishment is gruesome. A long green stick is heated in the fire and forced up the victim's rectum all the way to his throat forcing blood and flesh to come out of his mouth. The victim is then sent groaning among the people to die as a warning to others to avoid a like fate" [Stern 1934:86].

Because this same punishment is threatened against anyone who reveals the secrets of this society, little is known of their activity. They paint their bodies black from the waist up except for a vertical, approximately 8-inch-wide strip up the middle front of the body. This form of painting is used because the ceremony "is animated by the spirit of the blackfish. The blackfish travel in packs like wolves, and scour the bottom of the sea, swimming close against submerged sea cliffs, brushing off animals from the gorges in the rocks. After they get their prey out into deep water, they circle around and eat it. As the members of the secret society come to the place of festivity, they land [in their canoes] in the group formation of the blackfish" [Stern 1934:87].

Xwthlaxwap
Twana, *Northwest Coast*
A strong healing power obtained from the Otter. The following is an account of the use of *xwthlaxwap* by a shaman named Doctor Charley, circa 1850:

Now this sick man was a big man among the Nisqually, his name was puyu´ixʷ. He was a doctor himself.

They put the sick man in the middle of the floor . . . and Doctor Charley knelt beside him and sang, with his elbow over his eyes. . . . That's his otter power now. And he quit singing and said, "This man's power has disappeared. It's off somewhere or somebody has captured it." And the sick man said, feebly, "Yes, yes, my power's been gone a long time." So Doctor Charley went on with his [otter] song and everybody there sang with him, helping him. And again he stopped and said, "Well, I'm going to look for your power, wherever I'll find it." And he went on singing again. He used a skin drum and beat it while he sang, and he had two or three tamánamis [see entry] poles that he set young fellows to beating on an overhead cedar board with. And the people sitting around the house beat on (drumming planks) with sticks while they helped him sing.

And now Doctor Charley stopped and told the people, "This man's power is up . . . Mount Rainier. Four slaha´l [gambling game] hand-game bones have it tied up there. And it was another doctor, a slaha´l man, took his power. That doctor's slaha´l power took this man's power. That doctor wanted to kill him. And this man's power has been up the mountain a long time, it's getting dry up there. But now I've found it."

And now Doctor Charley asked the sick man, "What am I going to do with those slaha´l gaming bones? Shall I kill them or let them go?" The sick man said, "I'll give you two horses to kill those slaha´l. That's a man that has always tried to kill me. And I'll give you two horses to kill them!" So Doctor Charley asked his brother Tenas Charley to come and help him. . . . And now those two brothers go to catch those slaha´l bones now. And they make motions of grabbing them and holding them in their hands, and they twist their fists together, and blood pours down from those slaha´l when they twist them. . . .

And now those two brothers sang again and went after the sick man's power. And they got hold of that power and brought it back and Doctor Charley bathed it in a basket of water, holding the tamánamis in his hands. They took water in their hands now and blew it through their hands like a tube at that power to give it more life. . . . Owl is his [the patient's] doctor power that Doctor Charley and Tenas Charley brought back. And now that sick man is all right [Frank Allen in Elmendorf 1993:215–216].

Yabaicini

Keres, *Southwest*

The wooden-slat altar used in Acoma curing ceremonies [White 1930:610]. "The use of a slat altar by a curing society is a comparatively recent practice" [White 1930:610, n. 11]. Thus at Santo Domingo and San Felipe (also possibly Cochiti), the healing ceremony altar, which goes by this same name, is instead a meal painting on the floor upon which stone fetishes, usually in the shape of animals, are set. Although they have wooden-slat altars, they are used "at retreats and solstice ceremonies, but not at cures" [White 1930:610].

Yaholi

Seminole, *Southeast*

Powerful shaman. See *aiyik-comi*.

Yak

Tlingit, *Northwest Coast*

A shaman's helping spirit, which can also be the spirit of a former shaman [L. Jones 1914:159]. A shaman can acquire a helping spirit either through inheritance from another shaman or through a vision quest.

See also *ichta*.

Yalbixw

Twana, *Northwest Coast*

Sunfish. The name given to a powerful *cshalt* (see entry) power that descended through three generations in a single Skokomish family during the nineteenth century. The power of this spirit enabled its owner to bring forth runs of smelt and herring. The *cshalt* became extinct in the 1870s when it "swam up the river and died" [Elmendorf 1960:499].

Yampavinyukwi

Paiute, *Basin*

Literal translation: "Mockingbird Runner" [Laird 1976: 36]. A Chemehuevi (Southern Paiute) shaman from around the turn of the twentieth century, whose English name was Johnny Moss. Only brief mention is made of him in the literature, referencing the unusual manifestations of skulls that occurred during his healing ceremonies. "When his patient was too far gone for his ministrations, when the case was hopeless, he would find himself juggling two skulls. Everyone present would see the skulls" [Laird 1976:36].

Yanpavinuk
Paiute, *Basin*

Literal translation: "Runs-Like-Mockingbird" [Kelly 1939:163]. A Las Vegas (Southern Paiute) shaman from the early part of the twentieth century whose English name was John Moss. His guardian spirit was an eagle, and he was renowned for his shamanic feats. "While this man sang he would pick up some sort of plant, and as he held it in his hand, it flowered and bore fruit. The latter he gave the patient to eat. . . . The same man would suddenly produce the (amnion?) sack of an unborn calf and turn it over and over in front of the fire for everyone to see. He was able, too, to restore life to dead animals—quail, desert tortoise, and rabbits. He picked up the dead body, gave it life, and the animal ran over the hill, out of sight. But always on the far side of the hill it would be found dead" [unidentified informant in Kelly 1939:163]. (Note: probably same person as in preceding entry.)

Yapaitu
Wintun, *California*

Spirit. By the 1930s the Wintu and Nomlaki were giving various descriptions of this spirit. Some felt it could be any kind, while others felt it was a big animal spirit. Goldschmidt [1951:351] guessed "that *yapaitu* was a spirit (or spirits) associated with the Huta initiation and the secret society." However, Du Bois stated that it was the term for a shaman's guardian spirit [Du Bois 1935:72] as did Kroeber [1932:360], where he noted that in Patwin the word means dancer. Curtin [1898:513] mentioned that it is one of three causes for sickness since "when a good yapaitu spirit is angry with a man [it] strikes him with his spirit point."

The word *lehs* (see entry) is the Wintu term for "the souls of living persons and the spirits of deceased ones" [Du Bois 1935:77]. Often a *lehs* will serve as a shaman's guardian spirit as well as a *yapaitu*.

One informant made the following distinction between these two forms of spirits: "Yapaitu is something in the hills, they are never people. You never see them. Lεs is somebody who is dead. It is what a person has with him. Maybe it is somewhere in the back of the head. When a person is alive his Lεs is always around the house. If you travel your Lεs follows you but doesn't get there until evening. Your Lεs is always about a day or half a day behind you. When somebody buries a man he always sees his Lεs sometime soon after. It is like a whirlwind. Your hair stands on end and you feel a chill. Not everybody can see a Lεs" [unidentified informant in Du Bois 1935:77]. It was reported that, in former times, a ghost was heard as well as seen [Du Bois 1935:78].

When a *lehs* does manifest as a ghost, it may be referred to as a *loltcit* [Du Bois 1935:78], the common Wintu word for ghost. Contact with a *loltcit* can cause illness. Indicators of this particular type of illness are loss of strength [Du Bois 1935:78], an inability to talk, hysterical behavior, laughing, sobbing, and drooling [Du Bois 1935:67]. However, *lehs* may also be used to designate a ghost [Du Bois 1935:77].

In other contexts *yapaitu* is best translated as "poison." For example, the phrase *yapaitu dokos* (see *dokos* entry) is used to refer to the small disease object, also called "pain," that an offended spirit or sorcerer sends into the body of its victim to cause illness or death [Knudtson 1975:12]. Du Bois [1935:93] rendered *yapaitu dokos* as "dangerous obsidian or arrowpoint." In addition, Wintu shaman Fanny Brown said *yapaitu dokos* was a "big pain" and looked "like a sliver of bone" [Du Bois 1935:93]. "I always get out a yapaitu dokos, but they are of different colors—red, white, black. There is no particular color for each sickness. One sickness may have different colors" [Fanny Brown in Du Bois 1935:93]. In order to cure the patient, a shaman must remove this object by sucking on the patient's body at the "seat" or location of the "pain."

"A doctor may have twenty or thirty spirits, but he rarely calls on more than two or three, and it is seldom that any great number are fit-ted to work together in a given case" [Curtin 1898:513].

Also, the phrase *yapaitu wintun* translates as "poison people" [Knudtson 1975:13] and is used to refer to whites, mainly because of the new diseases they brought when populating California.

Yayatü Society
Hopi, *Southwest*

Also: *yayaat* [Levy 1994:314]. One of two curing societies among the Hopi. The name of this soci-ety comes from the Keresan (Cochiti) term *yaya* (EONAH, pp. 325–326), literally "mother," which refers to the corn fetishes used by this soci-ety. The tutelary spirit of the society is the Hawk, from whom their shamans obtained "the power to withstand death by fire and falls from heights" [Voth in Levy 1994:314]. Consequently, they are adept at fire eating and walking on fire, but they also have the power of "flying, and instanta-neously transporting themselves long distances" [Levy 1994:314]. They treat individuals—for ex-ample, a treatment for a person with burns in-cludes the shaman swallowing burning embers [Stephen 1936:460] and in times of drought or pestilence, shamans also conduct public cere-monies for the entire community.

Many of their power feats are identical to those performed by the shamans of the Zuni Fire society. Overall, they are capable of performing spectacular power feats.

Yayatü could parachute off a cliff in a basket, transform inanimate things into living creatures, and once after eating a rabbit stew they laid the bones together, covered them over, and changed them into four rabbits which ran up the ladder and jumped across the kiva hatch and off to the valley. Another time the Yayatü terrified a visitor from Isleta who wore a black hat and fancy garters. They covered the hat and garters with a white blanket, and soon something was seen to move under it, and when it was removed, the hat was found transformed into a raven and the garters into a snake. They called to the Isletan to come and get his hat and garters, but he ran off afraid, crying he did not want them.

Fire tricks were among the feats of the Yayatü society. They once took a Walpi man below the mesa and trussed him up by hands and feet in a squat posture. They dug a hole in the sand large enough to hold him, and in it they made a big fire, and, after it was reduced to embers, they put the man in this hot pit and covered him with embers and with an airtight covering of sandy clay. The victim's brother came among the Yayatü, lashing at them with a rope and clamoring for his brother. They disclaimed all knowledge of him and told him to look in the pit and see for himself, which he did but found nothing in it but embers. The man went on to Walpi where the Yayatü were dancing and found his brother dancing with them. His brother was not entirely unharmed for he showed marks of roasting on shoulders and hips, and his queue was burned off [Parsons 1939:440–441].

The other curing society of the Hopi is the *Poswimkya* (see entry).

Yechu
Zuni, *Southwest*

Ritual paraphernalia [Parsons 1933:91]. These could include offerings, such as *oneane* (see entry) or *klo'o* (see entry), or a ritual fetish such as the *mikyapani,* "mother corn" [Parsons 1956:326], or double ear of corn.

Yega
Coyukon, *Mackenzie-Yukon*

A shaman's helping spirit, most often in the form of an animal [Krech 1981:90].

Yellow Bear
Hopi, *Southwest*

The English name of Sikyá Hónauüh, a shaman during the latter part of the nineteenth century. He was one of the last three surviving members of the *Poboctü* (see entry), "eye-seekers," society [Stephen 1894:212]. In February 1894 Alexander M. Stephen (see entry), only two months prior to his death, was treated by Sikyá Hónauüh for chest pains. Despite his condition Stephen, who by then had worked among the Hopi for fourteen years, provided an unusually detailed account of Sikyá Hónauüh's treatment.

The shaman began by making a visit to Stephen. The shaman asked him, "not at all in a solicitous manner, but rather as a friendly suggestion," if he would like him to take a look to see what was the matter with him [Stephen 1894:212]. Stephen consented and gave him several yards of cloth as payment. Sikyá Hónauüh then got a bowl from the house and filled it with water and proceeded to seat himself on the floor next to the pallet upon which Stephen was lying.

Opening a small pouch that he constantly wears, he took out four quartz and other pebbles, typical of the emblematic cardinal colors, although I could not see much difference between them, but they represented Yellow, for the northwest; Blue, for the southwest; Red, for the southeast; and White, for the northeast. Beginning with the yellow pebble, he dropped them into the bowl [of water], one at a time, with low muttered prayers to Bear, Badger, Horn-toad and Wú-yak Có-hü, Broad Star (Aldebaron). . . . He then crushed a small fragment of dry herb roots between his fingers and sprinkled it upon the surface of the water in the bowl, and this he told me made the ñá-kü-yi, charm water. He now took from his pouch a beautiful leaf-shaped knife, about three inches long, made of a pale green stone of compact texture, and laid it on the pallet close to my left side. He then drew from the pouch an irregular shaped lump of quartz crystal, about the size of a walnut, retaining it in his hand.

"Now," said he to me, "take off your shirt and sit up, and I will try to see what makes you ill." He seated himself on the foot of the pallet, which brought him under the window in the southwest wall, while I sat up on the other end of the pallet, facing him. Taking the crystal between finger and thumb, sometimes one hand, sometimes the other, he placed it close to his eye and looked intently at me; then he would hold the crystal at

arm's length toward me; then he would bend over so as to bring it close up to me; and thus he swayed back and forth, in silence, occasionally making passes with his arms to and fro and towards me, for about four or five minutes. Suddenly he reached over me and pressed the crystal against my right breast, and just upon the region of a quite severe pain, and which I may have described to him; but whether or no[t] he located the seat of pain exactly. He at once put the crystal in his pouch, and told me to lie down again, and after I had done so he took up the pretty green knife and began sawing the skin up and down, *i.e.,* lengthwise, over the spot where he had set the crystal.

It was a mere scarification, just enough to draw blood, which being effected, he put the knife back in his pouch, and sipped a little of the charm-water. He then bent over me, and placing his lips against the wound, he *exhaled* twice upon it, and the effect was to send an icy chill through me from head to foot. . . . After each of these exhalations he raised himself on his knees, and breathed ostentatiously from me; he again bent over me, and placing his lips again on the wound he *inhaled* twice, no marked sensation following the inhalation. But after the second time he carried my left hand to his mouth and spat into my palm an abominable looking, arrow-shaped, headless sort of centipede. It was about an inch and a quarter long; of a dark-brown color, and seemed to be covered with a visoid [sic] substance; it had no head that I could make out, but its legs certainly moved, and it seemed to be a living insect. This, said Yellow Bear, is Tü'-kyai-ni (that causes sickness); it is also called po-wá-ka ho-adta, sorcerer, his arrow; as I understood him, it may come to one through mishap, but usually it is sent (shot) by a sorcerer; it bores through the flesh until it reaches the heart, which it also bores and causes death. Yellow Bear only permitted me to look at it briefly, because it must be instantly carried forth to the cliff edge and there exorcised. This rite he performed alone. . . . On coming in again he made me drink part of the charm-water, and gave the rest to my two friends, who sat awe-struck, and as they afterwards confessed, rather badly scared. He then munched between his teeth the dried roots of four herbs, spitting them into a bowl of cold water, and the compound was very fragrant and somewhat mucilaginous. This he told me to drink from time to time for four days, which I did, and I really received much benefit, but whether from the cold infusion or the scarification I am still in doubt, at any rate the pains in my chest ceased [Stephen 1894:213–214].

Yidwas

Twana, *Northwest Coast*

Soul. Literal translation: "heart" [Elmendorf 1960:513]. The Twana view holds that an individual possesses two souls. The heart soul is "a vague concept, undefined in form or nature. It had its seat in the heart and perished with its owner's death; it could not become detached from or leave its owner's body. The heart soul seems to have been a mere belief item without other cultural associations" [Elmendorf 1960:513].

The other Twana soul is known as *shula* (see entry).

Yiwakwayau

Diegueño, *Peninsula*

Cocopa scalp keeper. Great warriors were selected to keep the scalp of a slain enemy, and for each scalp a different *yiwakwayau* was selected. Because the soul of the victim was associated with the scalp, great care was needed in handling it. The *yiwakwayau* had to bathe early each morning and just before sundown and also abstain from eating meat, fish, and salt for four days after receiving a scalp. In addition he could not smoke. If any of the taboos associated with scalp keeping were broken, the warrior would lose his power to be a great warrior [Gifford 1933:301].

Following the ceremonial purification of the scalp over a period of eight days, it was then stored in a sealed olla placed in a special hut erected outside the home of the *yiwakwayau*.

Yoktco

Miwok, *California*

A Plains Miwok prophet/shaman during the latter part of the nineteenth century. Little is known of his life. "[His] home was near Pleasanton in Alameda county, where he resided in a mixed settlement of indigenous Costanoans and transplanted Northern San Joaquin Yokuts and Plains Miwok. This mixed assemblage represented the last of the Indians and their descendants once collected at Mission San Jose in Alameda county" [Gifford 1927:220]. Around 1872 Yoktco introduced eight new Kuksu cult (EONAH, p. 140) dances into the Southern Maidu region, where he had become the *temaya* (dance leader). Yoktco often dreamed of the various spirits (*nedi*—see entry) associated with each dance but was "reported to have said that he learned in his youth dances which he in turn taught to the Southern Maidu" [Gifford 1927:229].

"At dancing time Yoktco spoke a strange language," which led Gifford [1927:230] to suggest that it was "perhaps" Yokuts or Costanoan because the shaman had lived among those people as a youth. However, it is well known that shamans often use a "secret" language that is nonintelligible to the audience when speaking to their helping spirits. One of the dances introduced by Yoktco was the *hiweyi* (EONAH, p. 107) dance, known elsewhere in central California and referred to as "a shaman's curing dance" [Gifford 1927:231].

Yoktco died around 1873 or 1874 and was succeeded by an old blind man named Rice, who continued as *temaya* until his death around 1888 [Gifford 1927:230].

Yómto

Wappo, *California*

Shaman [Sawyer 1965:90]. See *yomto* in EONAH, p. 329.

Yomuse

Maidu, *California*

Also: *yommüse*. Dialectical variant: *yomta* (Miwok) (EONAH, p. 329). Plural: *yomi* [Kroeber 1925:

423]. The most common Nisenan (Southern Maidu) term for shaman. Dixon [1905:271] gave *yomi* as the singular form of the word for the Northern Maidu. Variations on this term among the Nisenan are as follows: *yomuze* and *yomuse maiduk,* Amador County forms; *yomedaidu,* Placerville form; *yomen maidu,* Nevada City form; and *eyum* or *eyumunwak,* Forest Hill, Placer County form [Beals 1933:390]. Other Southern Maidu variations include: *yomin, yomuzu,* and *yumizi* [Gifford 1927:243].

Maidu shamans are usually divided into three groups: valley shamans, hill or foothill shamans, and mountain shamans, and slight variations exist with regard to techniques and procedures. Gifford [1927:243] suggested that the Southern Maidu dance named *yomuse* was really "an outright performance by shamans."

Although some Nisenan become shamans directly through dreaming, most shamans receive instructions from older shamans. Those clairvoyants who only dream and undergo no formal instruction are known as *netdi* among the foothill Maidu [Kroeber 1925:423]. Among the foothill Nisenan, novice shamans are instructed as young boys by other shamans, usually in groups composed of four or five boys. Females may become shamans through dreaming but receive no formal training like that given to the boys. The training lasts from six to seven months and is conducted at a camp in the nearby hills. "During training period, boys painted black with pitch, charcoal. Every night fire built, doctor presses boy against him, first breast to breast, then breast against boy's back, rendering unconscious for 2–3 hrs. After neophytes recover, dance, about 11 o'clock, sleep. At daybreak dance around fire 4 times, blowing whistle while doctors sing. During day shamans take boys in woods, show herbs" [unidentified informant in Beals 1933:386]. During this training the boys are forbidden to eat salt, meat, or grease. The shaman can tell if a forbidden substance is in their food by touching his hand on the bowl [Beals 1933:386].

Among the mountain Nisenan the training is similar: "Novices and shaman camp far in woods, eat no meat, salt, fat. Stay 8 days learning doctor song. Shaman sings; 4 neophytes, naked except for loin cloth of wire grass pounded soft, dance around him blowing double whistles of alder wood. Shaman shows herbs, medicines, how to 'shoot' medicine. Shaman really proficient in latter art can smash stone pestle ¼ miles away. Informant had seen this done. Neophytes also practice killing people. After 8 days, shaman leaves, novices stay in woods several months, shaman visiting several times" [Beals 1933:389]. When the novice does acquire shamanic power, it is usually indicated by bleeding from the nose, the ears, or both.

Most Nisenan shamans become sucking doctors. However, with the onset of the Kuksu cult (EONAH, p. 140) in 1872, most healing was transferred to the latter group, which has a healing dance performance. Persons suffering from dreams or spirit visitations, for instance, are cured through the Kuksu cult healing dance [Beals 1933:387]. When an individual shaman is called upon, the "patient [is] often taken to round house [ceremonial house], laid on drum, feathers on. Shaman chews medicine, blows on patient and presses with medicine in hands until finds seat of illness [called "pain"], then sucks, spits out flint, lizard, frog, other object. Bowl full [of] medicine also given; if effect violent, patient will recover. If no reaction, shaman hangs head, cries, goes away [meaning cure not successful]" [Beals 1933:387].

This last technique is actually the initial diagnostic technique. "For medicines, diagnosis first made. Infusion of herbs cooked with quartz crystal; shaman always tastes, gives patient. If nauseated, faints, shaman delighted, if medicine no apparent effect, shaman tries another or more usually shakes head, perhaps cries, goes away. Another may be called" [Beals 1933:387]. The objects ("pains") that are removed from the patient's body through the shaman's sucking technique are "exhibited—if animals, always still alive—and then buried" [Kroeber 1925:424]. In addition, Maidu shamans frequently use a *sokot* (see entry) to accompany their singing.

Among the mountain Nisenan, "pains" are called *itu* [Kroeber 1925:422].

In addition some shamans cure their patients in the sweat lodge (see *weni* for an example). Another technique used is to bleed a patient. "For headache shaman sometimes cuts skin over seat of pain with flint knife until bleeds" [Beals 1933:389]. Successful shamans are paid, while those who fail to heal are not paid for their services.

Other types of Maidu shamans include weather shamans, Rattlesnake shamans, and *kopati* (see entry), or Bear shamans [Kroeber 1925:427].

For the most part, successful shamans are feared because they are known to have been trained in sorcery as well. Such training is mainly designed to teach the shaman how to "shoot" medicine into the enemies of the Nisenan, but it certainly could be used locally by an ill-tempered shaman.

Yua
Yupik, *Arctic Coast*
Plural: *yuat.* A shaman's guardian spirit [Carey 1992:144].

Yugûk
West Alaska Eskimo, *Arctic Coast*
A wooden doll in the form of a human being that is the central figure in this people's annual *Yugiyhik* ceremony. During the ceremony the doll is empowered by the shamans, then it "is wrapped in birch-bark and hung in a tree in some retired spot until the following year.... The place where the image is concealed is not generally known by the people of the village, but is a secret to all except the shamans and, perhaps, some of the oldest men who take prominent parts in the festival" [Nelson 1899:494].

During the following year shamans make visits to this secret location to consult the *yugûk,*

usually regarding the acquisition of game. Because the *yugûk* is a living spirit, "small offerings of food in the shape of fragments of deer fat or of dried fish are placed within the wrappings" [Nelson 1899:494]. If, during a visitation, the shaman discovers deer hairs deposited within the wrappings, this is seen as an indicator of success in deer hunting. Fish scales within the wrappings indicate success in fishing.

Yupa
Wintun, *California*
To speak from trance. Anthropologist Dorothy Lee "rendered this word somewhat inadequately as *to speak prophetically*" [Lee 1941:406]. The term refers to the speech of a shaman during trance possession by one of his helping spirits. "When the shaman is in trance, he may speak generally about the world, either foretelling events, or merely describing events with clairvoyance.... In both cases of prophetic speech which I recorded, the spirit is conceived of as speaking directly through the mouth of the shaman" [Lee 1941:406].

Yupa is therefore a term used to distinguish the shaman's altered state of consciousness during sacred ceremonies. "When, on the other hand, the shaman makes a diagnosis, or speaks about the subject in hand, it is he who describes what the spirit-power communicates to him through his general sensation. As Sadie [Marsh, Lee's informant] explained, 'His spirit makes him feel all this'" [Lee 1941:406]. The shaman's "feeling" of information may well be acquired from his helping spirit during a trance state, and when he returns to normal waking consciousness, he tells others what his spirits have said to him. Thus within the structure of the Wintun language, the shaman's altered state of being is recognized and identified as such.

Yutir
West Alaska Eskimo, *Arctic Coast*
A Nunivak Island term for mana (see entry). This word was used by Najagneq, a shaman from

this area whom Rasmussen [1969:384] interviewed near the end of October 1924.

Yuwadab
Twana, *Northwest Coast*

Doctoring, shaman-curing procedures. "Curing by Twana shamans involved a complex set of procedures based on an equally complex theory of disease causes and the specialization of certain spirit powers for specific curing operations" [Elmendorf 1960:504].

Healing begins with the shaman using his power to "see into" the patient in order to diagnose the cause of illness. The shaman sings a *swadash* (see entry) song "while covering his eyes with the crook of an elbow" [Elmendorf 1960:505]. After some time he announces his findings. Most often the cause is diagnosed as the intrusion into the patient's body of a harmful object, the loss of the patient's soul, a taboo violation, or contact with a harmful spirit power.

Healing sessions are open to the public. Assistants include singers, drummers, and members of the audience. In a case of object intrusion, the shaman removes the intrusive object either by sucking on the patient or by withdrawing the object with his hands. It is then disposed of in some way—by smashing it, cutting it in two, etc. For soul loss the shaman will travel to recover the lost soul and return it to the patient. However, there is a time limit on how long a soul can remain out of one's body. If the limit is surpassed, the soul will keep leaving the patient's body no matter how many times it is returned by a shaman.

Fees are paid for successful treatment. Upper-class patients "often paid in any case to avoid the stigma of lack of generosity" [Elmendorf 1960:507].

References

Aberle, David F.
1966 "Religo-Magical Phenomena and Power, Prediction, and Control." In *Southwestern Journal of Anthropology* 22(3):221–230.

Adams, E. Charles
1994 "The Katsina Cult: A Western Pueblo Perspective." In *Kachinas in the Pueblo World,* Polly Schaafsma, ed., pp. 35–46. Albuquerque: University of New Mexico Press.

Amoss, Pamela T.
1977 "The Power of Secrecy Among the Coast Salish." In *The Anthropology of Power: Ethnographic Studies from Asia, Oceania, and the New World,* Raymond D. Fogelson and Richard N. Adams, eds., pp. 131–140. New York: Academic Press.
1978 *Coast Salish Spirit Dancing.* Seattle: University of Washington Press.

Anson, Bert
1970 *The Miami Indians.* Norman: University of Oklahoma Press.

Aquila, Richard
1974 "Plains Indian War Medicine." In *Journal of the West* 13(2):19–43.

Armitage, Peter
1991 *The Innu (The Montagnais-Naskapi).* New York: Chelsea House Publishers.

Babcock, Barbara A.
1993 "'Not in the Absolute Singular': Rereading Ruth Benedict." In *Hidden Scholars: Women Anthropologists and the Native American Southwest,* Nancy J. Parezo, ed., pp. 107–128. Albuquerque: University of New Mexico Press.

Bahr, Donald
1977 "Breath in Shamanic Curing." In *Flowers of the Wind: Papers on Ritual, Myth, and Symbolism in California and the Southwest,* Thomas C. Blackburn, ed., pp. 29–40. Socorro, NM: Ballena Press.

Baker, Paul E.
1955 *The Forgotten Kutenai: A Study of the Kutenai Indians, Bonners Ferry, Idaho, Creston, British Columbia, Canada, and Other Areas in British Columbia Where the Kutenai Are Located.* Boise, ID: Mountain States Press.

Barnett, Homer G.
1955 *The Coast Salish of British Columbia.* University of Oregon Monographs, Studies in Anthropology, No. 4, pp. 1–320.

Barnouw, Victor
1977 *Wisconsin Chippewa Myths & Tales, and Their Relation to Chippewa Life.* Madison: University of Wisconsin Press.

Barrett, S. A.
1917 "Ceremonies of the Pomo Indians." In *University of California Publications in American Archaeology and Ethnology* 12(10):307–441.

Beals, Ralph L.
1933 "Ethnology of the Nisenan." In *University of California Publications in American Archaeology and Ethnology* 31(6):335–414.

Bean, Lowell John
1976 "Power and Its Applications in Native California." In *Native Californians: A Theoretical Retrospective,* Lowell John Bean and Thomas C. Blackburn, eds., pp. 407–420. Socorro, NM: Ballena Press.

Benedict, Ruth
1922 "The Vision in Plains Culture." In *American Anthropologist* 24(1):1–23.

Birket-Smith, Kaj
1924 "Ethnography of the Egedesminde District." In *Meddelelser om Grønland* 64:1–484.

1953   *The Chugach Eskimo.* Nationalmuseets Skrifter, Etnografisk Raekke No. 4. Copenhagen: Nationalmuseets Publikationsfond.

Black Elk, Wallace, and William S. Lyon
1990   *Black Elk: The Sacred Ways of a Lakota.* San Francisco: Harper & Row.

Bloomfield, Leonard
1934   *Plains Cree Texts.* Publications of the American Ethnological Society, vol. 6.

Boas, Franz
1894   *Chinook Texts.* Bureau of American Ethnology, Bulletin 20.
1912   "Tsimshian Texts." In Publications of the American Ethnological Society 3:65–284.
1918   *Kutenai Tales.* Bureau of American Ethnology, Bulletin 59.
1922   Unpublished manuscripts and field notes. Library, American Philosophical Society, Philadelphia, PA.
1928   *Keresan Texts.* In Publications of the American Ethnological Society, vol. 8, part 1.

Boatman, John F.
1992   *My Elders Taught Me: Aspects of Western Great Lakes American Indian Philosophy.* Lanham, MD: University Press of America.

Boscana, Geronimo (Fray)
1969   "Chinigchinich: A Historical Account of the Origin, Customs, and Traditions of the Indians at the Missionary Establishment of St. Juan Capistrano, Alta, California." In *Life in California,* Alfred Robinson, ed., pp. 225–341. New York: Da Capo Press.

Bourgeois, Arthur P., ed.
1994   *Ojibwa Narratives: Of Charles and Charlotte Kawbawgam and Jacques LePique, 1893–1895.* Detroit: Wayne State University Press.

Bourke, John G.
1884   *The Snake Dance of the Moquis of Arizona.* New York: Charles Scribner's Sons. (London: S. Low) (reissued in 1962 by Rio Grande Press.)

Boyd, Robert
1996   *People of the Dalles: The Indians of Wascopam Mission.* Lincoln: University of Nebraska Press.

Brandt, Elizabeth
1977   "The Role of Secrecy in a Pueblo Society." In *Flowers of the Wind: Papers on Ritual, Myth and Symbolism in California and the Southwest,* Thomas C. Blackburn, ed., pp. 11–28. Socorro, NM: Ballena Press.

Brown, Jennifer S. H., and Robert Brightman
1988   *"The Orders of the Dreamed": George Nelson on Cree and Northern Ojibwa Religion and Myth, 1823.* St. Paul: Minnesota Historical Society Press.

Brown, Joseph Epes
1953   *The Sacred Pipe: Black Elk's Account of the Seven Rites of the Oglala Sioux.* Norman: University of Oklahoma Press.
1964   *The Spiritual Legacy of the American Indian.* Pendle Hill Pamphlet no. 135. Lebanon, PA: Sowers Printing.

Buechel, Rev. Eugene
1970   *Lakota-English Dictionary.* Pine Ridge, SD: Red Cloud Indian School.

Bunzel, Ruth L.
1932a   "Introduction to Zuñi Ceremonialism." In *Forty-seventh Annual Report of the Bureau of American Ethnology.* 467–544.
1932b   "Zuñi Origin Myths." In *Forty-seventh Annual Report of the Bureau of American Ethnology.* 545–610.
1932c   "Zuñi Ritual Poetry." In *Forty-seventh Annual Report of the Bureau of American Ethnology.* 611–835.

Callahan, Alice Anne
1990   *The Osage Ceremonial Dance I'n-Lon-Schka.* Norman: University of Oklahoma Press.

Carey, Richard Adams
1992   *Raven's Children.* Boston: Houghton Mifflin.

Casanowicz, I. M.
1925   "Shamanism of the Natives of Siberia." In *Smithsonian Institution, Annual Report for the Year Ending June 30, 1924,* 415–434.

Catlin, George
1857   *Letters and Notes on the Manners, Customs, and Condition of the North American Indians.* Philadelphia: Willis P. Hazard.

Chapman, John W.
1914   *Ten'a Texts and Tales.* Publications of the American Ethnological Society, vol. 6.

Clark, Ella E., ed.
1956   "George Gibbs' Account of Indian Mythology in Oregon and Washington." In *Oregon Historical Quarterly* 57(2):125–167.

Cline, Walter
1938   "Religion and World View." In *The Sinkaietk or Southern Okanagon of Washington,* Leslie Spier, ed., pp. 131–182. General Series in Anthropology, Number 6. Contributions from the Laboratory of Anthropology, 2. Menasha, WI: George Banta Publishing.

Coale, George
1958   "Notes on the Guardian Spirit Concept among the Nez Perce." In *National Archives of Ethnography* 48:135–148.

Coleman, Sister Bernard
1937   "The Religion of the Ojibwa of Northern Minnesota." In *Primitive Man* 10(3 and 4):33–57.

Colson, Elizabeth
1953   *The Makah Indians: A Study of an Indian Tribe in Modern American Society.* Minneapolis: University of Minnesota Press.

Conklin, Harold C., and William C. Sturtevant
1953   "Seneca Indian Singing Tools at Coldspring Longhouse: Musical Instruments of the Modern Iroquois." In *Proceedings of the American Philosophical Society* 97(3):262–290.

Coolidge, Dane, and Mary Roberts Coolidge
1939   *The Last of the Seris.* New York: E. P. Dutton.

Cooper, John M.
1930   "Field Notes on Northern Algonkian Magic." In *Proceedings of the Twenty-third International Congress of Americanists,* pp. 513–518.
1933   "The Cree Witiko Psychosis." In *Primitive Man* 6(1):20–24.
1936   *Notes on the Ethnology of the Otchipwe of Lake of the Woods and Rainy Lake.* Anthropological Series No. 3. Washington, DC: Catholic University of America.

Cove, John J., and George F. MacDonald, eds.
1987   *Tsimshian Narratives I: Tricksters, Shamans and Heroes.* Collected by Marius Barbeau and William Beynon. Mercury Series, Paper No. 3. Ottawa: Canadian Museum of Civilization.

Covington, James W.
1993   *The Seminoles of Florida.* Gainsville: University Press of Florida.

Culin, Stewart
1901   "A Summer Trip among the Western Indians." In *University of Pennsylvania, Bulletin, Free Museum of Science and Art* 3(3):143–175.

Curtin, Jeremiah
1898   *Creation Myths of Primitive America: In Relation to the Religious History and Mental Development of Mankind.* Boston: Little, Brown.

DeMallie, Raymond J., ed.
1984   *The Sixth Grandfather: Black Elk's Teachings Given to John G. Neihardt.* Lincoln: University of Nebraska Press.

Dempsey, Hugh A.
1994   *The Amazing Death of Calf Shirt and Other Blackfoot Stories.* Norman: University of Oklahoma Press.

Densmore, Frances
1910   *Chippewa Music.* Bureau of American Ethnology, Bulletin 45.
1922   *Northern Ute Music.* Bureau of American Ethnology, Bulletin 75.
1929   *Chippewa Customs.* Bureau of American Ethnology, Bulletin 86.
1949   "A Study of Some Michigan Indians." In *Anthropological Papers, Museum of Anthropology, University of Michigan* 1:1–41.

Dièreville, le Sieur de
1933   *Relation of the Voyage to Port Royal in Acadia or New France,* John Clarence Webster, ed. Toronto: Champlain Society. (First French edition published in 1708.)

Dixon, Roland B.
1904   "Some Shamans of Northern California." In *Journal of American Folklore* 17:23–27.

1905   "The Northern Maidu." In *Bulletin of the American Museum of Natural History* 17:119–346.

Doll, Don
1994   *Vision Quest: Men, Women and Sacred Sites of the Sioux Nation.* New York: Crown Publishers.

Dorsey, George A.
1902   "The Dwamish Indian Spirit Boat and Its Use." In *University of Pennsylvania, Bulletin, Free Museum of Science and Art* 3(4):227–238.
1903   "How the Pawnee Captured the Cheyenne Medicine Arrows." In *American Anthropologist* 5(4): 644–658.
1904   *Traditions of the Arikara.* Carnegie Institution of Washington Publication No. 17. Washington, DC: Carnegie Institution of Washington.
1905   "The Cheyenne: 1, Ceremonial Organization." In *Publications of the Field Columbian Museum, Anthropological Series* 9(1):1–55.

Dorsey, George A., and H. R. Voth
1901   "The Oraibi Soyal Ceremony." In *Publications of the Field Columbian Museum, Anthropological Series* 3(1):1–59.
1902   "The Mishongnovi Ceremonies of the Snake and Antelope Fraternities." In *Publications of the Field Columbian Museum, Anthropological Series* 3(3):1–261.

Douglass, William Boone
1917   "Notes on the Shrines of the Tewa and Other Pueblo Indians of New Mexico." In *Proceedings of the Nineteenth International Congress of Americanists,* pp. 344–374.

Draper, William R.
1946   *Indian Dances, Medicine Men, and Prophets.* Girard, KS: Haldeman-Julius.

Driver, Harold E., and William C. Massey
1957   "Comparative Studies of North American Indians." In *Transactions of the American Philosophical Society* 47(2):163–456.

Drucker, Philip
1937   "The Tolowa and Their Southwest Oregon Kin." In *University of California Publications in American Archaeology and Ethnology* 36(4):221–300.

1939   "Contributions to Alsea Ethnography." In *University of California Publications in American Archaeology and Ethnology* 35(7):81–102.
1940   "Kwakiutl Dancing Societies." In *University of California Anthropological Records* 2(6):201–230.

Drury, Clifford
1958   *The Diaries and Letters of Henry H. Spalding and Asa Bowen Smith Relating to the Nez Perce Mission, 1838–1842.* Glendale, CA: Arthur H. Clark.

Du Bois, Cora
1935   "Wintu Ethnography." In *University of California Publications in American Archaeology and Ethnology* 36(1):1–148.
1938   *The Feather Cult of the Middle Columbia.* General Series in Anthropology, Number 7. 1–45. Menasha, WI: George Banta Publishing.

Dumont, M.
1753   *Memoires Historiques sur la Louisiane.* Paris: J. B Bauche. (Partially reprinted in vol. 5 of the *Louisiana Historical Collections.*)

Dunbar, John G.
1880   "The Pawnee Indians: Their Habits and Customs, Part 1." In *Magazine of American History* 5(5):320–342.
1882   "The Pawnee Indians: Their Habits and Customs, Part 2." In *Magazine of American History* 8(10):734–754.

Dusenberry, Verne
1959   "Visions Among the Pend d'Oreille Indians." In *Ethnos* 24(1–2):52–57.
1961   "The Significance of the Sacred Pipes to the Gros Ventre of Montana." In *Ethnos* 26 (1–2):12–29.

Eckstorm, Fannie Hardy
1945   *Old John Neptune and Other Maine Indian Shamans.* Portland, ME: Southworth-Anthoensen Press.

Eells, Rev. Myron
1889   "The Twana, Chemakum, and Klallam Indians, of Washington Territory." In *Smithsonian Insti-*

tution, Annual Report for the Year Ending June 30, 1887, Part 1, 605–681.

Eliade, Mircea
1964   *Shamanism: Archaic Techniques of Ecstasy.* Bollingen Series 74. New York: Pantheon Books.

Elmendorf, William W.
1960   *The Structure of Twana Culture.* Monographic Supplement No. 2, *Research Studies* 28(3):1–576. Pullman, WA: Washington State University. (Reprinted in 1974 in *Coast Salish and Western Washington Indians 4.* New York: Garland Publishing.)
1984   "Coast Salish Concepts of Power: Verbal and Functional Categories." In *The Tsimshian and Their Neighbors of the North Pacific Coast,* Jay Miller and Carol M. Eastman, eds., pp. 281–291. Seattle: University of Washington Press.
1993   *Twana Narratives: Native Historical Accounts of a Coast Salish Culture.* Seattle: University of Washington Press.

Fahey, John
1986   *The Kalispel Indians.* Norman: University of Oklahoma Press.

Fenton, William N.
1936   "An Outline of Seneca Ceremonies at Coldspring Longhouse." In *Yale University Publications in Anthropology* 9:1–23.
1937   "The Seneca Society of Faces" In *Scientific Monthly* 44:215–238.
1941   "Masked Medicine Societies of the Iroquois." In *Smithsonian Institution, Annual Report for the Year Ending June 30, 1940,* 397–430.
1942   "Songs from the Iroquois Longhouse: Program Notes for an Album of American Indian Music from the Eastern Woodlands." In *An Iroquois Source Book,* Vol. 3, 1985, Elisabeth Tooker, ed., 34 pp. in unpaginated text. New York: Garland Publishing.

Fenton, William N., and Gertrude P. Kurath
1951   "The Feast of the Dead, or Ghost Dance at Six Nations Reserve, Canada." In *Symposium on Local Diversity in Iroquois Culture,* William F. Fenton, ed. Bureau of American Ethnology, Bulletin 149, pp. 139–165.

Fletcher, Alice C., and Francis La Flesche
1911   "The Omaha Tribe." In *Twenty-seventh Annual Report of the Bureau of American Ethnology.* 17–672.

Fogelson, Raymond D.
1977   "Cherokee Notions of Power." In *The Anthropology of Power: Ethnographic Studies from Asia, Oceania, and the New World,* Raymond D. Fogelson and Richard N. Adams, eds., pp. 185–194. New York: Academic Press.
1980   "The Conjuror in Eastern Cherokee Society." In *Journal of Cherokee Studies* 5(2):60–87.

Ford, Clellan S.
1967   "Charlie Nowell Recalls the Winter Ceremonies." In *Indians of the North Pacific Coast,* Tom McFeat, ed., pp. 198–208. Seattle: University of Washington Press.

Forde, C. Daryll
1931   "Ethnography of the Yuma Indians." In *University of California Publications in American Archaeology and Ethnology* 28(4):83–278.

Forrest, Earle R.
1961   *The Snake Dance of the Hopi Indians.* Los Angeles: Westernlore Press.

Fortune, R. F.
1932   *Omaha Secret Societies.* Columbia University Contributions in Anthropology, vol. 14. New York: Columbia University Press.

Fowler, Catherine S., ed.
1989   *Willard Z. Park's Ethnographic Notes on the Northern Paiute of Western Nevada, 1933–1944.* University of Utah, Anthropological Papers, Number 114. Salt Lake City: University of Utah Press.

Fowler, Don D., and Catherine S. Fowler, eds.
1971   *Anthropology of the Numa: John Wesley Powell's Manuscripts on the Numic Peoples of Western North America 1868–1880.* Smithsonian Contributions to Anthropology, Number 14. Washington, DC: Smithsonian Institution Press.

Fox, Jennifer
1993   "The Women Who Opened Doors: Interviewing Southwestern Anthropologists." In *Hidden*

Scholars: Women Anthropologists and the Native American Southwest, Nancy J. Parezo, ed., pp. 294–310. Albuquerque: University of New Mexico Press.

Freed, Stanley A., and Ruth S. Freed
1963   "A Configuration of Aboriginal Washo Culture." In *The Washo Indians of California and Nevada,* Warren L. d'Azevedo, ed., pp. 41–56. University of Utah, Anthropological Papers, Number 67. Salt Lake City: University of Utah Press.

Freeland, L. S.
1923   "Pomo Doctors and Poisoners." In *University of California Publications in American Archaeology and Ethnology* 20:57–73.

Frisbie, Charlotte J.
1987   *Navajo Medicine Bundles or JISH: Acquisition, Transmission, and Disposition in the Past and Present.* Albuquerque: University of New Mexico Press.

Frost, John
1845   *The Book of the Indians of North America.* New York: D. Appleton.

Garfield, Viola E.
1939   "Tsimshian Clan and Society." In *University of Washington Publications in Anthropology* 7(3): 167–340.
1951   *The Tsimshian and Their Neighbors.* In Publications of the American Ethnological Society, Vol. 18.

Gatschet, Albert S.
1893   "Medicine Arrows of the Oregon Indians." In *Journal of American Folklore* 6(21):111–112.

Gayton, A. H.
1930   "Yokuts-Mono Chiefs and Shamans." In *University of California Publications in American Archaeology and Ethnology* 24(8):361–420.

Gibbs, George
1956   "An Account of Indian Mythology in Oregon and Washington." Edited by Ella E. Clark. In *Oregon Historical Quarterly* 57(2):125–167.

Giddings, J. L.
1961   *Kobuk River People.* Department of Anthropology and Geography, University of Alaska, Studies of Northern Peoples, Number 1, pp. 1–159.

Gifford, E. W.
n.d. a   "Central Miwok Shamans." Unpublished manuscript, Museum and Department of Anthropology Archives, Ethnological Document no. 179 (Archive no. CU-23.1), Bancroft Library, University of California, Berkeley.
n.d. b   "Southern Miwok Ceremonies." Unpublished manuscript, Museum and Department of Anthropology Archives, Ethnological Document no. 181 (Archive no. YB97–0442 853:8), Bancroft Library, University of California, Berkeley.
1927   "Southern Maidu Religious Ceremonies." In *American Anthropologist* 29(3):214–257.
1932   "The Northfork Mono." In *University of California Publications in American Archaeology and Ethnology* 31(2):15–65.
1933   "The Cocopa." In *University of California Publications in American Archaeology and Ethnology* 31(5):257–334.
1936   "Northeastern and Western Yavapai." In *University of California Publications in American Archaeology and Ethnology* 34(4):247–354.
1940   "Hupa Notes." Unpublished manuscript (described as "Ethnographic Notes on Hupa Ceremonies and Rituals"), Museum and Department of Anthropology Archives, Ethnological Document no. 171 (Archive no. CU-23–1), Bancroft Library, University of California, Berkeley.

Gill, Sam
1987   *Native American Religious Action: A Performance Approach to Religion.* Columbia: University of South Carolina Press.

Gillette, J. M.
1906   "The Medicine Society of the Dakota Indians." In *Collections of the State Historical Society of North Dakota* 1:459–474.

Gilmore, Melvin R.
1932   "The Sacred Bundles of the Arikara." In *Papers of the Michigan Academy of Science Arts and Letters* 16:33–50.

Goddard, Pliny Earle
1903 "Life and Culture of the Hupa." In *University of California Publications in American Archaeology and Ethnology* 1(1):1–88.
1911 "Jicarilla Apache Texts." In *Anthropological Papers of the American Museum of Natural History* 8:1–276.
1916 "The Beaver Indians." In *Anthropological Papers of the American Museum of Natural History* 10(4):201–293.
1917 "Beaver Texts (Part 5) and Beaver Dialect (Part 6)." In *Anthropological Papers of the American Museum of Natural History,* 10(5 and 6):295–546.

Goldschmidt, Walter
1951 *Nomlaki Ethography.* Berkeley: University of California Press.

Goodwin, Grenville
1938 "White Mountain Apache Religion." In *American Anthropologist* 40(1):24–37.

Graves, Charles S.
1929 *Lore and Legends of the Klamath River Indians.* Yreka, CA: Press of the Times.

Green, Jesse, ed.
1979 *Selected Writings of Frank Hamilton Cushing.* Lincoln: University of Nebraska Press.

Greenlee, Robert F.
1944 "Medicine and Curing Practices of the Modern Florida Seminoles." In *American Anthropologist* 46(3):317–328.

Grinde, Jr., Donald A.
1977 *The Iroquois and the Founding of the American Nation.* San Francisco: Indian Historian Press.

Grinnell, George Bird
1910 "The Great Mysteries of the Cheyenne." In *American Anthropologist* 12(4):542–575.
1922 "The Medicine Wheel." In *American Anthropologist* 24(3):299–310.
1923 *The Cheyenne Indians.* 2 vols. New Haven: Yale University Press.

Grossman, Captain F. E.
1873 "The Pima Indians of Arizona." In *Smithsonian Institution, Annual Report for the Year Ending June 30, 1871,* 407–419.

Haeberlin, Herman K.
1918 "SBeTeTDA´Q, A Shamanistic Performance of the Coast Salish." In *American Anthropologist* 20(3):249–257.

Hale, Horatio
1846 *Ethnology and Philology: Narratives of the United States Exploring Expedition, by Charles Wilkes.* Vol. 1. Philadelphia: Lea and Blauchard (reprinted in 1968 by Gregg Press).

Hall, C. L.
1906 "Autobiography of Poor Wolf, Head Soldier of the Hidatsa or Grosventre Tribe." In *Collections of the State Historical Society of North Dakota* 1:439–443.
1942 *The Role of Conjuring in Saulteaux Society.* Philadelphia: University of Pennsylvania Press.

Hallowell, A. Irving
1992 *The Ojibwa of Berens River, Manitoba: Ethnography into History.* Fort Worth, TX: Harcourt Brace Jovanovich College Publishers.

Handy, E. S. Craighill
1968 "Dreaming in Relation to Spirit Kindred and Sickness in Hawaii." In *Essays in Anthropology,* A. L. Kroeber, ed., pp. 119–127. Freeport, NY: Books for Libraries Press.

Hardin, Margaret Ann
1993 "Zuni Potters and *The Pueblo Potter:* The Contributions of Ruth Bunzel." In *Hidden Scholars: Women Anthropologists and the Native American Southwest,* Nancy J. Parezo, ed., pp. 259–269. Albuquerque: University of New Mexico Press.

Harrington, M. R.
1914 "Sacred Bundles of the Sac and Fox Indians." In *University of Pennsylvania, The University Museum, Anthropological Publications* 4(2):125–262.

Harrington, Mark W.
1896 "Weather Making, Ancient and Modern." In *Smithsonian Institution, Annual Report for the Year Ending July 30, 1894,* 249–270.

Harrod, Howard L.
1987   *Renewing the World: Plains Indian Religion and Morality.* Tuscon: University of Arizona Press.

Hawkes, E. W.
1914   "The Dance Festivals of the Alaskan Eskimo." In *University of Pennsylvania, The University Museum, Anthropological Publications* 6(2):1–41.
1916   *The Labrador Eskimo.* In Canada Department of Mines, Geological Survey, Memoir 91, Anthropological Series, No. 14.

Hays, Kelly Ann
1994   "Kachina Depictions on Prehistoric Pueblo Pottery." In *Kachinas in the Pueblo World,* Polly Schaafsma, ed., pp. 47–62. Albuquerque: University of New Mexico Press.

Heckewelder, J. G. E.
1819   *An Account of the History, Manners, and Customs of the Indian Nations, Who Once Inhabited Pennsylvania and the Neighbouring States.* American Philosophical Society, Historical and Literary Committee, Transaction no. 1, pp. 1–348. (For this encyclopedia the 1971 reprint edition by Arno Press and the *New York Times* was used.)

Hewitt, J. N. B.
1917   "Some Esoteric Aspects of the League of Iroquois." In *Proceedings of the Nineteenth International Congress of Americanists,* pp. 322–326.

Hieb, Louis A.
1993   "Elsie Clews Parsons in the Southwest." In *Hidden Scholars: Women Anthropologists and the Native American Southwest,* Nancy J. Parezo, ed., pp. 63–75. Albuquerque: University of New Mexico Press.
1994   "The Meaning of *Katsina:* Toward a Cultural Definition of 'Person' in Hopi Religion." In *Kachinas in the Pueblo World,* Polly Schaafsma, ed., pp. 23–33. Albuquerque: University of New Mexico Press.

Hill, W. W.
1982   *An Ethnography of the Santa Clara Pueblo New Mexico.* Edited and annotated by Charles H. Lange. Albuquerque: University of New Mexico Press.

Hill-Tout, Charles
1903   "Ethnological Studies of the Mainland Halkomelem, a Division of the Salish of British Columbia." In *Report of the 72nd Meeting of the British Association for the Advancement of Science* 72:355–490.

Hines, Donald M.
1992   *Ghost Stories: Yakima Indian Myths, Legends, Humor and Hunting Stories.* Issaquah, WA: Great Eagle Publishing.
1993   *Magic in the Mountains, The Yakima Shaman: Power & Practice.* Issaquah, WA: Great Eagle Publishing.

Hodge, Frederick Webb
1907   *Handbook of American Indians North of Mexico, Part 1.* Bureau of American Ethnology, Bulletin 30.
1910   *Handbook of American Indians North of Mexico, Part 2.* Bureau of American Ethnology, Bulletin 30.

Hoebel, E. Adamson
1960   *The Cheyennes: Indians of the Great Plains.* New York: Holt, Rinehart and Winston.

Hoffman, W. J.
1891   "The Mide′wiwin or 'Grand Medicine Society' of the Ojibwa." In *Seventh Annual Report of the Bureau of Ethnology.* 143–300.
1896   "The Menomini Indians." In *Fourteenth Annual Report of the Bureau of Ethnology.* 3–328.

Holm, Bill
1990   "Kwakiutl: Winter Ceremonies." In *Handbook of North American Indians, Northwest Coast, Volume 7,* Wayne Suttles, ed., pp. 378–386. Washington, DC: Smithsonian Institution.

Honigmann, John J.
1946   "Ethnography and Acculturation of the Fort Nelson Slave." In *Yale University Publications in Anthropology* 33:1–169.
1954   "The Kaska Indians: An Ethnographic Reconstruction." In *Yale University Publications in Anthropology* 51:1–163.

Howard, James H.
1953   "Notes on Two Dakota 'Holy Dance' Medicines and Their Uses." In *American Anthropologist* 55(4):608–609.

1954 "An Arikara Bear Society Initiation Ceremony." In *North Dakota History* 21(4):169–179.

1974 "The Arikara Buffalo Society Medicine Bundle." In *Plains Anthropologist* 19(1):241–271.

1984 *The Canadian Sioux.* Lincoln: University of Nebraska Press.

Hudson, Charles M., ed.
1979 *Black Drink: A Native American Tea.* Athens: University of Georgia Press.

Hultkrantz, Åke
1992 *Shamanic Healing and Ritual Drama: Health and Medicine in Native North American Religious Traditions.* New York: Crossroad.

Isaacs, Hope L.
1977 "*Orenda* and the Concept of Power among the Tonawanda Seneca." In *The Anthropology of Power: Ethnographic Studies from Asia, Oceania, and the New World,* Raymond D. Fogelson and Richard N. Adams, eds., pp. 167–184. New York: Academic Press.

Jacobsen, Johan Adrian
1977 *Alaskan Voyage 1881–1883.* Chicago: University of Chicago Press.

Jenness, Diamond
1933 "An Indian Method of Treating Hysteria." In *Primitive Man* 6(1):13–20.

1970 *The Life of the Copper Eskimos.* New York: Johnson Reprint. (First published in 1922.)

Jennings, Francis, William N. Fenton, Mary A. Druke, and David E. Miller, eds.
1985 *The History and Culture of Iroquois Diplomacy: An Interdisciplinary Guide to the Treaties of the Six Nations and Their League.* Syracuse, NY: Syracuse University Press.

Jewell, Donald P.
1987 *Indians of the Feather River: Tales and Legends of the Concow Maidu of California.* Menlo Park, CA: Ballena Press.

Johnson, Frederick
1943 "Notes on Micmac Shamanism." In *Primitive Man* 16(3 and 4):53–80.

Jones, Livingston F.
1914 *A Study of the Thlingets of Alaska.* London: Fleming H. Revell.

Jones, Peter
1861 *History of the Ojebway Indians.* London: A. W. Bennet.

Jones, William
1939 *Ethnography of the Fox Indians.* Edited by Margaret Welpley Fisher. Bureau of Ethnology, Bulletin 125.

Jorgensen, Joseph G.
1972 *The Sun Dance Religion: Power for the Powerless.* Chicago: University of Chicago Press.

Judd, Neil M.
1967 *The Bureau of American Ethnology.* Norman: University of Oklahoma Press.

Kelly, Isabel T.
1932 "Ethnography of the Surprise Valley Paiute." In *University of California Publications in American Archaeology and Ethnology* 31(3):67–210.

1936 "Chemehuevi Shamanism." In *Essays in Anthropology,* Robert H. Lowie, ed., pp. 129–142. Berkeley: University of California Press.

1939 "Southern Paiute Shamanism." In *University of California Anthropological Records* 2(4):151–167.

1964 "Southern Paiute Ethnography." In *University of Utah Anthropological Papers,* No. 69, pp. 1–194.

Keppler, Joseph
1941 "Comments on Certain Iroquois Masks." In *Contributions from the Museum of the American Indian, Heye Foundation* 12(4):1–40.

Kirk, Ruth
1986 *Tradition & Change on the Northwest Coast.* Seattle: University of Washington Press.

Kluckhohn, Clyde
1959 "The Philosophy of the Navaho Indians." In *Readings in Anthropology,* Morton H. Fried, ed., pp. 424–449. New York: Thomas Y. Crowell.

Knudtson, Peter M.
1975 "Flora, Shaman of the Wintu." In *Natural History* 84(5):6–17.

Kraft, Herbert C.
1986   *The Lenape: Archaeology, History, and Ethnography.* Newark: New Jersey Historical Society.

Krause, Aurel
1956   *The Tlingit Indians.* Seattle: University of Washington Press.

Krech III, Shepard
1981   "'Throwing Bad Medicine': Sorcery, Disease, and the Fur Trade among the Kutchin and Other Northern Athapaskans." In *Indians, Animals, and the Fur Trade: A Critique of Keepers of the Game,* Shepard Krech III, ed., pp. 73–108.

Kroeber, A. L.
1900   "The Eskimo of Smith Sound." In *Bulletin of the American Museum of Natural History* 12:265–327.
1907   "The Religion of the Indians of California." In *University of California Publications in American Archaeology and Ethnology* 4(6):319–356.
1925   *Handbook of the Indians of California.* Bureau of American Ethnology, Bulletin 78.
1931   "The Seri." In *Southwest Museum Papers* 6:1–60.
1932   "The Patwin and Their Neighbors." In *University of California Publications in American Archaeology and Ethnology* 29(4):253–423.

Kurath, Gertrude P.
1954   "The Tutelo Fourth Night Spirit Release Singing." In *Midwest Folklore* 4(2)87–105.

Laird, Carobeth
1976   *The Chemehuevis.* Banning, CA: Malki Museum Press.

Lake, Jr., Robert G.
1982   *Chilula: People from the Ancient Redwoods.* Lanham, MD: University Press of America.

Landes, Ruth
1968   *Ojibwa Religion and the Midéwiwin.* Madison: University of Wisconsin Press.

Lamphere, Louise
1969   "Symbolic Elements in Navajo Ritual." In *Southwestern Journal of Anthropology* 29(3):279–305.

Lange, Charles H.
1959   *Cochiti: A New Mexico Pueblo, Past and Present.* Austin: University of Texas Press.

Lantis, Margaret
1946   "The Social Culture of the Nunivak Eskimo." In *Transactions of the American Philosophical Society* 35(3):1–323.
1947   *Alaskan Eskimo Ceremonialism.* Monographs of the American Ethnological Society, number 11. New York: J. J. Augustin Publishers.

Latta, Frank
1949   *Handbook of the Yokuts Indians.* Oildale, CA: Bear State Books.

Le Page du Pratz
1763   *The History of Louisiana, or of The Western Parts of Virginia and Carolina.* London: T. Becket. (First French edition published in 1758.)

Lee, D. Demetracopoulou
1941   "Some Indian Texts Dealing with the Supernatural." In *Review of Religion* 5(4):401–411.

Levy, Jerrold E.
1994   "Hopi Shamanism: A Reappraisal." In *North American Indian Anthropology: Essays on Society and Culture,* Raymond J. DeMallie and Alfonso Ortiz, eds., pp. 307–327. Norman: University of Oklahoma Press.

Levy, Jerrold E., Raymond Neutra, and Dennis Parker
1987   *Hand Trembling, Frenzy Witchcraft, and Moth Madness: A Study of Navajo Seizure Disorders.* Tucson: University of Arizona Press.

Linton, Ralph
1923   "Annual Ceremony of the Pawnee Medicine Men." In *Field Museum of Natural History,* Leaflet Number 8, pp. 53–72.

Loeb, Edwin M.
1926   "The Creator Concept among the Indians of North Central California." In *American Anthropologist* 28(3):467–493.
1932   "The Western Kuksu Cult." In *University of California Publications in American Archaeology and Ethnology* 33(1):1–138.

1933 "The Eastern Kuksu Cult." In *University of California Publications in American Archaeology and Ethnology* 33(2):139–232.

Loftin, John D.
1986 "Supplication and Participation: The Distance and Relation of the Sacred in Hopi Prayer Rites." In *Anthropos* 81:177–201.

Long, John S.
1989 "The Cree Prophets: Oral and Documentary Accounts." In *Journal of the Canadian Church Historical Society* 31(1):3–13.

Long, Max Freedom
1936 *Recovering Ancient Magic.* London: Rider & Co.

Lopatin, Ivan A.
1945 *Social Life and Religion of the Indians in Kitimat, British Columbia.* The University of Southern California, Social Science Series no. 26. 1–107. Los Angeles: The University of Southern California Press.

Lowie, Robert H.
1909 "The Assiniboine." In *Anthropological Papers of the American Museum of Natural History* 4(1):1–270. (Published in 1910.)
1913a "Dance Associations of the Eastern Dakota." In *Anthropological Papers of the American Museum of Natural History* 11(2):101–142.
1913b "Societies of the Crow, Hidatsa and Mandan Indians." In *Anthropological Papers of the American Museum of Natural History* 11(3):143–358.
1915a "Societies of the Arikara Indians." In *Anthropological Papers of the American Museum of Natural History* 11(8):645–678.
1915b "Dances and Societies of the Plains Shoshone." In *Anthropological Papers of the American Museum of Natural History* 11(10):803–835.
1922 "Takes-the-Pipe, A Crow Warrior." In *American Indian Life,* Elsie Clews Parsons, ed., pp. 17–33. New York: B. W. Huebsch.
1939 "Ethnographic Notes on the Washo." In *University of California Publications in American Archaeology and Ethnology* 36(5):301–352.

Lyon, William S.
1984 "The Significance of the Experience of Transcendence in the Practice of Shamanism." In *Proceedings of the (First) International Conference on Shamanism,* Ruth-Inge Heinge, ed., pp. 139–156. University of California, Berkeley: Center for South and Southeast Asia Studies.
1987 "The Role of Vison Questing among North American Shamans." In *Proceedings of the Third International Conference on the Study of Shamanism and Alternate Modes of Healing,* Ruth-Inge Heinze, ed., pp. 271–278. Madison, WI: A-R Editions.
1989 "North American Indian Perspectives on Working with Sacred Power." In *Shaman's Drum* 16:32–39.
1996 "Back from the Edge of Chaos: A Psychotherapeutic Use of the Lakota Yuwipi." In *Shaman's Drum* 40:56–64.

Malouf, Carling
1951 "The Gosiute Indians." In *Shoshone Indians,* 1974, pp. 1–136. New York: Garland Publishing.

Mandelbaum, David G.
1940 "The Plains Cree." In *Anthropological Papers of the American Museum of Natural History* 37(2):155–316.

Marquis, Thomas B.
1928 *Memoirs of a White Crow Indian.* New York: Century Company.
1978 *The Cheyennes of Montana.* Edited by Thomas D. West. Algonac, MI: Reference Publications.

Mason, J. Alden
1946 "Notes on the Indians of the Great Slave Lake Area." In *Yale University Publications in Anthropology* 34:1–46.

Mavor, Jr., James W., and Byron E. Dix
1989 *Manitou: The Sacred Landscape of New England's Native Civilization.* Rochester, VT: Inner Traditions International.

McDowell, Jim
1997 *Hamatsa: The Enigma of Cannibalism on the Pacific Northwest Coast.* Vancouver, BC: Ronsdale Press.

McIlwraith, T. F.
1948   *The Bella Coola Indians,* 2 vols. Toronto, Canada: University of Toronto Press.

Meighan, Clement W., and Francis A. Riddell
1972   *The Maru Cult of the Pomo Indians: A California Ghost Dance Survival.* Southwest Museum, Paper Number 23. Los Angeles: Southwest Museum.

Merkur, Daniel
1987   "Eagle, the Hunter's Helper: The Cultic Significance of Inuit Mythological Tales." In *History of Religions* 27(2):171–188.
1989   "Arctic: Inuit." In *Witchcraft and Sorcery of the American Native Peoples,* Deward E. Walker, Jr., ed., pp. 11–21.
1991   *Powers Which We Do Not Know: The Gods and Spirits of the Inuit.* Moscow: University of Idaho Press.

Merriam, C. Hart
1955   *Studies of California Indians.* Berkeley: University of California Press.

Meyer, Roy W.
1977   *The Village Indians of the Upper Missouri: The Mandans, Hidatsas, and Arikaras.* Lincoln: University of Nebraska Press.

Michelson, Truman
1927   *Contributions to Fox Ethnology.* Bureau of American Ethnology, Bulletin 85.

Middleton, J., and E. Winter
1963   *Witchcraft and Sorcery in East Africa.* London: Routledge and Paul.

Miller, Bruce W.
1988   *Chumash: A Picture of Their World.* Los Osos, CA: Sand River Press.

Miller, Jay
1984   "Tsimshian Religion in Historical Perspective: Shamans, Prophets, and Christ." In *The Tsimshian and Their Neighbors of the North Pacific Coast,* Jay Miller and Carol M. Eastman, eds., pp. 137–147. Seattle: University of Washington Press.

Miller, Virginia P.
1979   *Ukomnom: The Yuki Indians of Northern California.* Ballena Press Anthropological Papers No. 14. Socorro, NM: Ballena Press.

Mironov, N. D., and S. M. Shirokogoroff
1924   "Shramana-Shaman: Etymology of the Word 'Shaman.'" In *Journal of the North-China Branch of the Royal Asiatic Society* 55:105–130.

Mitchell, D. D.
1962   "Indian Feats of Legerdemain." In *Bulletin of the Missouri Historical Society* 18:310–312. (First published in 1835.)

Mooney, James
1891   "The Sacred Formulas of the Cherokees." In *Seventh Annual Report of the Bureau of Ethnology.* 301–397.
1896   "The Ghost-Dance Religion and the Sioux Outbreak of 1890." In *Fourteenth Annual Report of the Bureau of Ethnology.* 641–1110.

Moore, James T.
1982   *Indian and Jesuit: A Seventeenth-century Encounter.* Chicago: Loyola University Press.

Morgan, William
1931   "Navaho Treatment of Sickness: Diagnosticians." In *American Anthropologist* 33(3):390–402.

Moriarty, James Robert
1965   "Cosmogony, Rituals, and Medical Practice among the Diegueno Indians of Southern California." In *Anthropological Journal of Canada* 3(3):2–16.

Murie, James R.
1914   "Pawnee Indian Societies." In *Anthropological Papers of the American Museum of Natural History* 11(7):543–644.

Nabokov, Peter
1978   *Native American Testimony: An Anthology of Indian and White Relations.* New York: Harper & Row.

Neihardt, John G.
1932   *Black Elk Speaks: Being the Life Story of a Holy Man of the Oglala Sioux.* New York: William Morrow.

Nelson, Edward William
1899   The Eskimo about the Bering Strait." In *Eighteenth Annual Report of the Bureau of American Ethnology.* 3–518.

Olbrechts, Frans M.
1930   "Some Cherokee Methods of Divination." In *Proceedings of the Twenty-third International Congress of Americanists,* pp. 547–552.

Olson, Ronald L.
1936   "The Quinault Indians." In *University of Washington Publications in Anthropology* 6(1):1–190.
1940   "The Social Organization of the Haisla of British Columbia." In *Anthropological Records* 2(5):169–200. Berkeley: University of California Press.

Opler, Marvin K.
1941   "A Colorado Ute Indian Bear Dance." In *Southwestern Lore* 7(2):21–30.

Opler, Morris Edward
1941   *An Apache Life-Way: The Economic, Social, and Religious Institutions of the Chiricahua Indians.* Chicago: University of Chicago Press.
1943   "The Character and Derivation of the Jicarilla Holiness Rite." In *University of New Mexico Bulletin, Anthropological Series* 4(3):1–98.

Osgood, Cornelius
1936   "Contributions to the Ethnography of the Kutchin." In *Yale University Publications in Anthropology* 14:13–189.
1937   "The Ethnography of the Tanaina." In *Yale University Publications in Anthropology* 16:1–229.
1958   "Ingalik Social Culture." In *Yale University Publications in Anthropology* 53:1–289.

Ostermann, H., ed.
1952   "The Alaskan Eskimos: As Described in the Posthumous Notes of Dr. Knud Rasmussen." In *Report of the Fifth Thule Expedition 1921–24* 10(3):1–292. Nordisk Forlag, Copenhagen: Gyldendalske Boghandel.

Parezo, Nancy J.
1993   "Matilda Coxe Stevenson: Pioneer Ethnologist." In *Hidden Scholars: Women Anthropologists and the Native American Southwest,* Nancy J. Parezo, ed., pp. 38–62. Albuquerque: University of New Mexico Press.

Parsons, Elsie Clews
1926   "Notes on Ceremonialism at Laguna." In *Anthropological Papers of the American Museum of Natural History* 19(4):85–131.
1929   *Kiowa Tales.* Memoirs of the American Folklore Society, vol. 22.
1932   "Isleta, New Mexico." In *Forty-seventh Annual Report of the Bureau of American Ethnology,* pp. 193–466.
1933   "Hopi and Zuñi Ceremonialism." In *Memoirs of the American Anthropological Association* 39:1–108.
1939   *Pueblo Indian Religion.* Chicago: University of Chicago Press.
1956   "A Note on Zuñi Deer-Hunting." In *Southwestern Journal of Anthropology* 12(3):325–326.

Pepper, George H., and Gilbert L. Wilson
1908   "An Hidatsa Shrine and the Beliefs Respecting It." *Memoirs of the American Anthropological Association,* 2(4):275–328.

Pinnow, Heinz-Jüen
1964   *Die Nordamerikanischen Indianersprachen.* Wiesbaden, Germany: Otto Harrassowitz.

Posinsky, S. H.
1965   "Yurok Shamanism." In *The Psychiatric Quarterly* 39(2):225–243.

Powell, Peter J.
1969   *Sweet Medicine: The Continuing Role of the Sacred Arrows, the Sun Dance, and the Sacred Buffalo Hat in Northern Cheyenne History,* 2 vols. Norman: University of Oklahoma Press.

Powers, William K.
1977   *Oglala Religion.* Lincoln: University of Nebraska Press.
1990   *Voices from the Spirit World.* Kendall Park, NJ: Lakota Books.

Radin, Paul
1911   "The Ritual and Significance of the Winnebago Medicine Dance." In *Journal of American Folklore* 24(92):149–208.
1922   "Thunder-Cloud, a Winnebago Shaman, Relates and Prays." In *American Indian Life,* Elsie Clews Parsons, ed., pp. 75–80. New York: B. W. Huebsch.

Rainey, Froelich G.
1947   "The Whale Hunters of Tigara." In *Anthropological Papers of the American Museum of Natural History* 41(2):229–283.

Rasmussen, Knud
1929   "Intellectual Culture of the Iglulik Eskimos." In *Report of the Fifth Thule Expedition 1921–24* 2(1):1–305.
1941   "Alaskan Eskimo Words." Edited by H. Ostermann. In *Report of the Fifth Thule Expedition 1921–24* 3(4):1–83.
1969   *Across Arctic America: Narrative of the Fifth Thule Expedition.* New York: Greenwood Press Publishers.

Reichard, Gladys A.
1950   *Navaho Religion: A Study of Symbolism.* Bollingen Series 28. New York: Pantheon Books.

Riddell, Francis A.
1960   "Honey Lake Paiute Ethnography." In *Nevada State Museum, Anthropological Papers,* Number 4, pp. 1–87. Carson City, NV: State Printing Office.

Ritzenthaler, Robert E.
1953a   "The Potawatomi Indians of Wisconsin." In *Bulletin of the Public Museum of the City of Milwaukee* 19(3):99–174.
1953b   "Chippewa Preoccupation with Health: Change in a Traditional Attitude Resulting from Modern Health Problems." In *Bulletin of the Public Museum of the City of Milwaukee* 19(4): 175–258.

Rodnick, David
1938   "The Fort Belknap Assiniboine of Montana." Ph.D. diss., University of Pennsylvania.

Ruby, Robert H., and John A. Brown
1996   *John Slocum and the Indian Shaker Church.* Norman: University of Oklahoma Press.

Saler, Benson
1964   "Nagual, Witch, and Sorcerer in a Quiché Village." In *Ethnology* 3(3):305–328.

Sandner, Donald F.
1979   "Navaho Indian Medicine and Medicine Men." In *Ways of Health: Holistic Approaches to Ancient and Contemporary Medicine,* David S. Sobel, ed., pp. 117–146. New York: Harcourt Brace Jovanovich.

Sapir, Edward
1909   *Wishram Texts.* In Publications of the American Ethnological Society, vol. 2.

Sarris, Greg
1994   *Mabel McKay: Weaving the Dream.* Berkeley: University of California Press.

Savage, Stephen
1962   *A Dictionary of the Maori Language of Raratonga.* Wellington, New Zealand: Department of Island Territories.

Sawyer, Jesse O.
1965   "English-Wappo Vocabulary." In *University of California Publications in Linguistics* 43:1–128.

Schaeffer, Claude E.
1969   *Blackfoot Shaking Tent.* Occasional Paper Number 5. Calgary, Alberta: Glenbow-Alberta Institute.

Schlesier, Karl H.
1987   *The Wolves of Heaven: Cheyenne Shamanism, Ceremonies, and Prehistoric Origins.* Norman: University of Oklahoma Press.

Schmalz, Peter S.
1991   *The Ojibwa of Southern Ontario.* Toronto: University of Toronto Press.

Schukies, Renate
1993   *Red Hat: Cheyenne Blue Sky Maker and Keeper of the Sacred Arrows.* Hamburg, Germany: Lit.

Schuster, Helen
1975 "Yakima Indian Traditions: A Study in Continuity and Change." Ph.D. diss., University of Washington.

Scully, Vincent
1975 *Pueblo: Mountain, Village, Dance.* New York: Viking Press.

Simmons, Leo W., ed.
1942 *Sun Chief: The Autobiography of a Hopi Indian.* New Haven, CT: Yale University Press.

Skinner, Alanson
1911 "Notes on the Eastern Cree and Northern Saulteaux." In *Anthropological Papers of the American Museum of Natural History* 9(1):1–116.
1914 "Political Organization, Cults, and Ceremonies of the Plains-Ojibway and Plains-Cree Indians." In *Anthropological Papers of the American Museum of Natural History* 11(4):475–542.
1915a "Societies of the Iowa." In *Anthropological Papers of the American Museum of Natural History* 11(9):679–740.
1915b "Kansa Organizations." In *Anthropological Papers of the American Museum of Natural History* 11(9):741–775.
1915c "Ponca Societies and Dances." In *Anthropological Papers of the American Museum of Natural History* 11(9):777–801.
1915d "Associations and Ceremonies of the Menomini Indians." In *Anthropological Papers of the American Museum of Natural History* 13(2):167–215.
1919a "The Sun Dance of the Plains Cree." In *Anthropological Papers of the American Museum of Natural History* 16(4):287–293.
1919b "The Sun Dance of the Plains-Ojibway." In *Anthropological Papers of the American Museum of Natural History* 16(4):311–315.
1924 "The Mascoutens or Prairie Potawatomi Indians: Part 1, Social Life and Ceremonies." In *Bulletin of the Public Museum of the City of Milwaukee* 6(1):1–262.

Smith, Anne M.
1974 *Ethnography of the Northern Utes.* Museum of New Mexico, Papers in Anthropology, Number 17. Albuquerque: Museum of New Mexico.

Smith, David Merrill
1973 *Inkonze: Magioco-Religious Beliefs of Contact-Traditional Chipewan Trading at Fort Resolution, NWT, Canada.* National Museum of Man, Mercury Series, Ethnology Division, Paper Number 6. Ottawa: National Museums of Canada.

Smith, J. L.
1967 "A Short History of the Sacred Calf Pipe of the Teton Dakota." In *Museum News* 28(7–8):1–37. The W. H. Over Dakota Museum. Vermillion: University of South Dakota.

Smithson, Carma Lee, and Robert C. Euler
1964 *Havasupai Religion and Mythology.* University of Utah Anthropological Papers, Number 68. Salt Lake City: University of Utah Press.

Speck, Frank G.
1907 "The Creek Indians of Taskigi Town." In *Memoirs of the American Anthropological Association* 2(2):99–164.
1928 "Chapters on the Ethnology of the Powhatan Tribes of Virginia." In *Indian Notes and Monographs* 1(5):221–455.
1931 *A Study of the Delaware Indian Big House Ceremony.* Publications of the Pennsylvania Historical Commission, Vol. 2. Harrisburg: Commonwealth of Pennsylvania, Bureau of Publications.

Spier, Leslie
1928 "Havasupai Ethnography." In *Anthropological Papers of the American Museum of Natural History* 29(3):83–392.
1930 "Klamath Ethnography." In *University of California Publications in American Archaeology and Ethnology* 30:1–338.
1935 *The Prophet Dance of the Northwest and Its Derivitives.* General Series in Anthropology, Number 1. Menasha, WI: George Banta Publishing Company.

Spier, Leslie, and Edward Sapir
1930 "Wishram Ethnography." In *University of Washington Publicatons in Anthropology* 3(3):151–300.

Spinden, Herbert Joseph
1964 "The Nez Percé Indians." In *Memoirs of the American Anthropological Association* 2(3):165–274.

Springer, James Warren
1981   "An Ethnohistoric Study of the Smoking Complex in Eastern North America." In *Ethnohistory* 28(3):217–235.

Stefánsson, Vilhjálmur
1914   "The Stefánsson-Anderson Arctic Expedition of the American Museum: Preliminary Ethnological Report. In *Anthropological Papers of the American Museum of Natural History* 14(1):1–395.

Stephen, Alexander M.
1894   "The Po-boc-tu among the Hopi." In *American Antiquarian and Oriental Journal* 16:212–214.
1936   *Hopi Journals of Alexander M. Stephen.* Edited by Elsie Clews Parsons. 2 vols. Columbia University Contributions to Anthropology, vol 23. New York: Columbia University Press.

Stern, Bernhard J.
1934   *The Lummi Indians of Northwest Washington.* New York: Columbia University Press.

Stevenson, Matilda Coxe
1904   "The Zuñi Indians." In *Twenty-third Annual Report of the Bureau of American Ethnology.* 3–634.

Steward, Julian H.
1933   "Ethnography of the Owens Valley Paiute." In *University of California Publications in American Archaeology and Ethnology* 33(3): 233–350.

Stoot, Margaret A.
1975   *Bella Coola Ceremony and Art.* National Museum of Man, Mercury Series, Canadian Ethnology Service, Paper Number 21. Ottawa: National Museums of Canada.

Sturtevant, William C.
1954a   "The Medicine Bundles and Busks of the Florida Seminole." In *Florida Anthropologist* 7(2): 31–70.
1954b   "The Mikasuki Seminole: Medical Beliefs and Practices." Ph.D. diss., Yale University. (Also University Microfilms 67–11, 355.)
1955   "Note on Modern Seminole Traditions of Osceola." In *Florida Historical Quarterly* 33:206–217.

Swanton, John R.
1908   "Haida Texts—Masset Dialect." In *Memoirs of the American Museum of Natural History* 14(2):273–812. (Reprint from vol. 10, part 2, of the Jesup North Pacific Expedition.)
1911   *Indian Tribes of the Lower Mississippi Valley and Adjacent Coast of the Gulf of Mexico.* Bureau of American Ethnology, Bulletin 43.
1928   "Religious Beliefs and Medical Practices of the Creek Indians." In *Forty-second Annual Report of the Bureau of American Ethnology.* 473–672.

Tarasoff, Koozma J.
1980   *Persistent Ceremonialism: The Plains Cree and Saulteaux.* National Museum of Man, Mercury Series, Canadian Ethnology Service, Paper Number 69. Ottawa: National Museums of Canada.

Tedlock, Dennis
1994   "Stories of Kachinas and the Dance of Life and Death." In *Kachinas in the Pueblo World,* Polly Schaafsma, ed., pp. 161–174. Albuquerque: University of New Mexico Press.

Teit, James A.
1898   *Traditions of the Thompson River Indians of British Columbia.* Memoirs of the American Folklore Society, vol. 6.
1900   "The Thompson Indians of British Columbia." In *Memoirs of the American Museum of Natural History* 2(4):163–390.
1909   "The Shuswap." In *Memoirs of the American Museum of Natural History* 4(7):447–758.

Thalbitzer, William
1914   *The Ammassalik Eskimo: Contributions to the Ethnology of the East Greenland Natives, in Two Parts.* Copenhagen: Bianco Luno. (Published in *Meddelelser om Grønland,* 1917/1921, 39:113–564 and 569–739.)
1931   "Shamans of the East Greenland Eskimo." In *Source Book in Anthropology,* A. L. Kroeber and T. T. Waterman, eds., pp. 430–436. New York: Harcourt, Brace.

Tiller, Veronica E.
1983   "Jicarilla Apache." In *Handbook of North American Indians, Southwest, Vol. 10,* Alfonso Ortiz,

ed., pp. 440–461. Washington, DC: Smithsonian Institution.

Titiev, Mischa
1943 "Notes on Hopi Witchcraft." In *Papers of the Michigan Academy of Science Arts and Letters* 28:549–557.
1972 *The Hopi Indians of Old Oraibi: Change and Continuity.* Ann Arbor: University of Michigan Press.

Toffelmier, Gertrude, and Katharine Luomala
1936 "Dreams and Dream Interpretation of the Diegueno Indians in Southern California." In *Psychoanalytic Quarterly* 4(2):195–225.

Tooker, Elizabeth
1970 *The Iroquois Ceremonial of Midwinter.* Syracuse, NY: Syracuse University Press.

Trowbridge, C. C.
1938 *Meearmeear Traditions.* Edited by Vernon Kinietz. Occasional Contributions from the Museum of Anthropology of the University of Michigan, Number 7. Ann Arbor: University of Michigan Press.

Turner, Edith
1996 *The Hands Feel It: Healing and Spirit Presence among a Northern Alaskan People.* DeKalb: Northern Illinois University Press.
1997 "The Reality of Spirits." In *Shamanism* 10(1):22–25.

Turner, Lucien M.
1894 "Ethnology of the Ungava District, Hudson Bay Territory." In *Eleventh Annual Report of the Bureau of Ethnology.* 159–350.

Turner, Victor
1967 *The Forest of Symbols: Aspects of Ndembu Ritual.* Ithaca, NY: Cornell University Press.

Turney-High, Harry Holbert
1937 "The Flathead Indians of Montana." In *Memoirs of the American Anthropological Association* 48:1–161.

Underhill, Ruth Murray
1938 *Singing for Power: The Song Magic of the Papago Indians of Southern Arizona.* Berkeley: University of California Press.
1939 *Social Organization of the Papago Indians.* Columbia University Contributions to Anthropology, vol. 30. New York: Columbia University Press. (Reissued by AMS Press in 1969.)

Underhill, Lonnie E., and Daniel F. Littlefield, Jr., eds.
1976 *Hamlin Garland's Observations on the American Indian, 1895–1905.* Tucson: University of Arizona Press.

Underhill, Ruth M., Donald M. Bahr, Baptisto Lopez, Jose Pancho, and David Lopez
1979 *Rainhouse and Ocean: Speeches for the Papago Year.* American Tribal Religions, vol. 4. Flagstaff: Museum of Northern Arizona Press.

Vallee, Frank G.
1966 "Eskimo Theories of Mental Illness in the Hudson Bay Region." In *Anthropologica* 8(1): 53–83.

Valory, Dale
1966 "The Focus of Indian Shaker Healing." In *Kroeber Anthropological Society Papers* 35:67–111.

Vestal, Stanley
1934 *New Sources of Indian History, 1850–1891.* Norman: University of Oklahoma Press.

Vizenor, Gerald
1981 *Summer in the Spring.* Minneapolis, MN: Nodin Press.

Voegelin, C. F.
1936 "The Shawnee Female Deity." In *Yale University Publications in Anthropology* 10:1–21.

Voth, H. R.
1901 "The Oraibi Powamu Ceremony." In *Publications of the Field Columbian Museum, Anthropological Series* 3(2):60–158.
1903 "The Oraibi Summer Snake Ceremony." In *Publications of the Field Columbian Museum, Anthropological Series* 3(4):262–385.

Walker, Jr., Deward E.
1967   "Nez Perce Sorcery." In *Ethnology* 6(1): 66–96.
1968   *Conflict and Schism in Nez Perce Accultura- tion: A Study of Religion and Politics.* Pullman: Wash- ington State University Press.

Walker, James R.
1980   *Lakota Belief and Ritual.* Edited by Ray- mond J. DeMallie and Elaine A. Jahner. Lincoln: University of Nebraska Press.

Wallis, Wilson D.
1947   "The Canadian Dakota." In *Anthropologi- cal Papers of the American Museum of Natural History* 41(1):1–225.

Wallis, Wilson D., and Ruth Sawtell Wallis
1955   *The Micmac Indians of Eastern Canada.* Minneapolis: University of Minnesota Press.
1957   *The Malecite Indians of New Brunswick.* National Museum of Canada, Bulletin Number 148, Anthropological Series Number 40. Ottawa: Minister of Northern Affairs and National Resources.

Waterman, T. T.
1924   "The Shake Religion of Puget Sound." In *Smithsonian Institution, Annual Report for the Year Ending June 30, 1922,* 499–507.
1930   "The Paraphernalia of the Duwamish 'Spirit Canoe' Ceremony." In *Museum of the American Indian, Heye Foundation, Indian Notes* 7(2):129–148; 7(3):295–312; 7(4):535–561.

Waterman, T. T., and A. L. Kroeber
1938   "The Kepel Fish Dam." In *University of California Publications in American Archaeology and Ethnology* 35(6):49–80.

Weatherford, Jack
1988   *Indian Givers: How the Indians of the Ameri- cas Transformed the World.* New York: Crown Publishers.
1991   *Native Roots: How the Indians Enriched America.* New York: Crown Publishers.

Wherry, Joseph H.
1969   *Indian Masks and Myths of the West.* New York: Bonanza Books.

White, Leslie A.
1930   "A Comparative Study of Keresan Medi- cine Societies." In *Proceedings of the Twenty-third In- ternational Congress of Americanists,* pp. 604–619.

Whiting, Alfred F.
1939   *Ethnobotany of the Hopi.* Museum of Northern Arizona, Bulletin Number 15. Flagstaff: Museum of Northern Arizona. (Reissued in 1966.)

Whitman, William
1937   *The Oto.* Columbia University Contribu- tions to Anthropology, vol. 23. New York: Columbia University Press.

Will, George F.
1928   "Magical and Slight of Hand Performances by the Arikara." In *North Dakota Historical Quarterly* 3(1):50–65.
1930   "Arikara Ceremonials." In *North Dakota Historical Quarterly* 4(4):245–265.
1934   "Notes on the Arikara Indians and Their Ceremonies." In *The Old West Series* 3:1–48.

Will, George F., and H. J. Spinden
1906   "The Mandans: A Study of Their Culture, Archaeology and Language." In *Papers of the Peabody Museum of American Archaeology and Ethnology* 33(4):79–219.

Wilson, Birbeck
1968   "Ukiah Valley Pomo Religious Life, Super- natural Doctoring, and Beliefs: Observations of 1939–1941." In *Reports of the University of California Archaeological Survey* 72:1–92.

Wilson, Gilbert Livingstone
1928   "Hidatsa Eagle Trapping." In *Anthropologi- cal Papers of the American Museum of Natural History,* 30(4):1–245.

Winick, Charles
1968   *Dictionary of Anthropology.* Totowa, NJ: Littlefield, Adams.

Winter, Keith
1975   *Shananditti: The Last of the Beothucks.* North Vancouver, BC: J. J. Douglas.

Wissler, Clark
1907   "Some Protective Designs of the Dakota." In *Anthropological Papers of the American Museum of Natural History* 1(2):19–53.
1912a   "Ceremonial Bundles of the Blackfoot Indians." In *Anthropological Papers of the American Museum of Natural History* 7(Part 2):65–298.
1912b   "Societies and Ceremonial Associations in the Oglala Division of the Teton-Dakota." In *Anthropological Papers of the American Museum of Natural History* 11(1):1–99.
1913   "Societies and Dance Associations of the Blackfoot Indians." In *Anthropological Papers of the American Museum of Natural History* 11(4):359–460.
1916   "General Discussion of Shamanistic and Dancing Societies." In *Anthropological Papers of the American Museum of Natural History* 11(12):853–876.

1922   "Smoking-Star, a Blackfoot Shaman." In *American Indian Life,* Elsie Clews Parsons, ed., pp. 45–62. New York: B. W. Huebsch.

Wyman, Leland C., and Flora L. Bailey
1943   "Navaho Upward-reaching-Way: Objective Behavior, Rationale, and Sanction." In *University of New Mexico Bulletin,* Anthropological Series 4(2):1–47.
1944   "Two Examples of Navaho Physiotherapy." In *American Anthropologist* 46(3):329–337.

Wyman, Leland C., and W. W. Hill
1942   "Navajo Eschatology." In *University of New Mexico Bulletin,* Anthropological Series 4(1):1–48.

Zigmond, Maurice
1977   "The Supernatural World of the Kawaiisu." In *Flowers of the Wind: Papers on Ritual, Myth and Symbolism in California and the Southwest,* Thomas C. Blackburn, ed., pp. 59–95. Socorro, NM: Ballena Press.

Ethnobotany Bibliography

Note: *SI-BAE* is an abbreviation for Smithsonian Institution, Bureau of American Ethnology.

Ager, Thomas A. and Lynn Price Ager. "Ethnobotany of the Eskimos of Neldon Island, Alaska." *Arctic Anthropology* 27, no. 1 (1980): 26–48.

Akana, Akaiko. *Hawaiian Herbs of Medicinal Value.* Honolulu, HI: Pacific Book House,1922.

Aller, Wilma F. "Aboriginal Food Utilization of Vegetation by the Indians of the Great Lakes Region as Recorded in the Jesuit Relations." *Wisconsin Archaeologist* 35 (1954): 59–73.

Anderson, J. P. "Plants Used by the Eskimo of the Northern Bering Sea and Arctic Regions of Alaska." *American Journal of Botany* 26 (1939): 714–716.

Arnason, Thor, Richard J. Hebda, and Timothy Johns. "Use of Plants for Food and Medicine by Native Peoples of Eastern Canada." *Canadian Journal of Botany* 59, no. 11(1981): 2189–2325.

Baker, Marc A. "The Ethnobotany of the Yurok, Tolowa, and Karok Indians of Northwest California." Master's thesis, Humboldt State University, 1981.

Bank, Theodore P., II. "Botanical and Ethnobotanical Studies in the Aleutian Islands, I. Aleutian Vegetantion and Aleut Culture." *Botanical and Ethnobotanical Papers, Michigan Academy of Science, Arts, and Letters* 37 (1951): 13–30.

———. "Botanical and Ethnobotanical Studies in the Aleutian Islands, II. Health and Medical Lore of the Aleuts." *Botanical and Ethnobotanical Papers, Michigan Academy of Science, Arts, and Letters* 38 (1953): 415–431.

Barrett, S.A. "Pomo Indian Basketry." *University of California Publications in American Archaeology and Ethnology* 7 (1908): 134–308.

———. "The Washoe Indians." *Bulletin of the Public Museum of the City of Milwaukee* 2, no. 1 (1917): 1–52.

———. "Material Aspects of Pomo Culture." *Bulletin of the Public Museum of the City of Milwaukee* 20 (1952): 1–508.

Barrett, S. A., and E. W. Gifford. "Miwok Material Culture." *Bulletin of the Public Museum of the City of Milwaukee* 2, no. 4 (1933): 117–376.

Barrows, David Prescott. *The Ethno-Botany of Coahuilla Indians of Southern California.* Chicago, IL: University of Chicago Press, 1900. Reprint. Banning, CA: Malki Museum Press, 1967.

Basehart, Harry W. *Apache Indians XII. Mescalero Apache Subsistence Patterns and Socio-Political Organization.* New York, NY: Garland Publishing, Inc., 1974.

Bean, Lowell John, and Katherine Siva Saubel. *Temalpakh (from the Earth): Cahuilla Indian Knowledge and Usage of Plants.* Banning, CA: Malki Museum Press, 1972.

Beardsley, Gretchen. "Notes on Cree Medicines, Based on Collections Made by I. Cowie in 1982." *Papers of the Michigan Academy of Science, Arts, and Letters* 28 (1941): 483–496.

Bell, Willis H., and Edward F. Castetter. "Ethnobiological Studies in the Southwest, VII. The Utilization of Yucca, Sotol and Beargrass by the Aborigines in the American Southwest." *University of New Mexico Bulletin* 5, no. 5 (1941): 1–74.

Black, Meredith Jean. *Algonquin Ethnobotany: An Interpretation of Aboriginal Adaptation in South Western Quebec.* Mercury Series No. 65. Ottawa, Ontario: National Museums of Canada, 1980.

Blankinship, J. W. "Native Economic Plants of Montana." *Bozeman Montana Agricultural Experimental Station Bulletin* 56 (1905): 1–38.

Boas, Franz. *Kwakiutl Ethnography.* Chicago, IL: University of Chicago Press, 1966.

Bocek, Barbara R. "Ethnobotany of Costanoan Indians, California, Based in Collections by John P. Harrington." *Economic Botany* 38, no. 2 (1984): 240–255.

Bradley, Will T. "Medical Practices of the New England Aborigines." *Journal of the American Pharmaceutical Association* 25, no. 2 (1936): 138–147.

Brugge, David M. "Navajo Use of Agave." *Kiva* 31, no. 2 (1965): 88–98.

Burgesse, J. Allen. "The Woman and the Child Among the Lac-St.-Jean Montagnais." *Primitive Man* 17 (1944): 1–18.

Bushnell, David I., Jr. "The Choctaw of Bayou Lacomb, St. Tammany Parish, Louisiana." *SI-BAE Bulletin* 48 (1909).

Buskirk, Winfred. *The Western Apache: Living with the Land Before 1950.* Norman, OK: University of Oklahoma Press, 1986.

Camazine, Scott, and Robert A Bye. "A Study of Medical Ethnobotany of the Zuni Indians of New Mexico." *Journal of Ethnopharmacology* 2 (1980): 365–388.

Campbell, T. N. "Medicinal Plants Used by Choctaw, Chickasaw, and Creek Indians in the Early Nineteenth Century." *Journal of the Washington Academy of Sciences* 41, no. 9 (1951): 285–290.

Carlson, Gustav G., and Volney H. Jones. "Some Notes on Uses of Plants by the Comanche Indians." *Papers of the Michigan Academy of Science, Arts, and Letters* 25 (1940): 517–542.

Carr, Lloyd G., and Carlos Westey. "Surviving Folktales & Herbal Lore Among the Shinnecock Indians." *Journal of American Folklore* 58 (1945):113–123.

Carrier Linguistic Committee. *Plants of Carrier Country.* Fort St. James, BC, Canada: Carrier Linguistic Committee, 1973.

Castetter, Edward F. "Ethnobiological Studies in the American Southwest, I. Uncultivated Native Plants Used as Sources of Food." *University of New Mexico Bulletin* 4, no. 1 (1935): 1–44.

Castetter, Edward F., and Willis H. Bell. "Ethnobiological Studies in the American Southwest IV. The Aboriginal Utilization of the Tall Cacti in the American Southwest." *University of New Mexico Bulletin* 5 (1937): 1–48.

———. *Pima and Papago Indian Agriculture.* Albuquerque, NM: University of New Mexico Press, 1942.

———. *Yuman Indian Agriculture.* Albuquerque, NM: University of New Mexico Press, 1951.

Castetter, Edward F., and M. E. Opler. "Ethnobiological Studies in the American Southwest, III. The Ethnobiology of the Chiricahua and Mescalero Apache." *University of New Mexico Bulletin* 4, no. 5 (1936): 1–63.

Castetter, Edward F., and Ruth M. Underhill. "Ethnobiological Studies in the American Southwest II.

The Ethnobiology of the Papago Indians." *University of New Mexico Bulletin* 4, no. 3 (1935): 1–84.

Chamberlain, Ralph V. "Some Plant Names of the Ute Indians." *American Anthropologist* 11 (1909): 27–40.

Chamberlain, Ralph V. "The Ethno-Botany of the Gosiute Indians of Utah." *Memoirs of the American Anthropological Association* 2, no. 5 (1911):331–405.

Chandler, R. Frank, Lois Freeman, and Shirley N. Hooper. "Herbal Remedies of the Maritime Indians." *Journal of Ethnopharmacology* 1 (1979): 49–68.

Chesnut, V. K. "Plants Used by the Indians of Mendocino County, California." *Contributions from the U.S. National Herbarium* 7, no. 6 (1902): 295–408.

Colton, Harold S. "Hopi History and Ethnobotany." In *Hopi Indians,* D. A. Horr, ed. New York, NY: Garland Press, 1974.

Compton, Brian Douglas. "Upper North Wakashan and Southern Tsimshian Ethnobotany: The Knowledge and Usage of Plants." Ph.D. dissertation, University of British Columbia, 1993.

Cook, Sarah Louise. "The Ethnobotany of the Jemez Indians." Master's thesis, University of New Mexico, 1930.

Coville, Frederick V. "Notes on the Plants Used by the Klamath Indians of Oregon." *Contributions from the U.S. National Herbarium* 5, no. 2 (1897): 87–110.

———. "Wokas, A Primitive Food of the Klamath Indians." *Reports of the U.S. National Museum* (1902): 725–739.

Curtin, L. S. M. *By the Prophet of the Earth.* Santa Fe, NM: San Vicente Foundation, 1949.

———. "Some Plants Used by the Yuki Indians, I. Historical Review and Medicinal Plants." *The Masterkey* 31, no. 2 (1957): 40–48.

———. "Some Plants Used by the Yuki Indians II. Food Plants." *The Masterkey* 31, no. 3 (1957): 85–94.

Dawson, E. Yale. "Some Ethnobotanical Notes on the Seri Indians." *Desert Plant Life* 9 (1944): 133–138.

Densmore, Frances "Chippewa Music—II." *SI-BAE Bulletin* 53 (1913).

———. "Menominee Music." *SI-BAE Bulletin* 102 (1932).

———. "Teton Sioux Music." *SI-BAE Bulletin* 61 (1918).

———. "Uses of Plants by the Chippewa Indians." *SI-BAE Annual Report* 44 (1928):275–379.

Elmore, Francis H. *Ethnobotany of the Navajo.* Santa Fe, NM: School of American Research, 1944.

Fewkes, J. Walter. "A Contribution to Ethnobotany." *American Anthropologist* 9 (1896): 14–21.

Fleisher, Mark S. "The Ethnobotany of the Clallam Indians of Western Washington." *Northwest Anthropological Research Notes* 14, no. 2 (1980): 192–210.

Fletcher, Alice C., and Francis La Flesche. "The Omaha Tribe." *SI-BAE Annual Report* 27 (1911): 17–654.

Fowler, Catherine S. *Willard Z. Park's Ethnographic Notes on the Northern Paiute of Western Nevada 1933–1940.* Salt Lake City, UT: University of Utah Press, 1989.

———. *Tule Technology: Northern Paiute Uses of Marsh Resources in Western Nevada.* Washington, DC: Smithsonian Institution Press, 1990.

Garth, Thomas R. "Atsugewi Ethnography." *University of California Anthropological Records* 14, no. 2 (1953): 123–212.

Gifford, E.W. "The Cocopa." *University of California Publications in American Archaeology and Ethnology* 31, no. 5 (1933): 257–334.

———. "Ethnographic Notes on the Southwestern Pomo." *University of California Anthropological Records* 25 (1967): 1–47.

———. "The Kamia of Imperial Valley." *SI-BAE Bulletin* 97 (1931).

———. "Northeastern and Western Yavapi." *University of California Publications in American Archaeology and Ethnology* 34, no. 4 (1936): 247–354.

———. "The Southeastern Yavapi." *University of California Publications in American Archaeology and Ethnology* 29, no. 3 (1932): 177–252.

Gill, Steven J. "Etnobotany of the Makah and Ozette People, Olympic Peninsula, Washington (USA)." Ph.D. dissertation, Washington State University, 1983.

Gilmore, Melvin R. *Some Chippewa Uses of Plants.* Ann Arbor, MI: University of Michigan Press, 1933.

———. "Some Native Nebraska Plants with Their Uses by the Dakota." *Nebraska State Historical Society Collections* 17 (1913): 358–370.

———. "A Study in the Ethnobotany of the Omaha Indians." *Nebraska State Historical Society Collections* 17 (1913): 314–357.

———. "Uses of Plants by the Indians of Missouri River Region." *SI-BAE Annual Report* 33 (1919): 43–154.

Goodrich, Jennie, and Claudia Lawson. *Kashaya Pomo Plants.* Los Angeles, CA: University of California American Indian Studies Center, 1980.

Gottesfeld, Leslie M. J. "The Importance of Bark Products in the Aboriginal Economies of Northwestern British Columbia, Canada." *Economic Botany* 46, no. 2 (1992): 148–157.

Gottesfeld, Leslie M. J., and Beverly Anderson. "Gitskan Traditional Medicine: Herbs and Healing." *Journal of Ethnobiology* 8, no. 1 (1988): 13–33.

Grinnell, George Bird. *The Cheyenne Indians—Their History and Ways of Life,* 2 volumes. Lincoln, NE: University of Nebraska Press, 1972.

———. "Some Cheyenne Plant Medicines." *American Anthropologist* 7 (1905): 37–43.

Guédon, Marie-Françoise. *People of Tetlin, Why Are You Singing?* Mercury Series no 9. Ottawa: National Museums of Canada, 1974.

Gunther, Erna. *Ethnobotany of Western Washington.* Rev. ed. Seattle, WA: University of Washington Press, 1973.

———. *Klallam Ethnography.* Seattle, WA: University of Washington Press, 1927.

Hamel, Paul B., and Mary U. Chiltoskey. *Cherokee Plants and Their Uses—A 400 Year History.* Sylva, NC: Herald Publishing Co., 1975.

Hann, John H. "The Use and Processing of Plants by Indians of Spanish Florida." *Southeastern Archaeology* 5, no. 2 (1986): 1–102.

Hart, Jeff. *Montana Native Plants and Early Peoples.* Helena, MT: Montana Historical Society Press, 1992.

———. "The Ethnobotany of the Northern Cheyenne Indians of Montana." *Journal of Ethnopharmacology* 4 (1981): 1–55.

Heller, Christine. *Edible and Poisonous Plants of Alaska.* Fairbanks: University of Alaska, 1953.

Hellson, John C. *Ethnobotany of the Blackfoot Indians.* Mercury Series. Canadian Ethnology Service, Paper No. 19. Ottawa: National Museums of Canada, 1974.

Herrick, James William. "Iroquois Medical Botany." Ph.D. dissertation, State University of New York, Albany, 1977.

Hinton, Leanne. "Notes on La Huerta Diegueno Ethnobotany." *Journal of California Anthropology* 2 (1975): 214–222.

Hocking, George M. "From Pokeroot to Penicillin." *The Rocky Mountain Druggist* (Nov. 1949).

———. "Some Plant Materials Used Medicinally and Otherwise by the Navaho Indians in the Chaco Canyon, New Mexico." *El Palacio* 63 (1956): 146–165.

Hoffman, W. J. "The Midewiwin or 'Grand Medicine Society' of the Ojibwa." *SI-BAE Annual Report* 7 (1891): 143–300.

Holmes, E. M. "Medicinal Plants Used by Cree Indians, Hudson's Bay Territory." *The Pharmaceutical Journal and Transactions* 15 (1884): 302–304.

Holt, Catharine. "Shasta Ethnography." *University of California Anthropological Records* 3, no. 4 (1946): 308.

Howard, James. "The Ponca Tribe." *SI-BAE Bulletin* 195 (1965).

Hrdlicka, Ales. "Physiological and Medical Observations Among the Indians of the Southwestern United States and Northern Mexico. *SI-BAE Bulletin* 34 (1908).

Jenness, Diamond. *The Ojibwa Indians of Parry Island, Their Religious and Social Life.* Anthropological Series 17. *National Museums of Canada Bulletin* 78 (1935).

Johnston, Alex. *Plants and the Blackfoot.* Lethbridge, Alberta: Lethbridge Historical Society, 1987.

Jones, Anore. *Nauriat Niginaqtuat = Plants That We Eat.* Kotzebue, AK: Maniilaq Association Traditional Nutrition Program, 1983.

Jones, David E. "Comanche Plant Medicine." *University of Oklahoma, Department of Anthropology, Papers in Anthropology* 9 (1968): 1–13.

Jones, Volney H. "An Ancient Food Plant of the Southwest and Plateau Regions." *El Palacio* 44 (1938): 41–53.

———. "The Ethnobotany of the Isleta Indians." Master's thesis, University of New Mexico, 1931.

Kari, Priscilla Russe. *Upper Tanana Ethnobotany.* Anchorage, AK: Alaska Historical Commission, 1985.

Kelly, Isabel T. "Etnography of the Surprise Valley Paiute." *University of California Publications in American Archaeology and Ethnology* 31, no. 3 (1932): 67–210. Reprint. New York: Krauss Reprint, 1965.

———. "Yuki Basketry." *University of California Publications in American Archaeology and Ethnology* 24, no. 9 (1930): 421–444.

Kirk, R. E. "Panamint Basketry." *Masterkey* 26 (1952): 78–86.

Kraft, Shelly Katheren. "Recent Changes in the Ethnobotany of Standing Rock Indian Reservation." Master's thesis, University of North Dakota, 1990.

Krause, Aurel. *The Tlingit Indians.* Translated by Erna Gunther. Seattle, WA: University of Washington Press, 1956.

Lantis, Margaret. "Folk Medicine and Hygiene." *Anthropological Papers of the University of Alaska* 8, no. 1 (1959):1–75.

Leighton, Anna L. *Wild Plant Use by the Woods Cree (Nihithawak) of East-Central Saskatchewan.* Mercury Series. Canadian Ethnology Service, Paper No. 101. Ottawa: National Museums of Canada, 1985.

Lynch, Regina H. *Cookbook.* Chinle, AZ: Navajo Curriculum Center, Rough Rock Demonstration School, 1986.

Mahar, James Michael. "Ethnobotany of the Oregon Paiutes of the Warm Springs Indian Reservation." Bachelor's thesis, Reed College, 1953.

Malo, David. *Hawaiian Antiques.* Honolulu, HI: Hawaiian Gazette Co., Ltd., 1903.

Mandelbaum, David G. "The Plains Cree." *Anthropological Papers of the American Museum of Natural History* 37, no. 2 (1940): 202–203.

McClintock, Walter. "Meizinal- und Nutzpflanzen der Schwarzfuss Indianer." *Zeitschriff für Ethnologie* 41 (1909): 273–279.

McKennan, Robert A. "The Upper Tanana Indians." *Yale University Publications in Anthropology* 55 (1959): 1–223.

Mechling, W. H. "The Malecite Indians with Notes on the Micmacs." *Anthropologica* 8 (1959):239–263.

Merriam, C. Hart. "Ethnographic Notes in California Indian Tribes." Robert F. Heizer, ed. 3 pts. *University of California Archaeological Survey Reports* 68, 1966.

Murphey, Edith Van Allen. *Indian Uses of Native Plants.* 1959. Reprint. Glenwood, IL: Meyerbooks, 1990.

Nelson, Richard K. *Make Prayers to the Raven—A Koyukon View of the Northern Forest.* Chicago, IL: University of Chicago Press, 1983.

Nequatewa, Edmund. "Some Hopi Recipes for the Preparation of Wild Plant Foods." *Plateau* 16 (1943): 18–20.

Nickerson, Gifford S. "Some Data on Plains and Great Basin Indian Uses of Certain Native Plants." *Tebiwa* 9, no. 1 (1966): 45–51.

Oswalt, W. H. "A Western Eskimo Ethnobotany." *Anthropological Papers of the University of Alaska* 6 (1957): 17–36.

Palmer, Gary. "Shuswap Indian Ethnobotany." *Syesis* 8 (1975): 29–51.

Parker, Arthur Caswell. "Iroquois Uses of Maize and Other Food Plants." *New York State Museum Bulletin* 144, no. 482 (1910): 5–113.

Perry, F. "Ethno-Botany of the Indians in the Interior of British Columbia." *Museum and Art Notes* 2, no. 2 (1952): 36–53.

Perry, Myra Jean. "Food Uses of 'Wild' Plants by Cherokee Indians." Master's thesis, University of Tennessee, 1975.

Porsild, A. E. "Edible Plants of the Arctic." *Arctic* 6 (1953): 15–34.

———. *Edible Roots and Berries of Northern Canada.* National Museum of Canada, Department of Mines and Resources, 1937.

Powers, Stephen. "Aboriginal Botany." *Proceedings of the California Academy of Science* 5 (1875): 373–379.

Radin, Paul. "The Winnebago Tribe." *SI-BAE Annual Report* 37 (1923): 35–550.

Ray, Verne F. "The Sanpoil and Nespelem: Salishan Peoples of Northeastern Washington." *University of Washington Publications in Anthropology* 5 (1932): 1–237.

Raymond, Marcel. "Notes Éthnobotaniques sur les Têtes-de Boules de Manouan." *Contributions de l'Institut botanique de l'Université de Montréal* 55 (1945): 113–134.

Rea, Amadeo M. "Gila River Pima Dietary Reconstruction." *Arid Lands Newsletter* 31 (1991): 3–10.

Reagan, Albert. "Plants Used by the Bois Fort Chippewa (Ojibwa) Indians of Minnesota." *Wisconsin Archaeologist* 7, no. 4 (1928): 230–248.

———. "Plants Used by the Hoh and Quileute Indians." *Kansas Academy of Science* 37 (1936): 55–70.

———. "Plants Used by the White Mountain Apache Indians of Arizona." *Wisconsin Archaeologist* 8 (1929): 143–161.

———. "Various Uses of Plants by West Coast Indians." *Washington Historical Quarterly* 25 (1934): 133–137.

Robbins, W. W., J. P. Harrington, and B. Freire-Marreco. "Ethnobotany of the Tewa Indians." *SI-BAE Bulletin* 55 (1916).

Rogers, Dilwyn J. *Lakota Names and Traditional Uses of Native Plants by Sicangu (Brule) People in the Rosebud Area, South Dakota.* St. Francis, SD: Rosebud Educational Society, 1980.

Romero, John Bruno. *The Botanical Lore of the California Indians.* New York, NY: Vantage Press, Inc., 1954.

Rousseau, Jacques. "Éthnobotanique Abénakise." *Archives de Folklore* 2 (1947): 145–182.

———. *Éthnobotanique et Éthnozoölogie Gaspésiennes.* *Archives de Folklore* 3 (1948): 51–64.

———. "Le Folklore botanique de Caughnawaga." *Contributions de l'Institut botanique de l'Université de Montréal* 55 (1945): 7–72.

———. "Le Folklore botanique de l'Île aux Coudres." *Contributions de l'Institut botanique de l'Université de Montréal* 55 (1945): 75–111.

———. Notes sur l'Éthnobotanique d'Anticosti." *Archives de Folklore* 1 (1946): 60–71.

Russell, Frank. "The Pima Indians." *SI-BAE Annual Report* 26 (1908): 3–389.

Sapir, Edward, and Leslie Spier. "Notes on the Culture of the Yana." *University of California Anthropological Records* 3, no. 3 (1943): 239–298.

Schenck, Sara M., and E. W. Gifford. "Karok Ethnobotany." *University of California Anthropological Records* 13, no. 6 (1952): 377–392.

Smith, G. Warren. "Arctic Pharmacognosia." *Arctic* 26 (1973): 324–333.

Smith, Harlan I. "Materia Medica of the Bella Coola and Neighboring Tribes of British Columbia." *National Museum of Canada Bulletin* 56 (1929): 47–68.

Smith, Huron H. "Ethnobotany of the Menomini Indians." *Bulletin of the Public Museum of the City of Milwaukee* 4, no. 1 (1923): 1–174.

———. "Ethnobotany of the Meskwaki Indians." *Bulletin of the Public Museum of the City of Milwaukee* 4, no. 2 (1928): 175–326.

———. "Ethnobotany of the Ojibwe Indians." *Bulletin of the Public Museum of the City of Milwaukee* 4(3) (1932): 327–525.

———. "Ethnobotany of the Forest Potawatomi Indians." *Bulletin of the Public Museum of the City of Milwaukee* 7, no. 1 (1933): 1–230.

Sparkman, Philip S. "The Culture of the Luiseño Indians." *University of California Publications in American Archaeology and Ethnology* 8, no. 4 (1908): 187–234.

Speck, Frank G. "Catawba Medicines and Curative Practices." *Publications of the Philadelphia Anthropological Society* 1 (1937): 179–197.

———. "A List of Plant Curatives Obtained from the Houma Indians of Louisiana." *Primitive Man* 14 (1951): 49–73.

———. "Medicine Practices of the Northeastern Algonquins." *Proceedings of the 19th International Congress of Americanists* (1917): 303–321.

Speck, Frank G., and R. W. Dexter. "Utilization of Animals and Plants by the Malecite Indians of New Brunswick." *Journal of the Washington Academy of Sciences* 42 (1952): 1–7.

Speck, Frank G., and R. W. Dexter. "Utilization of Animals and Plants by the Micmac Indians of New Brunswick." *Journal of the Washington Academy of Sciences* 41 (1951): 250–259.

Speck, Frank G., R. B. Hassbrick, and E. S. Carpenter. "Rapahannock Herbals, Folk-Lore, and Science of Cures. *Proceedings of the Delaware County Institute of Science* 10(1) (1942): 7–55.

Spier, Leslie. " Havasupai Ethnography." *Anthropological Papers of the American Museum of Natural History* 29, no. 3 (1928): 83–392.

———. "Klamath Ethnography." *University of California Publications in American Archaeology and Ethnology* 30 (1930): 1–338.

Steedman, E. V. "The Ethnobotany of the Thompson Indians of British Colombia." *SI-BAE Annual Report* 45 (1930): 441–522.

Steggerda, Morris. "Navajo Foods and Their Preparation." *Journal of the American Dietetic Association* 17, no. 3 (1941): 217–225.

Stevenson, Matilda Coxe. "Ethnobotany of the Zuñi Indians." *SI-BAE Annual Report* 30 (1915): 31–302.

Steward, Julian H. "Ethnography of the Owens Valley Pauite." *University of California Publications in American Archaeology and Ethnology* 33, no. 3 (1933): 233–350.

Stewart, Kenneth M. "Mohave Indian Gathering of Wild Plants." *Kiva* 31, no. 1 (1965): 46–53.

Sturtevant, William. "The Mikasuki Seminole: Medical Beliefs and Practices." Ph.D. dissertation, Yale University, 1954.

Swan, James Gilchrist. "The Indians of Cape Flattery at the Entrance to the Strait of Fuca, Washington Territory." *Smithsonian Contributions to Knowledge* 16, no. 8 (1870): 1–106. Reprint. Seattle, WA: Shorey Publications, 1982.

Swank, George R. "The Ethnobotany of the Acoma and Laguna Indians." Master's thesis, University of New Mexico, 1932.

Swanton, John R. "Religious Beliefs and Medical Practices of the Creek Indians." *SI-BAE Annual Report* 42 (1928): 473–672.

Swartz, B.K., Jr. "A Study of Material Aspects of Northeastern Maidu Basketry." *Kroeber Anthropological Society Publications* 19 (1958): 67–84.

Tantaquidgeon, Gladys. *Folk Medicine of the Delaware and Related Algonkian Indians.* Harrisburg: Pennsylvania Historical Commission, Anthropological Papers No. 3, 1972.

———. "Mohegan Medical Practices, Weather-Lore, and Superstitions." *SI-BAE Annual Report* 43 (1928): 264–270.

———. *A Study of Delaware Indian Medicine Practice and Folk Beliefs.* Harrisburg, PA: Pennsylvania Historical Commission, 1942.

Taylor, Linda Averill. *Plants Used as Curatives by Certain Southeastern Tribes.* Cambridge, MA: Botanical Museum of Harvard University, 1940.

Theodoratus, Robert J. "Loss, Transfer, and Reintroduction in the Use of Wild Plant Foods in the Upper Skagit Valley." *Northwest Anthropological Research Notes* 23, no. 1 (1989): 35–52.

Train, Percy, James R. Henrichs, and W. Andrew Archer. *Medicinal Uses of Plants by Indian Tribes of Nevada.* Washington, DC: U.S. Department of Agriculture, 1941.

Turner, Lucien M. "Ethnology of the Ungava District, Hudson Bay Territory." *SI-BAE Annual Report* 11 (1894): 159–350.

Turner, Nancy Chapman, and Marcus A. M. Bell. "The Ethnobotany of the Coast Salish Indians of Vancouver Island, I and II." *Economic Botany* 25, no. 1 (1971): 63–104, 335–339.

———. The Ethobotany of the Southern Kwakiutl Indians of British Columbia." *Economic Botany* 27, no. 3 (1973): 257–310.

Turner, Nancy J., and Barbara S. Erfat. *Ethnobotany of the Hesquiat Indians of Vancouver Island.* Victoria, BC: British Columbia Provincial Museum, 1982.

Turner, Nancy J., R. Bouchard, and Dorothy I. D. Kennedy. *Ethnobotany of the Okanagan-Colville Indians of British Columbia and Washington.* Victoria, BC: British Columbia Provincial Museum, 1980.

Turner, Nancy J., John Thomas, Barry F. Carlson, and Robert T. Ogilvie. *Ethnobotany of the Nitinaht Indians of Vancouver Island.* Victoria, BC: British Columbia Provincial Museum, 1983.

Turner, Nancy J., Laurence C. Thompson, and M. Terry Thompson et al. *Thompson Ethnobotany: Knowledge and Usage of Plants by the Thompson Indians of British Columbia.* Victoria, BC: Royal British Columbia Museum, 1990.

Veniamenov, I. *Notes on the Islands in the Unalaska District.* St. Petersburg: Russian-American Company, 1840. Reprint. Kingston, Ontario: The Limestone Press, 1985.

Vestal, Paul A. "The Ethnobotany of the Ramah Navaho." *Papers of the Peabody Museum of American Archaeology and Ethnology* 40, no. 4 (1952): 1–94.

———. "Notes on a Collection of Plants from the Hopi Indian Region of Arizona Made by J. G. Owens in 1891." *Harvard University, Botanical Museum Leaflets* 8, no. 8 (1940): 153–168.

Vestal, Paul A., and Richard Evans Schultes. *The Economic Botany of the Kiowa Indians.* Cambridge, MA: Botanical Museum of Harvard University, 1939.

Voegelin, Ermine W. "Tübatulabal Ethnography." *University of California Anthropological Records* 2, no. 1 (1938): 1–84.

Wallis, Wilson D. "Medicines Used by the Micmac Indians." *American Anthropologist* 24 (1922): 24–30.

Watahomigie, Lucille J. *Hualapai Ethnobotany.* Peach Springs, AZ: Hualapai Bilingual Program, Peach Springs School District 8, 1982.

Waugh, F. W. *Iroquois Foods and Food Preparation.* Ottawa: Canada Department of Mines, 1916.

Weber, Steven A., and P. David Seaman. *Havasupai Habitat: A. F. Whiting's Ethnography of a Traditional Indian Culture.* Tucson, AZ: University of Arizona Press, 1985.

White, Leslie A. "Notes on the Ethnobotany of the Keres." *Papers of the Michigan Academy of Arts, Sciences, and Letters* 30 (1945): 557–568.

———. "The Pueblo of Sia, New Mexico." *SI-BAE Bulletin* 184 (1962).

Whiting, Alfred F. "Ethnobotany of the Hopi." *Museum of Northern Arizona Bulletin* 15 (1939).

Willoughby, C. "Indians of the Quinaielt Agency, Washington Territory." *Smithsonian Institution Annual Report for the Year 1886* (1889): 267–287. Reprint. Seattle, WA: Shorey Book Store, 1969.

Wilson, Michael R. "Notes on Ethnobotany in Inuktuit." *The Western Canadian Journal of Anthropology* 8 (1978): 180–196.

Witthoft, John. "Cherokee Indian Use of Potherbs." *Journal of Cherokee Studies* 2, no. 2 (1977): 250–255.

———. "An Early Cherokee Ethnobotanical Note." *Journal of the Washington Academy of Sciences* 37, no. 3 (1947): 73–75.

Wyman, Leland C., and Stuart K. Harris. *The Ethnobotany of the Kayenta Navaho.* Albuquerque, NM: University of New Mexico Press, 1951.

Zigmond, Maurice L. *Kawaiisu Ethnobotany.* Salt Lake City, UT: University of Utah Press, 1981.

Illustration Credits

Index